Security
in
Computing

Charles P. Pfleeger

Trusted Information Systems, Inc.

Prentice Hall, Englewood Cliffs, New Jersey 07632

Library of Congress Cataloging-in-Publication Data

Pfleeger, Charles P. (date)
    Security in computing / Charles P. Pfleeger.

      p.   cm.
    Bibliography: p.
    Includes index.
    ISBN 0-13-798943-1
    1. Computers—Access control.   2. Data protection   3. Privacy,
Right of.   I. Title.
QA76.9.A25P45 1989
005.8—dc19   88-12411
                                        CIP

Editorial/production supervision: Nancy Havas Farrell
Cover design: Lungren Graphics, Ltd.
Manufacturing buyer: Mary Ann Gloriande
Cover Art: Dave Shannon

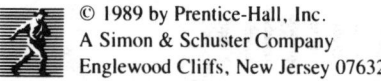

The publisher offers discounts on this book when ordered
in bulk quantities. For more information, write:

    Special Sales/College Marketing
    College Technical and Reference Division
    Prentice Hall
    Englewood Cliffs, New Jersey 07632

Printed in the United States of America

10 9 8 7 6 5

ISBN 0-13-798943-1

Prentice-Hall International (UK) Limited, *London*
Prentice-Hall of Australia Pty. Limited, *Sydney*
Prentice-Hall Canada Inc., *Toronto*
Prentice-Hall Hispanoamericana, S.A., *Mexico*
Prentice-Hall of India Private Limited, *New Delhi*
Prentice-Hall of Japan, Inc., *Tokyo*
Simon & Schuster Asia Pte. Ltd., *Singapore*
Editora Prentice-Hall do Brasil, Ltda., *Rio de Janeiro*

Contents

12 PHYSICAL PROTECTION—PLANNING AND PRODUCTS   437

Preface

In 1987, a group of West German youths obtained unauthorized access to a NATO computing system with links to U.S. computers. During 1986 someone penetrated a computing system at a secure scientific research laboratory in the U.S. In 1983, juveniles from Milwaukee, Wisconsin, called the "414s," broke into many computing systems, including Sloan-Kettering hospital and Security Pacific Bank. Attacks such as these are not uncommon, nor are all the successful attacks publicized in the news media.

Computer security is an important topic for professionals in computing. Users and managers of large mainframe computing systems of the 1960s and 1970s developed computer security techniques that were reasonably effective against the threats of that era. However, two factors have made those security procedures outdated:

1. *Personal computer use.* Vast numbers of people have become dedicated users of personal computing systems. These users may not be especially conscious of the security threats involved in computer use; even if they are aware, however, they may not know what to do to reduce their risk.

2. *Networked remote-access systems.* Machines are being linked in large numbers. A user of a mainframe computer may not realize that access to the same machine is allowed to people throughout the world from an almost uncountable number of computing systems.

It is imperative for every computing professional to understand the threats and the countermeasures currently available in computing. This book addresses that need.

This book is designed for the student or professional in computing. Beginning at a level appropriate for an experienced computer user, this book describes the security pitfalls that are inherent in many important computing tasks today. Then, the book explores the controls that can check these weaknesses. The book also points out where existing controls are inadequate and serious consideration needs to be given to the risk present in the computing situation

Uses of This Book

The chapters of this book progress in an orderly manner. After an introduction, the topic of encryption—the process of disguising something written to conceal its meaning—is presented as the first tool in computer security. The book continues through the different kinds of computing applications, their weaknesses, and their controls. The applications areas include:

- o general programs

- o operating systems

- o data base management systems

- o personal computers

- o remote access computing

- o multi-computer networks

These sections begin with a definition of the topic, continue with a description of the relationship of security to the topic, and conclude with a statement of the current state-of-the-art of computer security research related to the topic. The book concludes with an examination of risk analysis and planning for computer security, and a study of the relationship of law and ethics to computer security.

Background required to appreciate the book is an understanding of programming and computer systems. Someone who is a senior or graduate student in computer science, or a professional who has been in the field for a few years would have the appropriate level of understanding. Although some facility with mathematics is useful, all important mathematical background is developed in the book. Similarly, the necessary material on design of software systems, operating systems, data bases, or networks is given in the relevant chapters. One need not have a detailed knowledge of these areas prior to reading this book.

The book is designed to be a textbook for a one-or two-semester course in computer security. The book functions equally well as a reference for a computer professional. The introduction and the chapters on encryption are fundamental to the understanding of the rest of the book. After studying those pieces, however, the reader can study any of the later chapters in any order. Furthermore, many chapters follow the format of introduction, then security aspects of the topic, then current work in the area. Someone who is interested more in background than in current work can stop in the middle of one chapter and go on to the next.

This book has been used in classes both at The University of Tennessee and at George Washington University. Roughly half of the book can be covered in a semester. Therefore, an instructor can design a one-semester course that considers some of the topics of greater interest.

Acknowledgments

Many people have contributed to the content and structure of this book. First, the computer Science Department of the University of Tennessee and Systems/Software, Inc., have made available time and resources for me to do the research, analysis, and writing necessary for this book. Second, the following colleagues supplied advice and suggestions during the development of the book: Lance Hoffman, Dorothy Denning, Virgil Gligor, Dick Kemmerer, Jan Cook, Richard Baskerville, Dave Fox, Joe Turner, Dave Hsiao, Charlie Reynolds, and Glenn Graber. Similarly, these people from outside of academia were very encouraging: Terry Mayfield, Steve Walker, Carolyn Deverin, Gene Davenport, and Bruce Barnes. I apologize if I have forgotten to mention someone else; the oversight is accidental.

Lance Hoffman deserves special mention. He used a preliminary copy of the book in a course at George Washington University. Not only did he provide me with suggestions of his own, his students supplied invaluable comments from the student perspective of sections that did and did not communicate effectively. I want to thank them for their constructive criticisms.

My two assistants at Systems/Software, Laura Davis and Debra Pyatt-Poore, were outstanding at helping to handle the seemingly endless revisions on three separate computing systems. Laura, especially, caught errors that I would never have found.

Finally, if someone alleges to have written a book alone, distrust the person immediately. While an author is working 16-hour days on the writing of the book, someone else needs to see to all the other aspects of life, from simple things like food, clothing, and shelter, to complex things like social and family responsibilities. My wife, Shari Lawrence Pfleeger, took the time from her professional schedule so that I could devote my full energies to writing. Furthermore, she soothed me when the schedule inexplicably slipped, when the computer went down, when I had writer's block, or when some other crisis beset this project. On top of that, she reviewed the entire manuscript, giving the most thorough and constructive review this book has had. Her suggestions have improved the content, organization, readability, and overall quality of this book immeasurably. Therefore, it is with great pleasure that I dedicate this book to Shari, the other half of the team that caused this book to be written.

Charles P. Pfleeger
Washington DC

1

Is There a Security
Problem in Computing?

You seldom hear of bank robberies these days. In the wild west, banks kept large amounts of cash as well as gold and silver, which could not be traced. Cash was much more commonly used than checks. Communications and transportation facilities were such that it might be hours before the legal authorities were informed of a robbery and days before they could actually arrive at the scene of the crime, by which time the robbers would be long gone. A single guard for the night was only marginally effective. Robbery might require a little common sense and perhaps several days spent analyzing the situation, but it did not require much sophisticated training; one usually learned on the job in a form of apprenticeship. All of these factors led to a balance tipped very much in the favor of the criminal, so that bank robbery used to be fairly profitable.

Today, however, many factors work against the potential criminal. Very sophisticated alarm systems protect the bank silently while people are around or not. The techniques of criminal investigation have become very effective, so that a person can be identified by fingerprint, voice recognition, composite sketch, ballistics evidence, or other hard-to-mask characteristics. Many bank branches carry less cash than some large retail stores, since much of a bank's business is now conducted with checks. Places that do store large amounts of cash or currency are protected with many levels of security: several layers of physical systems, complex locks, two-party systems requiring agreement of two people to allow access, and many more schemes. Transportation and communication mean that police can be at the scene of a crime in minutes and can alert other officers to suspects to watch for in seconds. The risk and required sophistication are so high that the average criminal will often turn to an easier target than a bank.

This book is about security for computing systems, not banks. Consider the security differences between computing systems and banks.

- *Size and portability.* The physical devices in computing are so small that a thousand dollars of computing gear will fit comfortably in a briefcase, and ten thousand dollars' worth can be carried comfortably in two arms.

- *Ability to avoid physical contact.* Electronic funds transfers account for most transfers of money between banks. For example, private companies pay employees by direct computer transfer instead of check. Utilities, insurance companies, and mortgage companies automatically process deductions against their clients' bank accounts. Customers can even bank at home, moving funds between accounts and arranging withdrawals by touch-tone phone access to a computer.

- *Value of assets.* The value of the information stored in a computer is also high. Some computers contain confidential information about a person's taxes, investments, medical history, or education. Other computers contain very sensitive information about new product lines, sales figures, marketing strategy, or military targets, troop movements, weapons capabilities and so forth.

In terms of security, computing is very close to the wild west days. At some installations, computers and their data have been recognized as a valuable and vulnerable resource, and appropriate protection has been applied. Other installations are dangerously deficient in their security measures. But, unlike the "wild west" bankers, some computing professionals and managers do not even recognize the value of the resources they use or control.

Worse yet, in the event of a crime, some companies will not investigate or prosecute, for fear that it will damage their public image. For example, would you feel safe depositing your money in a bank that had just suffered a five million dollar loss through computer embezzlement? In fact, that bank has just been made painfully aware of its security weaknesses. That bank will probably enhance its security substantially so that it could be safer than a bank that had not been recently victimized.

Criminal investigation and prosecution are hindered by statutes that do not recognize electromagnetic signals as property. The news media have recently pictured computer intrusion by teenagers as pranks no more serious than tipping over an outhouse.

Obviously, security in computing is a very important issue. It is an area that deserves study by computer professionals, managers, and even many computer users. This book is written for all of those people. By studying this book, you will learn what are the security problems in computing and what methods are available to deal with those problems.

The purpose of this book is to examine the risks of security in computing, to consider available countermeasures, and to identify areas where more work is needed. In this chapter, we start by examining the *what,* the kinds of vulnerabilities to which computing systems are prone. We then consider *how* these vulnerabilities are exploited: different kinds of attacks that are possible. The third area we will look at in this chapter is *who,* the kinds of people who contribute to the security problem in computing. Finally, we introduce *controls,* ways to prevent the attacks on systems.

1.1 Characteristics of Computer Intrusion

The target of a crime involving computers may be any piece of the computing system. A **computing system** is a collection of hardware, software, storage media, data, and persons that an organization uses to do computing tasks. Whereas the obvious target of a bank robbery is cash, a list of names and addresses of depositors might be valuable to a competing bank. The list might be on paper, recorded on a magnetic medium, stored in internal computer memory, or transmitted electronically across a medium such as a telephone line. This multiplicity of targets makes computer security difficult.

In any security system, the *weakest point* is the most serious vulnerability. A robber intent on stealing something from your house will not attempt to penetrate a two-inch thick metal door if a window gives easier access. A sophisticated perimeter physical security system does not compensate for unguarded access by means of a simple telephone line and a modem. The "weakest point" philosophy can be restated as the following principle.

Principle of Easiest Penetration.   An intruder must be expected to use any available means of penetration. This will not necessarily be the most obvious means, nor will it necessarily be the one against which the most solid defense has been installed.

This principle says that computer security specialists must consider all possible means of penetration, because strengthening one may just make another means more appealing to intruders. We now consider what these means of penetration are.

1.2 Kinds of Security Breaches

In security, an **exposure** is a form of possible loss or harm in a computing system; examples of exposures are unauthorized disclosure of data, modification of data, or denial of legitimate access to computing. A **vulnerability** is a weakness in the security system that might be exploited to cause loss or harm. A human who exploits a vulnerability perpetrates an **attack** on the system. **Threats** to computing systems are circumstances that have the potential to cause loss or harm; human attacks are examples of threats, as are natural disasters, inadvertent human errors, and internal hardware or software flaws. Finally, a **control** is a protective measure—an action, a device, a procedure, or a technique—that reduces a vulnerability.

The major assets of computing systems are **hardware**, **software**, and **data**. There are four kinds of threats to the security of a computing system: **interruption, interception, modification**, and **fabrication**. The four threats all exploit vulnerabilities of the assets in computing systems. These four threats are shown in Figure 1.1.

1. In an *interruption*, an asset of the system becomes lost or unavailable or unusable. An example is malicious destruction of a hardware device, erasure of a program or data file, or failure of an operating system file manager so that it cannot find a particular disk file.

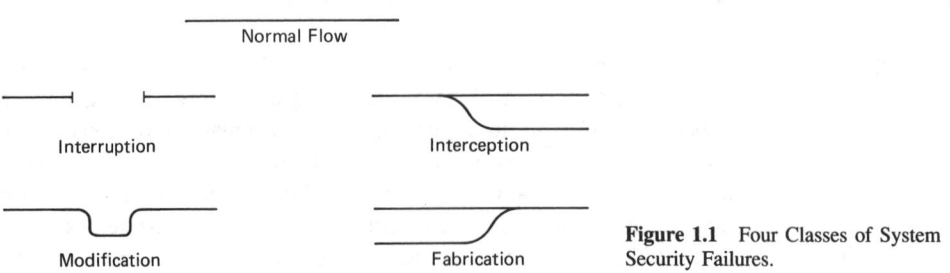

Figure 1.1 Four Classes of System Security Failures.

2. An *interception* means that some unauthorized party has gained access to an asset. The outside party can be a person, a program, or a computing system. Examples of this type of failure are illicit copying of program or data files, or wiretapping to obtain data in a network. While a loss may be discovered fairly quickly, a silent interceptor may leave no traces by which the interception can be readily detected.

3. If an unauthorized party not only accesses but tampers with an asset, the failure becomes a *modification*. For example, someone might modify the values in a data base, alter a program so that it performs an additional computation, or modify data being transmitted electronically. It is even possible for hardware to be modified. Some cases of modification can be detected with simple measures, while other more subtle changes may be almost impossible to detect.

4. Finally, an unauthorized party might *fabricate* counterfeit objects for a computing system. The intruder may wish to add spurious transactions to a network communication system, or add records to an existing data base. Sometimes these additions can be detected as forgeries, but if skillfully done, they are virtually indistinguishable from the real thing.

These four classes of interference with computer activity—interruption, interception, modification, and fabrication—can describe the kinds of exposures possible. Examples of these kinds of interferences are shown in Figure 1.2. The problems are described below.

1.3 The Points of Security Vulnerability

Computer security consists of maintaining three characteristics: **secrecy**, **integrity**, and **availability**.

- *Secrecy* means that the assets of a computing system are accessible only by authorized parties. The type of access is "read"-type access: reading, viewing, printing, or even just knowing the existence of an object.

- *Integrity* means that assets can be modified only by authorized parties. In this context, modification includes writing, changing, changing status, deleting, and creating.

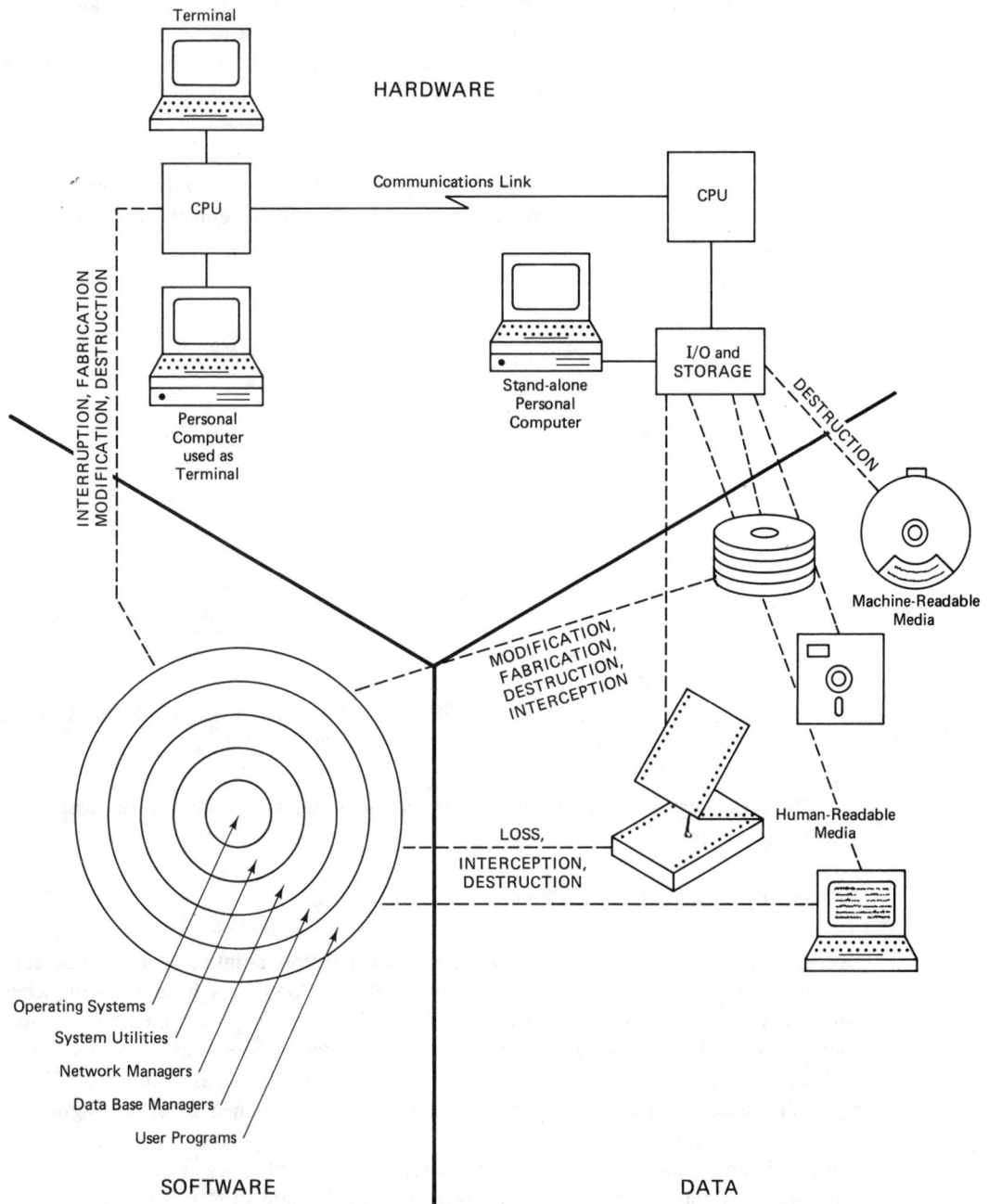

Figure 1.2   Types of Abuse in Computing Systems.

- *Availability* means that assets *are* available to authorized parties. An authorized party should not be prevented from accessing those objects to which he or she or it has legitimate access. For example, a security system could preserve perfect secrecy by preventing everyone from reading a particular object. However, this system does not meet the requirement of availability for proper access.

Figure 1.3 shows these three security responsibilities as they apply to the assets of hardware, software, and data. These three assets, and the connections between them, are all potential security weak points.

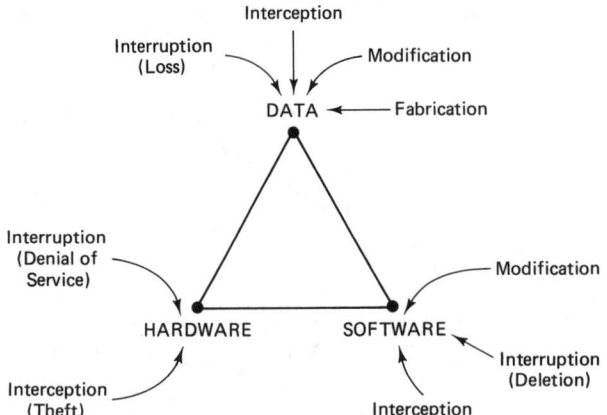

Figure 1.3 Computing System Weak Points.

The following few sections address the vulnerabilities of each specific asset of a computing system.

Attacks on Hardware

Because a physical device is so visible, it is a rather simple point to attack; fortunately, however, reasonable safeguards are usually in place. Computers have been drenched with water, burned, gassed, and electrocuted with lightning or power surges from other sources. People have spilled soft drinks, corn chips, ketchup, beer, and many other kinds of food on computing devices. Mice have chewed through cables. Particles of dust, especially particles of ash from cigarette smoke, have threatened precisely-engineered moving parts. Computers have been kicked, slapped, bumped, jarred, and punched. All of this abuse might come under the category of "involuntary machine-slaughter": accidental acts not intended to do serious damage to the hardware involved.

A more serious attack could be called "voluntary machine-slaughter" or "machine-icide," in which someone actually wishes to do harm to the computer. Machines have been shot with guns and stabbed with knives. Bombs, fires, and collisions have destroyed computer rooms. Ordinary keys, pens, and screwdrivers have been used to short out circuit boards and other components. Machines have been carried off by thieves. The list of human attacks on computers goes on almost without end.

We have just mentioned some of the many accidental and intentional ways people have attacked computer equipment in order to limit availability. Theft and destruction are the primary techniques. Managers of major computing centers long ago recognized the vulnerability of their machines and installed physical security systems to protect them. However, the proliferation of microcomputers in offices has left people with several thousands of dollars of equipment sitting unattended on desks outside the computer room. (Curiously, the supply cabinet, containing only a couple hundred dollars of pens, stationery, and paper clips, is often locked.) Sometimes the security of hardware components can be enhanced greatly by simple physical measures, such as locks or guards.

Attacks on Software

Computing equipment is worthless without the *software* (the operating system, utility programs, and applications programs) that users expect. Software can be destroyed maliciously, or it can be modified or deleted or misplaced accidentally. The result is the same, however, regardless of the motive: a loss of software becomes apparent when one tries to run it. These attacks are all problems of availability of software.

More subtle is software that runs but has been altered. Physical equipment usually shows some mark of inflicted injury, but the loss of one crucial line of source or object code may not leave an obvious mark in a program. Furthermore, it is possible to change a program so that it does all it did before, and then some. In this case, it is very hard to detect that the software has been changed, let alone to determine the extent of the change.

Software Deletion

Software is surprisingly easy to delete. Probably every programmer has accidentally erased a file, or saved a bad copy of a program, destroying a good previous copy. Because of software's high value to a commercial computing center, access to software is usually carefully controlled, through a process called **configuration management**, so that software is not deleted, destroyed, or replaced accidentally.

Software Modification

In this attack, a working program is modified, either to cause it to fail during execution or to cause it to do some unintended task. Software is relatively easy to modify: changing a bit or two can convert a working program into one that fails. Depending on which bit was changed, the program may crash when it begins, or it may execute for some time before it crashes.

With a little work, the change can be much more subtle, so that the program works well most times but fails in specialized circumstances. This change produces a program effect known as a **logic bomb**. For example, a disgruntled employee may modify a crucial program so that it accesses the system date and halts abruptly after July 1. The employee might quit on May 1 and plan to be at a new job miles away by July.

Another type of change can extend the functioning of a program so that an innocuous program has a hidden side effect. For example, a program that ostensibly structures a listing of files belonging to a user may also modify the protection of all those files to permit access by another user.

The category of software modification includes

1. a **Trojan horse**, a program that overtly does one thing while covertly doing another

2. a **trapdoor**, a secret entry point to a program

3. a program that **leaks information**, making this information accessible to unintended people or programs

It is, of course, possible to invent a new program and install it on a computing system. Inadequate control over the programs that are installed on and run on a computing system permit this kind of software security breach.

Software Theft

This attack includes unauthorized copying of software. Software authors and distributors are entitled to fair compensation for use of their product, as are musicians or book authors. Unauthorized copying of software has not been stopped satisfactorily, although several steps in this direction are described in Chapter 10.

Attacks on Data: A Special Concern

Hardware security is usually the concern of a relatively small staff of computing center professionals. Software security is a larger problem, extending to all programmers and analysts who create or modify programs. Computer programs are written in a dialect intelligible primarily to computer professionals, so that a "leaked" source listing of a program would be meaningless to the general public.

Printed data, however, can be readily interpreted by the general public. Because of its public nature, data attack is a more widespread and serious problem than either hardware or software attack. Thus, data items have a greater public value than hardware and software, because more people know how to use or interpret data.

Data has essentially no intrinsic value. For this reason, it is hard to measure the value of data. However, data does have a cost, perhaps measurable by the cost to reconstruct or redevelop lost data. Confidential data leaked to a competitor may narrow a competitive edge. Finally, inadequate security may lead to a financial liability if certain personal data is made public. Thus, data has a definite value, although that value is often difficult to measure.

Both hardware and software have a relatively long life, with a gradual decline in value over that time. The value of data may be high, but some data items are of interest only for a short period of time. Consider the following example.

Government analysts periodically generate data on the national economy; the results will be released to the public at a predetermined time and date. Prior to that time, access to the data could allow someone to profit from advance knowledge of the probable effect of the data on the stock market. Suppose the analysts develop the data 24 hours before its release, and they wish to communicate their results to other analysts for independent verification prior to release. A protection scheme expected to take an outsider more than 24 hours to break is adequate for this data, since after 24 hours there is no further need for confidentiality.

Study of the security of data raises the second principle of computer security.

Principle of Timeliness.   Computer items need to be protected only until they lose their value.

This principle says that things that have a short life can be protected with security measures that are effective only for that short lifetime. This principle applies primarily to data, since it is the element in computer security that usually has the shortest life.

Figure 1.4 shows three factors of the security of data: **secrecy** (preventing unauthorized disclosure), **integrity** (preventing unauthorized modification), and **availability** (preventing denial of authorized access).

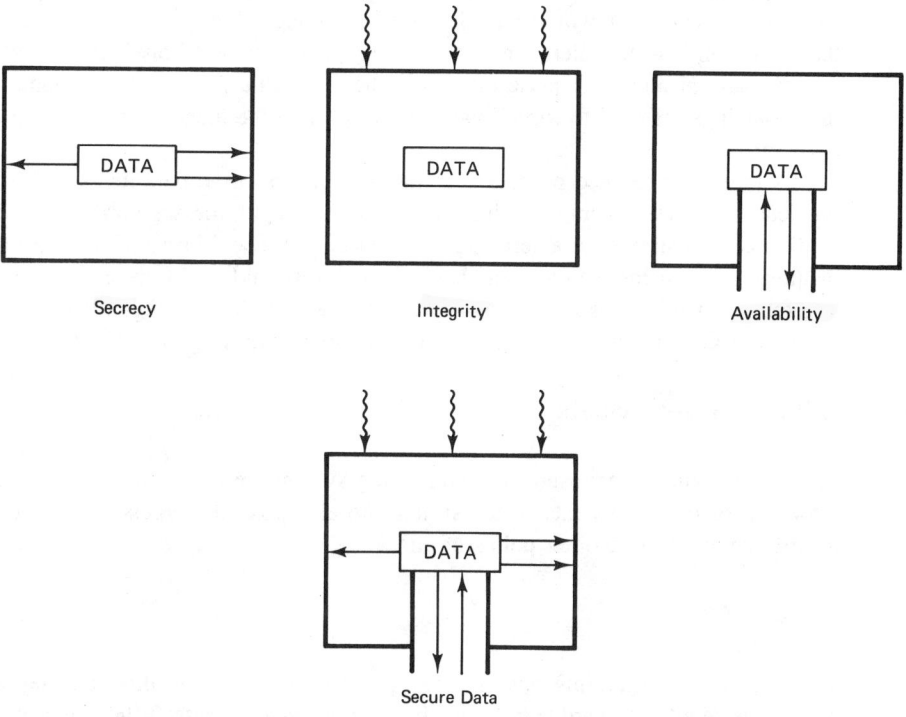

Figure 1.4   Security of Data.

Data Secrecy

Data can be gathered by tapping wires, planting bugs in output devices, sifting through trash receptacles, monitoring electromagnetic radiation, bribing key employees, inferring one data point from other values, or simply requesting it. Because data is often available in a form humans can read, the secrecy of data is a major concern in computer security.

Data Integrity

Stealing or buying or finding or hearing data requires no computer sophistication, while modifying or making new data requires an understanding of the technology by which the data is transmitted or stored, as well as the format in which the data is maintained. Thus, a higher level of sophistication is needed to modify existing data or to fabricate new data than to intercept existing data. The most frequent sources of this kind of problem are malicious programs, errant file system utilities, or flawed communication facilities.

Data is especially vulnerable to modification. Small and skillfully-done modifications may not be detected in ordinary ways. For example, a criminal could write a program to reduce the value of interest paid on a bank's savings accounts by one cent per customer, and then credit the collected pennies to one particular account. It is unlikely that a customer would calculate interest independently, and even more unlikely that a customer would alert the bank to a suspected error of one cent. This attack is called a **salami** attack, because the crook shaves a little from many accounts and puts these shavings together to form a valuable result, like the meat scraps joined together in a salami.

A more complicated process is trying to reprocess used data items. With telecommunications between banks, a fabricator might intercept a message ordering one bank to credit a certain amount to a certain person's account. The fabricator might try to **replay** that message, causing the receiving bank to think it should credit the same account again. The fabricator might also try to modify the message slightly, changing the account to be credited or the amount, and then transmit this revised message.

Other Exposed Assets

The major points of exposure in a computing system are hardware, software, and data. However, other components of the system are also possible targets. In this section we identify some of these other points of attack.

Storage Media

The storage media holding data are also potential loss points, although they are more often considered with hardware, since they are physical objects. Effective security plans consider adequate backups of data and physical protection for the media containing these backups.

Networks

Networks are really collections of hardware, software, and data, the three fundamental assets of computing systems. Each node of the network is a computing system with all the normal security problems. To these, a network adds the problems of communication, which may be via a very exposed medium, and access from distant, and potentially untrustable, computing systems.

Networks simply multiply the problems of computer security. Lack of physical proximity, use of insecure, shared media, and need to identify remote users are all security problems that are made more difficult in computer networks.

Access

Another exposure is access to computing equipment. First, the intruder may steal computer time just to do computing. Theft of computer services is analogous to theft of electricity or any other utility; the value of the services stolen may be substantially higher than electricity, however. This unpaid access spreads the true costs of maintaining the computing system to the other legitimate users. Second, malicious access to a computing system can destroy software or data. Finally, unauthorized access may deny service to a legitimate user. For example, a user who has a time-critical task to perform may depend on the availability of the computing system. For all three of these reasons, unauthorized access to a computing system must be prevented.

Key People

Finally, people can be crucial weak points in security. If only one person knows how to use or maintain a particular program, trouble can arise if that person gets sick, has an accident, or leaves. Trusted individuals, such as operators and systems programmers, are usually carefully selected because of their potential ability to affect all computer users.

Summary of Exposures

In this section, the three basic vulnerabilities of computing systems—secrecy, integrity, and availability—have been applied to the assets of a computing system. Problems such as loss of data, leakage of data, theft of services, failure of hardware, and modification of software fit the framework of these three vulnerabilities.

The rest of this book is an analysis of how these vulnerabilities operate, and how they can be controlled. Most controls work on the humans who exploit these vulnerabilities. The next section describes people who pose threats to computer security.

1.4 The People Involved

In TV westerns, the "bad guys" always wore shabby clothes, had mean and sinister looks, and lived in gangs somewhere out of town. By contrast, the sheriff dressed well, stood proud and tall, and was known and respected by everyone in town, not to mention striking fear in the hearts of most criminals.

Some computer criminals, to be sure, are mean and sinister types. Many more wear business suits, have college degrees, and are the pillars of their community. Some are teenagers or college students. Others are middle-aged business executives. Some are mentally deranged, or overtly hostile, or extremely committed to a cause, and they attack computers as a symbol. Others are ordinary people presented with temptation for personal profit, revenge, challenge, advancement, or job security.

Whatever their motivations, computer criminals have access to enormous amounts of hardware, software, and data; they have the potential to cripple much of effective business and government throughout the world.

Let us define "computer crime" as any crime involving or aided by the use of a computer (admittedly a pretty broad definition).

The FBI uniform crime statistics do not separate computer crime from crime of other sorts. Furthermore, many companies do not report computer crime, because of fear of damage to reputation, because of shame, or because of an agreement not to prosecute if the criminal will "go away." Therefore, dollar estimates of computer crime losses are only vague suspicions. Estimates range from $300 million to $500 billion per year.

Most experts acknowledge that computer security is a major problem, however. Studies have been made to determine characteristics of people who commit computer crime. These studies are intended to help spot likely criminals and prevent crime. Here are some of the kinds of people who commit computer crimes.

Amateurs

Amateurs have committed most of the computer crimes reported to date. Most embezzlers are not career criminals but are normal people who observe a flaw in a security system that allows them access to cash or other valuables. In the same sense most computer criminals are ordinary computer professionals or users, doing their jobs, when they discover they have access to something valuable.

When nobody objects to private use of computing facilities, the amateur may start using the computer at work to write letters, maintain soccer league team standings, or do accounting. The situation may expand until the employee is carrying on a business in accounting, stock portfolio management, or desktop publishing on the side, using the employer's computing facilities. Alternately, amateurs may become disgruntled over a negative work situation (such as a reprimand or denial of a promotion) and vow to "get even" with management by wreaking havoc on a computing installation.

The problem with amateur computer criminals is that there is very little in their background or profile that would lead one to suspect them.

Hackers, Crackers, Whiz Kids

System hackers are usually university or high school students who attempt to access computing facilities for which they have not been authorized. A common thread is that these people tend to have few friends and have trouble developing relationships. They are usually very intelligent but are unable to express themselves verbally with other people. They turn to computers instead of people. They know computers will not reject them, and so computers provide them with social gratification. Bulletin board communication with other similar people is another form of social relationship, but it is one behind an electronic wall, safe and secure.

Cracking a computer's defenses is seen as the ultimate victimless crime. Nobody is hurt, or even endangered, by stealing a little machine time, or even trying to log on, just to see if it can be done. Most cracking can be done without confronting anybody, not even a human voice. In the absence of explicit warnings not to trespass in a system, hackers infer that access is permitted. A network of hackers helps to pass along secrets of success; as with a jigsaw puzzle, a few isolated pieces joined together may produce a large effect. The news media have reduced the public perception of the seriousness of hacking to the level of a harmless childhood prank.

Hacking and cracking are serious offenses that have caused millions of dollars in damages. They are prosecuted seriously with harsh penalties. They continue to be appealing crimes, however, especially to juveniles.

Career Criminals

By contrast, the career computer criminal understands the targets of computer crime. The career computer criminal seldom changed fields from arson, murder, or auto theft to computing; more frequently he or she started as a computer professional who engaged in computer crime, and found the prospects and the payoff good.

As mentioned earlier, some companies are reticent to prosecute computer criminals; in fact, after having discovered a computer crime, the companies are often thankful if the criminal will quietly resign. The criminal is then free to continue the same illegal pattern with another company.

1.5 Methods of Defense

Computer crime is certain to continue. The goal of computer security is to institute controls that preserve secrecy, integrity, and availability. Sometimes these controls are able to prevent attacks; other less powerful methods can only detect a breach as or after it occurs.

Controls

In this section we will survey the controls that attempt to prevent exploitation of the vulnerabilities of computing systems.

Encryption

The most powerful tool in providing computer security is coding. By transforming data so that it is unintelligible to the outside observer, the value of an interception and the possibility of a modification or a fabrication are almost nullified.

Encryption provides secrecy for data. Additionally, encryption can be used to achieve integrity, since data that cannot be read generally also cannot be changed. Furthermore, encryption is important in protocols, which are agreed-upon sequences of actions to accomplish some task. Some protocols ensure availability of resources. Thus, encryption is at the heart of methods for ensuring all three goals of computer security.

Encryption is an important tool in computer security, but one should not overrate its importance. Users must understand that encryption does not solve all computer security problems. Furthermore, if encryption is not used properly, it can have no effect on security or can, in fact, degrade the performance of the entire system. Thus, it is important to know the situations in which encryption is useful and to use it effectively.

Software Controls

Programs themselves are the second link in computer security. Programs must be secure enough to exclude outside attack. They must also be developed and maintained so that one can be confident of the dependability of the programs.

Program controls include the following kinds of things:

1. *Development controls,* which are standards under which a program is designed, coded, tested, and maintained

2. *Operating system controls,* which are limitations enforced by the operating system to protect each user from all other users

3. *Internal program controls* that enforce security restrictions, such as access limitations in a data base management program

Software controls may use tools such as hardware components, encryption, or information gathering. Software controls generally affect users directly, and so they are often the first aspects of computer security that come to mind. Because they influence the way users interact with a computing system, software controls must be carefully designed. Ease of use and potency are often competing goals in the design of software controls.

Hardware Controls

Numerous hardware devices have been invented to assist in computer security. These devices range from hardware implementations of encryption to locks limiting access to theft protection to devices to verify users' identities.

Policies

Some controls on computing systems are achieved through added hardware or software features, as described above. Other controls are matters of policy. In fact, some of the simplest controls, such as frequent changes of passwords, can be achieved at essentially no cost but with tremendous effect.

Legal and ethical controls are an important part of computer security. The law is slow to evolve, and the technology involving computers has emerged suddenly. Although legal protection is necessary and desirable, it is not as dependable in this area as it would be in more well-understood and long-standing crimes.

The area of computer ethics is likewise unclear, not that computer people are unethical, but rather that society in general and the computing community in particular have not adopted formal standards of ethical behavior. Some organizations are attempting to devise codes of ethics for computer professionals. Although these are important, before codes of ethics become widely accepted and therefore effective, the computing community and the general public need to understand what kinds of behavior are inappropriate and why.

Physical Controls

Some of the easiest, most effective, and least expensive controls are physical controls. Physical controls include locks on doors, guards at entry points, backup copies of important software and data, and physical site planning that reduces the risk of natural disasters. Often the simple physical controls are overlooked while more sophisticated approaches are sought.

Effectiveness of Controls

Merely having controls does no good unless they are used properly. The next section contains a survey of some factors that affect the effectiveness of controls.

Awareness of Problem

People using controls must be convinced of the need for security; people will willingly cooperate with security requirements only if they understand why security is appropriate in each specific situation. Many users, however, are unaware of the need for security, especially in situations in which a group has recently undertaken a computing task that was previously performed by a central computing department.

Likelihood of Use

Of course, no control is effective unless it is used. The lock on a computer room door does no good if people block the door open. During World War II code clerks used outdated codes because they had already learned them and could encode messages rapidly. Unfortunately, the opposite side had already broken some of those codes and could decode those messages easily.

Principle of Effectiveness.   Controls must be used to be effective. They must be efficient, easy to use, and appropriate.

This principle implies that computer security controls must be efficient enough, in terms of time, memory space, human activity, or other resources used, so that using the control does not seriously affect the task being protected. Controls should be selective so that they do not exclude legitimate accesses.

Overlapping Controls

Several different controls may apply to one exposure. For example, security for a micro-computer application may be provided by a combination of controls on program access to the data, on physical access to the microcomputer and storage media, and even by file locking to control access to the processing programs. This situation is shown in Figure 1.5.

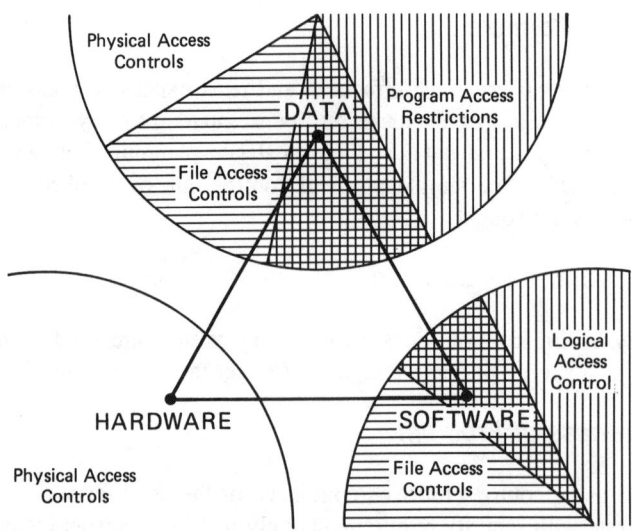

Figure 1.5   Overlapping Controls.

Periodic Review

Few controls are permanently effective. Just when the security specialist finds a way to secure assets against certain kinds of attacks, the opposition doubles its efforts in an effort to defeat the security mechanism. Thus, judging the effectiveness of a control is an ongoing task.

1.6 Plan of Attack

This book is a study of all aspects of security in computing. By studying it, you will become acquainted with the major problem areas of computer security, the controls that are effective against those problems, and the directions of current study in computer security.

This book has four parts that span the field of computer security. The first part of the book is an analysis of encryption. Encryption is defined, several different methods of encryption are explained, and the strengths and weaknesses of those methods are presented. The second part contains material on the hardware and software components of computing systems, the types of problems to which each is subject, and the kinds of protection that can be implemented for each component. The third part continues the study of hardware and software components by considering communications systems between computers and network systems. Finally, the fourth part of the book contains an analysis of the factors outside the hardware, software, and data of the system. The fourth part contains a study of physical factors in security and characteristics of the humans that use the system.

Following is a brief description of the contents of each of these parts.

Encryption

In the next two chapters you will study the techniques of data encryption, beginning with simple encryption methods and progressing to the current standard practices in the field. Then in the following chapter you will study different protocols, which are algorithms or procedures that use encryption to accomplish certain higher-level security goals.

Security in Single-Computer Systems

In the second part of this book, you will consider general programs, operating systems, data base management systems, and personal computers. The security problems and features of programs are introduced in Chapter 5.

Operating systems play a major role in security, since they are fundamental to the use of computers. Operating systems both provide security features to protect one user from another and introduce security vulnerabilities themselves. Chapter 6 addresses the security facilities for users, and Chapter 7 presents security consideration for the design of operating systems.

Data base management systems are really applications programs that also permit many users to share access to one common set of data. These systems are partially responsible for the secrecy, integrity, and availability of the shared data. In this way, they have characteristics both of user programs and of operating systems. These issues are described in Chapter 8.

Part two concludes with a study of the security aspects of personal computers, particularly the programs that run on personal computers, particularly the programs that run on personal computers. The chapter will show why personal computers lack many of the security features of multiuser mainframe computers.

Security in Multi-Computer Systems

The third part of the book is concerned with computer networks. The basis developed in the second part of this book extends naturally to the third. In one sense, a system of several computers is like a single computer system: It still contains hardware, software, data, and the connections between them. However, the connections become harder to secure as the distances between components extend from inches to miles, and as the responsibility shifts from a single person to several unrelated organizations.

Chapters 10 and 11 contain material on security problems and solutions particular to computer networks. Chapter 10 addresses computer networks, and Chapter 11 covers the communications media by which networked computers are connected.

Human Factors in Security

The first three parts of this book form a progression from security tools to security in complex multi-user, multi-computer systems. The security methods described are rather sophisticated. However, most security problems of computing systems are caused either by human or by environmental factors. Thus, another approach to computer security is to treat the causes (humans and the environment) rather than the symptoms (attacks and vulnerabilities). The fourth part of this book describes procedures that can be implemented in spite of, or in addition to, any controls built into hardware and software.

Chapter 12 is about some of the different hardware and software components that can be purchased to enhance computer security. That chapter also explains physical security mechanisms that can be used to protect computing systems against human attacks or natural disasters.

In Chapter 13, the topic of managing computer security is introduced. By using the technique of risk analysis, it is possible to identify the most serious vulnerabilities of a computing system and to select the controls that will provide the greatest improvement in security.

Finally, Chapters 14 and 15 consider the human controls of law and ethics. Although computer law is a relatively new field, its use is evolving rapidly, and it is an important tool in the defense of computing systems. Ethics covers some situations where the law is ineffective or inappropriate.

Thus, the organization of this book is from basic tools; through single-user computations, multi-user systems, and multi-system systems; and finally to human and environmental factors that apply to the gamut of computer configurations. The book raises the important problems of computer security, shows some solutions that are known, and tries to identify work in progress.

Computer security is a relatively new field. It seems as if each advance in computing has brought new security problems. In a sense, this is true. However, a more optimistic view of the field is appropriate. The fundamental work in security provides tools (such as encryption and operating system features) that form the basis of controls for these new problems as the problems arise. Part of the challenge and excitement of computer security is that new problems arise continually.

1.7 Summary

Computer security is assuring the secrecy, integrity, and availability of components of computing systems. The three principal pieces of a computing system subject to attacks are hardware, software, and data. These three pieces, and the communications between them, constitute the basis of computer security vulnerabilities. This chapter has identified four kinds of attacks on computing systems: interruption, interception, modification, and fabrication.

Three principles affect the direction of work in computer security. By the principle of easiest penetration, a computing system penetrator will use whatever means of attack is the easiest; therefore, all aspects of computing system security need to be considered at once. By the principle of timeliness, a system needs to be protected against penetration only long enough so that penetration is of no value to the penetrator. The principle of effectiveness states that controls must be usable and used in order to serve their purpose.

Controls can be applied at the levels of data, programs, the system, physical devices, communications links, the environment, and personnel. Sometimes several controls are needed to cover a single vulnerability, and sometimes one control addresses several problems at once.

1.8 Terms Used

The following list includes some terms that may be new to the reader, as well as the major concepts introduced in this chapter. Although they will be expanded upon in future chapters, it is good to begin now to learn the terms and the underlying concepts.

risks of security
countermeasures
computing system
threat
vulnerability
attack
control
principle of weakest point
penetration
interruption of flow
interception
modification of transmission
message fabrication
hardware attack
physical security
attack on software
software deletion
software modification
configuration management

logic bomb
Trojan horse
trapdoor
software theft
principle of timeliness
secrecy
integrity
availability
data interception
loss of data
data fabrication
data modification
leakage of data
salami attack
replay
computer crime
hacker or cracker
encryption/decryption
network
software control
operating system
data base management system
file controller
security device
procedural control
legal control
ethical control
backup
contingency plan
access limitation
principle of usability

1.9 Exercises

1. Distinguish between a vulnerability, a threat, and a control.

2. Describe two examples of vulnerabilities of automobiles for which auto manufacturers have instituted controls. Tell whether you think these controls are effective, somewhat effective, or ineffective.

3. One control against accidental software deletion is to save all old versions of a program. This control, of course, is prohibitively expensive in terms of cost of storage. Suggest a less costly control against accidental software deletion. Is your

control effective against all possible causes of software deletion? If not, what threats does it not cover?

4. On a typical mainframe computing system (for example, a central computing system at a university or an industry) who can modify the code (software) of the operating system? Of a major applications program, such as a payroll program or a statistical analysis package? Of a program developed and run by a single user? Who should be able to modify each of these examples of code?

5. Suppose a program to print paychecks secretly leaks a list of names of employees earning more than a certain amount each month. What controls could be instituted to limit the vulnerability of this leakage?

6. Preserving secrecy, integrity, and availability of data is a restatement of the concern over interruption, interception, modification, and fabrication. How do the first three concepts relate to the last four? That is, is any of the four equivalent to one or more of the three? Is a concern from the three encompassed by one or more of the four?

7. Describe an example (other than the one mentioned in this chapter) of data whose secrecy has a short timeliness, say a day or less. Describe an example of data whose secrecy has a timeliness of over a year.

8. Describe an example where absolute denial of service to a user (that is, the user gets no response from the computer) is a serious problem to that user. Describe another example where 10 percent denial of service to a user (that is, the user's computation progresses, but at a rate 10 percent slower than normal) is a serious problem to that user. Could access by unauthorized persons to a computing system result in a 10 percent denial of service to the legitimate users? How?

2

Basic Encryption and Decryption

Suppose we have a message to communicate, but our message might fall into the wrong hands. By using encryption we disguise the message so that even if the transmission is diverted, the message will not be revealed. Encryption is a means of maintaining secure data in an insecure environment. In this chapter you will learn the basic principles of encryption. Two basic methods of encryption—substitution and transposition—will be introduced. Along with these, you will study the analysis techniques used to reveal encrypted data.

This chapter contains a discussion of many aspects of encryption, including several examples of encryption systems and the theoretical foundations of encryption. Not all of this material has direct bearing on computer security. However, studying some of the classical methods of encryption can make it easier to learn the more complex forms that are useful in computing.

2.1 Terminology and Background

Suppose S wants to send a message to R; we will call S the **sender** and R the **receiver**. S entrusts the message to T, who will deliver it to R; T then becomes the **transmission medium**. If an outsider, O, wants the message and tries to obtain access to the message, we will call O an **interceptor** or **intruder**. Any time after S transmits it via T, the message is exposed, so O might try to access the message in any of the following ways:

- *interrupt* it, by preventing its reaching R, thereby affecting the availability of the message

- *intercept* it, by being able to see or listen to the message, thereby affecting the secrecy of the message

- *modify* it, by seizing the message and changing it in some way

- *fabricate* an authentic-looking message, arranging for it to be delivered as if it came from S, thereby affecting the integrity of the message

Notice that this list is just a restatement of the four possible failures of security listed in Chapter 1. Encryption is a technique to address all three of these problems.

Terminology

Encryption is a process of encoding a message so that the meaning of the message is not obvious; **decryption** is the reverse process: transforming an encrypted message back into its normal form. Alternately, the terms **encode** and **decode** or **encipher** and **decipher** are used instead of the verbs encrypt and decrypt.[1] A system for encryption and decryption is called a **cryptosystem**.

Encryption Algorithms

The original form of a message is known as **plaintext,** and the encrypted form is called **ciphertext**. This situation is shown in Fig 2.1. For convenience in explanations, we may denote a plaintext message P as a sequence of individual characters $P = [p_1, p_2, \ldots, p_n]$; similarly ciphertext can be written as $C = [c_1, c_2, \ldots, c_m]$. Formally, the transformations between plaintext and ciphertext are denoted $C = E(P)$ and $P = D(C)$, where C represents the ciphertext, E is the encryption algorithm, P is the plaintext, and D is the decryption algorithm. Obviously, we want a cryptosystem for which $P = D(E(P))$.

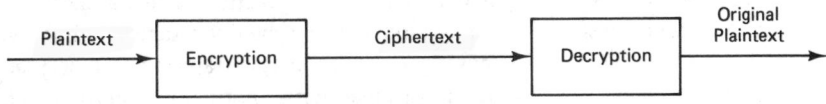

Figure 2.1   Encryption.

Some encryption algorithms use a **key** K, so that the ciphertext message depends on both the original plaintext message and the key value, denoted $C = E(K, P)$. Essentially, E is a *set* of encryption algorithms, and the key K selects one specific algorithm. Sometimes the encryption and decryption keys are the same, so that $P = D(K, E(K, P))$. Other times encryption and decryption keys come in pairs. Then a decryption key, K_D,

---

[1]   There are slight differences in the meanings of these three pairs of words, although they are not significant in this context. Strictly speaking, **encoding** is the process of translating entire words or phrases to other words or phrases, while **enciphering** is translating letters or symbols individually; **encryption** is the group term that covers both encoding and enciphering.

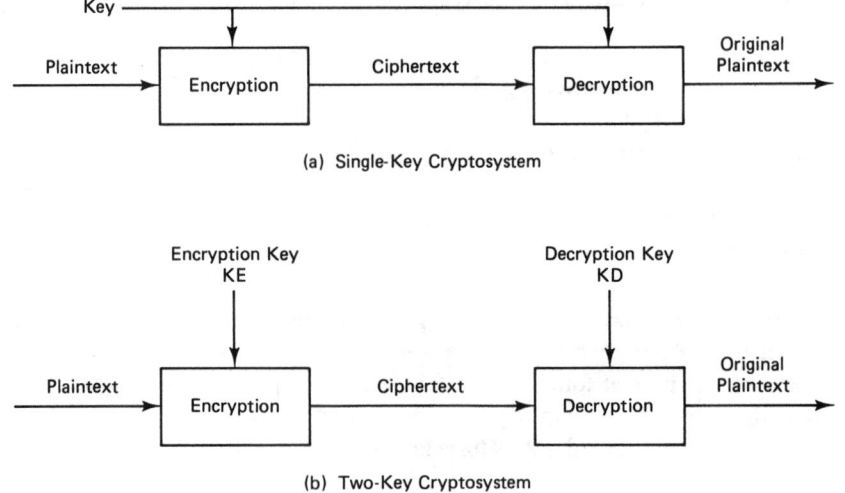

(a) Single-Key Cryptosystem

(b) Two-Key Cryptosystem

Figure 2.2   Encryption with keys.

inverts the encryption of key K_E, so that $P = D(K_D, E(K_E, P))$. These two cases are shown in Figure 2.2.

A key allows different encryptions of one plaintext message just by changing the key. Use of a key provides additional security. If the encryption algorithm should fall into the interceptor's hands, future messages can still be kept secret because the interceptor will not know the key value. A cipher that does not require the use a key is called a **keyless cipher**.

Cryptography means hidden writing, the practice of using encryption to conceal text. A **cryptanalyst** studies encryption and encrypted messages, with the goal of finding the hidden meanings of the messages. Both a cryptographer and a cryptanalyst attempt to translate coded material to its original form; normally a cryptographer works on behalf of a legitimate sender or receiver, while a cryptanalyst works on behalf of an unauthorized interceptor. Finally, **cryptology** is the research into and study of encryption and decryption; it includes both cryptography and cryptanalysis.

Cryptanalysis

A cryptanalyst's chore is to **break** an encryption; this means that the cryptanalyst will attempt to deduce the meaning of a ciphertext message, or to determine a decrypting algorithm that matches an encrypting algorithm. The analyst can do any or all of three different things:

1. attempt to break a single message

2. attempt to recognize patterns in encrypted messages, in order to be able to break subsequent ones by applying a straightforward decryption algorithm

3. attempt to find general weaknesses in an encryption algorithm, without necessarily having intercepted any messages

An analyst works with encrypted messages, known encryption algorithms, intercepted plaintext, data items known or suspected to be in a ciphertext message, mathematical or statistical tools and techniques, properties of languages, computers, and plenty of ingenuity and luck.

Breakable Encryption

An encryption algorithm may be **breakable**, meaning that given enough time and data, an analyst could determine the algorithm. However, practicality is also an issue. A particular cipher scheme may have an inverse deciphering scheme that requires 10^{30} operations. On a current-technology computer performing on the order of 10^{10} operations per second, this decipherment would require 10^{20} seconds, or roughly 10^{12} years. In this case, although we know that theoretically a deciphering algorithm exists, the deciphering algorithm can be ignored as infeasible using current technology.

Note two things about the breakability of encryption algorithms. First, the cryptanalyst cannot be expected to try just the hard, long way. In the example above, the obvious decryption might require 10^{30} machine operations, but a more ingenious approach might require only 10^{15} operations. At the speed of 10^{10} operations per second, 10^{15} operations take slightly more than one day. The ingenious approach is certainly feasible. Some of the algorithms we will study are based on known "hard" problems. But, the cryptanalyst does not necessarily have to solve the underlying problem to break the encryption of a single message.

Second, estimates of breakability are based on current technology. An enormous advance in the technology of computers has occurred within the last forty years. Things that were infeasible in 1940 became possible in the mid 1950s, and every succeeding decade has brought greater improvements. Operating characteristics of computers, such as numbers of operations per second and numbers of bits stored, have regularly increased by an order of magnitude every few years. It is risky to pronounce an algorithm secure just because it cannot be broken with *current* technology.

Representation of Characters

Ultimately we will want to study ways of encrypting any computer material, whether it is ASCII or EBCDIC characters, binary data, object code, or a control stream. However, to simplify the explanations, we will begin with the encryption of messages written in the standard English[2] alphabet,

$$A \ldots Z.$$

---

[2]   Because this book is written in English, the explanations will refer to English. However, with slight variations, the techniques are applicable to most other written languages as well.

In this chapter plaintext will usually be written in uppercase letters, while ciphertext will be in lowercase.

Most encryption algorithms are mathematical in nature, or can be explained or studied easily in mathematical form. Therefore, we will switch back and forth between uppercase letters and the numeric encoding of each letter as shown here.

letter:	A	B	C	D	E	F	G	H	I	J	K	L	M
code:	0	1	2	3	4	5	6	7	8	9	10	11	12

letter:	N	O	P	Q	R	S	T	U	V	W	X	Y	Z
code:	13	14	15	16	17	18	19	20	21	22	23	24	25

This representation allows arithmetic to be performed on letters. Addition and subtraction on letters will be performed on the corresponding code number. Expressions such as $A + 3 = D$ or $K - 1 = J$ have their natural interpretation. Arithmetic is performed as if the alphabetic table were circular. That is, addition wraps around from one end of the table to the other, so that $Y + 3 = B$. Thus, every result is between 0 and 25.

This form of arithmetic is called **modular arithmetic**, written mod n, which means that any result greater than n is reduced by n as many times as necessary to bring it back into the range $0 \leq result < n$. Another way to obtain this result is to use the remainder after dividing the number by n. The value of 95 mod 26 is the remainder of 95/26, which is 17, while $95 - 26 - 26 - 26 = 17$; alternately, starting at position 0 (A) and counting ahead 95 positions (and returning to position 0 each time after passing position 25) also arrives at position 17.

The remainder of this chapter concentrates on two forms of encryption: **substitutions**, where one letter is exchanged for another, and **transpositions**, where the order of the letters is rearranged. The goal of studying those two forms of encryption is to become familiar with the concept of encryption and decryption, to learn some of the terminology and methods of cryptanalysis, and to study some of the weaknesses to which encryption is prone. The chapter concludes with a discussion of characteristics of good encryption algorithms.

2.2 Monoalphabetic Ciphers (Substitutions)

Children sometimes devise "secret codes" that use a correspondence table with which to substitute each character by another character or symbol. Such a technique is called a **monoalphabetic cipher** or a **simple substitution**. A substitution is an acceptable way of encrypting text. In this section we study several kinds of monoalphabetic ciphers.

The Caesar Cipher

The **Caesar cipher** is named for Julius Caesar, said to be the first to employ it. In the Caesar cipher, each letter is translated to the letter a fixed number of letters after it in the alphabet. Caesar used a shift of 3, so that plaintext letter p_i was enciphered as ciphertext letter c_i by the rule

$$c_i = E(p_i) = p_i + 3.$$

A full translation chart of the Caesar cipher is shown below.

plaintext letter: `ABCDEFGHIJKLMNOPQRSTUVWXYZ`
ciphertext letter: `defghijklmnopqrstuvwxyzabc`

Using this encryption, the message

`TREATY IMPOSSIBLE`

would be encoded as

`TREATY IMPOSSIBLE`
`wuhdwb lpsrvvleoh`

Advantages and Disadvantages of the Caesar Cipher

Early ciphers had to be easy to perform in the field. Any cipher that was so complicated that its algorithm had to be written out was at risk of being revealed if the interceptor caught a sender with the written instructions. Then the interceptor could readily decode any ciphertext messages intercepted (until the encryption algorithm could be changed).

The Caesar cipher is quite a simple cipher. (Remember that in the era of Julius Caesar, anything written, even in plaintext, was rather well protected, because few people could read.) The pattern $p_i + 3$ was easy to memorize; a sender in the field could write out a plaintext and a ciphertext alphabet, encode a message to be sent, and then destroy the paper containing the alphabets.

That obvious pattern is also the major weakness of the Caesar cipher. A secure encryption should not have the characteristic that an interceptor can use a little piece to predict the entire pattern of the encryption.

Cryptanalysis of the Caesar Cipher

Look at the result of the encryption. Clues from the plaintext shine through, like the break between the two words, the `SS` which is translated to `vv`, and the repeated letters `T`, `I`, and `E`, which always translate to `w`, `l`, and `h`. These clues make this cipher easy to break.

Suppose you were trying to break the following ciphertext message.

`wklv phvvdjh lv qrw wrr kdug wr euhdn`

The message has actually been enciphered with a 27-symbol alphabet—A through Z and the "blank" character or separator between words. Worst of all, the blank h is been translated to itself! This is an exceptional piece of information, because it shows which are the small words. (In encryption, spaces between words often are deleted, under the assumption that a legitimate receiver can breakmostmessagesintowordsfairlyeasily. For ease of writing and decoding, messages are often then arbitrarily broken into blocks of a uniform size, such as every five characters, so that it is clear to an interceptor that there is no significance to the places where the message is broken.)

In English there are relatively few small words, such as "am", "is", "to", "be", "he", "we", …, and "and", "are", "you", "she", and so on. Therefore, one attack is to substitute known short words at appropriate places in the ciphertext and try substituting for matching characters other places in the ciphertext.

A stronger clue is the repeated r in the word wrr. Two very common three-letter words having the pattern *xyy* are "see" and "too"; other less common possibilities are "add", "odd", and "off". (Of course, there are also obscure possibilities like "woo" or "gee", but it makes more sense to try the common cases first.)

If wrr is SEE, wr would have to be SE, which is unlikely, but if wrr is TOO, wr would be TO, which is quite reasonable. Substituting T for w and O for r, the message becomes

```
wklv phvvdjh lv qrw wrr kdug wr euhdn
T---  -------  --  -OT TOO ----  TO  -----
```

The -OT could be "cot" or "dot" or "got" or "hot" or "lot" or "not" or "pot" or "rot" or "tot"; a likely choice is "not". Unfortunately, q = N does not give any more clues, since q appears only once in this sample.

The word lv is also the end of the word wklv, which probably starts with T. Likely two-letter words that can also end a longer word include SO, IS, IN, etc. However, SO is unlikely, since the form T-SO is not recognizable; IN is ruled out because of the previous assumption that q is N. A better approach is to substitute IS for lv throughout, and continue to analyze the message in that way.

The ciphertext letters uncovered are just three positions away from their plaintext counterparts. A cryptanalyst might try that same pattern on all the unmatched ciphertext. The completion of this decryption is left as an exercise.

The cryptanalysis described here is *ad hoc*, using deduction based on guesses instead of solid principles. Another approach is to consider which letters commonly start words, which letters commonly end words, and which prefixes and suffixes are common. Cryptanalysts have published lists of common prefixes, common suffixes, and words having particular patterns (such as "sleeps" is a word that follows the pattern *abccda*). A different analysis technique will be introduced in the next section.

Other Monoalphabetic Substitutions

In monoalphabetic substitutions, the alphabet is scrambled, and each plaintext letter maps to a unique ciphertext letter. Formally, a **permutation** is a reordering of the elements of a series. Two examples of permutations of the numbers 1 to 10 are $\pi_1 = 1, 3, 5, 7, 9, 10, 8, 6, 4, 2$; and $\pi_2 = 10, 9, 8, 7, 6, 5, 4, 3, 2, 1$. A permutation is a function, so we can write $\pi_1(3) = 5$ or $\pi_2(7) = 4$. If $a_1, a_2, \ldots, a_k$ are the letters of the plaintext alphabet, and π is a permutation of the numbers $1, 2, \ldots k$, in a monoalphabetic substitution each c_i is $a_{\pi(p_i)}$.

For example, $\pi(a)$ might be the function $\pi(a) = 25 - a$, so that A would be encoded as z, B as y, and Z would be encoded as a. This permutation is easy to write out from memory, so it could be used in the field. However, each plaintext-ciphertext pair maps both ways: $E(F) = u$ and $E(U) = f$. This double correspondence gives unnecessary aid to the interceptor.

An alternative is to use a **key**, a word that controls the enciphering. If the keyword is *key*, the sender or receiver first writes the alphabet and then writes the key under the first few letters of the alphabet.

```
ABCDEFGHIJKLMNOPQRSTUVWXYZ
key
```

The sender or receiver then fills in the remaining letters of the alphabet, in some easy-to-remember order, after the keyword.

```
ABCDEFGHIJKLMNOPQRSTUVWXYZ
keyabcdfghijlmnopqrstuvwxz
```

In this example, since the key was short, most plaintext letters were only one or two positions off from their ciphertext equivalents. With a longer keyword, the distance is greater and less predictable, as shown below. Since π must map one plaintext letter to exactly one ciphertext letter, duplicate letters in a keyword such as spectacular are dropped.

```
ABCDEFGHIJKLMNOPQRSTUVWXYZ
spectaulrbdfghijkmnoqvwxyz
```

Near the end of the alphabet replacements are rather close, and the last five characters map to themselves. Conveniently, the last characters of the alphabet are among the least frequently used, so that this exposure gives little help to the interceptor.

A less regular rearrangement of the letters is desirable. One possibility is to count by 3s (or 5s or 7s or 9s) and rearrange the letters in that order. For example, one encryption uses a table that starts with

```
ABCDEFGHIJKLMNOPQRSTUVWXYZ
adgj
```

using every third letter. At the end of the alphabet, the pattern continues *mod* 26, as shown below.

```
ABCDEFGHIJKLMNOPQRSTUVWXYZ
adgjmpsvybehknqtwzcfilorux
```

This permutation is $\pi(i) = (3 * i) \bmod 26$. For example, $\pi(\text{K}) = (3 * 10) \bmod 26 = 30 - 26 = 4 = \text{e}$.

Complexity of Monoalphabetic Encryption and Decryption

Encryption and decryption with this algorithm can be performed by direct lookup in a table like the ones above. Transforming a single character can be done in a constant amount of time, so the time to encrypt a message of n characters is proportional to n.

Cryptanalysis of Monoalphabetic Ciphers

The techniques described above for breaking the Caesar cipher can also be used on other monoalphabetic ciphers. Short words, words with repeated patterns, and common initial and final letters all give clues for guessing the permutation.

Of course, this is a lot like working a crossword puzzle: you try a guess, and continue to work to substantiate that guess until you have all the words in place, or until you reach a contradiction. For a long message this process can be extremely tedious. Fortunately there are other approaches.

Frequency Distributions

In English, some letters are used more frequently than others. The letters E, T, and A occur far more frequently than J, Q, and Z, for example. The text being analyzed also affects the distribution. (For example, a medical article in which the term *x-ray* was used often would have an uncommonly high frequency of the letter *x*.)

Table 2.1 shows the counts and relative frequencies of letters in a chapter of a book on computing. These frequencies are quite close to published counts from other sources. The table also shows the counts and relative frequencies of letters from a Pascal source program. Notice that the Pascal frequencies are similar, as one might expect, since Pascal uses English keywords and most variables at least resemble English words.

This table can be used to analyze the following passage of ciphertext.

```
hqfubswlrq lv d phdqv ri dwwdlqlqj vhfxuh frpsxwdwlrq
ryhu lqvhfxuh fkdqqhov
eb xvlqj hqfubswlrq zh glvjxlvh wkh phvvdjh vr wkdw
hyhq li wkh wudqvplvvlrq lv glyhuwhg
wkh phvvdjh zloo qrw eh uhyhdohg
```

The counts shown in Table 2.2 are obtained by counting the frequencies of the letters of the text.

The relative frequencies of these counts are shown in Figure 2.3, where they have been plotted against the relative frequencies from English text in the previous tables. Notice that this plot matches the first closely, except that the second is shifted right by three positions. This encryption used the Caesar cipher.

```
ENCRYPTION IS A MEANS OF ATTAINING SECURE COMPUTATION
OVER INSECURE CHANNELS
BY USING ENCRYPTION WE DISGUISE THE MESSAGE SO THAT
EVEN IF THE TRANSMISSION IS DIVERTED
THE MESSAGE WILL NOT BE REVEALED

hqfubswlrq lv d phdqv ri dwwdlqlqj vhfxuh frpsxwdwlrq
ryhu lqvhfxuh fkdqqhov
eb xvlqj hqfubswlrq zh glvjxlvh wkh phvvdjh vr wkdw
hyhq li wkh wudqvplvvlrq lv glyhuwhg
wkh phvvdjh zloo qrw eh uhyhdohg
```

Table 2.3 shows the counts and relative frequencies of letters in the cipher examined in the previous section.

```
wklv phvvdjh lv qrw wrr kdug wr euhdn
```

TABLE 2.1 LETTER FREQUENCY
DISTRIBUTIONS IN ENGLISH
AND PASCAL.

Letter	English		Pascal	
	Count	Percent	Count	Percent
a	3312	7.49	664	4.70
b	573	1.29	197	1.39
c	1568	3.54	878	6.22
d	1602	3.62	511	3.61
e	6192	14.00	1921	13.60
f	966	2.18	504	3.57
g	769	1.74	294	2.08
h	1869	4.22	478	3.39
i	2943	6.65	1215	8.60
j	119	0.27	6	0.04
k	206	0.47	87	0.61
l	1579	3.57	722	5.11
m	1500	3.39	270	1.91
n	2982	6.74	1157	8.19
o	3261	7.37	835	5
p	1074	2.43	340	2.41
q	116	0.26	12	0.08
r	2716	6.14	1147	8.12
s	3072	6.95	594	4.21
t	4358	9.85	1311	9.28
u	1329	3.00	377	2.66
v	512	1.16	127	0.89
w	748	1.69	193	1.36
x	123	0.28	139	0.98
y	727	1.64	137	0.96
z	16	0.04	5	0.03
ALL	44232		14121	

The message was only 23 letters long, and there were only 13 distinct letters, so there cannot be a great frequency variation. Thus, it is not certain that v, the most frequent ciphertext letter, is E, the most frequently occurring English letter. Counts do help to narrow the possibilities, however. The frequently occurring letters in the ciphertext are likely to be among the more frequently occurring letters in English.

Recall the earlier statement that cryptanalysts are going to try every tool at their disposal and are not necessarily going to attack hard problems to solve encryptions. At face value, monoalphabetic ciphers seem secure, since there are 26! possible different encipherments. By a brute force attack, the cryptanalyst could try all 26! decipherments of a particular ciphertext message. Working at one decipherment per microsecond (assuming the cryptanalyst had the patience to review the probable-looking plaintexts produced by some of the decipherments), it would still take over 10^3 years to test all 26! decipherments.

TABLE 2.2 FREQUENCIES IN EXAMPLE CIPHER.

Letter	Count	Percent	Letter	Count	Percent
a	0	0.00	n	0	0.00
b	3	1.80	o	4	2.41
c	0	0.00	p	5	2.99
d	11	6.59	q	16	9.58
e	2	1.20	r	9	5.39
f	6	3.61	s	3	1.80
g	4	2.40	t	0	0.00
h	26	15.56	u	8	4.79
i	2	1.20	v	17	10.18
j	5	2.99	w	14	8.38
k	5	2.99	x	5	2.99
l	16	9.58	y	4	2.40
m	0	0.00	z	2	1.20
ALL	167				

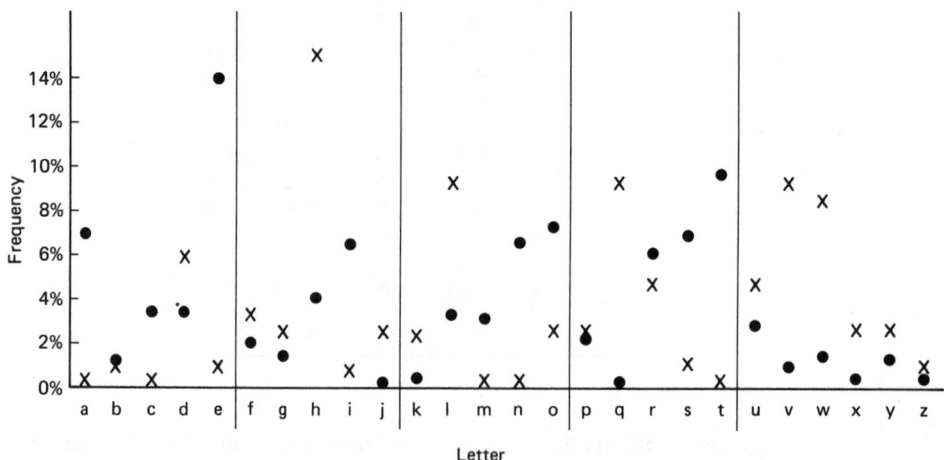

● = English Frequency Distribution

X = Frequency Distribution in Example Cipher

Figure 2.3 Frequencies of Sample Cipher against Normal Text.

However, for messages that are long enough, the frequency distribution analysis betrays quickly many of the letters of the plaintext. In this and other ways, a good cryptanalyst finds easier approaches to bypass hard problems. An encryption based on a hard problem is not secure just because of the difficulty of the problem.

TABLE 2.3 FREQUENCIES OF LETTERS IN
`wklv...` CIPHER.

Letter	Count	Percent	Letter	Count	Percent
w	2	8.70	k	2	8.70
l	2	8.70	v	4	17.39
p	1	4.34	h	2	8.70
d	2	8.70	j	1	4.34
q	1	4.34	r	3	13.04
s	1	4.34	u	1	4.34
g	1	4.34			

The Cryptographer's Dilemma

As with many analysis techniques, having very little ciphertext inhibits the usefulness of the technique. A cryptanalyst works by finding patterns. Short messages give the cryptanalyst little to work with, and so they are fairly secure with even simple encryption.

Monoalphabetic encryption displays the cryptographer's dilemma: An encryption algorithm has to be regular in order for it to be algorithmic and in order for cryptographers to be able to remember it. Unfortunately, the regularity gives clues to the cryptanalyst.

There is no solution to this dilemma. In fact, cryptography/cryptanalysis at times seems like a dog chasing its tail—the cryptographer invents a new encryption algorithm. The cryptanalyst studies the algorithm and finds its patterns and its weaknesses, which the cryptographer then sets out to try to secure by inventing a new algorithm. The principle of timeliness from Chapter 1 applies throughout cryptography: A security measure must be strong enough to keep out the attacker for the life of the data. Data with a short time value can be protected with simple measures.

2.3 Polyalphabetic Substitution Ciphers

The weakness of monoalphabetic ciphers is that their frequency distribution reflects the distribution of the underlying alphabet. A cipher that is more cryptographically secure would display a rather flat distribution, which gives no information to a cryptanalyst.

One way to flatten the distribution is to combine distributions that are high with ones that are low. If T is sometimes enciphered as a and sometimes as b, and if X is also sometimes enciphered as a and sometimes as b, the high frequency of T mixes with the low frequency of X to produce a more moderate distribution for a and b. In Figure 2.4, $E_1(\text{T}) = \text{a}$ and $E_2(\text{T}) = \text{b}$ while $E_1(\text{X}) = \text{b}$ and $E_2(\text{X}) = \text{a}$.

We can combine two distributions by using two separate encryption alphabets, the first for all the characters in odd positions of the plaintext message, the second for all the characters in even positions. This just requires alternating between two translation tables. An example of this technique is shown as follows.

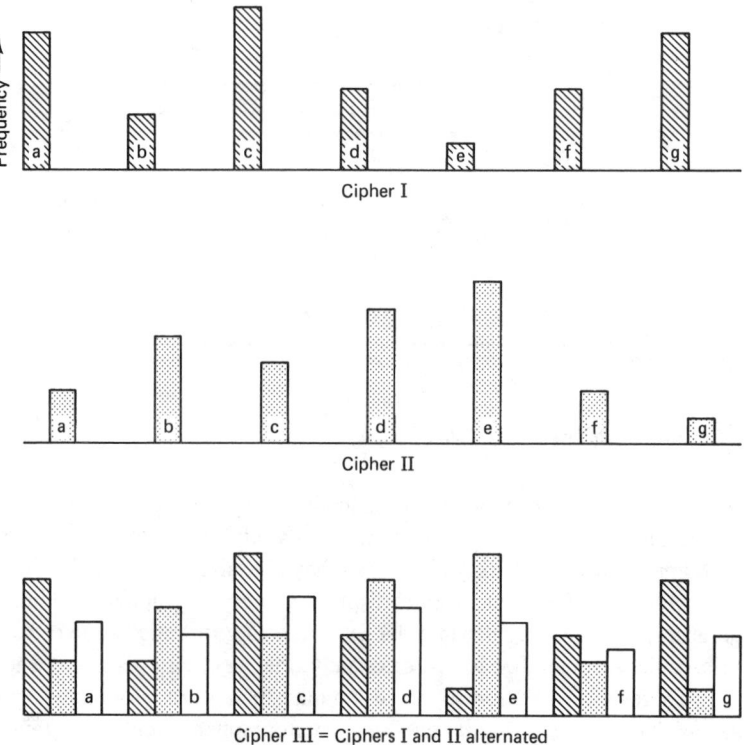

Figure 2.4   Polyalphabetic Substitution.

Suppose the two encryption algorithms are as shown below.

```
ABCDEFGHIJKLMNOPQRSTUVWXYZ
adgjmpsvybehknqtwzcfilorux
```

Table for Odd Positions

```
ABCDEFGHIJKLMNOPQRSTUVWXYZ
nsxchmrwbglqvafkpuzejotydi
```

Table for Even Positions

(The first table uses the permutation $\pi_1(a) = (3 * a) \bmod 26$, while the second uses the permutation $\pi_2(a) = ((5 * a) + 13) \bmod 26$.)

Encryption with these tables would proceed as follows. For the message TREATY IMPOSSIBLE,

```
                    TREAT YIMPO SSIBL E
```

the encryption would be

```
                    fumnf dyvtf czysh h.
```

Notice that the double S becomes cz, and that the two Es are enciphered as m and h, respectively. The two Ts of TREATY happen to encipher to f, and similarly the two Is encipher to ys. On the other hand, the final two hs come from two different letters, L and E. Because of alternating tables, half of the time repeated ciphertext letters are the result of identical plaintext letters, but half of the time not.

Polyalphabetic encryption flattens the frequency distribution of the plaintext considerably. Table 2.4 is the frequency analysis of Dickens' opening paragraph of *A Tale of Two Cities*. ("It was the best of times, it was the worst of times ...”). This example uses two very easy monoalphabetic substitutions. The first substitution is $\pi_1(a) = a$, where each letter goes to itself, and the second is $\pi_2(a) = 25 - a$, where each letter goes to the letter the same distance from the opposite end of the alphabet. The use of a second alphabet smoothes the distribution. Notice that e loses some of its strength to v, while g and h help to dissipate the frequency of s and t.

TABLE 2.4 TWO-ALPHABET ENCRYPTION LETTER FREQUENCIES

Letter	Count	Percent	Letter	Count	Percent
a	14	2.95	n	20	4.22
b	4	0.84	o	25	5.27
c	3	0.63	p	7	1.48
d	17	3.59	q	0	0.00
e	35	7.38	r	39	8.23
f	14	2.95	s	27	5.70
g	31	6.54	t	30	6.33
h	43	9.07	u	10	2.11
i	33	6.96	v	39	8.23
j	0	0.00	w	18	3.80
k	5	1.05	x	3	0.63
l	31	6.54	y	5	1.05
m	7	1.48	z	14	2.95
ALL	474				

Vigenère Tableaux

The distribution of Table 2.4 shows how some of the peaks and valleys of normal frequency distribution can be smoothed by allowing plaintext letters to "share" ciphertext equivalents. Of course, this has to be done in a systematic way so that the receiver can know how to decrypt a message.

The table also shows the effect of the accidental collision of two low-frequency letters, such as J and Q, which both mapped to j and q. The remaining variance in the frequency table, is attributed to the accidental collision of letters of similar high or low frequency.

One approach to this situation is to select any permutation as π_1, and then carefully choose π_2 to complement π_1; if π_1 maps a high frequency letter such as E to x, then π_2

should map a low frequency letter to *x*. This technique requires a little planning, but it is not too difficult.

Another approach is to extend the number of permutations. With three permutations, used in rotation, the chances of a flat distribution increase. But if three permutations are good, four should be better, and five should be great. The ultimate extension is 26 permutations, so that a plaintext letter can be enciphered as any ciphertext letter.

A **Vigenère tableau** is a collection of 26 permutations. Usually these permutations are written as a 26 × 26 matrix, with all 26 letters in each row and each column. Such an arrangement is shown in Table 2.5.

TABLE 2.5   VIGENÈRE TABLEAU

```
columns      0          1          2
         01234567890123456789012345

         abcdefghijklmnopqrstuvwxyz
      A  abcdefghijklmnopqrstuvwxyz   0
      B  bcdefghijklmnopqrstuvwxyza   1
      C  cdefghijklmnopqrstuvwxyzab   2
      D  defghijklmnopqrstuvwxyzabc   3
      E  efghijklmnopqrstuvwxyzabcd   4
      F  fghijklmnopqrstuvwxyzabcde   5
      G  ghijklmnopqrstuvwxyzabcdef   6
      H  hijklmnopqrstuvwxyzabcdefg   7
      I  ijklmnopqrstuvwxyzabcdefgh   8
      J  jklmnopqrstuvwxyzabcdefghi   9
      K  klmnopqrstuvwxyzabcdefghij  10
      L  lmnopqrstuvwxyzabcdefghijk  11
rows  M  mnopqrstuvwxyzabcdefghijkl  12
      N  nopqrstuvwxyzabcdefghijklm  13
      O  opqrstuvwxyzabcdefghijklmo  14
      P  pqrstuvwxyzabcdefghijklmop  15
      Q  qrstuvwxyzabcdefghijklmnop  16
      R  rstuvwxyzabcdefghijklmnopq  17
      S  stuvwxyzabcdefghijklmnopqr  18
      T  tuvwxyzabcdefghijklmnopqrs  19
      U  uvwxyzabcdefghijklmnopqrst  20
      V  vwxyzabcdefghijklmnopqrstu  21
      W  wxyzabcdefghijklmnopqrstuv  22
      X  xyzabcdefghijklmnopqrstuvw  23
      Y  yzabcdefghijklmnopqrstuvwx  24
      Z  zabcdefghijklmnopqrstuvwxy  25
```

plain text   cyphertext

# of chars in keyword =
# of alphabets

Keeping track of which column to use is the principal disadvantage rotating through all 25 permutations. A useful modification is to use a keyword, and let the letters of the keyword select the columns for encipherment.

For example, suppose you want to encipher the message BUT SOFT, WHAT LIGHT THROUGH YONDER WINDOW BREAKS, using the keyword *juliet*. You would write the message and write one character of the keyword above each message character, repeating the keyword as often as necessary.

column
Specify

```
julie tjuli etjul ietju lietj uliet julie tjuli e
BUTSO FTWHA TLIGH TTHRO UGHYO NDERW INDOW BREAK S
```

Specify
row

For reference, assume that the characters in the line of keys have been numbered $k_1, k_2, \ldots, k_n$, to correspond to the letters of the plaintext. Each plaintext letter p_i is then converted to the ciphertext letter in row p_i, column k_i of the tableau. For example, the first letter (B) is converted to the ciphertext letter in row 1 (B), column 9 (j), in this tableau. The letter in that position is k. The encryption of this message starts as shown below.

```
julie tjuli etjul ietju lietj uliet julie tjuli e
BUTSO FTWHA TLIGH TTHRO UGHYO NDERW INDOW BREAK S

koeas ycqsi ...
```

With a six-letter keyword such as *juliet* this algorithm effectively spreads the effect of the frequency of each letter onto six others, which flattens the distribution substantially. Long keywords can be used, but a keyword of length three usually suffices to smooth out the distribution.

Cryptanalysis of Polyalphabetic Substitutions

With a little help from frequency distributions and letter patterns, it is not too difficult to break a monoalphabetic substitution by hand. Therefore, with the aid of computer programs, and with an adequate amount of ciphertext, a good cryptanalyst can break such a cipher in an hour. Even an untrained but diligent interceptor could probably determine the plaintext in a day or so. Nevertheless, in some applications, the prospect of one day's effort, or even the appearance of a sheet full of text that makes no sense, may be enough to protect the message. Encryption, even in a simple form, will deter the casual observer.

As we have seen, polyalphabetic substitutions are apparently more secure than monoalphabetic substitutions. The casual observer has little hope of breaking one without some knowledge of cryptanalysis, and the cryptanalytic tools are tedious enough that use of a computer is necessary for all but the most patient people.

Unfortunately, polyalphabetic substitutions are not immune to breaking. The method to break such an encryption is to determine the number of alphabets employed, break the ciphertext into pieces that were enciphered with the same alphabet, and solve each piece as a monoalphabetic substitution. In fact, there are two powerful tools that can decrypt messages written even with a large number of alphabets. The two tools we will study are the Kasiski method, to determine when a pattern of encrypting permutations has repeated, and the index of coincidence, to predict the number of alphabets used for substitutions.

The Kasiski Method for Repeated Patterns

The **method of Kasiski,** named for its developer, a Prussian military officer, is a way of finding the number of alphabets that were used for encryption.

The method relies again on the regularity of English. Not only letters but also letter groupings and full words are repeated. For example, English uses endings -*th*, -*ing*, -*ed*, -*ion*, -*tion*, -*ation*, beginnings *im*-, *in*-, *un*-, *re*-, and patterns -*eek*-, -*oot*-, -*our*-, and so forth, disproportionately often. Furthermore, words such as *of*, *and*, *to*, *with*, *are*, *is*, and *that* also appear with high frequency.

The Kasiski method follows this rule: If a message is encoded with n alphabets in cyclic rotation, and if a particular word or letter group appears k times in a plaintext message, it should be encoded approximately k/n times from the same alphabet. As an example, if a keyword is six characters long, there are only six different ways to position the keyword over the plaintext word. A plaintext word or letter group that appears more than six times must be encrypted at least twice by the same position of the keyword, and those occurrences will all be enciphered identically.

The Dickens *It was the best of times...* example has much repetition so it will demonstrate this argument quickly. Suppose the keyword is *dickens*.

```
dicke nsdic kensd icken sdick ensdi ckens dicke
ITWAS THEBE STOFT IMESI TWAST HEWOR STOFT IMESI

nsdic kensd icken sdick ensdi ckens dicke nsdic
TWAST HEAGE OFWIS DOMIT WASTH EAGEO FFOOL ISHNE

kensd icken sdick ensdi ckens dicke nsdic kensd
SSITW ASTHE EPOCH OFBEL IEFIT WASTH EEPOC HOFIN
```

The phrase IT WAS THE is enciphered with keyword *nsdicken* once in the first line and twice in the third line. These three cases all appear as identical 8-character patterns in the ciphertext.

The Kasiski approach works on duplicate fragments in the ciphertext. In order for a plaintext phrase to be enciphered the same way twice, the key must have gone through a whole number of rotations and be back at the same point. Therefore, the distance between the repeated patterns must be a multiple of the keyword length.

To use the Kasiski approach, you identify all repeated patterns in the ciphertext. Short repeated patterns, such as two letters, are often accidental, so it is more trouble to consider them than to ignore them. Any pattern over three characters is almost certainly not accidental. (The likelihood of two four-letter sequences *not* being from the same plaintext segment is $1/26^4$, which is approximately 0.0000021).

For each instance of a pattern, you write down its starting position; you then compute the distance between successive starting positions. The distance between repeats must be a multiple of the key length, so you then determine all the factors of each distance.

The three repeated sequences in the example above have the following characteristics.

Starting Position	Distance from Previous	Factors
20	—	—
83	63 (83–20)	3, 7, 9, 21, 63
104	21 (104–83)	3, 7, 21

From this short example, we may guess that a keyword of 21 is improbable. Thus the key length is probably either 3 or 7. With more repeats you could reduce the number of possibilities for key length. Let us continue with the key length possibilities of 3 and 7.

For the Kasiski method, the steps are

1. Identify repeated patterns of three or more characters.

2. For each pattern write down the position at which each instance of the pattern begins.

3. Compute the difference between the starting points of successive instances.

4. Determine all factors of each difference.

5. If a polyalphabetic substitution cipher was used, the key length will be one of the factors that appears often in step 4.

Index of Coincidence

With key length possibilities of 3 and 7, the next step is to try to divide the message into pieces enciphered with the same alphabet. If you want to try the assumption that the key length is 3, for example, you would form sets of the letters 3 positions apart in the ciphertext, $S_1 = \{c_1, c_4, c_7, c_{10}, \cdots\}$, $S_2 = \{c_2, c_5, c_8, c_{11}, \cdots\}$, and $S_3 = \{c_3, c_6, c_9, c_{12}, \cdots\}$. If all characters in one of these sets have been enciphered with the same alphabet, they should have a frequency distribution similar to English, and they should have a distribution similar to the other sets (although with high values at different letters, of course).

The other cryptanalytic tool we will study is a way to rate how well a particular distribution matches the distribution of letters in English. Suppose we have a body of text that we suspect was encrypted with a monoalphabetic substitution. If our suspicion is correct, the frequencies of ciphertext letters should be the same as the frequencies of the corresponding English letters. The **index of coincidence** is a measure of the variation between frequencies in a distribution. (This description follows the lines of Sinkov [SIN66].)

As we have seen, English plaintext has a predictable nonuniform distribution. With a monoalphabetic substitution, this same distribution appears in the ciphertext. With two alphabets, however, high- and low-frequency letters blend, so that high-frequency letters are not as high, and low-frequency letters are not as low. With more alphabets the highs are even less high, and the lows are even less low. Ultimately, if the distributions all blended perfectly, every letter would appear just as often as every other letter.

We will now derive a measure that describes how high are the highs and how low are the lows in any distribution. With this measure we can tell whether a sample is encrypted with just one substitution (monoalphabetic), or with two, or more alphabets. This measure is the index of coincidence. Notice that the index just measures distribution; we do not need to know *which* ciphertext letter matches plaintext a or b.

Let us try to measure the nonuniformity of a distribution. Suppose we pick a letter at random from an English text. From the distribution in Table 2.1, there is a probability of 0.0985 that it is a *t*, or probability of 0.0028 that it is an *x*. In general, let $Prob_a$ be the probability of an *a*, $Prob_b$ of a *b*, ... and $Prob_z$ of a *z*. The random letter is certain to be either an *a*, or a *b*, ..., or a *z*, and so

$$Prob_a + Prob_b + \cdots + Prob_z = \sum_{i=a}^{i=z} Prob_i = 1.$$

We will imagine the graph of a distribution with the letters along the horizontal axis and their relative frequency of occurrence along the vertical axis. For a perfectly flat distribution,

$$Prob_a = Prob_b = Prob_c = \cdots = Prob_z = \frac{1}{26} \simeq 0.0384.$$

The graph of such a distribution would be a horizontal straight line. If a distribution is not flat, the difference between $Prob_a$ and 1/26 is its variance from the flat distribution. The graph of such a distribution would have peaks and valleys at the letters that occur with high and low frequencies, respectively.

Sinkov defines a **measure of roughness**, which is a measure of the size of the peaks and valleys. If $1/26 \simeq 0.0384$ is a baseline, a peak is a relative frequency above 0.0384, while a valley is a relative frequency below 0.0384. The graph of Figure 2.5 shows the roughness of the distribution of English text against 0.0384 as a baseline.

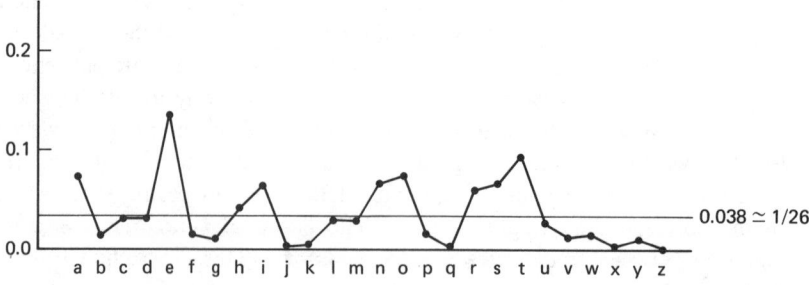

Figure 2.5   Roughness of Distribution of English Text.

The roughness or nonuniformity of a distribution is how much it varies from flat. If $RFreq_a$ is the relative frequency of *a*, $RFreq_a - (1/26)$ is the size of an observed peak or valley for *a*, and $Prob_a - (1/26)$ is its expected size.

We want to compute a measure that shows the nonuniformity of a whole distribution, not individual letters. Because a peak is positive and a valley is negative, simply summing these values would cause peaks to cancel valleys. Using $(Prob_a - (1/26))^2$ prevents these cancellations.

The measure of roughness or variance is then

$$var = \sum_{i=a}^{i=z} \left(Prob_i - \frac{1}{26} \right)^2$$

$$= \sum_{i=a}^{i=z} \left(Prob_i^2 - \frac{2}{26} Prob_i + \left(\frac{1}{26}\right)^2 \right)$$

$$= \sum_{i=a}^{i=z} Prob_i^2 - \frac{2}{26} * \sum_{i=a}^{i=z} Prob_i + \sum_{i=a}^{i=z} \left(\frac{1}{26}\right)^2$$

$$= \sum_{i=a}^{i=z} Prob_i^2 - \frac{2}{26} * 1 + 26 * \left(\frac{1}{26}\right)^2$$

$$= \sum_{i=a}^{i=z} Prob_i^2 - 0.0384$$

If a distribution were perfectly flat, each of the probabilities would be 1/26, and *var* would be $26 * (1/26^2) - 0.0384 = 0.0384 - 0.0384 = 0$. Using the frequencies of Table 2.1 as probabilities gives $var = 0.0680 - 0.0384 = 0.0296$.

Each term in the sum of $Prob_i^2$ is the probability of two events occurring at once: $Prob_i^2$ is the probability that any two given characters from the text will both be i. The variance can be estimated from a sample by counting the number of pairs of identical letters and dividing by the total number of pairs possible.

But we do not know how often a particular letter *ought* to occur without knowing the algorithm from which the letters were generated. We will approximate the probability from observed frequencies.

In an observed sample of n ciphertext letters, suppose there are $Freq_i$ instances of the character i. We want to know the likelihood of picking i twice at random. There are $Freq_i$ ways to choose the first i and $(Freq_i - 1)$ remaining occurrences of i from which to choose the second i. There are thus $Freq_i * (Freq_i - 1)$ ways of choosing the letter i twice. Since the pair (a,b) is the same as the pair (b,a), the product above counts each pair twice. Thus, there are $Freq_i * (Freq_i - 1)/2$ ways to select a pair of *is*. In total, there are $n * (n - 1)/2$ pairs of letters in a ciphertext of n characters.

Therefore,

$$\frac{Freq_i * (Freq_i - 1)}{n * (n - 1)}$$

represents the likelihood that any two letters picked randomly would both be i. But the likelihood of picking the letter i twice is approximately $Prob_i^2$.

The **index of coincidence**, written IC, is a way to approximate variance from observed data.

$$IC = \sum_{i=a}^{i=z} \frac{Freq_i * (Freq_i - 1)}{n * (n - 1)}$$

The index of coincidence ranges from 0.0384, for a polyalphabetic substitution with a perfectly flat distribution, to 0.068, for a monoalphabetic substitution from common English.

If the amount of ciphertext is large and the underlying plaintext has a fairly normal distribution of letters, the index of coincidence can be used to predict the number of alphabets. Table 2.6 shows IC values for several numbers of alphabets used in a polyalphabetic substitution. Notice that the IC drops rapidly from one to three alphabets, but that its change tapers off for many alphabets. The index of coincidence is a good predictor of how many alphabets were used when the number is small, but cannot discriminate well for large number of alphabets.

TABLE 2.6 NUMBER OF ENCIPHERING
ALPHABETS VS. INDEX OF COINCIDENCE.

alphabets	1	2	3	4	5	10	large
IC	.068	.052	.047	.044	.044	.041	.038

the more alphabets used, the smaller the IC the flatter the distribution

Return to the previous example in which the Kasiski method was used to predict possible key lengths. In that example, the suspected key length was 3 or 7, which represents the number of alphabets used. The index of coincidence might not differentiate successfully between three or seven alphabets.

Remember, however, that to test 3 as a possible key length, the three sets $S_1 = \{c_1, c_4 \ldots\}$, $S_2 = \{c_2, c_5 \ldots\}$, $S_3 = \{c_3, c_6 \ldots\}$ were formed. If the key length is 3, each of these sets represents one enciphering alphabet, and so $IC(S_1)$, $IC(S_2)$, and $IC(S_3)$ should all be close to 0.068. If that were not so, you would test a key length of 7 by forming sets $S_1 = \{c_1, c_8, \ldots\}$, $\ldots S_7 = \{c_7, c_{14}, \ldots\}$ and computing $IC(S_1)$, $\ldots$, $IC(S_7)$. When you use the correct key length, you will find all IC values close to 0.068.

Concluding Remarks on Polyalphabetic Ciphers

The steps in analyzing a polyalphabetic cipher are

1. Use the Kasiski method to predict likely numbers of enciphering alphabets. If no numbers emerge fairly regularly, the encryption is probably not simply a polyalphabetic substitution.

2. Compute the index of coincidence to validate the predictions from step 1.

3. Where steps 1 and 2 indicate a promising value, separate the ciphertext into appropriate subsets and independently compute the index of coincidence of each subset.

The Kasiski method of analysis of a polyalphabetic cipher assumes that there is some regular period to the use of alphabets. It attempts to find this period through analysis of repeated plaintext that happens to fall at the same point with respect to the key.

The index of coincidence can be used in two ways. First, it can help to confirm a suspicion that a given body of ciphertext has been enciphered with a polyalphabetic cipher. Second, given a guess as to the number of alphabets used and the frequency counts for the pieces supposedly enciphered using those alphabets, the index can confirm that the frequency distribution resembles a standard English distribution.

Both the Kasiski method and the index of coincidence depend on having available a large quantity of ciphertext. They work well when the enciphering alphabets are applied repeatedly at periodic intervals.

The "Perfect" Substitution Cipher

The ideal substitution would use many alphabets for an unrecognizable distribution and no apparent pattern for the choice of an alphabet at a particular point. What would happen if a text were enciphered with an unlimited number of alphabets? In this section we will consider ways to extend the number of alphabets.

The Vigenère tableau is fairly rigid in form, allowing the use of only 26 different permutations. However, suppose there were a way to generate an unlimited sequence of numbers between 0 and 25. Then each member of that sequence could select an alphabet (column) to be used to encipher the next plaintext character.

An infinite *nonrepeating* sequence of alphabets would confound the Kasiski method. First, a repeated plaintext phrase would not be encrypted the same way twice, since there is no repeating pattern to the choice of alphabets. Second, suppose some piece of ciphertext was a duplicate of a previous piece. That duplicate would almost certainly be accidental. The distance between two duplicate passages of plaintext would not denote a period in the encryption pattern, because there is no pattern and hence no period. The index of coincidence for such a body of ciphertext would be close to 0.038, indicating a large number of enciphering alphabets. But counting the frequencies for characters k positions apart in the ciphertext, for $k = 1, 2, \ldots$ would yield nothing, since the characters k positions apart would not necessarily have been enciphered with the same alphabet.

Thus, a nonrepeating selection of encryption alphabets would confound the cryptanalyst using tools we have seen so far. In the following sections we explore some ways of obtaining an unlimited, nonrepeating series of numbers.

One-Time Pads

This is the idea behind the "perfect" cipher, also called a **one-time pad**. The name comes from an encryption method in which a large nonrepeating set of keys is written on sheets of paper, glued together into a pad. If the keys are, for example, 20 characters long and a sender needs to transmit a message 300 characters in length, the sender would tear off the next 15 pages of keys. The sender would write them one at a time above the letters of the plaintext, and encipher the plaintext with a chart like a Vigenère tableau. The sender would then destroy the used keys.

The receiver needs a pad identical to that of the sender. Upon receiving a message, the receiver takes the appropriate number of keys and deciphers the message as if it were a plain polyalphabetic substitution with a long key. Essentially this algorithm gives the effect of a key as long as the number of characters in the pad.

There are two problems with this method the need for absolute synchronization between sender and receiver, and the need for an unlimited number of keys. Although generating a large number of random keys is no problem, there is a problem printing, distributing, storing, and accounting for such keys.

Long Random Number Sequences

A close approximation of a one-time pad for use on computers is a random number generator. In fact, computer random numbers are not random; they really form a sequence with a very long period. In practice, a generator with a long period can be acceptable for a limited amount of time.

The sender with a 300 character message would interrogate the computer for the next 300 random numbers, scale them to lie between 0 and 25, and use one number to encipher each character of the plaintext message.

Most computer random number generators are of the multiplicative type: number $r_{i+1} = c * r_i + b \bmod w$ where c and b are constants and w is a large integer, often the largest integer that can be stored in a computer word. Given enough terms, it is possible to determine c and b from the known r_i sequence, especially if w can be guessed to be the maximum integer. If the stream of random numbers is not long, this generator is fairly secure.

The Vernam Cipher

The **Vernam Cipher** is a type of one-time pad devised by Gilbert Vernam for AT&T. The Vernam cipher is immune to most cryptanalytic attacks. The basic encryption involves an arbitrarily long nonrepeating sequence of numbers that are combined with the plaintext. Vernam's invention used an arbitrarily long punched paper tape that fed into a teletype machine. The tape contained random numbers which were combined with characters typed into the teletype. The sequence of random numbers was nonrepeating, and each tape was used only once. As long as the key tape does not repeat or is not reused, this type of cipher is immune to cryptanalytic attack, because the available ciphertext does not display the pattern of the key. A model of this process is shown in Figure 2.6.

As an example, we will perform a Vernam encryption in decimal notation. Assume that the alphabetic letters are combined by sum mod 26 with a stream of random two-digit numbers. If the message is

VERNAM CIPHER

the letters would first be converted to their numeric equivalents, as shown here.

V	E	R	N	A	M	C	I	P	H	E	R
21	4	17	13	0	12	2	8	15	7	4	17

Next we need some random numbers to combine with the letter codes. Suppose the following series of random two-digit numbers is generated.

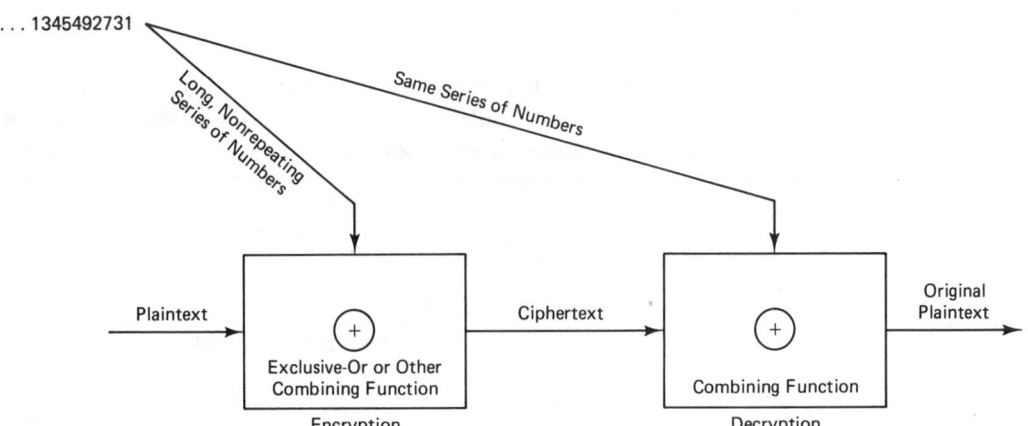

Figure 2.6   Vernam Cipher.

76 48 16 82 44 03 58 11 60 05 48 88

The encoded form of the message is the sum mod 26 of each coded letter with the corresponding random number. The result is then encoded in the usual base-26 alphabet representation.

plaintext	V	E	R	N	A	M	C	I	P	H	E	R
numeric equivalent	21	4	17	13	0	12	2	8	15	7	4	17
+ random number	76	48	16	82	44	3	58	11	60	5	48	88
= sum	97	52	33	95	44	15	60	19	75	12	52	105
≡ mod 26	19	0	7	17	18	15	8	19	23	12	0	1
ciphertext	T	A	H	R	S	P	I	T	X	M	A	B

Thus, the message

VERNAM CIPHER

is encoded as

tahrspitxmab

In this example, the repeated random number 48 happened to fall at the places of repeated letters, accounting for the repeated ciphertext letter a; such a repetition is highly unlikely. The repeated letter t comes from different plaintext letters, a much more likely occurrence. Duplicate ciphertext letters are generally unrelated with this encryption algorithm.

The Binary Vernam Cipher

This scheme works just as well with an "alphabet" of any other base. In order to encrypt a binary string (perhaps a series of words of binary data), random binary digits can be combined mod 2 with bits from the binary string. The result is another binary string.

For example, the binary number

$$1011011001010111001011010101100101$$

can be encoded with the random binary stream

$$1011110111101101011001001001110001$$

to produce the following ciphertext.

$$0000101110111010010010011111010100$$

Binary addition mod 2 can be calculated by the "exclusive or" function by or "add without carry." These functions are often supplied as machine instructions on computers, making it easier to implement this algorithm. Adding 0 produces no change, while adding 1 "complements" or reverses a bit.

Cracking Random Number Generators

Notice that many encryption algorithms, like the Vernam cipher, incorporate random numbers. The safety of the encryption depends on the randomness of the numbers used. A random sequence for a Vernam cipher has to be truly random, meaning without any discernible pattern. For example, the binary string 01010101... changes exactly every other bit. Such a string would make a very bad choice for a random stream because of the discernible pattern.

Where can we get truly random numbers, especially in a form easy to use with computers? The two-digit decimal numbers used in the Vernam cipher example above are middle digits from a list of phone numbers in a residential directory. As such, they would be expected to be free from patterns. (There may still be some nonuniformity, since many easy-to-remember sequences, like *ddd-d*000, *ddd*-1234, or *ddd*-1212, are assigned to businesses. Exploiting that nonuniformity would require the interceptor to acquire and analyze great amounts of ciphertext.) A telephone directory is rather limited as a source of random numbers, and the numbers may not be available in a machine-readable format.

A more common source of random numbers is a pseudo-random number generator computer program. Contrary to their name, these programs generate numbers from a predictable, repeating sequence. In this section we will examine typical random number generators.

The most common type, the **linear congruential random number generator**, begins with an initial value or "seed", r_0. Each successive random number r_{i+1} is generated by

$$r_{i+1} = (a * r_i + b) \bmod n,$$

where a, b, and n are constants. (In formulas that follow, we will drop the parentheses, so that mod will apply to the entire formula.) Often, n is chosen as 1 more than the maximum number that can be stored in a computer word, so that this computation can be performed by discarding any portion of the intermediate result that exceeds storage. This generator produces random integers between 0 and $n - 1$. (See [KNU69] for a thorough study of random number generators.)

If r_0 and a are relatively prime to n, each number between 0 and $n - 1$ will be generated before the sequence repeats. Once the repetition begins, the entire sequence repeats in order.

The problem with this form of random number generator is its dependability. Since each number depends only on the previous number, it is possible to determine constants by solving a series of equations.

$$r_1 = a * r_0 + b \bmod n$$
$$r_2 = a * r_1 + b \bmod n$$
$$r_3 = a * r_2 + b \bmod n$$

If an interceptor has r_0, r_1, r_2, and r_3, it is possible to solve for a, b, and n.

An interceptor can get r_0, r_1, r_2, and r_3 by a **probable word** attack. With a Vernam cipher, each ciphertext letter comes from the formula

$$c_i = r_i + p_i \bmod n$$

If an interceptor of the ciphertext guesses that the message starts with "MEMO" ("M" = 12, "E" = 4, "O" = 14), the interceptor can try to substitute probable values of p_i and solve for values of r_i.

$$r_0 = c_0 - 12 \bmod n$$
$$r_1 = c_1 - 4 \bmod n$$
$$r_2 = c_2 - 12 \bmod n$$
$$r_3 = c_3 - 14 \bmod n$$

With these values of r_0 to r_3, the interceptor may be able to solve the three equations for a, b, and n. Given those, the interceptor can generate the full sequence of random numbers and obtain plaintext directly.

Long Sequences from Books

Another source of supposedly "random" numbers is any book, piece of music, or other object of which the structure can be analyzed. A possible one-time pad is a telephone book. The sender and the receiver both need access to identical telephone books. They might agree, for example, to start at page 35, and use two middle digits (ddd-DDdd) of each phone number, mod 26 as a key letter for a polyalphabetic substitution cipher using a preagreed form of Vigenère tableau. This approach would not provide an unlimited number of key digits, but it might hold out for a year until a new telephone book became available.

A similar idea is the use of any book of prose as a key. Then, the key is the letters of the text, in order. For example, one might select a passage from Descarte's meditation: *What of thinking? I am, I exist, that is certain.* The meditation goes on for a great length, certainly long enough to encipher many very long messages. If you wanted to encipher the message MACHINES CANNOT THINK you would write the message under enough of the key, and encode the message, again as with a conventional polyalphabetic cipher.

```
iamie xistt hatis cert
MACHI NESCA NNOTT HINK
```

It would seem as if this cipher, too, would be impossible to break. Unfortunately that is not true. The flaw lies in the fact that neither the message nor the key text is evenly distributed and, in fact, the distributions of both cluster around high-frequency letters. For example, the four letters A, E, O, and T, account for approximately 40 percent of all letters used in standard English text. Each ciphertext letter is really the intersection of a plaintext letter and a key letter. But if the probability of the plaintext or the key letter's being A, E, O or T is 0.4, the probability of *both* being one of the four is $0.4 * 0.4 = 0.16$, nearly 1/6. The top six letters, adding N and I, increases the sum of the frequencies to 50 percent and increases the probability for a pair to 0.25.

Assuming a standard Vigenère tableau has been used, given a piece of ciphertext, we look for frequent letter pairs that could have generated each ciphertext letter. The encrypted version of the message MACHINES CANNOT THINK is

```
uaopm kmkvt unhbl jmed
```

To break the cipher, assume that each letter of the ciphertext comes from a situation in which the plaintext letter (row selector) and the key letter (column selector) are both one of the six most frequent letters. (This guess will be correct approximately 25 percent of the time.) The trick is to work the cipher inside out. For a ciphertext letter, look in the body of the table for the letter to appear at the intersection of one of the six rows with one of the six columns. Find combinations in the Vigenère table that could yield each ciphertext letter as the result of two high-frequency letters.

The ciphertext u in the above message could be in row A, column u, but that is not a pair of frequent letters, or it could be row B, column t, but that is not a common pair, nor is Cs, Dr, Eq, Fp, or any other pair. Thus, we cannot say much about the plaintext letter that produced u. The second letter, a, could come from row A, column a, but that is the only plaintext-keytext combination of AEOTNI that can produce an a. The likelihood is 0.25 that a represents A.

It will help to build a reduced table of the six frequent letter rows and columns.

	a e i n o t
A	a e i n o t
E	e i m r s x
I	i m r w x c
N	n r w b c h
O	o s x c d i
T	t x b g h m

This table is more useful "inside out": a could represent A, b could stand for N or T, and so on.

Searching through this table for possibilities, we transform the cryptogram.

```
uaopm kmkvt unhbl jmed
-AA-E -E-A -ANN-  -EA-
 O I   I  T  NTT   IE
   T   T            T
```

This technique does not reveal the entire message, or even enough of it to make the message MACHI NESCA NNOTT HINK easy to identify. The technique did, however, make predictions in ten letter positions, and there was a correct prediction in seven of those ten positions. The algorithm made 20 assertions about probable letters, and seven of those 20 were correct. (Seven out of 20 is 35 percent, even better than the 25 percent expected.) The algorithm does not come close to solving the cryptogram, but it reduces the 26^{19} possibilities for the analyst to consider. Giving this much help to the cryptanalyst is significant. A similar technique can be used even if the order of the rows is permuted.

Dual-Message Entrapment

It is possible to encipher two messages at once so that an interceptor cannot distinguish between the messages. One message is the real message, and another is a realistic-looking spurious message, called the "dummy." Assume that the sender and receiver both know the dummy message. The dummy is then used as a key.

The cryptanalyst may deduce both key (dummy) and plaintext messages, but it is impossible to tell from the messages which is which. This occurs because the encryption of letter x with key y is the same as the encryption of letter y with key letter x. For instance, the message and key

disregardthismessage	**key (dummy)**
THISMESSAGEISCRUCIAL	**message**

can be interchanged. The encryption of either the key or message with the other as the key is

wpajqejvdzlqkovvmuigp

Thus, it is impossible to distinguish the key from the message.

Summary of Substitutions

Substitutions are effective cryptographic devices. In fact, they were the basis of many cryptographic algorithms used for diplomatic communication through the first half of this century. They show up in mysteries by Arthur Conan Doyle, Edgar Allan Poe, Agatha Christie, and others.

The presentation of substitution ciphers has also introduced several cryptanalytic tools:

1. frequency distribution

2. index of coincidence

3. consideration of highly likely letters and probable words

4. repeated pattern analysis and the Kasiski approach

5. persistence, organization, ingenuity, and luck

The following section will introduce the other basic cryptographic invention: the transposition (permutation). Substitutions and permutations together form a basis for one of the most secure encryption algorithms known today, the Data Encryption Standard, which will be described and analyzed in Chapter 3.

2.4 Transpositions (Permutations)

The goal of a substitution is confusion, an attempt to make it difficult to determine how a message and key were transformed into ciphertext. A **transposition** is an encryption in which the letters of the message are rearranged. With a transposition the goal is diffusion, spreading the information from the message or the key out widely across the ciphertext. Transpositions try to break established patterns. Because a transposition is a rearrangement of the symbols of a message, it is also known as a **permutation**.

Columnar Transpositions

As with substitutions, we begin this study of transpositions with an easy one. The **columnar transposition** is a rearrangement of the characters of the plaintext into columns.

The following example is a five-column transposition. The plaintext characters are separated into blocks of five and arranged one block after another, as shown here.

$$
\begin{array}{ccccc}
c_1 & c_2 & c_3 & c_4 & c_5 \\
c_6 & c_7 & c_8 & c_9 & c_{10} \\
c_{11} & c_{12} & \text{etc.}
\end{array}
$$

The resulting ciphertext is formed by transversing the columns.

$$c_1 c_6 c_{11} \ldots c_2 c_7 c_{12} \ldots c_3 c_8, \text{ etc.}$$

As an example, you would write the plaintext message as

```
T H I S I
S A M E S
S A G E T
O S H O W
H O W A C
O L U M N
A R T R A
N S P O S
I T I O N
W O R K S
```

The resulting ciphertext would then be read off as

```
tssoh oaniw haaso lrsto imghw
utpir seeoa mrook istwc nasns
```

The length of this message happened to be a multiple of five, so all columns came out the same length. If the message length is not a multiple of the length of a row, the last columns will be a letter short. An infrequent letter, such as X is sometimes used to fill in any short columns.

Encipherment/Decipherment Complexity

This cipher involves no additional work beyond arranging the letters and reading them off again. Therefore, the algorithm is constant in the amount of work per character, and the time for the algorithm is proportional to the length of the message.

However, the other ciphers we have seen so far require only a constant amount of space (admittedly up to 26^2 locations). This algorithm requires storage for all characters of the message, so the space required is not constant but depends directly on the length of the message.

Furthermore, output characters cannot be produced until all characters of the message have been read. This restriction occurs because all characters must be entered in the first column before output of the second column can begin, but the first column is not complete until all characters have been read. Thus, the delay associated with this algorithm also depends on the length of the message, as opposed to the constant delay we have seen in previous algorithms.

Because of the storage space and the delay involved, this algorithm is not especially appropriate for long messages.

Digrams, Trigrams, and Other Patterns

Just as there are characteristic letter frequencies, there are also characteristic patterns of pairs of adjacent letters, called **digrams**. Letter pairs such as "-re-", "-th-", "-en-", and "-ed-" appear very frequently. Table 2.7 lists the ten most common digrams and trigrams (groups of three letters) in English. (They are shown with the most frequent ones first.)

Digram combinations like "-vk-" and "-qp-" occur very infrequently. (The infrequent combinations can occur in acronyms, in foreign words or names, or across word boundaries.) The frequency of appearance of letter groups can be used to match up plaintext letters that have been separated in a ciphertext. Table 2.8 shows the frequencies of all letter pairs. These counts and relative frequencies were obtained from a representative sample of English, not counting digrams that consist of the last latter of one word and the first letter of the next word. The character "space" (denoted by "SP") is used to show the beginnings and endings of words. For example, the entry for SP-T shows the relative occurrence of T as the first letter of a word.

TABLE 2.7 MOST COMMON DIGRAMS AND TRIGRAMS.

Digrams	Trigrams
EN	ENT
RE	ION
ER	AND
NT	ING
TH	IVE
ON	TIO
IN	FOR
TF	OUR
AN	THI
OR	ONE

TABLE 2.8 FREQUENCIES OF DIGRAMS IN ENGLISH.

	A	B	C	D	E	F	G	H	I	J	K	L	M
A	0	15	27	8	1	2	8	0	14	1	4	56	51
B	4	0	0	0	45	1	0	0	9	4	0	15	1
C	45	0	8	0	32	0	0	40	11	0	4	8	0
D	10	0	0	3	62	0	1	0	27	0	0	1	0
E	31	0	47	72	20	8	9	1	5	0	0	25	41
F	6	0	0	0	6	7	0	0	26	0	0	3	0
G	3	0	0	0	17	0	0	8	11	0	0	0	0
H	55	0	0	0	199	0	0	0	22	0	0	1	1
I	9	9	30	14	16	22	15	0	0	0	1	22	21
J	0	0	0	0	4	0	0	0	0	0	0	0	0
K	0	0	0	0	6	0	0	0	5	0	0	0	0
L	27	0	1	3	69	2	1	0	23	0	1	27	0
M	35	11	0	0	47	0	0	0	16	0	0	0	6
N	13	0	25	65	33	5	69	0	12	0	1	3	1
O	5	7	11	35	2	77	39	0	7	1	1	12	33
P	17	0	0	0	28	0	0	5	3	0	0	21	2
Q	0	0	0	0	0	0	0	0	0	0	0	0	0
R	70	0	4	9	113	6	5	0	28	0	5	6	15
S	7	0	9	0	68	3	0	6	34	0	2	1	1
T	39	1	1	0	161	0	0	253	102	0	0	3	0
U	10	4	10	3	11	1	6	0	7	0	0	37	11
V	9	0	0	0	56	0	0	0	16	0	0	0	0
W	15	0	0	0	34	0	0	21	17	0	0	0	0
X	9	0	0	0	5	0	0	0	2	0	0	0	0
Y	0	0	1	0	4	0	0	0	2	0	0	0	1
Z	0	0	0	0	3	0	0	0	0	0	0	0	0
SP	195	64	104	68	74	61	14	28	140	2	6	32	69

TABLE 2.8   FREQUENCIES OF DIGRAMS IN ENGLISH—CONTINUED.

	N	O	P	Q	R	S	T	U	V	W	X	Y	Z	SP
A	108	0	10	0	56	46	107	6	12	1	2	16	0	61
B	0	9	0	0	5	3	0	5	0	0	0	10	0	2
C	0	55	0	0	8	2	38	20	0	0	0	2	0	8
D	0	10	0	0	3	7	0	28	1	2	0	1	0	123
E	70	4	10	9	132	154	22	0	26	7	24	2	0	397
F	0	38	0	0	6	0	9	6	0	0	0	2	0	84
G	7	3	0	0	45	1	0	5	0	0	0	1	0	64
H	3	22	0	0	5	4	1	5	0	0	0	2	0	43
I	168	47	3	3	15	65	55	0	16	0	2	0	2	2
J	0	1	0	0	0	0	0	1	0	0	0	0	0	1
K	3	0	0	0	0	3	0	0	0	0	0	0	0	6
L	0	25	1	0	0	11	7	6	3	1	0	24	0	43
M	0	35	20	0	0	10	1	9	0	0	0	1	0	66
N	3	22	6	0	0	31	56	8	5	0	0	7	0	149
O	89	12	16	0	100	19	22	47	11	24	2	0	0	65
P	0	20	7	0	67	2	8	14	0	0	0	0	0	13
Q	0	0	0	0	0	0	0	14	0	0	0	0	0	1
R	3	101	3	0	32	34	11	8	1	0	0	6	0	102
S	0	23	10	0	0	26	128	17	0	0	0	23	0	253
T	2	69	6	0	21	22	6	10	0	10	0	13	0	160
U	18	0	9	0	29	35	35	0	0	0	0	0	0	7
V	0	2	0	0	0	0	0	0	0	0	0	0	0	0
W	4	8	0	0	4	2	0	0	0	0	0	0	0	14
X	0	0	5	0	0	0	3	0	0	0	0	0	0	9
Y	1	11	2	0	0	22	0	0	0	0	0	0	1	81
Z	0	0	0	0	0	0	0	0	0	0	0	0	0	0
SP	36	120	98	4	35	112	366	22	8	76	3	15	1	0

Total characters: 94785

Cryptanalysis by Digram Analysis

The basic attack on columnar transpositions is not as precise as the attack on substitution ciphers. Even though transpositions look less secure than substitutions, because transpositions leave the plaintext letters intact, the work for the cryptanalyst is more exhausting, because more relies on a human judgment of what "looks right."

The first step in analysis of the transposition is to compute the letter frequencies. The fact that all letters will appear with their normal frequencies implies that a transposition has been performed. Given a string of text, the trick is to break it into columns.

Two different strings of letters from a transposition ciphertext can represent pairs of adjacent letters from the plaintext. See Figure 2.7, which shows where adjacent plaintext characters end up in a ciphertext string. The problem is to find where in the ciphertext a pair of adjacent columns lies, and where the ends of the columns are.

t s s o h o a n i w h a a s o l r s t o i m g h w · · ·

Figure 2.7   Positions of Adjacent Letters in Ciphertext.

The process involves exhaustive comparison of strings of ciphertext. The process will compare a block of ciphertext characters against characters successively farther away in the ciphertext. Imagine a moving window that locates a block of characters for checking. Assume the block being compared is seven characters. The first comparison is c_1 to c_8, c_2 to c_9, ..., c_7 to c_{14}. Then the window of comparison shifts, and c_1 is compared to c_9, c_2 to c_{10}, and so forth. The window shifts again to c_1 against c_{10}. This process is shown in Figure 2.8.

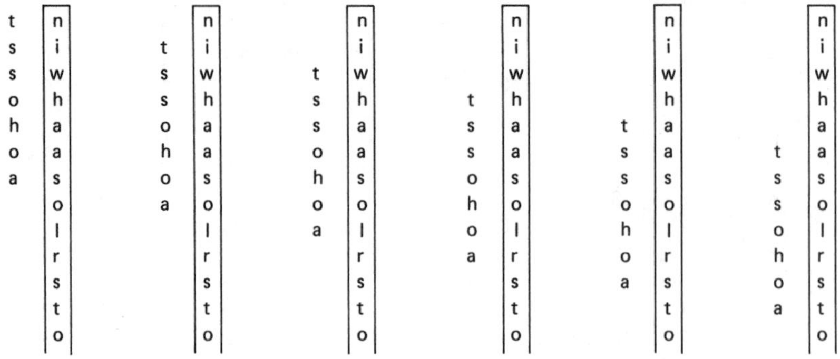

t	n		t	n			n			n			n			n
s	i		s	i		t	i			i			i			i
s	w		s	w		s	w		t	w			w			w
o	h		o	h		s	h		s	h			h			h
h	a		h	a		o	a		s	a		t	a			a
o	a		o	a		h	a		o	a		s	a		t	a
a	s		a	s		o	s		s	s		s	s		s	s
	o			o		a	o		o	o		o	o		o	o
	l			l			l		h	l		h	l		h	l
	r			r			r		o	r		o	r		o	r
	s			s			s		a	s		a	s		o	s
	t			t			t			t			t		a	t
	o			o			o			o			o			o

Figure 2.8   Moving Comparisons.

Two questions must be asked for each window position. First, do common digrams appear, and second, do most of the digrams look reasonable? The first question is answered by recording, for each of the ten pairs of digrams, the frequency of that digram in normal English. The second question is answered by computing the variance between the seven recorded digram frequencies. (To be manageable, this example demonstrates the technique using only eight characters in the block being compared. In practice, however, this technique would be implemented by computer, using a much longer block length.)

As another example, consider again the cryptogram from the beginning of this section.

```
tssoh oaniw haaso lrsto imghw
utpir seeoa mrook istwc nasns
```

The first comparison is of the first seven characters against the next seven: TSSOHOA to NIWHAAS. Some of the digrams produced that way are likely: -SI- and -SW-, but -TN- and -OH- are unlikely.

The next window places TSSOHOA against IWHAASO. Again, there are some likely digrams, but -AO- is very suspicious. The third window's comparison also has some suspicious points.

We know the next window will be the correct one, since the column length was ten. The comparison there is TSSOHOA against HAASOLR. We see that all the digrams are reasonable. In Table 2.9, we have listed the relative frequency of all of the digrams for a given window position. That table also shows the mean and standard deviation of each list of frequencies. A high mean implies that the digrams are likely; a low standard deviation implies that all of the digrams are likely, so that the mean is not being raised artificially by a few popular digrams.

TABLE 2.9 MATCHING POSSIBLE COLUMN POSITIONS.

First Letter	Second Letter, Digram, Relative Frequency			
c_1 t	n tn 17	i ti 1024	w tw 99	h th 529
c_2 s	i si 339	w sw 2	h sh 61	a sa 69
c_3 s	w sw 2	h sh 61	a sa 69	a sa 69
c_4 o	h oh 3	a oa 45	a oa 45	s os 262
c_5 h	a ha 555	a ha 555	s hs 41	o ho 216
c_6 o	a oa 45	s os 262	o oo 124	l ol 123
c_7 a	s as 460	o ao 1	l al 559	r ar 560
Mean	203	279	143	261
Std. Dev.	223	356	172	191

When digrams indicate a possible match for a fragment of ciphertext, the next step is to try to extend the match.

Also, the distance between c_1 and c_{k+1} (the distance is k) implies that another column might begin k positions later. To test that theory, c_{k+1} is checked against c_{2k+1}, and so on.

Double Transposition Algorithm

The **double transposition** cipher involves two columnar transpositions, with different numbers of columns, applied one after the other. The first transposition displaces adjacent letters, and the second breaks up the adjacency of short series of letters that happened to appear in adjacent columns of the first transposition. Table 2.10 is a duplicate of the columnar transposition from the earlier section. Letters from the third column have been preceded with a '(, and letters from the fourth column have been followed by a ')' to make them easy to locate in the resulting ciphertext.

TABLE 2.10 SINGLE COLUMNAR TRANSPOSITION.

T	H	(I	S)	I
S	A	(M	E)	S
S	A	(G	E)	T
O	S	(H	O)	W
H	O	(W	A)	C
O	L	(U	M)	N
A	R	(T	R)	A
N	S	(P	O)	S
I	T	(I	O)	N
W	O	(R	K)	S

produces:

```
tssoh oaniw haaso lrsto (i(m(g(h(w
(u(t(p(i(r s)e)e)o)a) m)r)o)o)k) istwc nasns
```

Since there were 50 characters, they fit perfectly into a 10 by 5 matrix. For the second transposition the ciphertext is written in an 8 by 7 matrix, as shown in Table 2.11. The symbols (and) have been retained to show the original locations of these characters. Since 50 characters do not fill an 8 by 7 matrix, the extra positions must be filled with a padding character, such as X.

TABLE 2.11 SECOND COLUMNAR PATTERN.

T	S	S	O	H	O	A
N	I	W	H	A	A	S
O	L	R	S	T	O	(I
(M	(G	(H	(W	(U	(T	(P
(I	(R	S)	E)	E)	O)	A)
M)	R)	O)	O)	K)	I	S
T	W	C	N	A	S	N
S	X	X	X	X	X	X

The result from the second columnar transposition is shown here.

```
tno(m(i m)tssi l(g(rr)w xswr(h s)o)cxo
hs(we)o nxhat (ue)k)ax oao(to) isxas
(i(pa)sn x
```

Even letters from adjacent columns of the first transposition, such as the (i m) pair at the beginning, come from widely separated letters. The i is the last "i" of "transposition," while the m is from the earlier word "columnar."

The six extra xs filling the last row stand out. A better way of padding is to use letters that would occur frequently anyway, such as a, e, i, n, o, or s, so that it would not be possible to identify the padding characters easily.

Cryptanalysis

There is a functional relationship between plaintext and ciphertext character positions. With single transposition, the plaintext character in position i moves to position $E(i) = 10 * \big([(i-1) \bmod 5] + (i-1)/5 + 1\big)$, so that

$$c_{10*\big([(i-1)\bmod 5]+(i-1)/5+1\big)} = p_i$$

With the second transposition, the relationship uses 8s and 7s instead of 10s and 5s, with a similar formula.

Double transpositions are an example of product ciphers, in which one encryption is applied to the result of another. Product ciphers resemble the product or composition of two functions in mathematics. If E_1 and E_2 are two transposition ciphers following a regular pattern, their product is also a regular pattern, $E_2(E_1(p))$. The product cipher formed by using the output of E_1 as the input to E_2 is a complicated function, but it is still regular.

This encryption algorithm can be broken with a chosen plaintext attack or a probable plaintext attack. It may even be broken by analysis of letters that appear together very often (such as Q followed by U, or X preceded by E). In all three cases, the cryptanalyst locates pairs of ciphertext letters that probably appear together in the plaintext. From these pairs the analyst tries to infer a mathematical relationship that would account for the placement of those letters in the ciphertext. The analyst then tries this same relationship on other ciphertext letters to see if they produce probable digrams.

A serious problem with this encryption algorithm is that once the analyst discovers the relationship between one plaintext character and its ciphertext position, that same relationship holds for all characters. The complexity of the relationship makes it hard to discern, but a small result reveals the entire scheme.

Generalized Transpositions

Transpositions are somewhat difficult to analyze because they move plaintext to unpredictable places in the ciphertext. A columnar transposition is just another example of a permutation. In fact, any permuting algorithm can be used, as long as it is reversible. For example, if the plaintext message is n characters long, the series [3, 6, 9, 12, ... to n, 4, 8, 16, 20, 28, ... to n, 5, 10, 25, ... to n, ..., 2, 1] permutes the letters, but it foils a possible digram analysis.

2.5 Fractionated Morse

The last encryption to consider in this chapter is an old form of cipher, called "fractionated Morse." The encryption algorithm amounts to little more than a keyed monoalphabetic cipher. The result is subsequently blocked. This cipher has Morse code as its basis.

Morse code is a means of representing letters as sequences of dots and dashes, used with telegraphs, flashing lights, and semaphore flags. The Morse code representation is shown in Table 2.12. Morse code was designed for human encoding, so that frequently used characters were assigned short codes (such as A, T, E), or easy patterns (such as S, O).

TABLE 2.12 MORSE CODE.

A .-	H	O ---	U ..-
B -...	I ..	P .--.	V ...-
C -.-.	J .---	Q --.-	W .--
D -..	K -.-	R .-.	X -..-
E .	L .-..	S ...	Y -.--
F ..-.	M --	T -	Z --..
G --.	N -.		

Morse Code

To encode a message in Morse code, you replace each letter with its counterpart in dashes and dots (or long and short ashes of light, or long and short pulses with a telegraph key). In all of these forms there is also a break or pause between separate letters; the pause will be represented by a vertical bar.

For example, the message

FRACTIONATED MORSE

would be encoded as

```
 F  |  R  |  A  |  C  |  T  |  I  |  O  |  N  |  A  |  T  |  E  |  D  |
..-.|.-. | .- |-.-.| -  | .. |--- |-.  | .- | -  | .  |-.. |

 |  M  |  O  |  R  |  S  |  E  |
 | -- |--- |.-. |... | .  |
```

or

```
..-.|.-.|.-|-.-.|-|..|---|-.|.-|-|.|-..||--|---|.-.|...|.
```

(Note that a break between words becomes | |, or a long pause.)

Morse Code for Encryption

Morse code is really a three-symbol coding scheme using the symbols dash," dot," and separator." There are 26 letters in the English alphabet, and $3^3 = 27 = 26 + 1$. Thus, all but one of the possible groups of dashes, dots, and separators can be associated with an English letter.

To use this fact for encryption, we select a keyword, such as *wovenflax*, and assign the letters of the alphabet to combinations of dash, dot, and separator in order,

TABLE 2.13 ENGLISH LETTERS ASSOCIATED WITH MORSE CODE SYMBOLS.

w ...	a .|-	i --|	r |.|
o ..-	x .||	j -|.	s |-.
v ..|	b -..	k -|-	t |--
e .-.	c -.-	m -||	u |-|
n .--	d -.|	p |..	y ||.
f .-|	g --.	q |.-	z ||-
l .|.	h ---		

starting with the keyword letters. Such a pattern is shown in Table 2.13. This table lacks only the combination | | |."

To encrypt a message using fractionated Morse requires three steps. First the English plaintext is converted to Morse code, using a separator between letters and an extra separator to represent a space between words. Next, the Morse code message is divided into blocks of three symbols. Finally, each block is encoded as the letter corresponding to that three-symbol pattern. An example of that encryption follows.

Example

As shown previously, the message

FRACTIONATED MORSE

is represented in Morse code as

table 2.12 { ..-.|.-.|.-|-.-.|-|..|---|-.|.-|-|.|-..||--|---|.-.|...|.

We begin fractionated Morse by breaking this message into blocks of three symbols. If the last block does not have three symbols, we fill it with the separator, |.

```
..- .|. -.| .-| -.- .|- |.. |-- - |- .|. -|- |.|
-.. ||- -|- --| .-. |.. .|.
```

The encryption is completed by replacing each block of three symbols by its letter equivalent from Table 2.13.

table 2.13 {
```
..- .|. -.| .-| -.- .|- |.. |-- -|- .|. -|- |.|
 o   l   d   f   c   a   p   t  k   l   k   r
```
```
-.. ||- -|- --| .-. |.. .|.
 b   z   k   i   e   p   l
```

The final transmitted message is

oldfcaptklkrbzkiepl

Cryptanalysis of Fractionated Morse

As with many historical ciphers, this one depends on having experience in some field other than encryption. Although a trained telegrapher might recognize patterns in this code, few other people would. The change of base from base-26 (alphabet) to base-2 (Morse code) to base-3 (Morse code with divisions between letters) back to base-26 (alphabet) will also forestall an interceptor.

This cipher has some of the same characteristics of the polyalphabetic cipher, since a single letter is encoded in several different ways. Unlike polyalphabetic encodings, however, there is no necessary fixed repetition of the key between similar representations. If the plaintext letter T (–) appears in a message, its encoding depends on the letters that precede and follow T, and where the dash appears in a block of three symbols.

This encryption is not very secure. If the basic algorithm is known, but not the code-word, frequent ciphertext letters will indicate frequent patterns. For example, common word endings are -g, -e, -d and -s, which end in Morse Code as – . | | , . | | , – . . | | , and . . . | | , respectively. All of these end in . | | , which will skew the distribution of that pattern. For this reason, certain patterns will show up disproportionately often, giving these and other clues.

A worse problem is repeated words and phrases. Common words, such as "is", "and", and "the", show up very frequently. There are only three ways for any of these to be encoded, depending on whether the word begins at the first, second, or third position of a block of three. In a long document these and other longer repeats will produce several adjacent repeated blocks, giving the analyst clues as to the positions of repeated words and phrases. A document that used a long term such as "encipherment" four times would be guaranteed at least one repetition of that whole block.

2.6 Stream and Block Ciphers

Most of the ciphers studied in this chapter were stream ciphers; that is, they convert one symbol of plaintext immediately into a symbol of ciphertext. (The exception is the columnar transposition cipher.) The transformation depends only on the symbol, the key, and control information of the encipherment algorithm. A model of stream enciphering is shown in Figure 2.9.

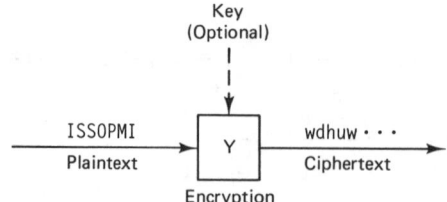

Figure 2.9   Stream Encryption.

Advantages of stream encryption are

+ *Speed of transformation.* Since each symbol is encrypted without regard for any other plaintext symbols, each symbol can be encrypted as soon as it is read. Thus, the time to encrypt each symbol depends only on the encryption algorithm itself, not on the time it takes to receive more plaintext.

+ *Low error propagation.* Since each symbol is separately encoded, an error in the encryption process affects only that character. For example, suppose the encryption algorithm is $c_i = (a * p_i + b)\ mod\ k$, where a, b, and k are constants. If the encryptor makes a mistake in arithmetic, the conversion of later characters is not affected. Or, with conventional Morse code, if either the sender or receiver makes a mistake on a particular letter, both the sender and receiver are resynchronized correctly by the separator after the mistaken letter. A receiver can often guess the correct replacement for a single garbled letter.

By contrast, the disadvantages of a stream cipher system are

- *Low diffusion.* Each symbol is separately enciphered. Therefore, all the information of that symbol is contained in one symbol of the ciphertext. A cryptanalyst can consider each ciphertext symbol as a separate entity and attempt to break it by analyzing the characteristics of all individual symbols of the ciphertext, using tools such as frequency distribution counts, digram analysis, the index of coincidence, and the Kasiski method.

- *Susceptibility to malicious insertions and modifications.* Since each symbol is separately enciphered, an active interceptor who has broken the code can splice together pieces of previous messages and transmit a spurious new message that may look authentic. For example, an interceptor might receive a message generating a credit to one account. The interceptor who can locate the account number portion can create a new message authorizing transfer of money to a new account.

Some kinds of errors, such as skipping a character in the key during encryption, will affect the encryption of all future characters. Errors such as this, however, can sometimes be recognized during decryption, because the plaintext will be properly recovered up to a point, and then all following characters will be wrong. If that is the case, the receiver may be able to recover from the error by dropping a character of the key on the receiving end. Once the receiver has successfully recalibrated the key with the ciphertext, there will be no further effects from this error.

Block ciphers encrypt a *group* of plaintext symbols as *one* block. The columnar transposition and other transpositions are examples of block ciphers. In the columnar transposition, the entire message is translated as one block. The block size need not have any particular relationship to the size of a character. Block ciphers work on blocks of plaintext and produce blocks of ciphertext, as shown in Figure 2.10.

In fractionated Morse, parts of characters are enciphered separately as a block. In this case, a block could consist of part of a four-symbol letter, one complete three-symbol letter, a two-symbol letter plus a space (before or after), a one-symbol letter surrounded by spaces, part of a letter plus a space, two one-symbol letters and a space, a one-symbol letter plus a space and part of an other letter, or parts of two letters and a space. For example, the letter T (–) could be represented in four different ways, depending whether the T falls at the start, middle, or end of a block and what comes before and after the T.

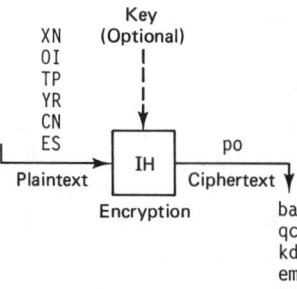

Figure 2.10 Block Cipher Systems.

Block ciphers have advantages that stream ciphers lack, but the disadvantages of block ciphers are the strengths of stream ciphers. First we list the advantages:

+ *Diffusion*. Information from the plaintext is diffused into several ciphertext symbols. One ciphertext block may depend on several plaintext letters.

+ *Immunity to insertions*. Since blocks of symbols are enciphered, it is impossible to insert a single symbol into one block. The length of the block would then be incorrect, and the decipherment would quickly reveal the insertion. Furthermore, one character from the plaintext does not produce just one ciphertext character. Therefore, an active interceptor cannot simply cut one ciphertext letter out of a message and paste a new one in to change an amount, a time, a date, or a name in a message.

On the other hand, block ciphers are subject to

— *Slowness of encryption*. Block ciphers must wait until an entire block of plaintext symbols has been received before starting the encryption process. The columnar transposition is the extreme case; there this delay must be for the entire message. In shorter cases, as with fractionated Morse, the delay is only until the next one or two characters fill the block. Clearly, block encryption schemes where the delay is limited to a small, fixed number of characters are preferable to unbounded delay.

— *Error propagation*. An error will affect the transformation of all other characters in the same block. In a stream cipher message it may be possible to interpret the message correctly with one character irretrievably garbled. With a block cipher, one error will cause loss or misinterpretation of an entire block, which may be part of one character, parts of two characters, or all or parts of many characters.

2.7 Characteristics of "Good" Ciphers

At this point we can reconsider what we have learned in this chapter about encryption. We have looked at two broad classes of algorithms—substitutions and transpositions.

Substitutions "hide" the letters of the plaintext. Polyalphabetic substitutions dissipate high letter frequencies. Transpositions scramble text so that adjacent-character analysis fails. We have also noted drawbacks to each type of algorithm.

How do we choose an encryption algorithm for a particular application? What does it mean for a cipher to be "good"? The meaning of *good* depends on the intended use of the cipher. A cipher to be used by military personnel in the field has different requirements from one that will be used in a secure installation with substantial computer support. This section contains some discussion on different characteristics of ciphers.

Shannon Characteristics

In 1949, Claude Shannon [SHA49] proposed characteristics of a good cipher. These criteria are listed here.

> **1.** The amount of secrecy needed should decide the amount of labor appropriate for the encryption and decryption.

Principle 1 is a reiteration of the principle of timeliness from Chapter 1, and of the earlier observation that even a simple cipher may be strong enough to deter the casual interceptor or to hold off any interceptor for a short time.

> **2.** The set of keys or the enciphering algorithm should be free from complexity.

This principle implies that it is wrong to restrict the choice of keys or the types of plaintext on which the algorithm can work. An algorithm that works only on plaintext having an equal number of As and Es is useless. Similarly, it would be very difficult to select keys such that the sum of the values of the letters of the key was a prime number. Restrictions such as these make the use of the encipherment prohibitively complex. If the process is too complex it will not be used. Furthermore, the key must be transmitted, stored, and remembered, so that it must be short.

> **3.** The implementation of the process should be as simple as possible.

Principle 3 was formulated with hand implementation in mind: A complicated algorithm is prone to error or likely to be forgotten. With the development and popularity of digital computers, algorithms far too complex for hand implementation became feasible. Still, the issue of complexity is important. People will avoid an encryption algorithm that severely hinders message transmission, which undermines security.

> **4.** Errors in ciphering should not propagate and cause corruption of further information in the message.

Principle 4 acknowledges that humans will make errors in their use of enciphering algorithms. One error early in the process should not throw off the entire remaining ciphertext. For example, dropping one letter in a columnar transposition throws off the entire remaining encipherment. Unless the receiver can guess where the letter was dropped, the remainder of the message will be unintelligible. By contrast, reading the wrong row or column for a polyalphabetic substitution affects only one character—remaining characters are unaffected.

5.   The size of the enciphered text should be no larger than the text of the original message.

The idea behind principle 5 is that a ciphertext that expands dramatically in size cannot possibly carry more information that the plaintext, yet it gives the cryptanalyst more data from which to infer a pattern. Furthermore, a longer ciphertext implies more space for storage and more time to communicate.

These principles were developed before the ready availability of digital computers, although Shannon was aware of computers and the computation power they represented. Some of the concerns of hand implementation are not limitations on computers. For example, a cipher's implementation need not be simple, as long as the time complexity of the implementation is tolerable.

Confusion and Diffusion

Two additional concepts relate to the amount of work to perform an encryption. An encrypting algorithm should take the information from the plaintext and transform it so that the interceptor cannot readily recognize the message. The interceptor should not be able to predict what changing one character in the plaintext will do to the ciphertext. This characteristic is called **confusion**. An algorithm providing good confusion will have a complex functional relationship between the plaintext/key pair and the ciphertext. In this way, it will take an interceptor a long time to determine the relationship among plaintext, key, and ciphertext; therefore, the code will take a long time to break.

As an example, the Caesar cipher is not good for providing confusion, since an analyst who deduces the transformation of a few letters can also predict the transformation of the remaining letters, with no additional information. By contrast, a polyalphabetic substitution with a key longer than the message length provides good confusion, since one plaintext letter can be transformed to any ciphertext letter at different places in the output. There is no apparent pattern to the ways of transforming a single plaintext letter.

The cipher should also spread the information from the plaintext over the entire ciphertext. Changes in the plaintext should affect many parts of the ciphertext. This principle is called **diffusion**, the characteristic of distributing the information from single plaintext letters over the entire output. Good diffusion means that the interceptor needs access to much ciphertext to infer the algorithm.

The fractionating scheme presented earlier demonstrates good diffusion. However, the substitution and permutation ciphers do not provide good diffusion (because one plaintext character has an effect on only one ciphertext character).

Information Theoretic Tests

A **secure** system is one where an interceptor cannot recover a plaintext message from its ciphertext, regardless of the amount of work performed. The perfect transformation, the one-time pad, is immune to cryptanalytic attack, but it fails if one assumes collusion, coercion, or bribery between the interceptor and a sender or receiver.

Perfect security defined this way is hard to achieve. A more reasonable interpretation of security is "secure enough," defined as follows. The cryptanalyst will try to find a transformation h that converts ciphertext into plaintext. The cryptographer hopes that the transformation h is not exact; that is, it can produce many possible plaintexts. For example, recall the frequent-letters analysis of the cipher that gets its key from a prose passage. The analysis predicted several possibilities for some character positions of the message, and no possibilities for other positions. Therefore, the cryptanalyst has a transformation that maps one ciphertext to none, one, or several possible plaintexts.

Suppose $C = E(P)$ is the encipherment, and h is the cryptanalyst's suspected decipherment. Then, let $h(C)$ be a set of possible plaintexts, $h(C) = \{Poss_1, Poss_2, \cdots\}$. The actual plaintext, P, may or may not be one of the possibilities $Poss_i$.

An encryption is **effectively secure** if the probability that $h(C)$ is P is arbitrarily small; that is,

$$Prob\,(h(C) = P) < \epsilon$$

for some arbitrarily small value ϵ. For example, the dual-message entrapment scheme just described produces a probability no larger than $1/2$. The analyst deducing the one message will also find the other, but the analyst cannot determine which is authentic.

As another example, consider the encryption system shown in Figure 2.11. The figure shows a situation where five plaintext messages, P_1 through P_5, are encrypted with the five keys, k_1 through k_5. Suppose it happened that those five encryptions produced only five different ciphertexts, C_1 through C_5. (Normally five plaintexts under five keys would produce about 25 distinct ciphertexts.) An interceptor might obtain one of the ciphertexts, say C_1, and might even have access to the keys $k_1 \ldots k_5$ and the

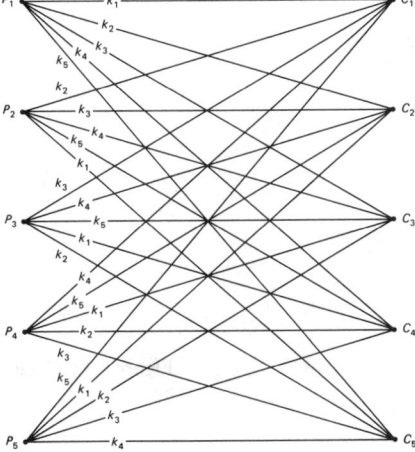

Figure 2.11 Example of Perfect Secrecy, Adapted from [SHA49].

matching plaintexts $P_1 \ldots P_5$. Having C_1 gives the interceptor no additional information about which plaintext was sent, since any of the five plaintexts could have produced ciphertext C_1. In this case,

$$Prob_{C_1}(h(C_1) = P) = Prob(h(C_1) = P) = Prob(P)$$

That is, the probability that any particular plaintext P was sent is not influenced by the fact that ciphertext C_1 was sent.

By contrast, consider the more common case in which a single ciphertext is the encipherment of very few plaintext-key combinations. Here, knowing all the ks, all the Ps, and which C was sent instantly reveals the corresponding plaintext. This situation is shown in Figure 2.12. For example, knowing that C_1 was sent reveals that the plaintext could only have been P_2 or P_3. Thus, it is possible to deduce more information about the cipher, such as

$$Prob_{C_1}(h(C_1) = P_1) = 0$$

since there is no key k for which $E(k, P_1) = C_1$.

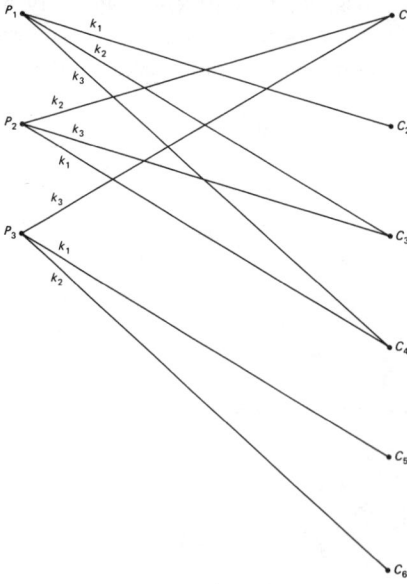

Figure 2.12 Example of Imperfect Secrecy.

Redundancy

Languages are inherently redundant. The minimum number of bits of information needed to represent the unique letters of an alphabet is $A = \lceil log_2(k) \rceil$ where k is the number of letters in the alphabet and $\lceil\ \rceil$ denotes rounding up to the nearest integer. This measure is called the **absolute rate** of the language. For example, English has a 26-letter alphabet. Therefore, $\lceil log_2(26) \rceil$, or 5, bits are needed to represent all letters uniquely.

The number of possible n-letter messages in the language is 2^{An}. Some of these are meaningful, but most are not. Let 2^{Rn} be the number of meaningful messages. The **rate** of the language is R. The **redundancy** of the language is $D = A - R$; in other words, D is the number of excess bits available that are not needed to represent meaningful messages.

As an example, imagine writing out all strings that are 20 characters long. (There are $26^{20} \simeq 2*10^{28}$ such strings.) Most of them, like AAA..AA, AAA..AB, AAA..AC, ..., ZZZ..ZZ are meaningless, but all meaningful messages 20 letters long will be there (see Figure 2.13). If you had a list of all and only the meaningful messages, a more economical way of referring to one would be to number them and use just the number of the one you want. If there were 1,000 meaningful messages, $\lceil log_2(1000) \rceil = 10$ bits would suffice to refer to a single message, instead of the $20*5 = 100$ bits to write it in letters. This difference between the conventional representation and the most economical representation in a language is the redundancy of the language.

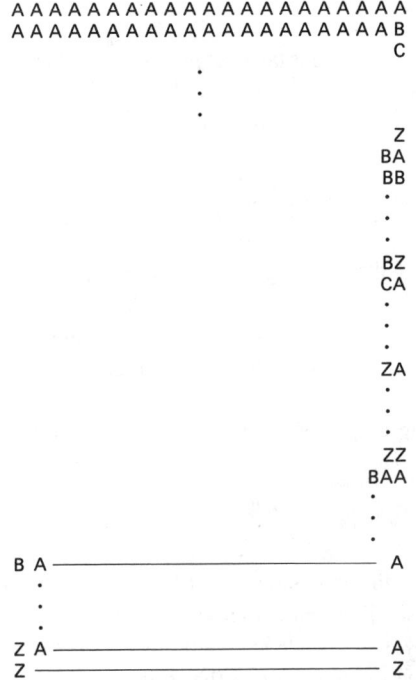

Figure 2.13 All messages of length 20.

If an encryption algorithm encrypts two or more different messages to the same ciphertext, an interceptor cannot determine which of two or more possible meaningful plaintext messages is the authentic one. When the number of such multiple-message encodings is high, the encryption system is also secure. If a language is highly redundant, the number of possible multiple-message encodings can be high.

For example, if you could identify meaningless plaintext, you could devise an encryption algorithm to encrypt nine meaningless plaintext messages and one meaningful one to each ciphertext. An interceptor, presumably unable to distinguish meaningful from meaningless messages, would have a probability of only 1/10 of selecting the right decipherment. Note that the phrasing here is *can be* high; the number is not necessarily high.

Unicity Distance

Define *Prob*(P) as the probability of plaintext message P having been sent. Given that C was received, let *Prob$_C$*(P) be the probability that P was the message sent. (That is, *Prob$_C$*(P) is the probability that $C = E(P)$.) Perfect secrecy occurs only if *Prob$_C$*(P) = *Prob*(P). In other words, knowing that C was received gives the analyst no additional information about what message was sent.

Shannon defined a concept, called the **unicity distance**, that describes the amount of ciphertext needed in order to break a cipher. Define

$$H_C(P) = \sum_P Prob_C(P) log_2 \left(\frac{1}{Prob_C(P)} \right)$$

The unicity distance is the smallest message length n for which $H_C(P)$ is close to 0. For some systems, like the one-time pad systems, $H_C(P)$ is never close to 0.

If an encryption has $2^{H(P)}$ keys, the unicity distance is

$$N = \frac{H(P)}{D}$$

where D is the redundancy of the language, as described earlier. If there are as many keys as messages, the cipher is theoretically unbreakable. This situation occurs with the dual message entrapment and the Vernam cipher, as well as the other infinite-length key systems. It also explains why it is possible to break standard substitutions given enough ciphertext.

The probability of getting a spurious decryption of a ciphertext is

$$q = \frac{2^{Rn}}{2^{An}} = 2^{(R-A)n} = 2^{-Dn}$$

where D is the redundancy of the language, described earlier. This is so because there are 2^{An} possible ways of encoding n characters, but there are only 2^{Rn} meaningful messages; therefore, the leftover $(2^{An} - 2^{Rn})$ encodings represent nothing. Therefore, q is the likelihood of getting one of these things that represents nothing.

2.8 What the Cryptanalyst Has to Work With

Four possible situations confront the cryptanalyst, depending on what information is available. These four cases suggest five different approaches the analyst can take.

Ciphertext Only

In most of the discussions so far, it was assumed that the analyst had only the ciphertext with which to work. The decryption had to be done based on probabilities, distributions, and characteristics of the available ciphertext, plus publicly available knowledge. This method of attack is called a **ciphertext-only attack**.

Full or Partial Plaintext

The analyst may be fortunate enough to have a sample message and its decipherment. For example, a diplomatic service may have intercepted an encrypted message, suspected to be the text of an official statement. If the official statement (in plaintext) is subsequently released, the interceptors have both C and P and only need to deduce the E for which $C = E(P)$. In this case the analysts are attempting to find E (or D) using a **known plaintext** attack.

The analyst may have additional information, too. For example, the analyst may know that the message was intercepted from a diplomatic exchange between Germany and Austria. From that information, the analyst may guess that the words Bonn, Vienna, and Chancellor appear in the message. Alternatively, the message may be a memorandum to the sales force from a corporate president, and the memo would have a particular form (To: Sales Force, From: The President, Date: —, Subject: New Product Pricing Schedule).

In these cases, the analyst can use what is called a **probable plaintext** analysis. After doing part of the decryption, the analyst may find places where the known message fits with the deciphered parts, thereby giving more clues about the total translation.

After cryptanalysis has provided possible partial decipherments, a probable plaintext attack may permit a cryptanalyst to fill in some blanks. For example, letter frequencies may suggest a substitution for the most popular letters, but leave gaps such as SA_ES _OR_E. With a probable plaintext, the cryptanalyst can expect SALES FORCE to appear somewhere in the memo and could easily fill in these blanks.

Ciphertext of any Plaintext

The analyst may have infiltrated the sender's process so as to be able to cause messages to be encrypted and sent at will. This attack is called a **chosen plaintext** attack. For instance, the analyst may be able to insert and delete records into a data base, and observe the change in statistics after the insertions. Linear programming will sometimes enable such an analyst to infer data that should be kept confidential in the data base. Alternatively, an analyst may have tapped wires in a network and be able to notice the effect of sending a particular message to a particular user on the network. A chosen plaintext attack is very favorable to the analyst.

Algorithm and Ciphertext

Finally, the analyst may have available the encryption algorithm and the ciphertext. In a **chosen ciphertext** attack, the analyst can run the algorithm on massive amounts of plaintext in order to find one plaintext message that encrypts as the ciphertext. The purpose of a chosen ciphertext attack is to deduce the sender's encryption key in order to decrypt future messages by simply applying the sender's decryption key to intercepted ciphertext. This approach fails if two or more distinct keys can produce the same ciphertext as the result of encrypting (different) meaningful plaintext.

2.9 Summary of Basic Encryption

This chapter has examined the basic processes of encryption and cryptanalysis. The two basic methods of encipherment—substitution and transposition or permutation—have been introduced in this chapter. These methods will be used again in Chapter 4 in the study of other encryption methods.

Several cryptanalytic tools have also been introduced in this chapter. These tools include frequency distribution, digram (and trigram) study, index of coincidence, searching for repeated patterns, and study of probable letters. Five classic cryptanalytic attacks have been presented; these are the ciphertext-only, known plaintext, probable plaintext, chosen plaintext, and chosen ciphertext methods. Finally, the chapter has presented some of the formal material on cryptanalysis and cryptography, including notions of redundancy, entropy in a language, and the unicity distance.

2.10 Terms and Concepts

encryption
secure communication
channel
sender
receiver
transmission medium
intercept
modify
fabricate
interceptor
intruder
encryption/decryption
encipher/decipher
encode/decode
plaintext
ciphertext

key
keyless cipher
cryptography
cryptanalyst
cryptology
cryptosystem
breakable encryption
substitution
transposition
monoalphabetic cipher
Caesar cipher
permutation
frequency distribution
brute force attack
polyalphabetic substitution
Vigenère tableau
Kasiski method
index of coincidence
measure of roughness
one-time pad
long random key
Vernam cipher
long prose key
dual-message entrapment
transposition ciphers
columnar transposition
digram analysis
secrecy
error propagation
diffusion
confusion
secure system
effectively secure
rate of a language
absolute rate of a language
redundancy
unicity distance
ciphertext-only attack
known plaintext attack
probable plaintext attack
chosen plaintext attack
chosen ciphertext attack

2.11 Bibliographic Notes

This chapter does not present much of the history of encryption. Because encryption has been used for military and diplomatic communications, many of the stories are fascinating, but some of the stories have not been made public. David Kahn's thorough study of encryption [KAH67] still stands as the masterpiece. Other interesting sources are [CLA77]; the works by Friedman [FRI76a], [FRI76b], and [FRI76c]; [DEA85]; [BAM82]; and [YAR31].

The highly-readable presentation of elementary cryptography by Sinkov [SIN66] is well worth study. A more precise and mathematical analysis is done by Konheim [KON80] and Meyer and Matyas [MEY82]. A description of the unicity distance can be found in [DEA77]. Many more encryption algorithms are presented in [FOS82].

2.12 Exercises

The first several exercises ask you to decrypt a piece of ciphertext. Each of these is an English prose quotation. More important than the precise quotation is the *process* you use to analyze the encryption. Justify your answer by describing the various tests you performed and the results you obtained for those tests.

1. Decrypt the following encrypted quotation.

   ```
   fqjcb rwjwj vnjax bnkhj whxcq nawjv nfxdu mbvnu
   ujbbf nnc
   ```

2. Decrypt the following encrypted quotation.

   ```
   oczmz vmzor jocdi bnojv dhvod igdaz admno ojbzo
   rcvot jprvi oviyv aozmo cvooj ziejt dojig toczr
   dnzno jahvi fdiyv xcdzq zoczn zxjiy
   ```

3. Decrypt the following encrypted quotation.

   ```
   pbegu uymiq icuuf guuyi qguuy qcuiv fiqgu uyqcu
   qbeme vp
   ```

4. Decrypt the following encrypted quotation.

   ```
   jrgdg idxgq anngz gtgtt sitgj ranmn oeddi omnwj
   rajvk sexjm dxkmn wjrgm ttgdt gognj ajmzg ovgki
   nlaqg tjamn xmsmj jrgko jtgnw jrgnj rgvat tmgta
   wamno jjrgw izgtn sgnji babgu
   ```

5. Decrypt the following encrypted quotation.

   ```
   ejitp spawa qleji taiul rtwll rflrl laoat wsqqj
   atgac kthls iraoa twlpl qjatw jufrh lhuts qataq
   itats aittk stqfj cae
   ```

6. Decrypt the following encrypted quotation.

   ```
   auqrq rkrzd dmhxk ageho kfalu hkmog rlagm hznhf
   fhglm hkrlh mvzmr znvir klhgl vhodw krnra przgr
   ```

```
jozdl vzkra gmvrw almka xomah gmvrf zbhka mtqho
dwxre dzwmh mzcro imvra khqgz gwwri zkm
```

7. Decrypt the following encrypted quotation.

```
jmjmj gsmsg lrjgu csqyj quflr mfajq erdmc cmqlv
lqyhg gawgq arpgq sblce jrlrj lnemc cyjqu flrmf
ajqer d
```

8. Decrypt the following encrypted quotation.

```
vcwpc kwblm smljy glbgu gbtwj jyats lwsgm lwjjy
vcrfc rikwl qjwte fscpw lbgqm jwscb ktpbc pqats
vfwsm dvwpw lbsfc ktrfu wtlsc brpgk cmdqj wtefs
cpgle vfmjc ncmnj cq
```

9. Decrypt the following encrypted quotation.

```
ptgpz ggprf bdkrg pequt tngtf ggpzf zfqgp tukrw
wkzfg kquyd qxwzu ltuet zfrfl ptgpz ggprf bdkrg
pequt dhmgw tgokr wwdtt bxqug tuedq xequt fraty
rdaur erfzg rqfot gjzfr gorfa wrftd hdgqx rfyxz
hwgdz fokpt utuzg ptugp zfrfq hudtw jtdpt gpzgu
tzydz fyluq kdfqk rdtud hdcta gdfqg prdqk fytxr
artfa omhga qecwz rfdqx pzuyk quydz fyqmd ahutd
tfgtf atdzf yzdbd kpomq qbdzu tkurg gtfkp rapaz
ffqgm thfyt udgqq y
```

10. Decrypt the following encrypted quotation.

```
mszkx ijddj nzatm lrkdj mlwmc qrktj tnwir zatnj
bxdrj amlrs zxrzd dbjbk wsrir mlrxc icnic qrkza
tmlrb cbriz mlkco mnizx r
```

11. Decrypt the following encrypted quotation.

```
gahzh zgaff irfcc fqgmx eefsp xmgaf bxscy gadgb
afqbf dsfzh rvhqm xsgnq fxmgf qgafz nsmfh gxmxn
sxbqk faduh xnsbf jdvft nhcgp xmxns yhzdz gfszg
afznq gafjx xqdqy gafzg dszdz hmbfb fsfuh ccdhq
zkpqf rfzzh gpmxx czkpa fdufq cprxj enczh xq
```

12. Decrypt the following encrypted quotation.

```
gasaz afxfk hqbzp zbqnq hfkqf zdfgr gsaaf afdfz
fzujz fhhxh irxxg rvnqp fhsdm cqbqx cmfyx fxjgc
qsdaz ggvfk mnfzp xqtga efndf exhsd fmczu sggdf
pfpzq xqxhc mgmmp gaxbr afnfx bzsbj bnyfe xshsn
smzfc cfduz yhzhh gggcx axfcq dmsdi
```

13. What characteristics would make an encryption absolutely unbreakable? What characteristics would make an encryption impractical to break?

14. Does a substitution need to be a permutation of the plaintext symbols? Why or why not?

15. Why is it better to use a permutation that is not regular instead of a permutation that follows a pattern, such as $\pi(i) = i + 3$ or $\pi(i) = 5 * i \bmod 26$?

16. Suppose the rows of a Vigènere tableau have been scrambled. For example, row A might be jklmno.... How could you determine the table of the six frequent letters (AEINOT)?

17. Explain why the index of coincidence decreases as the number of enciphering alphabets increases.

18. Explain why the index of coincidence for five alphabets is close to that for ten alphabets, which is close to that for many alphabets.

19. Suppose a six-symbol alphabet is used for encryption, and the relative frequencies of the six ciphertext symbols (denoted a, b, c, d, e, f) are 1/4, 1/4, 3/16, 1/8, 1/8, and 1/16, respectively. Compute the variance of this system. Compute the index of coincidence for this system.

20. Suppose a Kasiski analysis identifies the following pairs of repeated sequences.

Location of	
First Occurence	Second Occurence
10	34
21	62
37	109
49	105
58	162
72	132

   What can you conclude about the number of alphabets used to encrypt this message? Explain your answer.

21. Explain why $Freq_i * (Freq_i - 1)/n * (n - 1)$ is approximately $Prob_i^2$.

22. What is the plaintext message of Table 2.3? What encryption algorithm was used?

23. Explain why two substitution ciphers, applied one after another, may provide no more security than one substitution. (Such a cipher is called the **product** of the two underlying ciphers.)

24. Explain why the product of two relatively simple ciphers, such as a substitution and a transposition, can achieve a high degree of security.

25. What will be the value of the index of coincidence of the ciphertext of a transposition cipher applied to some English text?

26. In a particular language there are 12 letters. Two of these are used with relative frequency 3; four are used with relative frequency 2, and the remaining six are used with relative frequency 1. Compute the index of coincidence for monoalphabetic substitutions in this language.

3

Secure Encryption Systems

The previous chapter introduced the concepts of encryption and cryptanalysis. The encryption methods described have been relatively simple, since they were designed many years ago for use before the invention of computers. They are reasonably secure for short messages, for short periods of time, or for messages where the interceptor is not expected to want to work too hard to break the code. However, it should be evident that these methods are inappropriate for situations affecting national security, for bank transfer operations involving millions of dollars, or for other times when a high degree of security is important.

Cryptanalysts now have new tools for analyzing codes. Even such simple tasks as frequency counts are very tedious and error-prone by hand, while they are fast, simple, and reliable by computer. The computer has made a host of cryptanalytic approaches feasable that were effectively impossible in the past.

Fortunately, the same can be said of encryption. Previous algorithms had to be carried out exclusively by hand, which was both tedious and error-prone. Some algorithms were just too difficult to implement by hand. The next step was slow, awkward encryption machines, used in the first half of the 20th century for military and diplomatic purposes. Now the computer has revolutionized the process of encryption within a relatively few years.

This chapter will survey three important encryption algorithms, which represent the state of the art of public encryption algorithms. All three of these algorithms require extensive computation. Interestingly, all three algorithms were presented about the same time—in the middle 1970s.

The first algorithm, the Merkle-Hellman knapsack, is an example of a good method based on a solid foundation. Unfortunately, within a few years of its presentation, a way was found to break the algorithm. It still stands, however, as illustrative of a class of algorithms based on very difficult problems. The second algorithm, the Rivest-Shamir-Adelman (RSA) algorithm, appeared about the same time as the Merkle-Hellman algorithm but, to date, it has withstood much cryptanalytic attack from the research community. The difficulty with RSA is that it can be very costly to implement in software, although it has been implemented in hardware. The third algorithm, the Data Encryption Standard (DES), was designed with support from the U.S. National Bureau of Standards in order to provide the public with a secure encryption method for use in commercial applications. Questions about the soundness of this algorithm have been raised since its introduction, and further government support for it has recently been withdrawn for certain kinds of applications. Nevertheless, there are still applications for which it is appropriate.

This chapter begins with a study of hard problems that can form the basis of secure encryption schemes. Following that discussion are a few mathematical concepts needed for the encryption schemes that follow. The three sophisticated schemes are presented and analyzed next. Finally, this chapter concludes the study of encryption with a survey of encryption algorithms in general and a discussion of where the field of encryption/cryptanalysis is likely to lead.*

3.1 "Hard" Problems: Complexity

The encryption algorithms described so far have been based on very simple problems: substituting characters, permuting their order, and performing relatively minor changes at the bit level. A disadvantage with these kinds of algorithms is that not very much work is involved with a "brute force" attack. (A **brute force** attack is one that tries all possible solutions.) For example, if it is known that a single transposition was used, the interceptor might print all $n!$ permutations of an n-character message if the message is short enough. By scanning these, the interceptor can locate the one that looks right. Of course, this attack is feasible by hand only up to about five or six characters. The use of a computer increases the value of n for which a brute force attack is feasible.

We would like the interceptor to have to solve a hard problem, such as figuring out the *algorithm* that selected one of $n!$ permutations. In fact, however, the interceptor may simply generate all possible permutations and scan them visually (or with some computer assistance), looking for probable text. Thus, the interceptor need not solve our hard problem (determine how one permutation of the $n!$ was chosen); the interceptor can solve the easier problem of determining which permutation was used *in this instance*.

---

* *Note to the reader:* It is possible to study this chapter at two levels. For each of the three major encryption schemes presented—Merkle-Hellman, RSA, and DES—there is an introductory section describing the method in understandable terms but without all the detail of how the algorithm actually works. Some people who read this chapter need to know only the rudiments of each algorithm. These people may want to have background knowledge of current encryption practices, but they do not need a working ability. For these people the introduction to each algorithm may be adequate. Other people want a more detailed understanding of how these three schemes work. For example, these people may want to judge the suitability of the algorithm for a particular situation or to do further work in cryptanalysis of these or similar algorithms. These people should read the introductory sections and then study the detailed sections following. In this way, practitioners and researchers can both use this important material in whatever way suits their needs.

Principle of Easiest Work: We cannot expect the interceptor to choose the hard way to do something.

A recent trend in encryption has been to consider problems that are known to be hard to solve, and for which the number of possible solutions is large. Then, even with computer support, an exhaustive brute force solution is expected to be infeasible. Concurrent with this effort, there has been an analysis of the inherent complexity of problems. The goal is to say that not only is a *particular* solution (or algorithm) time-consuming, there simply isn't *any* easy solution. Substantial progress occurred in this area, not coincidentally, in the early 1970s. We will begin our study of secure encryption systems by developing a foundation in problem complexity and some mathematical concepts we will need.

NP-Complete Problems

An important investigation of the complexity of problems explored what are called **NP-complete** problems, based on work by Cook [COO71] and Karp [KAR72]. We will try to approach the notion of NP-complete problems intuitively, by studying three problems. Each of the problems is easy to state, not hard to understand, and straightforward to solve. Each also happens to be NP-complete. After the problems are displayed, the precise meaning of NP-completeness will be studied.

Satisfiability

The problem is to determine whether any given logical formula is satisfiable, that is, whether there is a way of assigning the values *TRUE* and *FALSE* to the variables so that the result of the formula is *TRUE*. Formally, the problem is presented as follows.
    Given a formula

- composed of the variables $v_1, v_2, \ldots, v_n$ and their logical complements $\bar{v}_1, \bar{v}_2, \ldots, \bar{v}_n$

- represented as a series of clauses in which each clause is the logical *OR* ($\vee$) of variables and their logical complements

- expressed as the logical *AND* ($\wedge$) of the clauses

is there a way to assign values to the variables so that the value of the formula is *TRUE*? If there is such an assignment, the formula is said to be **satisfiable**.
    For example, the formula

$$(v_1) \wedge (v_2 \vee v_3) \wedge (\bar{v}_3 \vee \bar{v}_1)$$

is satisfiable, while

$$(v_1) \wedge (v_2 \vee v_3) \wedge (\bar{v}_3 \vee \bar{v}_1) \wedge (\bar{v}_2)$$

is not. Both of these formulas are in the form prescribed.

Knapsack

The name of the problem relates to packing items into a knapsack. Is there a way to select some of the items to be packed such that their "sum" (the amount of space they take up) exactly equals the knapsack capacity (the target)? The problem can be expressed as a case of adding integers. Given a set of nonnegative integers and a target, is there a subset of the integers whose sum equals the target?

Formally, given a set $S = \{c_1, c_2, \ldots, c_n\}$ and a target sum T, where each $c_i \geq 0$, is there a selection vector, $V = [v_1, v_2, \ldots, v_n]$, each of whose elements is 0 or 1, such that $\sum_{i=1}^{n}(c_i * v_i) = T$? (The selection vector records a 1 for each element chosen for the sum and a 0 for each not chosen.)

For example, the set S might be $\{4, 7, 1, 12, 10\}$. A solution exists for target sum $T = 17$, since $17 = 4 + 12 + 1$. The selection vector is $V = [1, 0, 1, 1, 0]$. No solution is possible for $T = 25$.

Clique

Given a graph G and an integer n, is there a subset of n vertices such that every vertex in the subset shares an edge with every other vertex in the subset? (A graph in which each vertex is connected to every other vertex is called a **clique**.)

Formally, we are given a graph $G = (V, E)$ where V is a set of vertices and $E \subseteq V \times V$ is the set of edges, and given a number $n > 0$. The problem is to determine whether there is a subset of n vertices, $V_S \subseteq V$, such that for each pair of vertices v_i, v_j in V_S, the edge (v_i, v_j) is in E.

As an example, consider Figure 3.1. Vertices $\{v_1, v_2, v_7, v_8\}$ form a clique of size 4, but there are no cliques of 5 vertices.

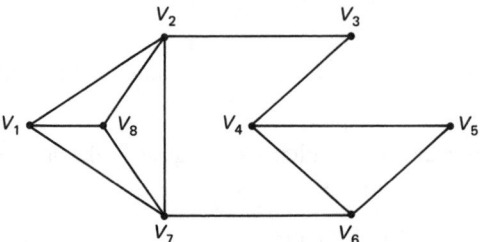

Figure 3.1 Clique Subgraphs in a Graph.

Characteristics of NP-Complete Problems

The problems just listed are reasonable representatives of the class of NP-complete problems. Notice the following characteristics of these problems.

1. Each problem *is* solvable, and it is solvable by a relatively *simple* approach (although the approach may be time-consuming). For each of them, we can simply enumerate all the possibilities: all ways of assigning the logical values of n variables, all

subsets of the set S, all subsets of n vertices in G. If there is a solution, it will appear in the enumeration of all possibilities; if there is no solution, testing all possibilities will demonstrate that.

2. There are 2^n cases to consider if we use the approach of enumerating all possibilities (where n depends on the problem). Each possibility can be tested in a relatively small amount of time, so the time to test all possibilities and answer *yes* or *no* is proportional to 2^n.

3. The problems are apparently unrelated, having come from logic, number theory, and graph theory, respectively.

4. If it were possible to "guess" perfectly, each problem could be solved in relatively little time. For example, if someone could guess the correct assignment or the correct subset, it would be simple to verify that the formula had been satisfied or a correct sum had been determined, or a clique had been identified. The verification process could be done in time bounded by a polynomial function of the size of the problem.

The Classes P and NP

Let **P** be the collection of all problems for which there is a solution that runs in time bounded by a polynomial function of the size of the problem. For example, determining if an item is in a list can be done in time proportional to the size of the list (simply by examining each element in the list to determine if it is the correct one), and items in a list can be sorted into ascending order in time bounded by the square of the number of elements in the list (using the well-known bubble sort algorithm.) There may also be faster solutions; that is not important here. Both the searching problem and the sorting problem would be in **P**, since they can be solved in time n and n^2, respectively.

For most problems, polynomial time algorithms are about the limit of feasible complexity. Any problem that could be solved in time $n^{1,000,000,000}$ would be in **P**, even though for large values of n, the time to perform such an algorithm might be prohibitive. Notice also that we do not have to know an explicit algorithm, we just have to be able to say that such an algorithm exists.

By contrast, let **NP** be the set of all problems that can be solved in time bounded by a polynomial function of the size of the problem, *assuming the ability to guess perfectly*. (In the literature, this "guess function" is called an **oracle machine** or a **nondeterministic Turing machine**). This guessing is called **nondeterminism**.

Of course, it is impossible to guess perfectly. Guessing is simulated by cloning an algorithm and applying one version of it to each possible outcome of the guess, as shown in Figure 3.2. Essentially, the idea is equivalent to a computer programming language in which IF statements could be replaced by GUESS statements: Instead of testing a known condition and branching depending on the outcome of the test, the GUESS statements would cause the program to split, following two or more paths concurrently.

The ability to guess can be useful. For example, instead of deciding whether to assign the value *TRUE* or *FALSE* to variable v_1, the nondeterministic algorithm can

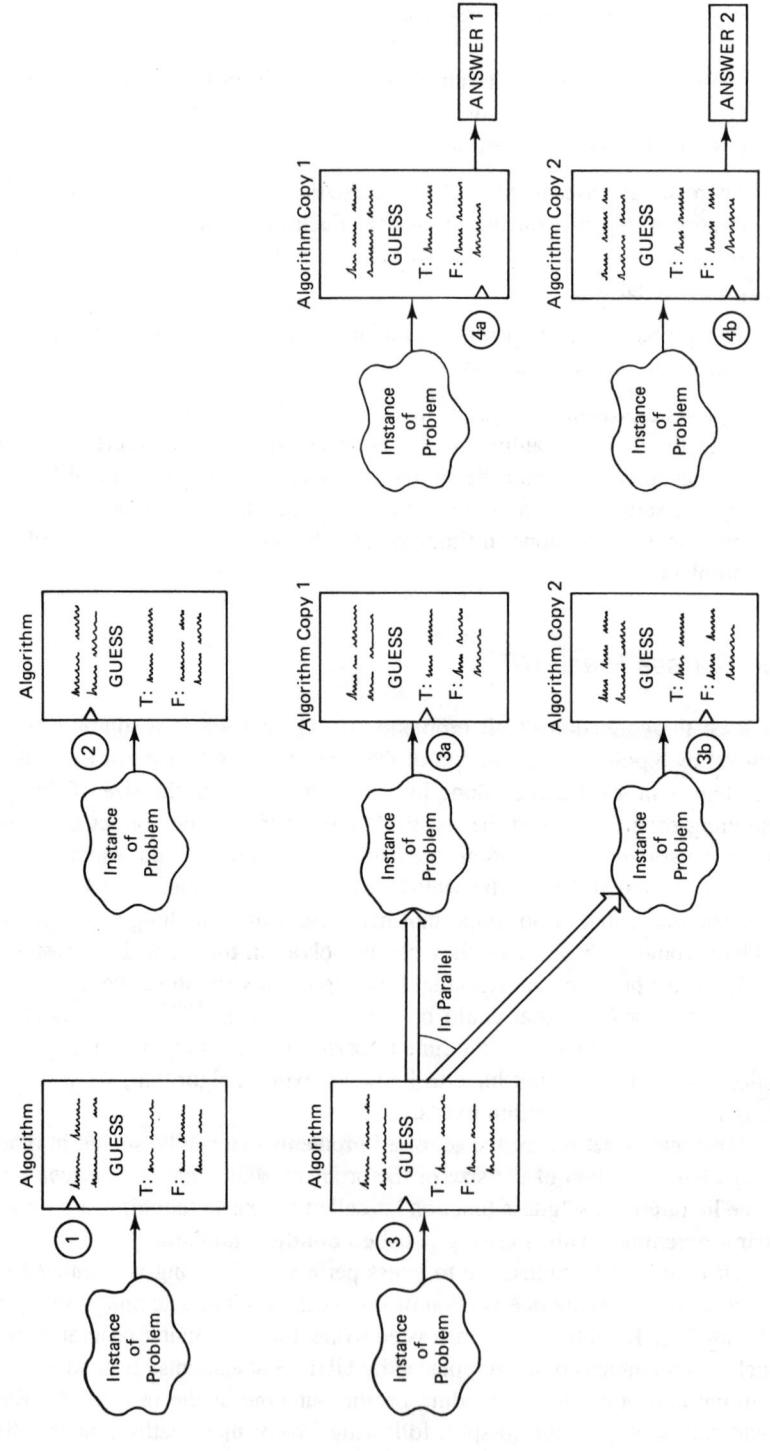

Figure 3.2 Simulating Nondeterminism.

proceed in two directions: one assuming *TRUE* had been assigned to v_1, and the other assuming *FALSE*. As the number of variables increases so does the number of possible paths to be pursued concurrently.

Certainly every problem in **P** is also in **NP**, since the guess function does not have to be invoked. There is also a class **EXP**, which consists of problems for which a deterministic solution exists in exponential time, c^n for some constant c. As noted earlier, every NP-complete problem has such a solution. Every problem in **NP** is also in **EXP**.

The Meaning of NP-Completeness

Cook [COO71] showed that the satisfiablity problem is **NP-complete**, meaning that it can represent the entire class **NP**. His important conclusion was that if there is a *deterministic*, polynomial time algorithm (one without guesses) for the satisfiability problem, then there is a deterministic, polynomial time algorithm for *every* problem in **NP**; that is, **P** = **NP**.

Karp [KAR72] extended Cook's result by identifying a number of other problems, all of which shared the property that if any one of them could be solved in a deterministic manner in polynomial time, then all of them could. The knapsack and clique problems were identified by Karp. The results of Cook and Karp included the converse: if for even *one* of these problems (or any NP-complete problem) it could be shown that there was *no* deterministic algorithm that ran in polynomial time, then no deterministic algorithm could exist for *any* of them.

It is important to distinguish between a problem and an instance of a problem. An **instance** is a specific case: one formula, one specific graph, or one particular set S. Certain simple graphs or simple formulas may have solutions that are very easy and fast to identify. A **problem** is more general; it is the description of all instances of a given type. For example, the formal statements of the satisfiability, knapsack, and clique sections are statements of problems, since they tell what each specific instance of that problem must look like. Solving a problem requires finding *one* general algorithm that will solve *every* instance of that problem.

Essentially the problem space (that is, the classification of all problems) looks like Figure 3.3. There are problems known to be solvable deterministically in polynomial time (**P**), and there are problems known *not* to have a polynomial time solution (**EXP** and beyond). The class **NP** fits somewhere between **P** and **EXP**. It may be that **P** = **NP**, or that **P** $\neq$ **NP**.

The significance of Cook's result is that NP-complete problems have been studied for a long time by many different groups of people—logicians, operations research specialists, electrical engineers, number theorists, operating systems specialists, and communications engineers. If there were a practical (reasonably fast) solution to any one of these problems, you would hope that someone would have found it by now. Currently, several hundred problems have been identified as NP-complete. (Garey and Johnson [GAR79] enumerate many NP-complete problems.) The more problems in the list, the stronger the reason to believe that there is no simple (polynomial time) solution to any (all) of them.

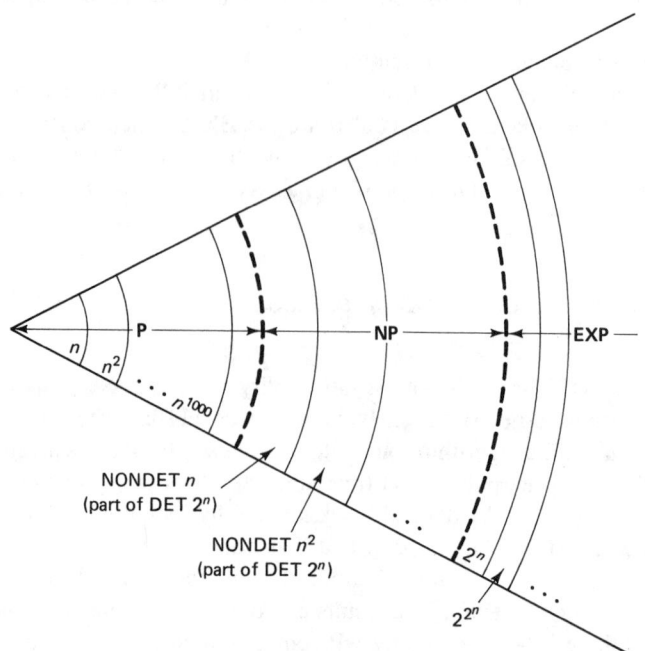

Figure 3.3   Hierarchies of Complexity Classes.

NP-Completeness and Cryptography

Hard-to-solve problems are fundamental to cryptography. Basing an encryption algorithm on one of these hard problems would seem to be a way to require the interceptor to do a prodigious amount of work to break the encryption. There are four fallacies with this line of reasoning.

1. An NP-complete problem does not *guarantee* that there is *no* solution easier than exponential; it merely indicates that an easier solution is unlikely to be found. This distinction means that the basis of the difficulty to crack the encryption algorithm might deteriorate if it is later shown that **P = NP**. This is the least serious of the fallacies.

2. Every NP-complete problem has a deterministic exponential time solution, that is, one that runs in time proportional to 2^n. For small values of n, 2^n is not large, and so the work of the interceptor using a brute force attack may not be prohibitive. This difficulty can be addressed by designing the algorithm so that the instance of the problem has a very large size, that is, if n is large, 2^n will be appropriately deterring.

3. Continuing advances in hardware make problems of larger and larger size tractable. For example, parallel processing machines are now being designed with a finite but

large number of processors running together. With a GUESS program, two processors could follow the paths from a GUESS point simultaneously. A large number of processors could complete certain nondeterministic programs in deterministic mode in polynomial time. However, we can select the problem's setting so that the value of n is large enough to require an unreasonable number of parallel processors. What seems unreasonable now may become reasonable in the future.

4. Even if an encryption algorithm is based on a hard problem, it is not always necessary for the interceptor to solve the hard problem in order to crack the encryption. To be useful for encryption, these problems have to have a secret, easy solution. An interceptor may look for the easy way instead of trying to solve a hard underlying problem. An example of this type of exposure will be described later with respect to the Merkle-Hellman knapsack algorithm.

Other Inherently Hard Problems

Another source of inherently difficult problems is number theory. These problems are appealing because they relate to numeric computation, so their implementation is natural on computers. Number theory problems appear as important tasks. Since these problems have been the subject of much research recently, the lack of easy solutions inspires confidence in their basic complexity. Although most of these number theory problems are not NP-complete, the known algorithms are very time-consuming.

Two such problems that form the basis for secure encryption systems are computation in Galois fields and factoring large numbers. In the next section we will review some topics in algebra and number theory that will allow us to understand and use these problems.

3.2 Properties of Arithmetic

We begin with a study of properties of multiplication and division on integers. In particular, we investigate prime numbers, divisors, and factoring, since these topics have major implications in the secure encryption algorithms. We also study a restricted arithmetic system, called a "field." The fields we consider are finite and have convenient properties that make them very useful for representing cryptosystems.

Unless we explicitly state otherwise, in this section we will consider only arithmetic on integers. Also, unless explicitly stated otherwise, all arithmetic in this section will be conventional, *not* mod n.

Inverses

Let $\odot$ be an operation on numbers. For example, $\odot$ might be $+$ or $*$. A number i is called an **identity** for $\odot$ if $x \odot i = x$ and $i \odot x = x$ for every number x. For example, 0 is an identity for $+$, since $x + 0 = x$ and $0 + x = x$. Similarly, 1 is an identity for $*$.

Let i be an identity for $\odot$. The number b is called the **inverse** of a under $\odot$ if $a \odot b = i$. An identity holds for an entire operation; an inverse is specific to a single number. The identity element is always its own inverse, since $i \odot i = i$. The inverse of an element a is sometimes denoted a^{-1}.

Using the example of addition again, we see that the inverse of any element a is $(-a)$, since $a + (-a) = 0$. When we consider the operation of multiplication on the rational numbers, the inverse of any element a (except 0) is $1/a$, since $a * (1/a) = 1$. However, under the operation of multiplication on the *integers*, there are no inverses (except 1). Consider, for example, the integer 2. There is no other integer b such that $2 * b = 1$. The positive integers under the operation $+$ have no inverses, either.

Primes

To say that one number **divides** another, or that the second is **divisible by** the first, means that the remainder of dividing the second by the first is 0. Thus, we say that 2 divides 10, since $10/2 = 5$ with remainder 0. However, 3 does not divide 10, since $10/3 = 3$ with remainder 1. Also, the fact that 2 divides 10 does not necessarily mean that 10 divides 2; $2/10 = 0$ with remainder 2.

A **prime number** is any positive number that is divisible (with remainder 0) only by itself and 1.[1] For example, 2, 3, 5, 7, 11, and 13 are primes, while 4 $(2 * 2)$, 6 $(2 * 3)$, 8 $(2 * 2 * 2)$, and 9 $(3 * 3)$ are not. A number that is not a prime is a **composite**.

Greatest Common Divisor

The **greatest common divisor** of two numbers, a and b, is the largest integer that divides both a and b. The greatest common divisor is often written $\gcd(a, b)$. For example, $\gcd(15, 10) = 5$ since 5 divides both 10 and 15, and nothing larger than 5 does. If p is a prime, for any number $q < p$, $\gcd(p, q) = 1$. Clearly, $\gcd(a, b) = \gcd(b, a)$.

Euclidean Algorithm

The **Euclidean algorithm** is a procedure for computing the gcd of two numbers. This algorithm exploits the fact that if x divides a and b, x also divides $a - (k * b)$ for every k. To see why, suppose x divides both a and b; then $a = x * a_1$ and $b = x * b_1$. But

$$a - (k * b) = x * a_1 - (x * k * b_1)$$
$$= x * (a_1 - k * b_1)$$
$$= x * d$$

so that x divides (is a factor of) $a - (k * b)$.

This result leads to a simple algorithm for computing gcd. Suppose we want to find x, the gcd of a and b, where $a > b$. Rewrite a as

$$a = m * b + r$$

---

[1]   We disregard -1 as a factor, since $(-1) * (-1) = 1$

where $0 \le r < b$. (In other words, compute $m = a/b$ with remainder r.) If $x = \gcd(a, b)$, x divides a, x divides b, and x divides r. But $\gcd(a, b) = \gcd(b, r)$ and $a > b > r \ge 0$. Therefore, the search for gcd can be simplified, by working with b and r instead of a and b:

$$b = m' * r + r'$$

where $m' = b/r$ with remainder r'. This leads to a simple iterative algorithm, which terminates when a remainder 0 is found.

Example

For example, we will compute $\gcd(3615807, 2763323)$.

$$3,615,807 = (1) * 2,763,323 + 852,484$$
$$2,763,323 = (3) * 852,484 + 205,871$$
$$852,484 = (4) * 205,871 + 29,000$$
$$205,871 = (7) * 29,000 + 2,871$$
$$29,000 = (10) * 2,871 + 290$$
$$2,871 = (9) * 290 + 261$$
$$290 = (1) * 261 + 29$$
$$261 = (9) * 29 + 0$$

Thus, $\gcd(3615807, 2763323) = 29$.

Modular Arithmetic

In Chapter 2, modular arithmetic was introduced as a way of confining results to a particular range; in that instance we wanted to perform some arithmetic operations on a plaintext character[2] and guarantee that the result would be another character. Modular arithmetic has the required property: Results stay in the underlying range of numbers. An even more useful property is that the operations $+$, $-$, and $*$ can be applied before or after the modulus is taken with similar results.

Recall that a modulus applied to a nonnegative integer means *remainder after division*, so that $11 \bmod 3 = 2$ since $11/3 = 3$ with remainder 2. If $a \bmod n = b$ then

$$a = c * n + b$$

for some integer c. Two different integers can have the same modulus: $11 \bmod 3 = 2$ and $5 \bmod 3 = 2$. Any two integers are **equivalent** under modulus n if their results mod n are equal. This is denoted

$$x \equiv_n y \qquad \text{if and only if} \qquad (x \bmod n) = (y \bmod n)$$

---

[2]   Strictly speaking, these operations were on a numeric value associated with the character.

Alternately

$$x \equiv_n y \qquad \text{if and only if} \qquad (x - y) = k * n \quad \text{for some } k$$

In the following sections, unless we use parentheses to indicate otherwise, a modulus will apply to a complete expression. Thus $a + b \bmod n$ should be interpreted as $((a + b) \bmod n)$, not $a + (b \bmod n)$.

Properties of Modular Arithmetic

Modular arithmetic on the nonnegative integers forms a construct called a **commutative ring** with operations $+$ and $*$ (addition and multiplication). Furthermore, if every number other than 0 has an inverse under $*$, the group is called a **Galois field**. All rings have the properties of associativity and distributivity; commutative rings, as their name implies, also have commutativity. Inverses under multiplication produce a Galois field. The integers mod n are a Galois field. The properties of this arithmetic system are listed here.

Property	Example
associativity	$a + (b + c) \bmod n = (a + b) + c \bmod n$
	$a * (b * c) \bmod n = (a * b) * c \bmod n$
commutativity	$a + b \bmod n = b + a \bmod n$
	$a * b \bmod n = b * a \bmod n$
distributivity	$a * (b + c) \bmod n = ((a * b) + (a * c)) \bmod n$
existence of identities	$a + 0 \bmod n = 0 + a \bmod n = a$
	$a * 1 \bmod n = 1 * a \bmod n = a$
existence of inverses	$a + (-a) \bmod n = 0$
	$a * (a^{-1}) \bmod n = 1$ if $a \neq 0$
reducibility	$(a + b) \bmod n = ((a \bmod n) + (b \bmod n)) \bmod n$
	$(a * b) \bmod n = ((a \bmod n) * (b \bmod n)) \bmod n$

Example

As an example, consider the field of integers mod 5 shown here. These tables show one way of computing the sum or product of any two integers mod 5. However, the reducibility rule gives a method that may be easier to use. To compute the sum or product of two integers mod 5, we compute the regular sum or product and then reduce this result by subtracting 5 until the result is between 0 and 4. Alternatively, we divide by 5 and keep only the remainder after division.

For example, let us compute $3 + 4 \bmod 5$. Since $3 + 4 = 7$ and $7 - 5 = 2$, we can conclude that $3 + 4 \bmod 5 = 2$. This fact is confirmed by the table. Similarly, to compute $4 * 4 \bmod 5$, we compute $4 * 4 = 16$. We can compute $16 - 5 = 11 - 5 = 6 - 5 = 1$, or we can compute $16/5 = 3$ with remainder 1. Either of these two approaches shows that

+	0	1	2	3	4
0	0	1	2	3	4
1	1	2	3	4	0
2	2	3	4	0	1
3	3	4	0	1	2
4	4	0	1	2	3

*	0	1	2	3	4
0	0	0	0	0	0
1	0	1	2	3	4
2	0	2	4	1	3
3	0	3	1	4	2
4	0	4	3	2	1

inverse mod n

$a * (a^{-1}) \mod n = 1$

$4 * 4 \mod 5 = 1$, as proven by the table. Since it is complicated to construct the tables for large values of the modulus, the remainder technique is especially helpful.

Computing Inverses

In the ordinary system of multiplication on rational numbers, the inverse of any number a is $1/a$, since $a * (1/a) = 1$. Finding inverses is not quite so easy in the finite fields just described. In this section we will find how to determine the multiplicative inverse of any element.

The inverse of any element a is that element b such that $a*b = 1$. The multiplicative inverse of a may be written a^{-1}. Looking at the table for multiplication mod 5, we find that the inverse of 1 is 1, the inverse of 2 is 3 and, since multiplication is commutative, the inverse of 3 is also 2; finally, the inverse of 4 is 4. These values came from inspection, not from any systematic algorithm.

To perform one of the secure encryptions, we need a procedure for finding the inverse mod n of any element, even for very large values of n. An algorithm to determine a^{-1} directly is likely to be faster than searching a table, especially for large values of n. Also, although there is a pattern to the elements in the table, it is not easy to generate the elements of a particular row, looking for a 1, each time we need an inverse. Fortunately there is an algorithm which is reasonably simple to compute.

Fermat's Theorem

In number theory, Fermat's theorem states that for any prime p and any element $a < p$,

$$a^p \mod p = a$$

or

$$a^{p-1} \mod p = 1$$

This result leads to the inverses we want. For a prime p and an element $a < p$, the inverse of a is that element x such that

$$ax \mod p = 1$$

Combining the last two equations, we obtain

$$ax \mod p = 1 = a^{p-1} \mod p$$

so that

Inverse of ω

$$x = a^{p-2} \bmod p$$

This method is not a complete method for computing inverses, in that it only works for a prime p and an element $a < p$.

Example

We can use this formula to determine the inverse of 3 mod 5:

$$3^{-1} \bmod 5 = 3^{5-2} \bmod 5$$
$$= 3^3 \bmod 5$$
$$= 27 \bmod 5$$
$$= 2$$

as we determined earlier from the multiplication table.

Algorithm for Computing Inverses

Another method to compute inverses is shown in the following algorithm. This algorithm, adapted from [KNU69], is a fast approach that uses Euclid's algorithm for finding the greatest common divisor.

$\{** \text{ Compute } x = a^{-1} \bmod n \text{ given } a \text{ and } n \ **\}$
$c_0 := n$
$c_1 := a$
$b_0 := 0$
$b_1 := 1$
$i := 1$
repeat
    $c_{i+1} := c_{i-1} \bmod c_i$
    $t := c_{i-1} \ \mathbf{div} \ c_i$
    $b_{i+1} := b_{i-1} - t * b_i$
    $i := i + 1$
until $c_i = 0$
if $(b_{i-1} \geq 0)$ **then** $a := b_{i-1}$ **else** $a := n + b_{i-1}$

We will use these mathematical results in the next sections as we examine two encryption systems based on arithmetic in finite fields.

3.3 Public-Key Systems

In 1976, Diffie and Hellman [DIF76] proposed a new kind of encryption system: With a **public key** encryption system, each user would have a key that did not have to be kept secret. The public nature of the key would not inhibit the secrecy of the system. The public key transformation is essentially a one-way encryption with a secret (private) way to decrypt.

Motivation

Public key systems have an enormous advantage over the conventional key systems: anyone can send a secret message to a user, while the message remains adequately protected from being read by an interceptor. With a conventional key system, a separate key is needed for each pair of users.

A **channel** is a pathway for information flow; in a private environment, a channel is a pathway for information flow with protection against access by anyone outside the channel. Assume that three users, A, B, and C want to set up communication channels in pairs: A and B want to be able to exchange information that C cannot interpret, A and C want to be able to exchange information concealed from B, and B and C want to be able to exchange information without its being available to A. To handle this situation, three keys are necessary; call these keys k_{AB}, k_{AC} and k_{BC}.

If a fourth user, D, is to be added to the system, and there are to be channels established with the other three users, another three keys are needed: one to connect D to each of the existing users. Each time a new user is added to a system of n users, n additional keys are needed. Adding a sixth user is shown in Figure 3.4.

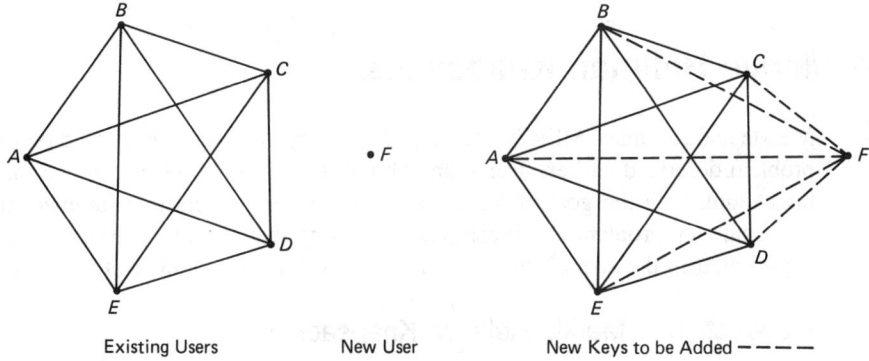

Figure 3.4   Creating New Private Channels.

In general, an n-user system will require $n * (n - 1)/2$ keys. As the number of users grows, the number of keys increases very rapidly. Determining and distributing these keys is a problem; more serious is maintaining security for the keys already distributed, because it is unreasonable to expect users to memorize so many keys.

Characteristics

With a public key system, each user has two keys: a public key and a private key. The user may publish the public key freely. The keys operate as inverses. Let k_{PRIV} be a user's private key, and let k_{PUB} be the corresponding public key. Then,

$$P = D(k_{\text{PRIV}}, E(k_{\text{PUB}}, P))$$

That is, a user can decode with a private key what someone else has encrypted with the corresponding public key. Furthermore, with the second public key encryption algorithm,

$$P = D(k_{\text{PUB}}, E(k_{\text{PRIV}}, P))$$

so that a user can encrypt a message with a private key, and the message can be revealed only with the corresponding public key. (We will see an application of this second case in the next chapter on digital signature protocols.)

These two properties imply that public and private keys can be applied in either order. (With the RSA system, there is no distinction between private and public keys. Either key of a pair can be used as the private or as the public key.) Ideally, the decryption function D can be applied to any argument, so that it is possible to decrypt first and then encrypt. With conventional encryption, one seldom thinks of decrypting *before* encrypting. With public keys, it simply means to apply the private transformation first, and then the public one.

With public keys, only two keys are needed per user: one public and one private. B, C, and D can all encrypt messages for A using A's public key. If B has encrypted a message using A's public key, C *cannot* decrypt it, even if C knew it was encrypted with A's public key. Applying A's public key twice, for example, would not decrypt the message. (We assume, of course, that A's private key remains secret.)

3.4 Merkle-Hellman Knapsacks

Merkle and Hellman [MER78] developed an encryption algorithm based on the knapsack problem described earlier. The knapsack problem posed a set of positive integers and a target sum, with the goal of finding a subset of the integers that summed to the target. The knapsack problem is NP-complete, implying that to solve it probably requires time exponential in the size of the problem—in this case, the number of integers.

Introduction to Merkle-Hellman Knapsacks

This section contains an outline of the operation of the Merkle-Hellman knapsack encryption method.

The idea behind the Merkle-Hellman knapsack scheme is to encode a binary message as a solution to a knapsack problem, reducing the ciphertext to the target sum obtained by adding terms corresponding to 1s in the plaintext. That is, blocks of plaintext will be converted to a knapsack sum by adding into the sum those terms that match with 1 bits in the plaintext, as shown in Figure 3.5.

A knapsack is represented as a vector of integer terms in which the order of the terms is very important. There are actually two knapsacks—an easy one, to which a fast (linear time) algorithm exists, and a hard one, derived by modifying the elements of the easy knapsack. The modification is such that a solution with the elements of either knapsack is a solution with the other one as well. This modification is a **trapdoor**,

Plaintext Binary Message	1 0 1 0 0 1	0 1 1 0 1 0	1 1 0 1 0 0	0 0 0 0 0 0	0 1 1 1 1 1 · · ·
Knapsack	1 2 5 9 20 43	1 2 5 9 20 43	1 2 5 9 20 43	1 2 5 9 20 43	1 2 5 9 20 43
Ciphertext Encrypted Message Target Sum	1 + 5 + 43 = 49	2 + 5 + 20 = 27	1 + 2 + 9 = 12	0 0	2 + 5 + 9 + 20 + 43 = 79

Figure 3.5   Knapsack for Encryption.

permitting legitimate users to solve the problem simply. Thus, the general problem is NP-complete, but there is a restricted version of it that has a very fast solution.

The algorithm begins with a knapsack set each of whose elements is larger than the sum of all previous elements. Suppose we have a sequence where each element a_k is larger than $a_1 + a_2 + \ldots + a_{k-1}$. If a sum is between a_k and a_{k+1}, it must contain a_k as a term, because no combination of the values $a_1, a_2, \ldots, a_{k-1}$ could produce a total as large as a_k. Similarly, if a sum is less than a_k, clearly it cannot contain a_k as a term.

The modification of the algorithm disguises the elements of the easy knapsack set by changing this increasing size property in a way that preserves the underlying solution. The modification is accomplished using multiplication by a constant mod n.

Detailed Explanation of the Merkle-Hellman Technique

In this section we explain the Merkle-Hellman technique in full detail. This section is intended for people who want a detailed understanding of the algorithm.

General Knapsacks

The knapsack problem examines a sequence $a_1, a_2, \cdots, a_n$ of integers and a target sum, T. The problem is to find a vector of 0s and 1s such that the sum of the integers associated with 1s equals T. That is, given $S = [a_1, a_2, \cdots, a_n]$, and T, find a vector V of 0s and 1s such that

$$\sum_i a_i * v_i = T$$

For example, consider the list of integers [17,38,73,4,11,1] and the target number 53. The problem is to find which of the integers should be selected for the sum, that is, which should correspond with 1s in C. Clearly 73 cannot be a term, so we can ignore it. Trying 17, the problem reduces to finding a sum for $(53 - 17 = 36)$. With a second target of 36, 38 cannot contribute, and 4+11+1 are not enough to make 36. We then conclude that 17 is not a term in the solution.

If 38 is in the solution, then the problem reduces to the new target $(53 - 38 = 15)$. With this target, a quick glance at the remaining values shows that 4 and 11 complete the solution, since $4 + 11 = 15$. A solution is thus $38 + 4 + 11$.

This solution proceeded in an orderly manner. We considered each possible integer as contributing to the sum and reduced the problem correspondingly. When one solution did not produce the desired sum, we backed up, discarding recent guesses and trying alternatives. This backtracking seriously impaired the speed of solution.

With only six integers, it did not take long to determine the solution. Fortunately, one of the integers (73) could be discarded immediately as too large, and in a subproblem another integer (38) could be dismissed immediately. With many integers, it would have been much more difficult to find a solution, especially if they were all of similar magnitude so that none could be dismissed immediately.

Superincreasing Knapsacks

Suppose this problem has an additional restriction: The integers of S must form a **superincreasing sequence**, that is, one where each integer is greater than the sum of all preceding integers. Then, every integer a_k would be of the form

$$a_k > \sum_{j=1}^{k-1} a_j$$

In the previous example, [1,4,11,17,38,73] is a superincreasing sequence. If we restrict the knapsack problem to superincreasing sequences, it is easy to tell whether a term is included in the sum or not. No combination of terms less than a particular term can yield a sum as large as the term. For instance, 17 is greater than 1+4+11 (=16). If a target sum is greater than or equal to 17, 17 or some larger term must be a term.

The solution of a **superincreasing knapsack** (also called a **simple knapsack**) is easy to find. Start with T. Compare the largest integer in S to it. If this integer is larger than T, it is not in the sum, so let the corresponding position in C be 0. If the largest integer is less than or equal to T, that integer is in the sum, so let the corresponding position in C be 1 and reduce T by the integer. Repeat for all remaining integers in S. An algorithm for solving a simple knapsack is shown in Figure 3.6.

96:	73? Yes		95:	73? Yes ⟵
96 − 73 = 23:	38? No		95 − 73 = 22:	38? No
23:	17? Yes		22:	17? Yes ⟵
23 − 17 = 6:	11? No		22 − 17 = 5:	11? No
6:	4? Yes		5:	4? Yes ⟵
6 − 4 = 2:	1? Yes		5 − 4 = 1:	1? Yes ⟵
1:	−		1 − 1 = 0	
No Solution			Solution	

Figure 3.6 Example of Solving a Simple Knapsack.

The Encryption Technique

The Merkle-Hellman encryption technique is a public-key cryptosystem. That is, each user has a public key, which can be distributed to anyone, and a private key, which is kept secret. The public key is the set of integers of a knapsack problem (*not* a superincreasing knapsack); the private key is a corresponding superincreasing knapsack. The contribution of Merkle and Hellman was the design of a technique for converting a superincreasing knapsack into a regular one. The trick is to change the numbers in a nonobvious but reversible way.

Principles of Modular Arithmetic

In normal arithmetic, adding to or multiplying a superincreasing sequence preserves its superincreasing nature, so that the result is still a superincreasing sequence. That is, if $a > b$ then $k * a > k * b$ for any positive integer k.

However, in arithmetic mod n the product of two large numbers may in fact be smaller than the product of two small numbers, since results larger than n are reduced to between 0 and $n - 1$. Thus, the superincreasing property of a sequence may be destroyed by multiplication by a constant mod n.

Consider a system mod 11. The product $3 * 7 \bmod 11 = 21 \bmod 11 = 10$, while $3 * 8 \bmod 11 = 24 \bmod 11 = 2$. Even though $7 < 8$, $3 * 7 \bmod 11 > 3 * 8 \bmod 11$. Multiplying a sequence of integers mod some base may destroy the superincreasing nature of the sequence.

Modular arithmetic is sensitive to common factors. If all products of all integers are mapped into the space of the integers mod n, clearly there will be some duplicates, that is, two different products can produce the same result mod n. If $w * x \bmod n = r$, then $w * x + n \bmod n = r$, $w * x + 2n \bmod n = r$, and so on. Furthermore, if w and n have a factor in common, then not every integer between 0 and $n - 1$ will be a result of $w * x \bmod n$ for some x.

Look at the integers mod 5. If $w = 3$ and $x = 1, 2, 3, \ldots$, the multiplication of $x * w \bmod 5$ produces all the results from 0 to 4, as shown in Table 3.1. Notice that after $x = 5$, the modular results repeat.

TABLE 3.1 $3 * x \bmod 5$

x	$3 * x$	$3 * x \bmod 5$
1	3	3
2	6	1
3	9	4
4	12	2
5	15	0
6	18	3
7	21	1

However, if we choose $w = 3$ and $n = 6$, not every integer between 0 and 5 is used. This occurs because w and n share a common factor, 3. Table 3.2 shows the results of $3 * x \bmod 6$.

Thus, there may be some values that cannot be written as the product of two integers mod n for certain values of n. To produce all values between 0 and $n - 1$, n must be relatively prime to w.

If w and n are relatively prime, w has a multiplicative inverse mod n. That means that for every integer w, there is another integer w^{-1} such that $w * w^{-1} = 1 \bmod n$. A

TABLE 3.2 $3 * x \bmod 6$

x	$3*x$	$3*x \bmod 6$
1	3	3
2	6	0
3	9	3
4	12	0
5	15	3
6	18	0
7	21	3

multiplicative inverse is a way of undoing the effect of multiplication: $(w*q)*w^{-1} = q$. (Remember that multiplication is commutative and associative in the group mod n so that $w * q * w^{-1} = (w * w^{-1}) * q = q \bmod n$.)

With these results from modular arithmetic, Diffie and Hellman found a way to break the superincreasing nature of a sequence of integers. The pattern can be broken by multiplying all integers by a constant w, and taking the result mod n where w and n are relatively prime.

Transforming a Superincreasing Knapsack

In order to perform an encryption using the Merkle-Hellman algorithm, we need a superincreasing knapsack that can be transformed into a hard knapsack. In this section we will show just how to do that.

We begin by picking a superincreasing sequence S of m integers. Such a sequence is easy to find. Select an initial integer (probably a relatively small one).Choose the next integer to be larger than the first. Then select an integer larger than the sum of the first two. Continue this process by choosing new integers larger than the sum of all integers already selected.

For example,

$$
\begin{array}{lll}
[1, & & \\
[1, & ? > 1: & 2 \\
[1, 2, & ? > 1 + 2: & 4 \\
[1, 2, 4, & ? > 1 + 2 + 4: & 9 \\
[1, 2, 4, 9, & ? > 1 + 2 + 4 + 9: & 19
\end{array}
$$

is such a sequence.

The superincreasing sequence just selected is called a **simple knapsack**. Any instance of the knapsack problem formed from that knapsack has a solution that is easy to find.

After selecting a simple knapsack $S = [s_1, s_2, \ldots, s_m]$, we choose a multiplier w and a modulus n. The modulus should be a number greater than the largest integer, s_m. The multiplier should have no common factors with the modulus. One easy way to guarantee this is to choose a modulus that is a prime number, since no number smaller than it will have any common factors with it.

Finally, we replace every integer s_i in the simple knapsack with the term

$$h_i = w * s_i \bmod n$$

Then $H = [h_1, h_2, \ldots, h_m]$ is a hard knapsack. We will use both the hard and simple knapsacks in the encryption.

For example, start with the superincreasing knapsack $S = [1, 2, 4, 9]$ and transform it by multiplying by w and reducing mod n where $w = 15$ and $n = 17$.

$$
\begin{array}{rcrcc}
1*15 & = & 15 \bmod 17 & = & 15 \\
2*15 & = & 30 \bmod 17 & = & 13 \\
4*15 & = & 60 \bmod 17 & = & 9 \\
9*15 & = & 135 \bmod 17 & = & 16
\end{array}
$$

The hard knapsack derived in this example is $H = [15, 13, 9, 16]$.

Example Using Merkle-Hellman Knapsacks

Now we show how to use Merkle-Hellman encryption on a plaintext message P. The encryption algorithm using Merkle-Hellman knapsacks starts with a binary message. The message is envisioned as a binary sequence $P = [p_1, p_2, \ldots, p_k]$. Divide the message into blocks of m bits, $P_0 = [p_1, p_2, \ldots, p_m]$, $P_1 = [p_{m+1}, \ldots, p_{2m}]$, and so forth. The value of m is the number of terms in the simple or hard knapsack.

The encipherment of message P is a sequence of targets, where each target is the sum of some of the terms of the hard knapsack H. The terms selected are those corresponding to 1 bits in P_i, so that P_i serves as a selection vector for the elements of H. Each term of the ciphertext is $P_i * H$, the target derived using block P_i as the selection vector.

Encrypting a Message

For this example, we use the knapsacks $S = [1, 2, 4, 9]$ and $H = [15, 13, 9, 16]$ obtained in the previous section. With those knapsacks, $w = 15$, $n = 17$, and $m = 4$. The public key (knapsack) is H, while S is kept secret.

The message

$$P = 0100101110100101$$

is encoded with the knapsack $H = [15, 13, 9, 16]$ as follows.

$$P = 0100\ 1011\ 1010\ 0101$$

$$
\begin{array}{l}
[0, 1, 0, 0] * [15, 13, 9, 16] = 13 \\
[1, 0, 1, 1] * [15, 13, 9, 16] = 40 \\
[1, 0, 1, 0] * [15, 13, 9, 16] = 24 \\
[0, 1, 0, 1] * [15, 13, 9, 16] = 29
\end{array}
$$

The message is encrypted as the integers 13, 40, 24, 29, using the public knapsack $H = [15, 13, 9, 16]$.

Decryption Algorithm

The legitimate recipient knows the simple knapsack and the values of w and n that transformed it to a hard public knapsack. The legitimate recipient determines the value w^{-1} so that $w * w^{-1} = 1 \bmod n$. In our example, $15^{-1} \bmod 17$ is 8, since $15 * 8 \bmod 17 = 120 \bmod 17 = (17 * 7) + 1 = 1$.

Remember that H is the hard knapsack derived from the simple knapsack S. H is obtained from S by

$$H = w * S \bmod n$$

(This notation, in which a constant is multiplied by a sequence, should be interpreted as $h_i = w * s_i \bmod n$ for all i, $1 \le i \le m$.)

The ciphertext message produced by the encryption algorithm is

$$C = H * P = w * S * P \bmod n$$

To decipher, it is necessary to multiply C by w^{-1}, since

$$w^{-1} * C = w^{-1} * H * P = w^{-1} * w * S * P = S * P \bmod n$$

To recover the plaintext message P, the legitimate recipient would solve the simple knapsack problem with knapsack S and target $w^{-1} * C_i$ for each ciphertext integer C_i. Since $w^{-1} * C_i = S * P \bmod n$, the solution for target $w^{-1} * C_i$ is plaintext block P_i, which is the message originally encrypted.

Example of Decryption

We continue our example, in which the underlying simple knapsack was $S = [1, 2, 4, 9]$, and $w = 15$ and $n = 17$. The transmitted messages were 13, 40, 24, and 29.

To decipher, these messages are multiplied by 8 mod 17 since 8 is $15^{-1} \bmod 17$. It is then easy to solve the simple knapsacks, as shown here:

$$
\begin{aligned}
13 * 8 &= 104 \bmod 17 = 2 = [0100] \\
40 * 8 &= 320 \bmod 17 = 14 = [1011] \\
24 * 8 &= 192 \bmod 17 = 5 = [1010] \\
29 * 8 &= 232 \bmod 17 = 11 = [0101]
\end{aligned}
$$

The recovered message is thus `0100101110100101`.

Cryptanalysis

In this example, because m is 4, it is easy to determine the solution to the knapsack problem for 13, 40, 24, and 29. Longer knapsacks (larger values of m), which also imply larger values of the modulus n, are not so simple to solve.

Practical Implementation

Typically, the value of n is chosen to be 100 to 200 binary digits long. If n is 200 bits long, the s_i are usually chosen to be about 2^{200} apart. That is, there are about 200 terms in the knapsacks, and each term of the simple knapsack is between 200 and 400 binary digits long. More precisely, s_0 is chosen so that $1 \leq s_0 < 2^{200}$, $2^{200} \leq s_1 < 2^{201}$, $2^{201} \leq s_2 < 2^{202}$, and so on, so that there are approximately 2^{200} choices for each s_i.

A sequence of random numbers can be used to generate the simple knapsack just described. A sequence of m random numbers, $r_1, r_2, r_3, \ldots, r_m$ is generated. Each r_i must be between 0 and 2^{200}. Then each value s_i of the simple knapsack is determined as by

$$s_i = 2^{200+i-1} + r_i$$

for $i = 1, 2, \ldots, m$.

With such large terms for S (and H), it is infeasible to try all possible values of s_i in order to infer S given H and C. Even assuming a machine could do one operation every microsecond, it would still take 10^{47} years to try every one of the 2^{200} choices for each s_i. A massively parallel machine with 1000 or even 1,000,000 parallel elements would not reduce this work factor enough.

Weaknesses of the Merkle-Hellman Encryption Algorithm

The Merkle-Hellman knapsack method seems secure. With appropriately large values for n and m, the chances of someone's being able to crack the method by brute force attack are slim.

However, an interceptor does not have to solve the basic knapsack problem in order to break the encryption, since the encryption depends on specially selected instances of the problem. In 1980, Shamir found that if the value of the modulus n is known, it may be possible to determine the simple knapsack. The exact method is beyond the scope of this book, but the method of attack will be outlined. For more information, see the article of Shamir and Zippel, [SHA80].

First, notice that since all elements of the hard knapsack are known, it is simple to determine which elements correspond with which elements of the simple knapsack. Consider h_0 and h_1, the first two elements of a hard knapsack, corresponding to simple knapsack elements s_0 and s_1.

Let

$$\rho = h_0/h_1 \bmod n$$

Since $h_0 = w * s_0 \bmod n$ and $h_1 = w * s_1 \bmod n$, it is also true that

$$\rho = (w * s_0)/(w * s_1) = s_0/s_1 \bmod n$$

Given the ratio ρ, determine the sequence

$$\Delta = \rho \bmod n, \ 2 * \rho \bmod n, \ 3 * \rho \bmod n, \ \ldots k * \rho \bmod n, \ \ldots, 2^m * \rho \bmod n$$

For some k, k and s_1 will cancel each other mod n; that is $k * (1/s_1) = 1 \bmod n$. Then

$$k * \rho \bmod n = k * s_0 * 1/s_1 \bmod n = s_0 \bmod n = s_0$$

It is reasonable to expect that s_0 will be the smallest element of Δ. Once s_0 is known, it is simple to determine w, then w^{-1} and each of the s_i.

A more serious flaw was identified later by Shamir [SHA82]. The actual argument is beyond the scope of this book, but again it can be sketched fairly briefly. The approach tries to deduce w and n from the h_i alone.

The approximate size of n can be deduced from the fact that it will be longer than any of the h_i, since they have been reduced mod n; however, n will not be substantially longer than the longest h_i, since it is likely that the results after taking the modulus will be be fairly evenly distributed between 1 and n.

Assume you are trying to guess w. You might iteratively try different candidate values $\tilde{w} = 1, 2, 3, \ldots$ for w. The graph of $\tilde{w} * h_i \bmod n$ as a function of $\tilde{w}$ would increase steadily until a value of $\tilde{w} * h_i$ was greater than n. At that point, the graph of $\tilde{w} * h_i$ would be discontinuous and have a small value. The values of $\tilde{w} * h_i$ would then resume their steady increase as $\tilde{w}$ increased until $\tilde{w} * h_i$ exceeded n again. The graph would form a progression of jagged peaks, resembling the teeth of a saw. The slope of each "tooth" of the graph is h_i. (See Figure 3.7 for a graphical representation of this process.)

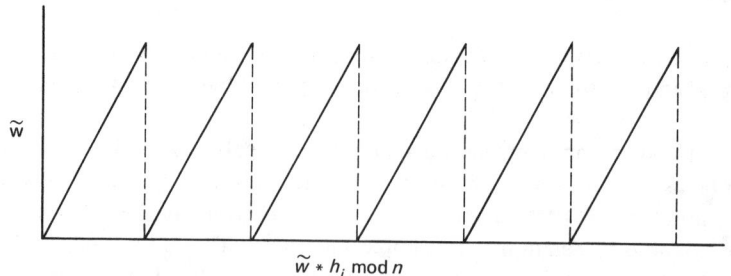

Figure 3.7   Graph of Change of Merkle Knapsack Function.

The correct value of $\tilde{w} = w$ occurs at one of the points of discontinuity of the graph of $\tilde{w} * h_i \bmod n$. This same pattern occurs for all values h_i: h_1, h_2, and so forth. Since w is a discontinuity point of $\tilde{w} * h_1 \bmod n$, it is also a discontinuity of $\tilde{w} * h_2 \bmod n$, of $\tilde{w} * h_3 \bmod n$, and so forth. To determine w superimpose the graph of $\tilde{w} * h_1 \bmod n$ on $\tilde{w} * h_2 \bmod n$ and superimpose those graphs on $\tilde{w} * h_3 \bmod n$, and so on. Then w will be at one of the places where all of the curves are discontinuous and fall from a high value to a low one. Two such graphs are shown in Figure 3.8. The problem of determining w is thus reduced to finding the point where all of these discontinuities coincide.

The actual process is a little more difficult. The value of n has been replaced by real number N. Since n and N are unknown, the graphs are scaled by dividing by N, and then approximating by successive values of the real number $\tilde{w}/N$ in the function $(\tilde{w}/N) * h_i \bmod 1.0$. Fortunately, this reduces to the solution of a system

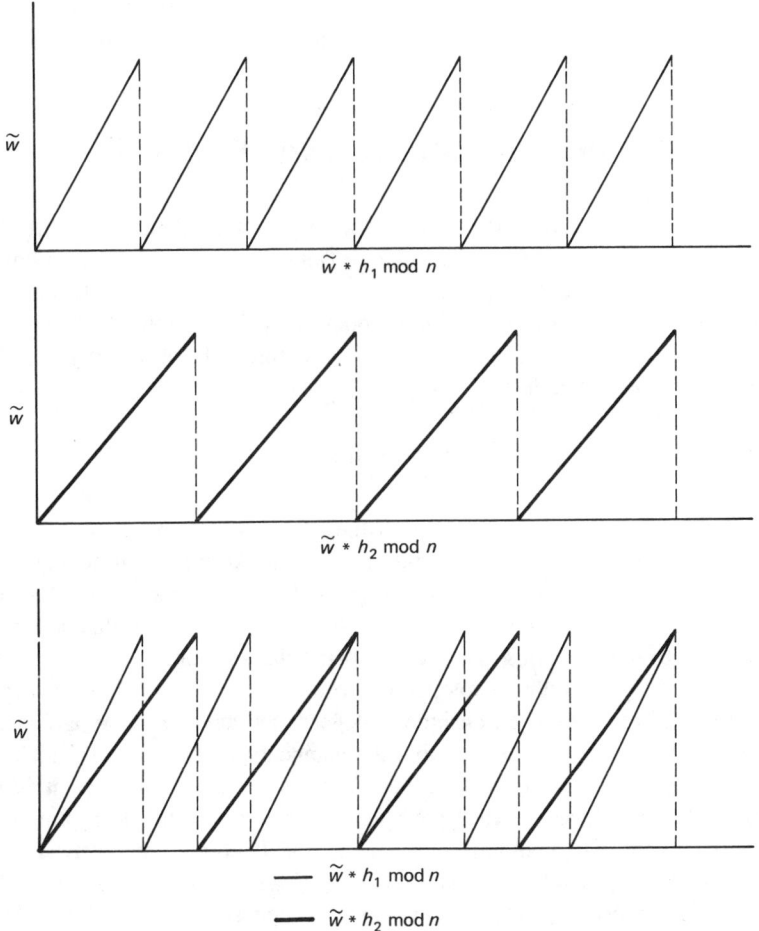

$\widetilde{w} * h_1 \bmod n$

$\widetilde{w} * h_2 \bmod n$

——— $\widetilde{w} * h_1 \bmod n$

——— $\widetilde{w} * h_2 \bmod n$

Figure 3.8   Coinciding Discontinuities.

of simultaneous linear inequalities. That problem can be solved in polynomial time. Therefore, the Merkle-Hellman knapsack problem can be broken in reasonable time.

Notice that this solution does not apply to the general knapsack problem; it applies only to the special class of knapsack problems derived from superincreasing sequences by multiplication by a constant modulo another constant. Thus, the basic knapsack problem is intact; it is only this restricted form that has been solved. This result underscores the point that a cryptosystem based on a hard problem is not necessarily as hard to break as the underlying problem.

Since it has become known that the Merkle-Hellman knapsack can be broken, other workers have analyzed variations of Merkle-Hellman knapsacks. (See, for example, [BRI83] and [LAG83].) To date, transformed knapsacks do not seem secure enough for an application where a concerted attack can be expected. The Merkle-Hellman algorithm or a variation would suffice for certain low-risk applications. However, because it is fairly complicated to use, the Merkle-Hellman method is not often recommended.

3.5 Rivest-Shamir-Adelman (RSA) Encryption

Another cryptosystem based on an underlying hard problem is the RSA algorithm, named after its three inventors, Rivest, Shamir, and Adelman. This algorithm was introduced in 1978 and, to date, it remains secure. As with the Merkle-Hellman algorithm, RSA has been the subject of extensive cryptanalysis. No serious flaws have yet been found. Although the amount of analysis is no guarantee of the security of a method, it does suggest a confidence level.

Intoduction to the RSA Algorithm

This section contains an overview of the RSA encryption scheme.

The RSA encryption algorithm incorporates results from number theory, combined with the difficulty of determining the prime factors of a target. On the surface, then, the RSA algorithm is similar to the Merkle-Hellman method, in that solving the encryption amounts to finding terms that add to a particular sum or multiply to a particular product.

The RSA algorithm also operates with arithmetic mod n. In this approach, a plaintext block is treated as an unsigned integer. Two keys, d and e, are used for decryption and encryption. They are actually interchangeable. The plaintext block, P, is encrypted as P^e mod n. Because the exponentiation is performed mod n, it is very difficult to factor P^e to uncover the encrypted plaintext. However, the decrypting key d is carefully chosen so that $(P^e)^d$ mod $n = P$. Thus, the legitimate receiver who knows d simply computes $(P^e)^d$ mod $n = P$ and recovers P without having to factor P^e.

The underlying problem on which the encryption algorithm is based is that of factoring large numbers. The factorization problem is not even known to be NP-complete; the fastest known algorithm is exponential in time.

Detailed Description of the Encryption Algorithm

In this section we present in detail the background and implementation of the RSA algorithm.

With the RSA algorithm, there are two keys, d and e, that work in pairs for decryption and encryption, respectively. A plaintext message P is encrypted to ciphertext C by

$$C = P^e \bmod n$$

The plaintext is recovered by

$$P = C^d \bmod n$$

Because of symmetry in modular arithmetic, encryption and decryption are mutual inverses and commutative. Therefore,

$$P = C^d \bmod n = (P^e)^d \bmod n = (P^d)^e \bmod n$$

This means that one can apply the encrypting transformation and then the decrypting one, or the decrypting one followed by the encrypting one.

Choosing Keys

The encryption key consists of the pair of integers (e, n), and the decryption key is (d, n). The starting point in finding keys for this algorithm is to select a value for n. The value of n should be quite large, a product of two primes p and q. Both p and q should be large themselves. Typically p and q are approximately 100 digits each, so that n is approximately 200 digits long. This length effectively inhibits factoring n to infer p and q.

Next a relatively large integer e is chosen so that e is relatively prime to $(p-1) *$ $(q-1)$. (Recall that "relatively prime" means that e has no factors in common with $(p-1)*(q-1)$.) An easy way to guarantee that e is relatively prime to $(p-1)*(q-1)$ is to choose e as a prime that is larger than both $(p-1)$ and $(q-1)$.

Finally, select d such that

$$e * d \equiv 1 \bmod (p-1) * (q-1)$$

$$d = e^{-1} \bmod (p-1)*(q-1)$$

Mathematical Foundations of the RSA Algorithm

The Euler totient function $\varphi(n)$ is the number of positive integers less than n that are relatively prime to n. If p is prime, then

$$\varphi(p) = (p-1)$$

Furthermore, if $n = p * q$, where p and q are both prime,

$$\varphi(n) = \varphi(p) * \varphi(q) = (p-1) * (q-1)$$

An identity devised by Euler and Fermat indicates that

$$x^{\varphi(n)} \equiv 1 \bmod n$$

for any integer x if n and x are relatively prime.

Suppose we encrypt a plaintext message P by the RSA algorithm, so that $E(P) = P^e$. We need to be sure we can recover the message. The value e is selected so that its inverse d can be found easily. Because e and d are inverses mod $\varphi(n)$,

$$e * d \equiv 1 \bmod \varphi(n)$$

or

$$e * d = k * \varphi(n) + 1 \tag{0}$$

for some integer k.

Because of the Euler/Fermat result,

$$P^{p-1} \equiv 1 \bmod p$$

and, since $(p-1)$ is a factor of $\varphi(n)$,

$$P^{k*\varphi(n)} \equiv 1 \bmod p$$

Multiplying by P produces

$$P^{k*\varphi(n)+1} \equiv P \bmod p$$

The same argument holds for q, so

$$P^{k*\varphi(n)+1} \equiv P \bmod q$$

Combining these last two results with (0) produces

$$(P^e)^d = P^{e*d}$$
$$= P^{k*\varphi(n)+1}$$
$$\equiv P \bmod p$$
$$\equiv P \bmod q$$

so that

$$(P^e)^d \equiv P \bmod n$$

and e and d are inverse operations.

Example

Let $p = 11$ and $q = 13$, so that $n = p*q = 143$ and $\varphi(n) = (p-1)*(q-1) = 10*12 = 120$. Next, an integer e is needed, and e must be relatively prime to $(p-1)*(q-1)$. Choose $e = 11$.

The inverse of 11 mod 120 is also 11, since $11 * 11 = 121 = 1 \bmod 120$. Thus, both encryption and decryption keys are the same: $e = d = 11$.

Let P be a "message" to be encrypted. For this example we use $P = 7$. The message is encrypted as follows: $7^{11} \bmod 143 = 106$, so that $E(7) = 106$. (Note: This result can be computed fairly easily with the use of a common pocket calculator. $7^{11} = 7^9 * 7^2 // 7^9 = 40\,353\,607,$ but it is not necessary to work with figures that large. Because of the reducibility rule, $a * b \bmod n = (a \bmod n) * (b \bmod n) \bmod n$. Since our final result will be reduced mod143, we can reduce any term, such as 7^9, which is 8 mod 143. Then, $8 * 49 \bmod 143 = 392 \bmod 143 = 106$.)

This answer is correct, since $D(106) = 106^{11} \bmod 143 = 7$.

Practical Implementation of the Algorithm

The user of the RSA algorithm chooses primes p and q, from which the value $n = p*q$ is obtained. Next e is chosen to be relatively prime to $(p-1)*(q-1)$; e is usually a prime larger than $(p-1)$ or $(q-1)$. Finally, d is computed as the inverse of $e \bmod \varphi(n)$.

The user distributes e and n, and keeps d secret; p, q, and $\varphi(n)$ may be discarded (but not revealed) at this point. Notice that even though n is known to be the product of two primes, if they are relatively large (such as 100 digits long), it will not be possible to determine the primes, p and q, or the private key, d, from e. Therefore, this scheme provides adequate security for d.

It is not even practical to verify that p and q themselves are primes, since that would require considering on the order of 10^{50} possible factors. A heuristic algorithm from Solovay and Strassen [SOL77] can determine the probability of primality to any desired degree of confidence.

Every prime number passes two tests. If p is prime and r is any number less than p,

$$gcd(p, r) = 1$$

(where gcd is the greatest common divisor function) and

$$J(r, p) \equiv r^{(p-1)/2} \bmod p$$

where $J(r, p)$ is the Jacobi function defined as follows.

$$J(r,p) = \begin{cases} 1 & \text{if } r = 1 \\ J(r/2, p) * (-1)^{(p^2 - 1)/8} & \text{if } r \text{ is even} \\ J(p \bmod r, r) * (-1)^{(r-1)*(p-1)/4} & \text{if } r \text{ is odd and } r \neq 1 \end{cases}$$

If a number is suspected to be prime but fails either of these tests, it is definitely *not* a prime. If a number is suspected to be a prime and passes both of these tests, the likelihood that it is prime is at least $1/2$.

The problem relative to the RSA algorithm is to find two large primes p and q. With the Solovay and Strassen approach, one first guesses a large candidate prime, p. One then generates a random number r and computes $gcd(p, r)$ and $J(r, p)$. If either of these tests fails, p was not a prime, and the procedure stops. If both pass, the likelihood that p was not prime is at most $1/2$. The process repeats with a new value for r chosen at random. If this second r passes, the likelihood that a nonprime p could pass both tests is at most $1/4$. In general, after repeating the process k times without either test failing, the likelihood that p is not a prime is at most $1/2^k$.

Zimmerman [ZIM86] gives a method for computing RSA encryptions efficiently.

Cryptanalysis of the RSA Method

Like the Merkle-Hellman knapsack algorithm, the RSA method has been scrutinized intensely by professionals in computer security and cryptanalysis. Several minor problems have been identified with it, but there have been no flaws as serious as those for the Merkle-Hellman method.

3.6 Single Key (Conventional) Systems

The Merkle-Hellman and RSA algorithms are both **public key** algorithms. They provide users with two keys, one for encryption and another for decryption, so that one key can be made available to anyone wishing to send encrypted information, and the other key—which is kept secret—is the only key that can decrypt that information.

The algorithms presented in the last chapter were all **single key** or **conventional encryption** algorithms, in which both the encryptor and the decryptor use the same key, which must be kept secret. Single key systems are sometimes called **private key** systems. Because of the possibility of confusing that term with the private key of a public key system, we will use "single key" throughout the rest of this book.

Advantages and Disadvantages

The single key systems provide a two-way channel to their users: A and B share a secret key, and they can both encrypt information to send to the other as well as decrypt information from the other. The symmetry of this situation is a major advantage.

As long as the key remains secret, the system also provides **authentication**, proof that a message received was not fabricated by someone other than the declared sender. Authenticity is insured because only the legitimate sender can produce a message that will decrypt properly with the shared key.

Problems of Single Key Systems

There are several difficulties with single key systems.

1. With all key systems, if the key is revealed (stolen, guessed, bought, or otherwise compromised), the interceptors can immediately decrypt all encrypted information they have available. Furthermore, an imposter using an intercepted key can produce bogus messages under the guise of a legitimate sender. For this reason, in secure encryption systems, the keys are changed fairly frequently so that a compromised key will reveal only a limited amount of information.

2. Distribution of keys becomes a problem. Keys must be transmitted with utmost security, since they allow access to all information encrypted under them. For applications that extend throughout the world, this can be a complex task. Often couriers are used to distribute the keys securely by hand. Another approach is to distribute the keys in pieces under separate channels, so that any one discovery will not produce a full key. This approach is shown in Figure 3.9.

3. As described earlier, the number of keys increases with the square of the number of people exchanging secret information. This problem is usually contained by having only a few people exchange secrets directly so that the network of interchanges is relatively small. If people in separate networks need to exchange secrets, they may do so through a central "clearing house" or "forwarding office," which accepts secrets from one person, decrypts them, reencrypts them using another person's key, and transmits them. This technique is shown in Figure 3.10.

4. The single key encryption systems described so far have been relatively weak, vulnerable to various cryptanalytic attacks. Both the Merkle-Hellman and the RSA

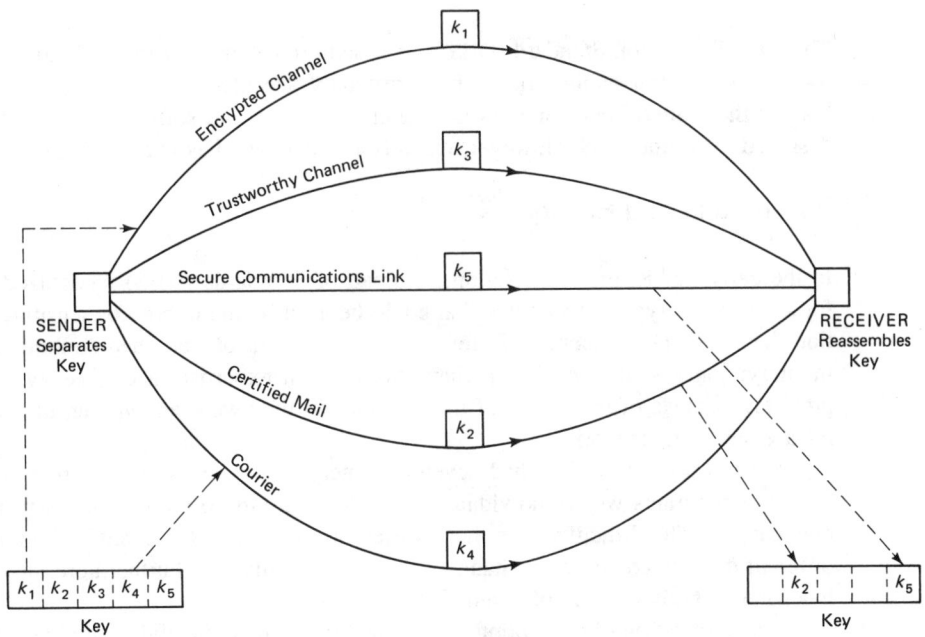

Figure 3.9   Key Distribution in Pieces.

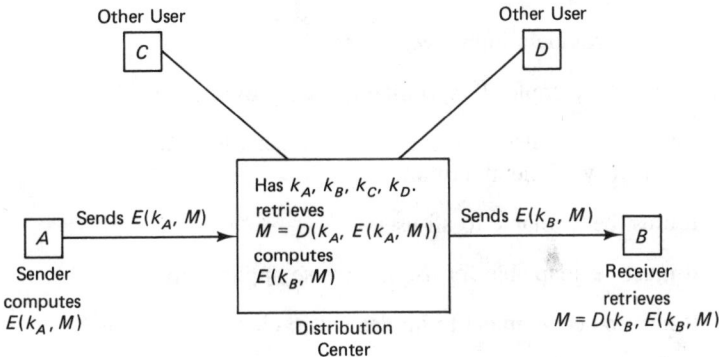

Figure 3.10   Distribution Center for Encrypted Information.

algorithms are based on much more complex problems, problems that have interested mathematicians for years. A secure single key system must be based on an equally solid approach.

3.7 The Data Encryption Standard (DES)

The Data Encryption Standard (DES) is a system developed for the U.S. government for use by the general public. It has been officially accepted as a cryptographic standard both in the United States and abroad. Many hardware and software systems have been designed using the DES. However, recently its adequacy has been questioned.

Background and History

In the early 1970s, the U.S. National Bureau of Standards (NBS) recognized the need for a secure encryption technique that could be used by the public for sensitive information. The U.S. Department of Defense and Department of State had continuing interest in encryption systems and had perhaps the greatest expertise in cryptology. However, precisely because of the nature of the information they were encrypting, they could not release any of their work.

Several private vendors had developed encryption devices, using either mechanical means or programs which individuals or firms could buy to protect their sensitive communications. The difficulty with this proliferation was one of exchange: Two users with different devices could not exchange encrypted information. Furthermore, there was no independent body capable of extensive testing of these devices.

Standardization of encryption was needed to promote the ability of unrelated parties to exchange encrypted information and to provide a single encryption system that could be rigorously tested and publicly certified. In 1972 the NBS issued a call for proposals for a public encryption algorithm. The call specified desirable criteria for such an algorithm.

1. It must provide a high level of security.

2. It must be completely specified and easy to understand.

3. The algorithm itself must provide the security; the security should not depend on the secrecy of the algorithm.

4. It must be available to all users.

5. It must be adaptable for use in diverse applications.

6. It must be economical to implement in electronic devices.

7. It must be efficient to use.

8. It must be able to be validated.

9. It must be exportable.

Clearly, from criterion 6 the NBS envisioned an algorithm that could be provided as a separate hardware device. From criterion 3, the NBS wanted to be able to reveal the algorithm itself, basing the security of the system on the keys (which would be under the control of the users).

Response to the call was not promising, and so the NBS issued a second call in August 1974. The idea judged the most promising was the "Lucifer" algorithm on which IBM had been working for several years. This idea had been published earlier, so that the basic algorithm was public and open to scrutiny and validation. Although lengthy, the algorithm was straightforward, a natural candidate for iterative implementation in a computer program. Furthermore, unlike the Merkle-Hellman and RSA algorithms, which use arithmetic on 100- or 200-digit binary numbers (far larger than most machine instructions would handle as a single quantity), Lucifer used only simple logical operations on relatively small quantities. Thus, the algorithm could be implemented fairly efficiently in either hardware or software on conventional computers.

A data encryption algorithm based on Lucifer was developed by IBM for the NBS; this algorithm became known as the DES (Data Encryption Standard), although its proper name is DEA (Data Encryption Algorithm) in the U.S. and DEA1 (Data Encryption Algorithm-1) in other countries. The NBS negotiated with IBM to determine a fair compensation for public release and distribution of the product IBM had developed. The NBS called upon the Department of Defense through its National Security Agency (NSA) to analyze the strength of the encryption algorithm. Finally, the NBS released the algorithm for public scrutiny and discussion.

After these steps, the DES was officially adopted as a Federal standard on November 23, 1976. It was authorized for use on all public and private sector unclassified communication. It was later accepted as an international standard by the International Standards Organization.

Overview of the DES Algorithm

The DES algorithm is a careful and complex combination of two of the fundamental building blocks of encryption: substitution and permutation (transposition). The algorithm derives its strength from repeated application of these two techniques, one on top of the other, for a total of 16 cycles. The sheer complexity of tracing a single bit through 16 iterations of substitutions and permutations has so far stopped researchers in the public from identifying more than a handful of general properties of the algorithm.

Plaintext is encrypted as blocks of 64 bits. Although the key is 64 bits long, in effect the key can be any 56-bit number. The key can be changed at will by the user any time security of the old key may be uncertain.

The two ciphers of the DES are substitutions and permutations. The substitutions, just like the substitutions of Chapter 2, provide confusion by systematically substituting some bit patterns for others. The transpositions, just like the transpositions of Chapter 2, provide diffusion by reordering the bits. Plaintext is affected by a series of cycles of a substitution then a transposition. The iterative substitutions and permutations are performed as outlined in Figure 3.11.

The algorithm uses only standard arithmetic and logical operations on up to 64-bit numbers, so it is suitable for implementation in software on most current computers. Although complex, the algorithm is repetitive, making it suitable for implementation on a single-purpose chip. In fact, several such chips are available on the market for use as basic components in devices that use DES encryption in an application.

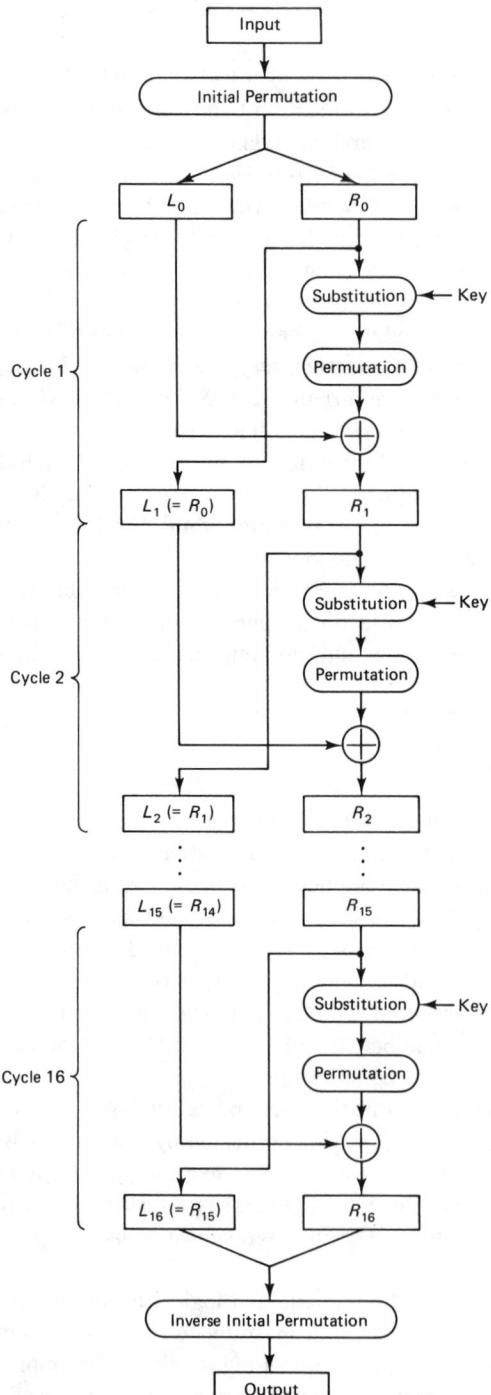

Figure 3.11 Iterative Substitution and Transposition.

Details of the Encryption Algorithm

The algorithm is derived from two concepts of Shannon's theory of information secrecy, published in 1949 ([SHA49]). Shannon identified two techniques to conceal information: confusion and diffusion. Recall from Chapter 2 that in **confusion** a piece of information is changed, so that the output bits have no obvious relationship to the input bits. **Diffusion** attempts to spread the effect of one plaintext bit to other bits in the ciphertext.

Thus, the basis of Lucifer and of the DES is two different ciphers, applied alternately. Shannon noted that two relatively weak ciphers can be made more secure by applying them together, called the "product" of the two ciphers alternately. The product of two ciphers is depicted in Figure 3.12.

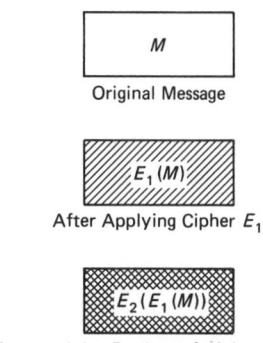

M

Original Message

$E_1(M)$

After Applying Cipher E_1

$E_2(E_1(M))$

After Applying Product of Ciphers $E_1 \cdot E_2$ **Figure 3.12** Product Ciphers.

Outline of the DES

After initialization the DES algorithm operates on blocks of data. It splits a data block in half, scrambles each half independently, combines the key with one half, and swaps the two halves. This process is repeated 16 times. It is an iterative algorithm using just table lookups and simple bit operations. Although the bit-level manipulations of the algorithm are quite complex, the algorithm itself can be implemented quite efficiently. The rest of this section identifies the individual steps of the algorithm. In the next section each step is described in full detail.

Input to the DES is divided into blocks of 64 bits, which are transformed using a 64-bit key. The 64 data bits are permuted by a so-called "initial permutation." The key is reduced from 64 bits to 56 bits by dropping bits 8, 16, 24, . . . , 64. These bits are assumed to be parity bits that carry no information in the key.

Next begins the sequence of operations known as a **cycle**. The 64 permuted data bits are broken into a left half and a right half of 32 bits each. The key is shifted left by a number of bits and permuted. The key is combined with the right half, which is then combined with the left half. The result of these combinations becomes the new right half; the old right half becomes the new left half. This sequence of activities, which

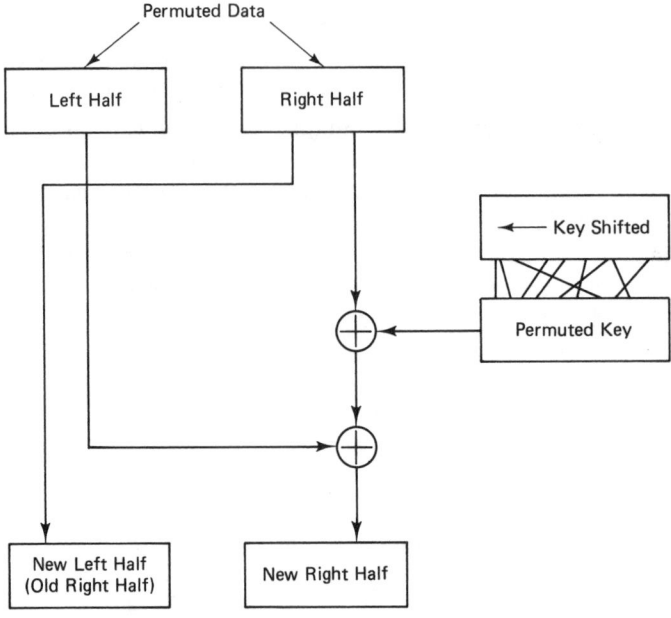

Figure 3.13   A Cycle in the DES.

constitutes a cycle, is shown in Figure 3.13. The cycles are repeated 16 times. After the last cycle there is a final permutation, which is the inverse of the initial permutation.

In order to combine a 32-bit right half with a 64-bit key, two changes are needed. First, the 32-bit half is expanded to 48 bits by repeating certain bits, while the 64-bit key is reduced to 48 bits by choosing only certain bits. These last two operations, called **expansion permutations** and **permuted choices** are shown in the diagram of Figure 3.14.

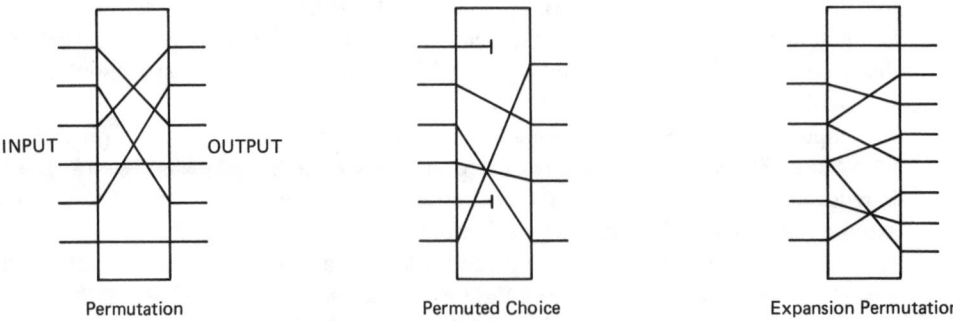

Figure 3.14   Types of Permutations.

Details of Each Cycle of the Algorithm

Each cycle of the algorithm is really four separate operations. First a right half is expanded from 32 bits to 48. Then it is combined with a form of the key. The result of this operation is then substituted for another result and condensed to 32 bits at the same time. The 32 bits are permuted, and then combined with the left half to yield a new right half. This whole process is shown in Figure 3.15.

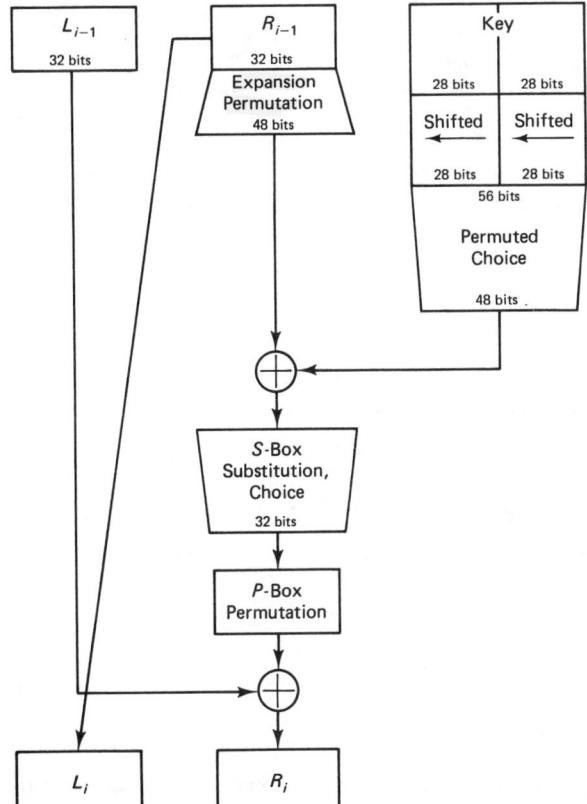

Figure 3.15   Detail of a Cycle.

Expansion Permutation

Each right half is expanded from 32 to 48 bits by means of the expansion permutation. The expansion permutes the order of the bits and also repeats certain bits. The expansion has two purposes: to make the intermediate halves of the ciphertext comparable in size to the key, and to provide a longer result that can later be compressed.

The expansion permutation is defined by Table 3.3. For each 4-bit block, the first and fourth bits are duplicated, while the second and third are used only once. This table shows *to which* output position(s) the input bits move. Since this is an expansion

TABLE 3.3 EXPANSION PERMUTATION.

Bit	1	2	3	4	5	6	7	8
Moves to	2,48	3	4	5,7	6,8	9	10	11,13
Bit	9	10	11	12	13	14	15	16
Moves to	12,14	15	16	17,19	18,20	21	22	23,25
Bit	17	18	19	20	21	22	23	24
Moves to	24,26	27	28	29,31	30,32	33	34	35,37
Bit	25	26	27	28	29	30	31	32
Moves to	36,38	39	40	41,43	42,44	45	46	47,1

permutation, some bits move to more than one position. Each row of the table shows the movement of eight bits. The interpretation of this table is that bit 1 moves to positions 2 and 48 of the output, while bit 10 moves to position 15. A portion of the pattern is also shown in Figure 3.16.

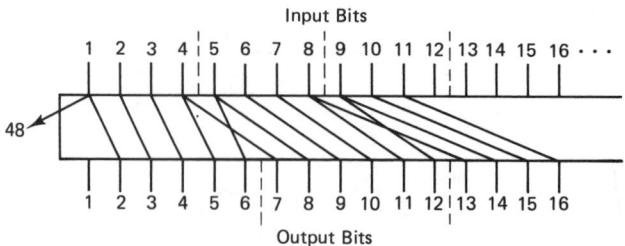

Figure 3.16   Pattern of Expansion Permutation.

Key Transformation

As just described, the 64-bit key immediately becomes a 56-bit key by deletion of every eighth bit. At each step in the cycle, the key is split into two 28-bit halves, the halves are shifted left by a specified number of digits, the halves are pasted together again, and 48 of these 56 bits are permuted to use as a key during this cycle.

The key for the cycle is combined by an exclusive-or function with the expanded right half from the section above. That result moves into the S-boxes described in the next step.

At each cycle, the halves of the key are independently shifted left circularly by a specified number of bit positions. The number of bits shifted is given in Table 3.4.

After being shifted, 48 of the 56 bits are extracted for the exclusive-or combination with the expanded right half. The choice permutation that selects these 48 bits is shown in Table 3.5. From this table, for example, bit 1 of the shifted key goes to output position 5, while bit 9 is ignored in this cycle.

TABLE 3.4 NUMBER OF BITS OF
CIRCULAR SHIFTS FOR EACH CYCLE.

Cycle number	Bits Shifted
1	1
2	1
3	2
4	2
5	2
6	2
7	2
8	2
9	1
10	2
11	2
12	2
13	2
14	2
15	2
16	1

TABLE 3.5 CHOICE PERMUTATION TO SELECT 48 KEY BITS.

Key bit	1	2	3	4	5	6	7	8	9	10	11	12	13	14
Selected for position	5	24	7	16	6	10	20	18	–	12	3	15	23	1

Key bit	15	16	17	18	19	20	21	22	23	24	25	26	27	28
Selected for position	9	19	2	–	14	22	11	–	13	4	–	17	21	8

Key bit	29	30	31	32	33	34	35	36	37	38	39	40	41	42
Selected for position	47	31	27	48	35	41	–	46	28	–	39	32	25	44

Key bit	43	44	45	46	47	48	49	50	51	52	53	54	55	56
Selected for position	–	37	34	43	29	36	38	45	33	26	42	–	30	40

S-Boxes

Substitutions are performed by eight **S-boxes**. An S-box is a table by which six bits of data are replaced by four bits. The 48-bit input is divided into eight 6-bit blocks, identified as $B_1 B_2 \ldots B_8$; block B_i is operated on by S-box S_i, as shown in Figure 3.17.

The S-boxes are substitutions based on a table of 4 rows and 16 columns. Suppose that block B_i is the six bits $b_1 b_2 b_3 b_4 b_5 b_6$. Bits b_1 and b_6, taken together, form a two-bit binary number $b_1 b_6$, having a decimal value from 0 to 3. Call this value r. Bits b_2, b_3, b_4, and b_5 taken together form a four-bit binary number $b_2 b_3 b_4 b_5$, having a decimal value from 0 to 15. Call this value c. The substitutions from the S-boxes transform each 6-bit block B_i into the 4-bit result shown in row r, column c of section S_i of Table

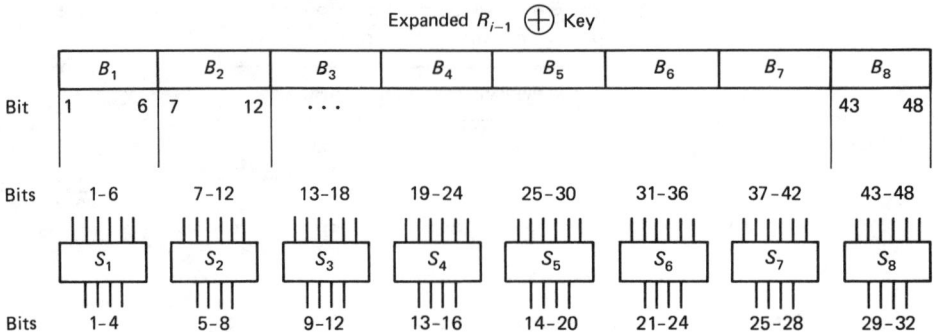

Figure 3.17   S-Boxes Operating on Eight 6-bit Blocks.

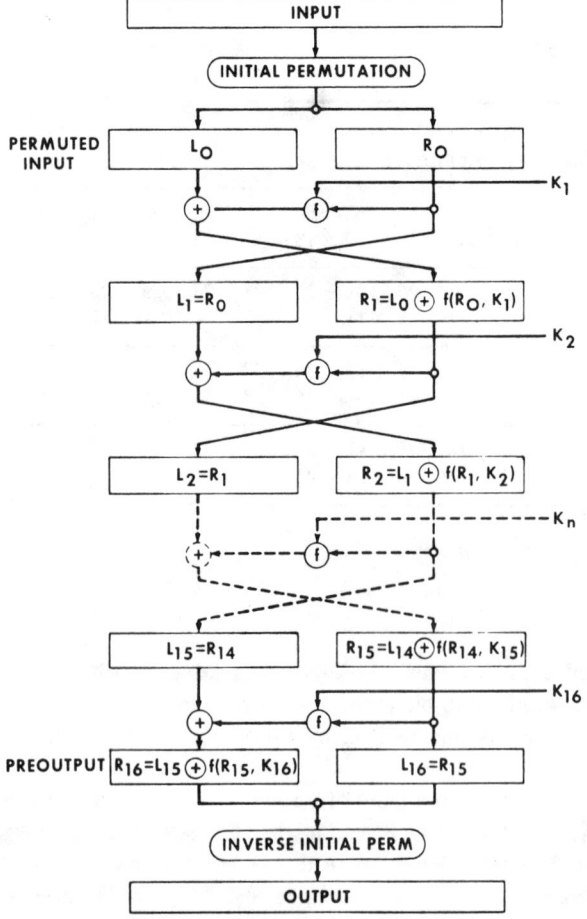

Figure 3.18   Complete Representation of the DES.

TABLE 3.6   S-BOX TABLE FOR THE DES.

$b_2 b_3 b_4 b_5 \Rightarrow c$

$b_1 b_6 \Rightarrow r$

Row	0	1	2	3	4	5	Column 6	7	8	9	10	11	12	13	14	15
S_1																
0	14	4	13	1	2	15	11	8	3	10	6	12	5	9	0	7
1	0	15	7	4	14	2	13	1	10	6	12	11	9	5	3	8
2	4	1	14	8	13	6	2	11	15	12	9	7	3	10	5	0
3	15	12	8	2	4	9	1	7	5	11	3	14	10	0	6	13
S_2																
0	15	1	8	14	6	11	3	4	9	7	2	13	12	0	5	10
1	3	13	4	7	15	2	8	14	12	0	1	10	6	9	11	5
2	0	14	7	11	10	4	13	1	5	8	12	6	9	3	2	15
3	13	8	10	1	3	15	4	2	11	6	7	12	0	5	14	9
S_3																
0	10	0	9	14	6	3	15	5	1	13	12	7	11	4	2	8
1	13	7	0	9	3	4	6	10	2	8	5	14	12	11	15	1
2	13	6	4	9	8	15	3	0	11	1	2	12	5	10	14	7
3	1	10	13	0	6	9	8	7	4	15	14	3	11	5	2	12
S_4																
0	7	13	14	3	0	6	9	10	1	2	8	5	11	12	4	15
1	13	8	11	5	6	15	0	3	4	7	2	12	1	10	14	9
2	10	6	9	0	12	11	7	13	15	1	3	14	5	2	8	4
3	3	15	0	6	10	1	13	8	9	4	5	11	12	7	2	14
S_5																
0	2	12	4	1	7	10	11	6	8	5	3	15	13	0	14	9
1	14	11	2	12	4	7	13	1	5	0	15	10	3	9	8	6
2	4	2	1	11	10	13	7	8	15	9	12	5	6	3	0	14
3	11	8	12	7	1	14	2	13	6	15	0	9	10	4	5	3
S_6																
0	12	1	10	15	9	2	6	8	0	13	3	4	14	7	5	11
1	10	15	4	2	7	12	9	5	6	1	13	14	0	11	3	8
2	9	14	15	5	2	8	12	3	7	0	4	10	1	13	11	6
3	4	3	2	12	9	5	15	10	11	14	1	7	6	0	8	13
S_7																
0	4	11	2	14	15	0	8	13	3	12	9	7	5	10	6	1
1	13	0	11	7	4	9	1	10	14	3	5	12	2	15	8	6
2	1	4	11	13	12	3	7	14	10	15	6	8	0	5	9	2
3	6	11	13	8	1	4	10	7	9	5	0	15	14	2	3	12
S_8																
0	13	2	8	4	6	15	11	1	10	9	3	14	5	0	12	7
1	1	15	13	8	10	3	7	4	12	5	6	11	0	14	9	2
2	7	11	4	1	9	12	14	2	0	6	10	13	15	3	5	8
3	2	1	14	7	4	10	8	13	15	12	9	0	3	5	6	11

3.6. For example, assume that block B_7 in binary is 010011. Then $r = 01 = 1$ and $c = 1001 = 9$. The transformation of block B_7 is found in row 1, column 9 of section 7 of Table 3.6. The value $3 = 0011$ is substituted for the value 010011.

TABLE 3.7 PERMUTATION BOX P.

Bit	1	2	3	4	5	6	7	8	9	10	11	12	13	14	15	16
Goes to position	9	17	23	31	13	28	2	18	24	16	30	6	26	20	10	1

Bit	17	18	19	20	21	22	23	24	25	26	27	28	29	30	31	32
Goes to position	8	14	25	3	4	29	11	19	32	12	22	7	5	27	15	21

P-Boxes

After an S-box substitution, all 32 bits of a result are permuted by a straight permutation, P. Table 3.7 shows the position to which bits are moved. For example, bit 1 of the output of the substitution moves to bit 9, while bit 10 moves to position 16.

Decryption of the DES

The substitutions and the permutations of the DES seem like numbers chosen at random; there is no apparent pattern to the tables describing the various changes. However, the changes, which were chosen with extreme care, produce a surprising but intended result. The same DES algorithm is used both for encryption *and decryption.*

This result is true because cycle j derives from cycle $(j - 1)$ in the following manner:

$$L_j = R_{j-1} \tag{1}$$
$$R_j = L_{j-1} \oplus f(R_{j-1}, k_j) \tag{2}$$

where $\oplus$ is the exclusive-or operation, and f is the function computed in an expand-shift-substitute-permute cycle. These two equations show that the result of each cycle depends only on the previous cycle.

By rewriting these equations in terms of R_{j-1} and L_{j-1}, we get

$$R_{j-1} = L_j \tag{3}$$

and

$$L_{j-1} = R_j \oplus f(R_{j-1}, k_j). \tag{4}$$

Substituting (3) into (4) gives

$$L_{j-1} = R_j \oplus f(L_j, k_j). \tag{5}$$

Equations (3) and (5) show that these same values could be obtained from the results of *later* cycles. It is this property that makes the DES a reversible procedure; we can encrypt a string and also decrypt the result to derive the plaintext again.

With the DES it is possible to go forward and encrypt or to go backwards and decrypt using the same function f. The only change is that the keys must be taken in reverse order (k_{16}, k_{15}, ..., k_1) for decryption. That one algorithm can be used either to encrypt or to decrypt is very convenient for a hardware or software implementation of the DES.

Questions about the Security of the DES

Since its first announcement, there has been controversy concerning the security provided by the DES. Although much of this controversy has appeared in the open literature, certain features of the DES have neither been revealed by the designers nor inferred by outside analysts.

Design of the Algorithm

Initially, there was concern with the basic algorithm itself. During development of the algorithm, the National Security Agency (NSA) indicated that key elements of the algorithm design were "sensitive" and would not be made public. These elements include the rationale behind transformations by the S-boxes, the P-boxes, and the key changes. There are many possibilities for the S-box substitutions, but one particular set was chosen for the DES.

Two issues arose about the secrecy of the design. The first involved a fear that certain "trapdoors" have been imbedded in the DES algorithm, so that a covert, easy means is available to decrypt any DES-encrypted message. Such trapdoors would give NSA the ability to inspect private communications.

After a Congressional inquiry, the results of which are classified, an unclassified summary exonerates NSA from any improper involvement in the DES design.

The second issue addresses the possibility that a design flaw will be (or perhaps has been) discovered by a cryptanalyst, this time giving an interceptor the ability to access private communications.

Both Bell Laboratories [MOR77] and the Lexar Corporation [LEX76] scrutinized the operation (not the design) of the S-boxes. Neither analysis revealed any weakness that impairs the proper functioning of the S-boxes. The DES algorithm has been studied extensively and, to date, no serious flaws have been publicized.[3]

In response to criticism, the NSA released certain information on the selection of the S-boxes ([KON81], [BRA77]).

- No S-box is a linear or affine function of its input; that is, the four output bits cannot be expressed as a system of linear equations of the six input bits.

- Changing one bit in the input of an S-box results in changing at least two output bits; that is, the S-boxes diffuse their information well throughout their outputs.

- The S-boxes were chosen to minimize the difference between the number of 1s and 0s when any single input bit is held constant; that is, holding a single bit constant as a 0 or 1 and changing the bits around it should not lead to disproportionately many 0s or 1s in the output.

---

[3]   Curiously, the NSA has recently withdrawn further support of the DES. See the subsequent section.

Number of Iterations

Many analysts wonder whether 16 iterations are sufficient. Since each iteration diffuses the information of the plaintext throughout the ciphertext, it is not clear that 16 cycles diffuse the information sufficiently. For example, with only one cycle, a single ciphertext bit is affected only by a few bits of plaintext. With more cycles, the diffusion becomes greater, so that ideally there is no dependence of any one ciphertext bit on any subset of plaintext bits.

Experimentation with both the DES and its IBM predecessor Lucifer was performed by the NBS and by IBM as part of the certification process of the DES algorithm. These experiments have shown [KON81] that 8 iterations are sufficient to eliminate any observed dependence. Thus, the 16 iterations of the DES should surely be adequate.

Key Length

The length of the key is the most serious objection raised. The key in the original IBM implementation of Lucifer was 128 bits, while the DES key is effectively only 56 bits long. The argument for a longer key centers around the feasibility of an exhaustive search for a key.

Given a piece of plaintext known to be enciphered as a particular piece of ciphertext, the goal for the interceptor is to find the key under which the encipherment was done. This attack assumes that the same key will be used to encipher other (unknown) plaintext. Knowing the key will allow the interceptor to decipher intercepted ciphertext easily.

The attack strategy is the "brute force" attack: Encipher the known plaintext with an orderly series of keys, repeating with a new key until the enciphered plaintext matches the known ciphertext. There are 2^{56} 56-bit keys. If it were possible to test one every 100 ms, the time to test all keys would be $\approx 7.2 \times 10^{15}$ sec., or about 228 million years. If the test took only 1 μs, then the total time for the search is (only!) about 2,280 years. Even supposing the test time to be 1 ns, infeasible on current technology machines, the search time is still in excess of two years, working full time with no hardware or software failures!

Diffie and Hellman [DIF77] suggest a parallel attack. With a parallel design, multiple processors can be assigned the same problem simultaneously. If one chip, working at a rate of one key per microsecond, can check about 8.6×10^{10} keys in one day, it would take 10^6 days to try all $2^{56} \approx 7 \times 10^{16}$ keys. However, 10^6 chips working in parallel at that rate could check all keys in one day.

One estimate of the cost of such a machine is $50 million. Assuming a "key shop" existed where people would bring their plaintext/ciphertext pairs to obtain keys, and assuming that there was enough business to keep this machine busy 24 hours a day for five years, the proportionate cost would be only about $20,000 per solution. As hardware costs continue to fall, the cost of such a machine becomes lower. The stumbling block in the economics of this argument is prorating the cost over five years: If such a device became available at affordable prices, use of the DES would cease for important data.

An alternate criticism is the table lookup argument [HEL80]. For this attack, assume a chosen plaintext attack, that is, the to ability insert a given plaintext block into the encryption stream and obtain the resulting ciphertext under a still-secret key. Hellman argues that with enough advance time and enough storage space, it would be possible to compute all of the 2^{56} results of encrypting the chosen block under every possible key. Then determining which key was used is a matter of looking up the output obtained.

By a heuristic algorithm, Hellman suggests an approach that will limit the amount of computation and data stored to 2^{37}, or about 6.4×10^{11}. Again assuming many DES devices working in parallel, it would be possible to precompute and store all results. As the cost of hardware decreases and the speed of hardware increases, Hellman argues that implementing such a machine may become feasible.

How to Use the DES

Although the key length is *believed* by most analysts to be long enough, some people are still unsure about its 56-bit length. There is a method for increasing the effective length of the key. The method requires no change to the algorithm itself, which is convenient in case the algorithm is to be implemented by a hardware device or in an unmodifiable piece of software.

Two Keys Give the Effect of a 112-bit Key

Because there is considerable concern for the security available with only one 56-bit key, a reasonable approach may involve using two keys. If somehow an exhaustive search defeats one key, the second lock should double the time required to break in (or so the analogies to the physical world would imply.) Unfortunately, this is not quite so. Merkle ([MER81]) argues that two 56-bit keys in series can be broken with a chosen plaintext attack in 2^{57} tries, instead of the 2^{112} that would be expected. Therefore, the second encryption adds almost no security.

Tuchman ([TUC79]) counters that two keys used in a special way enhances security. Tuchman uses a technique invented by Matyas and Meyer for use by IBM in encrypting master keys in some of their encryption systems. With two keys, K_1 and K_2, the sender encrypts with K_1, decrypts with K_2, and encrypts with K_1 again. The receiver decrypts with K_1, encrypts with K_2, and decrypts with K_1 again.

This approach is desirable for use with an automatic encrypting device (which might be either hardware or software). If the device expects two keys and the user wants to use only one, the user supplies k_1 twice. The device encrypts with k_1, decrypts with k_1 (which returns the original plaintext), and finally encrypts with k_1. In that way one device can produce both single and double encryptions.

Weaknesses of the DES

There are known weaknesses of the DES, but these weaknesses are not believed to limit the effectiveness of the algorithm seriously.

Complements

The first known weakness concerns complements. (Throughout this discussion, "complement" means "ones complement," the result obtained by replacing all 1s by 0s and 0s by 1s.) If a message is encrypted with a particular key, the complement of that encryption will be the encryption of the complement message under the complement key. Stated formally, let p represent a plaintext message and k a key, and let the symbol $\bar{x}$ mean the complement of the binary string x. If $c = \text{DES}(p, k)$ (meaning c is the DES encryption of p using key k), then $\bar{c} = \text{DES}(\bar{p}, \bar{k})$. Since most applications of encryption do not deal with complement messages, and since users can be warned not to use complement keys, this is not a serious problem.

Weak Keys

A second known weakness concerns choice of keys. Because the initial key is split into two halves, and the two halves are independently shifted circularly, if the value being shifted is all 0s or all 1s, the key used for encryption in each cycle is the same as for all other cycles. Remember that the difference between encryption and decryption is that the key shifts are applied in reverse. Key shifts are right shifts and the number of positions shifted is taken from the bottom of the table up, instead of top down. But if the keys are all 0s or all 1s anyway, right or left shifts by 0, 1, or 2 positions are all the same. For these keys, encryption is the same as decryption: $c = \text{DES}(p, k)$, and $p = \text{DES}(c, k)$. These keys are called "weak keys." The same thing happens if one half of the key is all 0s and the other half is all 1s. Since these keys are known, they can simply be avoided, so this is not a serious problem.

The four weak keys are shown in hexadecimal notation in Table 3.8. (The initial key permutation extracts every eighth bit as a parity bit and scrambles the key order slightly. Therefore, the "half zeros, half ones" keys are not just split in the middle.)

TABLE 3.8   DES WEAK KEYS.

Left Right	Weak Key Value
zeros zeros	0101 0101 0101 0101
ones ones	FEFE FEFE FEFE FEFE
zeros ones	1F1F 1F1F 0E0E 0E0E
ones zeros	E0E0 E0E0 F1F1 F1F1

Semi-Weak Keys

A third difficulty is similar: There are identifiable pairs of keys that have more than one identical decryption. That is, there are two different keys k_1 and k_2 for which $c = \text{DES}(p, k_1)$ and $c = \text{DES}(p, k_2)$. This implies that k_1 can decrypt a message encrypted under k_2. These so-called "semi-weak" keys are shown in Table 3.9. Other key patterns have been investigated with no additional weaknesses found to date. It is, however, sensible to avoid any key having an obvious pattern such as these.

TABLE 3.9   DES SEMI-WEAK KEY PAIRS

01FE 01FE 01FE 01FE	FE01 FE01 FE01 FE01
1FE0 1FE0 0EF1 0EF1	E01F E01F F10E F10E
01E0 01E0 01F1 01F1	E001 E001 F101 F101
1FFE 1FFE 0EFE 0EFE	FE1F FE1F FE0E FE0E
011F 011F 010E 010E	1F01 1F01 0E01 0E01
E0FE E0FE F1FE F1FE	FEE0 FEE0 FEF1 FEF1

Design Weaknesses

In another analysis of the DES, [DAV83] shows that the expansion permutation E repeats the first and fourth bits of every 4-bit series, crossing bits from neighboring 4-bit series. This paper further indicates that in S-box S_4 the last three output bits can be derived the same way as the first by complementing some of the input bits. This small weakness, of course, raises the question whether there are similar weaknesses in other S-boxes or in pairs of S-boxes.

It has also been shown that two different, but carefully chosen, inputs to S-boxes can produce the same output (see [DAV83]). In [DES84] the point is made that in a single cycle, by changing bits only in three neighboring S-boxes, it is possible to obtain the same output; that is, two slightly different inputs, encrypted under the same key, will produce identical results at the end of just one of the 16 cycles.

Key Clustering

Finally, the researchers in [DES84] investigate a phenomenon called "key clustering." They seek to determine whether there are two different keys that can generate the same ciphertext from the same plaintext, that is, two keys that produce the same encryption. The semi-weak keys are key clusters, but the researchers seek others. Their analysis is very involved, looking at ciphertexts that produce identical plaintext with different keys in one cycle of the DES, then looking at two cycles, then three, and so forth. Up through three cycles, they found key clusters. Because of the complexity involved, they had to stop the analysis after three cycles.

Security of the DES

There are two arguments on a collision course: Hellman argues that because of increasing hardware speed and decreasing hardware cost, it may be feasible to perform an exhaustive key search in a known plaintext attack. Other researchers show that some keys may not work differently from others, thus reducing the proportion of keys to consider in an exhaustive key search. When hardware power surpasses number of keys to search, the exhaustive key search becomes a real threat.

Does this mean the DES is insecure? No, not yet. Nobody has yet shown serious flaws in the DES, nor do people really believe that hardware power has reached the point of feasibility.

NSDD-145 and Support of the DES

DES was accepted by the NBS in 1978 and was approved later by the American National Standards Institute (ANSI) as a standard in the private sector. In 1988 NBS is scheduled to review the standard.

However, the National Security Agency (NSA) has veto power over the NBS in matters of cryptography. This power comes under a controversial executive directive called NSDD-145 which gave NSA the authority to develop a national policy on computer and communications security. The directive extends the authority of the NSA beyond government agencies to the private sector. "In cases where the implementation of security measures to nongovernmental systems would be in the national security interest, the private sector shall be encouraged, advised, and where appropriate, assisted in undertaking the application of such measures."

NSA has already announced that it will not recertify the standard in 1988. The problem with DES is not that it is known, or even suspected, to *have been* broken; it is just becoming more likely that it *could be* broken. The extensive debate about the feasibility of an exhaustive key search machine, coupled with the exhaustive analysis of the DES algorithm, has made DES too risky.

In the same way that users should change passwords, encryption keys, and procedures periodically—even without suspecting a security lapse—the NSA seems to think the DES has become too obvious a target.

The NSA has already indicated that future generations of encryption will be in the form of "black boxes," sealed encryption devices to which NSA will not disclose the algorithms. NSA will distribute devices and keys to users. Without access to the algorithm, it will be substantially more complex to analyze the devices in an attempt to uncover weaknesses. DES equipment can still be sold to and used by government and private agencies. NSA expects to have its new encryption devices available sometime in 1988.

Public reaction to NSDD-145 and NSA's announcement that it plans not to recertify DES in 1988 has identified several problems.

- o Export of the new devices to foreign countries will be prohibited, because of national security concerns. This raises serious problems for U.S. companies doing business abroad or having foreign affiliates.

- o Security of communications and data currently protected by DES is in question.

- o Some companies have invested substantial sums in hardware that uses DES. Replacing this machinery will be expensive. Other companies that manufacture DES-based devices may have produced merchandise that they will be unable to sell.

- o NSA's plan to distribute the devices *and the keys* constitutes government control of who can use encryption. In addition, if the government retains records of who has received what keys, the government then has the capability to decrypt any intercepted encrypted data, within the private or public sector.

Computer Security Act of 1987

In a piece of legislation approved late in 1987, the National Bureau of Standards has been given responsibility for improving computer security in civilian government agencies. This responsibility is taken from the NSA, which had been given that authority under NSDD-145. Under the new law, NBS must create security standards, design security measures, and develop training programs for computer security.

Each federal agency will identify computing systems that process or maintain sensitive information. Information that is sensitive is "any information, the loss, misuse or unauthorized access to or modification of which could adversely affect the national interest or the conduct of federal programs or an individual's rights under the Privacy Act." Previously "national interest" was taken to mean just defense activities or affairs of state; this new legislation indicates that the national interest could include commerce, such as banking and securities trading, as well as areas such as energy and health care. These documents will be reviewed by NBS, working with the technical support of NSA.

An important point of the new law is that it places an entirely new emphasis on computer security. This comfirmation from Congress of the importance of unclassified information advises upper level management of civilian agencies to develop stronger computer security programs.

3.8 Conclusions on Secure Encryption

In this chapter we have studied three formidable encryption algorithms: Merkle-Hellman, RSA, and DES. The first had serious design weaknesses discovered about five years after its introduction; the latter two have remained essentially unassailed. Both RSA and DES have been implemented in both hardware and software, and their popularity is growing within the security community. During the time since the development of these three, several dozen alternate public key and single key encryption schemes have been introduced; serious errors have been discovered with many of these within three years of their first announcement. This situation is certainly not any "proof" of the security of either RSA or DES, but it does lead to more confidence in their security.

Now a new class of algorithms is proposed. These algorithms would be distributed as sealed encryption devices, so that neither the algorithm nor its implementation or analysis would be made public. In doing this, the NSA hopes to make it harder for someone to discover a flaw in an algorithm: First you have to infer the algorithm before you can begin to analyze it. Although this does provide an extra measure of security, it limits the ability of the research community to inspire confidence in the devices because there can be no rigorous analysis of the algorithm. The important issue of trust in scientific invention is supported by public analysis and criticism. Public scrutiny and security are by their very nature conflicting goals.

3.9 Summary of Secure Encryption

In this chapter we have studied three encryption algorithms. The Merkle-Hellman algorithm is based on the NP-complete knapsack problem of finding a set of numbers that add to a specific sum. The underlying problem is known to be at least of polynomial difficulty to solve, and it is likely to require exponential work. Unfortunately, there is a technique to solve the restricted version of the knapsack problem (without solving the underlying knapsack problem) in reasonable time.

The RSA algorithm is based on the underlying hard problem of factoring large numbers. The factoring problem is not even NP-complete. The algorithm is conceptually simple: To encrypt and to decrypt you treat a plaintext as a number and raise it to a particular power. Also encryption and decryption can be performed in either order, and multiple encryptions and decryptions commute with one another. These properties make this a very desirable algorithm. The principal difficulty with this algorithm is its implementation: Raising 200-digit numbers to a 200-digit power is not easy to implement on popular computers. Hardware devices have been produced to implement this algorithm efficiently.

The DES algorithm was designed for the U.S. government and has been officially certified as a standard for encryption. It uses a series of 16 iterations of a loop involving simple arithmetic and logical operations. It can be implemented reasonably easily on any popular computer. Certain minor design faults have been uncovered, but there has been nothing conclusive published regarding a major vulnerability. Still, controversy has raged about its security since its introduction.

Under the premise that periodically even secure algorithms should be replaced, the NSA has withdrawn support of the DES. The NSA would like to distribute sealed devices for the next generation of encryptions, where even the algorithm remains secret. Although this presumably improves the security of these encryption mechanisms, there is considerable concern about the government's role in security in the private sector.

3.10 Terms and Concepts

brute force attack
exhaustive attack
NP-complete problem
satisfiability problem
knapsack problem
clique problem
solvable problem
P
polynomial time algorithm
NP
guess function
oracle machine

nondeterministic Turing machine
EXP
modular arithmetic
associativity
commutativity
distributivity
inverse
reducibility
gcd (greatest common divisor)
relative prime
modulus
public key cryptography
channel
Merkle-Hellman knapsack
knapsack
superincreasing sequence
superincreasing knapsack
simple knapsack
RSA encryption
inverse mod n
privacy
authentication
lost key
single key encryption
key distribution
channel
distribution center for secrets
NBS
public encryption algorithm
hardware encryption
Lucifer
DES
confusion
diffusion
product cipher
cycle
permutation
expansion permutation
permuted choice
left half
right half
S-box
P-box
trapdoor

exhaustive key search
brute force attack
parallel attack
chosen plaintext attack
two DES keys
key weaknesses
key complements
weak keys
semi-weak keys
S-box
DES weakness
key clustering
NSDD-145
NSA
national policy on computer and communications security
sealed encryption device

3.11 Bibliographic Notes

Konheim [KON81] and Denning [DEN83] both present the three secure encryption systems described in this chapter. Lempel [LEM79] also covers this material. Cryptanalysis of the Merkle-Hellman method is given in [SHA80], [SHA82], and [ADL82]. An attack on the RSA method is given in [WAG83]. Discussion of the security of the DES appears in [HEL79], [MOR77], [LEX76], [DAV82], and [DAV83]. Other public key cryptosystems are given in [GOO84] and [LAG83].

3.12 Exercises

1. Show that formula $F = (v_1) \wedge (v_2 \vee v_3) \wedge (\bar{v}_3 \vee \bar{v}_1)$ is satisfiable, and justify that formula $G = (v_1) \wedge (v_2 \vee v_3) \wedge (\bar{v}_3 \vee \bar{v}_1) \wedge (\bar{v}_2)$ is not.

2. Are there any other cliques in the graph of Figure 3.1?

3. Give a procedure for locating a clique of size n in any given graph. What is the time complexity of your algorithm?

4. An algorithm with a GUESS statement can be replaced by two clones of procedures executing the algorithm, one clone executing as if TRUE had been the correct guess, and the other executing as if FALSE had been correct. If one of these clones later encounters another guess, it clones itself again, so that two clones become three. Suppose an algorithm executes in n steps. What is a limit to the number of cloned processes needed to simulate that algorithm?

5. Differentiate between a problem and an instance of a problem. Cite an example of each.

6. Suppose an encryption algorithm is based on the satisfiability problem. Estimate the number of machine instructions necessary to solve the satisfiability problem by testing all cases. Using current technology hardware, how many variables are needed in the formula so that the time to solve this problem exceeds one year? What is the corresponding figure for hardware of five years ago? Ten years ago? Assuming similar speed improvements in the next five years, how long will it take to solve today's one-year-sized problem?

7. Compute $\gcd(1875, 405)$.

8. Justify that $(a * b) \bmod n = ((a \bmod n) * (b \bmod n)) \bmod n$.

9. Write the addition and multiplication tables for the integers mod 4 and for the integers mod 7.

10. By Fermat's theorem, what is the multiplicative inverse of 2 in the field of integers mod 11?

11. With a public key encryption, suppose A wants to send a message to B. Let A_{PUB} and A_{PRIV} be A's public key and private key, respectively; similarly for B. Suppose C knows both public keys, but neither private key. If A sends a message to B, what encryption should A use so that only B can decrypt the message. (This property is called secrecy.) Can A encrypt a message so that anyone receiving the message will be assured the message came only from A? (This property is called authenticity.) Can A achieve both secrecy and authenticity for one message? How or why not?

12. Given the knapsack $[17, 38, 23, 14, 11, 21]$ is there a solution for the target 42? Is there a solution for the target 43? Is there a solution for the target 44?

13. Convert the superincreasing knapsack $[1, 3, 5, 11, 23, 47, 97]$ to a hard knapsack by multiplying by 7 mod 11; by 7 mod 29.

14. Encrypt the message 10110110100101 by each of the two hard knapsacks of the previous exercise.

15. Encrypt the message 10110110100101 by each of the two simple knapsacks of the above exercise.

16. Is the Merkle-Hellman algorithm an "onto" algorithm? That is, is every number k, $0 \le k < n$, the result of encrypting some number using a fixed knapsack?

17. Explain why the graph of $\tilde{w} * h_i$ is discontinuous when $\tilde{w} * h_i > n$.

18. Find keys d and e for the RSA cryptosystem where $p = 7$ and $q = 11$.

19. Find primes p and q so that 12-bit plaintext blocks could be encrypted with RSA.

20. Is the DES an onto function; that is, is every 64-bit binary string the result of encrypting some string?

21. Prove the complement property for the DES.

22. Suppose you are designing a processor that would compute with encrypted data. For example, given two encrypted data values $E(x)$ and $E(y)$, the processor would compute $E(x) \oplus E(y)$, where $\oplus$ is an encrypted addition operator that performs addition on encrypted numbers. $D(E(x) \oplus E(y))$ must be the same as $x + y$. None of the encryption algorithms of this chapter has the property that $E(x) + E(y) = E(x + y)$, although the encrypted addition operator does not necessarily have to be $+$. For the three algorithms of this chapter, is there a relationship between $E(x)$, $E(y)$, $E(x + y)$?

4

Using Encryption:
Protocols and Practices

In Chapter 3 we considered two examples of encryption systems believed to be secure. There are hundreds of other encryption methods, but the DES and the RSA are the two most widely acclaimed secure single key and public key systems in general distribution today.

But simply having or using an encryption system believed to be secure does not mean that all transactions using the system *will* be secure. There are right and wrong ways to use these methods of encryption. Furthermore, these algorithms can be used to solve problems for which secrecy or authenticity is only a part of the solution. In this chapter we study and evaluate techniques, called protocols, that use encryption to establish secure communication between two users. We also explore appropriate ways to use encryption.

4.1 Protocols: Using Encryption to Solve Problems

Encryption systems provide an important tool in computer security: They give a user the ability to transmit information in a concealed form. Their obvious use is in transmitting documents and data over a channel that may be intercepted. By use of established conventions between two parties, cryptosystems can be used for purposes other than just secret communication. These conventions, called protocols, are the topic of the next section.

Definition of Protocols

A **protocol** is an orderly sequence of steps taken by two or more parties to accomplish some task. Everyone using a protocol must know the protocol and agree to it before using it. The order of the steps is important, as is the activity of each step. People use protocols to regulate behavior for mutual benefit.

Using a telephone is a simple example of a protocol. The person dialing hears both the ringing sound and when the connection is established. Protocol, standard practice, is that the receiver speaks first, saying "hello," or something similar. The originator answers this with a greeting that identifies him- or herself. The two parties then alternate pieces of the conversation. Without this standard practice, both people might speak at once when the connection was established, and neither would hear the other.

The sequence of steps described is an example of a protocol. As with the example, a protocol has the following characteristics:

o *Established in advance:* The protocol is completely designed before it is used.

o *Mutually subscribed:* All parties to the protocol agree to follow its steps, in order.

o *Unambiguous:* No party can fail to follow a step properly because the party has misunderstood the step.

o *Complete:* For every situation that can occur there is a prescribed action to be taken.

Protocols are also used in computer-to-computer communication. A computer needs to know when to "speak," when to "listen," with whom it is communicating, whether it has received all of a particular communication, and so forth. There are also protocols for communications between computers. In a two-computer communication, both computers need to follow the same protocol in order for either to participate.

Motivation for Studying Protocols

Certain tasks, such as negotiating contracts, voting, distributing information, and even playing poker are simple human activities. However, many of these tasks depend on a witness' presence to ensure fairness. Would you trust someone who said he was going to shuffle cards, not look at them, and mail you your hand? Would you trust the person if you did not know him, or if the stakes were thousands or millions of dollars?

Modern society requires the use of computers and communications as tools of commerce. Many users of computers are not personally acquainted with the managers or other users of a system. In many cases the computer communication is over a long distance. Because of anonymity and distance, one user will not, and often should not, trust the managers or other users of a system. In order to use computers effectively, we must develop protocols by which two suspicious parties can interact with each other and be convinced of fairness.

In addition to regulating behavior, protocols serve another very important purpose: Protocols separate the *process* of accomplishing a task from the *mechanism* by which it is done. A protocol specifies only the rules of behavior. In this way, we can examine a protocol to convince ourselves that it achieves the desired result. We verify the correctness of the process at a high level.

After becoming convinced of the correctness of the design, we can implement the protocol using some mechanism, that is, using some particular language or encryption system. The implementation is separate from the design. Therefore, we need only verify that the mechanism correctly reflects the design; we do not need to reverify that the implementation solves the problem for which the protocol was originally designed. Furthermore, we can later change the implementation without affecting the design. Separating *design* from *implementation* is an important advantage of using protocols.

Arbitrated Protocols

An **arbiter** is a disinterested third party trusted to complete a transaction between two distrusting parties. If you sell a car to a stranger and the stranger gives you a check, you have no way to know that the check is good. You would like to deposit the check and hold the car for a few days until you are sure the check has cleared. A suspicious buyer would not tolerate this, since you have both the car and the check and could leave town with both.

A solution is to use a trusted third party, such as a banker or a lawyer, as an arbiter. You give the car's title and keys to the arbiter, and the buyer gives the arbiter a check. You three agree on a time for the check to clear. The arbiter deposits the check to your account. If the check clears within the specified time, the arbiter turns the car over to the buyer. If the check doesn't clear, you show evidence of that to the arbiter, who returns your car to you. In a computer protocol, an arbiter is a trustworthy third party who ensures fairness. The arbiter might be a person, a program, or a machine. For example, in a network an arbiter might be a program running on one machine of the network. The program receives and forwards messages between users. The users trust that when the arbiter forwards a message saying it came from A, the message really did come from user A.

The notion of an arbiter is the basis for a type of secure protocol called an **arbitrated protocol**.

Arbitrated computer protocols have several disadvantages.

o The two sides may not be able to find a neutral third party that both sides trust. Suspicious users are rightfully suspicious of an unknown arbiter in a network.

o Maintaining the availability of an arbiter is a cost of the users or the network; that cost may be high.

o Arbitration causes a time delay in communication, because a third party must receive, act on, and then forward every transaction.

o If the arbitration service is heavily used, it may become a bottleneck in the network as many users try to access a single arbiter.

o Secrecy becomes vulnerable, since the arbiter has access to much sensitive information.

For these reasons, an arbitrated protocol is avoided if possible.

Adjudicated Protocols

Similar to the arbiter is the idea of an **adjudicator**: a third party that can judge whether a transaction was performed fairly. For example, a **notary public** is a trusted, disinterested third party who attests that a document was signed voluntarily and that the notary has taken reasonable care to ascertain that the signer is authentic. A notary's signature is often required for legal documents whose authenticity might later be challenged. The notary adds nothing to the transaction other than as a witness who could testify later, in the event of a challenge.

Some computer protocols use the equivalent of a notary to build evidence of fairness. With **adjudicable** protocols enough data is available for a disinterested third party to judge fairness based on the evidence. Not only can a third party determine if two disputing parties acted fairly, that is, within the rules of the protocol, but the third party can also determine who cheated.

Adjudicated protocols involve the services of a third party only in case of a dispute. Therefore, they are usually less costly, in terms of machine time or access to a trusted third-party software judge, than arbitrated protocols. However, adjudicated protocols detect a failure to cooperate only after the failure has occurred.

Self-Enforcing Protocols

A **self-enforcing protocol** is one that guarantees fairness. If either party tries to cheat, that fact becomes evident to the other party. No outsider is needed to ensure fairness. Obviously, self-enforcing protocols are preferable to the other types. However, there is not a self-enforcing protocol for every situation.

There are thus three levels of protocols.

1. *Arbitrated protocols*, in which a trusted third party participates in each transaction to ensure that both sides act fairly,

2. *Adjudicated protocols*, in which a third party could judge after the fact whether both parties had acted fairly and if not, which party had not, and

3. *Self-enforcing protocols*, in which either party's attempt to cheat becomes immediately obvious to the other party.

These three types of protocols are shown in Figure 4.1.

Next we turn our attention to the use of protocols to solve problems in computer security.

Digital Signatures

Let us examine a typical computer situation: an order to transfer funds from one person to another. This is, in essence, a computerized check. We understand how this transaction is handled in the conventional, paper mode:

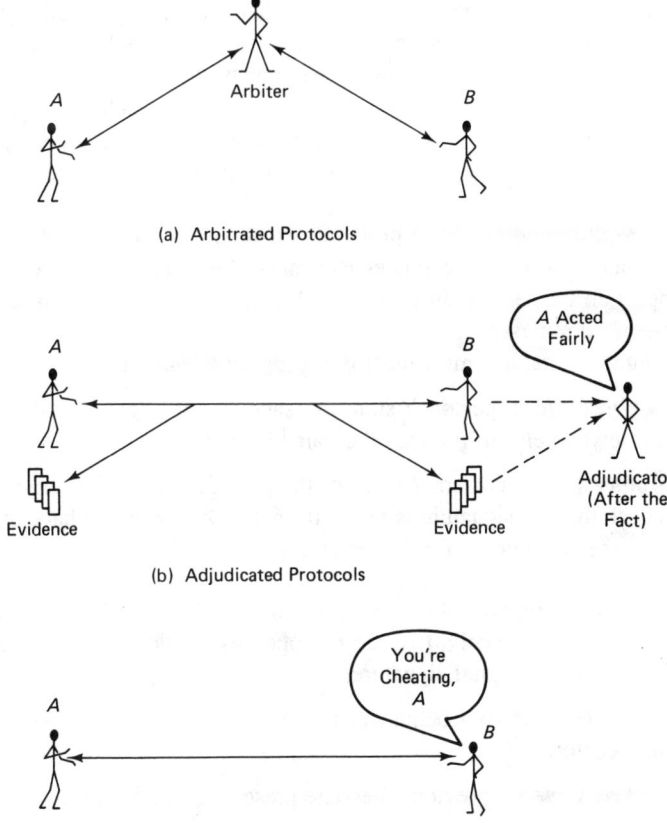

Figure 4.1   Types of Protocols.

o A check is a *tangible object* authorizing a financial transaction.

o The signature on the check *confirms authenticity,* since (presumably) only the legitimate signer can produce that signature.

o In the case of an alleged forgery, a third party can be called in to *judge authenticity.*

o A check is cancelled, so that it *cannot be reused.*

o The paper check is *not alterable.* Or, most forms of alteration are easily detected.

Transacting business by check depends on *tangible objects* in a *prescribed form.*

Tangible objects do not exist for transactions on computers. Therefore, authorizing payments by computer requires a different model. Let us consider the requirements of such a situation, both from the standpoint of a bank and from the standpoint of a user.

Sandy sends her bank a message authorizing it to transfer $100 to Tim. Sandy's bank must be able to verify and prove that the message really came from Sandy, if she should later disavow sending the message. The bank also wants to know that the message is entirely Sandy's, that it has not been altered along the way. On her part, Sandy wants to be certain that her bank cannot forge such messages. Both parties want to be sure that the message is new, not a reuse of a previous message, and that it has not been altered during transmission. Using electronic signals instead of paper complicates this transaction.

A **digital signature** is a protocol that produces the same effect as a real signature: It is a mark that only the sender can make, but others people can easily recognize as belonging to the sender. Just like a real signature, a digital signature is used to confirm agreement to a message.

Digital signatures must meet two primary conditions:

- *Unforgeable*. If person P signs message M with signature $S(P, M)$, it is impossible for anyone else to produce the pair $[M, S(P, M)]$.

- *Authentic*. If a person R receives the pair $[M, S(P, M)]$ purportedly from P, R can check that the signature is really from P. Only P could have created this signature, and the signature is firmly attached to M.

The first two requirements, shown in Figure 4.2, are the major hurdles in computer transactions. Additionally, two more properties are desirable for transactions completed through the aid of digital signatures:

- *Not alterable*. After being transmitted, M cannot be changed by S, by R, or by an interceptor.

- *Not reusable*. A previous message presented will be instantly detected by R.

Initially, we present a mechanism that meets the first two requirements. Then we add to that solution to satisfy the other requirements.

Conventional Key Digital Signatures

With a private key encryption system, the secrecy of the key guarantees the authenticity of the message, as well its secrecy. If Sandy and the bank have an encryption key in common, she can encrypt her request to transfer money. The bank can be sure of the authenticity of this message, because nobody else has Sandy's key.

Conventional key encryption does not prevent forgery, however; the bank can create an identical message, since it also has access to the key. With conventional encryption such as DES, an arbiter is needed to prevent forgery.

Here is an outline of the digital signature protocol. Let S be the sender (Sandy), A be the arbiter, and R be the recipient (the bank). The sender has key K_S in common with the arbiter, and the recipient has key K_R in common with the arbiter. Assume that S and R have previously agreed to a format for a digital signature. S wants to send a message M to R, with the added requirements that the message is unforgeable and that its authenticity can be verified.

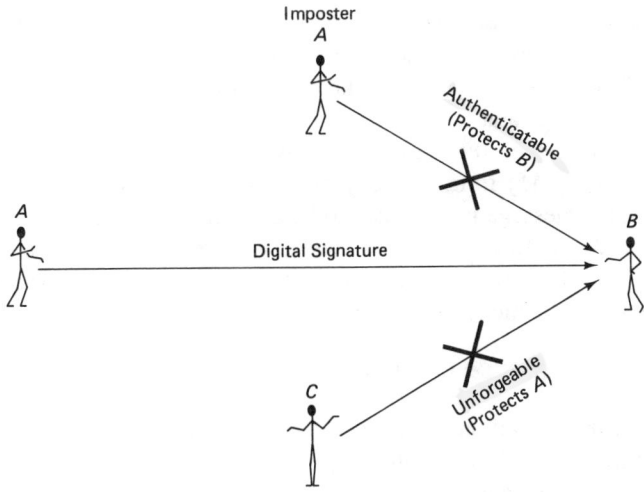

Figure 4.2   Requirements for a Digital Signature.

S first sends $E(M, K_S)$ to the arbiter, A. The arbiter decrypts M using K_S. After verifying that the message is actually from S, the arbiter sends $E((M, S, E(M, K_S)), K_R)$ to R. In this way, R receives all of M encrypted under K_R so that R can decrypt the message and act on it. R receives the arbiter's message S, showing that the arbiter will attest the message came from S. R also receives $E(M, K_S)$ which R cannot decipher, since it is encrypted with K_S. However, R files a copy of M and $E(M, K_S)$ in case there is a future dispute.

The authentication condition is met, since the receiver trusts the arbiter who says the message came from the sender. The no forgery property is satisfied, because if S later claims that there was a forgery, R produces M and $E(M, K_S)$. The arbiter can reencrypt M using K_S and certify that only S (or the arbiter, who we presume is honest) could have produced $E(M, K_S)$, since it is encrypted with K_S. Therefore, the arbiter can attest that S (or someone with K_S) sent M.

Digital Signatures without Encryption

This protocol produces a system that is actually stronger than required: The message is transmitted in encrypted form, even though secrecy is not needed in every situation. As we have seen, some encryption algorithms are time-consuming, and their use could degrade the speed of message transmission. Therefore, we would like another protocol that did not require encryption of the entire message.

If S and R are not concerned with secrecy, they can agree upon a **cryptographic sealing function** to use as a signature. A seal is a stamp, mark, or imprint permanently bound to a document to prove its authenticity. A sealing function is a mathematical function affected by every bit of its input. For example, the bytes of a message can be used as numbers, and the sum of all bytes of a message can be computed. This sum is unique to the message, since a change to the message will produce a change to the sum as well. The sealing function can be a one-way encryption function, or it can be any other function that depends on the entire input and is easy to compute.

Suppose S and R have each registered a personal sealing function with the arbiter; let f_S and f_R be these two functions. Then S sends M and $f_S(M)$ to A. A also computes $f_S(M)$ from the copy of M received from S. If the two values of $f_S(M)$ match, the message is presumed to be authentic, from S. Then, A sends M, S, $f_S(M)$, and $f_R(M, S)$ to R. Again, R cannot interpret $f_S(M)$, but R retains this as evidence that S sent the original message. R does verify the correctness of $f_R(M)$, in order to know the authenticity of the message.

Preventing Reuse or Alteration

Both of these solutions meet the requirements for authenticity and preventing forgeries; therefore, they are acceptable digital signature protocols. However, we also want to prevent reuse or alteration of an old message. Although R cannot create *new* messages under K_S of f_S, the receiver can reuse old ones. For example, the receiver can save an old order to pay Tim \$100 and process it every month. Furthermore, knowing the encryption technique but not the encryption key, the receiver may be able to cut pieces from old messages and paste them together to form a new message. Paper checks solve this problem— the bank cancels the check and returns it to the sender, so that the sender knows it cannot be reused. We need a way to create a similarly self-destructing computer signature, one that cannot be reused.

To document the use of a message, we make part of the signature into a **time stamp**. For example, if Sandy's message shows the date and time sent, the bank cannot reprocess that same message a week later without Sandy or anyone else detecting the forgery. The time stamp need not be literally the time or date; any nonrepeating code, such as an increasing series of numbers, will do. This solves the reprocessing difficulty.

To prevent cutting the message into pieces and reusing a single piece, Sandy can make each piece depend on the time stamp. For example, with DES which encrypts 64-bit text blocks into a 64-bit output, Sandy could encrypt the date and time in the first 8 bits of each block, leaving 56 bits of each block for message. Since all 64 bits of a DES output block depend on all 64 input bits, the bank cannot combine the 56 message bits with a different 8-bit time stamp. This process is shown in Figure 4.3. As we will see in the end of this chapter, the cipher block chaining mode of DES is another way to prevent reuse of a block of one message in another message.

These solutions are somewhat complicated. They require an active arbiter on each transaction, and ensuring secrecy requires the message to be encrypted twice. Fortunately, the public key protocol is simpler.

Public Key Protocol

Public key encryption systems are ideally suited to digital signatures. For simple notation, let us assume that the public key encryption for user U is accessed through $E(M, K_U)$, and that the private key transformation for U is written as $D(M, K_U)$. We can think of

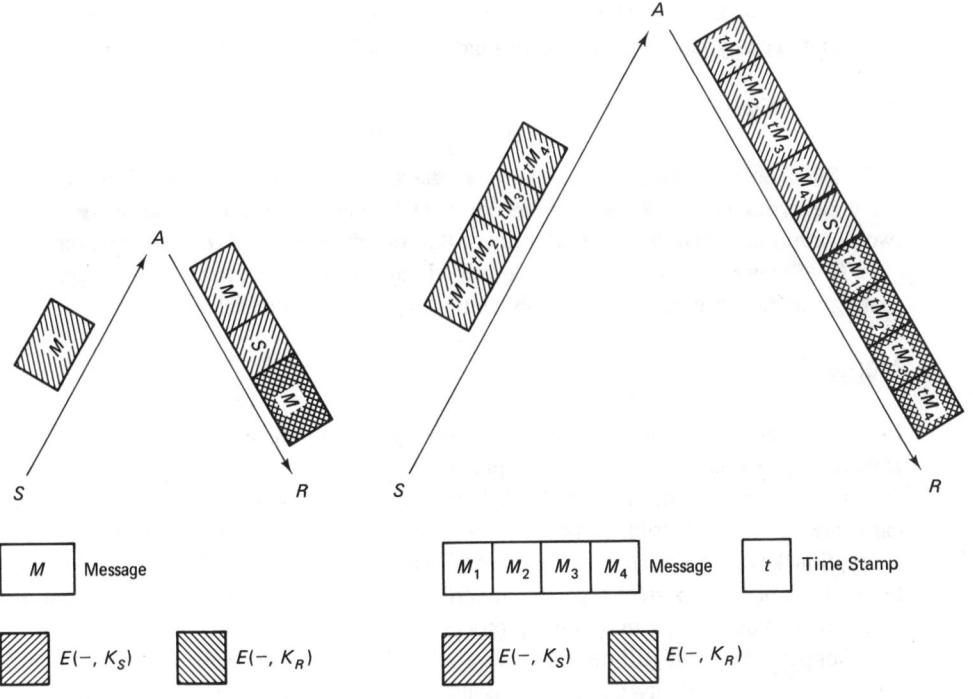

Figure 4.3   Conventional Key Digital Signature with Time Stamp.

E as the *privacy* transformation (since only U can decrypt it), and D as the *authenticity* transformation (since only U can produce it). Remember, however, that under RSA D and E are commutative, and either one can be applied to any message. Thus,

$$D(E(M, -), -) = M = E(D(M, -), -)$$

If S wishes to send M to R, S uses the authenticity transformation to produce $D(M, K_S)$. S then sends $D(M, K_S)$ to R. R decodes the message with the public key transformation of S, computing $E(D(M, K_S), K_S)$. Since only S can create a message that makes sense under $E(-, K_S)$, the message must genuinely have come from S. This test satisfies the authenticity requirement.

R will save $D(M, K_S)$. If S should later allege that the message is a forgery (not really from S), R can simply show M and $E(M, K_S)$. Anyone can verify that since $D(M, K_S)$ is transformed to M using the public key transformation of S—but only S could have produced $D(M, K_S)$—therefore, $D(M, K_S)$ must be from S. This test satisfies the unforgeable requirement.

The public key solution is obviously much less cumbersome than the private key solution. One disadvantage of this approach is that the message is authentic but not private; that is, anyone who knows the public key of S can translate the message. We can overcome this disadvantage by using two encryptions.

Since S is sending M to R, authenticity can be achieved through the private key of S, and secrecy can be achieved through the public key of R. For example, S could send

$$E(D(M, K_S), K_R)$$

to R. Since only S can produce $D(-, K_S)$, the message must be from S. But, since only R can decrypt $E(-, K_R)$, the message content remains private until R transforms it. With two encryptions, then, we have a protocol that provides both privacy and authenticity.

Time stamps as we have just described can be used to guard against replays. A sealing function can also prevent substitution of pieces of ciphertext.

Mental Poker

In this section we consider a similar situation involving the need for both secrecy and authenticity. Consider a poker game played by people who cannot see each other, for example, by mail. The most difficult part of playing poker by mail is ensuring that cards are dealt and distributed fairly. In a later section we use this protocol to distribute encryption keys, in which case the "cards" become keys. Even though playing poker by mail is not an important task, the underlying protocol has some very important uses. The card-playing setting makes the protocol easy to explain.

Suppose Ann and Bill decide to play poker by mail. Ann is the dealer and shuffles the cards. (For simplicity the deck is assumed to contain only ten cards, of which each player will get five. The protocol can be extended easily to conventional 52-card decks by replacing 10 by 52, or any other number, in the following explanation.

Distribution Protocol

To shuffle the cards, Ann puts them in an arbitrary order, places each card in an unmarked box, and puts a lock on each box. Ann then sends all ten boxes to Bill. Since the boxes appear indistinguishable, Bill selects any five boxes, and puts a second lock on these boxes. These five boxes constitute Bill's hand. Bill leaves the other five boxes untouched, so they have only Ann's locks on them. Bill then sends all ten boxes back to Ann.

Upon receiving the boxes, Ann can see that Bill has so far acted fairly—he has selected only five boxes and has not peeked at the cards (since Ann's locks are intact). Ann removes all ten locks. Now Ann has access to the five cards Bill left alone; these constitute Ann's hand.

Ann returns the remaining five boxes, still bearing Bill's lock. Bill removes his five locks from the five boxes containing the cards of his hand. Ann does not know these cards, since Bill's locks have not been tampered with. Bill, satisfied by the fairness of the deal, continues to play. This sequence of events is shown in Figure 4.4.

Conventional Key Implementation

This protocol works easily with conventional encryption systems. Clearly it is not limited to ten cards. Each "card" might be any individual message, such as an encryption key,

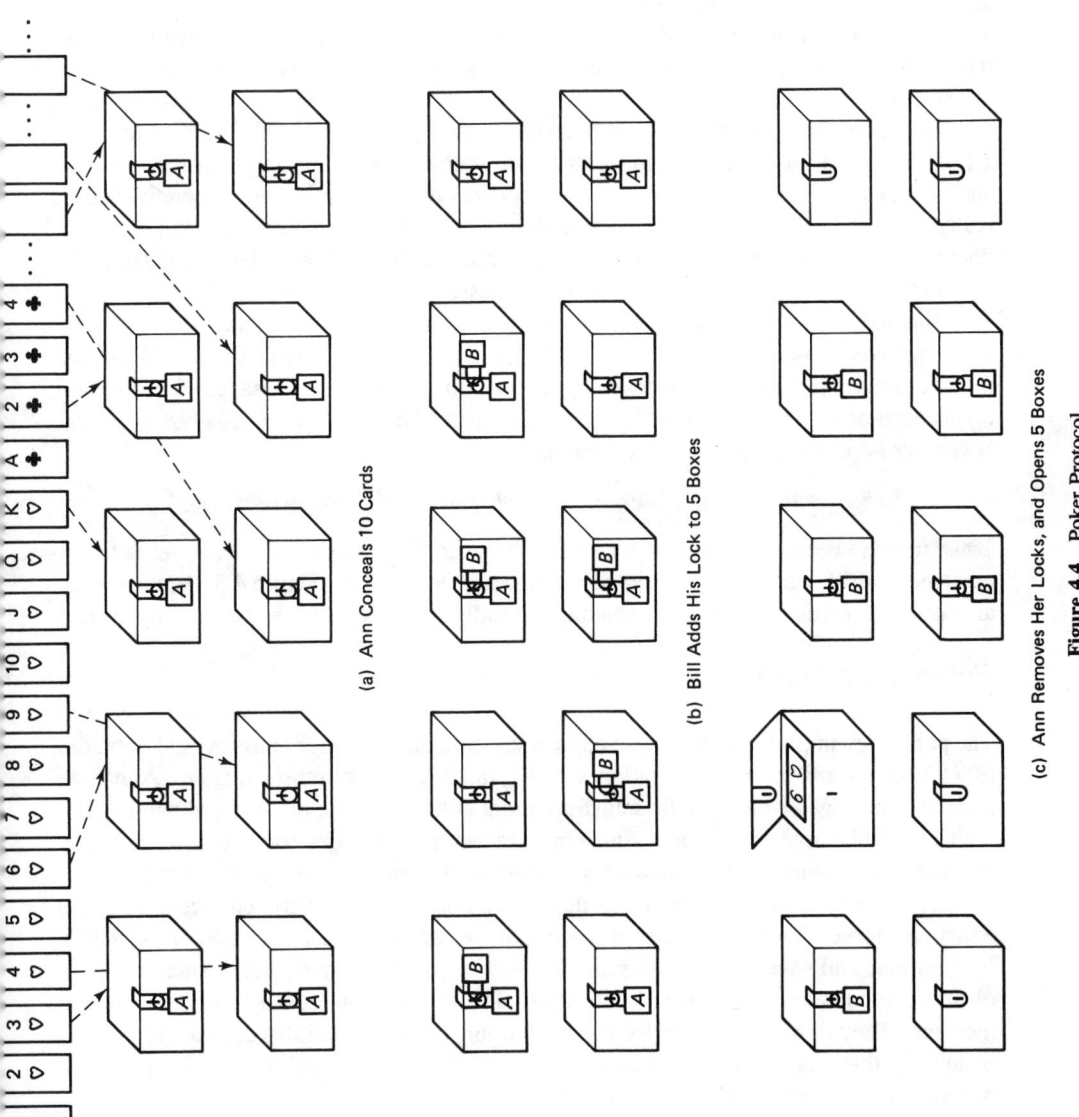

(a) Ann Conceals 10 Cards

(b) Bill Adds His Lock to 5 Boxes

(c) Ann Removes Her Locks, and Opens 5 Boxes

Figure 4.4 Poker Protocol.

instead of a playing card. For generality we will use the term "message" instead of "card" in the protocol. Furthermore, there can be fewer or more than ten messages without any substantial change to the protocol.

Ann "shuffles" the messages and encrypts each under K_A, Ann's key. Ann then sends all encrypted messages to Bill.

As the messages arrive Bill chooses five at random. Bill cannot identify these messages since they are encrypted under Ann's key. Bill sends these back to Ann untouched.

Bill takes the remaining five; call them B_1 to B_5. Bill sends $E(B_1, K_B)$ through $E(B_5, K_B)$ back to Ann. Remember that Ann sent encrypted messages to Bill, so that each B_i is really $E(c_j, K_A)$, message c_j encrypted with Ann's key. Therefore, Bill really sends $E(E(c_j), K_A), K_B)$ back to Ann. The encryption with Bill's key forms a double lock on these messages, in order to guarantee that Bill will get just these back and that Ann cannot know the content of the messages.

Ann has now received five messages encrypted once, $E(c_i, K_A)$, and five more messages encrypted under two keys, $E(E(c_j, K_A), K_B)$. Ann now unlocks the five messages that she is to keep; Ann does this by decrypting the five $E(c_i, K_A)$ messages. She also decrypts each of the five messages that Bill chose, producing $D(E(E(c_j, K_A), K_B), K_A)$. If encryption and decryption are commutative,

$$D(E(E(c_j, K_A), K_B), K_A) = E(D(E(c_j, K_A), K_A), K_B) = E(c_j, K_B)$$

Thus, these messages are now concealed only under Bill's key. Ann then returns these messages to Bill, who decrypts them and continues the game. In Figure 4.5, the messages are shown as cards with different shadings to indicate encryption by Ann and by Bill.

Public Key Implementation

The public key implementation is the natural substitution, using our conventional notation of $D()$ for the private transformation and $E()$ for the public transformation. Ann first locks the messages with a public transformation; Bill then locks his selected hand again with his public transformation. Ann removes her public lock, so that now they are concealed only under Bill's public lock. Finally Bill removes his lock, obtaining his messages. (In fact, this protocol has a flaw if Ann provides Bill only ten messages from which to choose. See the exercises at the end of the chapter for a description of the flaw.)

Fortune and Merritt [FOR84] point out that this protocol does leak a small amount of information when implemented with RSA. The information leaked is about 1 bit per message. They describe a patch for the RSA implementation and discuss the fact that it is unlikely that this information would be useful in real poker. Still, the weakness might be exploited in some similar use of the protocol.

Key Distribution: An Application of the Protocol

The protocol is not limited to the rather unrealistic situation of distributing playing cards by computer. Consider instead an encryption system that requires special keys, so that not every number is an acceptable key. (Some implementations of the DES require that

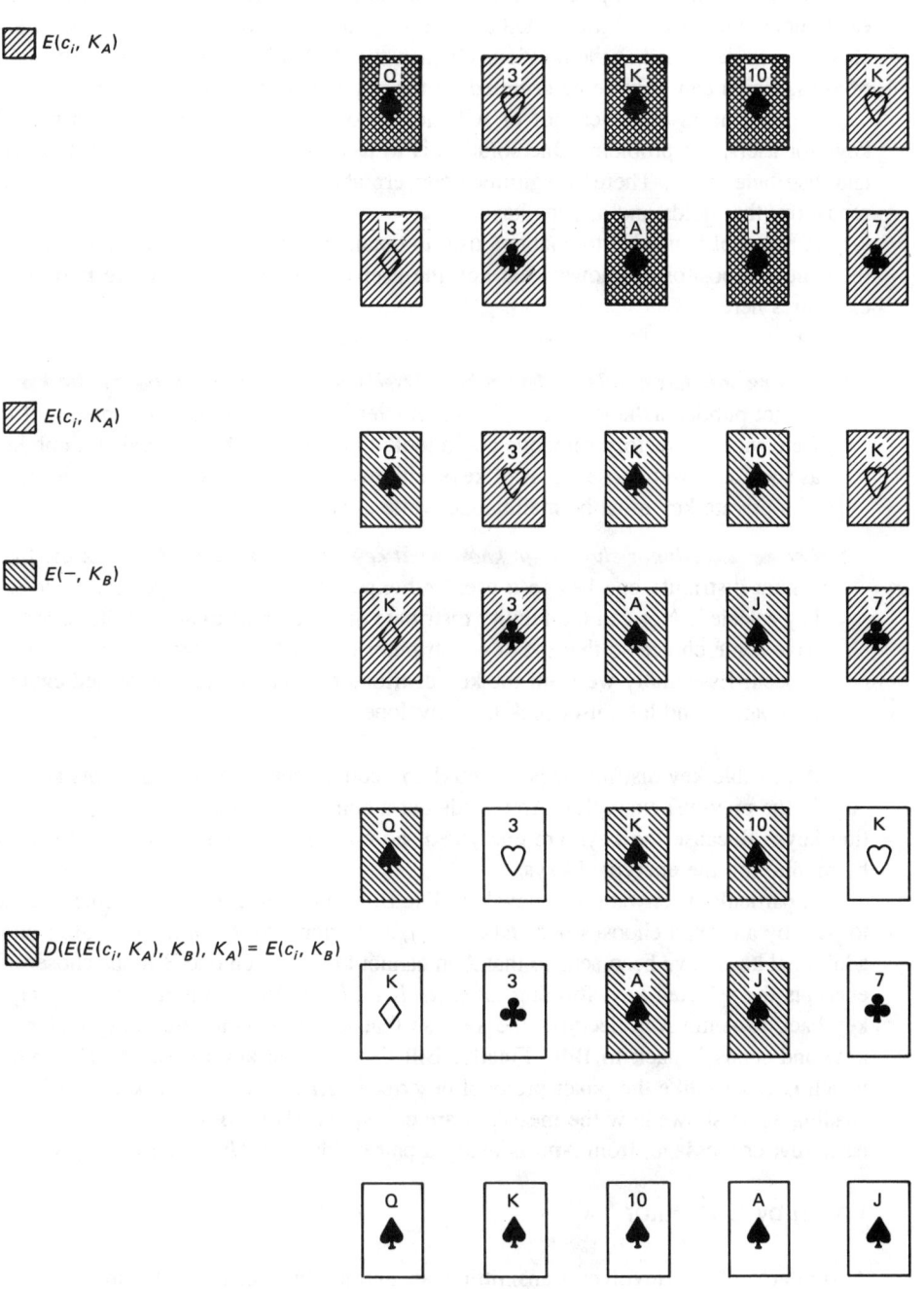

Figure 4.5   Poker Protocol with Encryption

every eighth bit of the key be a parity bit for the previous seven bits of the key. This is easily done with any 56-bit key. Other than that, any 56-bit binary number can be a key. However, as described in the previous chapter, the RSA algorithm requires a special pair of keys, which can only be determined by the implementer of the algorithm.)

General users either cannot or will not choose keys themselves. Thus providing keys for users is a problem. One solution is to have a central key server that generates and distributes keys. There is legitimate concern about maintaining secrecy for a central repository that holds and assigns keys.

A protocol is needed to enable a user to obtain a new key, while nobody—not even the central repository—knows what key the user has received. There are two possible exposures here.

1. *No one should be able to determine a user's private key given the public key.* We cannot publish a "key directory" and let everyone choose a key at random. If there were such a directory someone could look up the private key matching a public key as soon as a user chose a pair of keys and revealed the public key. Thus the privacy of a private key must be maintained while a user is selecting a new key.

2. *The key distributor should not know what key a user has selected.* Thus the facility cannot distribute one key to a user and expect the user to ask for the mate to the key selected. Nor can the facility distribute only one pair to a user; the user should have some choice so that the key distributor cannot be sure which key the user has chosen. Essentially we want the key distributor to put the keys in sealed envelopes in a barrel, and let a user pick one envelope.

A possible key distributor is a central source that generates and encrypts keys (like Ann in the previous example). Ann sends out a continuous stream of *encrypted* encryption keys. Because the keys are encrypted, no one can determine the keys themselves by monitoring the encrypted keys.

A particular user wanting a new key (like Bill) allows a few of Ann's encrypted keys to pass by and then chooses one, $E(k_i, K_A)$, at random. Some time later (after enough additional keys have been sent so that Ann cannot know which one Bill has chosen), Bill encrypts the selected key, forming $E(E(k_i, K_A), K_B)$. Bill sends this twice-encrypted key back to Ann. Ann decrypts the key, so that it is now concealed only under Bill's key, and sends it back to Bill. Finally, Bill decrypts the key to use it. This process, which is exactly like the poker protocol described earlier, is shown in Figure 4.6, where shading again shows how the messages are encrypted. (If used for a public key system, each key, or message, from Ann is really a pair of keys, $E((k_{PUB}, k_{PRIV}), K_A)$.)

Voting by Computer

A similar problem involves transmitting an untraceable yet authentic message. Such communication could, for example, allow human participants in an experiment to answer a confidential questionnaire anonymously. In another case, a computer might run an election. A third example involves automating private transactions (like Swiss bank

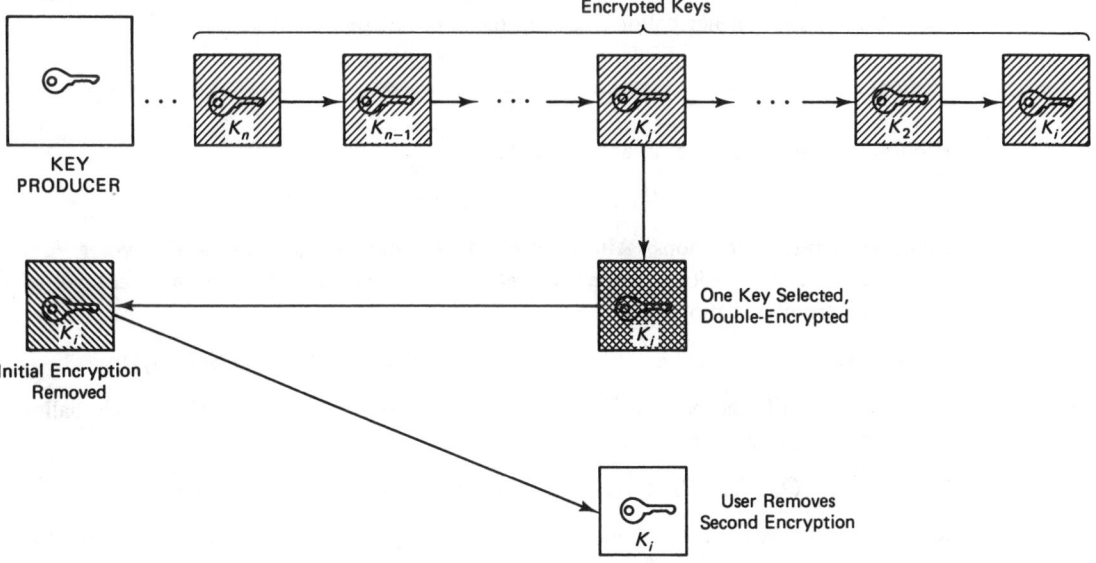

Encrypted Keys

Figure 4.6   Secure Key Distribution Protocol.

accounts), where financial transfers are authentic but cannot be traced back to their originators.

In all three cases, we need a protocol to ensure secrecy and legitimacy. Every message in the system must have come from some legitimate user, but no user can be associated with a particular message once the message is transmitted. The security requirements of this protocol are as follows.

- Only authorized users can transmit messages.

- Each user can transmit only one message at a time.

- Nobody can determine who sent a particular message.

To show how the protocol works we will consider a voting example. Suppose three voters, Jan, Keith, and Lee, are voting "yes" or "no" on one issue. Let each voter have two public key encryption functions. The first function, E, is a conventional public key encryption function, but the second, R, embeds the message in a random string and then encrypts the result. D will be the decrypting function for E and Q for R. Because there will be several layers of functions, we will change notation to E_U as the transformation for individual U.

Two people could have identical votes. The protocol must permit each user to recognize his or her vote, without being able to know which other votes, if any, are identical. The R encryption with a random string provides the desired secrecy and identifiability. Outwardly, the votes are concealed, because two identical votes have different random strings attached. However, each voter can uniquely identify his or her vote. Since each person's R decryption is known only to that person, only the sender can affirm that his or her ballot is among those to be counted.

Voting Protocol

Each voter chooses a vote, v, and computes

$$R_J(R_K(R_L(E_J(E_K(E_L(v))))))$$

using the public encryptions. All of the encrypted votes are sent to the first voter, Jan. Jan verifies that her ballot is among the set received. Jan then removes the first level of encryption from all ballots with

$$Q_J(R_J(R_K(R_L(E_J(E_K(E_L(v))))))) = R_K(R_L(E_J(E_K(E_L(v)))))$$

Now Jan forwards the ballots, in scrambled order, to Keith, who checks for his ballot and decrypts one level, producing

$$Q_K(R_K(R_L(E_J(E_K(E_L(v)))))) = R_L(E_J(E_K(E_L(v))))$$

Keith sends this result to Lee who sends $E_J(E_K(E_L(v)))$ for all the v to Jan. Lee also signs the votes with a digital signature, sending this signature to Jan and Keith.

Jan removes one more level of encryption, checks to verify that her vote is still in the set, forwards the ballots to Keith, and sends digital signatures of the ballots to Keith and Lee. Keith receives $E_K(E_L(v))$ from Jan which he decrypts to produce $E(L(v))$ for Lee. Lee removes E_L and publishes the results.

This protocol works because the analysis process is a six-link chain: $J \rightarrow K \rightarrow L \rightarrow J \rightarrow K \rightarrow L$. Results at each link of the chain can be made public without destroying the anonymity of any ballot. Furthermore, for the last three links of the chain, anyone can go "backward", but only one person can go "forward." That is, suppose Jan transforms the votes and passes them to Keith. Only Jan can perform this transformation. But Keith or anyone else can perform the reverse transformation, $J \leftarrow K$, to see if what Jan passed to Keith matches what Jan started with. This ability to check each other's work inhibits anyone from cheating.

Analysis of the Protocol

Let us analyze each step of this protocol. First, there is nothing that associates a vote with a single person, so the votes remain secret. Second, each person could have voted only once, since there are only three votes and everyone attests in the first round that his or her vote is among the three. Finally, nobody other than the three could have voted, since one of the three voters would find his or her vote missing.

Suppose during the second round someone decides to tamper with a vote. Once the results have been announced, the three voters can encrypt the result votes with R to see if these match the set originally sent around. Since each of the three signs the set of votes being passed forward, it is possible to detect who falsified the results.

Figure 4.7 depicts an example of this protocol. For simplicity, the E-type encryptions are shown with directed shadings, and the R-type encryptions are shown by Jan adding one random bit on the left, Keith adding two random bits on the right, and Lee adding three random bits on the left.

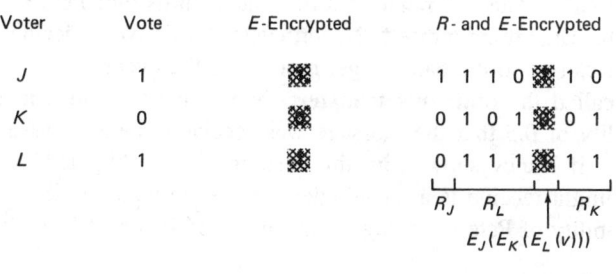

J, K, and L compute their encrypted votes; K and L send theirs to J

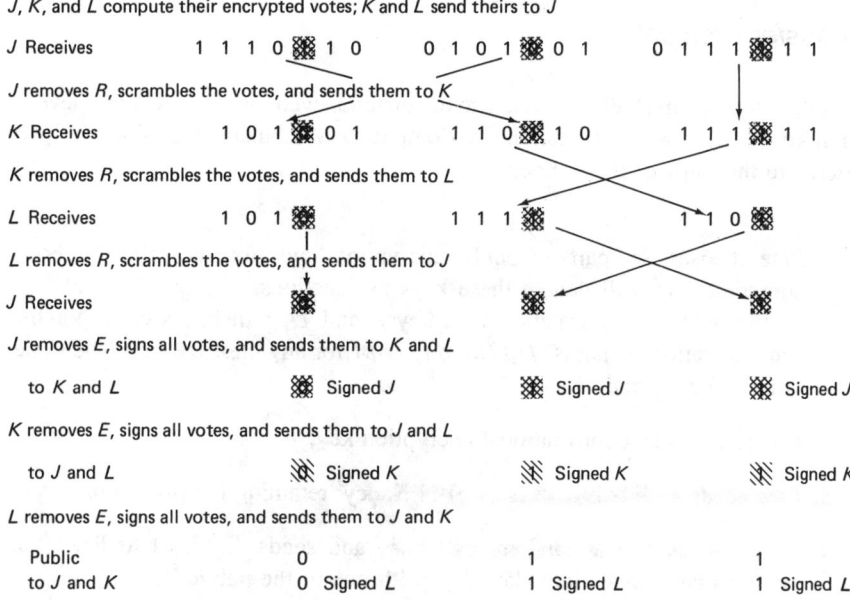

Figure 4.7   Voting Protocol.

Oblivious Transfer

The next protocol is a tool that will be used in later, more complicated protocols. The problem involves sending one of two messages, with the restriction that neither the sender nor the receiver will know until later which message was sent. An example of this problem is flipping a coin at some distance. One person ("the sender") flips a coin and writes down the result (heads or tails). The other ("the receiver") writes down a guess of how the coin landed. The two people meet later and exchange pieces of paper. In this case, if the words on the papers match, the receiver has won; otherwise the sender has won.

Suppose the two people cannot meet to exchange pieces of paper. Imagine this scenario. Pete and Nancy agree to go out one evening. On the telephone Pete suggests flipping a coin; if it turns out heads, Pete will pay for dinner and a movie, but if it is tails, Nancy will pay. Nancy replies that this is fine with her. Pete knows that if Nancy flips the coin, she will call it "heads" regardless of what it turns out; Pete knows this because he would do the same thing himself. Nevertheless, they have to decide over the phone so that the other can go to the bank to get money for the evening.

This problem is called the **oblivious transfer**; Pete wants to send a message to Nancy with a probability of 0.5 that the message was received. Pete's message could be "I will pay. –Pete." If Nancy shows him this message he is obligated to pay; the other message Nancy might receive is a meaningless garble, in which case she will be obligated. If the probability of Pete's message being received is 0.5, it is equivalent to flipping a coin fairly.

Transfer Protocol

A solution by Even [EVE82] is easy to understand, even though it requires several encryption keys. (© 1982, Association for Computing Machinery, Inc. Used by permission.) Here are the steps of the protocol.

1. Pete chooses two pairs of public encryption keys (four keys in all). For reference sometimes we will denote these keys as functions, E_i, D_i, E_j, and D_j. E_i will be the public transformation with key i, and D_i will be its corresponding private transformation. (That is, $D_i(E_i(M)) = M$ for any message M.) The same notation is used for E_j and D_j.

2. Nancy chooses a conventional encryption key, K_N.

3. Pete sends both public keys (i, j) to Nancy, retaining the private ones himself.

4. Nancy picks one at random, call it k, and sends $E_k(K_N)$ to Pete; that is, she encrypts her conventional key K_N with one of the public keys E_k.

5. Pete picks either i or j at random; suppose it is j. Pete computes $P = D_j(E_k(K_N))$. This is just a binary string to Pete, so he cannot tell whether j is the k Nancy chose. If $k = j$, the P is Nancy's key K_N; otherwise P is a meaningless binary string.

6. Pete computes $E(\text{"I will pay. –Pete"}, P)$, which he sends to Nancy, along with the value of j.

7. Nancy decrypts Pete's message with K_N. She picked k and Pete picked j; if $k = j$ she wins, for she properly decrypts Pete's message. If $k \neq j$, she loses, getting only a meaningless tangle of bits.

8. After the winner is known, Pete gives the private keys i and j to Nancy. From these keys, she can verify whether her k was i or j, and that the j Pete used was one of these two.

Analysis of the Protocol

How does this protocol work? Nancy first picks one of Pete's keys, which she disguises and returns to Pete. Pete cannot tell which Nancy has picked because he does not have access to K_N with which to decrypt it. Therefore, when he picks j, the chance that he picks the one Nancy picked is 1 in 2. He encrypts a message which Nancy must reproduce exactly in order to convince him that he picked her key. If they picked the same key, Nancy's K_N decrypts the message; if not, K_N produces a meaningless string. When they get together later, they can exchange keys and verify that each party lived up to the rules of the protocol.

Of course, flipping coins over a telephone is not a very important task. However, this protocol is the basis for the two protocols that we consider next.

Contract Signing

Suppose that Charles and Diane agree to something and wish to sign a contract to show their agreement. Both of them are committed to performing some act by the contract, but each wants to commit only if the other does also. Charles might, for example, commit to selling his car to Diane if Diane agrees to give him a part interest in her pizza franchise. Charles is in California and Diane is in New York. Charles will not sign the contract first and mail it to Diane, because that leaves him at Diane's mercy: He has agreed to sell the car, so he must take it off the market. But Diane could tear up the contract, leaving Charles with the car; on the other hand, Diane could sign the contract, forcing Charles to produce the car. Charles is bound by the contract as soon as he signs. However, he does not know if Diane will sign or not, so she is not bound by it. The situation is the same if Diane signs first: She is bound but not Charles.

In practice, this would be handled by both people signing together. We want to establish a protocol for signing contracts by computer. Physical proximity and written signatures are what we want to avoid with our solution.

Another approach would be to appeal to a trustworthy third party: Charles and Diane each sign a copy of the contract, which they forward to a trusted third party, who holds these two copies with one signature each. These constitute evidence of their willingness to enter into the contract. When the third party announces that a signed copy has been received from each, Charles signs another copy which he sends to Diane, and she signs a copy which she sends to him. Charles and Diane inform the third party that the contracts are in order, and the third party destroys the ones with only one signature each. We want to avoid appeal to a third party, too, if possible.

Thus, a contract protocol requires two things:

- *Commitment.* After a certain point both parties are bound by the contract; until then neither is.

- *Unforgeability.* The signatures on the contract must be demonstrably authentic; that is, it must be possible for either party to prove that the signature of the other is authentic.

The protocol must be able to achieve these two things *indirectly,* without face-to-face participation. An indirect protocol is suitable for use in a computerized situation.

Real-life Solution

A protocol without face-to-face cooperation might operate in the following manner. This protocol would probably not actually be used, but it is similar to a computer protocol that will be described in the next section. Charles and Diane pass at least three copies of the contract back and forth. Each holds one copy as proof of what has happened up until then; a copy can also be in transit. It is fairly clear who sends which copy to whom in order to hold onto a piece of evidence, so we will not describe the different copies that move back and forth.

Charles writes the first part of his name on the contract, "C", and sends it to Diane. She writes her first initial, "D," and sends it back. Charles writes the next part of his name, "h", and they continue trading the contract, each affixing a piece of the signature. With only the letter "C" on the contract, Charles knows that nobody could require him to fulfill the contract. However, the letter is an act of good faith that he shows to Diane. Diane responds with a similar act of good faith.

After several letters are in each signature, Diane knows that she could convince a judge that Charles should really be bound by the terms of the contract. She would explain the circumstances and hope the judge would agree. There is a measure of uncertainty in this: Charles is not bound by just the letter "C," but he is bound by his full signature. However, the point at which he becomes bound is not obvious: is it 1/2 of the letters? 2/3? 3/4?

Since they are uncertain at exactly what point they become bound, both Charles and Diane must fear they are bound at each point, so there is no reason not to continue the protocol. They also know that the longer they continue, the greater probability of proving the other is also bound, so again it is in their best interest to continue. Besides, both wanted to sign the contract anyway; they just wanted to be bound at the same time. This issue of uncertainty of point of commitment is the basis of the computer solution.

Overview of the Indirect Protocol

The computer solution works much the same way. The parties exchange a message of commitment in pieces, using the oblivious transfer protocol from the previous section. Remember that the oblivious transfer is a way of transmitting one of two messages, so that neither the sender nor the receiver is sure which message has been transmitted. Therefore, neither party knows when half of this message has been transmitted, because with oblivious transfer neither knows exactly what the other has received.

Suppose each person's signature is divided into four blocks, and that it is impossible to recognize the signature just by looking at it. Charles and Diane execute the oblivious transfer eight times each. Charles sends each block once under an i and once under the corresponding j; Diane does likewise.

For the first three times, Charles feels safe, since Diane cannot have all four blocks of his signature. Charles sends the fourth piece. With this, Diane may have a full signature, but she cannot tell that. In fact, the probability is low that she has received all four signature blocks. If she stops, Charles might have received 3/4 of her signature and be able to convince a judge that Diane had reneged on the contract. Diane has no choice but to continue. As Charles and Diane continue, they come closer and closer to assurance.

At any point after four rounds, neither can stop, because he or she might already have transmitted a full signature, thereby being bound by the contract anyway. Therefore, it is in the best interest of both to continue until the end, when the full signatures are definitely exchanged.

Indirect Contract-Signing Protocol

The following protocol, designed by Even, Goldreich and Lempel [EVE85], follows this outline. (© 1985, Association for Computing Machinery, Inc. Used by permission.)

1. Charles randomly selects $2n$ keys for a conventional key cryptosystem, such as DES. Let these keys be $c_1, c_2, \ldots, c_{2n}$. The keys are treated as pairs, (c_1, c_{n+1}), (c_2, c_{n+2}), and so forth. There is nothing distinctive about c_1 and c_{n+1} that marks them as a pair, however.

2. For each key, Charles computes $C_i = E_{c_i}(S)$ for some standard message S whose content is irrelevant. Charles sends C_1 through C_{2n} to Diane. That is, Diane has the encrypted version of the standard message under each key.

3. Charles agrees that he is committed to the contract if Diane can present *both* keys c_i and c_{n+i} for some i. (Note: In the description by Even *et al.* each C_i is called an "S-puzzle," and the key c_i is called its "solution.")

4. Diane repeats these three steps similarly, with keys d_i and encrypted messages D_i.

5. Charles sends each pair c_i and c_{n+i}, $1 \leq i \leq n$, to Diane via the oblivious transfer. That is, Charles sends either c_i or c_{n+i} to Diane, but neither he nor she is sure which has been received. Diane does the same with all d_i and d_{n+i} for $1 \leq i \leq n$. At this point, Charles and Diane each have half of the other's secrets.

6. Let l be the length of each c_i or d_i.

    For $1 \leq j \leq l$ begin
    Charles transmits the jth bit of all c_i, $1 \leq i \leq n$ to Diane.
    Diane transmits the jth bit of all d_i, $1 \leq i \leq n$ to Charles.
    end

7. Assuming neither stops early, at the end both have all l bits of all of the other's secrets, and the contract is signed.

When step 6 begins, both Diane and Charles have half of the other's secrets; however, it is infeasible to determine the key c_{n+i} from its encrypted message C_{n+i}, assuming Diane received c_i. As this step progresses, Diane receives one bit of c_{n+i}, then the next bit, then the next bit, etc. If Diane uses a brute force attack to determine c_{n+i}, each bit she receives cuts her work load in half.

At some point, she may think the work still to be done is easy enough that she will attempt to determine c_{n+i} for some c_i. Thus she may stop sending bits to Charles. At this same point, Charles has an equivalent amount of information about each d_i. If it is feasible for Diane to determine c_{n+i}, it is just as feasible for Charles to determine d_k or d_{n+k} for some k. Thus, the time Diane needs to cheat gives Charles time to match her solution, so that they are both bound to the contract.

Certified Mail

Sending certified mail is the last problem for which we will develop a protocol solution. Suppose Gina wants to send a message to Hal, but she wants proof that Hal received the message. She does not want to release the message to Hal without getting a receipt. He, of course, is not going to sign the receipt until he actually has the message. Postal employees and arbiters can solve this problem. However, as usual, we would like a solution that works without an arbiter. The solution is very much like the contract signing protocol just studied; in fact, this solution also comes from Even *et al.* in [EVE85].

Let Gina's message to Hal be M. She will transmit M to Hal in encrypted form and will give Hal the encryption key only when she has received an adequate acknowledgment from Hal of his having received M. Hal will acknowledge receiving M only when he receives a key that lets him obtain the plaintext M.

1. Gina randomly selects $n+1$ keys for a private cryptosystem (such as DES), naming them $g_0, g_1, g_2, \ldots, g_n$. She also computes $g_{n+i} = g_0 \oplus g_i$ for $1 \leq i \leq n$. (The symbol $\oplus$ denotes exclusive or.)

2. Gina computes $G = E_{g_0}(M)$, the encryption of her message M with key g_0. She sends G to Hal. Since for each i, $g_{n+i} = g_0 \oplus g_i$,

$$g_{n+i} \oplus g_i = g_0 \oplus g_i \oplus g_i = g_0 \oplus 0 = g_0.$$

Thus Hal can determine M given any pair g_i, g_{n+i}.

3. Gina computes and sends to Hal $G_i = E_{g_i}(S)$ for $1 \leq i \leq 2n$, where S is some standard message whose content is irrelevant. At this point Hal has the encrypted message G and a standard message S encrypted with each of Gina's $2n$ different keys.

4. Hal chooses $2n$ keys $h_1, h_2, \ldots, h_{2n}$. Hal computes $H_i = E_{h_i}(S)$ for $1 \leq i \leq 2n$. Hal sends all the H_i to Gina.

5. Hal sends a statement to Gina that he acknowledges receipt of the plaintext of message G if Gina can produce *both* one of Hal's pairs (h_i and h_{n+i}) *and* all g_j for $1 \leq j \leq 2n$.

Saying this, Hal acknowledges that if Gina has the time to determine one of his pairs, h_i and h_{n+i}, he would also have time to determine one of her pairs, g_m and g_{n+m}. Any time Hal gets a pair, Hal can compute the encryption key g_0 and obtain the message $M = D_{g_0}(G)$. The second condition on Hal's statement ensures that Gina acted fairly: that each pair does yield g_0.

6. As in the contract signing protocol, Gina and Hal exchange pairs (g_1, g_{n+1}), (g_2, g_{n+2}), and so forth, and (h_1, h_{n+1}), (h_2, h_{n+2}), and so forth, by oblivious transfer. That is, Hal receives either g_1 or g_{n+1}, but neither he nor Gina knows which; Gina receives half of each (h_i, h_{n+i}) pair, without knowing which.

7. As in the contract signing protocol, let l be the length of each key g_i.

   For $j = 1$ to l **begin**
       Gina sends Hal the jth bit of each g_i for $1 \leq i \leq 2n$.
       Hal sends Gina the jth bit of each h_i for $1 \leq i \leq 2n$.
   end

The amount of work to be done to break the other's code is the same as for contract signing, so the same rationale for continuing applies. Although both the contract signing and the certified mail protocol are too complicated for easy implementation by humans, they are easily suited for computer communication.

Protocol Summary

In the previous sections we have studied several examples of protocols for computer use. The protocols have solved problems that ordinarily require face-to-face interaction between humans. However, by careful design, we have been able to ensure properties of secrecy and authenticity while maintaining absolute fairness.

As noted earlier, separating design from implementation is desirable. Protocols, which can be analyzed and verified, are a good design medium, since the correctness of the protocol can be determined exclusive of any specific use of the protocol.

For each protocol, we first explored the *problem* to be solved. Then we identified the *security requirements* we wished to satisfy with the protocol. Next, we designed a *protocol* that met the security requirements. Finally, we performed an *analysis* of the protocol to confirm that it met the requirements.

In the next section we will study the practices of using encryption. Although these practices are not as formal as protocols, they do guide us in our use of encryption to perform tasks with computers.

4.2 Appropriate Uses of Encryption

We have examined protocols as orderly sequences of steps for interaction between two parties. The methods presented clever ways of exchanging information while preserving secrecy, anonymity, or privacy. The protocols used encryption as a tool to achieve secrecy, authenticity, or integrity, although the focus was on the protocol and the security properties to be achieved, not on the encryption itself. Protocols, which are independent of any specific encryption algorithm, assume only the existence of a particular type of encryption (conventional or public key), perhaps having a fairly general property (such as commutativity).

Some situations in computing involve only one user. No sequence of steps is needed, since there can be no disagreement about fairness or adherence to a rule. In these cases, secrecy or authenticity are of prime importance. These situations, called **encryption practices** or **encryption techniques,** are the subject of the remainder of this chapter.

We must be familiar with the characteristics, the advantages, and the disadvantages of encryption algorithms. In this way, we can select algorithms correctly and use appropriate methods of encryption. In this section we consider criteria by which to judge specific encryption systems. We study limitations of these systems and ways to avoid the limitations. The two major schemes to be considered are the RSA and the DES. We also study general limitations of public and private key systems.

Recall from Chapter 2 that Shannon suggested overall criteria for encryption systems. Although these criteria were developed before the popularity of modern computers, they, are still remarkably applicable to the problems encountered today. Shannons criteria are repeated here.

1. The degree of secrecy needed should determine the amount of labor appropriate for encryption and decryption.

2. The set of keys should be free from complexity.

3. The implementation of the process should be as simple as possible.

4. Errors in ciphering should not propagate and cause corruption of further information in the message.

5. The size of the enciphered text should be no larger than the text of the original message.

Criterion 1 is a basis of cryptosystems. Criterion 2 was more important when keys—and the entire encryption system—had to be applied by hand. With computers to perform the tedious or complicated work, complexity of key choice is not a concern. Distributing keys to users is difficult when a key change is due or desired, however. The implementation of an encryption scheme should still be as simple as possible. However, with the use of computers, previously infeasible algorithms can now be implemented. The propagation of errors described in criterion 4 is still a concern. Finally, size may or may not be a concern. We address each criterion in greater detail in the sections following.

Amount of Secrecy

The controversy concerning recertification of DES is a good example of the relevance of secrecy today. It has not been argued, or even suggested, that the DES *is* flawed, only that it *could be* compromised, given enough time and computing resources.

Hellman [HEL79b] argues that a dedicated attacker could break the secrecy of a message encrypted using DES. The argument centers around speed of computation on a dedicated, multiprocessor special purpose machine designed solely to discover DES keys. The number of processors needed for such a machine—several hundred thousand to a million—would certainly attract attention if bought on the open market, unless the purchase were done over a very long time. However, current hardware prices are lower than in the late 1970s when this argument was first raised. The cost to build such a machine would be very high, though, even at current prices. It is doubtful that any private company in the U.S. could amass the hardware resources or cash necessary to acquire such a machine. This reservation is also true for any underworld group or for any government agency that wants the ability to break DES encryptions.

Some uses of encryption are like padlocks: to keep out casual intruders, not to keep out someone really determined to break in. For example, a company might encrypt memoranda dealing with a new line of products in order to maintain an edge over the competition. Banks encrypt funds transfer information to prevent unauthorized modification and to detect spurious transmission errors more than to preserve privacy. A user may encrypt the file of a source program to prevent unauthorized modifications.

In these and other cases, the value of the encrypted information must be weighed against the value to others who might be able to break in. DES is still adequately safe to keep out most casual interceptors. The same may be said of RSA. In over a decade, no serious challenge to the security of RSA has been raised.

In summary, then, the security of the encryption system should be appropriate to the degree of confidentiality of the data being preserved. Users of encryption systems should consider the value of the data being encrypted when selecting an encryption system.

Key Distribution

Keys for the more complex encryption systems cannot simply be chosen at random. The public key systems, for example, require two keys in carefully determined pairs.

With this consideration, key distribution can be a major issue. When it is time to change keys, each possessor of a key must be informed of the key change, and all users must start to use the new key at the same time (in order to avoid having some messages encrypted with the old instead of the new key, and being unable to distinguish between them).

Selecting New Keys

Centralized key distribution is a protocol for facilitating the communication between pairs of users. In this approach, two users, A and B, both deposit private keys with a central repository. Therefore, n users need only n keys on file with the central repository. When A wishes to communicate something to B, A requests the repository to issue a new key to be used only for that one session. A and B are free to change their central keys any time they wish. Since a new session key is always issued for each session, one user does not need to know if the other may have changed central keys. Unfortunately, this protocol places much responsibility with the key repository.

As an alternative, A can choose a public key transformation, $E_A()$, and its corresponding private transformation, $D_A()$. A then sends $E_A()$ to B, who picks a conventional encryption key k. B sends $E_A(k)$ to A, who decrypts that to obtain k, which A and B then use for the current session. The disadvantage here is that although k remains hidden, an interceptor C, masquerading as B, could send a spurious k_C to A, tricking A into communicating a message under a key C can read.

This trick can be circumvented if A sends a secret message to B and B sends the same message back to A. For example, A would send something like

$$E_B(D_A(\text{"I am A: } date/time\text{"}))$$

to B. Only B can read this message, since only B has access to D_B. The date and time mark the message as current. Then B chooses a key, k, and sends back

$$E_A(D_B(k, \text{"I am A: } date/time, \text{ new } date/time\text{"}))$$

to A. Only B could have sent this message. Furthermore, B must have received the original message in order to have decrypted the "I am A" part and sent it back. Finally, only A can read the message to verify B's authenticity and to obtain k. A and B complete their session using k.

Lost (Revealed) Keys

Both public and private key systems are sensitive to lost, revealed, or stolen keys. The only known approach is time checking. A user must know when a key may have been compromised. If this is so, the user notifies a central repository, or all correspondents who might receive messages from the user, that the key is believed to have been revealed. All receivers of messages from the user are thereby notified that they should suspect any message received after the date of the loss; they are also notified that they should not send any further messages under the user's public key.

This procedure, which is not really optimal, is about the best available. A user who wishes to back out of a signed contract simply claims disclosure of the private key at some time before the date of the contract. Since the private key was allegedly not private at the time of the contract, anyone could have acted as the user whose key was supposedly lost.

Complexity to Encrypt

Consider next the complexity to perform an encryption. Two major complexity issues are the delay before the encryption algorithm can begin to produce ciphertext and the slowness of the encryption algorithm itself.

Delay to Encrypt

The delay before encryption commences depends on the type of encryption—block or stream—and the size of a block. As described in Chapter 2, stream ciphers are desirable, so that the encryption algorithm can encrypt each new character as it appears. Slightly less desirable, although usually adequate, are stream ciphers that work on blocks. Each character cannot be enciphered as it appears, but new characters are held until a block (for example eight 8-bit characters or 64 bits, with DES) has been received. The least desirable encryption functions are those for which the whole plaintext message, or an unbounded amount of the message, must be received before encryption can begin.

Both the RSA and the DES are block ciphers. With the DES, a block is 64 bits. With the RSA there is no required block length (although there is limited security with a short block). The maximum block length is also a matter of choice for the implementer. The developers of RSA propose a block of 100 to 200 bits. The lengths of both DES and RSA are reasonable for commercial use.

Speed of Encryption

Some encryption algorithms perform a constant amount of work per character encrypted. For example, the substitution ciphers, all of which are essentially table lookup processes, possess this property. The DES and RSA algorithms, although much more complicated, also use only a constant amount of work per block. Both algorithms operate in time proportional to the size of the plaintext message; only the constant of proportionality is different.

Speed is important, because it ensures that if an encryption algorithm can handle one block before the second one is received, the algorithm will not degrade the speed of the application. There are hardware (chip) implementations of both DES and RSA that work at reasonable speeds.

Propagation of Errors

Errors in transmission are prevalent and serious. As we will see in later chapters, local and remote networks are prone to errors of transmission. These errors may not indicate an interceptor. Ideally encryption algorithms should be immune to the network's errors. Often the network is responsible for detecting faulty communications and retransmitting faulty messages, so that the user will not know there had been a difficulty.

A true error (the result of an interceptor's attempted change) should be apparent in the ciphertext, so that any modification is readily noticed. Neither the DES or the RSA has any tamper-protection mechanism. With both of these, the encryption algorithm is so contorted that changing even a single output bit would lead to a severely garbled decrypted message. If the plaintext is prose, a change will be evident. If the plaintext is binary data with little or no pattern, a change may not be detected.

Size of Ciphertext

The size of the resulting ciphertext is also important. In some instances, the encrypted ciphertext is expected to fit back in the space previously occupied by the plaintext. If this is true, then even a slight increase in text size is intolerable. Note that both block ciphers, DES and RSA, must encrypt a full block at a time. Although it is easy to pad a short last block to bring it up to size, this padding increases the size of the output text.

4.3 Enhancing Cryptographic Security

The DES and RSA are believed to be secure encryption algorithms. Thus, an intruder is unlikely to discover the content of a message encrypted under one of them. However, the description of possible attacks on a secure system (described in Chapter 1) included many more potential security weaknesses than just breaking the secrecy of a message. In this section we consider some of these attacks.

Error Prevention and Detection

In the DES each block is an entity. An interceptor who understood the format of a sender's messages could modify messages without needing to break the encryption.

Block Replay

For example, consider the following situation. Two banks agree to electronic exchange of information about transfers of money between the two banks, using encrypted data for security. They agree to transmit records having a certain fixed format:

name of depositor	24 bytes
account number	8 bytes
amount of transfer	8 bytes

These records consist of 40 bytes = 320 bits = five 64-bit blocks, as shown in Figure 4.8. Suppose John is able to tap the data channel between these banks. The first day, John has his bank transfer $100. on his behalf from the one bank to the other. The next day he does the same thing. On both days he taps, intercepts, and records the transmission from the one bank to the other. Assume that both transmissions were sent under the same encryption key and that both transmissions begin at the start of a record. John knows that both transmissions will contain three blocks representing his name, one representing his account number, and one representing the amount, and that these five blocks in a row will be the same on both days. Identifying the data in these fields is merely a process of looking for duplicates, a tedious task that can be performed easily by computer.

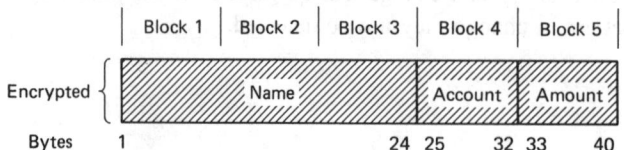

Figure 4.8   Blocks of DES Encryption.

The next day, John verifies his supposition by sending through another transaction for a different amount, again looking for four blocks identical to before, but with a different fifth block. If only one set of blocks fits this pattern, John has the encrypted form of his name, account number, and two amounts.

By *inserting* data onto the transmission line, instead of simply reading messages from it, John can now replace any person and account number with his own name and account number, leaving the amount alone. John does not need to know who should be getting the money or how much is being obtained; John simply changes names and account numbers to his own and watches the balance in his account grow. This technique is known as **block replay**, in which encrypted blocks from one transmission are sent in a second transmission. To use block replay, the interceptor does not necessarily have to break the encryption, as shown in this example.

At the end of each transmission, the banks probably send the total of all transfers in the transmission, but John leaves that alone, so the total will balance. If John is lucky, at least one of the altered transmissions will net John a substantial sum. Customers may not notice the lack of a transfer (which John has diverted to his own account) until a month after John begins his transmission interference. John carries on this game for slightly less than a month, withdraws all the money from his account in cash, and heads for another country.

John is probably an "insider," meaning that he knows the format of the transmissions, the frequency with which encryption keys are changed, how often these transmissions occur, and so forth. John also probably has ways to guarantee a good return in one tampering incident. The technique used here has been simplified somewhat, both to make the explanation easier, and to avoid a detailed guide to larceny.

Because they treat each block of plaintext independently, the DES and other block ciphers are prone to this type of attack. Fortunately, there is an easy solution, called **block chaining.**

Block Chaining

Recall that if you exclusive-or any binary string with itself the result is 0, and the exclusive-or operation is commutative. Therefore, for any strings a and b, letting $\oplus$ represent exclusive-or,

$$(a \oplus b) \oplus a = (a \oplus a) \oplus b$$
$$= 0 \oplus b$$
$$= b$$

With block chaining each block to be transmitted is combined with the exclusive-or of all blocks up to that block. If the blocks are B_1, B_2, B_3, and the encryption function is $E()$, the following blocks are transmitted.

$$C_1 = E(B_1),$$
$$C_2 = E(E(B_1) \oplus B_2) = E(C_1 \oplus B_2),$$
$$C_3 = E(E(E(B_1) \oplus B_2) \oplus B_3) = E(C_2 \oplus B_3),$$

This process is shown in Figure 4.9.

The receiver decrypts the first block received, C_1, as normal. The receiver decrypts the second received block (which is $E(C_1 \oplus B_2)$ or C_2), obtaining $C_1 \oplus B_2$. From the

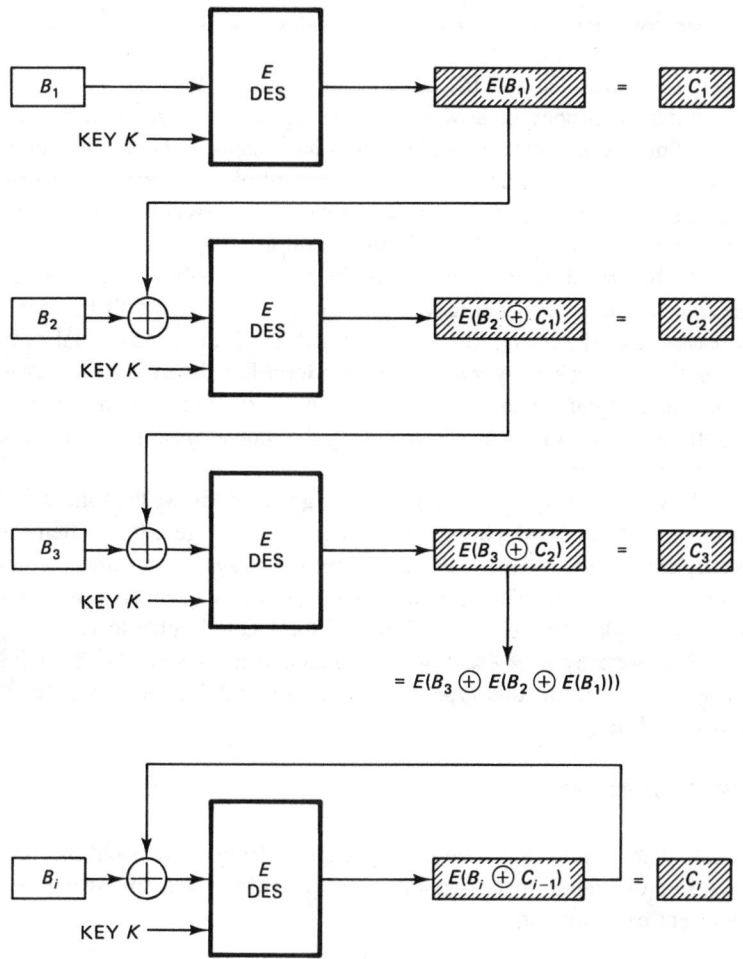

Figure 4.9   Example of Block Chaining.

previously obtained C_1, the receiver then computes $(C_1 \oplus B_2) \oplus C_1$. Thus this expression simplifies to

$$(C_1 \oplus B_2) \oplus C_1 = (C_1 \oplus C_1) \oplus B_2 = 0 \oplus B_2 = B_2$$

or the plaintext value of block 2. The receiver proceeds this way with all subsequent blocks.

As shown in Figure 4.10, identical plaintext blocks transmitted separately or within the same transmission do not necessarily produce the same ciphertext. The difference occurs because each block depends on all the blocks that precede it. Thus, it will be impossible for an interceptor to repeat certain blocks from one transmission in another or even to find blocks that come from identical plaintext.

For the DES, one block does not disclose another, since $E(C_1 \oplus B_2) \neq E(C_1) \oplus E(B_2)$. Even if the interceptor knows that $C_2 = E(C_1 \oplus B_2)$ and the interceptor has just obtained C_1, that information does not reveal B_2, or even $E(B_2)$.

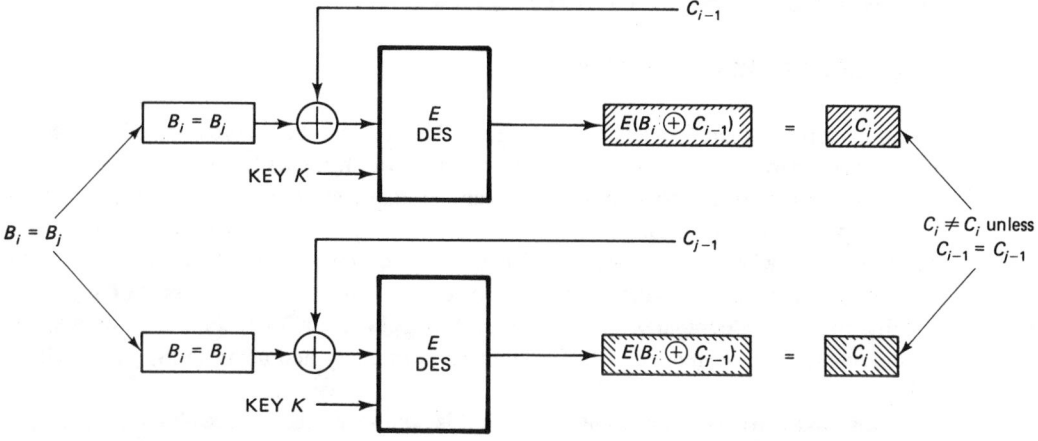

Figure 4.10   Encryption of Identical Plaintext Blocks.

Initial Chaining Value

Block chaining conceals identical blocks, as long as each is preceded by something unique. For some messages, however, the first few blocks may follow a set format (for example, memoranda that begin with the stock pattern "MEMORANDUM FROM: JANE BELL. TO: ALL EMPLOYEES. SUBJECT:"). With the same encryption key all such memoranda would produce the same ciphertext output.

If this exposure is unacceptable, added security is obtained by using an **initial chaining value**. This value is any random string used as the initial block. Any string can be used, such as the current time and date, or even a random number. The string must be different for every message encrypted. Both the sender and receiver know to decrypt this block but use it only in the exclusive-or of subsequent blocks; it carries no data of importance.

With the use of an initial chaining vector, the message $B_1 B_2 B_3 \ldots$ essentially becomes $I\ B_1 B_2 B_3 \ldots$. The first block sent is $E(I)$, where I is the initial chaining value. The next block sent is $E(E(I) \oplus B_1)$. Even if two identical blocks appear in different messages, for example B_1, they will not result in identical ciphertext. Since I is different for each message, $E(E(I) \oplus B_1)$ will be different, too.

One-Way Encryption

Some encryptions depend on a function that is difficult to compute. For a simple example, consider the cube function, $y = x^3$. It is relatively easy to compute x^3 by hand, with pencil and paper, or with a calculator. The inverse function, $\sqrt[3]{y}$ is much more difficult to compute. And the function $y = x^2$ has no inverse function, since there are two possibilities for $\sqrt{y}$: $+x$ and $-x$. Functions like these, which are much easier to compute than their inverses, are called **one-way functions.**

Uses of One-Way Encryption

One-way functions are especially useful in authentication. Passwords are often used to check that a particular user is the person trying to log in as that user. A public table of user passwords is risky in a computing system, so many systems use a one-way function to encrypt the password table. The system stores $f(pw)$ when a user obtains a new password, pw, where f is a one-way function. When the user later tries to log on, the system asks for the password. The user types ew, and the system computes $f(ew)$. Finally, the system compares $f(ew)$ to $f(pw)$ to authenticate the user. For example, the system could store $E(pw, pw)$, that is, the password encrypted using DES, with itself as a key.

The password system is secure because it is computationally infeasible or impossible to compute f^{-1}. An intruder might find the password table and detect that the encrypted form of a user's password is $f(pw)$. This information, however, does not allow the intruder to infer pw. Furthermore, the intruder could try different passwords with a brute force attack until finding a word w for which $f(w) = f(pw)$. With long passwords chosen from a large alphabet, this attack is effectively rendered infeasible.

Cryptographic Sealing

Another useful property of encryption is its ability to protect data from tampering. For example, in an ordinary data file, a value, a line, a record, or a whole file can be changed without detection. In this discussion we refer to files, although the same considerations apply to a record, field, or single byte.

Encryption is most commonly used for secrecy. In some cases, however, integrity is a more important concern than secrecy. For example, in a document retrieval system it may be important to know that the copy retrieved is exactly what was stored. Likewise, in a secure communications system, need for the correct transmission of messages may override secrecy concerns. Encryption can ensure integrity as well as secrecy.

In most files there is no force that binds the elements together. That is, each byte or bit or character is independent from every other one in the file. Changing one value affects the integrity of the file, but that one change can easily go undetected.

Cryptography can be used to **seal** a file, essentially encasing it in plastic, so that any change becomes apparent. One technique is to compute a cryptographic function, sometimes called a **checksum**, of the file. The function must depend on all bits of the file being sealed, so that any change to even a single bit will alter the checksum result.

The checksum value is stored with the file. Then each time the file is accessed or used, the checksum is recomputed. If the computed checksum matches the stored value, it is likely that the file has not been changed.

A cryptographic function, such as the DES, is especially appropriate for sealing values, since an outsider will not know how to modify the stored value to match with data being modified. As described earlier, chaining applied to DES produces a result where each block depends on the value of previous blocks. A file cryptographic checksum could be the last block of the chained DES encryption of a file, since that block will depend on all other blocks.

Authentication

Remember the folk legends in which two people would cut a coin in half, and one would take a half and then leave, saying "if a messenger brings something with this half of the coin, you'll know it is from me"? With encryption we can do something similar. With personal communication, when dealing with people we know, we have ways of being sure the person to whom we speak is who we think it is. We recognize voices, mannerisms, patterns of behavior. With computer communication, we do not have as many clues to assure us of identity.

The primary means of authentication is a password: a word or string that only one person knows. The computer system presumes that anyone knowing the password is the person to whom the password belongs. As we will see later, passwords can be secure, although if misused they offer little protection.

Another form of authentication is encryption. If you receive an encrypted message that can be decrypted with a key known only to you and one other person, the message is authentic. Assuming that the encryption scheme has not been broken, or that the key has not been compromised (both of which are unlikely), the message could have been created only by the one other person having the key.

This certainty extends to the entire message. With a strong encryption algorithm, it is impossible for someone else to substitute a desired phrase for part of the message, or to "paste together" pieces from two or more old messages. For example, cipher block chaining described earlier prevents substituting one block in a message. The message received was sent by the known person with no tampering before its receipt.

Time Stamps

Another security problem is the possibility that a message in its entirety might have been intercepted by someone else and is now being replayed. (This is the electronic equivalent of trying to negotiate a photocopy of a check, where the person cashing the copy does not detect it is a copy.) If this is a potential problem, the sender and receiver can identify each message with a message number or a time stamp.

A message number is a number embedded within the message. The interceptor has no way to know where within the message the message number bits appear, or how to change the bits to produce the enciphered version of the next number, or how to change these bits without corrupting the decryption of the rest of the message. Being embedded, message numbers cannot be substituted, modified, or forged.

The receiver keeps count of message numbers received. If two people use one set of numbers, the receiver can tell immediately if a message before the current one has been lost or delayed, because the number encrypted with the current message will be more than one higher than the number of the previous message.

Alternatively, a sender will have a single message number generator for messages to all recipients. If the sender sends messages to two people, A and B, message 1 might go to A, 2 to B, 3 and 4 to A, 5 to B, and so on. Neither recipient can tell if a particular message was lost, because the message numbers are only an ascending sequence, not necessarily all numbers in the range. However, a recipient can instantly spot a replay of a previous message. The message number should be encrypted or otherwise protected to inhibit modification.

A sender with many messages can run into the problem of extremely long message numbers. For this reason, it is usual to reset the message number counter when it gets too high, say after its length exceeds 30 bits. In this case all recipients must be informed (by a message) that the next message number sent will be reset to small numbers. Another problem is that a separate counter is maintained for each pair of sender and receiver. A popular sender or receiver must maintain many different counters for many different correspondents.

Time and date stamps are somewhat more flexible. They are markings of the time and date the message was sent, with enough precision that no two messages will have the same marking. They need not be reset.

The receiver must match the sender's time closely. In a fast transmission, if the sender's and receiver's clocks are not synchronized, the sender's time stamp could be later than the recipient's current time. It is typical to allow a small tolerance for unsynchronized times, or recognition that one sender's time stamps are all slightly fast.

We have now studied various aspects of encryption in specific applications, such as ensuring integrity, preventing replay, and assuring secrecy. These can be achieved with any encryption system, since they depend only on general properties of encryption.

Modes of Use of DES

Now we investigate different ways that the DES can be used. The version of DES presented in Chapter 3 is called the Electronic Code Book (ECB) use of DES. Essentially a message is translated one independent 64-bit block at a time, as if one had a huge code book of all 64-bit quantities and their DES encryption (for a particular key). However, we discussed the limitation of that mode of encryption with identical plaintext. In the following sections, we present other modes of use of the DES.

Cipher Block Chain

As described earlier, the Cipher Block Chain (CBC) mode of operation starts with a random initialization vector (IV). The initialization vector is combined by exclusive-or with the first plaintext block; this result is encrypted. Then the first ciphertext block

$(E(p_1 \oplus IV, k))$ is combined by exclusive-or with the second plaintext block, and that result is encrypted. Each ciphertext block is chained to the remainder of the message, so that it is impossible to substitute one ciphertext block for another without being discovered. Cipher block chaining is shown in Figure 4.11.

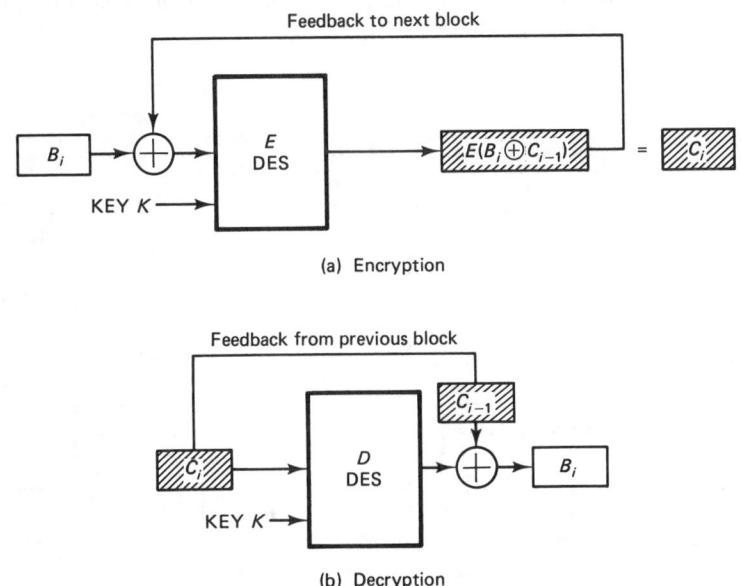

Figure 4.11   Cipher Block Chaining.

CBC mode also has the property of being self-healing, so that a change in block c_i affects the decryption of blocks p_i and p_{i+1}. However, blocks p_{i+2} and beyond are unaffected. After two blocks, the exclusive-or function cancels any error. (Recall that for any string x, $x \oplus x = 0$.) The self-healing property is convenient because an error in transmission or encryption will not damage a large amount of ciphertext.

Cipher Feedback

The block-oriented nature of DES is inconvenient for two reasons noted earlier. First, a partial final block must be padded. Thus, the size of the resulting ciphertext can be slightly larger than the size of the corresponding plaintext. Second, encryption cannot begin until all 64 bits of a block have been received. Therefore, the speed of encryption of one character can depend on how fast several later characters are received. Some applications require immediate encryption of each character. For example, in a secure network environment, a user must transmit each character as it is entered at the terminal.

The Cipher Feedback (CFB) mode of operation works on one character at a time. Therefore, the ciphertext is not expanded in order to fill the last block, and no delay is imposed because of needing 64 bits to encrypt.

The CFB algorithm operates on a 64-bit queue. Initially, the queue is filled with an initialization vector, like the IV of cipher block chaining mode. The queue is enciphered, and the leftmost eight bits of the result are combined by exclusive-or with the first character to be encrypted. These encrypted eight bits are transmitted. The eight bits also move into the rightmost eight bit positions of the queue, all other bits move eight bits left, and the leftmost eight bits are discarded. A similar process occurs at the receiving end. This procedure is shown in Figure 4.12.

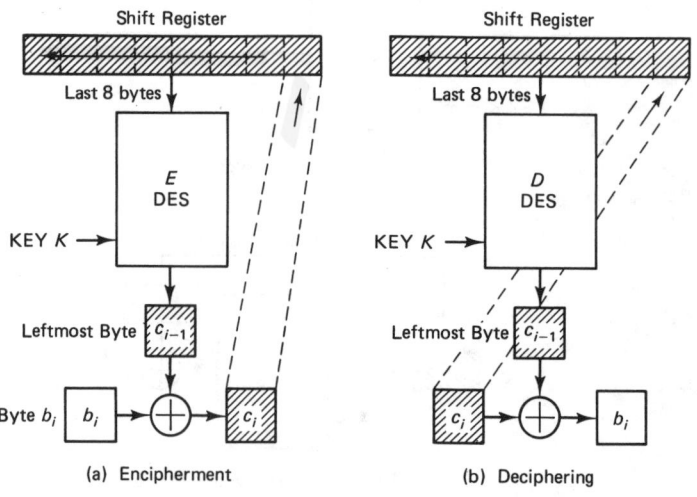

Figure 4.12   Cipher Feedback.

The advantage of CFB mode is the ability to encipher one character at a time. As with CBC mode, each character affects all succeeding characters, so that a change to any character during transmission affects subsequent characters. An error during encryption affects the character being transformed, as well as the next eight characters, since it will be in the queue for eight more character encryptions until the erroneous character is pushed off the left end of the queue.

These two modes extend the usefulness of the DES substantially. They overcome two major limitations on DES: the flaw of duplicate encryption of repeated plaintext and the delay from waiting to encrypt a block of text at once. Without these limitations, the DES has similar qualities to stream encryption algorithms.

4.4 Summary of Protocols and Practices

In this chapter we have looked at several problems important in the use of computers and communications systems. We have studied protocols that effectively separate design of a problem's solution from the implementation of that solution.

We have identified six tasks for which protocols have been designed. These tasks are

1. digital signature

2. random selection (poker protocol)

3. voting

4. transfer without knowledge (oblivious transfer)

5. contract signing

6. delivery with assurance of receipt

For each, the protocol specifies a set of steps; following these steps assures all parties that the operation has been accomplished fairly.

We have also looked at appropriate practices in the use of encryption. Just using encryption does not guarantee secrecy, privacy, or authenticity; it is the *correct* use of encryption that brings about these results. We evaluated DES and RSA encryption systems against the classic Shannon criteria and other standards of security. Finally, we investigated cryptographic techniques to limit undetected errors, such as replay, through techniques such as time stamps and chaining.

4.5 Terms and Concepts

protocol
arbiter
arbitrated protocol
notary
adjudicable protocol
self-enforcing protocol
digital signature
forgeable signature
authenticity
time stamp
mental poker
card distribution protocol
cryptographic key distribution
voting protocol
oblivious transfer
contract signing
commitment
certified mail
encryption practices
secrecy

key distribution
selecting new keys
revealed keys
encryption delay
encryption speed
error propagation
ciphertext size
error detection
block replay
block chaining
initial chaining vector (IV)
initial chaining value
one-way encryption
one-way function
cryptographic sealing cryptographic checksum
authentication
time stamp
DES modes of operation
electronic codebook
cipher block chain
cipher feedback

4.6 Bibliographic Notes

Two important surveys of computer protocols are by DeMillo and Merritt [DEM83] and Akl [AKL83]. Fundamental papers presenting protocols are by Merkle [MER80], Needham and Schroeder [SCH78], Popek and Kline [POP78], Rabin [RAB78], and Rivest, Shamir and Adelman [RIV78].

Additional uses of DES are described in [NBS80], and by Voydock and Kent in [VOY85].

4.7 Exercises

1. The first cryptographic sealing function suggested (the sum of the numeric values of all bytes of a message) has a serious flaw: Exchanging the places of two bytes of the message will not be detected by the sealing function. Suggest an alternate function that does not have that weakness.

2. The Merkle-Hellman knapsack encryption is not an "onto" function; that is, some binary number is *not* the result of applying the knapsack encryption to a piece of plaintext. With which protocols would this characteristic cause a problem? Explain the problem.

3. There is a flaw in the cryptographic sealing mechanism presented: If R can compute f_S to verify that document M has been received as it was transmitted, then R can also compute f_S to forge a digital signature. Suggest a solution to this flaw.

4. As initially described, the mental poker protocol has a flaw. If there are only ten cards, as soon as Ann sees her hand, she knows from set difference what cards Bill must have. Suggest an alternative protocol that does not have this flaw.

5. When used in cipher block chaining mode, the DES is said to be "self-healing": An error in transmission of one block does not cause faulty decryption of all the rest of the transmission. Explain how this is so.

6. Describe a protocol for fair exchange of secrets (in a human, that is, a noncomputer setting). Two people each wish to exchange secret information; neither wants to give up a secret without getting one in return. (a) What are the security requirements of this situation? (b) What is a protocol for fair exchange of secrets?

7. Why is an arbiter not desirable in a protocol for exchange of secrets?

8. Give an example of a self-enforcing protocol in real life.

9. List the requirements for a secret key digital signature scheme. Can any of these requirements be met with an adjudicated protocol? Why or why not? Can any of these requirements be met with a self-enforcing protocol? Why or why not?

10. Present a digital signature protocol using conventional key encryption so that the sender and receiver do not have to expose the contents of their message to the arbiter.

11. Explain why the digital signature protocol using public key encryption prevents a receiver from forging a message from the sender, using the sender's public key.

12. Show that RSA encryption has both commutative and onto properties. Why are these two properties necessary for the public key digital signature protocol.

13. What are the security properties necessary in the card distribution protocol? Explain how the protocol meets each of these properties.

14. In the card distribution protocol, what prevents Ann from cheating by putting five cards in one box and none in four boxes?

15. Describe a protocol to distribute ID numbers from an instructor to students so that each student can submit a piece of work to be graded anonymously, but the instructor can be assured that each piece of work comes from a legitimate person in the class.

16. In the voting protocol, explain how each user can be assured that his or her vote is still in the set to be counted.

17. In the voting protocol, if Jan knew there was at least one 1 vote and one 0 vote, could she remove a vote at random and replace it by $E_J(E_K(E_L(1)))$? Why or why not?

18. In the voting protocol, what prevents Lee (or anyone) from finding out the answers early by computing $E_J(E_K(E_L(1)))$ and $E_J(E_K(E_L(0)))$ and counting the images of these encrypted votes?

19. Design an oblivious transfer protocol that uses only conventional key encryptions.

20. Suppose one party, say Diane, decides to terminate the contract signing protocol early. She has one more bit of each c_i than Charles does of the d_i. Thus she has less work to do to break the c_i. What condition on the use of this protocol would nullify this advantage?

21. Design a protocol to allow a remote host on a network to identify itself and be authenticated by the other hosts on the network. What are the security requirements of this situation?

22. Design a protocol so that three different users can access certain secret information. There are four pieces of information, called W, X, Y, and Z; the three users are called A, B, and C. A should have access only to W and Z; B only to X and Z; and C only to Y and Z.

23. Suppose in the previous exercise, A was to have access to W and X; B to X and Y; and C to Y and Z. Would your protocol still work? If not, design a new one.

5

Security Involving Programs

This chapter contains information on ways that programs can be used to exploit vulnerabilities in computing systems. The term "program" means an ordinary user program, such as an inventory program; a "program" can also be a system utility program, such as a spreadsheet program, a compiler, a directory listing program, or a text editor. Although an operating system is, in a sense, just another program, we will defer consideration of operating systems until the next chapter. There are two reasons to defer operating systems. First, operating systems provide many of the protection facilities under which all programs run, and second, the size and complexity of an operating system make it a more difficult object to attack. Thus, we will consider operating systems as special types of programs, although many of the weaknesses of programs are also weaknesses of operating systems.

Programs can cause two kinds of difficulties: They can intercept or modify data on behalf of users who should not have access to that data, and they can exploit service flaws in computing systems—to allow system access to users who should not have it or to inhibit use by legitimate users. These two problems will be considered separately. The chapter concludes with a discussion of controls that can be used to cover program exposures.

Regretfully, the area of program flaws is much larger than the available techniques to control the exposures. There are two reasons for this distressing situation. First, program controls still apply at the level of the individual programmer; some of the more obvious difficulties may be detected, but a dedicated programmer can still hide flaws successfully. Second, operating systems have been asked to assume the protection needs of a computing system, but even the operating system must apply protection at a rather high level, screening out only major violations, in the interest of good service and sharing.

This chapter is not intended to serve as a "how-to" guidebook for would-be computer criminals. Therefore, the explanations will be slightly vague, although complete enough to identify the vulnerability.

5.1 Information Access Problems

Programs operate on data. By themselves programs are seldom security threats. However, since computer data is usually in a form not easily understood by humans, programs often serve unauthorized users as vehicles to access data. We begin by studying several kinds of programs that can be used for unauthorized access to data. This access can involve either interception or modification and fabrication.

Trapdoors

A **trapdoor** is a secret, undocumented entry point into a module. The trapdoor is inserted sometime during code development, perhaps to test the module, perhaps to provide "hooks" by which to connect future modifications or enhancements, and perhaps to allow access in the event of future errors. In addition to these legitimate uses, trapdoors can allow a programmer access into a program once it is placed into production.

Examples of Trapdoors

Because computing systems are complex structures, programmers usually develop and test systems in a modular manner. Each small component of the system is tested. Then components are grouped into logical clusters of a few components, and each cluster is tested individually.

Each component is initially tested without all surrounding routines that prepare input or work with output. To test a single module it may be necessary to write "stubs" and "drivers," simple routines to inject data into and extract results from the routine being tested. As testing continues, these stubs and drivers are discarded, because they are replaced by the actual routines whose functions they mimic. The two modules MODA and MODB in Figure 5.1 are being tested by stubs and drivers.

During program testing, flaws may be discovered in modules. Sometimes, when the source of the flaw is not obvious, debugging code is inserted into suspicious modules, causing these modules to display intermediate results of a computation or to perform extra computations to check the validity of previous modules.

To control stubs or invoke debugging code, special control sequences are embedded in the design of the module to be tested. For example, a module in a text formatting system might be designed to recognize commands such as .PAGE, .TITLE, and .SKIP. During program testing, the programmer may have inserted a command .DEBUG that has a series of parameters of the form $var = value$. This command allows the programmer to modify the values of program variables during execution, either to test corrections to this module or to supply values passed to modules this one calls.

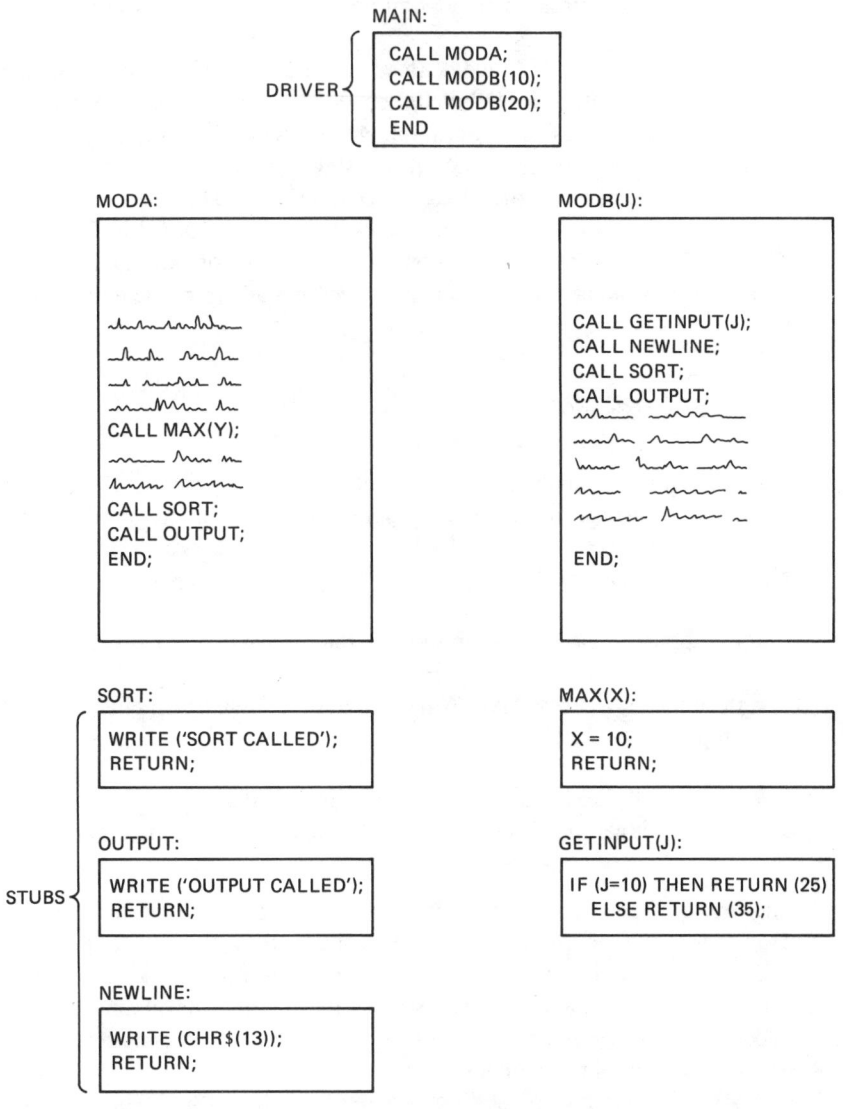

Figure 5.1   Stubs and Drivers.

Command insertion is a recognized testing practice. If left in place after testing, the extra commands can become a problem. They are undocumented control sequences that produce side effects and can be used as trapdoors.

Poor error checking is another source of trapdoors. In some poorly designed systems, unacceptable input may be not be caught and may be accepted. For example, a routine may look only for one of three expected sequences; finding none of the three it should recognize an error. If the three possibilities are tested in a CASE statement, a failure may simply fall through the CASE.

Another common example of this kind of flaw can be found in hardware processor design, where not all possible binary opcode values have matching machine instructions. The undefined opcodes sometimes implement peculiar instructions, either for testing the design of the processor or due to an oversight by the designer of the processor. This is the hardware counterpart of the software flaw described earlier.

Trapdoors are not always bad. They can be very useful in finding security flaws. Auditors sometimes request trapdoors in production programs so that they can insert fictitious but identifiable transactions into the system and trace the flow of these transactions through the system.

Causes of Trapdoors

The programmer usually removes trapdoors during program development. However, trapdoors can persist in production programs because the programmer:

- forgets to remove them

- intentionally leaves them in the program to assist in the rest of testing

- intentionally leaves them in the program to assist in maintenance of the finished program

- intentionally leaves them in the program in order to have a covert means of access to the routine after it becomes an accepted production program

The first of these cases is an unintentional security blunder; the next two are serious exposures of the security of a system, and the fourth is the first step in an outright attack. The fault is not the trapdoor; these are very useful techniques for program testing, correction, and maintenance. The fault is the program development environment. The trapdoor becomes a vulnerability if it is not noticed and no one acts to prevent or control its use in vulnerable situations.

Trapdoors are a vulnerability because they expose the system to modification during execution. The trapdoor can be exploited by the original programmer; it can also be used by anyone who discovers the trapdoor by accident or through exhaustive trials.

Trojan Horse

Recall from Greek mythology that the **Trojan horse** was a gift that carried an unannounced and unexpected visitor. A computing system can be visited by a Trojan horse as well. In a computer, a Trojan horse performs a hidden function in addition to its stated, obvious function.

Examples of Trojan Horses

As an example, suppose a programmer wants to modify the protection level associated with files belonging to other users. The programmer writes a program that ostensibly produces a listing of files in a desirable format. The programmer then offers it to the manager of the computing system, as a utility program for the benefit of all users. What the programmer doesn't say is that the utility will also alter the protection level of those files.

Since a user other than the original programmer calls this utility, the program will probably execute with the protection level of the user. Therefore, the utility will have access to the user's files, and it may have the right to alter the access rights to those files for other users, as shown in Figure 5.2. More complicated Trojan horses alter the access rights, signal the interceptor that a particular file can be accessed, pause, and reset the access right to its original value. If the interceptor performs the desired interception quickly, the Trojan horse can cover its tracks so that the user is unaware an access has occurred. Of course, the code in Figure 5.2 is very obvious; anyone looking at the procedure can see what it really does. This procedure can be disguised if it is embedded it in a very long and complex procedure, or distributed only as compiled object code.

```
$     IF NOT EXIST (SECRET_FILE.DAT) THEN GOTO SKIP
$          SET PROTECT SECRET_FILE.DAT RW;RW;RW
$          SEND USER (JONES) "READ IT FAST!!!"
$          PAUSE (30)
$          SET PROTECT SECRET_FILE.DAT RW;;
$     SKIP:
$     WRITE "FORMATTED FILE LISTING"
$     WRITE "FILE     DATE     SIZE"
      . . .
```

Figure 5.2 Trojan Horse.

How Trojan Horses Occur

In the easiest of cases, the programmer prepares a Trojan horse source program, compiles the source code, and gives the computing center staff only the object code and documentation on the overt use of the program. In this way the true operation of the utility program is hidden. Knowing this, some computing centers accept only source code and perform their own compilations before making a contributed utility public. Microcomputer users are not always so conscious of security, nor do they have the option of requiring the source code. One particularly cruel Trojan horse has been inadvertently distributed by microcomputer users' groups; this utility secretly erases all files on a system's disk drives, including hard disks.

A programmer may find a way to access and modify the stored source code of accepted utility routines. The modified source code is recompiled and installed when a new version of the computing system is brought up. Alternatively, the programmer may laboriously modify the binary object code of the system version of a utility program, changing instructions a bit at a time. This can occur either to an online version stored on some device between calls or to a version in memory during execution.

A clever programmer can cover the trail of a Trojan horse by scattering the instructions throughout the overt program or by creating a sequence of instructions that modify the overt program during its execution, or that branch off to some concealed routine. Instructions of a Trojan horse may be encrypted or otherwise concealed so that they are converted to plaintext only momentarily when they are executed. Trojan horses can be hidden quite effectively.

Salami Attack

Another kind of program attack is called a **salami attack**. This attack gets its name from the way odd bits of meat are formed together in a salami. Programs that compute amounts of money may be subject to a salami attack. In this attack, a small amount of money is shaved from each computation. The amount shaved is so small that an individual case is unlikely to be noticed. However, accumulated amounts can add up.

Examples of Salami Attacks

The classic, perhaps apocryphal, story of a salami attack involves computations of interest. The computation of 6.5% interest on $102.87 for 31 days is $31/365 * .065 * 102.87 =$ $0.5495726. Since banks deal only in full cents, a typical practice is to round down if an amount is less than half a cent above a full cent, and round up if an amount is half a cent or more. However, few people check their interest computation closely, and fewer still would complain about having the amount $0.5495 rounded down to $0.54, instead of up to $0.55. Most programs that perform computations on currency recognize that, because of rounding, a sum of individual computations may be a few cents different from the computation applied to the sum of the balances.

What happens to these fractional cents? The classic tale is told of a programmer who collected the fractional cents and credited them to a single account: hers! The interest program merely had to balance total interest paid to interest due on the total of the balances of the individual accounts. It is unlikely that auditors would notice one specific account. In a situation with many accounts, the roundoff error can be substantial, and the programmer's account pockets this roundoff.

Salami attacks that net more are more interesting. For example, instead of shaving fractional cents, the programmer may take a few cents from each account, again assuming that no individual has the desire or understanding to recompute the amount the bank reports. Most people finding a result a few cents different from that of the bank would accept the bank's figure, attributing the difference to an error in arithmetic or a misunderstanding of the conditions under which interest is credited. Or a program might record a $20. fee for a particular service, while the company standard is $15. If unchecked, the extra $5. could go to the credit of an account of the programmer's choice.

Why Salami Attacks Persist

Computer computations are notoriously subject to small errors involving rounding and truncation, especially when large numbers are to be combined with small numbers. Rather than document the exact errors, it is easier for programmers and users to accept a small amount of error as natural and unavoidable. To reconcile accounts, an error correction is included in computations. Inadequate auditing of these corrections is one reason why the salami attack may be overlooked.

Usually the source code of a system is too large or complex to be audited for salami attacks, unless there is reason to suspect one. Size is definitely on the side of the programmer.

Programs that Leak Information

In this section we will consider programs that communicate their information to people who should not receive that information. A general name for these extraordinary paths of communication is **covert channels**. In this section we describe how a programmer can create covert channels.

Covert Channels

In an environment in which data is sensitive, a programmer should not have access to the data on which a program operates after the program has been put into operation. For example, a programmer for a bank has no need to access the names or balances in depositors' accounts. Programmers for a securities firm have no need to know what buy and sell orders exist for the clients. During program testing, access to the real data may be justifiable, but not after the program has been accepted for regular use.

Still, a programmer might be able to profit from knowledge that a customer is about to sell a large amount of a particular stock, or that a large new account has just been opened. In many cases a programmer may want to develop a program that secretly communicates some of the data on which it operates. The programmer creates what is called a **covert channel**, a hidden means for the program to communicate information.

How To Create Covert Channels

A programmer can always find ways to communicate data values covertly. Running a program that produces a specific output report or displays a value may be too obvious. For example, in some installations, a printed report might occasionally be scanned by a security person before it is delivered to its intended recipient.

If printing the data values themselves is too obvious, the programmer can encode the data values in another innocuous report by varying the format of the output, changing the lengths of lines, or printing or not printing certain values. For example, changing the word "TOTAL" to "TOTALS" in a heading would not be noticed, but this creates a 1-bit covert channel. The absence or presence of the S conveys one bit of information. Numeric values can be inserted in insignificant positions of output fields, and the number of lines per page can be changed. These subtle channels are shown in Figure 5.3.

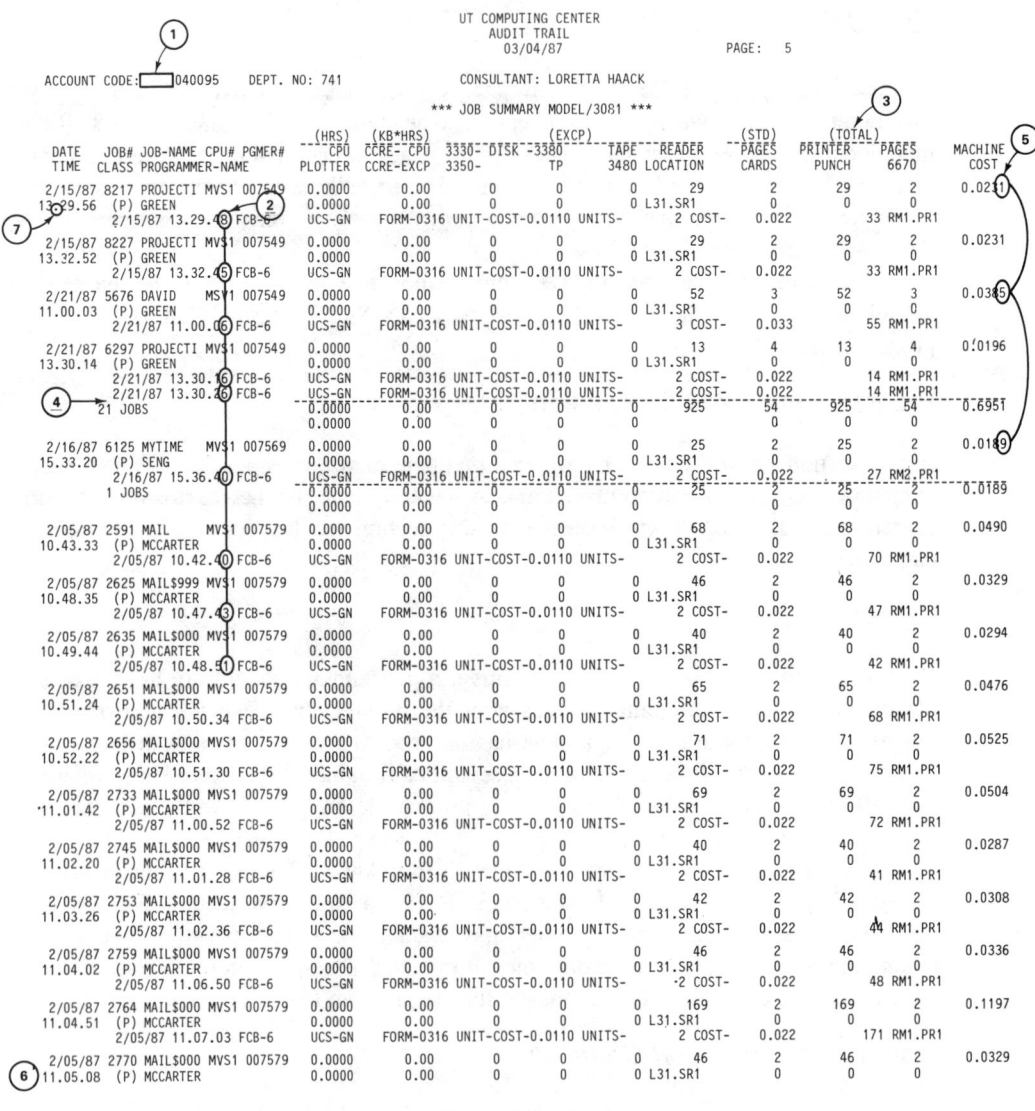

Figure 5.3   Covert Channels.

If the programmer should not have access to the data of the program, even printing a disguised report might be unacceptably obvious. One sensitive program can invoke a second less sensitive one. The first program passes sensitive data to the less noticeable program, which then leaks the data in a printed form. Other programs in execution or recognizable data in any output may alert the computing staff that a program is communicating data to someone not authorized to have that data.

A devious programmer can create a hidden channel for computation. For example, suppose a program has access to confidential data during its execution. The programmer cannot produce a printed report. However, if the programmer can see the computer during execution, the programmer can arrange for the program to pass the information through a binary code (for example, Morse code), where the bits of information come from starting and stopping a tape drive, from lighting a light on the system console, or from generating a message that causes the operator to do something.

These examples all require much human work to obtain a small amount of information. Such codes can leak small amounts of data; because of the volume of output produced, these codes are virtually impossible to detect, let alone to break. They are best suited to cases where a small amount of data is needed. For example, the existence of a particular file may be sensitive information. A file's existence may indicate whether or not another sequence of activities has taken place, which in turn may determine the success of another program to breach security. The data required to communicate the existence of a file is only one bit, which is not excessive using methods like the ones outlined here.

5.2 Service Problems

So far, all the methods described have been ways to access *data*, since that is often the most useful artifact of a computing system. However, programs can be used to affect computer service as well. In this section we consider types of programs that can block a computing system so that no other computation can go on. When legitimate users are excluded from access to a computing system, the security failure is called "denial of service."

Greedy Programs

Some computers, especially at research sites, have resident "background" tasks that perform meaningful but very low priority computation, only when nothing else is available to be computed. For example, one research computer has a program that computes the value of e or π to an extremely large number of digits. The result of this computation is not time dependent; the program merely soaks up machine cycles when the computer would otherwise be idle. Maliciously or erroneously altered, this background task can assume a foreground position, thereby blocking all other computation.

Loops

A simple example of a greedy program is one that loops indefinitely. Most multiprogrammed computing systems have clocks that limit program execution to some predetermined limit, to stop unintentional infinite loops. Individual programmers are allowed to specify an execution time limit, in case they have extremely long programs. The operating system generally has a built-in upper limit on time, such as 24 hours.

Time counted is usually just computing time (time spent using the CPU) since time waiting for I/O is unpredictable. Because I/O time depends on the load on the system caused by other programs, I/O time is not usually checked. On some systems once a process requests an I/O service, it waits for completion of the I/O activity, thereby stopping its CPU clock. The I/O activity goes on asynchronously, controlled and executed by an I/O processor. It is not too difficult to produce an I/O program that loops infinitely. Once this program is turned over to the I/O processor, the main (CPU) program waits for completion of the I/O activity, which will run indefinitely. This idea can be extended to many programs started on all or several I/O devices; once these all begin execution, the entire system is effectively monopolized.

Viruses

A computer virus is the logical extension of a greedy program. A **virus** is a program that can "infect" other programs by modifying them. The term *virus* arises because the infected program can be modified to include a copy of the virus program itself, so that the infected program then begins to act as a virus, infecting other programs. The infection spreads at a geometric rate. The viruses eventually overtake the entire computing system. (This section sounds like a low-grade science fiction plot, but the exposure identified here is real. Specific examples are identified in [COH84], in which a virus was planted and overtook an entire computing system in times ranging from 5 to 30 minutes.)

Examples of Viruses

Not all viruses are bad. For example, a virus might locate uninfected programs, compress them so that they occupy less memory, and insert a copy of a routine that decompresses the program when its execution begins, as well as spreading the compression function to other programs. This virus could substantially reduce the amount of storage required for stored programs, possibly by up to 50 percent. However, the compression would be done at the request of the virus, not at the request, or even knowledge, of the program owner.

A virus can be planted in shared system utilities to access common data, such as electronic mail, system news bulletins, and lists of users on the system. Because many users access these utilities, a virus planted in one can spread quickly.

The time to develop a virus can be surprisingly short. In one case a virus of 200 lines of Fortran code plus 50 lines of command files was developed in less than 24 hours with little experience of the machine under attack. In addition to speed of development, secrecy can keep viruses from being found until it is too late. A virus can be written to cover most traces of its spreading.

The Source of Viruses

Since a virus can be rather small, its code can be "hidden" inside other larger and more complicated programs. Two hundred lines of a virus could be separated into 100 packets of two lines of code and a jump each; these 100 packets could be easily hidden inside a compiler, a data base manager, a file manager, or some other large utility. Discovering a virus could be aided by a procedure to determine if two programs are equivalent. However, theoretical results are very discouraging because of the complexity of the equivalence problem. The question is undecidable in general, meaning that it may be extremely difficult to determine if an infected compiler and an uninfected one produce the same results. Therefore, we are unlikely to develop a screening program that can separate infected modules from uninfected ones.

It is possible to detect certain known viruses; that is, if you know that a particular virus may infect a computing system, it is possible to check for and detect that virus. Having found the virus, however, you are left with the task of cleansing the system of it. Removing the virus in a running system requires being able to detect and eliminate its instances faster than it can spread.

Limiting the Spread of Viruses

The spread of a virus depends on sharing and transitivity. The virus must be able to use shared information and to cause other programs to share its information. Thus, limiting sharing of information can limit viral infection. In the next chapter we will consider compartments through which data can be divided into separate unrelated groups. In some systems where information is compartmented, the effect of a virus can be confined to one compartment.

Similarly, information flows from one process to another. If there is an information flow from A to B, and one from B to C, then implicitly there is a flow from A to C. A bound on transitivity limits the extent to which a virus can spread by limiting the number of transitive information flows used.

Worms

The **worm** programs of Shoch and Hupp (described in [SHO82]) are network extensions of viruses. The worms use the network management mechanism of a computing system to identify free machines on the network, and to pass the worm program to the free machines. Once active, the worm tries to find another free machine to which it will transfer a segment of itself. As with viruses, worms can be embedded in almost any other meaningful computer programs.

Uses of Worms

Some worm programs have legitimate purposes—for example, running system bulletin boards or alarm clocks. Worms can also be applied to parallel computation on a network of serial machines. In these situations, the worm programs perform specific tasks and then exit. However, a general worm program can continue execution without limit, thereby denying access to other users.

Shoch and Hupp [SHO82] list several examples of worm programs, including examples that run on the ARPAnet. Control programs of the network itself are examples of worms, since the ARPAnet uses distributed control to manage resources and sharing within that network of thousands of users. All of the worm examples are positive uses of network facilities, in which multiple hosts are invoked to perform computations more extensive than a single host could support.

Causes of Worms

Worms multiply in situations of trust, such as network sites in which users are all assumed to be friendly and trustworthy. It does not require too much imagination, however, to construct scenarios in which these same trusting users could be duped.

The primary example of a "bad" worm from Shoch and Hupp is a network worm developed at one large, networked site. Because the possible operation of the worm was untrusted, the designers prudently included a means to annihilate worms if necessary. That control was used once when a worm became mutated (through some unknown hardware or software fluke), and replicated copies that would crash any system to which they transferred.

The developers had the foresight to include a means to stop a worm in case of an error. Clearly, not all developers of worm programs are so thoughtful or concerned. Without the planned escape, the only recourse would have been to locate a clean, worm-free copy of the full system of *each* machine on the network. A backup from before the worm was released would suffice, although if the worm had been running for some time, or if it was unknown exactly when the mutation occurred, all users of the network would suffer significant loss.

5.3 Program Development Controls Against Program Attacks

The picture just described is not very pretty: Programmers have numerous ways that they can subvert a system to their own advantage. In this section we consider controls used during software development—the design, writing, and testing of the program—to cover those sorts of exposures. Other controls, from operating systems to administrative procedures, are the subjects of later sections.

We begin by discussing the controls that can be applied during program development to help to ensure the quality and trustworthiness of code to be produced.

Description of the Programming Task

In the original model of programming, a programmer received a description of a task to be performed, went away independently to derive a program to perform the task, and returned with the program in hand. The programmer worked alone on this task. Arguments in favor of working alone were these:

- Programming is an individual task, requiring independent thought. Communicating these ideas to another takes more time, to no gain.

- Programs, being creative expressions on the part of programmers, are very individualistic. It is unreasonable to expect two different programmers to be able to work together on one project.

- Programmers are basically solitary individuals who prefer to work alone. Disrupting that preferred work style could have a negative influence on either the program or the programmer.

- Programming is an art understood only by programmers. Management is incapable of understanding programs (or management would prefer not to have to try to understand programs).

None of those arguments holds. The basic case against programming by the individual is size. The expected output of a good programmer in a single year is at most two thousand lines of code (perhaps modified by a factor of two or three depending on programming language, complexity of programming task, and environment). Some good programmers of complex tasks produce on the average only two or three lines of code per day! That level of output is insufficient to produce current major systems involving hundreds of thousands and even millions of lines of code.

The field called **software engineering** addresses the problem of "programming in the large," that is, writing code for enormous systems. The basic principles of software engineering are division of labor, reuse of code, use of standard preconstructed software "tools," and organized activity.

Peer Reviews

When a system is large enough that several people are programming it concurrently, all must have a precise design document that shows what each piece does and how each piece interfaces with other pieces. Because the design document is somewhat subject to the individual interpretation of each programmer, it is important to identify inconsistencies in understanding early. It is also important to locate programmers' flaws of logic.

A philosophy of software engineering is that correct code is the responsibility of all programmers on the team. For this reason, members of a team participate in **peer design reviews** and **peer code reviews**. When a designer or a programmer has completed a particular section of code, several other designers or programmers are invited to participate in a "walk-through" of the design or code. The original developer presents the material in an orderly manner, pausing for the comments, questions, and suggestions of others. These questions are designed to identify misunderstandings or errors.

This style of programming is also called "egoless" programming. It is recognized that the product belongs to the *group*, not to the *individual* who produced it. The review is not to chastise the programmer for having made errors, but to identify errors for the good of the product. The group succeeds only if its products are right; therefore, all members of the group have a vested interest in the correctness of the product.

Because all reviewers are designers or programmers themselves, they understand programming. They can distinguish between an error and a section that is correct but is not what they would have used. They know what things are suspicious in a program, or do not belong, or have a nonobvious side effect.

A rigorous design or code review can locate trapdoors, Trojan horses, salami attacks, worms, viruses, and other program flaws. A crafty programmer can conceal some of these flaws, but the chance of discovery rises when competent programmers review the code, especially at the level of a module of 30 to 60 lines. Management should use demanding code reviews throughout code development as a way of ensuring security of the programs produced.

Modularity, Encapsulation, and Information Hiding

The principles of software engineering recommend writing code in small, self-contained units, called **modules**. Modularity offers advantages for program development, as well as security advantages. A module can be isolated from the negative effects of other modules with which it interacts. This isolation occurs due to a design principle called **encapsulation**. **Information hiding** is another benefit of modularization. With information hiding other modules know that a module performs a certain task, but not *how* it performs that task. In this section we describe these three principles and their role in computer security.

Modularity

Modularization is the process of dividing a task into subtasks. Each module performs a separate, independent part of the task. Modularity is depicted in Figure 5.4.

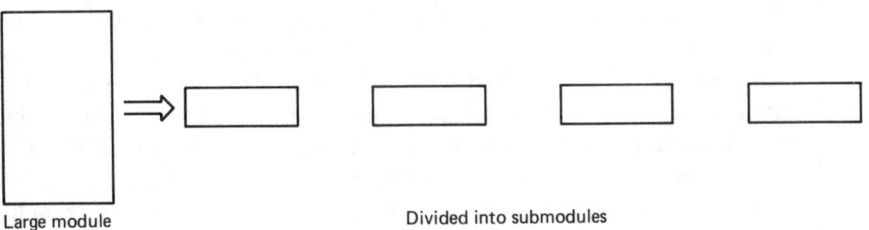

Large module   Divided into submodules

Figure 5.4   Modularity.

Program units should be only as large as needed to perform their required duties. There are several advantages to writing a program as a series of small, self-contained modules.

- *Maintainability.* If a function is implemented as a single module, the module can be replaced with a revised one, if necessary. The new module may be needed due to a change in requirements or hardware or the environment. Sometimes the replacement is just an enhancement that uses a smaller, faster, more correct, or otherwise better module. The interfaces between this module and the remainder of the program are few and well described, so the effects of the replacement are evident.

- *Understandability.* A program composed of many small modules will be easier to comprehend than one large, unstructured program.

- *Reusability.* Modules developed for one purpose can often be reused in other programs. Reuse of correct, existing program modules can significantly reduce the difficulty of programming and testing.

- *Correctability.* An error can be quickly traced to its cause if the modules perform only one task each.

- *Testability.* A single module with well-defined inputs, output, and function can be tested exhaustively by itself, without concern for its effects on other modules (other than the expected function and output, of course).

From a standpoint of security, it is important to be able to understand each module as an independent unit, and to be assured of its limited effect on other modules. Proper modularity leads to modules that have minimal interaction with other modules.

Encapsulation

Modularity leads to a form of independence in which each module functions as an independent object. A well-designed module has little **coupling** to other routines of the same program. The other routines are free of unwitting interference from other modules. This characteristic is called **encapsulation**, in which a module essentially operates as if it were surrounded by a shield that prevents unwanted access from the outside.

With encapsulation, modules interact only through certain well-defined interfaces. A module is entered only at specified entry points, and a module interacts with the fewest other modules possible. Encapsulation is shown in Figure 5.5.

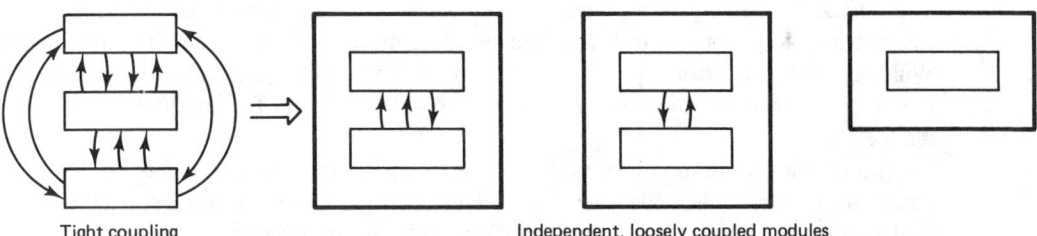

Tight coupling   Independent, loosely coupled modules

Figure 5.5   Encapsulation.

Encapsulation does not mean complete isolation. Modules need certain inputs and must exchange information with other modules. However, this sharing is carefully documented, so that a module is affected only in known ways by other modules in the system. Sharing is also minimized, so that the fewest interfaces possible are used. Limited interfaces reduce the number of covert channels that can be constructed.

Information Hiding

A modular design leads to modules with limited effects on other modules. Conversely, programmers who work where modularization is stressed can be sure that other modules will have limited effect on the ones they write. To carry this one step farther, a module can be seen as a form of black box, with certain well-defined inputs and outputs and a well-defined function. Other modules and other designers do not need to know *how* the module completes its function; it is enough to be assured that the module does its task in some correct manner.

Concealing the way that a module does its task is called **information hiding**. Information hiding is depicted in Figure 5.6. Information hiding is desirable, because programmers cannot maliciously alter the modules of others if they do not know how the modules work.

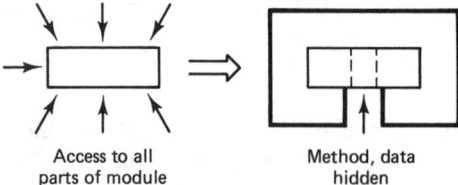

Access to all
parts of module

Method, data
hidden

Figure 5.6   Information Hiding.

The three characteristics of modularity, encapsulation, and information hiding are fundamental principles of software engineering. They are good practices for security because they lead to modules that can be understood, analyzed, and trusted.

Independent Testing

The purpose of testing is to certify the *correctness* of a program, not necessarily to assign blame for errors. A test that finds errors is more useful than one that finds none: With demonstrated errors, you know that the test was rigorous. When no errors are found, however, either the routine being tested was correct, or the test procedures were ineffective.

Programmers are too close to their code to test it effectively. For this reason, it is common to use an independent test team. This team begins to develop test data as soon as the program design is complete. Test data can be constructed without reference to the source code of the program itself. The test cases designed by the test team check whether the program does what its design says it *should*, not necessarily what the programmer *interpreted* the design to require. The test team and the programmer may differ in their interpretation of the design, but it is better to identify that ambiguity and resolve it than to combine a module with another whose programmer may expect something different.

From a security standpoint, independent testing is highly desirable, since a programmer attempting to hide something in a routine does not develop the tests that will be applied to the routine. Independent testing increases the likelihood that a test will expose the effect of a hidden feature.

Configuration Management

Configuration management is another aspect of software engineering that offers advantages in security. When configuration management is practiced, a person or system controls and records all changes to a program or documentation. A group of professionals, called a **change control board**, judges the desirability and correctness of all proposed changes.

The Major Need for Configuration Management

The goal of configuration management is to guarantee availability and usage of the correct version of all system components—software, design documents, documentation, control files, and so forth. Configuration management is simply strongly enforced organization and bookkeeping.

Virtually every programmer has "lost" a version of a program. After making one change, the programmer makes another change, then another, then another, and finally decides to abandon that approach. By this time, the original version may be deleted, confused with other versions, or merged with unrelated changes.

The situation is even worse if there are several parallel versions of a program. For example, suppose a company has a computer program for sale. After the first version is developed and sold, users report small errors, which the company fixes. So as not to distribute errors, the company updates its distribution version, fixing any known errors. Meanwhile, the company works on an enhanced version of the product, which will eventually be marketed. In this scenario, there are at least three separate versions of the product: the original, the one with some errors corrected, and the expanded one under development. Further error fixes or enhancements can cause even more versions.

As another example, consider a company that has developed a software product. The product runs in three different environments: VAX VMS, IBM-PC, and UNIX. Although these implementations are similar, there are differences among them. Every time a module is changed, the change must be installed in all three versions, which must then be tested. Changing one version may require changing other parts of that version. Therefore, for each version there is one copy in form for distribution and one copy being changed. These separate versions and the changes being applied to them must be documented and controlled.

If the program is large enough to consist of several modules produced by several programmers, all programmers must recognize when someone has changed a module, since that module might affect other modules. The person who wrote a program cannot be free to change that code at will, even if those changes correct known errors. Commonly programmers keep shadow copies of corrected or revised routines, waiting for an update cycle when all programmers will combine new versions of their code and retest the entire system. There are thus stable versions of modules and working versions belonging to programmers. As system development progresses, there may be several different stable versions, in various stages of testing or integration with other modules.

The situations just described have identified three purposes for configuration management:

1. To guard against inadvertent loss (deletion) of a version of a program

2. To manage the parallel development of several similar versions of one program

3. To provide facilities for controlled sharing of modules that combine to form one system

These goals can all be achieved through the systematic method of managing source code, object code, and documentation. The system must provide careful records so that someone knows where a copy of each version is located and what characteristics distinguish that version from all others. Companies commonly designate one or more configuration management specialists to do this job.

Typically a programmer "freezes" a module at some point in time and gives control of that copy to configuration management. The programmer no longer has the right or ability to modify that version. All changes from that point on are carefully monitored by a configuration management panel. The panel scrutinizes all change requests for correctness and for potential effect on other modules.

Security Advantages of Configuration Management

There are two security advantages to using configuration management. The first advantage protects against unintentional threats; the second guards against malicious ones.

Protecting the integrity of programs and documentation is the main security motivation for using configuration management. Because changes occur only after explicit approval from a configuration management authority, all changes are also carefully evaluated for side effects. With configuration management, previous versions of programs are archived, so that it is possible to retract a faulty change.

The other security advantage of configuration management is protecting a program from malicious modification. Once a reviewed program is accepted for a system, the programmer cannot sneak in and make small, subtle changes, such as inserting trapdoors. The programmer has access to the running production program only through the configuration management panel, and these people are alert to such security breaches.

In order to have intelligible, auditable control over changes, the configuration management team often accepts program changes only at the source code level. Even though the programmer has compiled and tested the program and could provide object code, the configuration management team accepts only source code changes: statement insertions, deletions, and replacements. The configuration management team keeps the original source code plus the individual changes to produce each version. When a new version is to be produced, the configuration management team creates a temporary source program to be compiled. In this way, there is a precise record of all changes, when they were made, and by whom.

Proofs of Program Correctness

A security specialist wants to be certain that a given program computes a particular result, computes it correctly, and does nothing more. Unfortunately, results in computer science theory indicate that security specialists can never be certain about every possible program. There can be no general decision procedure which, given any two programs, determines if the two are equivalent. This is a result of the "halting problem," which states that there is no general technique to determine whether an arbitrary program will halt when processing an arbitrary input.

In spite of this disappointing general result, a process called **program verification** can demonstrate formally the correctness of a certain specific program. Program verification involves making initial assertions about the inputs. Each program statement is translated into a logical statement about the contribution of that statement to the logical flow of the program. Finally, the terminal statement of the program is associated with the desired results of the program. Then, by applying a logic analyzer, it is possible to prove that the initial assumptions, through the implications of the program statements, produce the terminal conclusion. In this way, it is shown that the program achieves its goal. An example of program verification is given in Chapter 7.

Program correctness proofs are hindered by several factors.

- Correctness proofs depend on the programmer or the logician to translate a program's statements into logical implications. Just as programming is prone to errors, so also is this translation.

- It is complicated to derive the correctness proof from the initial assertions and the implications of statements. The logical engine to generate proofs thus runs slowly. The speed of the engine decreases as the size of the program increases, so that proofs of correctness are even less appropriate for large programs.

- The current state of program verification is less well developed than code production. Proofs of correctness have not been successfully applied to large production systems consistently.

Program verification systems are being improved constantly. Larger programs are being verified in less time than before. As program verification continues to mature, it will become a more important control to ensure the security of programs.

5.4 Operating System Controls on Use of Programs

Programmer controls like those just described are applied to large development projects in some software production environments. However, not every program is produced that way, and computer users cannot always be assured that all other users of the system have followed the proper standards of program development. Therefore, a more common standard of software security is enforcement by the operating system.

In the next two chapters we will examine operating systems in some detail in order to determine what security features they provide for their users. This section outlines the kinds of protection that an operating system can provide against the program flaws identified at the beginning of this chapter.

Trusted Software

By **trusted software** we mean code believed to be safe both by functional correctness— doing what it was designed to do and nothing more—and by enforcing its correctness on programs that run under it. An operating system may be a piece of trusted software. The developer is trusted to have designed the module correctly. Programmers are trusted to have included only necessary statements. More important, we may trust that the operating system correctly controls the accesses of modules run from that operating system. For example, the operating system might be expected to limit the accesses of the users to certain files.

Based on vigorous analysis and testing, trusted software has earned its reputation by several characteristics:

- *Functional correctness:* The program does what it is supposed to, and it works correctly.

- *Enforcement of integrity:* Even if presented erroneous commands or commands from unauthorized users, it maintains the correctness of the data with which it has contact.

- *Limited privilege:* The program is allowed to access secure data, but the access is minimized and neither the access right nor the data is passed along to other untrusted programs or back to an untrusted caller.

- *Appropriate security level:* The program has been examined and rated at a degree of trust appropriate for the kind of data and environment in which it is to be used.

Essentially trusted software becomes a safe way for general users to access sensitive data. Trusted programs are used to perform sensitive operations for users without allowing the users direct access to sensitive data.

As a simple example, think of a table ordered by hash coding. The placement of the entries is very important, since a misplaced entry may mean that not only that entry but also other entries can never be retrieved. Instead of allowing arbitrary access to the table, you write a module that correctly inserts and deletes entries. Then you limit access to the table so that all accesses to the table must occur through your module. Your module then becomes a trusted interface that you and everyone else must invoke in order to use the table.

Mutual Suspicion

Programs are not always trustworthy. Even with an operating system to enforce access limitations, it may be impossible or infeasible to bound the access privileges of an untested program effectively. In this case, the user U is legitimately suspicious of a new program P. However, program P may be invoked by another program, Q. There is no way for Q to know that P is correct or proper, any more than U knows that of P.

Therefore, the concept of **mutual suspicion** was developed to describe the relationship between two programs. Mutually suspicious programs operate as if other routines in the system were flawed. A calling program cannot trust its called subprocedures to be correct, and a called subprocedure cannot trust its calling program to be correct. Each protects its interface data so that the other has only limited access. For example, a procedure to sort the entries in a list cannot be trusted not to modify those elements, while that procedure cannot trust its caller to provide any list at all, or to supply the number of elements predicted.

Confinement

Confinement is a technique used by an operating system on a suspected program. A **confined** program is strictly limited in what system resources it can access.

The principle of confinement is similar to the military classification of data. Items are labeled with classification levels, such as "secret" or "top secret." An untrusted individual or program can access only items with labels appropriate for the clearance level of the accessor.

Compartmented Information

Compartmented information is similar to confinement. In a system with compartments, all data and programs are divided into exclusive groups, so that a program can access only programs and data within its same compartment. If a program is not trusted, the data it can access is strictly limited. Furthermore, the objects in the compartment all can access only other objects in the compartment. Essentially the compartments form a partition of the objects in the system, with each object belonging to and accessing things in only one compartment. If the program is faulty or malicious, it can only affect data (or other programs) within the same compartment.

Compartments would be helpful in limiting the spread of viruses. Since a virus spreads by means of transitivity and shared data, all the data and programs within a single compartment can affect only the data and programs in the same compartment. Therefore, the virus can spread only to things in that compartment; it cannot get outside the compartment.

Access Log

An **access log** is a listing of who accessed which computer objects, when, and for what amount of time. Commonly applied to files and programs, this is less a means of protection than an after-the-fact means of tracking down what has been done.

Typically an access log is a file or a dedicated output device (such as a printer), to which a log of activities is written. The logged activities may be such things as logins and logouts, accesses or attempted accesses to files or directories, execution of programs, and uses of other devices.

Failures are also logged. It may be less important to record that a particular user listed the contents of a permitted directory than that the same programmer tried to but was prevented from listing the contents of a protected directory. One failed login may result from a typing error, but a series of failures in a short time from the same device may result from the attempt of an intruder to break into the system.

Unusual events in the audit log should be scrutinized. For example, a new program might be tested in a dedicated, controlled environment. After the program has been tested, an audit log of all files accessed should be scanned to determine if there are any unexpected file accesses, which could point to a Trojan horse in the new program.

Each of these important aspects of operating system control will be expanded in the next two chapters.

5.5 Administrative Controls

Not all controls can be imposed automatically by the computing system. In this section we will consider controls that can be applied by administrative procedures.

Standards of Program Development

Major computing departments do not allow programmers to produce code at any time in any manner. In addition to correctness, there are concerns about maintainability and compatibility with other routines. Following are typical examples of administrative control over software development.

- Standards of *design,* including use of specified design tools, languages, or methodologies.

- Standards of *documentation, language,* and *coding style* (layout of code on the page, choices of names of variables, use of recognized program structures).

- Standards of *programming,* including mandatory programmer peer reviews and periodic code audits for correctness and compliance with standards.

- Standards of *testing*, such as use of program verification techniques, independent testing, and archiving of test results for future reference.

- Standards of *configuration management,* to control access to and changes of stable or completed program units.

Standardization of this kind is intended to improve the situation for all programmers by establishing a common framework within which everyone works so that anyone can assist or take over for another programmer. Standards also assist in maintenance, since the maintenance team can find required information in a well-organized source program.

Enforcing Program Development Standards

Standards must be enforced to be effective. Trivial though this idea sounds, it is sometimes not recognized by management. When a project falls behind schedule, or when key people leave a project team, the common reaction is to emphasize completing the project rather than following established standards.

Firms committed to following software development standards often perform **security audits**. In a security audit an independent security evaluation team checks each project on an unannounced basis. The team reviews designs, documentation, and code to verify that standards are being followed. Knowing that programs are routinely scrutinized, a programmer is unlikely to put suspicious code in a module in the first place.

Separation of Duties

Banks often break tasks into two or more pieces to be performed by separate employees. Employees are less tempted to do wrong if they need the cooperation of another employee to do so. In programming, the same practice can be used. Modular programming and design forces programmers to cooperate in order to achieve illicit results with programs. Independent test teams, not the programmers who wrote a piece of code, will test a module more rigorously. All of these forms of separation lead to a higher degree of security in programs.

Hiring Characteristics

It is common for a computing company to perform a background investigation of its employees prior to hiring them. A company would not want to hire a felon unknowingly, and might even carefully limit the access of an employee who had not developed a degree of trust from long-term service.

Investigation of Employees

After hiring an employee, companies may impose unusual standards of behavior for security reasons. For example, a bank may require its employees to keep their bank accounts at that bank, so that the auditors can monitor those accounts closely for unexplained gains or losses. The accounting programs written by an employee with a gambling habit, whose account balance is usually very low, might be carefully supervised. Alternatively, a bank might prohibit its employees from opening accounts at that bank, so that it would be more difficult for a programmer to extract funds and credit those funds to an account for the programmer's personal use. Certainly in both of these instances, the employee could open an account under a false name, but that adds to the difficulty of the enterprise, which may be a deterrent.

5.6 Summary of Program Controls

In this chapter we have considered two general classes of program flaws: programs that compromise or change data, and those that affect computer service. There are essentially three controls on such activities. Programmer controls limit the programming activity, to make it harder for a programmer to create malicious programs. These same controls are effective against inadvertent mistakes by programmers. The operating system provides some degree of control by limiting access to objects of the computing system. Finally, administrative controls limit the kinds of actions people can take.

It is wrong to consider these controls only for their negative aspects, that is, for actions they *prohibit*. All of these controls have positive effects which are, in fact, more important and more commonly used than their prohibiting features. Program controls coming from software engineering have as their primary purpose improving the quality of software produced. Operating systems limit access as a way of promoting the safe sharing of information between programs. And administrative controls and standards improve the usability and maintainability of code produced. For all of these controls, the security features are a secondary aspect.

Program controls are part of the more general problem of limiting the effect of one user on another. In the next chapter we will consider the role of the operating system in regulating the interaction between users.

5.7 Terms and Concepts

program
user program
utility program
operating system
data access
trapdoor
stub
driver
side effect
error checking
undefined operation
Trojan horse
salami attack
information leakage
covert channel
timing channel
denial of service

greedy program
loop
computer virus
computer worm
software engineering
peer review
program design
program [source] code
walk-through
egoless programming
modularity
maintainability
understandability
reusability
correctability
testability
encapsulation
coupling
controlled sharing
information hiding
independent test team
configuration management
shadow program copy
proof of program correctness
program verification
logic analyzer
initial assertion
logical implication
program goal
trusted software
functional correctness
enforcement of integrity
limited privilege
appropriate security level
mutual suspicion
confinement
compartmented information
access log
program development standards
design standards
documentation standards
programming standards
testing standards
configuration management standards

5.8 Bibliographic Notes

Programs that compromise data are some of the earliest examples of computer security vulnerabilities. Various examples of program flaws are described by Parker [PAR76] and [PAR83], Denning [DEN82], and Lobel [LOB86].

Software engineering principles of program development are described by numerous authors. The book by Pfleeger [PFL87] is good for readers unfamiliar with the field, while the book by Pressman [PRE87] contains more advanced material. The section on reliability in Shooman [SHO83] is also very good. Babich [BAB86] explains configuration management, and Chow [CHO85] contains an overview of software testing.

5.9 Exercises

1. Suppose you are a customs inspector. You are responsible for checking suitcases for secret compartments in which bulky items such as jewelry might be hidden. Describe the procedure you would follow to check for these compartments.

2. Your boss hands you a microprocessor and its technical reference manual. You are asked to check for undocumented features of the processor. Because of the number of possibilities, it is infeasible to test every operation code with every combination of operands. Outline the strategy you would use to identify and characterize unpublicized operations.

3. Your boss hands you a computer program and its technical reference manual. You are asked to check for undocumented features of the program. How is this activity similar to the task of Exercise 2? How does it differ? Which is the more feasible? Why?

4. Could a computer program be used to automate testing for trapdoors? That is, could you design a computer program that would be given the source or object version of another program and a suitable description of that other program, and the first program would reply *Yes* or *No* to show whether the second program had any trapdoors? Explain your answer.

5. A program is written to compute the sum of the integers from 1 to 10. The programmer, well-trained in reusability and maintainability, writes the program so that it computes the sum of the numbers from k to n. However, a team of security specialists scrutinizes the code. The team certifies that this program properly sets k to 1 and n to 10; therefore, the program is certified as being properly restricted in that it always operates on precisely the range 1 to 10. List different ways that this program can be sabotaged so that during execution it computes a different sum, for example, 3 to 20.

6. One means of limiting the effect of an untrusted program is confinement: controlling what processes have access to the untrusted program and what access the program

has to other processes and data. Explain how confinement would apply to the example presented in Exercise 5.

7. List three controls that could be applied to detect or prevent salami attacks.

8. Covert channels are sometimes also known as "timing channels." Explain why this name is appropriate for a particular class of covert channels.

9. List the limitations on the amount of information leaked per second through a covert channel in a multiaccess computing system.

10. An electronic mail system could be used to leak information. First, explain how the leakage could occur. Then identify controls that could be applied to detect or prevent the leakage.

11. Modularity can have a negative effect as well as a positive one. A program that is over-modularized performs its operations in very small modules, so that it is difficult to acquire a perspective. While it may be easy to see what many individual modules do, it is not easy to determine what they do together. Suggest an approach that can be used during program development to maintain this perspective.

12. You are given a program that purportedly manages a list of items through hash coding. The program is supposed to return the location of an item if the item is present, or return the location where the item should be inserted if the item is not in the list. Accompanying the program is a manual describing parameters such as the expected format of items in the table, the table size, and the specific calling sequence. You have only the object code of this program, not the source code. List the cases you would apply to test the correctness of the program's function.

13. You are writing a procedure to add a node to a doubly linked list. The system on which this procedure is to be run is subject to periodic hardware failures. The list your program is to maintain is of very high importance. It is necessary for your program to ensure the integrity of the list, even if the machine fails in the middle of executing your procedure. List the individual statements to update the list. (Your list should be about a half dozen statements long.) Tell the effect of a machine failure after each instruction. Describe a procedure to run that will restore the integrity of the basic list after a machine failure.

14. Explain how information in an access log could be used to identify the true identity of an imposter who has acquired unauthorized access to a computing system. Describe several different pieces of information in the log that combine to identify the imposter.

15. Several proposals have been made for a processor that could decrypt encrypted machine instructions and data and then execute the instructions on the data. The processor would then encrypt the results. How would such a processor be useful? What are the design requirements for such a processor?

6

Protection Services for
Users of Operating Systems

In this chapter and the next we will consider operating systems and their role in computer security. We begin by studying the contributions that operating systems have made to user security. Operating systems support multiprogramming, the concurrent use of a system by more than one user, and so they have developed ways to protect the computation of one user from inadvertent or malicious interference from another. Among the facilities that operating systems security provide are memory protection, file protection, general control of access to objects, and user authentication. This chapter is basically a survey on controls to provide those four features. In the next chapter we will see how operating system design is affected by security considerations.

6.1 Protected Objects and Methods of Protection

We begin by considering the history of protection in operating systems. From the history we determine what kinds of things operating systems can protect and what methods are available for protection.

History of Operating Systems

Originally in computing there were no operating systems: users entered their programs in binary through switches. Each user had exclusive use of the computing system, so that users scheduled blocks of time to use the machine. Users loaded their own libraries of support routines—assemblers, compilers, shared subprograms—and "cleaned up" after use by removing any sensitive data.

The first operating systems were simple utilities, called **executives**, to assist individual programmers and to smooth the transition for new users starting to use the machine.

The early executives provided linkers and loaders for relocation, easy access to compilers and assemblers, and automatic loading of subprograms from libraries. The executives handled the tedious aspects of support for programmers. The major function of these programs was support for a single programmer during execution.

With the development of multiprogramming, operating systems assumed an entirely different role—and a different name. When it was realized that two users could interleave access to the resources of a computing system, the concepts of scheduling, sharing, and parallel use developed. Multiprogrammed operating systems, also known as **monitors**, oversaw the execution of programs. Whereas an executive stayed passively in the background, waiting to be called into service by a requesting user, a monitor actively asserted control of the computing system and gave resources to the user only when it was consistent with general good use of the system. Whereas the executive provided service on demand, the monitor oversaw all computing and lent resources to users.

Multiprogramming brought another important change in computing. In the single user case, the only force to be protected against was oneself. The user felt foolish after making an error, but one user could not adversely affect the computation of any other user. With multiple users, however, a user would rightfully be angry if another user caused a negative effect on a program's execution. Therefore, protection of one user from another became an important issue in multiprogrammed operating systems.

Protected Objects

Several objects of a computing system required protection:

1. memory

2. sharable I/O devices, such as disks

3. serially reusable I/O devices, such as printers and tape drives

4. sharable programs and subprocedures

5. sharable data

The operating system had to protect these objects when it assumed responsibility for the controlled sharing of them. In the following sections we consider mechanisms by which operating systems have enforced protection for these objects.

Security Methods of Operating Systems

Rushby and Randell [RUS83] note that security in an operating system can occur from

- *Physical separation*, in which processes use different physical objects, such as separate printers for output requiring different levels of security

- *Temporal separation*, in which processes having different security requirements are executed at different times

- *Logical separation*, in which users operate under the illusion that no other processes exist, as when an operating system constrains a program's accesses so that it cannot access objects outside its permitted domain

- *Cryptographic separation*, in which processes conceal their data and computations in such a way that they are unintelligible to outside processes

Of course, combinations of two or more of these forms of separation are also possible.

The categories of separation are listed roughly in increasing order of complexity to implement, and in decreasing order of the security provided. However, the first two approaches are very stringent and can lead to poor resource utilization. Therefore, it is desirable to shift the burden of protection to the operating system to allow concurrent execution of processes having different security needs.

An operating system may offer protection at any of several levels.

1. *No protection.* These systems are appropriate when sensitive procedures are being run at separate times.

2. *Isolation.* When an operating system provides isolation, different processes running concurrently are unaware of the presence of each other. Each process has its own address space, files, and other objects. The operating system must confine each process to completely conceal the objects of the other processes.

3. *Share all or share nothing.* With this form of protection the owner of an object declares it to be "public" or "private." A public object is available to all users, while a private object is available only to its owner.

4. *Share via access limitation.* With protection by access limitation, the operating system checks the allowability of each potential access. Access control is implemented for a specific user and a specific object. By means of lists, the operating system determines if a particular user should have access to a particular object. The operating system acts as a guard between users and objects, ensuring that only authorized accesses occur.

5. *Share by capabilities.* An extension of limited access sharing, this form of protection allows dynamic creation of sharing rights for objects. The degree of sharing can depend on the owner or the subject, on the context of the computation, or on the object itself.

6. *Limit use of an object.* This form of protection limits not just the access to an object, but the use made of that object after it has been accessed. For example, a user may be allowed to view a sensitive document, but not to print a copy of it. More powerfully, a user may be allowed access to data in a data base in order to derive statistical summaries (for example, average salary at a particular grade level), but not to determine specific data values (salaries of individuals).

Again, these types of operating system support of sharing are arranged in increasing order of difficulty to implement, but also in increasing order of fineness of protection they provide. A given operating system may provide different levels of protection for different objects, users, or situations.

Granularity of control is also a concern. For data, access can be controlled at the level of the bit, the byte, the element or word, the field, the record, the file, or the volume. The larger the level of object controlled, the easier it is to implement access control. However, with large objects a user needing access only to part of an object (for example, a single record in a file) must be allowed access to the entire object (the whole file).

6.2 Protection of Memory and Addressing

The most obvious problem of multiprogramming is preventing one program from affecting the memory of other programs. Fortunately, protection can be built into the hardware mechanisms that provide for efficient use of memory, so that solid protection can be provided at essentially no additional cost.

Fence

The simplest form of memory protection was introduced in single-user systems in order to prevent a faulty user program from destroying part of the resident portion of the operating system. As its name implies, a **fence** is a method to confine users to one side of a boundary.

In one implementation, the fence was a predefined memory address, so that the operating system resided on one side and the user on the other. This situation is shown in Figure 6.1. Unfortunately, that implementation was very restrictive, since a fixed amount of space was reserved for the operating system. If less than that amount of space was required, the excess space was wasted, while the operating system could not grow beyond the fence boundary.

Another implementation used a hardware register, often called a **fence register**, that contained the address of the end of the operating system. Each time a user program generated an address for data modification, the address was automatically compared against the fence address. If the address was greater than the fence address (that is, in the user area), the instruction was executed; if it was less than the fence address (that is, in the operating system area), an error condition was raised. The use of fence registers is shown in Figure 6.2.

A fence register protects only in one direction. An operating system can be protected from a single user, but the fence cannot protect one user from another. Similarly, a user cannot identify certain areas of the program as inviolable (such as the code of the program itself or a read-only data area).

Relocation

If the operating system can be assumed to be of a fixed size, programmers can write their code assuming the program begins at a constant address. This makes it easy to determine

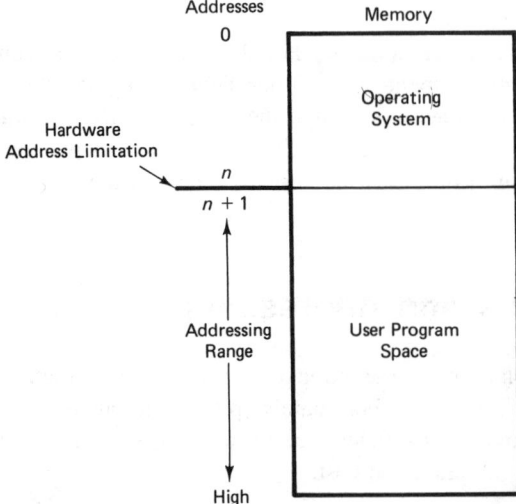

Figure 6.1 Fixed Fence.

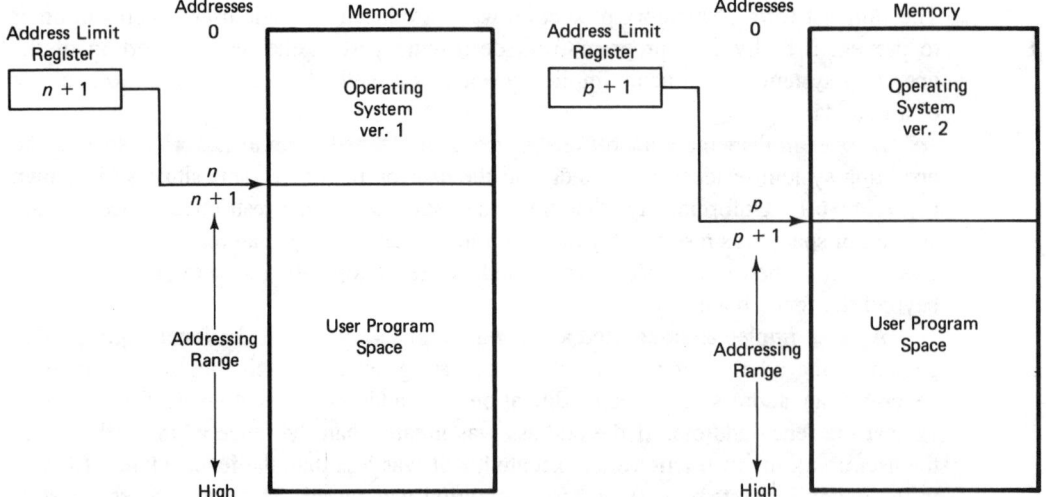

Figure 6.2 Variable Fence Register.

the address of any object in the program, but it also makes it essentially impossible to change the starting address if, for example, a new version of the operating system is larger or smaller than the old one. If the size of the operating system is allowed to change, then programs must be written in a way that does not depend on placement at a specific location in memory.

Relocation is the process of taking a program written as if it began at address 0 and changing all addresses to reflect the actual address at which the program is located in memory. In many instances, this merely entails adding a constant **relocation factor** to each address of the program. The relocation factor is the starting address of the memory assigned for the program.

Conveniently, the fence register can be used in this situation to provide an important extra benefit. The fence register can be a hardware relocation device. To each program address the contents of the fence register is added. This both relocates the address and guarantees that it is impossible to access a location lower than the fence address. (Addresses are treated as unsigned integers, so adding the value in the fence register to any number is guaranteed to produce a result at or above the fence address.) Special instructions can be added for the few times when a program legitimately intends to access a location of the operating system.

Base/Bounds Registers

The advantage of fence registers is the possibility of relocation just described, which is even more important in a multiuser environment. With two or more users, neither can know in advance where a program will be loaded for execution. The relocation register solves the problem by providing a base or starting address. All addresses inside a program are offsets from that base address. A variable fence register is generally known as a **base register**.

The difficulty with fence registers is that they provide a lower bound (a starting address), but not an upper one. To overcome the difficulty, a second register is often added, as shown in Figure 6.3. The second register, called a **bounds register**, is an upper address limit, in the same way that a base or fence register is a lower address limit. Each program address is forced to be above the base address, since the contents of the base register are added to the address; each address is also checked to ensure that it is below the bounds address. In this way, a program's addresses are neatly confined to the space between the base and the bounds registers.

This technique protects a program's memory from modification by another user. When execution changes from one user's program to another's, the operating system must change the contents of the base and bounds registers to reflect the true address space for that user. This change is part of the general preparation, called a **context switch**, that the operating system must perform when transferring control from one user to another.

With a pair of base/bounds registers, a user is perfectly protected from outside users or, more correctly, outside users are protected from errors in any other user's program. Erroneous addresses *inside* a user's address space can still affect that program, since the base/bounds checking guarantees only that each address is inside the user's address space. A possible user error would be a subscript out of range or an undefined variable which generates an address reference within the user's space but, unfortunately, inside the executable instructions of the user's program. Therefore a user can inadvertently store data on top of instructions. Such an error can let a user inadvertently destroy a program, but only the user's own program.

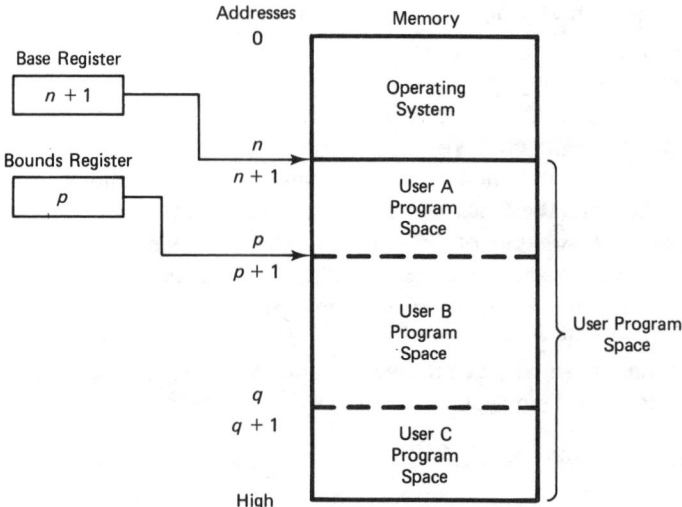

Figure 6.3   Base/Bounds Register Pairs.

A solution is to use another pair of base/bounds registers, one for the instructions (code) of the program and a second for the data space. Then, only instruction fetches (instructions to be executed) are relocated and checked with the first register pair, and only data accesses (operands of instructions) are relocated and checked with the second register pair. The use of two pairs of base/bounds registers is shown in Figure 6.4. Although two pairs of registers do not prevent all program errors, they do limit the effect of data-manipulating instructions to the data space. They offer another more important advantage—the ability to split a program into two pieces that can be relocated separately.

These two advantages seem to call for the use of three or more pairs of registers, one for code, one for read-only data, and one for modifiable data values. Although in theory this concept can be extended, two pairs of registers is the limit for practical computer design. For each additional pair of registers added, something in the machine code of each instruction must indicate which relocation pair is to be used to address the operands of the instruction. With two pairs, the decision can be automatic: instructions with one pair, data with the other. With more than two pairs, each instruction specifies one of two or more data spaces.

Tagged Architecture

Another problem with base/bounds registers for protection or relocation is their contiguous nature. Each pair of registers confines accesses to a consecutive range of addresses. It is relatively simple for a compiler or loader to rearrange a program so that all code sections are adjacent and all data sections are adjacent, too.

However, it may be desirable to protect *some* data values but not *all*. A programmer may want to ensure the integrity of certain data values by allowing them to be written

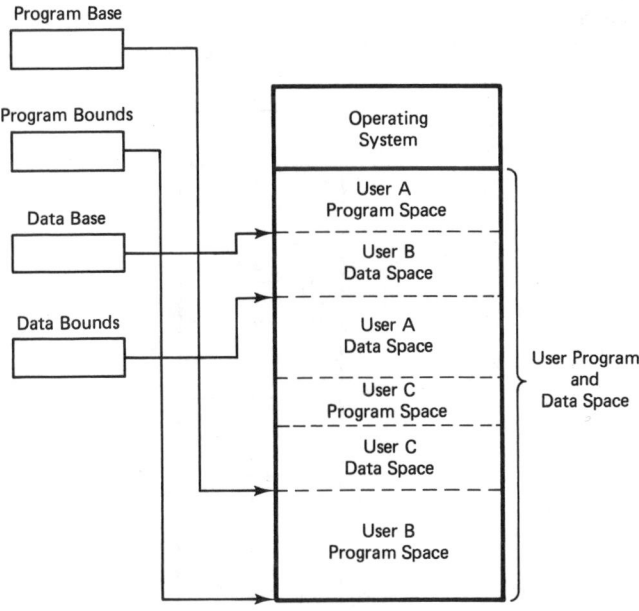

Figure 6.4   Two Pairs of Base/Bounds Registers.

when the program is initialized, but prohibiting the program from modifying them later. This protects against errors in the programmer's own code. A programmer may also want to invoke a shared subprogram from a common library. In Chapter 5 we studied information hiding and modularity in program design, good design characteristics. These characteristics dictate that one program module share with another module only the *minimum* amount of data necessary for both of them to do their work.

Base/bounds registers create an all-or-nothing situation for sharing: either a program makes all its data available to be accessed and modified, or it prohibits access to all. Even if there were a third set of registers for shared data, all data would need to be located together. A procedure could not effectively share data items A, B, and C with one module, A, C, and D with a second, and A, B, and D with a third. The only way to do this would be by moving the appropriate set of data values to some contiguous space, a solution that would not be acceptable if the data items were large records, arrays, or structures.

An alternative is **tagged architecture**, in which every word of machine memory has one or more extra bits to identify the access rights to that word. These access bits can be set only by privileged (operating system) instructions. The bits are tested every time an instruction accesses that location.

For example, as shown in Figure 6.5, one memory location may be protected as execute-only (object code of instructions), while another is protected for fetch-only (read) data access, and another accessible for modification (write). Two adjacent locations can have different access rights. Furthermore, with a few extra tag bits, different classes of data (numeric, character, address or pointer, and undefined) can be separated, and data fields can be protected for privileged (operating system) access only.

Tag Memory Word

Tag	Memory Word
R	0001
RW	0137
R	0099
X	〰〰
X	〰〰
X	〰〰
X	〰〰
X	〰〰
X	〰〰
X	〰〰
X	〰〰
X	〰〰
X	〰〰
R	4091
RW	0002

Code:

R = Read-Only
RW = Read/Write   **Figure 6.5**   Example of Tagged
X = Execute-Only   Architecture.

This protection technique has been used on a few systems, although the number of tag bits has been rather small. The Burroughs B6500-7500 system [HAU68] uses three tag bits to separate data words (three types), descriptors (pointers), and control words (stack pointers and addressing control words). The IBM System/38 uses a tag to control both integrity and access [BER78].

A variation that has also been used is one tag that applies to a group of consecutive locations, for example, 128 or 256 bytes. With one tag for a block of addresses, the added cost for implementing tags is not as high as with one tag per location.

A problem with the acceptance of a tagged architecture is compatibility of code. Major computer vendors are still working with operating systems that were designed and implemented 10 or 20 years ago for architectures of that era. The prices of memory have fallen so much recently that implementation of a tagged architecture is more feasible now than before. However, most manufacturers are locked into a more conventional memory architecture because of wide availability of components and desire to maintain compatibility among operating systems and machine families. A tagged architecture would require fundamental changes to substantially all of the operating system code, which is prohibitive.

Segmentation

The last two approaches for protection we present can be implemented on top of a conventional machine structure, so that they have a better chance of acceptance. These approaches have been developed and implemented for well over 20 years. Furthermore, they offer important advantages in addressing, with memory protection being a delightful bonus. Segmentation was developed as a feasible means to have the effect of an unbounded number of base/bounds registers: A program could be divided into many pieces having different access rights.

Segmentation is simply the notion of dividing a program into separate pieces. Each piece has a logical unity, a relationship among all of its code or data values. For example, a segment may be the code of a single procedure, or the data of an array, or the collection of all local data values used by a particular module. Segmentation is used in the Multics operating system.

Each segment has a unique name. A code or data item within a segment is addressed as the pair ⟨*name,offset*⟩, where *name* is the name of the segment containing the data item, and *offset* is its location within the segment, that is, its offset from the start of the segment.

Logically, the programmer pictures a program as a long collection of segments. Segments can be separately relocated, allowing any segment to be placed in any available memory locations. The relationship between a logical segment and its true memory position is shown in Figure 6.6.

The operating system must maintain a table of segment names and their true addresses in memory. When a program generates an address of the form ⟨*name,offset*⟩, the operating system must look up *name* in the segment directory and determine its real memory address. To that address the operating system adds *offset*, giving the true memory address of the code or data item. This translation is shown in Figure 6.7. For efficiency there is usually one operating system segment address table for each process in execution. Two processes that want to share access to a single segment would have the same segment name and address in their segment tables.

Thus, a user's program does not know what true memory addresses it uses. It has no way—and no need—to determine the actual address associated with a particular ⟨*name,offset*⟩. The ⟨*name,offset*⟩ pair is adequate to access any data or instruction to which a program should have access.

This hiding of addresses has three advantages for the operating system.

1. The operating system can move any segment to any location in memory. Since all address references are translated by the operating system using a segment address table, the operating system need only update the address in that one table when a segment is moved.

2. A segment can be removed from main memory (and stored on an auxiliary device) if it is not being used currently.

3. Every address reference passes through the operating system, so that there is an opportunity to check each for protection.

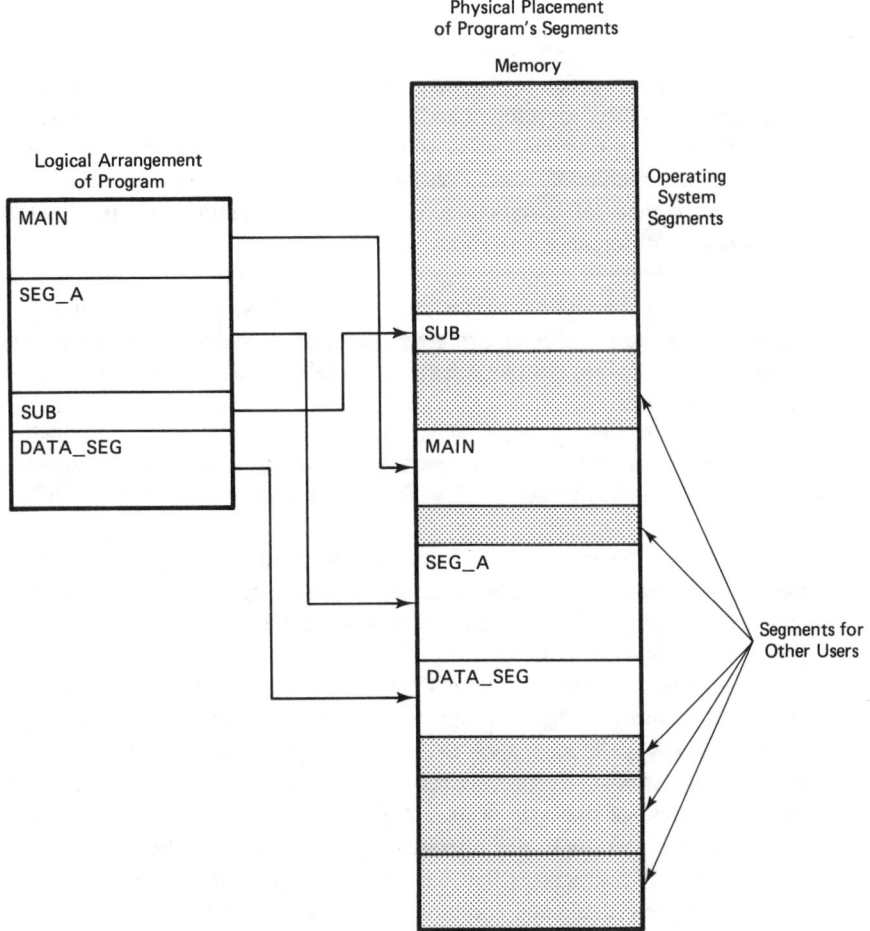

Figure 6.6   Logical and Physical Representation of Segments.

Because of the third characteristic, a process that does not have a segment name in its table is denied all access to that segment. The operating system controls which programs have entries for a particular segment in their segment address tables. This provides strong protection of segments from access by unpermitted processes. For example, program *A* might have access to segments *BLUE* and *GREEN* of another user, but not to other segments of that user or of any other user.

It is possible to assign different protection classes to segments of any user's program. The process of segmentation is handled by a combination of hardware and software. Therefore, it is feasible to associate certain levels of protection with certain segments, and to have the operating system/hardware check that protection on each access to the segment. For example, one segment might be read-only data, a second might be execute-

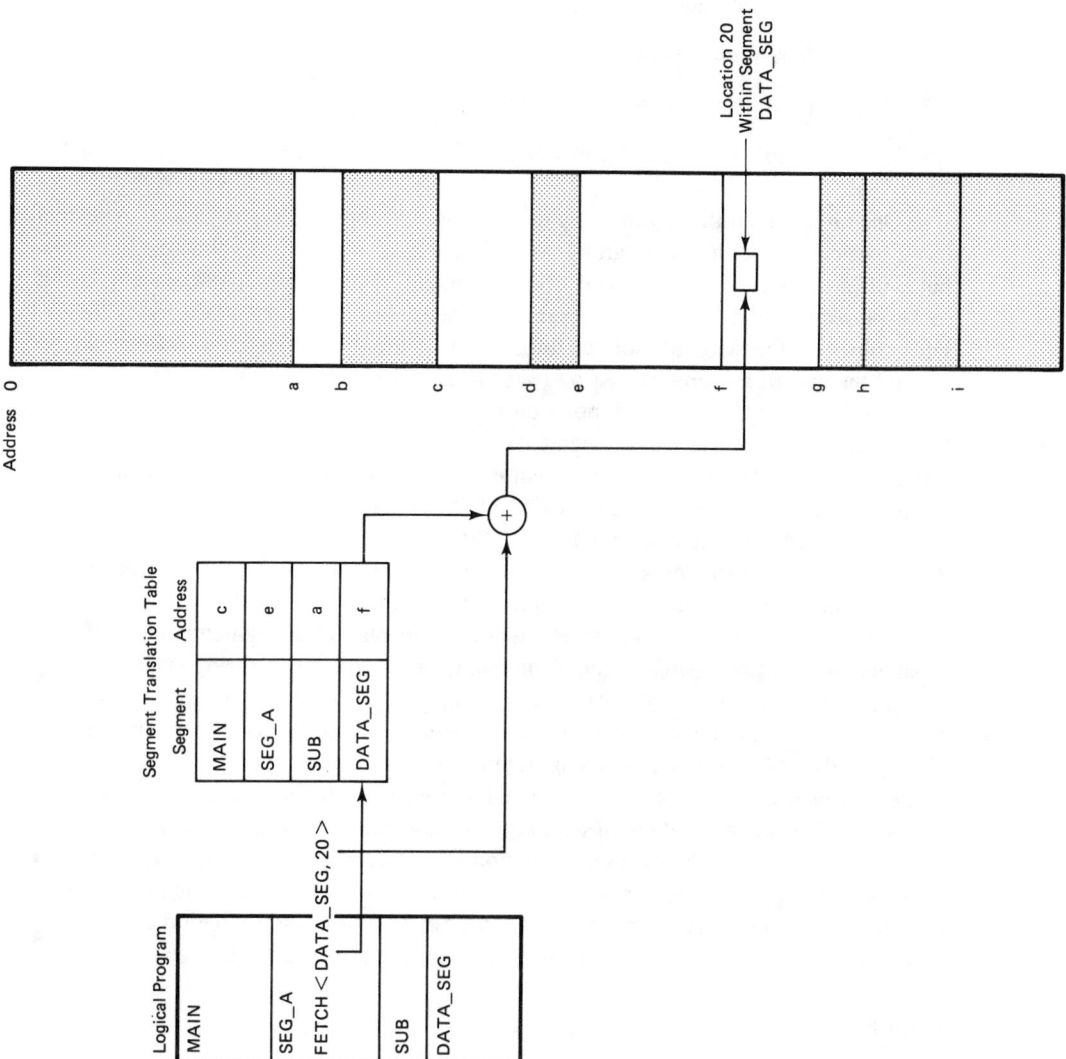

Figure 6.7 Translation of Segment Address.

only code, and a third might be writable data. This situation means that segmentation can approximate the goal of separate protection of different pieces of a program, as outlined in the previous section on tagged architecture.

Relative to protection, the benefits of segmentation are these.

1. Each address reference is checked for protection.

2. Many different classes of data items can be assigned different levels of protection.

3. Two or more users can share access to a segment, but with different access rights.

4. It is impossible for a user to generate an address or access to an unpermitted segment.

One protection difficulty inherent in segmentation concerns segment size. A segment has a particular size, but a program can generate a reference to a valid segment *name*, but with an *offset* beyond the end of the segment. For example, reference ⟨*A*,9999⟩ looks perfectly valid, although in reality segment *A* may be only 200 bytes long. If left unplugged, this security hole could allow a program to access any memory address beyond the end of a segment, just by using large values of *offset* in an address.

This problem cannot be stopped during compilation, or even when a program is loaded, because effective use of segments requires that they be allowed to grow in size during execution. For example, a segment might contain a dynamic data structure such as a stack. Therefore, secure implementation of segmentation requires checking an address generated to verify that it is not beyond the current end of the segment referenced. Although it is an extra expense, segmentation systems maintain the current segment length in the translation table and compare every address generated.

There are two difficulties with efficient implementation of segmentation. First, segment names are inconvenient to encode in instructions, and the operating system's lookup of the name in a table can be slow. To overcome this difficulty, segment names are often converted to numbers by the compiler when a program is translated; the compiler also appends a linkage table matching numbers to true segment names. This presents an implementation difficulty when two procedures wish to share the same segment, since the assigned segment numbers of data accessed by that segment must be the same.

The second difficulty of implementation is that segments can lead to fragmentation of main memory, since they are of varying sizes. After time, unused fragments of space can lead to poor memory utilization. A solution to fragmentation is periodic compaction of memory, but compaction and updating of appropriate tables takes time.

Paging

An alternative to segmentation is **paging**. Numerous operating systems, including VAX VMS and DEC System/10, use paging to manage memory. As with segmentation, each address is a two-part object, this time consisting of ⟨*page*,*offset*⟩. The program is divided into equal-sized pieces called **pages**, and memory is divided into the same sized units, called **page frames**. (For implementation reasons, the page size is usually chosen to be a power of two between 512 and 4096 bytes.)

Each address is again translated by a process similar to that of segmentation: The operating system maintains a table of user page numbers and their true addresses in memory. The *page* portion of every ⟨*page,offset*⟩ reference is converted to a page frame address by a table lookup; the *offset* portion is added to the page frame address to produce the real memory address of the object referred to as ⟨*page,offset*⟩. This process is shown in Figure 6.8.

Unlike segmentation, all pages are of the same fixed size, so fragmentation is not a problem: Each page can fit in any available page in memory. There is no problem of addressing beyond the end of a page. The binary form of a ⟨*page,offset*⟩ address is designed so that the *offset* values fill a range of bits in the address. Therefore, an *offset* beyond the end of a particular page results in a carry into the *page* portion of the address, which changes the address.

For example, with a page size of 1024 bytes ($1024 = 2^{10}$), 10 bits are allocated for the *offset* portion of each address. It is impossible to generate an *offset* value larger than 1023 in 10 bits. Moving to the next location after ⟨x,1023⟩ causes a carry into the *page* portion, thereby moving translation to the next page, that is, to address ⟨$x + 1, 0$⟩. During the translation, there is a check to verify that a ⟨*page,offset*⟩ reference does not exceed the maximum number of pages the process has defined.

A programmer has to be conscious of segments but remains oblivious to page boundaries. There is no logical unity to a page, and a page is just the next n bytes of the program. A change to a program, such as the addition of one instruction, will push all subsequent instructions to lower addresses, and move a few bytes from the end of each page to the start of the next. This is not something about which the programmer need be concerned, since the entire mechanism of paging and address translation is hidden from the programmer.

However, from the standpoint of protection, this is a serious loss. With segmentation, it is possible to protect different segments with separate protection rights, such as read-only or execute-only. This problem could be handled efficiently during address translation. With paging, since there is no necessary unity to the items on a page, there is no way to establish all values on a page as read-only or execute-only.

Combined Paging with Segmentation

Because of the efficiency of implementation of paging and the desirable logical protection characteristics of segmentation, these two approaches have been combined.

The MULTICS operating system (initially implemented on a GE/Honeywell-645 machine) applied paging on top of segmentation. Essentially, the approach allowed the programmer to divide a program into logical segments. Then each segment was broken into fixed-sized pages. The segment *name* portion of an address was an 18-bit number, with a 16-bit *offset*. The addresses were then broken into 1024 byte pages. The translation process is shown in Figure 6.9. This approach retained the logical unity of a segment and permitted differentiated protection for the segments, but it added an additional layer of translation for each address. Additional hardware improved the efficiency of the implementation.

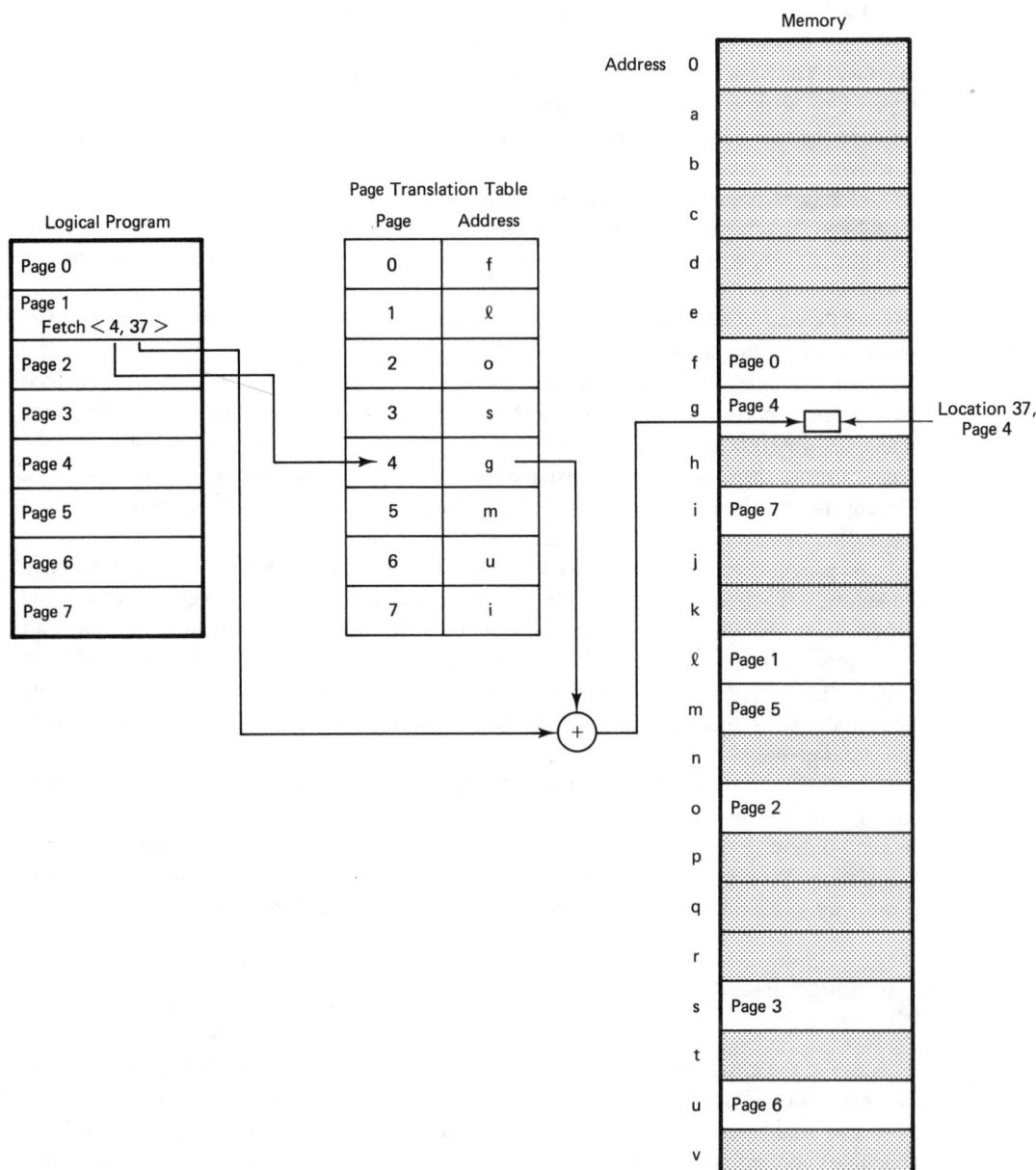

Figure 6.8   Page Address Translation.

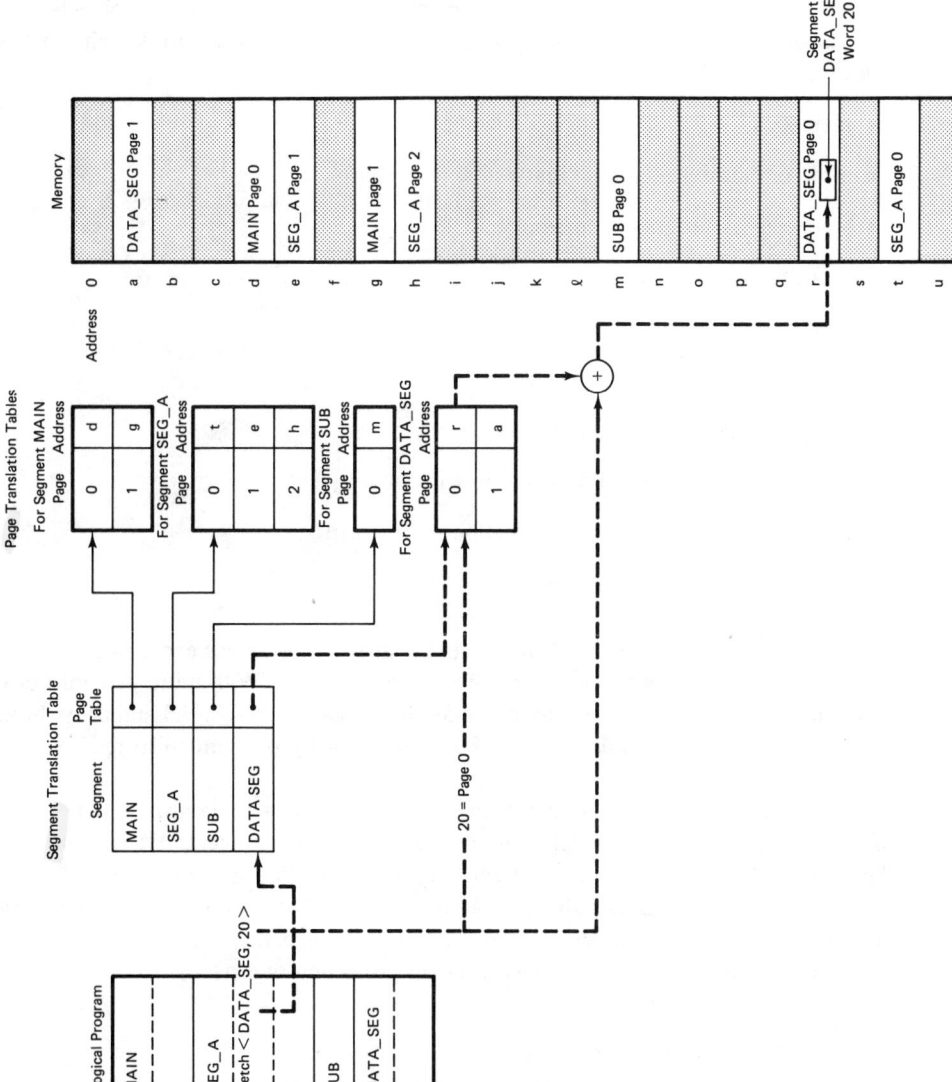

Figure 6.9 Paged Segmentation.

6.3 Protection of Access to General Objects

Protection of memory is a specific case of the more general problem of protection of *objects*. As multiprogramming has developed, the number and kind of objects shared have also increased. Here are some examples of the kinds of objects for which protection is desirable.

- memory

- a file or data set on an auxiliary storage device

- an executing program in memory

- a directory of files

- a hardware device

- a data structure, such as a stack

- a table of the operating system

- instructions, especially privileged instructions

- passwords and the user authentication mechanism

- the protection mechanism itself

The memory protection mechanism can be fairly simple, since every memory access is guaranteed to go through certain points in the hardware. With more general objects, the number of points of access may be larger, there may be no central authority through which all accesses pass, and the kind of access is not simply limited to read, write, or execute.

Furthermore, all accesses to memory occur through a program, so it is clear to refer to "the program" or "the programmer" as the accessing agent. We will use terms like "the user" or "the subject" in describing an access to a general object. This user or subject could be a person who uses a computing system, a programmer, a program, another object, or something else that seeks to use an object.

There are several complementary goals in protecting objects.

1. *Check every access.* It may be desirable to revoke a user's privilege to access an object. If the user has previously been authorized to access the object, it may be inappropriate for the user to retain indefinite access to the object. In fact, in some situations, it is important to prevent further accesses after authorization has been revoked. For this reason, every access by a user to an object should be checked.

2. *Allow least privilege.* The principle of least privilege states that a subject should have access to the smallest number of objects necessary to perform some task. Even if extra information would be useless to the subject, the subject should not have additional access. For example, a program should not have access to the absolute

memory address to which a page number reference translates, even though the program could not use that address in any effective way. Not allowing access to unnecessary objects guards against security weaknesses if a part of the protection mechanism should fail.

3. *Verify acceptable usage*. Ability to access is a yes-no decision. Of more interest is checking that the activity to be performed on an object is appropriate. For example, a data structure such as a stack has certain acceptable operations, including *push*, *pop*, *clear*, and so on. It may be appropriate not only to control who has access to a stack but to be assured that the accesses performed are legitimate stack accesses.

In the next section we consider protection mechanisms appropriate for general objects of unspecified types, such as the kinds of objects just listed. To make the explanations easier to understand, we sometimes use an example of a specific object, like a file. Note, however, that a mechanism can be used to protect any of the types of objects listed earlier.

Directory

One simple protection mechanism works like a file directory. Imagine the set of objects to be files and the set of subjects to be users of a computing system. (This description will be phrased in terms of files, although the concept generalizes easily to arbitrary subjects and objects.) Every file has a unique owner who posesses major access rights, including the rights to declare who has what access and to revoke access by any person at any time. Each user has a file directory, which lists all the files to which that user has access.

Clearly no user can be allowed to write in the file directory, since that would be a way to forge access to a file. Therefore, the operating system must maintain all file directories, under commands from the owners of files. The obvious rights to files are the common *read*, *write*, and *execute* familiar on many time sharing systems. Furthermore, another right, *owner*, is possessed by the owner, permitting that user to grant and revoke access rights. Figure 6.10 shows an example of a file directory.

This approach is easy to implement, since it uses one list per user, naming all the objects that user is allowed to access. The list, however, becomes too large if there are many shared objects, accessible to all users, such as libraries of subprograms or a common table of users. Then the directory of each user must have one entry for each such shared object, even if the user has no intention of accessing the object.

A second difficulty is revocation of access. If owner A has passed to user S right to read file F, an entry for F is made in the directory for S. This implies a level of *trust* between A and S. If A later questions that trust, A may want to revoke the access right of S. The operating system can respond easily to the single request to delete the right of B to access F, since that involves deleting one entry from a specific directory. If A wants to remove the access rights of *everyone* to F, the operating system must search each individual directory for the entry F, which can be time-consuming on a large system. For example, large time sharing systems have 5,000 to 10,000 active accounts. Then,

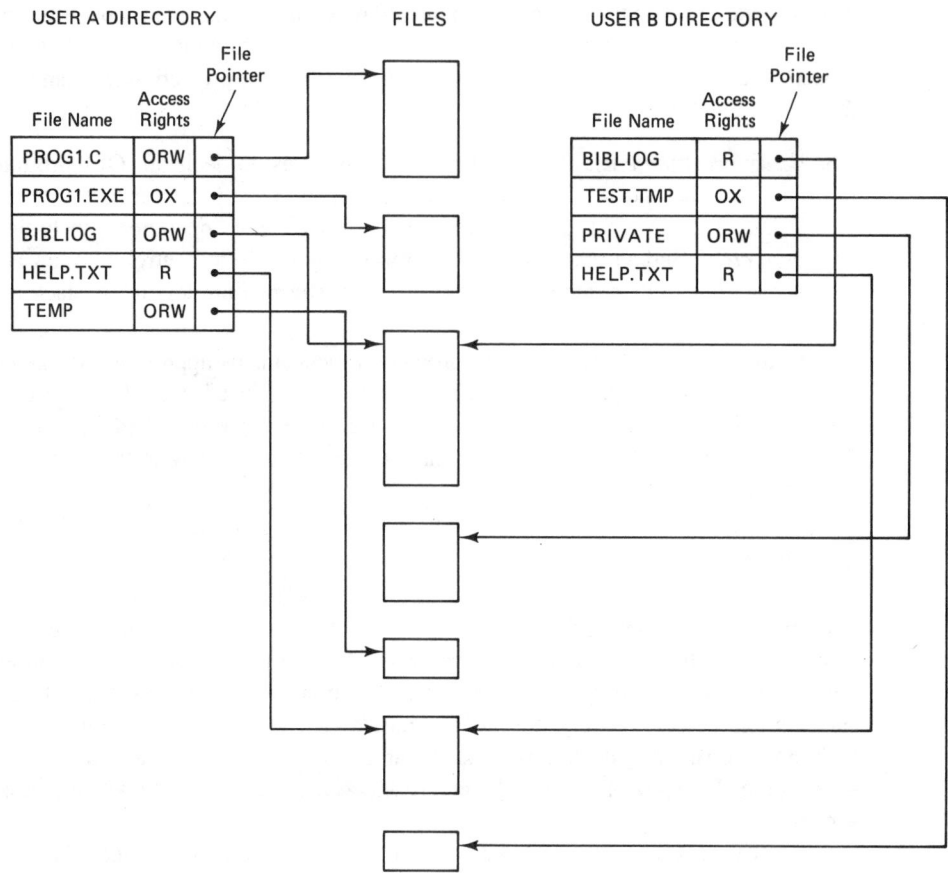

Figure 6.10 Directory Access.

too, if B passed the access right for F to another user, A may not know that access exists and should be revoked.

A third difficulty is pseudonyms. Two owners, A and B, may have two different files named F, and they may both want to allow access by S. Clearly the directory for S cannot contain two entries for the same file name. Therefore, S has to be able to uniquely identify the F from A (or B). One approach is to include the original owner's designation as if it were part of the file name, with a notation like $A : F$ (or $B : F$).

Suppose, however, that S has trouble remembering file contents from the name F. Another approach is to allow S to name F with any name unique to the directory of S. Then, F from A could be called Q to S. As shown in Figure 6.11, S may have forgotten that Q is F from A, and so S requests access again from A for F. By now, however, A trusts S more, and so A transfers F with greater rights than before. This leaves the possibility of one subject, S, having two distinct sets of access rights to F, once under the name Q and once under the name F. Allowing pseudonyms leads to the possibility of multiple permissions, which are not necessarily consistent. The directory approach, therefore, is too simple for most object protection situations.

Access Control List

An alternate representation is the **access control list**. There is one such list for each object, and the list shows all subjects who should have access to the object and what their access is. This differs from the directory list because there is one access control list per *object*, while a directory is created for each *subject*. Although this difference seems small, there are some significant advantages.

For example, if subjects A and S both have access to object F, the operating system will maintain just one access list for F showing the access rights for A and S, as in Figure 6.12. The access control list can have general default entries for any users. In this way, specific users can have explicit rights, and all other users can have a default set of rights. With this organization, a public file or program can be shared by all possible users of the system without needing an entry for the object in the individual directory of each user.

The MULTICS operating system uses a form of access control list in which each user belongs to three protection classes: a *user*, a *group*, and a *compartment*. The user designation identifies a specific subject; the group designation brings together subjects who have a common interest, such as coworkers on a project. The compartment is used to confine an untrusted object: a program executing in one compartment cannot access objects in another compartment without specific permission. The compartment is also a way to collect objects that are related, such as all files for a single project.

Suppose every user who initiates access to the system identifies a group and a compartment with which to work. If Adams logs on as user Adams in group Decl and compartment Art2, only those objects having Adams-Decl-Art2 in the access control list are accessible in the session.

By itself that mechanism would be too restrictive to be usable. Adams cannot create general files to be used in any session. Worse yet, shared objects would not only have to list Adams as a legitimate subject, they would have to list Adams under all acceptable groups and all acceptable compartments for each group.

The solution is the use of **wild cards**, placeholders meaning "any user" (or "any group" or "any compartment"). An access control list might specify access by Adams-Decl-Art1, giving specific rights to Adams if working in group Decl on compartment Art1. The list might also specify Adams-*-Art1, meaning that Adams can access the object from any group in compartment Art1. A notation of *-Decl-* would mean "any user in group Decl in any compartment." Different placements of the wildcard * have the obvious interpretations.

The access control list can be maintained in sorted order, with * sorted as coming after all specific names. Adams-Decl-* would come after all specific compartment designations for Adams. The search for access permission continues just until the first match. All explicit designations will be checked before wild cards in any position, and so a specific access right would take precedence over a wild card right. The last entry

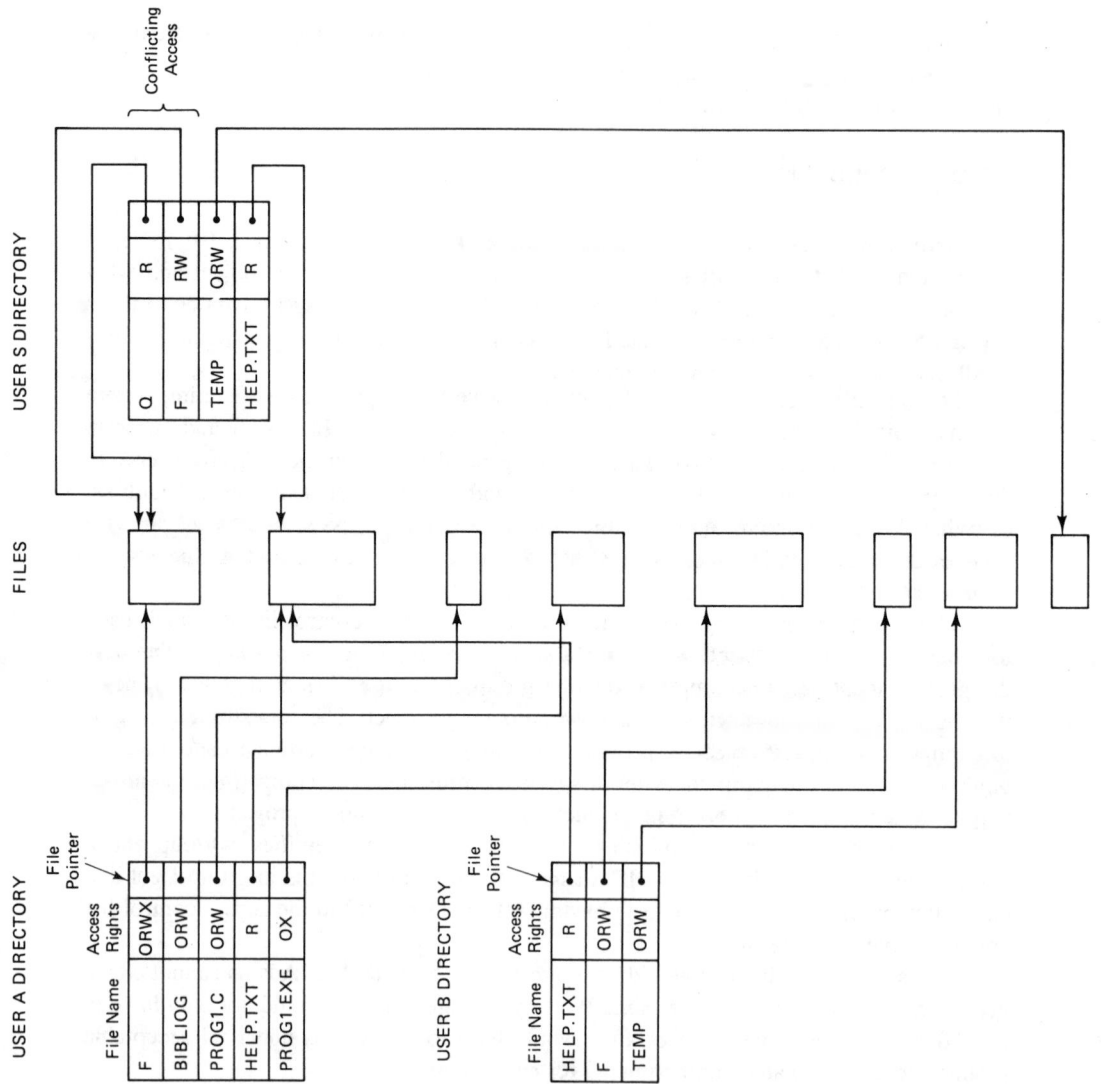

Figure 6.11 Alternate Access Paths.

216

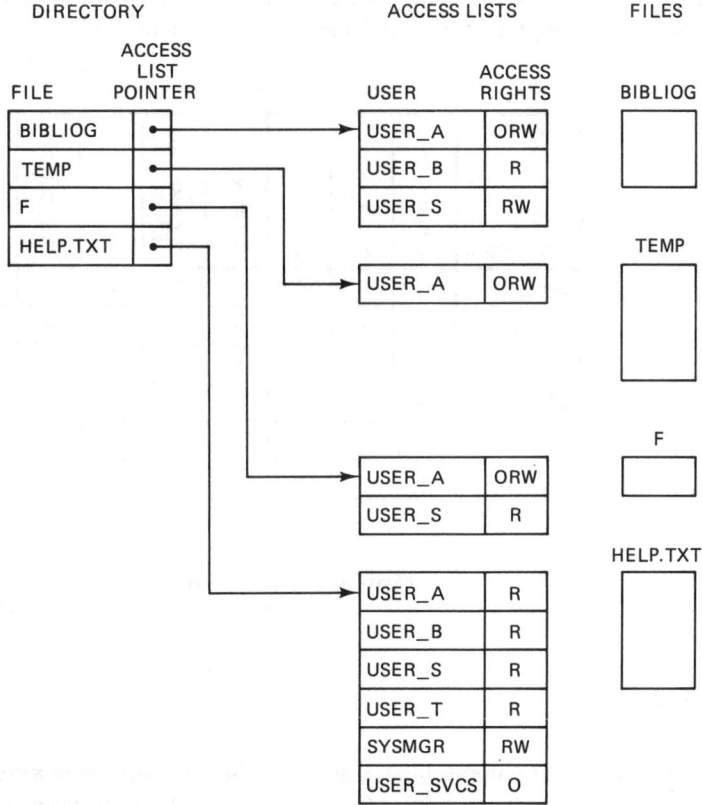

Figure 6.12   Access Control List.

on an access list could be *-*-*, specifying rights allowable to any user not explicitly on the access list. This device means that a shared public object can have a very short access list, explicitly naming those few subjects who should have access rights different from the default.

Access Control Matrix

Think of the directory as listing objects accessible by a single subject, and the access list as identifying subjects who can access a single object. The total data in these two representations is equivalent; the distinction is the ease of use in given situations.

An alternative is the **access control matrix**, which is a table in which each row represents a subject, each column represents an object, and each entry is the set of access rights for that subject to that object. A representation of an access control matrix is shown in Figure 6.13. In general, the access control matrix will be sparse: Most subjects will not have access rights to most objects. The access matrix can be represented as a list of triples, having the form ⟨*subject,object,rights*⟩. Searching a large number of these triples is inefficient enough that this implementation is seldom used.

Subjects \ Objects	BIBLIOG	TEMP	F	HELP.TXT	C_COMPILER	LINKER	SYS_CLOCK	PRINTER
User_A	ORW	ORW	ORW	R	X	X	R	W
User_B	R	–	–	R	X	X	R	W
User_S	RW		R	R	X	X	R	W
User_T	–	–	–	R	X	X	R	W
Sys MGR	–	–	–	RW	OX	OX	ORW	O
USER_Svcs	–	–	–	O	X	X	R	W

Figure 6.13   Access Control Matrix.

Capability

A **capability** is an unforgeable token giving the possessor certain rights to an object. A capability is analogous to a ticket to a movie or an ID card that cannot be duplicated. The MULTICS system [SAL74] and later CAL [LAM76] and HYDRA [WUL74] systems used capabilities for access control. The theory behind capabilities is that a subject can create new objects and can specify the operations allowable on those objects. Certainly users can create new objects such as files, data segments, or subprocesses; and it is reasonable for a user to specify the kinds of operations acceptable, such as read, write, or execute. But a user can also create completely new objects, such as new data structures, and define types of accesses previously unknown to the system.

A capability is a ticket giving permission to a subject to perform a certain type of access on an object. The ticket must be unforgeable. One way to make an unforgeable ticket is to not give the ticket directly to the user. Instead, the operating system holds all tickets on behalf of the users. A capability can be created only by specific request from a user to the operating system. Each capability also identifies the allowable accesses.

One possible access right to an object is *transfer* or *propagate*. A subject having this right can pass copies of capabilities to other subjects. Each of these capabilities also has a list of permitted types of accesses, one of which might also be *transfer*. In this instance, process A can pass a copy of a capability to B, who can then pass a copy to C. B can prevent further distribution of the capability (and therefore prevent further dissemination of the access right) by omitting the *transfer* right from the rights passed in the capability to C. B might still pass certain access rights to C, but not the right to propagate access rights to other subjects.

As a process executes, it operates in a **domain** or **local name space**. This is the collection of objects to which the process has access. A domain for a user at a given time might include some programs, files, data segments, and I/O devices such as a printer and a terminal. Such a domain is shown in Figure 6.14.

DOMAIN FOR MAIN

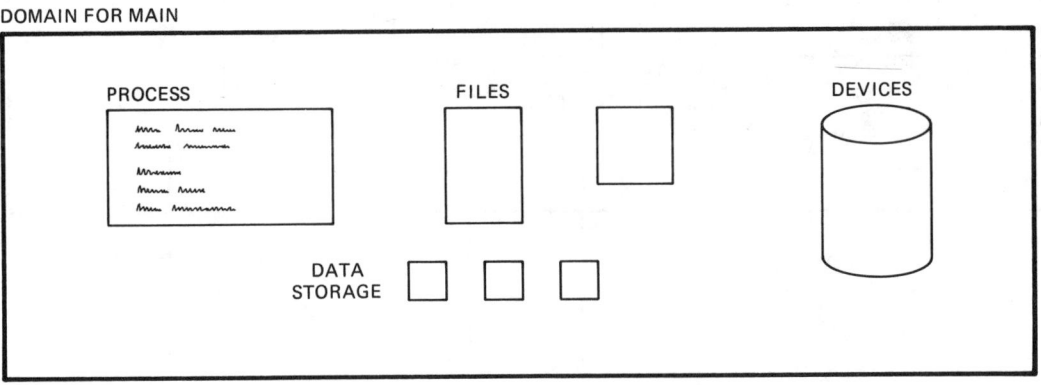

Figure 6.14   Process Execution Domain.

As execution continues, the process may call a subprocedure, passing some of the objects to which it has access as arguments to the subprocedure. The domain of the subprocedure is not necessarily the same as that of its calling procedure; in fact, a calling procedure may pass only some of its objects to the subprocedure, and the subprocedure may have access rights to other objects not accessible to the calling procedure. The caller may also pass only some of its access rights for the objects it passes to the subprocedure. For example, a procedure might pass to a subprocedure the right to read but not modify a particular data value.

Since each capability identifies a single object in a domain, the collection of capabilities defines the domain. When a process calls a subprocedure and passes certain objects to the subprocedure, the operating system forms a stack of all the capabilities of the current procedure. The operating system then creates new capabilities for the subprocedure, as shown in Figure 6.15.

Operationally, capabilities are a straightforward way to keep track of the access rights of subjects to objects during execution. The capabilities will be backed up by a more comprehensive table, such as an access control matrix or an access control list. Each time a process seeks to use a new object, the operating system examines the master list of objects and subjects to determine if the object is accessible. If so, the operating system creates a capability for that object.

Capabilities must be stored in memory inaccessible to normal users. One way of accomplishing this is to store capabilities in segments not pointed at by the user's segment table, or by enclosing them in protected memory as from a pair of base/bounds registers. Another approach is to use a tagged architecture machine to identify capabilities as structures requiring protection.

DOMAIN FOR MAIN

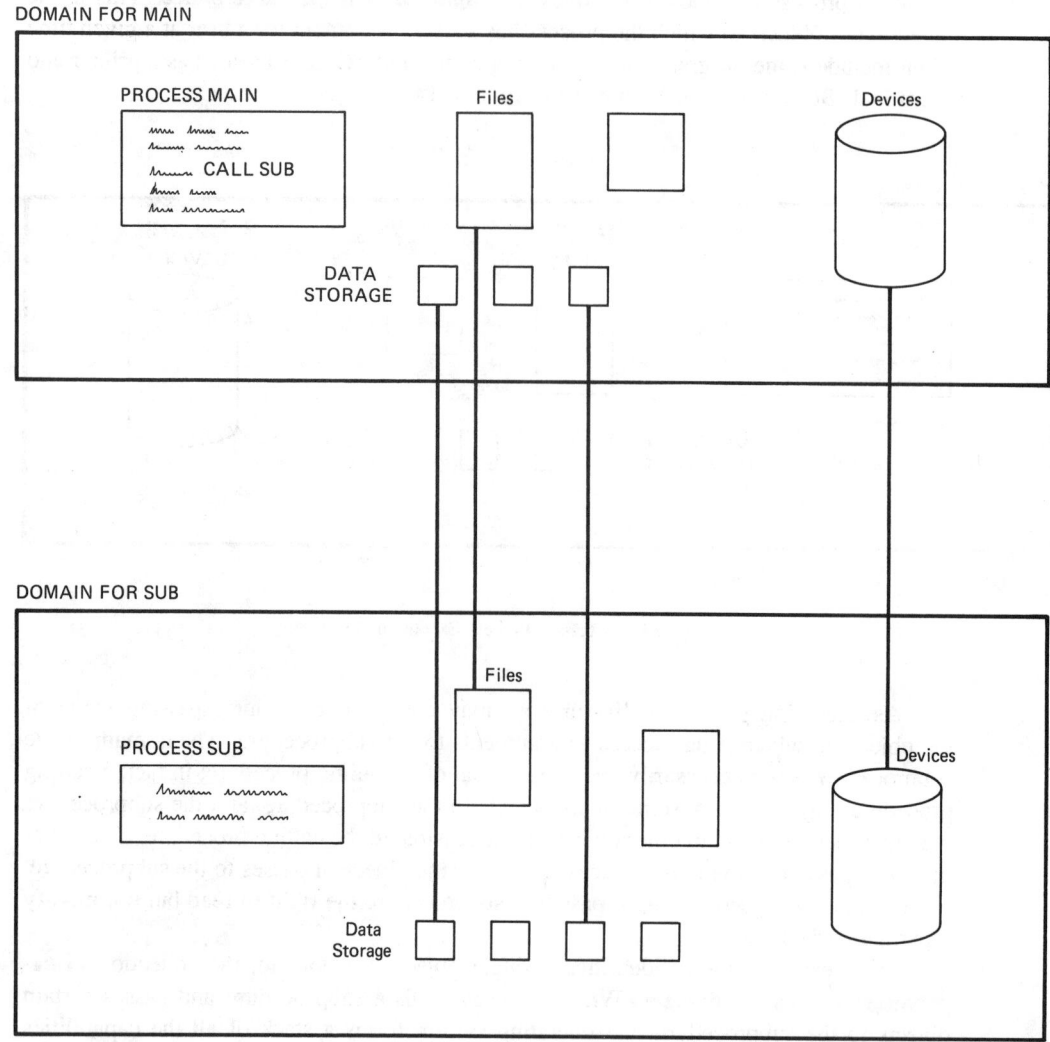

Figure 6.15   Passing Objects to a Subject.

During execution only the capabilities of objects that have been accessed by the current process are kept readily available. This restriction improves the speed with which access to an object can be checked. This approach is essentially the one used in MULTICS, as described in [FAB74].

A difficulty is that capabilities can be revoked. When an issuing subject revokes a capability, no further access under the revoked capability should be permitted. A capability table can contain pointers to the active capabilities spawned under it, so that the operating system can trace what access rights should be deleted if a capability is revoked. A similar problem is deleting capabilities for users who are no longer active.

Procedure-Oriented Access Control

A goal in access control is to restrict not just what subjects have access to an object, but also what they can *do* to that object. Read versus write access can be controlled rather readily by most operating systems, but more complex control is not so easy to achieve.

By **procedure-oriented** protection, we imply the existence of a procedure that controls access to objects (for example, by performing its own user authentication to strengthen that provided by the basic operating system). Essentially the procedure forms a capsule around the object, permitting only certain specified accesses.

Another feature of procedure-oriented protection is that the procedure can require that accesses to an object be done through a trusted interface. For example, neither users nor general operating system routines might be allowed direct access to the table of valid users. The only accesses might be through three procedures, one to add a user, one to delete a user, and one to check whether a particular name corresponds to a valid user. These procedures, especially add and delete, could employ their own checks to make sure that calls to them are legitimate.

Procedure-oriented protection implements the principle of information hiding, because the means of implementing an object is known only to the control procedure of the object. Of course, his degree of protection carries a penalty of efficiency. There can be no simple, fast access, even if the object is frequently used.

This survey of mechanisms for access control has intentionally progressed from simple to complex. As the mechanisms have provided greater flexibility, they have done so at the price of increased overhead. For example, implementing capabilities that must be checked on each access is far more difficult than implementing a simple directory structure that is checked only on a subject's first access to an object. This complexity is apparent both to the user and to the implementer. The user is aware of additional protection features, but the naive user may be frustrated or intimidated at having to select protection options with little understanding of their usefulness. The implementation complexity becomes apparent in slow response to users. The balance between simplicity and functionality is a continuing battle in security.

6.4 File Protection Mechanisms

Several existing programs or techniques for file protection are studied in this section. These examples are only representative; they do not cover all possible means of file protection on the market.

Basic Level Protection

As described earlier, all multiuser operating systems must provide some minimal protection to keep one user from maliciously or inadvertently accessing or modifying the files of another. As the number of users has grown, so also has the complexity of these protection schemes.

All-None Protection

In the original IBM OS operating systems, files were by default public. Any user could read, modify, or delete a file belonging to any other user. The principal protection was trust, combined with ignorance. The first supposition was that users could be trusted not to read or modify others' files, since the users would expect the same respect from others. Ignorance helped this situation, since a user could access a file only by name, and it was presumed that users knew the names of only those files to which they had legitimate access.

Certain system files were considered sensitive, and the system administrator could protect them with a password. A normal user could use this feature, but it was clearly most valuable for protecting files of the operating system. The password could control all accesses (read, write, or delete), or it could control only write and delete accesses, since only these had an effect on other users. The password mechanism required intervention by the system operator each time access to the file began.

This type of protection is unacceptable for several reasons.

- *Lack of trust:* The assumption about trustworthy users is not necessarily justified. For systems with few users who knew each other, mutual respect might suffice, but for large systems where not every user knows every other user, there is no basis for trust.

- *All or nothing:* Even if a user identifies a set of trustworthy users, there is no convenient way to allow access only to them.

- *Rise of timesharing:* This protection scheme is more appropriate for a batch environment, where users have little chance to interact with other users, and where users do their thinking and exploring off the system. On timesharing systems, users interact with other users. Since users choose when to execute programs, they are more likely to arrange computing tasks to be able to pass results from one program or one user to another.

- *Complexity:* Because (human) operator intervention is required, its use degrades the performance of the operating system. Its use is, therefore, discouraged by computing centers for all but the most sensitive data sets.

- *File listings:* For accounting purposes and to help users remember for what files they were responsible, various system utilities can produce a list of all files. Users are not ignorant of what files were on the system. Interactive users may try to browse through any unprotected files.

Group Protection

For reasons such as these, the next major development was the identification of *groups* of users who had some commonality. In a typical implementation, the world is divided into three classes: the user, a trusted working group associated with the user, and the rest of the users. For simplicity these can be called "user," "group," and "world." This form of protection is used on Digital Equipment Corp. DEC-10 computers, the UNIX system, and VAX VMS systems.

All authorized users are separated into groups. A group may be several members working on a common project, a department, a class, or a single user. The basis for selection of the group is *need to share*. The members of a group have some common interest and therefore are assumed to have files to share with the other members of the group. No user belongs to more than one group.

When creating a file, a user defines access rights to the file for the user, for other members of the same group, and for all other users in general. Typically the choices for access rights are a limited set, such as {read, write, execute, delete}. For a particular file, a user might declare read-only access to the general world, read- and write-access to the group, and all rights to the user. This would be appropriate for a paper being developed by a group, where the different members of the group might modify sections being written within the group, and the paper itself should be available for people outside the group to review but not change.

The implementation is easy. A user is recognized by two identifiers (usually numbers), a user ID and a group ID. These identifiers are stored in the file directory entry for each file and are obtained by the operating system when a user logs in. Therefore, it is simple to check whether a proposed access to a file is from someone whose group ID matched the group ID for the file to be accessed.

This protection scheme overcomes some of the shortcomings of the all-or-nothing scheme described earlier, and it has the advantage of being easy to implement. However, the scheme introduces some new difficulties of its own.

- *Group affiliation:* A single user cannot belong to two groups. Suppose Tom belongs to one group with Ann and a second group with Bill. If Tom indicates that a file is to be readable by the group, to which group(s) does this permission refer? Suppose a file of Ann's is readable by the group; does Bill have access to it? These ambiguities are most simply resolved by declaring that every user belongs to exactly one group. (This does not mean that all users belong to *the same* group.)

- *Multiple personalities:* To overcome the one-person one-group restriction, certain people could obtain multiple accounts, permitting them, in effect to be multiple users. This introduces new problems as a person can be only one user at a time. Suppose Tom obtains two accounts, thereby becoming Tom1 in a group with Ann and Tom2 in a group with Bill. Tom1 is not in the same group as Tom2, so any files, programs, or aids developed under the Tom1 account can be available to Tom2 only if they are available to the entire world. This solution leads to proliferation of accounts, redundant files, limited protection for files of general interest, and inconvenience to users.

- *Limited sharing:* Files can be shared only within groups or with the world. Users want to be able to identify sharing partners for a file on a per-file basis, for example, sharing one file with 10 people and another file with 20 others.

Single Permissions

The simplicity of implementing these schemes spawned other easy-to-manage methods that provided finer degrees of security. The next form of protection designed allowed a user to associate permission with a single file.

Password or Other Token

With the evolution of the IBM OS operating systems into MVS, a simpler form of password protection appeared. A user could assign a password to a file. User accesses were limited to those who supplied the correct password at the time the file was opened. The password could be required for any access or for modifications only.

Password access gives a user the effect of a different "group" for every file. However, file passwords suffer from difficulties similar to those of authentication passwords, such as the following:

- *Loss:* Depending on the implementation, it may be impossible to replace a lost (forgotten) password. The operator or system administrator can certainly intervene and unprotect or assign a particular password, but often they cannot determine what password a user has assigned; if the user loses the password, a new one will have to be assigned.

- *Disclosure:* If a password is disclosed to an unauthorized individual, the file becomes immediately accessible. If the user then changes the password to reprotect the file, all the other legitimate users must be informed of the new password, since their old password will fail.

- *Revocation:* To revoke one user's access right to a file, the password must be changed, which causes the same problems as disclosure.

Temporary Acquired Permission

An interesting permission scheme is provided by the UNIX operating system. As described previously, the basic protection is a three-level user-group-world hierarchy. One important addition is called the **set userid (suid)** permission. If this protection is set for a file to be executed, the protection level is that of the file's *owner*, not the *executor*. That is, if Tom owns a file and allows Ann to execute it, while Ann executes it she has the protection rights of Tom, not of herself.

This peculiar-sounding permission does have a useful application. It permits a user to establish data files to which access is allowed only through specified procedures.

For example, you might want to set up a computerized dating service that manipulates a data base of people available on particular nights. Sue might be interested in a date for Saturday, but she might have already refused a request from Jeff, saying she had other plans. Sue instructs the service not to reveal to Jeff that she is available. In order to use the service, Sue and Jeff and others must be able to read and write (at least indirectly) to the file to determine who is available or to post their availability. But if Jeff can read the file directly, he would find that Sue has lied. Therefore, your dating service must force Sue and Jeff (and all others) to access this file only through an access program that would screen the data Jeff obtains. But if the file access is limited to read and write by you, its owner, Sue and Jeff will never be able to enter data into it.

The solution is the UNIX SUID protection. You create the data base file, giving only you access permission. You also write the program that is to access the data base, and save it with the SUID protection. Then when Jeff executes your program, he temporarily acquires your access permission, only during execution of the program. Jeff never has direct access to the file, since your program will do the actual file access. When Jeff exits from your program, he regains his own access rights and loses yours. Thus, your program can access the file, but the program transfers only the data Jeff is allowed to see.

This mechanism is convenient for system functions which general users should be able to perform only in a prescribed way. For example, only the system should be able to modify the file of users' passwords, but individual users should be able to change their own passwords any time they wish. With the SUID feature, a password change program can be owned by the system, which will therefore have full access to the system password table. The program to change passwords also has SUID protection, so that when a normal user executes it, the program can modify the password file in a carefully constrained way on behalf of the user.

Per-Object and Per-User Protection

The primary limitation still existing with the protection schemes just described is the ability to create meaningful groups of related users who should have similar access to one or more data sets. The access control lists or access control matrices described earlier provide very flexible protection. Their disadvantage is for the user who wants to allow access to many users to many different data sets; such a user must still specify each data set to be accessed by each user. As a new user is added, that user's special access rights must be specified by all appropriate users.

VAX VMS/SE

Digital Equipment Corporation's VAX VMS-SE operating system (version 4.0 with security enhancements) provides access control lists (ACLs). A user can create an ACL for any file, specifying who has access to the file, and what type of access each person has.

Each user belongs to one group, as described earlier. Additionally, the system administrator can create effective groups by defining what are called "general identifiers." For example, a software project team might include Tom from group 1, Ann from group 2, and Bill and Sally from group 3; the system administrator can define a new general identifier, SOFTPROJ, which includes only those four people. A user can allow access to a file to people in the general identifier SOFTPROJ, without allowing access to any other users from groups 1, 2, or 3. The ACL lists specific users, groups, or general identifiers.

In VMS an ACL can also be applied to a specific device or device type, allowing users access only to certain printers, or restricting which users can enter the system through dialup (telephone) lines. Furthermore, network access and batch access to resources can also be limited through ACLs.

IBM RACF, ACF2

An IBM enhancement for the MVS operating system, RACF (Resource Access Control Facility) provides similar protection for its data sets. Two competitors are ACF2 and Top Secret. All of these systems allow the owner of a file to assign a default protection for a file (access allowed to any user), and then to refine that access for specific listed users.

The files can be identified individually or with a general file name. Once access has been given, it can also be revoked.

6.5 User Authentication

An operating system bases much of its protection on knowing who a user of the system is. In real life situations, people commonly ask for identification of people they don't know: a bank employee may ask for a driver's license before cashing a check, while library employees may require some identification before charging out books. Some universities do not give out grades over the telephone, because the office workers do not necessarily know the students calling. However, a professor who recognizes the voice of a certain student can give out that student's grades. People have developed systems of authentication using documents, voice recognition, and other trusted means of identification.

In computing, obviously, the situation is less secure. Anyone can attempt to login to a computing system. Unlike the professor who may recognize a student's voice, the computer cannot recognize electrical signals from one person as being any different from those of anyone else. Thus, most authentication systems must be based on some knowledge shared only by the computing system and the user.

The most common authentication mechanism is a **password**, a "word" known to computer and user. Although this would seem a relatively secure system, human practice sometimes degrades its quality. In this section we consider passwords, selection criteria, and authentication mechanisms. We conclude with the study of problems in the authentication process, notably Trojan horses masquerading as the computer authentication process, and other techniques of authentication.

Use of Passwords

Passwords are mutually agreed-upon code words, assumed to be known only to the user and the system. In some cases a user chooses passwords, while in other cases they are assigned by the system. The length and format of the password also vary from one system to another.

The use of passwords is fairly straightforward. A user enters some piece of identification, such as a name or an assigned user ID; this identification can be available to the public or easy to guess, because it does not provide the real security of the system. The system then requests a password from the user. If the password matches that on file for the user, the user is authenticated to the system. If the password match fails, the user may have mistyped, in which case the system requests the password again.

Loose-Lipped Systems

So far the process seems secure. Let us consider the actions of a would-be intruder. Authentication is based on knowing the ⟨*name*,*password*⟩ pair. A complete outsider is presumed to know nothing of the system. Suppose the intruder attempts to access a system in the following manner. (In the following examples, the system messages are in uppercase, while the user's responses are in lowercase.)

```
WELCOME TO THE XYZ COMPUTING SYSTEMS
ENTER USER NAME: adams
INVALID USER NAME--UNKNOWN USER
ENTER USER NAME:
```

We assumed that the intruder knew nothing of the system, but without having to do anything, the user found out that "adams" is not the name of an authorized user. The intruder could try other common names, first names, and likely generic names like "system" or "operator" to build a list of authorized users.

An alternate arrangement of the login sequence is shown here:

```
WELCOME TO THE XYZ COMPUTING SYSTEMS
ENTER USER NAME: adams
ENTER PASSWORD: john
INVALID ACCESS
ENTER USER NAME:
```

This system notifies a user of a failure only after accepting both the user name and the password. The failure message should not indicate whether it is the user name or password that is unacceptable. In this way, the intruder does not know which failed.

The previous examples also gave a clue as to which computing system is being accessed. The true outsider has no right to know that, while legitimate insiders already know what system they have accessed. In the following example, the user is given no information until the system is assured of the identity of the user.

```
ENTER USER NAME: adams
ENTER PASSWORD: john
INVALID ACCESS
ENTER USER NAME: adams
ENTER PASSWORD: johnq
WELCOME TO THE XYZ COMPUTING SYSTEMS
```

Additional Authentication Information

There is more information available to authenticate users. Suppose Adams works the shift between 8:00 am and 5:00 pm, Monday through Friday, and works in the accounting department. Any legitimate attempt by Adams should be during those times, through a terminal in the accounting department offices. By limiting Adams to logging in under those conditions, the system protects against two problems:

1. Someone from outside might try to impersonate Adams. This attempt would be thwarted either by the time of access or the port through which the access was attempted.

2. Adams might attempt to access the system from home or on a weekend, to use resources not allowed, or to do something that would be too risky with other people around.

Limiting users to certain terminals or to certain times of access can cause complications (as when a user legitimately needs to work overtime, or a person has to access the system while out of town on a business trip). However, some companies use those authentication techniques because the added security they provide outweighs these inconveniences.

Attacks on Passwords

How secure are passwords themselves? Passwords are somewhat limited as protection devices because of the relatively small number of bits of information they contain.
     Here are some ways you might be able to determine a user's password.

1. Try all possible passwords

2. Try many probable passwords

3. Try passwords likely for the user

4. Search for the system list of passwords

5. Ask the user

Of course, these are arranged in decreasing order of difficulty, although the later ones are, or at least should be, less likely to succeed.

Exhaustive Attack

In an **exhaustive** or **brute force** attack, the attacker tries all possible passwords. The number of possible passwords depends on the implementation of the particular computing system.
     If passwords are words, consisting of the 26 characters A–Z, and passwords can be of any length from 1 to 8 characters, there are 26^1 passwords of 1 character, 26^2

passwords of 2 characters, and 26^8 passwords of 8 characters. The system as a whole has $26^1 + 26^2 + \ldots + 26^8 = 26^9 - 1 \simeq 5 * 10^{12}$ possible passwords. That number seems intractable enough. At a rate of one password per millisecond (a very generous time estimate), it would still take on the order of 150 years to test all passwords.

Searching for a single particular password, however, does not necessarily require all those passwords to be tried. If the passwords were evenly distributed, half of the password space would be the expected number of searches to find any particular password. However, passwords are not evenly distributed. Since a password has to be remembered, people tend to pick simple passwords.

Probable Passwords

Think of a word.

Is the word you thought of long? Is it uncommon? Is it hard to spell or to pronounce? Likely the answer to all three of these questions is "no."

A penetrator searching for passwords realizes these characteristics of humans. Therefore, penetrators try techniques that are likely to lead to rapid success. If people prefer short passwords to long ones, the penetrator will try all passwords, but try them in order by length. There are only $26^1 + 26^2 + 26^3 = 18278$ passwords of length 3 or less. At the assumed rate of one password per millisecond, all of these passwords can be checked in 18.278 seconds, hardly a challenge with a computer. Even going to 4 or 5 characters raises the count to only 475 seconds (about 8 minutes) and 12,356 seconds (about 3.5 hours), respectively.

This approach assumes that people choose passwords such as "vxlag" and "msms" as often as they pick "enter" and "beer." However, people tend to choose names or words they can remember. Many computing systems have spelling checkers that can be used to check for spelling errors and typographic mistakes in documents. These spelling checkers sometimes carry on-line dictionaries of the most common English words. One contains a dictionary of 80,000 words. Trying all of these words takes only 80 seconds.

Passwords Likely for a User

If Sandy is picking a password, she is probably not choosing a word completely at random. Most likely Sandy's password is something meaningful to her. People typically choose personal passwords, such as the name of a spouse, a child, a brother or sister, a pet, a street name, or something similar. Selecting just names of people (first names), streets, projects, and so forth, produces a list of only a few hundred possibilities, at most. These can all be tried in under a second! Even a person working by hand could try ten likely candidates in a minute or two.

The likelihood of success in this approach is frightening. Morris and Thompson [MOR79] report on the results of having gathered passwords from many users over a long period of time. Table 6.1 (©1979, Association for Computing Machinery, Inc. Used by permission.) shows the characteristics of the 3289 passwords gathered. The results from that study are distressing, at the least. All of those passwords, 86% of the sample, could be uncovered in about one week's worth of 24-hour a day testing, using the very generous time of 1 millisecond per password check. But there is an even easier way to get passwords.

TABLE 6.1   DISTRIBUTION OF ACTUAL PASSWORDS

15 (0.5%)	were a single(!) ASCII character
72 (2%)	were two ASCII characters
464 (14%)	were three ASCII characters
477 (14%)	were four alphabetic letters
706 (21%)	were five alphabetic letters, all of the same case
605 (18%)	were six lower case alphabetic letters
492 (15%)	more were words in dictionaries or lists of names
2831 (86%)	total of all above categories

Finding a Plaintext System Password List

In order to validate passwords, the system must have a way of comparing entries with actual passwords. Rather than trying to guess a user's password, an attacker may instead target the system password file. Why guess when with one table you can determine passwords with total accuracy?

On some systems, the password list is a file, organized essentially as a two-column table of user ids and corresponding passwords. Certainly that is too obvious to leave out in the open. Various security approaches are used to conceal this table from those who should not see it.

One security device is to protect the table with strong access controls, limiting its access to the operating system. This is even looser than it should be, because not every module of the operating system needs or deserves access to this table. For example, the operating system scheduler, or accounting routines, or storage manager have no need to know the contents of that table. Unfortunately, in some systems, there are $n + 1$ known users: n regular users and the operating system. The operating system is not divided, so that all its modules have access to all privileged information. This implies that a user who exploits a flaw in one section of the operating system has access to all the deepest secrets of the system. A better approach, then, is to limit the access to this table to those modules who need access—the user authentication module and the parts associated with installing new users, for example.

Dumping memory at a convenient time is another way to get access to a password table if the table is stored in plain sight. A user who can time things carefully may be able to dump the contents of all of memory and, by exhaustive search, find values that look like the password table.

System backups can also be used to obtain the password table. In order to be able to recover from system errors, periodically the file space is backed up onto some auxiliary medium, often magnetic tape, for safe storage. In the unlikely event of a problem, the file system can be reloaded from a backup, with a loss of only those changes since the last backup. Backup tapes often contain only file contents; usually there is no protection mechanism to control access to the files on a backup tape. (Physical security and access controls to the tapes themselves are depended upon to provide security for the contents of backup tapes.) If a regular user can access these tapes, even ones from several weeks, months, or years ago, the password table stored in them may still contain some valid entries.

Encrypted Password File

It is safer to encrypt the password list so that reading it will not help the penetrator. Two commonly used ways to encrypt the password list are conventional encryption and one-way ciphers. These methods of protection are described in this section.

With conventional encryption, the entire password table is encrypted, or perhaps just the password column. When a user's password is received, the stored password is decrypted, and the two are compared.

There is still a slight exposure with this method. For an instant the user's password is available in plaintext in main memory. It is available to anyone who could obtain access to all of memory.

A safer approach uses one-way encryption—an encryption function for which encryption is relatively easy and decryption is relatively hard. For example, the function x^3 is easy to compute, but its inverse, $\sqrt[3]{x}$ is far harder. The password in the password table is stored in encrypted form. When the user enters a password, it too is encrypted, and the encrypted forms are compared. If the two forms are equal, the authentication succeeds. Of course, the encryption has to be such that it is unlikely that two passwords would encrypt to the same ciphertext, but this characteristic is true for most secure encryption algorithms.

With one-way encryption the password file can be stored in plain view; in fact, the password table for the UNIX operating system can be read by any user, unless special access controls have been installed. Backup copies of the password table are also not a problem.

Two people might choose the same password, which would create two identical entries in the password file. Even though these entries are encrypted, each user will know the plaintext equivalent. If Bill and Kathy both choose their passwords on April 1, they might choose APRILFOOL as a password. Bill might read the password file and notice that the encrypted version of his password is the same as that of Kathy.

UNIX circumvents this flaw by using a password extension, called the "salt." The salt is a 12-bit number formed from the system time and the process identifier. Thus, the salt is likely to be unique for each user. The salt is concatenated to Bill's password (pw) when he chooses it; $E(pw + \text{salt})$ is stored for Bill, and the salt value is also stored. When Kathy chooses her password, the salt is different, because the time or the process number is different. Call this new one salt_K. For her, $E(pw + \text{salt}_K)$ and salt_K are stored. When either tries to login, the system fetches the appropriate salt from the password table and combines that with the password before performing the encryption. The encrypted versions of pw+salt are very different for these two users. When Bill looks down the password list, the encrypted version of his password will not look at all like Kathy's.

Storing the password file in a disguised form relieves much of the pressure to secure it. Access may still be limited to those processes that have a legitimate need for access. However, securing the *contents* of the table as well as access to the table provides a second layer of security. Someone who successfully penetrates the outer security layer does not get access to useful information.

Asking the User

The easiest way to obtain unauthorized access may be simply to obtain the password directly from the user. It is not uncommon to find a password taped to the side of a terminal or written on a card just inside the top desk drawer. Users are afraid they will forget their passwords or cannot be bothered by trying to remember them. Users with several accounts are especially tempted to write the passwords down.

Users sharing work or data may also be tempted to share passwords. If someone needs a file, it is easier to say "my password is x; get the file yourself" than to arrange to share the file. This situation is certainly a result of user weakness, but it may be brought about by a system that makes sharing inconvenient.

Password Selection Criteria

The preceding discussion leads to some conclusions regarding appropriate passwords. Passwords should be hard to guess and hard to determine exhaustively. The security needs of the situation also affect password selection. Here are some suggestions regarding password selection.

- *Use more than A–Z.* If passwords are chosen from the letters A–Z, there are only 26 possibilities. Adding digits expands the number of possibilities to 36. Using both upper case and lower case letters plus digits expands the number of possibilities to 62. Although this change seems small, the effect is large when testing a full space of all possible combinations of characters. It takes about 100 hours to test all 6-letter words from letters of one case only, while it takes about two years to test all 6-symbol passwords from upper and lower case letters and digits. While 100 hours is reasonable, two years is oppressive enough to make this attack far less attractive.

- *Choose long passwords.* The combinatorial explosion of passwords begins at length 4 or 5. Choosing 6-character or longer passwords makes it less likely that a password will be uncovered. Remember that a brute force penetration can stop as soon as the password is found. Some penetrators will try the easy cases—known words and short passwords—and move on to another target if those attacks fail.

- *Avoid actual names or words.* Theoretically there are 26^6 or about 300 million "words" of length 6, but there are only about 150,000 words in a good collegiate dictionary, ignoring length. By picking one of the 99.95% nonwords, you force the attacker to use a longer brute force search, instead of the abbreviated dictionary search.

- *Choose an unlikely password.* Password choice is a double bind. In order to remember the password easily, you want one that has special meaning to you. However, you don't want someone else to be able to guess this special meaning. One easy-to-remember password is 2Brn2B. That unlikely-looking jumble is a simple transformation of "to be or not to be." The first letters of a line from a song, a few letters from different words of a private phrase, or a memorable football score are examples of reasonable passwords.

- *Change the password regularly.* Even if there is no reason to suspect that the password has been compromised, change is advised. A penetrator may break a password system by obtaining an old list or working exhaustively on an encrypted list.

- *Don't write it down.*

- *Don't tell anyone else.*

To help users select good passwords, some systems provide meaningless but pronounceable passwords. For example, the VAX VMS system randomly generates five passwords from which the user chooses one. They are pronounceable, so that the user should be able to repeat and memorize them. However, it is easy to interchange syllables or letters of a meaningless string.

Other systems encourage users to change their passwords regularly. The regularity of password change is usually a system parameter, which can be changed for the characteristics of a given installation. Suppose the frequency is set at 30 days. Some systems begin to warn the user after 25 days that the password is about to expire. Others wait until 30 days and inform the user that the password has expired. Some systems nag without end, while other systems cut off a user's access if a password has expired. Other systems force the user immediately into the password change utility on the first login after 30 days.

Morris [MOR84] argues that this process is not necessarily good. Choosing passwords is not difficult, but under pressure a user may adopt any password, just to satisfy the system's demand for a new password. Furthermore, if this is the only time when a password can be changed, a user who selects a bad password and realizes it cannot change until the next scheduled time.

Some systems force users to change passwords periodically. Users with favorite passwords alternate between two passwords each time a change is required. To prevent password reuse, IBM MVS systems refuse to accept any of the most recently used passwords. One user of such a system went through 24 password changes each month, just to cycle back to the favorite password.

One-Time Passwords

A **one-time password** is one that changes every time it is used. Instead of assigning a static phrase to a user, the system assigns a static mathematical function. The system provides an argument to the function, and the user computes and returns the function value. Such systems are also called **challenge-response** systems, since the system presents a challenge to the user and judges the authenticity of the user by the user's response. Here are some simple examples of one-time password functions; these functions are overly simplified just to make the explanation easier. Very complex functions can be used in place of these simple ones for host authentication in a network.

- $f(x) = x + 1$. With this function, the system prompts with a value for x, and the user enters the value $x + 1$. The kinds of mathematical functions used are limited only by the ability of the user to compute the response quickly and easily. Other similar possibilities are $f(x) = 3x^2 - 9x + 2$, $f(x) = p_x$ where p_x is the x-th prime number, or $f(x) = d * h$ where d is the date and h is the hour of the current time.

- $f(x) = r(x)$. For this function, the receiver uses the argument as the seed for a random number generator (available to both the receiver and host). The user replies with the value of the first random number generated. A variant of this scheme uses x as a number of random numbers to generate. The receiver generates x random numbers and sends the x-th of these to the host.

- $f(a_1 a_2 a_3 a_4 a_5 a_6) = a_3 a_1 a_1 a_4$. With this function, the system provides a character string, which the user must transform in some manner. Again many different character operations can be used.

- $f(E(x)) = E(D(E(x)) + 1)$. In this function, the computer sends an encrypted value, $E(x)$. The user must decrypt the value, perform some mathematical function, and encrypt the result to return it to the system. Clearly, for human use, the encryption function must be something that can be done easily by hand, unlike DES. For machine to machine authentication, however, an encryption algorithm such as DES is appropriate.

One-time passwords are very secure for authentication, since an intercepted password is useless. However, their usefulness is limited by the complexity of algorithms people can be expected to remember. A password generating device, similar to a pocket calculator, can implement more complex functions, but such a device can be lost or stolen.

The Authentication Process

Authentication usually operates in the manner outlined. Users, however, will occasionally mistype their passwords. A user who receives a message of INCORRECT LOGIN will carefully retype the login and gain access to the system. Even a user who is a terrible typist should be able to login successfully in three to five tries.

Some authentication procedures are intentionally slow. It is not inconvenient to a legitimate user if the login process takes 5 or 10 seconds. To a penetrator who is trying an exhaustive search or a dictionary search, though, 5 or 10 seconds per trial makes this class of attack generally infeasible.

Someone who continually fails to login may not be an authorized user. Systems commonly disconnect a user after three to five failed logins, forcing the user to reestablish a connection with the system. (This action will slow down a penetrator who is trying to penetrate the system by telephone. After a small number of failures, the penetrator must redial, which takes a few seconds.)

In more secure installations, stopping penetrators is more important than tolerating users' mistakes. For example, the developers of one system assume that all legitimate users can type their passwords correctly within three tries. After three successive password failures, the account for that user is disabled, and it can be reenabled only by the security administrator. This action identifies accounts that may be the target of attacks by penetrators.

Flaws in the Authentication Process

Password authentication assumes that anyone who knows a password is the user to whom the password belongs. As we have already seen, however, passwords can be guessed, deduced, or inferred. Some people will give out their passwords for the asking. Other passwords have been obtained just by watching a user typing in the password. The password, then, is a piece of evidence, but skeptics will want more convincing proof.

Challenge-Response Systems

The login is usually time-invariant. Except for password changes, each login looks like every other. A more sophisticated login requires a user id and password, followed by a **challenge-response** interchange. The system prompts the user for a reply that will be different each time the user logs in. For example, the system might display a four-digit number, and the user would have to correctly enter a function such as the sum or product of the digits. Each user is assigned a different challenge function to compute. Since there are many possible challenge functions, a penetrator who captures the user id and password cannot necessarily infer the proper function. A physical device similar to a calculator can be used to implement a more complicated response function. The user enters the challenge number, and the device computes and displays the response for the user to type in order to login.

Impersonation of Login

In the systems we have described, the proof is one-sided. The system demands certain identification of the user, but the user is supposed to trust the system. A programmer can easily write a program that displays the standard prompts for user id and password, captures the pair entered, stores the pair in a file, displays SYSTEM ERROR; DISCONNECTED and exits. This attack is a type of Trojan horse. The perpetrator sets it up, leaves the terminal unattended, and waits for an innocent victim to attempt a login. The naive victim may not even suspect that a security breach has occurred.

To foil this type of attack, the user should be sure the path to the system is reinitialized each time. On some systems turning the terminal off and on again or pressing the BREAK key generates a clear signal to the computer to halt any running process for the terminal. Not every computer recognizes power off or BREAK as an interruption of the current process, however.

Alternatively, the user can be suspicious of the computing system, just as the system is suspicious of the user. The user will not enter confidential data (such as a password) until convinced that the computer is legitimate. Of course, the computer acknowledges the user only after passing the authentication process. A computing system can display some information known only by the user and the system. For example, the system might read the user's name and reply "YOUR LAST LOGIN WAS 10 APRIL AT 09:47." The user can verify that the date and time are correct before entering a secret password. If higher security is desired, the system can send an encrypted time stamp. The user decrypts this and discovers that the time is current. The user then replies with an encrypted time stamp and password, in order to convince the system that a malicious intruder has not intercepted a password from some prior login.

Authentication without or in Addition to Passwords

Several physical devices to assist authentication are described in Chapter 12. These devices include handprint detectors, voice recognizers, and identifiers of patterns in the retina. Authentication with such devices uses unforgeable physical characteristics to authenticate users. Although expensive and experimental, these devices are useful in very high security situations.

More normal security needs can be handled by a combination of login and characteristics. As already described, a user may be restricted to terminals in certain physical locations or during certain hours. Another characteristic might be pattern of access. A user who sought access to files for which there was no justifiable reason might not be authentic. After a system detects such an access violation attempt, the system might disconnect the user and suspend access until a security administrator cleared the matter. Therefore, a penetrator who gets into the system as Jones has to continue to act like Jones in order to remain on the system.

Authentication is a very important matter for an operating system, because accurate identification of users is the key to individual access rights. Most operating systems and computing system administrators have applied reasonable but stringent security measures to lock out illegal users before they can access system resources.

6.6 Summary of Security for Users

This chapter has addressed four topics—memory protection, file protection, general object access control, and user authentication. Memory protection in a multiuser setting has evolved with advances in hardware and system design. Fences, base/bounds registers, tagged architecture, paging, and segmentation are all mechanisms designed both for addressing and for protection.

File protection schemes on general-purpose operating systems are often based on a three- or four-level format (for example, user-group-all). This format is reasonably straightforward to implement, but it restricts the granularity of access control to few levels.

Access control in general is addressed by the access control matrix or access control lists organized on a per-object or per-user basis. Although very flexible, these mechanisms can be difficult to implement efficiently.

User authentication is a serious issue which becomes even more serious when unacquainted users seek to share facilities by means of computer networks. The traditional authentication device is the password. A plaintext password file presents a serious vulnerability for a computing system. These files are usually either heavily protected or encrypted. The more serious problem, however, is establishing administrative procedures that make users' passwords adequately secure. Additional protocols are needed to perform mutual authentication in an atmosphere of distrust.

This chapter has concentrated on the user's side of protection. Protection mechanisms visible to and employed by users of operating systems have been presented. The next chapter addresses security from the perspective of the operating system designer. Chapter 7 includes material on how the security features of an operating system are implemented, and why security considerations should be a part of the initial design of the operating system.

6.7 Bibliographic Notes

The survey article by Denning and Denning [DEN77] presents a good background on access control in operating systems, and the paper by Linden [LIN76] describes operating systems components that affect protection. Lampson [LAM71], Graham and Denning [GRA72], Popek [PO74], and Saltzer [SAL74] and [SAL75] are good treatments of protection in operating systems.

Capability-based protection is described in Fabry [FAB74] and Wulf [WUL74]. Lampson and Sturgis [LAM76] discuss the subject in general.

Several other papers on different aspects of operating system design are cited in the bibliographic notes for Chapter 7.

6.8 Terms and Concepts

single-user system
sensitive data
executive
multiprogrammed system
protected objects
memory
sharable I/O devices
serially reusable I/O devices
sharable programs and data
physical separation
temporal separation
logical separation

cryptographic separation
isolation
memory protection
fence
fence register
relocation
base/bounds registers
tagged memory architecture
segmentation
logical program
segment address table
segment address translation
paging
page frame
page address translation
paged segmentation
directory
revocation of access
access control list
user-group-world protection
access control matrix
capability
domain
local name space
file protection
shared files
acquired permission
temporary access permission
per-object protection
per-subject protection
user authentication
password
password response
impersonation
exhaustive attack on password
brute force attack on password
probable password
likely password
system password list
one-way encryption
UNIX password salt
authentication
challenge-response
login impersonation
physical device authentication

6.9 Exercises

1. Give an example of the use of physical separation for security in a computing environment.

2. Give an example of the use of temporal separation for security in a computing environment.

3. Give an example of an object whose security level may change during execution.

4. Respond to the allegation, "An operating system requires no protection for its executable code (in memory) since that code is a duplicate of code maintained on disk."

5. Explain how a fence register is used for relocation of a user's program.

6. Can any number of concurrent processes be protected from each other by just one pair of base/bounds registers?

7. The discussion of base/bounds registers implies that program code is execute only, and data areas are read-write-only. Is this ever not the case? Explain your answer.

8. A design using tag bits presupposes that adjacent memory locations hold dissimilar things: a line of code, a piece of data, a line of code, two pieces of data, and so forth. Most programs do not look like that. How can tag bits be appropriate in a situation where programs have the more conventional arrangement of code and data?

9. What are some other levels of protection that users might want to apply to code or data, in addition to the common *read, write,* and *execute* permission?

10. If two users share access to a segment, they must do so by the same name. Must their protection rights to it be the same? Why or why not?

11. A problem with segmented and with paged address translation is I/O. Suppose a user wishes to read some data from an input device into memory. For efficiency during data transfer, often the actual memory address where the data is to be placed is provided to the I/O device. The real address is passed so that time-consuming address translation will not have to be performed during a very fast data transfer. What security problems does this approach bring?

12. A directory is also an object to which access should be controlled. Why is it *not* appropriate to allow a user to modify his or her own directory directly?

13. Why should the directory of one user not be generally accessible (for read-only access) to other users?

14. Describe each of the following four kinds of access control mechanisms in terms of *(a)* ease of determining authorized access during execution, *(b)* ease of adding access for a new subject, *(c)* ease of deleting access by a subject, and *(d)* ease of creating a new object to which all subjects by default have access.

1. Per-subject access control list. (That is, one list for each subject tells all the objects to which that subject has access.)
2. Per-object access control list. (That is, one list for each object tells all the subjects who have access to that object.)
3. Access control matrix.
4. Capability.

15. Suppose a per-subject access control list is used. Deleting an object in such a system is very inconvenient, since all changes must be made to the control lists of all subjects who did have access to the object. Suggest an alternate, less costly means of handling deletion.

16. File access control relates largely to the secrecy dimension of security. What is the relationship between an access control matrix and the integrity of the objects to which access is being controlled?

17. One feature of a capability-based protection system is the ability of one process to transfer a copy of a capability to another process. Describe a situation in which it is desirable for one process to be able to transfer a capability to another.

18. Describe a mechanism by which an operating system can enforce *limited* transfer of capabilities. That is, process A might transfer a capability to process B, but A wants to prevent B from transferring the capability to any other processes.
Your design should include description of the activities to be performed by A and B, as well as the activities performed by and the information maintained by the operating system.

19. List two disadvantages to using physical separation in a computing system. List two disadvantages to using temporal separation in a computing system.

20. Explain why asynchronous I/O activity is a problem with many memory protection schemes, including base/bounds and paging. Suggest a solution to the problem.

21. Suggest an efficient scheme for maintaining a per-user protection scheme. That is, the system maintains one directory per user, and that directory lists all the objects to which the user is allowed access. Your design should address the needs of a system with 1000 users, of whom no more than 20 are active at any time. Each user has an average of 200 permitted objects; there are 50,000 total objects in the system.

22. (a) If passwords are three uppercase alphabetic characters long, how long is needed to determine a particular password, assuming that testing an individual password requires 5 seconds.
(b) Argue for a particular amount of time as the starting point for "secure." That is, argue that an attacker would use a brute force attack to determine a password if the attack took less than x amount of time.
(c) If the cutoff between "insecure" and "secure" was x amount of time, how long would a secure password have to be? State and justify your assumptions regarding character set from which the password is selected and also about the amount of time required to test a single password.

23. Design a protocol by which two mutually suspicious parties can authenticate each other. Your protocol should be usable the first time these two parties try to authenticate each other.

24. A flaw in the protection system of many operating systems is argument passing. Often a common shared stack is used by all nested routines for arguments as well as the remainder of the context of each calling process.
   (a) Explain what vulnerabilities this flaw presents.
   (b) Explain how the flaw can be controlled. The shared stack is still to be used for passing arguments and storing context.

25. Outline the design of an authentication scheme that "learns." The authentication scheme would start with certain primitive information about a user, for example, name and password. As the use of the computing system continued, the authentication system would gather such information as commonly used programming languages; dates, times, and lengths of computing sessions; use of distinctive resources. The authentication challenges would become more individualized as the system learned more information about the user.
   Your design should include a list of many pieces of information about a user that the system could collect. It is permissible for the system to ask an authenticated user for certain additional information, such as favorite book, to use in subsequent challenges. Your design should also consider the problem of presenting and validating these challenges: Does the would-be user answer a true-false or a multiple-choice question? Does the system interpret natural language prose?

7

Design of Secure Operating Systems

Operating systems are the prime providers of security in computing systems. They support many programming concepts, permit multiprogramming and sharing of resources, and enforce restrictions on program behavior. Because they have such power, operating systems are also targets for attack, since breaking through the defenses of an operating system gives access to the secrets of computing systems.

In the last chapter we considered operating systems from the perspective of users: What security services does an operating system provide? The four services that we studied were:

1. memory protection

2. file protection

3. general object protection

4. access authentication

In this chapter we take the position of an operating system designer: What components of an operating system provide security services, and how are these components designed? The four parts of this chapter address four stages of the development of a secure operating system. These stages are:

1. *Models.* Before beginning to create a secure operating system, the designer must know what security is. The designer constructs a model of the environment to be secured and studies different ways of enforcing that security. In the first part of this chapter we consider several different models for operating system security.

2. *Design*. After having selected a model of security, the designer chooses a means to implement that model. The second part of this chapter addresses choices that can be made in the design of a secure operating system.

3. *Trust*. Assurance of correctness is closely related to design. Users and designers both want to know that a particular operating system enforces the security policies encompassed in the model. People from designers to users need assurance that the design correctly represents the model, and that the code correctly implements the design. In the third part of this chapter we explore what makes a particular design or implementation worthy of trust.

4. *Implementation*. Several secure operating systems have been written, and more are under development. Some secure systems were originally designed for security; in others, security features were added to existing operating systems. The fourth part of this chapter presents examples of both of these ways to produce a secure operating system.

7.1 Models of Security

In Chapter 1 we introduced security in computing systems and presented three basic security requirements, which were secrecy, integrity, and availability. These three requirements describe the *access* of users to computing systems. In this section we consider the properties we want a secure operating system to enforce. We construct **models** to describe security properties of computing systems and users. Because access is at the heart of the security requirements of computing systems, access control is the basis of these models.

Throughout this chapter we assume that some access control **policy** dictates whether a given user can access a particular object. We also assume that this policy is established outside of any model. That is, a policy decision determines whether a specific user should have access to a specific object; the model is only a mechanism that implements that policy. We begin the study of models by considering simple ways to control access by one user.

Single-Level Models

In this section we examine two different representations of access. Both models are appropriate for the basic situation in which the access policy specifies a simple "yes" or "no" for each user-object pair. An example of such a situation is one in which an access control matrix determines access.

Monitor Model

The simplest model of access control is the monitor. A **monitor** (also called a **reference monitor**) is a gate between a user and an object, as shown in Figure 7.1. The user seeks

a particular type of access to an object by invoking the monitor. The monitor takes the
user's request, consults access control information as necessary, and allows or disallows
the access. The concept of a monitor is presented by Brinch-Hansen [BRI72] and Hoare
[HOA74], although the same basic idea is inherent in the work of Lampson [LAM69]
and Graham and Denning [GRA72].

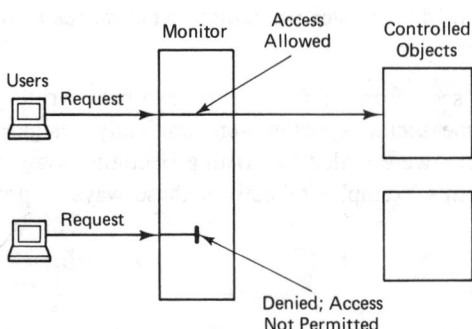

Figure 7.1   Monitor Model of Access.

A monitor is easy to implement. However, it suffers from two important limitations.
First, the monitor process will be heavily used, which may cause it to become a bottleneck
in the computing system. Each monitored access to an object must be checked, so that
the monitor will be invoked many times by many users. (To overcome this bottleneck,
some implementations of monitors retain data from an initial authorization of a user's
access; on subsequent accesses the monitors consult the retained data in order to improve
access speed.)

The second limitation of monitors is that they control only direct accesses. Consider
the example of the following program.

> **if** *profit* $<= 0$
> > **then** delete file T
> > **else begin**
> > > write file T, "*message*";
> > > close file T
> >
> > **end**

This program passes information about the value of *profit* through the existence of file
T. The user running this program presumably has legitimate access to *profit*. However,
some users may have access to T without having access to *profit*. In this example, the
existence of file T gives information about the value of *profit*. This weakness led to the
development of another model for access security.

Information Flow Model

Recognizing this weakness in the monitor model of access control, Denning [DEN76]
proposed the information flow model. Pictorially, this model acts as an intelligent filter

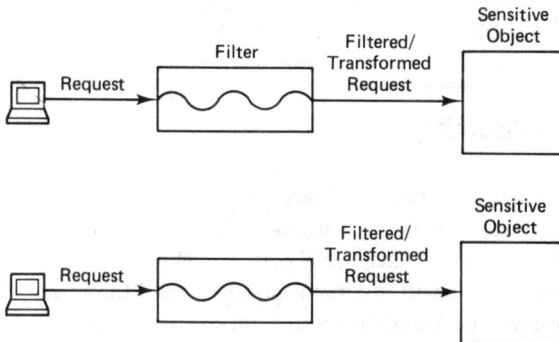

Figure 7.2   Information Flow Model.

to control the transfer of information permitted by access to a particular object. An information flow model of security is shown in Figure 7.2.

Denning was apparently the first to recognize that a user could infer information other than what the user explicitly requested. An example of information flow occurs at the level of data access within a program. Clearly in each of the following statements, information flows to a from b.

$$a := b;$$
$$a := b + c;$$
$$a := a + b;$$

However, the information flow in the following statement is more subtle. The user can learn whether the value of b was 0, without accessing b directly.

if $b = 0$ **then** $a := 0$ **else** $a := 1$

Information about b can be inferred from the value of a.

Suppose a module has access to sensitive data, but the module is to be called by users who should not have access to the sensitive data. For example, the module might perform password checking in a computing system. The module needs access to a table of all passwords for all users. However, a caller of the module should find out only that the supplied password matched or did not match the actual password of the user. Thus, the module has access to the sensitive password table, but should not be able to pass that sensitive data to any other modules or users.

Denning and Denning, in [DEN77], showed that the information flow model could be used to describe potential access as a program was *compiled*, that is, before running the program. Their procedure, which could be implemented by a compiler, involves analysis of the information flow for each statement in the program. This analysis can prove that supposedly nonsensitive outputs from a module are not affected in any way by accesses of the module to sensitive data. Therefore, the proof verifies that a user will not obtain unauthorized data as a result of calling the module.

The information flow model can be implemented on objects as small as single data items within a program. Naturally, it can also apply to larger objects, such as files, as well. Information flow analysis can assure us that operating system modules that have access to sensitive data cannot leak that data to calling modules. Therefore, recognizing information flow is an important step in developing trustworthy operating systems.

Lattice Model of Multi-Level Security

In the previous two models, security has been a binary property: An object was either sensitive or not, and a user was either authorized access or not. For a single user and a single object the access decision is still either "yes" or "no." However, in general we want to consider a range of degrees of sensitivity, both for objects and for users. We also want to model systems that concurrently handle pieces of information at several different degrees of sensitivity.

As an example of a range of sensitive data, consider an election. The names of the candidates are probably not sensitive. If the results have not yet been released, the name of the winner is somewhat sensitive. If one candidate received an embarrassingly low number of votes, the vote count may be more sensitive. Finally, the way any individual voted is extremely sensitive. Users, too, are ranked by the degree of sensitivity of information to which they can have access.

For obvious reasons, the military has developed extensive procedures for securing information. A generalization of the military model of information security has also been adopted as a model of data security within an operating system. The generalized model is called the **lattice model** of security, because its elements form a mathematical structure called a "lattice." In this section we describe the military example and then use it to explain the lattice model.

Military Security Model

In the military, each piece of information is ranked as *unclassified*, *confidential*, *secret*, or *top secret*. These ranks, which are disjoint, describe the sensitivity of the information. The ranks are shown in increasing order in Figure 7.3.

People use sensitive data to do work. One security principle we have previously identified is the principle of *least privilege:* A subject should have access to the fewest objects needed for the subject to work successfully. Therefore, people should not have access to all *top secret* information; they should have access only to that information necessary for them to do their work. Thus, an accountant would have reason to access certain sensitive financial data, but would not need to know the locations of all suspected terrorist camps. Information access is limited by the **need-to-know** rule: Access to sensitive data is allowed only to subjects who need to know that data to perform their jobs.

Each piece of classified information is associated with one or more projects, called **compartments**, describing the subject matter of the information. Compartments are used to enforce need-to-know restrictions, so that people can obtain access only to information whose content is relevant to their jobs.

Examples of compartments are *atomic*, *cryptographic*, and *USSR*. A single piece of information is coded with one, two, or more compartments, depending on the categories to which it relates. The association of information and projects is shown in Figure 7.4. For

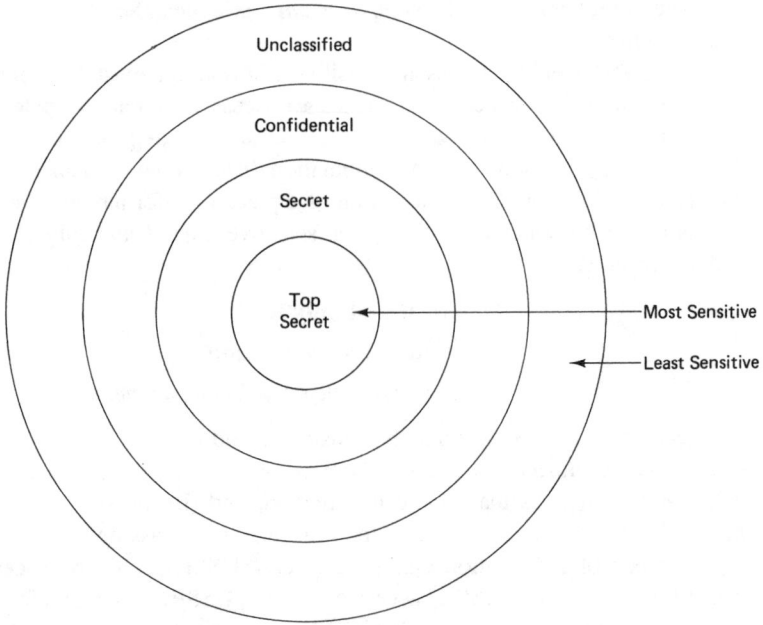

Figure 7.3   Hierarchy of Ranks.

example, one piece of information may be a list of publications on cryptography, while another may describe development of atomic weapons in the USSR. The compartment of this first piece of information is {*cryptographic*}, while the second is {*atomic, USSR*}.

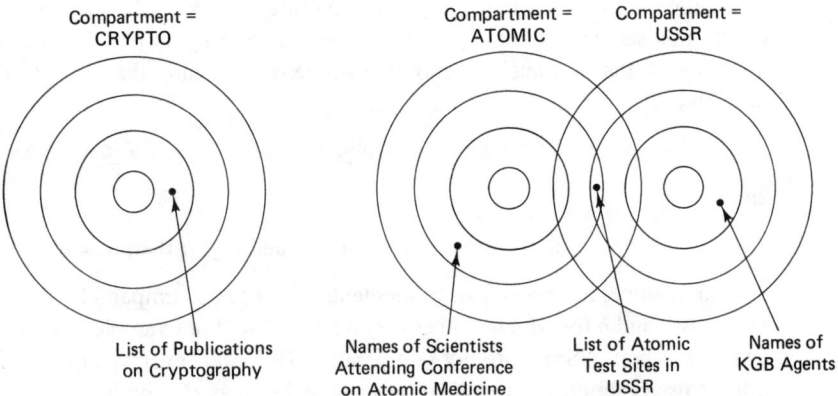

Figure 7.4   Association of Information and Compartments.

The combination $\langle rank; compartments \rangle$ is called the **class** or **classification** of a piece of information.

A person seeking access to sensitive information must be cleared. A **clearance** is an indication that a person is trusted to access information up to a certain level of sensitivity and that the person needs to know certain categories of sensitive information. The clearance of a subject is a combination $\langle rank; compartments \rangle$. This combination has the same form as the classification of a piece of information.

Now we introduce a relation $\leq$ on sensitive objects and subjects. For an object O and a subject S,

$$O \leq S \text{ if and only if}$$

$$rank_O \leq rank_S \text{ and}$$

$$compartments_O \subseteq compartments_S.$$

The relation $\leq$ is used to limit the sensitivity and content of the information a subject can access. A subject can access an object only if (a) the clearance level of the subject is *at least as high* as that of the information, and (b) the subject has a need to know about *all* compartments for which the information is classified.

A piece of information classified $\langle secret; USSR \rangle$ could be accessed by someone cleared for $\langle top\ secret; USSR \rangle$ access or $\langle secret; USSR, cryptographic \rangle$, but not by someone with a $\langle top\ secret; cryptographic \rangle$ clearance or someone cleared for $\langle confidential; USSR \rangle$.

The military security model enforces both sensitivity requirements and need-to-know requirements. Sensitivity requirements are known as **hierarchical** requirements; need-to-know restrictions are **nonhierarchical**.

Lattice Model of Access Security

The military security model is a representative of a more general scheme, called a lattice. A **lattice** is a mathematical structure of elements under a relational operator. The elements of a lattice are ordered under a partial ordering $\leq$. (We will also use the notation $\geq$ to denote this same relation: $b \geq a$ means the same thing as $a \leq b$.) A partial ordering is a relation $\leq$ that is transitive and antisymmetric, meaning that for every three elements a, b, and c,

$$\text{transitive:} \quad \text{if } a \leq b \text{ and } b \leq c \text{ then } a \leq c$$

and

$$\text{antisymmetric:} \quad \text{if } a \leq b \text{ and } b \leq a \text{ then } a = b.$$

In a lattice, not every pair of elements needs to be comparable; that is, there may be elements a and b for which neither $a \leq b$ nor $b \leq a$. For example, $\langle secret; cryptographic \rangle$ and $\langle top\ secret; USSR \rangle$ are not comparable. However, every pair of elements possesses a **least upper bound**, an element at least as large as ($\geq$) both a and b. Even though a and b may be incomparable under $\leq$, in a lattice there is an element u such that $a \leq u$ and $b \leq u$. Furthermore, in a lattice, every pair of elements possesses a **greatest lower bound**, an element dominated by both a and b; that is, $l \leq a$ and $l \leq b$.

Notice that the military security model is a lattice. The relation $\leq$ defined in the military model is the relation for the lattice. It is straightforward to verify that the relation $\leq$ is transitive and antisymmetric. The largest element of the lattice is the classification $\langle top\ secret; all\ compartments \rangle$, and the smallest element is $\langle unclassified; no\ compartments \rangle$. Therefore, the military model is a lattice.

However, many other schemes are lattices. For example, some companies classify the sensitivity of their data as PUBLIC, COMPANY CONFIDENTIAL, and HIGH SECURITY, with the natural ordering that public data is less sensitive than company confidential, which is less sensitive than high security. These three levels also form a lattice. A lattice is a fairly general structure; most common interpretations of the relation "greater than" form lattices.

Because a lattice is a natural representation of increasing degrees, security specialists have chosen to base security systems on lattices. A security system designed to implement lattice models of security can be used in a military environment. However, it can also be used in commercial environments with other labels for the security degrees. Thus, the lattice representation of sensitivity levels is a good security model for many different kinds of computing situations.

Information Flow Models

In this section, we consider models that describe the allowable transfer of information within a secure system. The Bell-LaPadula model implements secrecy, and the Biba model ensures integrity.

Bell-LaPadula Model

The Bell and LaPadula model [BEL73] is a formal description of the allowable paths of information flow in a secure system. The goal of the model is to identify allowable communication where it is important to maintain secrecy. The model has been used to define the security requirements for systems concurrently handling data at different sensitivity levels.

We are interested in secure information flows because they describe acceptable connections between subjects and objects of different levels of sensitivity. One purpose of analysis of security levels is to construct machines that can perform concurrent computation on data of two sensitivity levels. For example, one machine might be used for top secret and confidential data at the same time. The programs processing top secret data would be prevented from leaking data to the confidential data, and the confidential users would be prevented from accessing the top secret data. The Bell-LaPadula model is used as the basis for the design of systems that handle data of multiple levels.

Consider a security system with the following properties. The system covers a set of subjects S and a set of objects O. For each subject s in S and each object o in O there is a fixed security class $C(s)$ and $C(o)$. The security classes are ordered by a relation $\leq$. (Note: The classes may form a lattice, although the Bell-LaPadula model can apply to even less restricted cases.)

Two properties characterize the secure flow of information.

Simple Security Property.   A subject s may have *read* access to an object o only if $C(o) \leq C(s)$.

In the military model, this property says that the security class of someone receiving a piece of information must be at least as high as the class of the information.

∗-Property.   A subject s who has *read* access to an object o may have *write* access to an object p only if $C(o) \leq C(p)$.

The implications of these two properties are shown in Figure 7.5. The classifications of subjects (represented by squares) and objects (represented by circles) are indicated by their positions: As the classification of an item increases, it is shown higher in the figure.

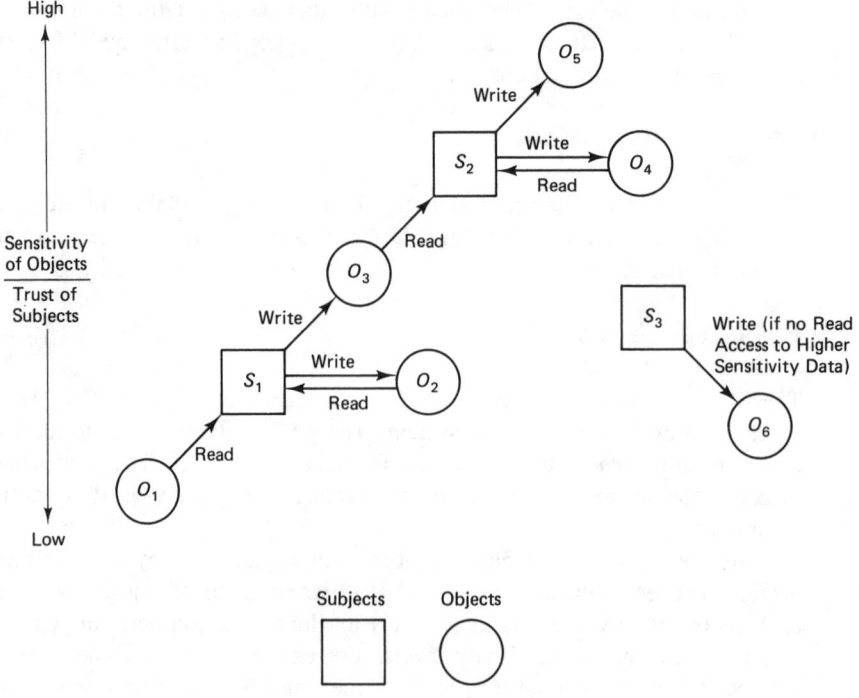

Figure 7.5   Secure Flow of Information.

In the military model, one interpretation of this property is that a person obtaining information at one level may pass that information along only to people at levels no lower than the level of the information. The ∗-property is used to prevent **write-down**, which occurs when a subject with access to high level data transfers that data by writing it to a low-level object.

Literally, the *-property requires that a person receiving information at one level not talk with people cleared at levels lower than the level of the information—not even about the weather! This example points out that this property is stronger than necessary to ensure security; the same is also true in computing systems. This property is relaxed when secure operating systems have been validated to allow write access if the data written does not depend on the data read. Similarly, in the human case, one person can talk to any other, as long as the conversation does not include information classified at a level greater than that of the listener.

Biba Model

The Bell-LaPadula model applies only to secrecy of information: The model identifies paths that could lead to inappropriate *disclosure* of information. However, the integrity of data is important, too. Biba [BIB77] constructed a model for preventing inappropriate modification of data.

The Biba model is the counterpart (dual) of the Bell-LaPadula model. Biba defines "integrity levels," which are analogous to the sensitivity levels of the Bell-LaPadula model. Subjects and objects are ordered by an integrity classification scheme, denoted $I(s)$ and $I(o)$. The properties are:

Simple Integrity Property.   If subject s can modify (have *write* access to) object o, $I(s) \geq I(o)$.

Integrity *-Property.   If subject s has *read* access to object o with integrity level $I(o)$, s can have *write* access to object p only if $I(o) \geq I(p)$.

These two rules cover untrustworthy information in a natural way. Suppose someone is known to be untruthful. If that person can create or modify a document, people should distrust the truth of the statements in the document. Thus, an untrusted subject who has write access to an object reduces the integrity of that object. Similarly, people are rightfully skeptical of a report based on unsound evidence. The low integrity of a source object implies low integrity for any object produced from the source object.

This model addresses the integrity issue that the Bell-LaPadula model ignores, but in doing so, the Biba model ignores secrecy. Secrecy-based security systems have been much more fully studied than integrity-based systems. The current trend is to join secrecy and integrity concerns in security systems, although no widely accepted formal models achieve this compromise.

The models described so far have been successfully used in the design of secure operating systems. The reference monitor model and the Bell-LaPadula model form the basis of the U. S. Department of Defense Trusted Computer System Evaluation standard (also called the "orange book"), which will be described later in this chapter.

Theoretical Limitations of Security Systems

Now we consider another class of models that formally addresses the question of what properties a security system can achieve. This new class of models is based on the general theory of computability. The results from these models show the limitations of abstract security systems.

Graham-Denning Model

Lampson [LAM71] and Graham and Denning [GRA72] introduced the concept of a formal system of protection rules. Graham and Denning constructed a model having generic protection properties. This model forms the basis for two later models of security systems.

The Graham-Denning model operates on a set of subjects S, a set of objects O, a set of rights R, and an access control matrix A. The matrix has one row for each subject, and one column for each subject and each object. The rights of a subject on another subject or an object are shown by the contents of an element of the matrix. For each object, one subject designated the "owner" has special rights; for each subject, another subject designated the "controller" has special rights.

In the Graham-Denning model, there are eight primitive protection rights. These rights are phrased as commands that can be issued by subjects, with effects on other subjects or objects.

o *create object:* allows the commanding subject to introduce a new object into the system

o *create subject, delete object, delete subject:* have the similar effect of creating or destroying a subject or object

o *read access right:* allows a subject to determine the current access rights of a subject to an object

o *grant access right:* allows the *owner* of an object to convey any access rights for an object to another subject

o *delete access right:* allows a subject to delete a right of another subject for an object, provided that the deleting subject is either the owner of the object or controls the subject from which access should be deleted

o *transfer access right:* allows a subject to transfer one of its rights for an object to another subject (Each right can be transferable or nontransferable. If a subject receives a transferable right, the subject can then transfer that right—either transferable or not—to other subjects. If a subject receives a nontransferable right, it can use the right, but cannot transfer that right to other subjects.)

These rules are shown in Table 7.1, which shows prerequisite conditions for the execution of each command and its effect. Table 7.1 is taken from [GRA72]. The access control matrix is $A[s, o]$, where s is a subject and o is an object. The subject executing each command is denoted x. A transferable right is denoted $r*$; a nontransferable right is written r.

This set of rules provides the properties necessary to model access control mechanisms of a protection system. For example, this mechanism can represent a reference

TABLE 7.1 PROTECTION SYSTEM COMMANDS.

Command	Condition	Effect
create object o	—	add column for o in A; place *owner* in $A[x, o]$
create subject s	—	add row for s in A; place *control* in $A[x, s]$
delete object o	*owner* in $A[x, o]$	delete column o
delete subject s	*control* in $A[x, s]$	delete row s
read access right of s on o	*control* in $A[x, s]$ or *owner* in $A[x, o]$	copy $A[s, o]$ to x
delete access right r of s on o	*control* in $A[x, s]$ or *owner* in $A[x, o]$	remove r from $A[s, o]$
grant access right r to s on o	*owner* in $A[x, o]$	add r to $A[s, o]$
transfer access right r or $r*$ to s on o	$r*$ in $A[x, o]$	add r or $r*$ to $A[s, o]$

monitor or a system of sharing between two untrustworthy, mutually suspicious subsystems.

Harrison-Ruzzo-Ullman Model

Harrison, Ruzzo, and Ullman [HAR76] proposed a variation on the Graham-Denning model. This revised model answered several questions concerning what protection systems can determine.

The Harrison-Ruzzo-Ullman model (called the HRU model) is quite similar to the Graham Denning model. The model is based on **commands**, where each command involves **conditions** and **primitive operations**.

The structure of a command is as follows.

$$\textbf{command } name(o_1, o_2, \ldots, o_k)$$
$$\textbf{if}\quad r_1 \text{ in } A[s_1, o_1] \text{ and}$$
$$r_2 \text{ in } A[s_2, o_2] \text{ and}$$
$$\cdots$$
$$r_m \text{ in } A[s_m, o_m]$$
$$\textbf{then}$$
$$op_1$$
$$op_2$$
$$\cdots$$
$$op_n$$
$$\textbf{end}$$

This command has a structure like a procedure, with parameters o_1 through o_k. The notation of the HRU model is slightly different from the Graham-Denning model: in HRU every subject is an object, too. Thus, the columns of the access control matrix are all the subjects *and* all the objects that are not subjects. For this reason, all the parameters of a command are labeled o, although they could be either subjects or nonsubject objects. Each r is a generic right, as in the Graham-Denning model. Each op is a primitive operation, as defined in the following material. The access matrix is shown in Figure 7.6.

Objects

Subjects	S_1	S_2	S_3	O_1	O_2	O_3
S_1	Control	Own Suspend Resume		Own	Own	Read Propagate
S_2		Control			Extend	Own
S_3			Control	Read, Write	Write	Read
. . .						

Figure 7.6   Access Matrix in HRU Model.

The primitive operations op, which are similar to those of the Graham-Denning model, are:

o *create subject s*

o *create object o*

o *destroy subject s*

o *destroy object o*

o *enter* right r into $A[s, o]$

o *delete* right r from $A[s, o]$

The interpretations of these operations are what their names imply. A **protection system** is a set of subjects, objects, rights, and commands.

Harrison *et al.* demonstrate that these operations are adequate to model several examples of protection systems, including the UNIX protection mechanism and an *indirect* access mode introduced by Graham and Denning [GRA72]. Thus, as with the Graham-Denning model, the HRU model can represent "reasonable" interpretations of protection.

Two important results derived by Harrison *et al.* have major implications for designers of protection systems. The proofs of these results will be omitted, although the methods of proof will be outlined here.

The first result applies when commands are restricted to contain just one operation each. In this case, it is possible to decide whether a given protection system, started with a given initial configuration of the access control matrix, can allow a given user to obtain a given access right to a given object. In other words, suppose one wants to know if a particular protection system can allow a subject s to obtain access right r to object o. (Harrison *et al.* say that such a system **leaks** the access right.)

As long as each command consists of only a single operation, there is an algorithm that can answer this question. The proof involves analysis of the minimum number of commands by which a right can be conferred. Certain operations, such as *delete* and *destroy* have no effect, and so they can be ignored. The shortest sequence of commands by which such a right can be conferred contains at most $m = |R| * (|S|+1) * (|O|+1) + 1$ commands, where $|R|$ is the number of rights, $|S|$ is the number of subjects, and $|O|$ is the number of objects in the protection system. The decision is made by testing all sequence of commands of length up to m. (There are 2^{km} such sequences, for some constant k.)

Thus, the first result from HRU indicates that it is possible to decide whether a given subject can ever obtain a particular right to an object. Therefore, it is decidable whether a low-level subject can ever obtain *read* access to a high level object, for example. The second result is less encouraging.

As a second result, Harrison *et al.* show that if commands are *not* restricted to one operation each, it is *not* decidable whether a given protection system can confer a given right. This result indicates that one cannot determine in general if a subject can obtain a particular right to an object.

The proof uses commands of an HRU protection system to represent operations of a formal system called a "Turing machine." Turing machines are general models of computing devices; any conventional computing system can be modeled with a Turing machine. Several decidable results about Turing machines are well known, including one that shows it is impossible to develop a general procedure to determine if a given Turing machine will halt when performing a given computation. The proof of the second HRU result follows by showing that a decision procedure for protection systems would also solve the halting problem for Turing machines, which is known to be unsolvable.

Since the UNIX protection scheme requires more than one operation per command in the HRU model, there can be no general procedure to determine whether a certain access right can be given to a subject. The UNIX protection scheme is relatively simple. Protection models for other systems are more complex.

The HRU result is bleak. In fact, the HRU result can be extended: There may be an algorithm to decide the access right question for a particular collection of protection systems, but even an infinite number of algorithms *cannot* decide the access right question for all protection systems. However, the negative results do not say that no decision process exists for any protection system. In fact, for certain specific protection systems, it is decidable whether a given access right can be conferred. Therefore, the HRU results are negative for general procedures but do not rule out the possibility of making decisions about given protection systems.

Take-Grant Systems

One final model of a protection system is the **take-grant** system, introduced by Jones [JON78] and expanded by Lipton and Snyder [LIP77], [SNY81].

In this model, there are only four primitive operations: create, revoke, take, and grant. Create and revoke are similar to operations from the Graham-Denning and HRU models; take and grant are new types of operations. These operations are presented most naturally through the use of graphs.

As in other systems, let S be a set of subjects and O be a set of objects; objects can be either active (subjects) or passive (nonsubject objects). Let R be a set of rights. Each subject or object is denoted by a node of a graph; the rights of a particular subject to a particular object are denoted by a labeled directed edge from the subject to the object. Figure 7.7 shows examples of subjects, objects, and rights.

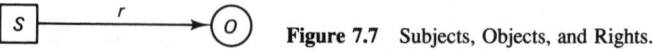

Figure 7.7   Subjects, Objects, and Rights.

Let s be the subject performing each of the operations. The four operations are defined as follows.

o *Create(o,r):* A new node with label o is added to the graph. From s to o there is a directed edge with label r, denoting the rights of s on o. Creation of an object is shown in Figure 7.8.

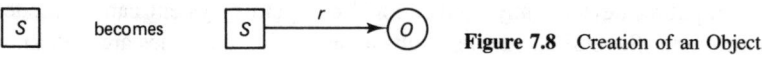

Figure 7.8   Creation of an Object.

o *Revoke(o,r):* The set of rights r is revoked from s on o. The edge from s to o was labeled $q \cup r$; the label is replaced by q. Informally, s can revoke its rights to do r on o. Revocation of access rights is shown in Figure 7.9.

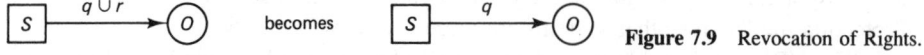

Figure 7.9   Revocation of Rights.

o *Grant(o,p,r):* s grants to o access rights r on p. A specific right is *grant*. Subject s can grant to o access rights r on p only if s has *grant* right on o, and s has r rights on p. Informally, s can grant (share) any of its rights with o, as long as s has the right to grant privileges to o. An edge from o to p is added, with label r. Granting of rights is shown in Figure 7.10.

Figure 7.10   Granting Access Rights.

    o *Take(o,p,r):* s takes from o access rights r on p. A specific right is *take*. Subject s can take from o access rights r on p only if s has *take* right on o, and o has r rights on p. Informally, s can take any rights o has, as long as s has the right to take privileges from o. An edge from s to p is added, with label r. Taking of rights is shown in Figure 7.11.

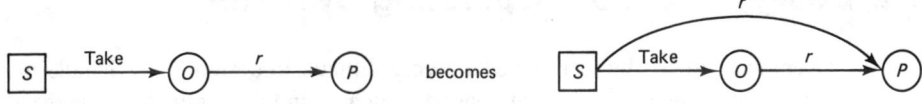

Figure 7.11   Taking Access Rights.

    This set of operations is even shorter than the operations of either of the two previous models. However, *take* and *grant* are more complex rights.

    Snyder shows that in this system certain protection questions are decidable; furthermore, they are decidable in reasonable (less than exponential) time. In [SNY81], Snyder considers two questions: First, can a given subject share an object with another subject, and second, can a given subject steal access to an object from another subject? Clearly these are important questions to answer about a protection system, for they show whether the access control mechanisms are secure against unauthorized disclosure.

    The answer to Synder's first question is "yes," if several other subjects together have the desired access to the object, and if the first subject is connected to each of the group of other subjects by a path of edges having a particular form. There is an algorithm to detect sharability that runs in time proportional to the size of the graph of the particular case.

    Snyder also answers the second question affirmatively for those situations heavily dependent on the ability to share. Thus, an algorithm can decide if access can be stolen by direct appeal to the algorithm to decide sharability.

    Landwehr [LAN81] points out that the take-grant model assumes the worst about users: If a user can grant access rights, the model assumes that the user will. Suppose a user can create a file and grant access to it to everyone. In that situation, every user could allow access to every object by every other user. This worst-case assumption limits the applicability of the model to situations of controlled sharing of information. In general, however, the take-grant model is useful because it identifies conditions under which a user can obtain access to an object.

Summary of Models of Protection Systems

There are two purposes to studying models of computer security. First, models are important in determining the policies a secure system should enforce. For example, the Bell-LaPadula and Biba models identify specific conditions to enforce in order to ensure secrecy or integrity. Second, the study of abstract models can lead to an understanding of the properties of protection systems. For example, the HRU model states certain characteristics that can or cannot be decided by an arbitrary protection system. These characteristics are important for designers of protection systems to know.

In the next section we study the design of secure operating systems. These designs follow from the policies established after analyzing models of protection systems.

7.2 Design of Secure Operating Systems

Operating systems by themselves are very difficult to design. They handle many duties, are subject to interruptions and context switches, and must minimize overhead so as not to slow user computations. Transferring the responsibility for security enforcement to the operating system substantially increases the difficulty of designing an operating system.

In this section we study the design of operating systems for a high degree of security. First we examine the basic design of a standard multipurpose operating system. Then we consider isolation, through which one operating system supports both sharing and separation of user domains. We look at the "kernel" design of an operating system, an effective way to provide security. There are actually two different interpretations of the kernel, both of which are studied. Finally, layered or ring structured designs are considered.

Basic Multiprogramming Operating System Features

An operating system performs several functions that relate to security, which we list here:

1. *Authentication of users*. The operating system must identify each user who requests access and ascertain that the user is actually who he or she purports to be. The most common authentication mechanism is password comparison.

2. *Protection of memory*. Each user's program must run in a portion of memory inaccessible to unauthorized users. The protection may also control a user's own access to restricted parts of the program space. Differential security, such as read, write, and execute, may be applied to parts of a user's memory space.

3. *File and I/O device access control*. The operating system must protect user and system files from access by unauthorized users. Similarly, I/O device use must be protected.

4. *Allocation and access control to general objects*. General objects, such as mechanisms to permit concurrency and allow synchronization, must be provided to users. However, use of these objects must be controlled so that one user does not have a negative effect on other users.

5. *Enforcement of sharing*. Resources should be made available to users as appropriate. Sharing brings about the need to guarantee integrity and consistency.

6. *Guarantee of fair service.* All users expect CPU usage and other service to be provided so that no user is indefinitely starved from receiving service. Hardware clocks combine with scheduling disciplines to provide this fairness.

7. *Interprocess communication and synchronization.* Executing processes sometimes need to communicate with other processes or to synchronize their accesses to shared resources. Operating systems provide these services by acting as a bridge between processes, responding to process requests for asynchronous communication with other processes or for synchronization.

Figure 7.12 relates these security concerns to the more traditional functions of an operating system.

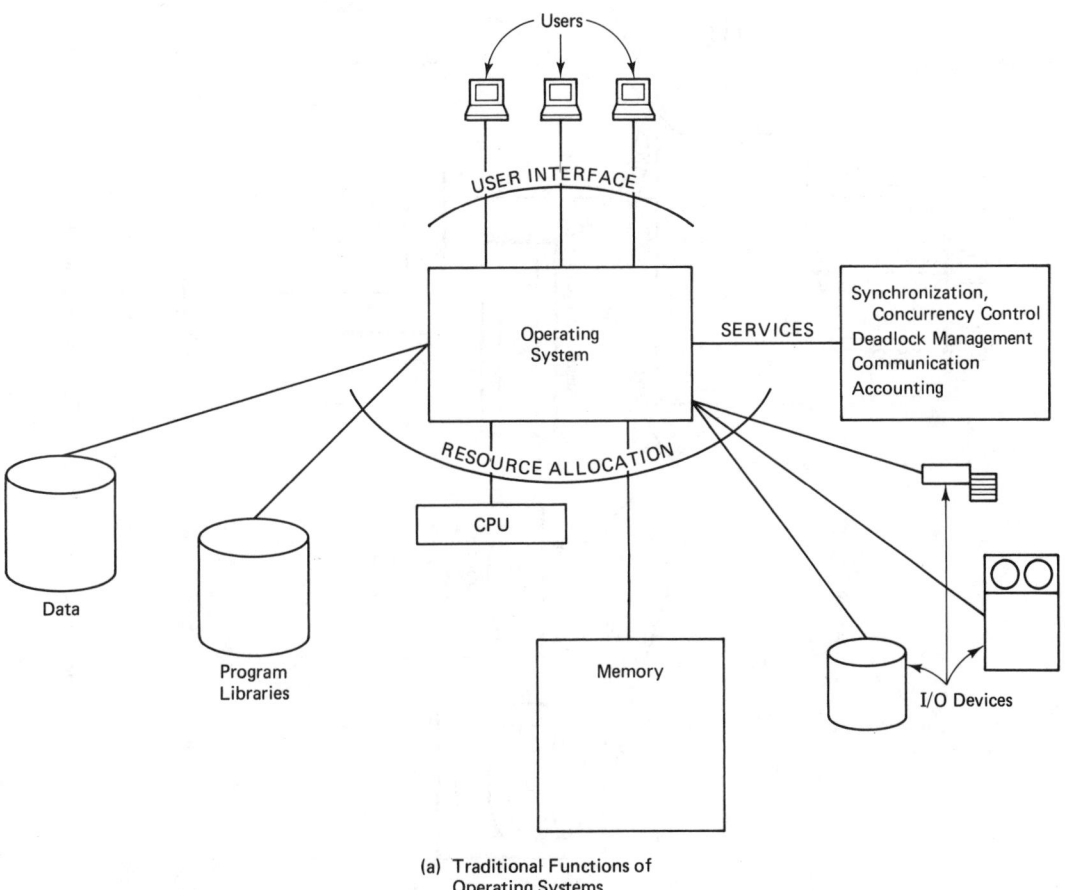

(a) Traditional Functions of
Operating Systems

Figure 7.12a   Security Properties in Operating Systems— Traditional Functions of Operating Systems.

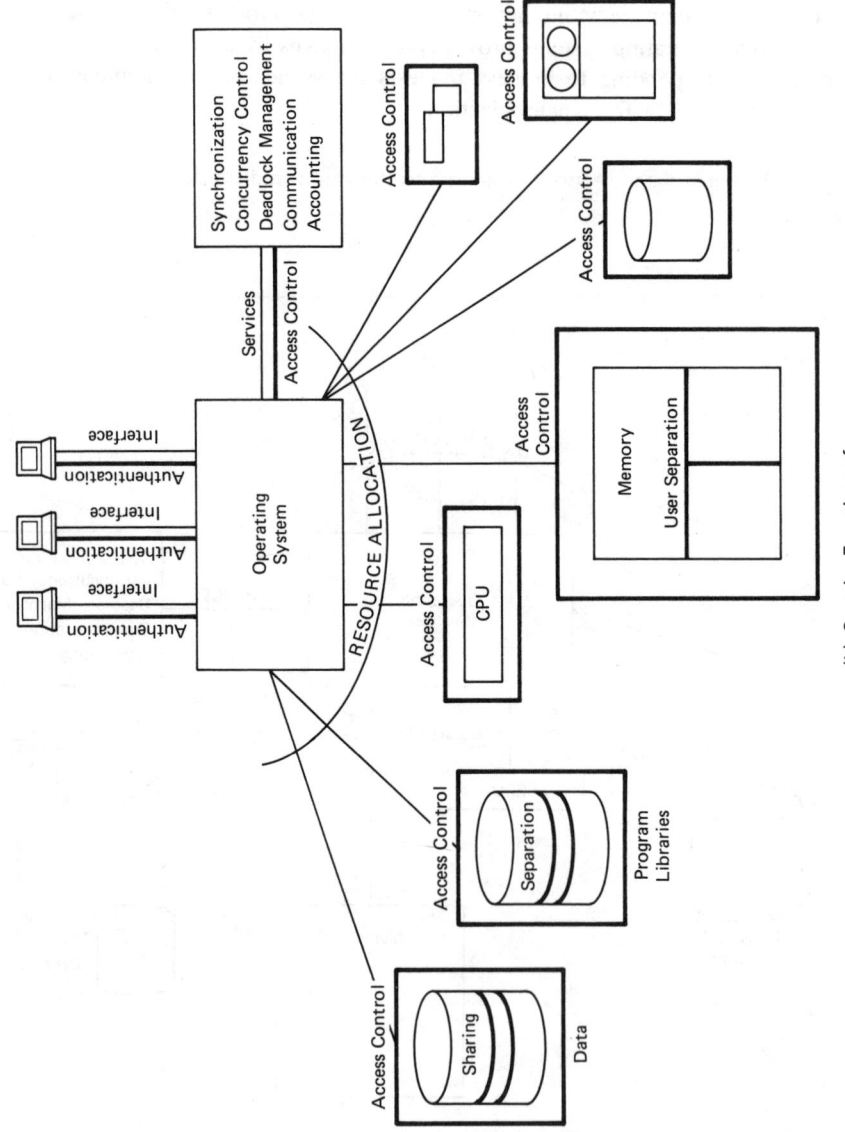

Figure 7.12b Security Properties in Operating Systems—Security Functions of Operating Systems.

(b) Security Functions of
Operating Systems

Security functions pervade the design and structure of operating systems, which implies two things about the design of secure operating systems. First, security must be considered in every aspect of the design of operating systems. When a section has been designed, it must be checked for the degree of security that it enforces or provides. Second, since security appears throughout an operating system, it is very difficult to add security features to an operating system designed with no or inadequate security. Security must be a part of the initial design of an operating system.

Saltzer [SAL74] and Saltzer and Schroeder [SAL75] listed the following principles of the design of secure protection systems.

o *Least privilege:* Each user and each program should operate using the fewest privileges possible. In this way, the damage from an inadvertent or malicious attack is minimized.

o *Economy of mechanism:* The design of the protection system should be small, simple, and straightforward. Such a protection system can be exhaustively tested, perhaps verified, and trusted.

o *Open design:* The protection mechanism must not depend on the ignorance of potential attackers; the mechanism should be public, depending on secrecy of relatively few key items, such as a password table. An open design is also available for extensive public scrutiny.

o *Complete mediation:* Every access must be checked.

o *Permission-based:* The default condition should be denial of access. A conservative designer identifies those items that *should* be accessible, rather than those that should *not*.

o *Separation of privilege:* Ideally, access to objects should depend on more than one condition, such as user authentication plus a cryptographic key. In this way, someone who defeats one protection system will not have complete access.

o *Least common mechanism:* Shared objects provide potential channels for information flow. Systems employing physical or logical separation reduce the risk from sharing.

o *Easy to use:* If a mechanism is easy to use, it is unlikely to be avoided.

In the remaining parts of this section, we examine successful implementations of security in the design of operating systems. We consider three properties: isolation (the logical extension of least common mechanism), kernelized design (a result of least privilege and economy of mechanism), and ring-structuring (an example of open design and complete mediation).

Separation/Isolation

There are four ways to separate one process from others: physical separation, temporal separation, cryptographic separation, and logical separation. With **physical separation**, processes use different hardware facilities. For example, sensitive computation may be performed on a reserved computing system; nonsensitive tasks are run on a public system. **Temporal separation** occurs when processes are run at different times. Some military systems run nonsensitive jobs between 8:00 am and noon, with sensitive computation only from noon to 5:00 pm. Encryption is used for **cryptographic separation**, so that unauthorized users cannot access sensitive data in a readable form. **Logical separation**, also called **isolation**, is provided when a process such as a reference monitor separates the objects of one user from those of another. Secure computing systems use all these forms of separation.

Multiprogramming operating systems should isolate each user from all others, allowing only carefully controlled interactions between the users. Most operating systems provide a single environment with one copy of the operating system for many users, as shown in Figure 7.13. There are often two pieces of the operating system, located at the highest and lowest addresses of memory.

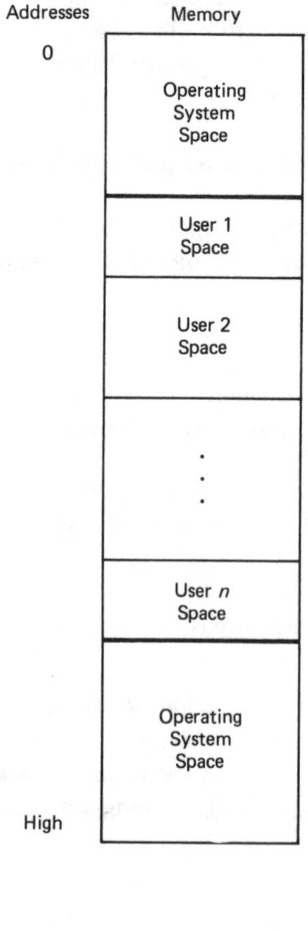

Addresses   Memory

0

Operating
System
Space

User 1
Space

User 2
Space

.
.
.

User *n*
Space

Operating
System
Space

High

Figure 7.13 Conventional Multiuser Operating System Memory.

Multiple Virtual Memory Spaces

The IBM MVS operating systems provide logical separation that gives the user the impression of physical separation. IBM MVS is a paging system, so that each user's logical address space is separated from that of other users by the page mapping mechanism. Additionally, MVS includes the operating system in each user's logical address space, so that a user runs on what seems to be a complete, separate machine.

Most paging systems present to a user only the user's virtual address space, which is independent of the operating system address space. However, the operating system is part of the logical space of each MVS user. Therefore, to the user MVS seems like a single-user system, as shown in Figure 7.14.

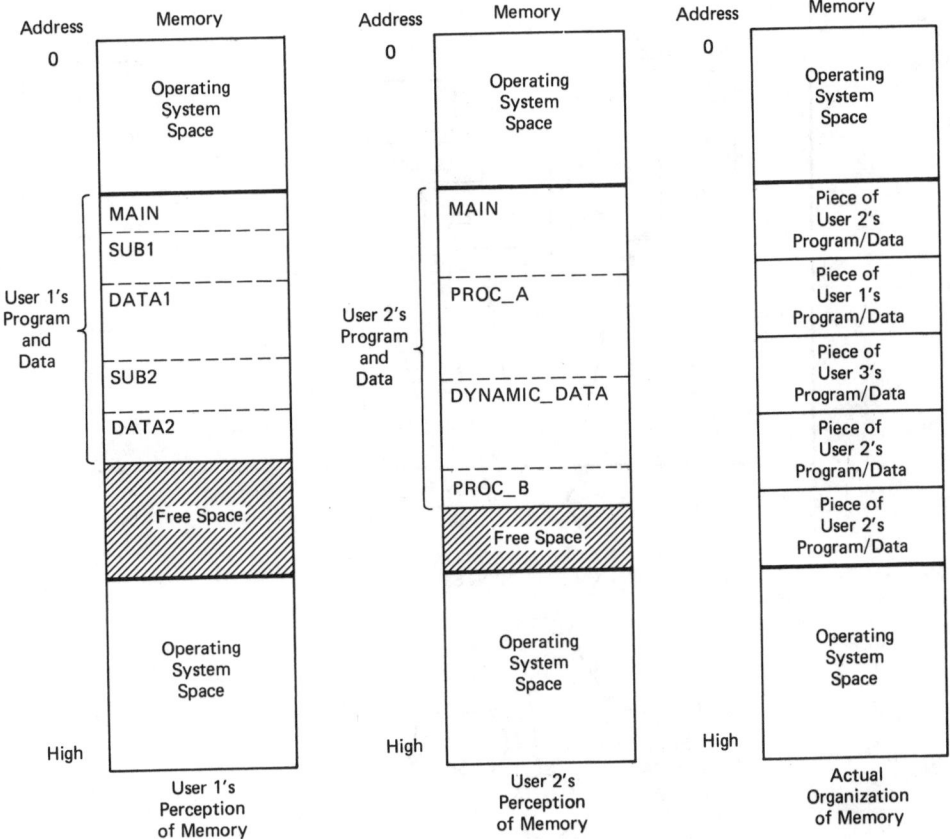

Figure 7.14   Multiple Virtual Addressing Spaces.

The primary advantage of MVS is memory management: Each user's virtual memory space can be as large as total addressable memory, in excess of 16 million bytes. However, a second advantage of this representation of memory is protection. Since each user's logical address space includes the operating system, the user has the illusion of running on a separate machine, which could even be true.

Virtual Machines

The IBM VM operating system provides a level of protection that is stronger still. A conventional operating system has hardware facilities and devices that are under the direct control of the operating system, as shown in Figure 7.15. The VM operating system provides an entire virtual machine to each user, so that each user has not only logical memory, but logical I/O devices, logical files, and other logical resources, too.

COMPUTING SYSTEM

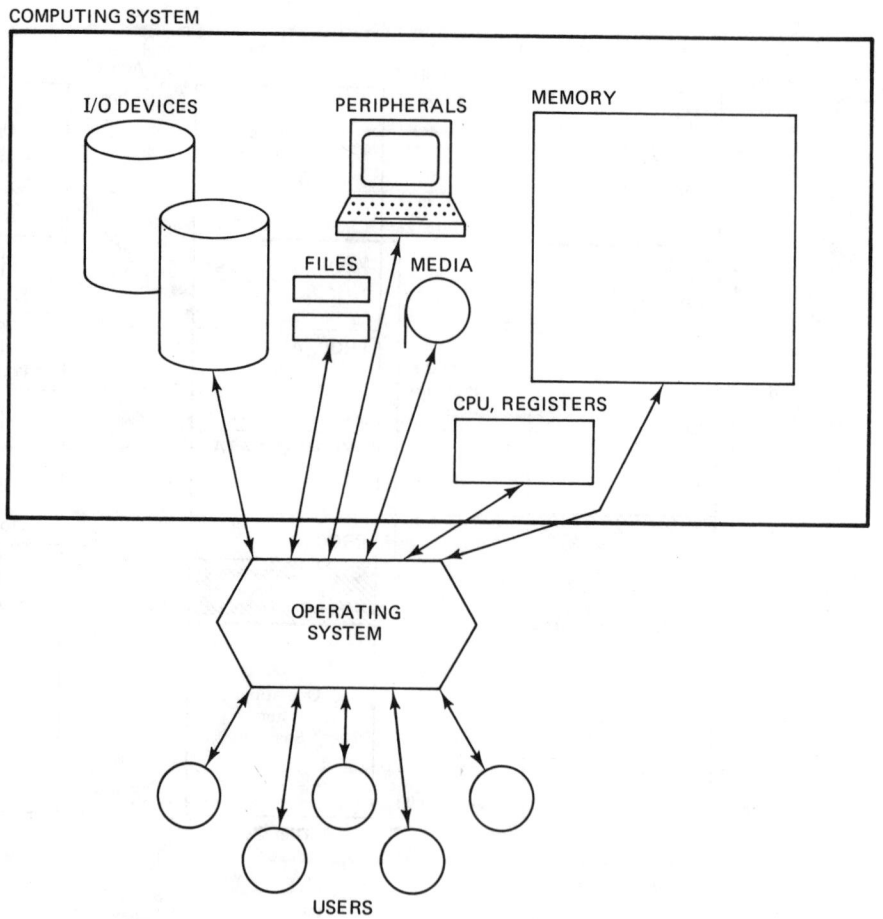

Figure 7.15   Conventional Operating System.

The VM system is a natural extension of the concept of virtual memory. Virtual *memory* gives the user a memory space that is logically separated from real memory and that is also usually larger than real memory. A virtual *machine* gives the user a full set of hardware features, that is, a complete machine that may be substantially different from the real machine. These virtual hardware resources are also logically separated from those of other users. The relationship of virtual machines to real is shown in Figure 7.16.

The VM operating system was designed to run other operating systems. The VM operating system consists of a **control program** (CP) that maps physical devices and hardware interactions to signals passed between CP and each subject operating system.

VM was intended as a way to support two or more different operating systems on a single computing system. Two systems might be desirable during a gradual changeover from one operating system to another, so that both systems could be available at the same time. Another reason for two systems is to be able to change and test one operating system in an environment where a system error would not affect other users.

Virtual memory was originally designed to provide flexibility in addressing and memory management; security was achieved as a bonus. The VM operating system turned out to have a security advantage as well. Because CP performs all actual interaction with hardware, it acts as a second security layer between the operating system and the hardware.

Suppose a user identifies and exploits a flaw in the operating system. Under VM, the user might get outside the user domain and reach the operating system domain (where MVS is run). The user still does not have access to the actual machine hardware, nor to users or domains running on other operating systems on other virtual machines. To penetrate another user or operating system, the user would have to find and exploit yet another flaw, this one in the security mechanism of VM itself.

Both MVS and VM separate the user from the actual computing system, thereby reducing the possible impact of a security flaw. These systems improve the isolation of each user from other users and from the hardware of the system. Of course, this added complexity increases the overhead incurred with these levels of translation and protection. In the next section we study alternate designs that reduce the complexity of providing security in an operating system.

Kernel

A **kernel** is the part of an operating system that performs the lowest-level functions. In standard operating system design, the kernel implements operations such as synchronization, interprocess communication, message-passing, and interrupt-handling. The kernel is also called a **nucleus** or **core**. The notion of designing an operating system around a kernel is described by Lampson [LAM76] and by Popek and Kline [POP78].

A **security kernel** is responsible for implementing the security mechanisms of the entire operating system. The security kernel provides the security interfaces among the hardware, the operating system, and the other parts of the computing system. Typically the security kernel is contained within the operating system kernel. Security kernels are discussed by Ames [AME83].

Security functions may be isolated in a security kernel for several reasons.

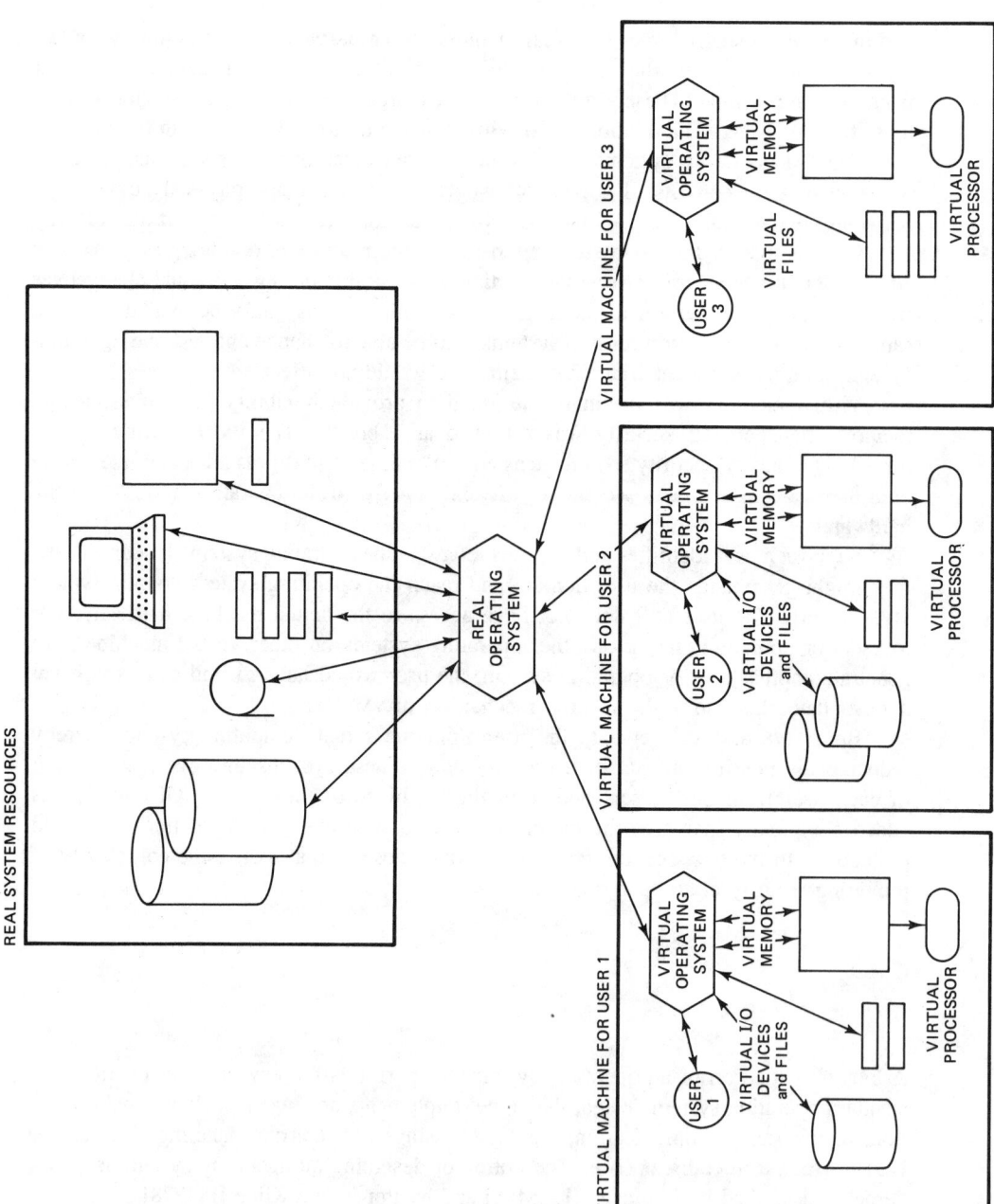

Figure 7.16 Virtual Machine.

266

1. *Separation:* By isolating security mechanisms from the rest of the operating system and from the user space, it is easier to protect them from penetration by the operating system or the users.

2. *Unity:* All security functions are performed by a single set of code.

3. *Modifiability:* Changes to the security mechanism are easier to make and easier to test.

4. *Compactness:* Because it performs only security functions, the kernel is likely to be relatively small.

5. *Verifiability:* Being relatively small, the security kernel may be proven correct in a rigorous, formal sense.

6. *Coverage:* Every access to a protected object must pass through the security kernel. This makes it possible to ensure that every access is checked.

Notice the similarity between these advantages and the design goals of operating systems from Saltzer and Schroder described earlier.

On the negative side, implementation of a security kernel may degrade system performance because the kernel adds yet another layer of interface between user programs and operating system resources. Presence of a kernel does not guarantee that it contains *all* security functions, or that it has been implemented correctly. And, in some cases, a security kernel can be quite large.

The design and usefulness of a security kernel depend somewhat on the design approach. The kernel can be designed as an addition to the operating system or it can be the basis of the entire operating system. These two design approaches are described in the next two sections.

Collect Security Functions in the Operating System Kernel

For an existing operating system (one not designed primarily for security), security-related activities are likely to be performed in a very large number of different places. Security is potentially related to every memory access, every I/O operation, every file or program access, every initiation or termination of a user, and every interprocess communication. In a modular operating system, these separate activities can be handled in independent modules. Each of these separate modules then has both security-related and other functions.

Collecting all security functions into the kernel may destroy the modularity of an existing operating system. A unified kernel may also be too large to be verifiable. Nevertheless, a designer may decide to separate the security functions of an existing operating system, creating a security kernel. This form of kernel is depicted in Figure 7.17.

Design the Security Kernel Functions First

A more sensible approach is to design the security kernel first, and then design the operating system around it. This technique was used by Honeywell in the design of

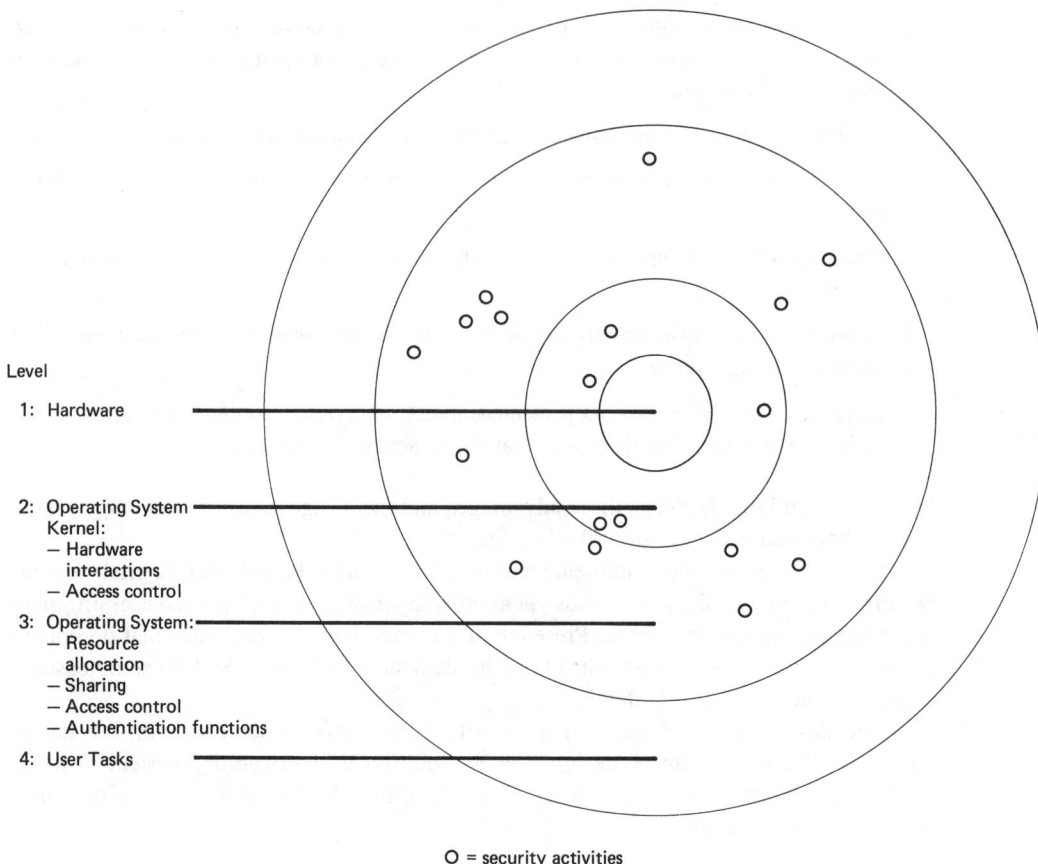

Level

1: Hardware

2: Operating System
   Kernel:
   — Hardware
     interactions
   — Access control

3: Operating System:
   — Resource
     allocation
   — Sharing
   — Access control
   — Authentication functions

4: User Tasks

O = security activities

Figure 7.17   Combined Security Kernel/Operating System.

a prototype system for SCOMP (a secure operating system to be described later). That prototype system contained only 20 modules to perform the primitive security functions, and consisted of fewer than 1,000 lines of higher-level language source code. The actual security kernel of SCOMP contains approximately 10,000 lines of source code.

In a security-based design, a security kernel is an interface layer, just on top of the system hardware. The security kernel monitors all operating system hardware accesses and performs all protection functions. The security kernel, which relies on support from hardware, allows the operating system to handle most functions not related to security. In this way, the security kernel can be small and efficient. A byproduct of this partitioning is that there are at least four execution domains of a computing system, as shown in Figure 7.18. These domains are hardware, security kernel, operating system, and user.

The security kernel, which must maintain the secrecy and integrity of each domain, monitors four basic interactions.

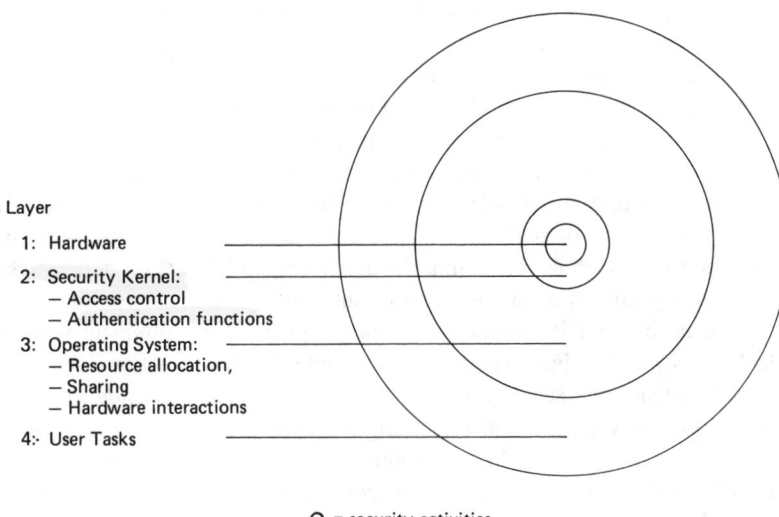

Layer

1: Hardware

2: Security Kernel:
   − Access control
   − Authentication functions

3: Operating System:
   − Resource allocation,
   − Sharing
   − Hardware interactions

4: User Tasks

O = security activities

Figure 7.18   Separate Security Kernel.

1. *Process activation:* In a multiprogramming environment, activation and deactivation of processes occur frequently. Changing from one process to another requires a complete change of registers, relocation maps, file access lists, process status information, and other pointers, much of which is security-sensitive information.

2. *Execution domain switching:* Processes running in one domain frequently invoke processes in other domains to obtain more sensitive data or services.

3. *Memory protection:* Since each domain includes code and data stored in memory, the security kernel must monitor memory references to ensure secrecy and integrity for each domain.

4. *I/O operation:* In some systems, software is involved as each character is transferred in an I/O operation. This software connects a user program, in the outermost domain, to an I/O device, in the innermost (hardware) domain. Thus, I/O operations can cross all domains.

Layered Design

As described earlier, a kernelized operating system consists of at least four levels: hardware, kernel, operating system, and user. Each of these layers may itself include sublayers. For example, in [SCH83a], the kernel has five distinct layers. At the user level, it is not uncommon to have quasi-system programs, such as data base managers or user interface shells, that constitute separate layers of security themselves.

This view of a secure operating system can be depicted as a series of concentric circles, where the most sensitive operations are in the innermost layers. The trustworthiness and access rights of a process can be judged by its proximity to the center: The more trusted processes are closer to the center. Such a system is shown in Figure 7.19.

In this design, some protection functions are performed outside the security kernel. For example, user authentication may include accessing a password table, challenging the user to supply a password, verifying the correctness of the password, and so forth. The disadvantage of performing all these operations inside the security kernel is that some of them (such as formatting the user terminal interaction and searching for the user in a table of known users) do not warrant high security.

In a common implementation, the security kernel interacts with modules known to be trustworthy. For example, many authentication functions can be performed in a module outside the security kernel. The trusted module outside the security kernel has been formally verified or at least scrutinized to give a high degree of confidence in its correctness. The security kernel monitors such actions as access to the password list, but it trusts the authentication module to perform certain mechanical parts of authentication properly.

A single logical function implemented in several modules is an example of a **layered design**. In the examples just described, trustworthiness and access rights are the basis of layering. A single function may be performed by a set of modules operating in different layers, as shown in Figure 7.20. The modules of each layer perform operations of a certain degree of sensitivity.

A layered approach is recognized as a good operating system design. Each layer uses the more central layers as services, and each layer provides a certain level of functionality to the layers farther out. In this way, it is possible to "peel off" each layer and still have a logically complete system with less functionality.

Ring Structured

The MULTICS operating system carries a layered design one step further. Protection during execution is implemented by a **ring structure**, specifying what access rights a process has. (Schroeder [SCH72] explains the ring structure in detail.) In MULTICS a ring is a domain in which a process executes. The rings are numbered, from 0 up, with the kernel being ring 0. Rings are implemented as if they were concentric bands around the hardware of a computing system.

Each executing process runs at a particular ring level. More trusted processes operate at lower numbered rings. The rings are overlapping, so that running at ring i includes privileges of all rings j where $j > i$. The lower the ring number, the more access a process has; correspondingly, the lower the ring number, the less protection covers its operation.

Each data area or procedure is called a **segment**. A segment is protected by means of three numbers, $b1, b2, b3$, where $b1 \leq b2 < b3$. The three numbers $\langle b1, b2, b3 \rangle$ are called the **ring bracket**; $(b1, b2)$ is called the **access bracket**, and $(b2, b3)$ is called the **call bracket** or **gate extension**. The range from $b1$ to $b2$ is the set of rings of processes that can access this segment freely. The rings beyond $b2$ up to $b3$ constitute the rings

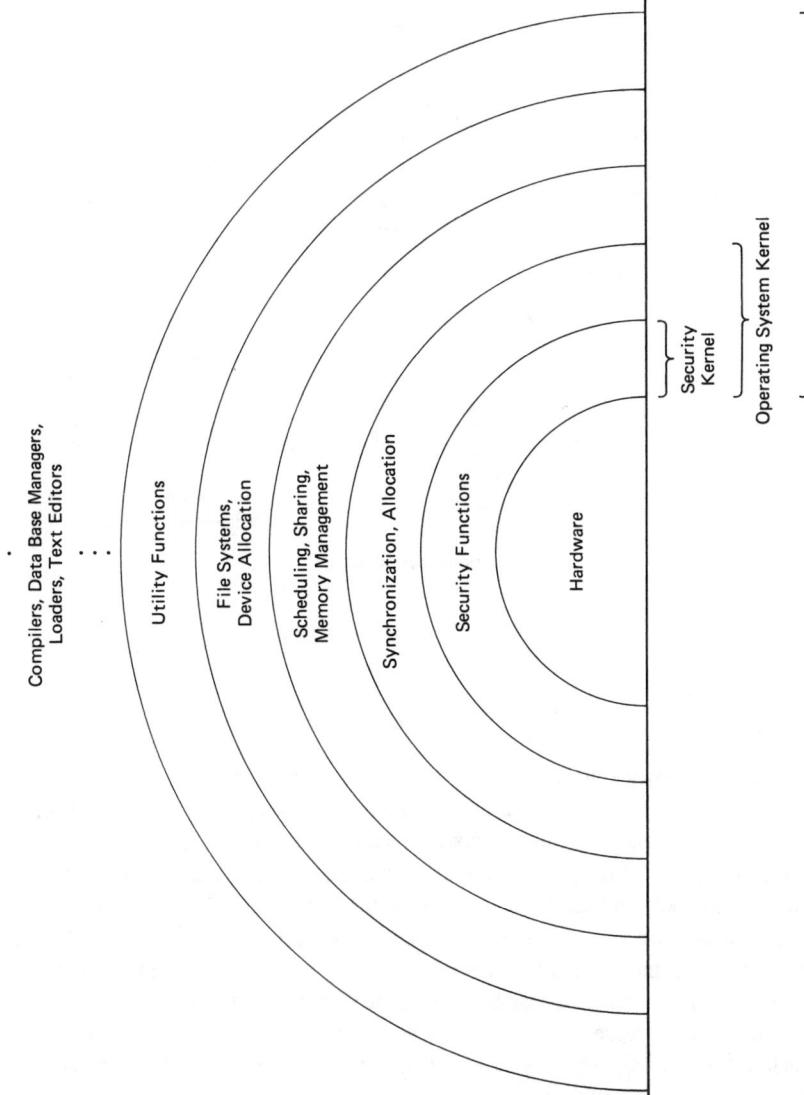

Subprocesses of User Processes

User Processes

Compilers, Data Base Managers,
Loaders, Text Editors

Utility Functions

File Systems,
Device Allocation

Scheduling, Sharing,
Memory Management

Synchronization, Allocation

Security Functions

Hardware

Security
Kernel

Operating System Kernel

Operating System

Figure 7.19 Layered Operating System.

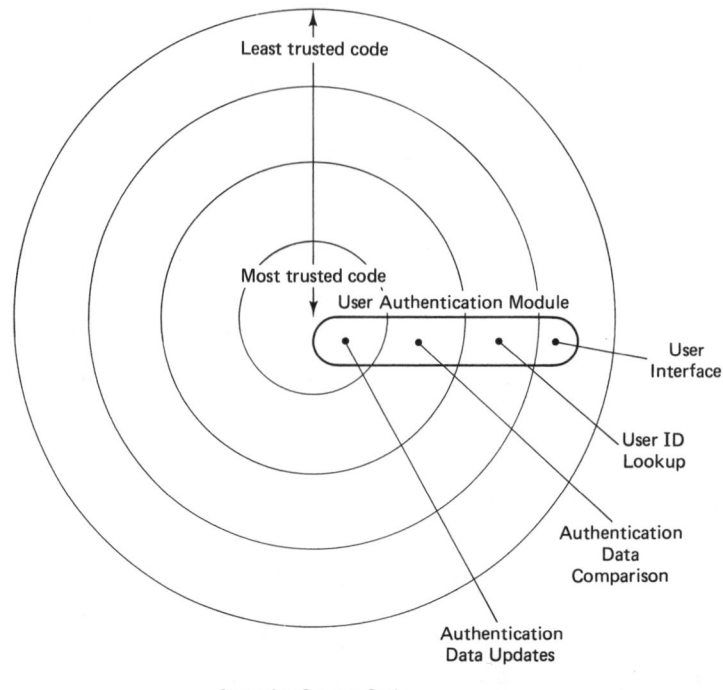

Figure 7.20   Modules Operating in Different Layers.

of processes that can call this segment only at certain distinguished entry points. The representation of a ring bracket is shown in Figure 7.21.

For example, a kernel segment might have an access bracket of (0,4), meaning that processes at levels 0 through 4 could execute it freely. A user segment might have an access bracket of (4,6), indicating that it is normally accessed by user processes only. The ring bracket indicates the degree of trust in a segment. Segments that are highly trusted to be correct have access brackets that start at low numbers. Segments that are less highly trusted are seldom called by highly trusted kernel processes; therefore, less reliable segments have access brackets that start at higher numbers.

Suppose a process p, executing at level k, wishes to call a procedure with ring bracket $\langle b1, b2, b3 \rangle$. If $b1 \leq k \leq b2$, the call occurs normally, because the process is invoking a segment within its accepted range of free (trusted) access. If $k < b1$, the call is acceptable, but p executes only a *copy* of the desired process. (The reason for the copy relates to data and will be clear shortly.) If $b2 < k \leq b3$, p can complete the call only if it calls a recognized entry point, called a **gate**. Otherwise, the call is not acceptable. The interpretation of ring brackets for procedure calls is shown in Figure 7.22.

The same kind of checking occurs for data references. For access to data segments numbered within the access bracket, full read and write access is allowed. For access

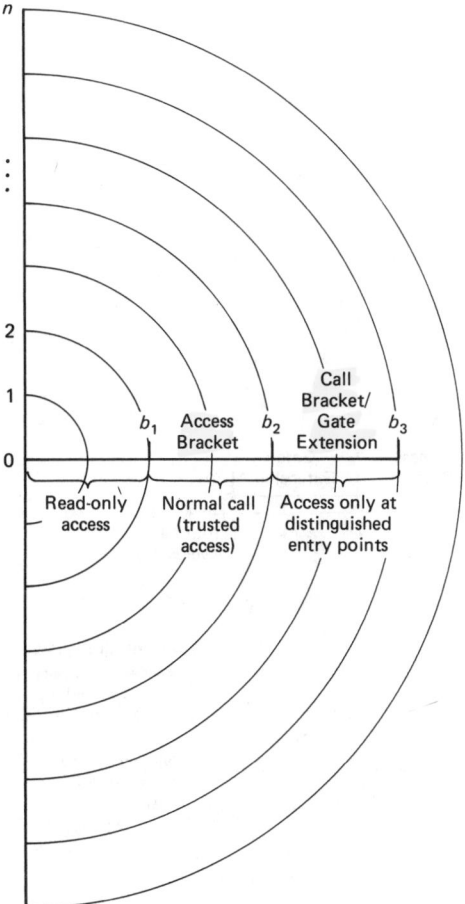

Figure 7.21 Ring Bracket.

to data segments with higher access brackets, write occurs to a *copy* of the data; a more privileged process can then decide whether or not it will accept that modified copy. This policy protects the integrity of data. That is, if a process at level k seeks access to a data segment, normal access occurs if $b1 \leq k \leq b2$; write to a copy of the segment occurs if $k < b1$; and no access occurs if $b2 < k$. The interpretation of ring brackets for data access is shown in Figure 7.23.

This implementation is a *minimal* security implementation; that is, all procedure calls and data fetches must follow these rules. Within these parameters, additional access conditions can be established. For example, a kernel segment with ring bracket (0,4) might implement a mechanism that screens callers operating at a ring of 3 or above. For example, only certain user processes could be allowed to invoke a routine that writes a data file for use by students in a class. This added mechanism is called a **discretionary control,** meaning that its use is optional, at the choice of the subject owning or managing an object. The basic ring bracket interpretation is a **nondiscretionary control** (also called

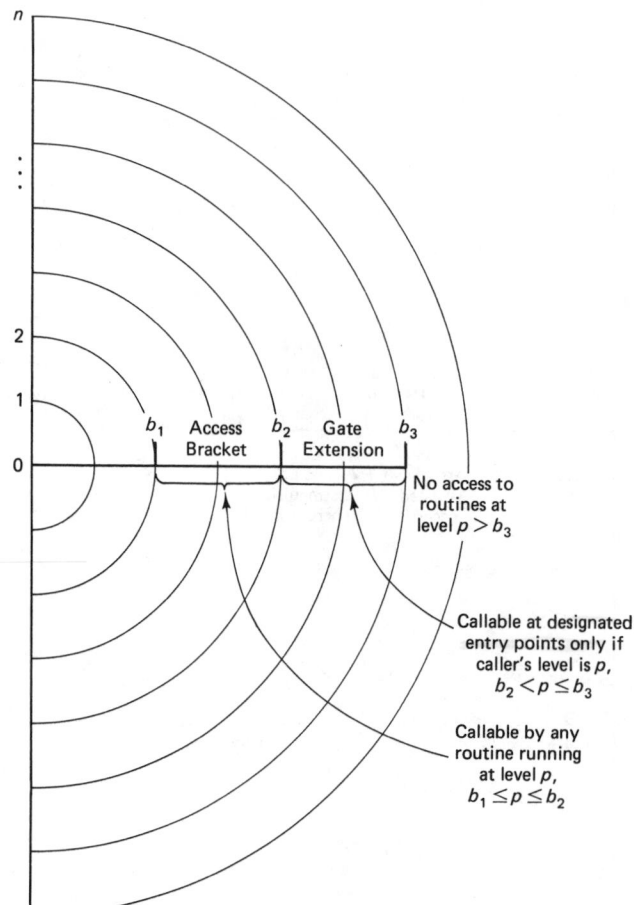

Figure 7.22   Interpretation of Ring Brackets for Procedure Calls.

a **mandatory control**), since it applies to all objects, regardless of contents or owner. Many operating systems implement both discretionary and nondiscretionary controls.

This chapter started with an study of different models of protection systems. In this section we have examined three design principles—isolation, security kernel, and layered structure—that are used in the design of secure operating systems. This presentation concludes the study of how operating systems are designed for security. In the next section we consider **trust**, convincing others that a model, design, and implementation are correct. We begin by examining how operating systems are tested, both before and after they are delivered. The first issue of testing involves users' attempts to defeat the controls of the system.

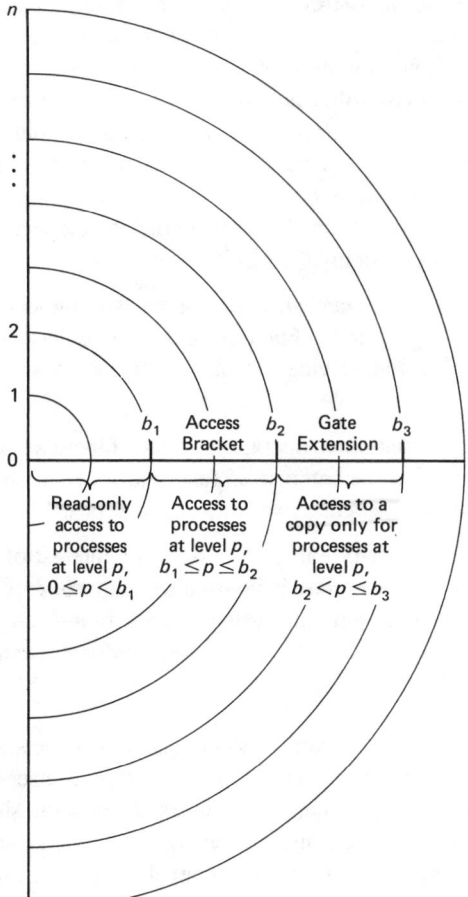

Figure 7.23 Interpretation of Ring Brackets for Data Access.

7.3 Penetration of Operating System

Periodically throughout this analysis of security features of operating systems, the term *exploit a flaw* has been used. Throughout the years many flaws have been uncovered in many operating systems. Gradually the flaws have been corrected, and the knowledge of likely weak spots has grown.

In this section we discuss typical flaws that have been uncovered in operating systems. The goal is not to provide a "how-to" guide for potential penetrators of operating systems. We study these flaws to understand the careful analysis necessary in the design and testing of operating systems.

Known Flaws

The largest single source of flaws has been I/O processing. There are probably several reasons why I/O is a weak spot.

o Independent intelligent devices, controllers, and channels often perform I/O activities. (An intelligent device has a certain amount of logic so that it can take some
   independent action of its own, for example, reordering disk requests in order to
   optimize head movement. A controller is a hardware device that oversees the operation of one or more I/O devices, buffers data and commands, and translates codes
   between memory and the device. A channel is an independent processor that executes a series of I/O operations asynchronously from the central processor.) These
   independent units often fall outside the security kernel or the security restrictions
   implemented by an operating system.

o The code to perform I/O is often much more complex than the code for any other
   component of the computing system. For this reason, it is harder to review I/O
   device drivers, access code, and service routines for correctness, let alone verify
   them formally.

o I/O activity sometimes bypasses other operating system functions, such as page or
   segment address translation, in the interest of fast data transfer. It may also thus
   bypass the protection features associated with those functions.

o I/O operations are often character-oriented. Again, in the interest of fast data transfer, the operating systems designers may have tried to take shortcuts by limiting the
   number of instructions executed by the operating system during actual data transfer.
   Sometimes the instructions eliminated are those that enforce security policies as
   each character is transferred.

A second prominent weakness in operating system security reflects an ambiguity in
access policy. On the one hand, it is important to have separation of users and protection
of their individual resources. On the other hand, users depend on shared access to
libraries, utility programs, common data, and system tables. The distinction between
isolation and sharing is not always clear at the policy level, so the distinction cannot be
sharply drawn at implementation.

A third difficulty with operating systems is incomplete mediation. Recall that Saltzer
recommended an operating system design in which every requested access was checked
for proper authorization. However, some systems check access only once per I/O operation, per process execution, or per machine interval. The mechanism is available to
implement full protection, but the policy decision on when to invoke the mechanism is
not complete. Therefore, in the absence of any explicit requirement, system designers
adopt the enforcement that will lead to the least use of machine resources.

A fourth protection weakness is generality, especially among commercial operating
systems for large computing systems. Operating system implementors try to provide
a means for users to customize their installation of an operating system and to allow
installation of software packages written by other companies. Some of these packages,
which operate as part of the operating system themselves, must execute with the same
access privileges as the operating system. Examples are programs that provide stricter
access control than the standard control available from the operating system. The "hooks"
by which these packages are installed are also trapdoors for any user to penetrate the
operating system.

Thus, there are several well-known points of security weakness common to many commercial operating systems. Now we consider several examples of actual flaws that have been exploited in order to penetrate operating systems.

Examples of Exploitations

As noted above, I/O is a weak point in many major operating systems. The first example of an exploited weakness involves I/O. On some systems, after access has been checked for an I/O operation, the operation continues without checking. Checking access permission with each character transferred is a substantial overhead for the protection system. The I/O command often resides in the user's memory space. Any user can alter the source or destination address of the command after the I/O operation has commenced. Since access has been checked once, it is not checked each time a piece of data is transferred, but the new address will be used. By exploiting this flaw, users have been able to transfer data to or from any memory address they desire. Complete mediation would have prevented this attack.

I/O is also involved in another example of illegal access. One operating system uses a common system buffer to retain data scheduled for delivery to all users. Any user can search this buffer and extract data that would be more carefully protected if it had been transferred to the user. In a particular attack, the data was the user authentication data, showing user IDs and passwords waiting to be read and validated by the operating system. Again, complete mediation would have eliminated this vulnerability.

Another example of exploitation involves a procedural flaw. In one system a special supervisor function was reserved for the installation of other security packages. When executed, this supervisor call returned control to the user in privileged mode. The operations allowable in that mode were not monitored closely, so that the supervisor call could be used for access control or for any other high-security system access. The particular supervisor call required some effort to execute, but it was fully available on the system. Additional checking should have been used to authenticate the program executing the supervisor request. As an alternative, the access rights for any subject entering under that supervisor request could have been limited to those objects necessary to perform the function of the added program.

Other penetrations have occurred by exploiting more complex combinations of flaws. In general, however, security flaws have resulted from a faulty analysis of a complex situation, such as I/O, or from an ambiguity or omission in the security policy. When simple security mechanisms are used to implement clear and complete security policies, the number of penetrations falls dramatically.

7.4 Certification of Secure Operating Systems

In previous sections we surveyed security features that operating systems must provide and different mechanisms for providing that security. We also studied models of protection systems, ways to design operating systems for security, and methods to penetrate flaws in operating systems.

Now we consider what it means to have confidence in the security features of an operating system—what justifies confidence and how confidence levels of operating systems have been rated. Since operating systems are used in different environments, various levels of security are acceptable among operating systems. However, we need ways of determining whether a particular operating system is appropriate for a certain set of needs.

Certification is the process of assessing the quality of the testing that has been performed and assigning a measure of confidence in the correctness of the system. The organization that has done the most for certifying the security of operating systems is the U.S. Department of Defense (DoD), working through its National Computer Security Center (NCSC). In this section, we examine the NCSC standard for evaluating trusted computing systems; this standard is known informally as the "orange book."

Methods of Evaluation

In this section we explore three ways to demonstrate the security of an operating system: formal verification, informal validation, and penetration analysis. These methods have been applied separately and in combination to assess the security of operating systems.

Formal Verification

The most precise method of analyzing security is through formal verification. In formal verification the operating system is reduced to a "theorem," which is then proven. The theorem asserts that the operating system is correct, that is, both that it provides the security features it should, and that it does not do anything else.

Proving correctness of an entire operating system is a formidable task, often requiring months or even years of effort by several people. Computer programs that apply rules of logic, called **theorem provers** can assist in this effort, although there is still much human activity needed. The amount of work required and the methods used are well beyond the scope of this book. However, we present an example of the use of proofs of correctness, as applied to a smaller program. (More extensive coverage of this topic is provided in [GRI81], [HAN76], and [CHE81].)

Consider the flow diagram of Figure 7.24, which determines the smallest of a set of n values, $A[1]$ through $A[n]$. The flow chart has a single identified beginning point, a single identified ending point, and five internal blocks, including an if-then structure and a loop.

In program verification, we begin with an initial assertion, a statement of conditions on entry to the module. We identify a series of intermediate assertions, associated with the work of the module. We also determine an ending assertion, a statement of the expected result of the flowchart. We then show that the initial assertion leads logically to the intermediate assertions, in order, which lead logically to the ending assertion.

Formally, we can prove the correctness of the algorithm in Figure 7.24 with four assertions. The first assertion, P, is a statement of initial conditions, assumed to be true on entry to the procedure.

$$n > 0 \hspace{4cm} (P)$$

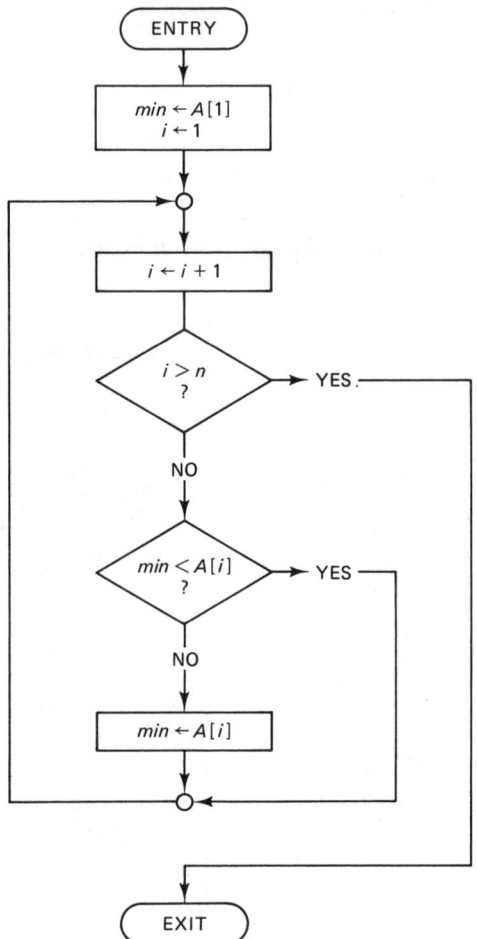

Figure 7.24 Flow Diagram for Finding the Minimum Value.

The second assertion, Q, is the result of applying the initialization code in the first box.

$$n > 0 \quad \text{and} \tag{Q}$$
$$1 \leq i \leq n \quad \text{and}$$
$$min \leq A[1]$$

The third assertion, R, is the loop assertion. It asserts what is true at the start of each iteration of the loop.

$$n > 0 \quad \text{and} \tag{R}$$
$$1 \leq i \leq n \quad \text{and}$$
$$\text{for all } j, \ 1 \leq j \leq i - 1 \quad min \leq A[j]$$

The final assertion, S, is the concluding assertion, the statement of conditions true at the time the loop exit occurs.

$$n > 0 \quad \text{and} \qquad\qquad\qquad (S)$$
$$i = n + 1 \quad \text{and}$$
$$\text{for all } j, \ 1 \le j \le n \quad min \le A[j]$$

These four assertions are shown overlaid on the flowchart in Figure 7.25.

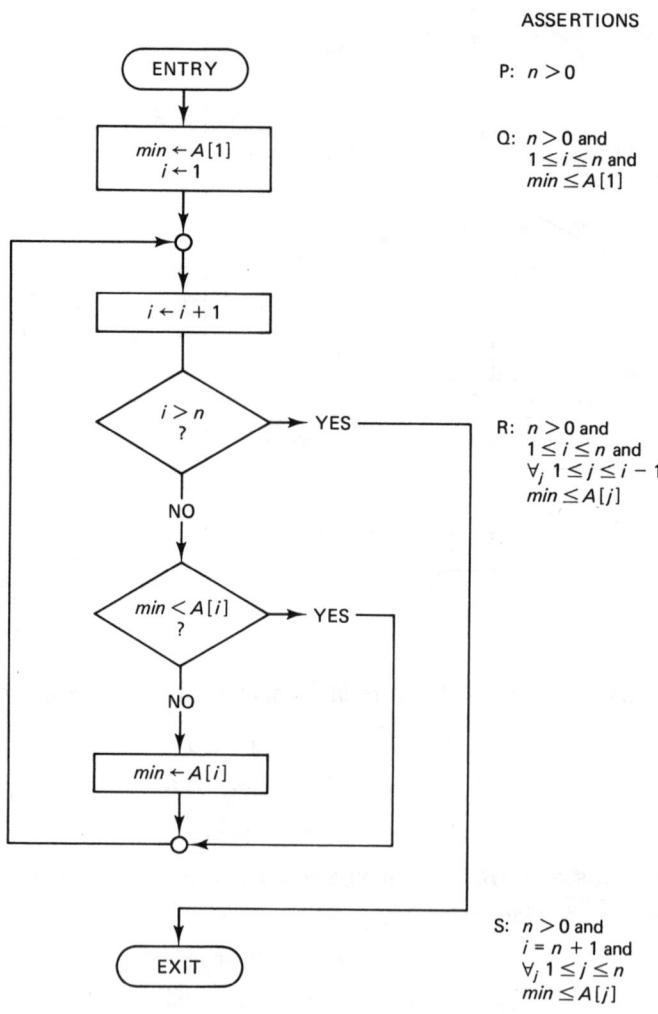

Figure 7.25   Verification Assertions.

These four assertions capture the essence of the work of the flowchart shown. Next in the verification process we must show the logical progression of these four assertions. That is, we must show that, assuming P is true on entry to this procedure, Q is true after completion of the initialization section; R is true both the first time the loop is entered and each time through the loop; and finally if R is true then S is true at the termination of the loop.

Clearly Q follows from P and the semantics of the two statements in the second box. The first time into the loop, $i = 2$, so $i - 1 = 1$. Thus, the assertion about *min* applies only for $j = 1$, which follows from Q. To prove that R remains true with each execution of the loop, we can use the principle of mathematical induction. The statement was true the first time through the loop, which forms a basis. With each iteration of the loop the value of i increases by 1, so it is necessary only to show that $min \leq A[i]$ for this new value of i. That proof follows from the meaning of the comparison and replacement statements. Therefore, R is true with each iteration of the loop. Finally, S follows from the final iteration value of R. This step completes the formal verification that this flowchart exits with the smallest value of $A[1]$ through $A[n]$ in *min*.

This algorithm (*not* the verification) is frequently used as an example in the first few weeks of introductory programming classes. It is quite simple; in fact after studying the algorithm for a short time, most students convince themselves that the algorithm is correct. The verification itself takes much longer to explain; it also takes far longer to write than the algorithm itself. There are two principal difficulties with formal verification methods:

1. *Time.* The methods of formal verification are time-consuming to perform. Stating the assertions at each step and verifying the logical flow of the assertions are both slow processes.

2. *Complexity.* Formal verification is a complex process. For some large systems it is hopeless to try to state and verify the assertions. This is especially true for systems that have not been designed with formal verification in mind.

These two difficulties reduce the number of situations in which formal verification is used successfully.

Validation

Validation is a more general term than verification. It includes verification, but it also includes other less rigorous methods of convincing people of the correctness of a program. There are several different ways to perform validation of an operating system.

o *Requirements checking.* One validation technique is to cross-check each requirement of the operating system with the source code or execution-time behavior of the system. The goal here is to demonstrate that the system does each thing listed in the functional requirements. This process tends to demonstrate only that the system does everything it should do, in at least one situation. The process seldom produces any result guaranteeing that the system does *not* do a host of things it should not.

o *Design and code reviews.* In this approach, the designers and programmers scrutinize the design or code of the system as it is being written to identify errors, incorrect assumptions, inconsistent behavior, or faulty logic. The success of this process depends on the rigor of the review.

o *Module and system testing.* During development of a program, the programmers or an independent test team select data to check the correctness of the system. This test data can be organized so as to examine each execution path, each conditional statement, each type of output report produced, each variable change, and so forth. The important point here is to make sure that all objects are checked in a methodical manner.

These and other techniques from software engineering can be applied to the validation of operating systems. Validation techniques from software engineering were studied in Chapter 5.

Tiger Team Penetration Testing

Another testing strategy is called **tiger team** analysis. In this approach, a team of experts in the use and design of operating systems tries to "crack" the system being tested. The tiger team knows typical flaws in operating systems and computing systems, as described in previous sections and chapters. With this knowledge, the team attempts to identify and exploit flaws in the system.

This approach is much like asking a mechanic to look over a used car on a sales lot. The mechanic knows potential weak spots and checks as many of them as possible. If the mechanic checks the fuel system, the cooling system, and the brakes, there is no guarantee that the muffler is good. Similarly, an operating system that *fails* a penetration test is known to have errors; a system that does *not* fail is not guaranteed to be error-free. Penetration testing is more useful to determine the presence of errors than their absence.

In summary, verification offers the most convincing demonstration of the correctness of an operating system, but it is also extremely difficult to apply. Various testing approaches justify a particular degree of confidence in the correctness of a system, but seldom can that confidence level approach 100 percent.

Qualities of Secure Systems

Given that it is infeasible to expect absolute assurance of the security of an operating system, what kinds of security measures should certifiers look for in evaluating operating systems or other computing systems? The U.S. Department of Defense has identified six requirements for secure computer systems.

1. *Security policy.* There must be an explicit and well-defined security policy enforced by the system.

2. *Identification.* Every subject must be uniquely and convincingly identified. Identification is necessary so that subject/object access request can be checked.

3. *Marking.* Every object must be associated with a "label" that indicates the security level of the object. The association, which is also known as "marking" the object, must be done so that the label is available for comparison each time an access to the object is requested.

4. *Accountability.* The system must maintain complete, secure records of actions that affect security. Such actions include introduction of new users to the system, assignment or change of the security level of a subject or an object, and denied access attempts.

5. *Assurance.* The computing system must contain mechanisms that enforce security, and it must be possible to evaluate the effectiveness of these mechanisms.

6. *Continuous protection.* The mechanisms that implement security must be protected against unauthorized change.

NCSC Certification

With these six requirements, DoD generated a set of standards for computing systems having different levels of security requirements. These were published in a document [DOD85] which has become known informally as the "orange book" because of the color of its cover. The actual name of the document is *Trusted Computer System Evaluation Criteria,* which is often abbreviated TCSEC. There are four basic divisions, A, B, C, and D, where A is the division with the most comprehensive degree of security. Within divisions there are additional distinctions, denoted with numbers, where the higher numbers indicate tighter security requirements. The complete set of ratings from lowest to highest assurance is D, C1, C2, B1, B2, B3, A1. Table 7.2 (from Appendix D of [DOD85]) shows the security requirements for each of the seven evaluated levels of NCSC certification. (Level D has no requirements, because it denotes minimal protection.)

The pattern of this table reveals that there are really four clusters: class D with no requirements; classes C1/C2/B1 that require security features common to many commercial operating systems; class B2 requiring a precise proof of security of the underlying model and a narrative specification of the trusted computing base (the security kernel); and classes B3/A1 that require more precisely proven descriptive and formal designs of the trusted computing base. This is not to imply that classes C1, C2, and B1 are equivalent. However, there are substantial increases of stringency between B1 and B2, and between B2 and B3. An operating system developer might be able to add security measures to an existing operating system in order to qualify for a C1 or C2 or B1 rating. However, security must be included in the *design* of the operating system for a B2 rating. Furthermore, the design of a B3 or A1 system must begin with construction and proof of a formal *model* of security. Thus, the distinctions between B1 and B2, and between B2 and B3 are significant.

TABLE 7.2   TRUSTED COMPUTER SYSTEM EVALUATION CRITERIA.

Criteria	Requirement						
	D	C1	C2	B1	B2	B3	A1
Security Policy							
Discretionary Access Control	■	⊗	⊗	⇒	⇒	⊗	⇒
Object Reuse	■	■	⊗	⇒	⇒	⇒	⇒
Labels	■	■	■	⊗	⊗	⇒	⇒
Label Integrity	■	■	■	⊗	⇒	⇒	⇒
Exportation of Labeled Information	■	■	■	⊗	⇒	⇒	⇒
Labeling Human-Readable Output	■	■	■	⊗	⇒	⇒	⇒
Mandatory Access Control	■	■	■	⊗	⊗	⇒	⇒
Subject Sensitivity Labels	■	■	■	■	⊗	⇒	⇒
Device Labels	■	■	■	■	⊗	⇒	⇒
Accountability							
Identification and Authentication	■	⊗	⊗	⊗	⇒	⇒	⇒
Audit	■	■	⊗	⊗	⊗	⊗	⇒
Trusted Path	■	■	■	■	⊗	⊗	⇒
Assurance							
System Architecture	■	⊗	⊗	⊗	⊗	⊗	⇒
System Integrity	■	⊗	⇒	⇒	⇒	⇒	⇒
Security Testing	■	⊗	⊗	⊗	⊗	⊗	⊗
Design Specification and Verification	■	■	■	⊗	⊗	⊗	⊗
Covert Channel Analysis	■	■	■	■	⊗	⊗	⊗
Trusted Facility Management	■	■	■	■	⊗	⊗	⇒
Configuration Management	■	■	■	■	⊗	⇒	⊗
Trusted Recovery	■	■	■	■	■	⊗	⇒
Trusted Distribution	■	■	■	■	■	■	⊗
Documentation							
Security Features User's Guide	■	⊗	⇒	⇒	⇒	⇒	⇒
Trusted Facility Manual	■	⊗	⊗	⊗	⊗	⊗	⇒
Test Documentation	■	⊗	⇒	⇒	⊗	⇒	⊗
Design Documentation	■	⊗	⇒	⊗	⊗	⊗	⊗

Legend: ■: no requirement; ⊗: additional requirement;
      ⇒: same requirement as previous class

    The descriptions of these levels and the qualities required for each rating are listed in the following sections. Within these descriptions, terms in quotation marks have been taken directly from the orange book in order to convey the spirit of the evaluation criteria.

Class D: Minimal Protection

This class is applied to systems that have been evaluated for a higher category but have failed that evaluation. No security characteristics are needed for a D rating.

Class C1: Discretionary Security Protection

Class C1 is intended for an environment of cooperating users processing data at the same level of sensitivity. A system evaluated as class C1 provides a separation of users from data. There must be controls that appear sufficient to implement access limitation in order to allow users to protect their own data. The controls of a C1 system may not have been stringently evaluated; the evaluation may be based more on the presence of certain features. In order to qualify for a C1 rating, a system must have a domain, including security functions, which is protected against tampering.

A key word in the classification is "discretionary." A user is "allowed" to decide when the controls apply, when they do not, and which named individuals or groups are allowed access.

The testing requirement indicates that the system shall be tested to ensure that it works as claimed in the documentation. Testing, such as penetration testing, shall be performed to ensure that there are no "obvious" ways for an unauthorized user to bypass or otherwise defeat the security protection mechanisms.

The IBM MVS operating system running the add-on package RACF (Resource Access Control Facility) has been certified C1.

Class C2: Controlled Access Protection

A class C2 system still implements discretionary control, although the granularity of control is finer: Protection must be implementable to the degree of a single user. The audit trail must be capable of tracking each individual's access (or attempted access) to each object.

An additional restriction imposed at the C2 level is elimination of residue exposure. **Residue** is the data that remains in primary or secondary memory or registers after a process terminates; it includes values existing in storage locations at termination, as well as data written to auxiliary storage devices but not retained after termination. Level C2 includes a requirement that this residue is to be erased, for example, by overwriting with 0s, before an object can be reused by another user.

The IBM MVS operating system running the add-on package ACF2 (Access Control Facility, version 2) is certified C2, as is the Digital Equipment Corp. VAX operating system VMS.

Class B1: Labeled Security Protection

All B-level certifications include *non*discretionary (mandatory) access control. At the B1 level, each controlled subject and object must be assigned a security level. (For class B1, the protection system does not need to control every object.)

Each controlled object must be individually labeled by security level, and these labels must be used as the basis for access control decisions. The access control must be based on a model employing both hierarchical levels and nonhierarchical categories. (The military model is an example of a system with hierarchical levels—unclassified, classified, secret, top secret—and nonhierarchical categories—need-to-know category sets.) The mandatory access policy is the Bell-LaPadula model. Thus, a B1 system must implement Bell-LaPadula controls for all accesses, and then user-discretionary access controls to further limit access.

The "design documentation, source code, and object code" shall be subjected to thorough analysis and testing. Any flaws discovered must be removed, and the system must be retested to ensure that the flaws have been eliminated and that new flaws have not been introduced. An "informal or formal model" of the security policy implemented by the system shall be available.

Class B2: Structured Protection

The major enhancement for B2 level is a design requirement: The design and implementation of a B2 system must enable a more thorough testing and review. A verifiable top-level design must be presented, and testing must confirm that the system implements this design. The system must be internally structured into "well-defined, largely independent modules." The principle of least privilege is to be enforced in the design.

Access control policies must be enforced on all objects and subjects, including devices. Analysis of covert channels is required. A person is to be designated as the security officer; this person implements the access control policy, while the operator performs only functions related to the continued operation of the system.

The protection system must maintain a protection domain for its own execution; the domain must guard the integrity of the system against external interference or tampering (for example, by modification of object code or data). The Honeywell operating system MULTICS has been rated B2.

Class B3: Security Domains

The security functions of a class B3 system must be small enough for extensive testing. A high-level design must be complete and conceptually simple, and a "convincing argument" must exist that the system implements this design. The implementation of the design shall "incorporate significant use of layering, abstraction, and information hiding."

Subject/object domains are required, with a capability to implement access protection for each object, indicating allowed subjects, kind of access allowed for each, and disallowed subjects. The full reference monitor concept shall be implemented, so that every access is checked.

The security functions must be tamperproof. The system must furthermore be "highly resistant to penetration." There is also a requirement that the system audit facility be able to identify when a violation of security is imminent.

Class A1: Verified Design

Class A1 requires a formally verified system design. The capabilities of the system are the same as for class B3. There are five important criteria for class A1 certification: (1) a formal model of the protection system and a proof of its consistency and adequacy, (2) formal top-level specification of the protection system, (3) a demonstration that the top-level specification corresponds to the model, (4) an implementation "informally" shown to be consistent with the specification, and (5) formal analysis of covert channels.

To date, only the Honeywell SCOMP system has been rated A1, although the developers of several other systems, including KVM/370 (kernelized VM/370, a security kernel retrofit to the IBM VM/370 system, produced by SDC for DARPA), PSOS (Provably Secure

Operating System, an ADA project of SRI), and KSOS (Kernelized Secure Operating System, a system from Ford Aerospace and Logicon, providing UNIX-like functions) have indicated they intend to seek that classification.

7.5 Examples of Security in General-Purpose Operating Systems

In the preceding sections you have studied the design of the security portions of operating systems. It is useful to understand the features of operating systems that can contribute to the overall security of a computing system. However, not every application requires security classified at an A1 level, which is fortuitous because few operating systems have the features needed to make them A1.

In this section we consider actual operating systems, looking at features such as access control, security kernel, and design. The focus here is on widely used, commercially available systems. In order to keep the descriptions short, only features relevant to security—and only *some* of those features—are presented.

UNIX

The UNIX operating system was never intended to have a high degree of security. It was designed in 1969 by two programmers, primarily for their own use to develop, test, and maintain programs. The system was intended for use in "nonhostile" environments, places such as research laboratories and universities, where the advantages of easy sharing of objects far outweighed the possibility of unfriendly access.

As a result, sharing of files, data, devices, and storage volumes is relatively simple, unencumbered by a strong protection mechanism. The UNIX system administrator is assumed to be a programmer who administers only part of the time and who does not, cannot, or should not perform many security functions.

UNIX grew essentially without plan. The UNIX designers, Ken Thompson, Dennis Ritchie, Doug McIlroy, and J.F. Ossanna, were programmers at Bell Laboratories when a decision was made to withdraw from the MULTICS project. Having grown used to the luxury of interactive use of a computing utility, they searched until they found an available machine on which to write their system. The design of UNIX was largely the product of Thompson, who designed the initial version and was heavily involved in the development of the system for over a decade.

Thompson's goal was to provide a simple toolbox in which a user could store and access a variety of tools that could be combined for individual uses. Generality and compactness were two qualities prominent in the design of the elementary UNIX functions, and that is still a hallmark of the operating system.

Simplicity and economy of design are virtues for users of the system, but they are a nightmare to the designer of a secure system. Security decisions permeate the UNIX commands.

There is one identified user, called the "superuser," who can perform essentially any operation in the system. Because the superuser is all-powerful, most system attacks are aimed at obtaining rights of the superuser. After having obtained this right once, even for only a few seconds, a penetrator can establish a trapdoor that permits superuser access at any time in the future.

A user sharing access to a system program can obtain high security rights if the system program runs in "setuid" mode; when a user executes such a program, the file access rights during execution of the program are the rights of the program's owner, not the program's user. The intended purpose of this feature is so that a user can use a utility program, such as `mail`, and through the program, access files at the level of `mail`. The difficulty is that most sensitive utility programs are "owned" by the superuser, so that a security flaw exploited in one utility program gives very wide access.

To UNIX all objects—directories, I/O devices, even parts of memory—are files and are accessed with the same structure. Again, this simplicity is good for the user, but it makes security difficult. File access permission is checked only once, when the file is opened. By changing the characteristics of the file or device after it has been opened, a user can obtain unchecked access permission.

UNIX provides reasonable security for the environment for which it was designed—essentially a friendly environment. However, the inherent lack of security in the basic UNIX system is evident from the fact that UNIX-based secure operating systems have actually been implemented by substantial rewrites of the UNIX kernel to provide a system that has the outward functionality of UNIX with a different internal structure. Sibert *et al.* [SIB87] describe the difficulties that would occur if UNIX were to be evaluated for B2 certification.

VAX/VMS

The Digital Equipment Corp. VAX/VMS operating system is an example of a mature, general-purpose operating system that has improved substantially over time. The original system provided moderate security features, but the current version (4) implements many desirable security features, and version 4.3 has been approved C2 under the "orange book" standards. Furthermore, advanced security features are planned.

The original system enforced moderate protection, primarily discretionary controls applied selectively by the users. The modifications that have led to C2 rating include

- o *access controls* that operate at the single subject/single object level

- o *password controls* that can be configured for the needs of a particular system

- o *auditing functions* that track selected security events

- o *monitoring functions* that warn security administrators of suspicious events or combinations of events

- o *encryption* available at the user's request

Furthermore, an additional security enhancement package is available.

IBM MVS

The IBM MVS operating system is another example of a system that has grown significantly. The underlying system design is OS/360, designed in the early 1960s for the 360 family of computers. The 360 architecture evolved into the 370 architecture, and the operating system evolved from OS/360-MVT to OS-VS2 release 2 and then to MVS.

Security features provided in IBM MVS include

- *access controls*, selected by the user, applying to individual files

- *virtual memory*, providing solid memory protection

- *access auditing*

The major enhancements have not been provided within the operating system itself, but rather within the environment in which the operating system runs. The original OS/360 MVT ran as a single operating system with multiple users. MVS was enhanced so that each user's virtual space included the operating system and no other users; in this way even if a user exploited a flaw in the operating system and broke out of the user area, the next layer of encapsulation was the operating system for that user alone. The principle of multiple virtual memories was described in Chapter 6.

VM/370

The VM/370 operating system from IBM is a good example of isolation within a multiprogramming environment. VM/370 was designed as an operating system's operating system: it runs other operating systems, which do not necessarily have to be similar. Essentially each operating system is isolated through logical separation so that it is completely unaware of the existence of other operating systems. Each operating system believes that it is executing alone on a complete machine.

VM/370 manages disk space, memory, access to hardware features such as interrupts, and processor use so that one resource can be logically shared among several different operating systems. The virtual machine concept was described in Chapter 6.

7.6 Operating Systems Designed for Security

All of the examples described so far are conventional, commercial, general-purpose operating systems. These systems are best suited to environments that are moderately safe, for example, where the users are reasonably friendly, and data and programs are of only moderate security value. Although their users expect reasonable security, the overhead and the difficulty of applying stringent security would exceed the benefit for most users. This is not to say that these systems should be easily penetrated, only that they do not have high security requirements.

Following are operating systems designed for environments having far greater security needs. In the design, security has been the foremost requirement, with such factors as usability and efficiency having lower importance. Such systems might be used for government security applications, diplomatic communication, or projects where the value of the assets of the system is high.

Honeywell SCOMP

There is a complementary relationship between the hardware and software for the Honeywell SCOMP (Secure Communications Processor) operating system, the first system to have been classified A1 by the National Computer Security Center. The software performs initial validation of a user's access request; it then builds a "descriptor," consisting of four words of security information, for use by the hardware in continuing the validation process. Reliance on hardware provides the advantages of speed and added security over a strictly software implementation.

The SCOMP operating system runs on a specially modified Honeywell Level 6/DPS 6, a 16-bit bus-structured minicomputer. Because of the bus structure, it is relatively easy to replace the standard processor with the security-enhanced one, and to add a special Security Protection Module (SPM).

Memory addressing uses a conventional paged segmentation scheme. Input and output are virtual processes, as well, using a translation process similar to memory. The SPM intercepts each I/O request, validates the request and memory addresses, and translates the request to an absolute memory address. The SPM then passes the real device designator and the real memory address to a device driver (software), which performs the I/O activity. Thus, checking the I/O access is done in the security kernel, but the actual data transfer can be done outside the kernel, reducing the size of the kernel. A reduced size is important for a kernel that must be formally verified.

The design of the operating system is ring-structured, using four rings. These rings are numbered from 0 (most privileged), in which the security kernel resides, to 3 (least privileged), in which user programs execute. A less privileged process can call a more privileged module to request a service. The more privileged module can access arguments passed to it using the access rights of the caller. In this way, a security function routine can receive arguments from a user, but not automatically transfer its more privileged access rights to the user's arguments.

Object access includes nondiscretionary security level and categories, as well as discretionary user-group-world access permissions. There are also ring brackets that limit the ring of privilege required to access an object.

The operating system uses the concept of *trusted software* to implement functions outside the security kernel. The software is trusted because the true security properties of the system are performed by the kernel, and because the kernel must depend on this software for the data it needs to implement security policies properly. There is a *trusted communications path* through which the user accesses trusted software. This path assures the user that the process at the other end of the path is the operating system, not a Trojan horse.

Another level of the operating system provides more common operating system features, such as a file system, process initiation and termination, subprocess creation, synchronization, and interface to the security kernel. These services reside in ring 2 of the operating system, with some of the facilities being utilities in ring 3 for use by the user.

UCLA Secure UNIX

The UCLA Data Secure UNIX [POP79] system chose a slightly different technique for assuring security. The system uses a three-level design, with hardware and an operating system security kernel at the lowest level, other operating systems tasks at the second level, and user processes and some utilities at the third.

At the user level, the software appears to be a standard implementation of UNIX. However, the standard UNIX operating system was not used; instead, a two-part package was written. One part is the user interface, which presents a UNIX environment to the user. The user UNIX interface interacts with the kernel through KISS, the Kernel Interface SubSystem. As shown in Figure 7.26, the kernel interface interacts with the user UNIX interface—through a conventional scheduler and network manager, and with a trusted policy manager and dialoguer. These last two routines are trusted because, as with SCOMP, they gather data or provide a user pathway that the kernel must trust in order to work.

For this system, too, the security kernel is relatively small, consisting of about 2000 lines of code. Significant improvements in efficiency and robustness occurred by collecting all security functions in one place, rather than having them distributed among many operating systems modules.

Kernelized VM/370

The SCOMP system was a development of an entirely new operating system, while UCLA Secure UNIX was an attempt to provide a UNIX environment to users, without necessarily using all or substantial parts of the UNIX operating system itself. However, the goal of Kernelized VM/370 (kvm/370) was to retrofit security features onto the existing VM/370 operating system. The experience of the KVM/370 system is described by Gold in [GOL77], [GOL79], and [GOL84]. The intention with KVM/370 was to leave at least half of the original operating system intact, a goal largely based on the substantial size and complexity of that system. The organization of the system is shown in Figure 7.27. Since VM/370 provides virtual *machines*, the KVM/370 system was expected to support multiple isolated machines, perhaps running at different security levels. The kernel would interact with trusted processes for user logon and authentication, as well as access to disks and directories. There was also a modified scheduler to perform allocation functions for the kernel.

A serious concern for the secure computations is to ensure that the user is communicating with a real system. SCOMP establishes a trusted communications path for the user. This was not feasible for KVM/370, so a three-way handshaking password system was used. The user initiates a logon by giving a user identification and a password. The system responds with a password known only by that particular user. The user must then respond with a third password. Thus, a program masquerading as the real user authentication system might be able to trick the user into revealing the first password,

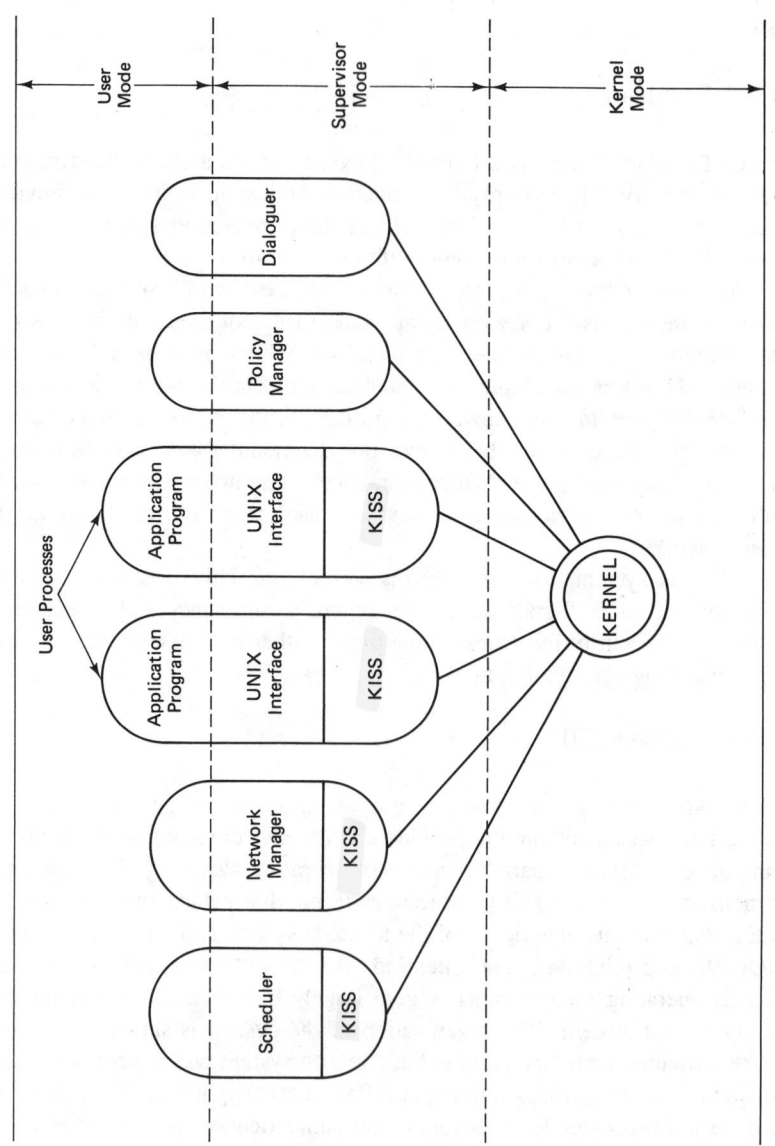

Figure 7.26 UCLA Secure Unix Interface.

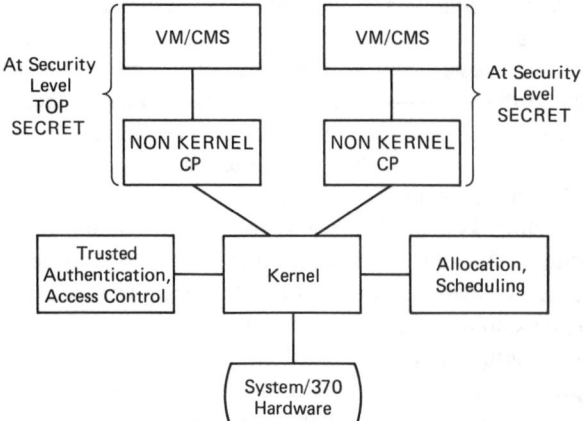

Figure 7.27   KVM/370 System Organization.

but since the masquerading program would not be able to send the second password, it could not trick the user into providing the third.

The support for KVM/370 was withdrawn in 1982, after roughly six years of work [GOL84]. The essential problems with the system were

- unverifiable design

- large and complex kernel

- hardware and software compatibility difficulties

- poor performance

The project suffered from trying to reuse existing nonsecurity-conscious code and from trying to maintain consistency with a very large, very general operating system.

7.7 Summary of Security in Operating Systems

Operating systems are at the heart of security systems for modern computers. Operating systems must provide the mechanisms for both separation and sharing; these mechanisms must be robust yet easy to use.

Development of secure operating systems involves four activities. First, the environment to be protected must be well understood. Through models, the essential components of systems are identified, and the interactions between these components can be studied. This chapter has presented a variety of models of security. These models ranged from reference monitors and information flow filters to multilevel security and integrity models. Models such as the one by Bell and LaPadula describe permissible access in a multilevel environment, while the HRU model demonstrates the limits of computer security.

After an environment is understood, a system must be designed to provide the desired protection. Certain design principles for secure operating systems were presented. Not surprisingly, features such as least privilege, openness of design, and economy of mechanism are quite similar to the software engineering design principles described in Chapter 5. Clearly, characteristics that lead to good design of an operating system apply to the design of other programs as well. Isolation or separation, layered design, and security kernel were studied in some detail.

After designing an operating system, one wants assurance that the design (and its implementation) are correct. This chapter considered three methods to demonstrate correctness: formal verification, validation, and penetration testing. The NCSC "Orange Book" evaluation criteria were examined in detail since they represent the current standard for certification of trusted computing systems.

Finally, several examples of the implementations of secure operating systems were studied. These examples included both widely available commercial systems and systems designed specifically for their security features.

In the next chapter, secure data base management systems are studied. Data base systems have many of the same requirements as operating systems: access control, availability, multilevel security. Data base management systems are implemented on top of operating systems, and thus they use some of the services provided by operating systems. Integrity and granularity are substantially different in those systems, however.

7.8 Terms and Concepts

model of security
access control policy
single-user model
monitor model
information flow model
military security model
sensitivity rank
least privilege
need-to-know principle
compartment
class/classification
clearance
lattice
lattice model of access security
least upper bound, greatest lower bound
information flow model
Bell-LaPadula model
simple security property
∗-property
write-down
simple integrity property

integrity ∗-property
Graham-Denning model
HRU model
protection system
Take-Grant system
least privilege
economy of mechanism
open design
complete mediation
permission-based
separation of privilege
least common mechanism
easy to use
physical separation
temporal separation
cryptographic separation
logical separation
isolation
multiple virtual memory space
virtual machine
control program
kernel
security kernel
separation of kernel
unity of kernel
modifiability of kernel
compactness of kernel
verifiability of kernel
coverage of kernel
layered design
ring structured protection
segment
ring bracket
call bracket
access bracket
gate extension
discretionary control
nondiscretionary control
trust
penetration
certification
formal verification
theorem prover
validation
tiger team penetration testing

security policy
identification
marking
accountability
assurance
continuous protection
residue
labelling
hierarchical level label
nonhierarchical category label
security domain
tamperproof
audit facility
covert channel
formal verification
UNIX
VAX VMS
IBM MVS
IBM VM/370
Honeywell SCOMP
UCLA Data Secure UNIX
Kernelized VM/370: KVM/370

7.9 Bibliographic Notes

The topic of secure computing systems includes fundamental papers such as Lampson [LAM71], Popek [POP74], Hoare [HOA74], Graham [GRA68], Saltzer and Schroeder [SAL75], and Jones [JON78]. Landwehr [LAN81] provides a good overview of models of protection systems. Additional information on models of security is provided by Bell [BEL83] and Harrison [Har85], and Goguen and Mesequer [GOG82].

The design of secure systems is discussed by Gasser [GAS88], Ames [AME83], and Landwehr [LAN83]. Certification of security systems is discussed by Neumann [NEU78] and Neugent [NEU82].

7.10 Exercises

1. There is another principle of the Bell-LaPadula model that was not mentioned in this chapter. This principle, called the **tranquility principle**, states that the classification of a subject or object does not change while it is being referenced. Explain the purpose of the tranquility principle. What are the implications of a model in which the tranquility principle is *not* true?

2. A subject can access another subject. Describe how a reference monitor would control access in the case of a subject acting on another subject. Describe how a reference monitor would control access in the case of two subjects interacting.

3. List the source and end of all information flows in each of the following statements.
   a. `sum := a+b+c;`
   b. `if a+b < c+d then q:=0 else q:=1;`
   c. `write (a,b,c);`
   d. `read (a,b,c);`
   e. `case (k) of`
   ```
        0: d:=10;
        1,2: d:= 20;
        other: d:= 30;
   end; /* case */
   ```
   f. `for i:=min to max do k:=2*k+1;`
   g. `repeat`
   ```
        a[i]:=0;
        i:=i-1;
   until i <= 0;
   ```

4. Does the system of all subsets of a finite set, under the operation "subset of" ($\subseteq$) form a lattice? Why or why not?

5. Can a user cleared for $\langle secret; \{dog, cat, pig\}\rangle$ have access to documents classified in each of the following ways under the military security model?
   a. $\langle top\ secret; dog\rangle$
   b. $\langle secret; \{dog\}\rangle$
   c. $\langle secret; \{dog, cow\}\rangle$
   d. $\langle secret; \{moose\}\rangle$
   e. $\langle confidential; \{dog,pig,cat\}\rangle$
   f. $\langle confidential; \{moose\}\rangle$

6. According to the Bell-LaPadula model, what restrictions would this rule place on two active subjects (for example, two processes) that wished to send and receive signals to each other? Justify your answer.

7. Write a set of rules combining the secrecy controls of the Bell-LaPadula model with the integrity controls of the Biba model.

8. Demonstrate a method for limited transfer of rights in the Graham-Denning model. A limit of one is adequate. That is, give a method by which A can transfer to B right r, with the provision that B can transfer that right to any other single subject. The subject to which B transfers the right cannot transfer the right, nor can B transfer it again.

9. How does the IBM VM operating system support the principle of least common mechanism?

10. Explain what is necessary to provide temporal separation. That is, what conditions must be met in order for two processes to be adequately separated?

11. Explain what action the system performs if a process running at level 3 on a MULTICS system wishes to call a process with ring bracket $\langle 0, 2, 5 \rangle$.

12. Assume in a MULTICS system that system processes run at levels 0 through 3, user processes run at levels 4 and 5, and levels 6 and 7 are unassigned. You have just received a piece of untrusted software. You wish to execute it, but you do not want it to be able to affect the integrity of certain data files. (a) What access bracket would you assign the procedure? (b) What access bracket would you assign to your data so that the untrusted procedure could access the data but not affect its integrity?

13. Does the standard UNIX operating system employ a nondiscretionary access control? Explain your answer.

14. Why is labeling of objects a security requirement? That is, why cannot the trusted computing base just maintain an access control table with entries for each object and each subject?

15. "Label integrity" means a technique that ensures that the label on each object is changed only by the trusted computing base. Suggest a method to implement label integrity for a data file. Suggest a method to implement label integrity for a callable procedure.

16. Describe a situation in which it is desirable to allow the security kernel to violate one of the security properties of the Bell-LaPadula model.

17. Explain the meaning of the term "granularity" in reference to access control. Discuss the tradeoff between granularity and efficiency.

18. Explain how a semaphore could be used to implement a covert channel in concurrent processing. Explain how concurrent processing primitives, such as *fork* and *join* could be used to implement a covert channel in concurrent processing.

19. The UNIX operating system structures files by use of a tree. Each file is at a leaf of the tree, and the file is identified by the (unique) path from the root to the leaf. Each interior node is a "subdirectory," which specifies the names of the paths leading from that node. A user can block access through a node by restricting access to the subdirectory. Devise a method that uses this structure to implement a discretionary access policy.

20. In the UNIX file system described earlier, could a nondiscretionary access policy be defined so that a user has access to a file only if the user has access to all subdirectories higher (closer to the root) in the file structure? What would be the effect of this policy?

21. I/O appears as the source of several successful methods of penetration. Discuss why I/O is hard to secure in a computing system.

8

Data Base Security

In this chapter we consider the security of data base management systems. This is an area of substantial interest in computing security because (1) the study of data bases is new relative to programming and operating systems, (2) the use of data bases is becoming very important in business and government, and (3) data bases contain information that is of far greater general interest than a piece of software. The value of information is just now being recognized as a major corporate asset.

The protection provided by data base systems has had mixed results. We have come closer to understanding the problems of data base security over the last ten years, and several good controls have been developed. However, there are still more security concerns than there are available controls.

We begin this chapter with a brief summary of data base terminology for those who may be unfamiliar. We then consider the security requirements for data base management systems. Two major security problems—integrity and secrecy—are explained in a data base context. The chapter concludes with a study of two major data base security problems, the inference problem and the multilevel problem, which are really related problems. Both of these problems are complex, and there are no immediate solutions. However, by understanding the problems we become more sensitive to ways of reducing the potential threat to the data.

8.1 Introduction to Data Bases

We begin by describing a data base and defining the terminology of data base use. We focus on what is called the **relational** data base, since it is the most widely used. We define the basic concepts first and then discuss security concerns. Additional detail on data bases is available from many sources, for example, [DAT81], [DAT83], [DEN82], and [ULL82].

Concept of a Data Base

A **data base** is a collection of *data* and a set of *rules* that organize the data by specifying certain relationships among the data. Through these rules, the user describes a *logical* format for the data. The data are stored in a file, but the precise *physical* format of the file is of no concern to the user. A **data base administrator** is a person who defines the rules that organize the data and also controls who should have access to what parts of the data. The user interacts with the data base through a program called a **data base manager** or a **data base management system (DBMS)**—informally known as a **front end**.

Components of Data Bases

The data base file consists of **records**, each of which contains one related group of data. As shown in Figure 8.1, a record in a name and address file would consist of one name and address. Each record consists of **fields** or **elements**, the elementary data items themselves. The fields in the name and address record are NAME, FIRST, ADDRESS, CITY, STATE, and ZIP. This data base may be viewed as a two-dimensional table, where a record is a row and each field of a record is an element of the table.

ADAMS	212 Market St.	Columbus	OH	43210
BENCHLY	501 Union St.	Chicago	IL	60603
CARTER	411 Elm St.	Columbus	OH	43210

Figure 8.1   Example of a Data Base.

Not every data base is easily represented as a single, compact table. The data base in Figure 8.2 logically consists of three files with possibly different uses. These three files could be represented as one large table, but that may not improve the utility or the access of the data.

The logical structure of a data base is called a **schema**. A particular user may have access to part of the data base, called a **subschema**. The overall schema of the data base in Figure 8.2 is pictured in Figure 8.3. The three separate blocks are examples of subschemas, although other subschemas of this data base can be defined.

The rules of a data base identify the columns with names. The name of each column is called an **attribute** of the data base. A **relation** is a set of columns. For example, using the data base in Figure 8.3, NAME-ZIP is a relation formed by taking the NAME and ZIP columns, as shown in Figure 8.4. The relation specifies clusters of related data values, in much the same way that the relation "mother of" specifies a relation among pairs of humans. In this example, each cluster contains a pair of elements, a NAME and a ZIP. Other relations have more columns, so that each cluster may be a triple, a 4-tuple, or an n-tuple (for some value n) of elements.

Queries

Users interact with data base managers through commands that retrieve, modify, add, or delete fields and records of the data base. A command is called a **query**. Data base

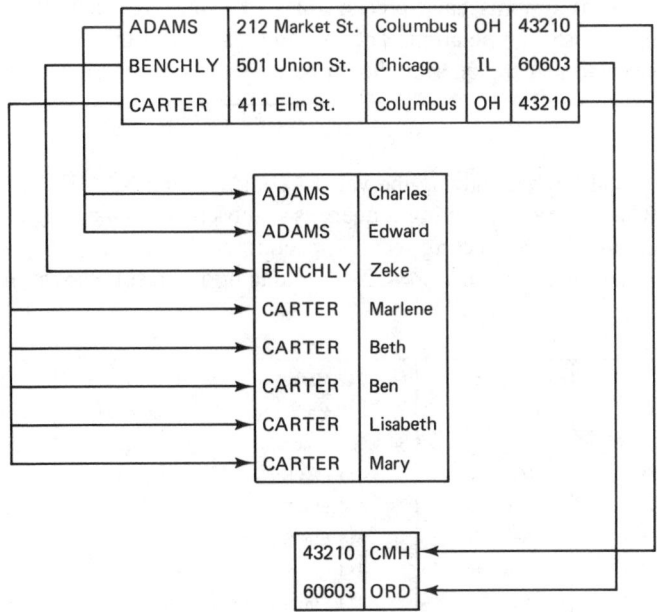

Figure 8.2   Related Parts of a Data Base.

NAME	FIRST	ADDRESS	CITY	STATE	ZIP	AIRPORT
ADAMS	Charles	212 Market St.	Columbus	OH	43210	CMH
ADAMS	Edward	212 Market St.	Columbus	OH	43210	CMH
BENCHLY	Zeke	501 Union St.	Chicago	IL	60603	ORD
CARTER	Marlene	411 Elm St.	Columbus	OH	43210	CMH
CARTER	Beth	411 Elm St.	Columbus	OH	43210	CMH
CARTER	Ben	411 Elm St.	Columbus	OH	43210	CMH
CARTER	Lisabeth	411 Elm St.	Columbus	OH	43210	CMH
CARTER	Mary	411 Elm St.	Columbus	OH	43210	CMH

Figure 8.3   Schema of Previous Data Base.

NAME	ZIP
ADAMS	43210
BENCHLY	60603
CARTER	43210

Figure 8.4   Relation in a Data Base.

management systems have precise rules of syntax for queries. Most query languages use an English-like notation. The example queries in this chapter will resemble English sentences so that the queries should be easy to understand. For example, the query

SELECT NAME='ADAMS'

retrieves all records having the value *ADAMS* in the NAME field.

The result of executing a query is a subschema. One way to form a subschema of a data base is by selecting records meeting certain conditions. For example, we might select records in which ZIP=43210, producing the result shown in Figure 8.5.

ADAMS	Charles	212 Market St.	Columbus	OH	43210	CMH
ADAMS	Edward	212 Market St.	Columbus	OH	43210	CMH
BENCHLY	Zeke	501 Union St.	Chicago	IL	60603	ORD
CARTER	Marlene	411 Elm St.	Columbus	OH	43210	CMH
CARTER	Beth	411 Elm St.	Columbus	OH	43210	CMH
CARTER	Ben	411 Elm St.	Columbus	OH	43210	CMH
CARTER	Lisabeth	411 Elm St.	Columbus	OH	43210	CMH
CARTER	Mary	411 Elm St.	Columbus	OH	43210	CMH

Figure 8.5   Result of Select Query.

Other more complex selection criteria are possible, using logical operators such as *and* (∧) and *or* (∨), and comparisons such as *less than* (<). An example of a select query is

SELECT (ZIP='43210') ∧ (NAME='ADAMS')

After having selected records, we may **project** these records onto one or more attributes. The select operation extracts certain rows from the data base, while a project operation extracts the values from certain fields (columns) of those records. The result of a select-project operation is the set of values of specified attributes for the selected records. For example, we might select records meeting the condition ZIP=43210 and project the results onto the attributes NAME and FIRST, as in Figure 8.6. The result is the list of first and last names of people whose addresses have zip code 43210.

Notice that it is not necessary to project onto the same attribute(s) on which the selection is done. An example of a project query is

SHOW FIRST WHERE (ZIP='43210') ∧ (NAME='ADAMS')

Finally, two subschema can be merged on a common element by a **join** query. The result of this operation is a subschema whose records have the same value for the common element. The example in Figure 8.7 shows that the subschema NAME-ZIP and the subschema ZIP-AIRPORT can be joined on the common field ZIP to produce the subschema NAME-AIRPORT.

ADAMS	Charles
ADAMS	Edward
CARTER	Marlene
CARTER	Beth
CARTER	Ben
CARTER	Lisabeth
CARTER	Mary

Figure 8.6 Results of Select-Project Query.

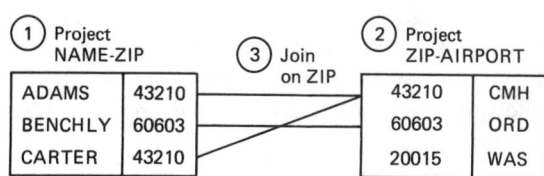

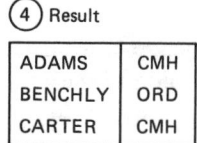

Figure 8.7 Results of Select-Project-Join Query.

Advantages of Using Data Bases

A data base is one collection of data, stored and maintained at one central location, to which many people have access as needed. (This is the logical principle of a data base; the actual implementation may involve some other physical storage arrangement or access, so long as the user's perception is as above.) The advantages of using a data base are:

- *shared access,* so that many users can use one common, centralized set of data

- *minimal redundancy,* so that individual users do not have to collect and maintain their own sets of data

- *data consistency,* so that a change to a data value affects all users of the data value

- *data integrity,* so that data values are protected against accidental or malicious incorrect changes

- *controlled access,* so that only authorized users are allowed to view or to modify data values

A DBMS is designed to provide these advantages efficiently. However, as often happens, the objectives can conflict with each other. In particular, as we shall see, security interests can conflict with performance. This should not be surprising, since measures to enforce security often increase the size or complexity of a computing system. What is surprising, however, is that security interests may also reduce the ability of the system to provide data to users, by limiting certain queries that seem innocuous by themselves.

8.2 Security Requirements

The basic security requirements of data base systems are not unlike the security requirements of other computing systems we have studied. The basic problems—access control, exclusion of spurious data, authentication of users, reliability—have appeared in many contexts so far in this book. Following is a list of requirements for security of data base systems.

- o *Physical data base integrity*, so that the data of a data base is immune to physical problems, such as power failures, and so that it is possible to reconstruct the data base if it is destroyed through a catastrophe.

- o *Logical data base integrity*, so that the structure of the data base is preserved. With logical integrity of a data base, a modification to the value of one field does not affect other fields, for example.

- o *Element integrity*, so that the data contained in each element is accurate.

- o *Auditability*, to be able to track who has accessed (or modified) the elements in the data base.

- o *Access control*, so that a user is allowed to access only authorized data and so that different users can be restricted to different modes of access (for example, read or write).

- o *User authentication*, to be sure that every user is positively identified, both for the audit trail and for permission to access certain data.

- o *Availability*, meaning that users can access the data base in general and all the data for which they are authorized.

We will examine each of these requirements briefly.

Integrity of the Data Base

If a data base is to serve as a central repository of data, users must be able to trust the accuracy of the data values. This implies that the data base manager must be assured that updates are performed only by authorized individuals. It also implies that the data must be protected from corruption, either by an outside illegal program action or by an outside force such as a fire or power failure. There are two situations affecting the integrity of a data base: (1) when the whole data base is damaged (as happens, for example, if a disk pack is dropped or otherwise damaged), or (2) when individual data items are unreadable.

Integrity of the data base as a whole is the responsibility of the DBMS, the operating system, and the computing system manager. From the perspective of the operating system and the computing system manager, data bases and DBMSs are files and programs, respectively. Therefore, one form of protection for the data base as a whole is regular backup copies of all files on the system. Periodic backups of a data base can be adequate controls against catastrophic failure.

If it is important to be able to reconstruct the data base at the point of an error, the DBMS must maintain a log of transactions. For example, a bank account data base manager might generate a printed message each time a transaction is processed. In the event of a system failure, accurate account balances can be obtained by starting with a backup copy of the data base and reprocessing all later transactions from the log.

Element Integrity

The **integrity** of elements of a data base refers to their correctness or accuracy. Ultimately, authorized users are responsible for putting correct data into data bases. However, users make mistakes collecting data, computing results, and entering values. Therefore, the DBMS must be able to help a user catch errors as they are entered and correct errors after they are inserted.

The DBMS maintains the integrity of each item in the data base in three ways. First, it can apply **field checks**, which are tests for appropriate values in a position. A field might be required to be numeric, or an uppercase letter, or one of a set of acceptable characters. The check ensures that a value falls within specified bounds or is not greater than the sum of the values in two other fields. These checks prevent simple errors as the data are being entered.

Integrity is also maintained by **access control**. A data base may contain data from several sources. Prior to the development of a data base, redundant data might have been stored in many places. For example, a student's address may be stored in many different campus files, some of which the student would not know. When the student moves, each separate file requires correction. Data bases have led to the collection and control of this data at one central source. This makes it easy for the student and users to be sure of having the correct address.

However, ownership of a shared central file is a question. Who has authorization to update which elements? What if two people apply conflicting modifications? What if modifications are applied out of sequence? How are duplicate records detected? What action is taken when duplicates are found? These are policy questions that must be resolved by the data base administrator.

The third means of maintaining the integrity of a data base is to maintain a **change log** for the data base. A change log is a list of every change made to the data base; the log contains both original and modified values. With this log a data base administrator can "undo" any changes that were in error. For example, a library fine might erroneously be posted against Charles W. Robertson, instead of Charles M. Robertson, flagging Charles W. Robertson as ineligible to participate in varsity athletics. Upon discovering this error, the data base administrator obtains Charles W.'s original eligibility value from the log and corrects the data base.

Auditability

In some applications it may be desirable to generate an audit record of all access (read or write) to a data base. Such a record can help to maintain the integrity of a data base or, at least, to discover after the fact who had affected what values and when. A second advantage, as discussed later, is that users can build up access to protected data incrementally: No single access reveals protected data, but a set of accesses taken together reveals the data like the clues to a mystery. In this case, an audit trail would be useful to identify which clues a user has already been given, as a guide to whether to tell the user more.

Granularity becomes an impediment in auditing. While audited events in operating systems are things like "open file" or "call procedure," they are seldom as specific as "write record" or "execute instruction." To be useful for the purposes just described, audit trails for data bases must include accesses at the record, field, and element levels. This level of detail is prohibitive for most data base applications.

Furthermore, a record may be accessed but not reported to a user, for example, when performing a select operation. (Accessing a record or an element without transferring the data received to the user is called the "pass through problem.") Also, it is possible to determine the values of some elements without accessing them directly. Thus, a log of all records accessed directly may both overstate and understate what a user actually knows.

Access Control

Data bases are often logically separated by user access privileges. For example, all users can be granted access to general data, while only the personnel department can obtain salary data, and only the marketing department can obtain sales data. Data bases are very useful since they centralize the storage and maintenance of data. Limited access is both a responsibility and a benefit of this centralization.

The data base administrator specifies who should be allowed access to which data, at the field, or record, or even element level. The DBMS must enforce this policy, granting access to all specified data or no access where prohibited. Furthermore, the number of modes of access can be many. A user or program may have the right to read, change, delete, or append to a value, add or delete entire fields or records, or reorganize the complete data base.

Superficially, access control for a data base seems like access control for operating systems or any other component of a computing system. However, the data base problem is more complicated, as we will see throughout the rest of this chapter. Operating system objects, such as files, are unrelated items, while records, fields, and elements are related. While a user cannot determine the contents of one file by reading others, a user might be able to determine one data element just by reading others. The problem of obtaining data values from others is called "inference"; that problem is considered later in this chapter.

It is possible to access data by inference, without needing to have direct access to the secure object itself. Restricting inference may mean prohibiting certain paths in order to prevent possible inferences. However, restricting access to control inference also limits queries from users who did not intend to access values not authorized. Access to the data base may also degrade in order to check requested accesses for possible unacceptable inferences.

Finally, size or granularity is different between operating system objects and data base objects. An access control list of several hundred files is much easier to implement than an access control list for a data base with several hundred files of perhaps a hundred fields each. Size has an effect on efficiency of processing.

User Authentication

The DBMS can require rigorous user authentication. For example, a DBMS might require a user to pass both specific password and time-of-day checks. This authentication is in addition to authentication performed by the operating system. Typically, the DBMS runs as an application program on top of the operating system. This means that it has no trusted path to the operating system, and it must be suspicious of any data it receives, including user authentication. Thus the DBMS must do its own authentication.

Availability

A DBMS has aspects of both a program and a system. It is a program that uses other hardware and software resources, yet to many users it is the only application run. The availability requirements of a DBMS are high. One availability problem stems from arbitrating two users' requests for the same record. A second problem comes from needing to withhold some nonprotected data in order to avoid revealing protected data. Both of these problems are described later.

Integrity/Secrecy/Availability

In this section we have outlined the three aspects of computer security—integrity, secrecy, and availability— as they relate to data base management systems. As we have described, integrity applies to the individual elements of a data base as well as to the data base as a whole. Thus, integrity is a major concern in the design of data base management systems. Integrity issues are covered in the next section.

Secrecy becomes a large issue with data bases because of inference. A user can access sensitive data indirectly. Inference and access control are covered in later sections of this chapter.

Finally, availability is important because of the shared access motivation underlying the development of data bases. However, availability can conflict with secrecy. The last sections of the chapter address availability in an environment where secrecy is also important.

8.3 Reliability and Integrity

Data bases are an amalgamation of data from many sources. Users entrust their data to a DBMS and rightfully expect protection of the data from loss or damage. Concern for reliability and integrity are general security issues, but they are more highly apparent with data bases.

Data bases really have three dimensions of reliability or integrity concerns:

1. *Data base integrity:* concern that the data base as a whole is protected against damage, as from the failure of a disk drive or the corruption of the master data base index. These concerns are addressed by operating system integrity controls and recovery procedures.

2. *Element integrity:* concern that the value of a specific data element is written or changed only by actions of authorized users. Proper access controls protect a data base from corruption by unauthorized users.

3. *Element accuracy:* concern that only correct values are written into the elements of a data base. Checks on the values of elements can help to prevent insertion of improper values. Also, constraint conditions can detect incorrect values.

There are several ways that a DBMS guards against the loss or damage of data. In this section we study methods to ensure data base integrity, element integrity, and element accuracy. However, these controls are not absolute: No control can prevent an authorized user from inadvertently entering an acceptable, but incorrect, value. Therefore, the ability to correct erroneous data in a data base is an important mechanism for ensuring accuracy.

Protection Features from the Operating System

In Chapter 6 we discussed the protection an operating system provides for its users. The files of a data base are backed up periodically, just as are other user files. The files are protected during normal execution against outside access by standard access control facilities of the operating system. Finally, the operating system performs certain integrity checks for all data as a part of normal read and write operations for I/O devices. These controls provide basic security for data bases, but the data base manager must enhance these controls.

Two-Phase Update

A serious problem for a data base manager is the failure of the computing system in the middle of modifying data. If the data to be modified was a long field, half of the field might show the new value, while the other half would contain the old. Even if errors of this type were spotted easily (which they are not), a more subtle problem occurs when updating several fields, where no single field appears in obvious error. The solution to this problem, proposed first by Lampson and Sturgis [LAM76] and adopted by most DBMSs, uses a two-phase update.

Update Technique

During the first phase, called the **intent** phase, the DBMS gathers the information and other resources it needs to perform the update. It may gather data, create dummy records, open files, lock out other users, and calculate final answers; in short, it does everything to prepare for the update, but it makes no changes to the data base. The first phase is repeatable an unlimited number of times, since it takes no permanent action. If the system should fail during execution of the first phase, there is no harm, since all of these steps can be restarted and repeated after the system resumes processing.

The last event of the first phase, called **committing**, involves writing a **commit flag** to the data base. The commit flag means that the DBMS has passed the point of no return—after committing, the DBMS begins making permanent changes.

The second phase is making the permanent changes. During the second phase, no actions from before the commit can be repeated, but the update activities of phase two can also be repeated as often as needed. If the system fails during the second phase, the data base may contain incomplete data, but this data can be repaired by performing all activities of the second phase. After the second phase has been completed, the data base is again complete.

Two-Phase Update Example

Suppose a data base contains an inventory of office supplies for a company. A central stockroom for the company stocks paper, pens, paper clips, and the like, and the different departments of the company requisition these items as they need them. The company buys in bulk to obtain the best prices. Each department has a budget for office supplies, and so there is a charging mechanism by which the cost of supplies is recovered from the department. Also, the central stockroom monitors quantities of supplies on hand so as to be able to order new supplies when the stock becomes low.

The process begins with a requisition, for example, from the accounting department, for 50 boxes of paper clips. Assume that there are 107 boxes in stock and a new order is placed if the quantity in stock ever falls below 100. Here are the steps followed after the stockroom has received the requisition.

1. The stockroom checks the data base to determine that 50 boxes of paper clips are on hand. If not, the requisition is rejected and the transaction is finished.

2. If there are enough paper clips in stock, the stockroom deducts 50 from the inventory figure in the data base. (107−50=57).

3. The stockroom charges accounting's supplies budget (also in the data base) for 50 boxes of paper clips.

4. The stockroom checks its remaining quantity on hand (57) to determine if the remaining quantity is below the reorder point. Since it is, a notice to order more paper clips is generated, and the item is flagged as "on order" in the data base.

5. A delivery order is prepared to cause 50 boxes of paper clips to be sent to accounting.

All five of these steps must be completed in order for the data base to be accurate and for the transaction to be processed correctly.

Suppose a failure occurs while these steps are being processed. If the failure occurs before step 1 is complete, there is no harm, since the entire transaction can be restarted. However, during steps 2, 3, and 4, changes are made to elements in the data base. If a failure occurs then, the values in the data base are inconsistent. Worse, the transaction cannot be reprocessed, since a requisition would be deducted twice, or a department would be charged twice, or two delivery orders would be prepared.

Using a two-phase commit, **shadow values** are maintained for key data points. A shadow data value is computed and stored locally during the intent phase, and it is copied to the actual data base during the commit phase. The operations on the data base would be performed as follows for a two-phase commit.

Intent:

1. Check the value of COMMIT_FLAG in the data base. If it is set, this phase cannot be performed. Compare number of boxes of paper clips on hand to number requisitioned; if more are requisitioned than on hand, halt.

2. Compute TCLIPS = ONHAND − REQUISITION.

3. Obtain BUDGET, current supplies budget remaining for accounting department. Compute TBUDGET = BUDGET − COST, where COST is the cost of 50 boxes of clips.

4. Check if TCLIPS is below reorder point; if so, set TREORDER = TRUE; else set TREORDER = FALSE.

Commit:

1. Set COMMIT_FLAG in data base.

2. Copy TCLIPS to CLIPS in data base.

3. Copy TBUDGET to BUDGET in data base.

4. Copy TREORDER to REORDER in data base.

5. Prepare notice to deliver paper clips to accounting department. Indicate transaction completed in log. Unset COMMIT_FLAG.

With this example, each step of the intent phase depends only on unmodified values from the data base and previous results of the intent phase. Each variable beginning with T is a shadow variable used only in this transaction. The steps of the intent phase can be repeated an unlimited number of times without affecting the integrity of the data base.

Once the DBMS begins the commit phase, it writes a COMMIT_FLAG. When this flag is set, the DBMS will not perform any steps of the intent phase. Intent steps cannot be performed after committing, because data base values are modified in the commit phase. Notice, however, that the steps of the commit phase can be repeated an unlimited number of times, again with no negative effect on the correctness of the values in the data base.

The one remaining flaw in this logic occurs if the system fails after writing the "transaction complete" message in the log, but before clearing the commit flag in the data base. It is a simple matter to work backward through the transaction log to find completed transactions for which the commit flag is still set and clear those flags.

Redundancy/Internal Consistency

Many data base managers maintain additional information to detect internal inconsistencies in data. The additional information ranges from a few check bits to duplicate or shadow fields, depending on the importance of the data.

Error Detection and Correction Codes

One form of redundancy is error detection and correction codes, such as parity, Hamming codes, and cyclic redundancy checks. These codes can be applied to single fields, to records, or to the entire data base. Each time data is placed in the data base, the appropriate check codes are computed and stored; each time data is retrieved, a similar check code is computed and compared to the stored value. If the values are unequal, they identify that an error has occurred in the data base. Some of these codes point out the place of the error, while others show precisely what the correct value should be. The more information provided, the more space required to store the codes.

Shadow Fields

Entire attributes or entire records can be duplicated in a data base. If the data are irreproducible, this second copy can provide an immediate replacement if an error is detected. Obviously redundant fields require substantial storage space.

Recovery

In addition to the processes just described for error correction, a DBMS can also maintain a log of accesses, particularly changes, by the users. Therefore, in the event of a failure, the data base is reloaded from a backup copy and all later changes are then applied from the audit log.

Concurrency/Consistency

Data base systems are often multiuser systems. Accesses by two users sharing the same data base must be constrained so that neither interferes with the other. Simple locking is done by the DBMS. If two users attempt to read the same data item, there is no conflict, since both obtain the same value.

If both users try to modify the same data items, there is no conflict since presumably each knows what to write; the value to be written does not depend on the previous value of the data item. However, this supposition is not quite accurate.

Suppose that the data base consists of seat reservations for a particular airline flight. Agent A, booking a seat for passenger Mock, submits a query to find what seats are still available. The agent knows that Mock prefers a right aisle seat, and the agent finds that seats 5D, 11D, and 14D are open. At the same time, Agent B is trying to book seats for a family of three traveling together. In response to a query, the data base indicates that 8A-B-C and 11D-E-F are the two remaining groups of three adjacent unassigned seats. Agent A submits the update command

```
            SELECT (SEAT_NO = '11D')
   ASSIGN 'MOCK,E' TO PASSENGER_NAME
```

while agent B submits the update sequence

```
            SELECT (SEAT_NO = '11D')
   ASSIGN 'LAWRENCE,S' TO PASSENGER_NAME
```

as well as commands for 11E and 11F. Then two passengers have been booked into the same one seat (which would be uncomfortable at least).

Both agents have acted properly: Each sought a list of empty seats, chose one seat from the list, and updated the data base to show to whom the seat was assigned. The difficulty in this situation is the time delay between reading a value from the data base and writing a modification of that value. During the delay time, another user has accessed the same data.

To resolve this problem, a DBMS treats the entire query-update cycle as a single atomic operation. The command from the agent must now resemble "read the current value of seat PASSENGER_NAME for seat 11D, if it is 'UNASSIGNED', modify it to 'MOCK,E' (or 'LAWRENCE,S')." The read-modify cycle must be completed as an uninterrupted item without allowing any other users access to the PASSENGER_NAME field for seat 11D. The second agent's request to book would not be considered until after the first agent's had been completed; at that time, the value of PASSENGER_NAME would no longer be 'UNASSIGNED.'

A final problem in concurrent access is read-write. Suppose one user is updating a value when a second user wishes to read. If the read is taken while the write is in progress, the reader may receive data that is only partly updated. The DBMS locks any read requests until a write has been completed.

Monitors

A **monitor** is a unit of a DBMS that is responsible for the structural integrity of the data base. A monitor can check values being entered to ensure their consistency with the rest of the data base, or with characteristics of the particular field. For example, a monitor might reject alphabetic characters for a numeric field. We discuss several forms of monitors.

Range Comparisons

A range comparison monitor tests each new value to ensure that the value is within an acceptable range. If the data value is outside the range, it is rejected and not entered into the data base. For example, the range of dates might be 1–12, '/', 1–31, '/', 00–99. An even more sophisticated range check might limit the day portion to 1–30 for months with 30 days, or might take into account leap year for February.

Range comparisons are also convenient for numeric quantities. For example, a salary field might be limited to $200,000, or the size of a house might be constrained to be between 500 and 20,000 square feet. Range constraints can also apply to other data having a predictable form.

Range comparisons can be used to ensure internal consistency of a data base. When used in this manner, the comparisons are between two elements of the data base. For example, a grade level from K–6 would be acceptable if the record described a student at an elementary school, while only 9–12 would be acceptable for a record of a student in high school. A person could be assigned a job qualification score of 75–100 only if the person had completed college or had had at least ten years work experience.

Checks of these types can control the data allowed in the data base. They can also be used to test existing values for reasonableness. If it is suspected that the data in a data base has been corrupted, a range check of all records could identify ones having suspicious values.

State Constraints

State constraints describe the condition of the entire data base. At no time should the data base values violate these constraints. Phrased differently, if these constraints are not met, some value of the data base is in error.

In the section on two-phase updates, we saw the use of a commit flag, which is set at the start of the commit phase and cleared at the completion of the commit phase. A state constraint for a data base would, therefore, be every transaction where the commit flag set is incomplete. We described a process to reset the commit flags in the event of a failure after a commit phase. Therefore, the status of the commit flag is an integrity constraint on the data base.

Another example of a state constraint is in a data base of employees' classifications. At any time, at most one employee is classified as "president." Furthermore, each employee has an employee number different from that of every other employee. If a mechanical or software error causes portions of the data base file to be repeated, one of these constraints might be violated. Testing the state of the data base would identify records with duplicate employee numbers or two records classified as "president."

Transition Constraints

State constraints describe the state of a correct data base. **Transition constraints** describe conditions necessary before changes can be applied to a data base. For example, before a new employee can be added to the data base, there must be a position number in the data base with status "vacant." (That is, an empty slot must exist.) Furthermore, after the employee is added, exactly one slot must be changed from "vacant" to the number of the new employee.

Simple range checks can be implemented within most data base management systems. However, the more sophisticated state and transition constraints can require special procedures for testing. Such user-written procedures are invoked by the DBMS each time an action must be checked.

Summary of Reliability

Reliability, correctness, and integrity are three closely related concepts in data bases. Users trust the DBMS to maintain their data correctly, and so integrity issues are very important in the security of data bases.

8.4 Sensitive Data

Some data bases contain what is called sensitive data. As a working definition let us say that **sensitive data** is data that should not be made public. Determining which data items are sensitive depends on the individual data base and the underlying meaning of the data. Obviously, some data bases, such as a public library catalog, contain no sensitive data, while other data bases, such as defense data bases, are totally sensitive. These two cases—nothing sensitive and everything sensitive—are the easiest to handle, since they can be covered by access controls to the data base itself. Someone either is or is not an authorized user. These controls are provided by the operating system.

The more difficult problem, which is also more interesting, is the case in which *some but not all* of the elements in the data base are sensitive. There may be varying degrees of sensitivity. For example, a university data base might contain student data consisting of name, financial aid, dorm, drug use, sex, parking fines, and race. Name is probably the least sensitive; financial aid, parking fines, and drug use the most; and sex and race somewhere in between. That is, many people may have legitimate access to name, some to sex and race, and relatively few to financial aid, parking fines, or drug use. An example of this data base is shown in Table 8.1.

Furthermore, although they are all highly sensitive, the financial aid, parking fines, and drug use fields may not have the same access restrictions—few people may be authorized to see each field, but nobody is authorized to see all three. The access control problem is to limit users' access so that they can obtain only the data to which they have legitimate access. Alternately, the access control problem is a challenge to ensure that sensitive data is not to be released to unauthorized people.

Several factors can make data sensitive.

- o *Inherently sensitive.* The value itself may be so revealing that it is sensitive. Examples are the locations of defensive missiles, or the median income of barbers in a town with only one barber.

- o *From a sensitive source.* The source of the data may indicate a need for confidentiality. An example is information from an informer whose identity would be compromised if the information were disclosed.

TABLE 8.1   SAMPLE DATA BASE.

Name	Sex	Race	Aid	Fines	Drugs	Dorm
Adams	M	C	5000	45.	1	Holmes
Bailey	M	B	0	0.	0	Grey
Chin	F	A	3000	20.	0	West
Dewitt	M	B	1000	35.	3	Grey
Earhart	F	C	2000	95.	1	Holmes
Fein	F	C	1000	15.	0	West
Groff	M	C	4000	0.	3	West
Hill	F	B	5000	10.	2	Holmes
Koch	F	C	0	0.	1	West
Liu	F	A	0	10.	2	Grey
Majors	M	C	2000	0.	2	Grey

○ *Declared sensitive.* The data base administrator or the owner of the data may have declared it to be sensitive. Examples are classified military data or the name of the anonymous donor of a piece of art.

○ *Of a sensitive attribute or a sensitive record.* In a data base, an entire attribute or record may be classified as sensitive. Examples are the salary attribute of a personnel data base, or a record describing a secret space mission.

○ *Sensitive in relation to previously disclosed information.* Some data becomes sensitive in the presence of other data. For example, the longitude coordinate of a secret gold mine reveals little, but the longitude coordinate in conjunction with the latitude coordinate pinpoints the mine.

All of these factors must be considered to determine the sensitivity of the data.

Access Decisions

Remember that a data base administrator is a *person* who decides *what* data should be in the data base and *who* should have access to it. The data base administrator considers the need for different users to know certain information and decides who should have what access. Decisions of the data base administrator are based on an access *policy.*

The data base manager or DBMS is a *program* that operates on the data base and auxiliary control information to implement the decisions of the access policy. We say that the data base manager "decides" to permit user x to access data y. Clearly, a program or machine cannot "decide" anything; it is more precise to say that the program performs the instructions by which x accesses y as a way of implementing the policy established by the data base administrator. (Now you see why we use the simpler wording.) To keep explanations concise, we occasionally describe programs as if they can carry out human thought processes.

The DBMS may consider several factors when deciding whether or not to permit an access. These factors include availability of the data, acceptability of the access, and authenticity of the user. We expand upon these three factors below.

Availability of Data

First, one or more required elements may be inaccessible. For example, if a user is updating several fields, other users' accesses to those fields must be blocked temporarily. This blocking assures that users do not receive inaccurate information, such as a new street address with an old city and state. This blocking should only be temporary. When performing an update, a user may have to block access to several fields or several records in order to ensure the consistency of data for others.

Notice, however, that if the updating user aborts while the update is in progress, the other users may be permanently blocked from accessing the record. This indefinite postponement is also a security problem, resulting in denial of service.

Acceptability of Access

The second point to be considered in making an access decision is that one or more values of the record may be sensitive and not accessible by the user. A DBMS should not release sensitive data to unauthorized individuals.

Deciding what is sensitive, however, is not as simple as it sounds, because the fields may not be directly requested. A user may have requested certain records which contain sensitive data, but the user's purpose may have been only to project the values from particular fields that are not sensitive. For example, a user of the data base shown in Table 8.1 may request the NAME and DORM of any student for whom FINES is not 0. The exact value of the sensitive field FINES is not disclosed, although "not 0" is a partial disclosure. Even when a sensitive value is not explicitly given, the data base manager may deny access on the grounds that it reveals information the user is not authorized to have.

Alternatively, the user may want to derive a nonsensitive statistic from the sensitive data; for example, if the average financial aid value does not reveal any individual's financial aid value, the data base manager can safely return the average. However, the average of one data value discloses that value.

Assurance of Authenticity

Third, certain characteristics of the user, external to the data base, may also be considered. To enhance security, the data base administrator may permit x to access the data base only at certain times, such as during working hours. Another characteristic to be considered is previous requests of the user. As we shall see, sensitive data can sometimes be revealed by combining results from several less sensitive queries.

Types of Disclosures

Data can be sensitive, but so also can characteristics of the data. In this section, we see that even information about data (such as its existence or whether it is zero) is a form of disclosure.

Exact Data

The most serious disclosure is the *exact value of the sensitive data* itself. The user may know that sensitive data is being requested, or the user may request general data, without knowing that some of it is sensitive. A faulty data base manager may even deliver sensitive data by accident, without the user's having requested it. In all of these cases the result is the same: The security of the sensitive data has been breached.

Bounds

Another exposure is disclosing bounds on a sensitive value, that is, indicating that a sensitive value, y, is between two values L and H. Sometimes by using a narrowing technique not unlike the binary search, the user may first determine that $L \leq y \leq H$ and then see if $L \leq y \leq H/2$, and so forth, thereby permitting the user to determine y to any desired precision. In another case, merely revealing that a value such as the athletic scholarship budget or the number of CIA agents exceeds a certain amount may be a serious breach of security.

Sometimes, however, bounds are a useful way to present sensitive data. It is not uncommon to release upper and lower bounds without identifying their specific records. For example, a company may announce that its salaries for programmers range from $20,000 to $32,000. If you are a programmer earning $29,700, you can presume that you are fairly well off, so you have the information you want; however, the announcement does not disclose who are the highest and lowest paid programmers.

Negative Result

Sometimes one can word a query to determine a negative result, that is, that z is *not* the value of y. For example, knowing that 0 is not the total number of felony convictions for a person reveals that the person was convicted of a felony. Typically the distinction between 1 and 2 or 47 felonies is not so sensitive as the distinction between 0 and 1. Therefore, disclosing that a value is not 0 is a significant disclosure. If a student does not appear on the Honors list, you can infer that the person's grade point average is below 3.50. This information is not too revealing, however, since the range of grade point averages from 0.0 to 3.49 is rather wide.

Existence

In some cases, the existence of data is itself a sensitive piece of data, regardless of the actual value. For example, an employer may not want employees to know that their use of long distance telephone lines is being monitored. In this case, discovering a LONG DISTANCE field in a personnel file would reveal sensitive data.

Probable Value

Finally, it may be possible to determine the probability that a certain element has a certain value. Suppose you want to find out if the President is a registered Communist. Knowing that the President is in the data base, you submit two queries to the data base:

How many people have 1600 Pennsylvania Avenue as their official residence? (Response: 4)

How many people have 1600 Pennsylvania Avenue as their official residence and have YES as the value of COMMUNIST? (Response: 1)

From these queries you conclude there is a 25 percent likelihood that the President is a registered Communist.

Summary of Partial Disclosure

In summary, a security problem may result if characteristics of sensitive data are revealed. Notice that some of the techniques discussed used information *about* the data, not even direct access to the data, to infer sensitive results. A successful security strategy must protect from both direct and indirect disclosure.

Security versus Precision

Through examples we have seen that it is not easy to determine what data is sensitive, and it is not easy to protect the sensitive data. The situation is complicated by a desire to share nonsensitive data. For reasons of **secrecy** we want to disclose only data that is not sensitive. Such an outlook encourages a conservative philosophy in determining what data to disclose.

Now consider the users of the data. The conservative philosophy says to reject any query that mentions a sensitive field. We may thereby reject many reasonable and nondisclosing queries. For example, a researcher may want a list of grades for all students using drugs, or a statistician may request lists of salaries for all men and for all women. These queries probably do not compromise the identity of any individual. We want to disclose as much data as possible so that users of the data base have access to the data they need. This goal, called **precision**, aims to protect all sensitive data while revealing as much nonsensitive data as possible.

We can depict the relationship between security and precision with concentric circles. As Figure 8.8 shows, the sensitive data in the middle should be carefully concealed. We willingly disclose data at the outside in response to queries. We know that the user may put together pieces of disclosed data and infer other, more deeply hidden data. Beneath that layer may be yet more nonsensitive data that the user cannot infer. Finally, on the inside is the sensitive data which we intend to keep secret.

The ideal combination of secrecy and precision allows us to maintain perfect secrecy with maximum precision, in other words, to disclose all and only the nonsensitive data. This is not as easy as it might seem, as shown in Section 8.5. In fact, we often must

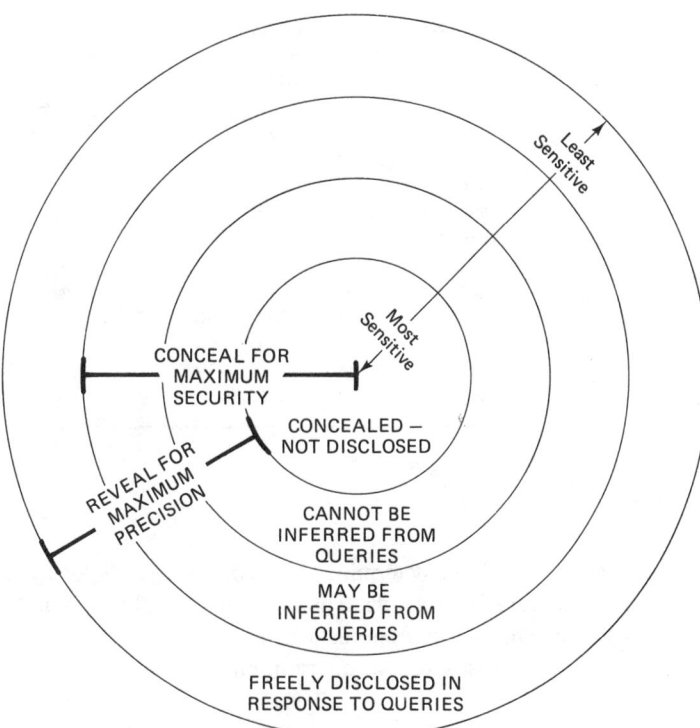

Figure 8.8   Security versus Precision.

sacrifice precision in order to maintain secrecy. In the next section we consider ways that sensitive data can be obtained from queries that appear harmless.

8.5 Inference Problem

In this section we study the **inference problem**, which is a way to infer or derive sensitive data from nonsensitive data. The inference problem is a subtle vulnerability in data base security.

The data base in Table 8.2 can help to illustrate the inference problem. Recall that AID is the amount of financial aid a student is receiving. FINES is the amount of parking fines still owed. DRUGS is the result of a drug-use survey: 0 means never used, and 3 means frequent user. Obviously this information should be kept confidential. We assume that AID, FINES, and DRUGS are sensitive fields, although only when the values are related to a specific individual. In this section we see that it is possible to determine sensitive data from the data base.

TABLE 8.2 SAMPLE DATA BASE

Name	Sex	Race	Aid	Fines	Drugs	Dorm
Adams	M	C	5000	45.	1	Holmes
Bailey	M	B	0	0.	0	Grey
Chin	F	A	3000	20.	0	West
Dewitt	M	B	1000	35.	3	Grey
Earhart	F	C	2000	95.	1	Holmes
Fein	F	C	1000	15.	0	West
Groff	M	C	4000	0.	3	West
Hill	F	B	5000	10.	2	Holmes
Koch	F	C	0	0.	1	West
Liu	F	A	0	10.	2	Grey
Majors	M	C	2000	0.	2	Grey

Direct Attack

In a direct attack one tries to determine values of sensitive fields by seeking them directly with queries that yield few records. The most successful technique is to form a query so specific that it matches exactly one data item.

In the table above, a sensitive query might be

$$\text{List NAME where}$$
$$\text{SEX=M} \wedge \text{DRUGS=1}$$

This query discloses that for record ADAMS, DRUGS=1. However, it is an obvious attack, since any name listed is one for whom DRUGS=1.

A less obvious query is

$$\text{List NAME where}$$
$$(\text{SEX=M} \wedge \text{DRUGS=1}) \vee$$
$$(\text{SEX} \neq \text{M} \wedge \text{SEX} \neq \text{F}) \vee$$
$$(\text{DORM=AYRES})$$

On the surface, this query looks as if it should conceal drug usage by selecting other non-drug-related records as well. However, this query still retrieves only one record, revealing a name that corresponds to the sensitive DRUG value. The DBMS needs to know that SEX has only two possible values, so that the second clause will select no records. Even if that were possible, the DBMS would also need to know that no records exist with DORM=AYRES, even though AYRES might be an acceptable value for DORM.

Organizations that publish personal statistics, such as the U. S. Census Bureau, do not reveal results where a small number of people make up a large proportion of the category. The rule of "n items, over k percent" means that data should be withheld if n items represent over k percent of the result reported. In the previous case, the one person selected represents 100 percent of the data reported, so that there is no ambiguity about which person matches the query.

Indirect Attack

Another procedure used by the U. S. Census Bureau and other people who gather sensitive data is to release only statistics. Therefore, they suppress individual names, addresses, or other characteristics by which a single individual can be recognized. Only neutral statistics, such as count, sum, and mean, are released.

The indirect attack seeks to infer a result based on one or more statistical results. It requires work outside the data base itself. A statistical attack seeks to use some apparently anonymous statistical measure to infer individual data. Following are several examples of indirect attacks based on data bases that report statistics.

Sum

An attack by sum tries to infer a value from a reported sum. For example, with our sample data base, it might seem safe to report student aid by sex and dorm. Such a report is shown in Table 8.3. This seemingly innocent report reveals that no female living in Grey is receiving financial aid. Thus, any female living in Grey (such as Liu) is certainly not receiving financial aid. This is another example of disclosure of a negative result.

TABLE 8.3   SUMS OF FINANCIAL
AID BY DORM AND SEX.

	Holmes	Grey	West	Total
M	5000	3000	4000	12000
F	7000	0	4000	11000
Total	12000	3000	8000	23000

Count

The count can be combined with the sum to produce some even more revealing results. Often these two statistics are released for a data base to allow users to determine average values. (Conversely, if count and mean are released, sum can be deduced.)

Table 8.4 shows the count of records for students by dorm and sex. This table is innocuous by itself. Combined with the sum table, however, this table demonstrates that the two males in Holmes and West are receiving financial aid in the amount of $5000 and $4000, respectively. The names can be obtained by selecting the subschema of NAME, DORM, which is not sensitive since it delivers only low-security data on the entire data base.

Median

By a slightly more complicated process, it is possible to determine an individual value from medians. The attack requires finding selections having one point of intersection, which happens to be exactly in the middle, as shown in Figure 8.9.

TABLE 8.4 COUNT OF STUDENTS
BY DORM AND SEX.

	Holmes	Grey	West	Total
M	1	3	1	5
F	2	1	3	6
Total	3	4	4	11

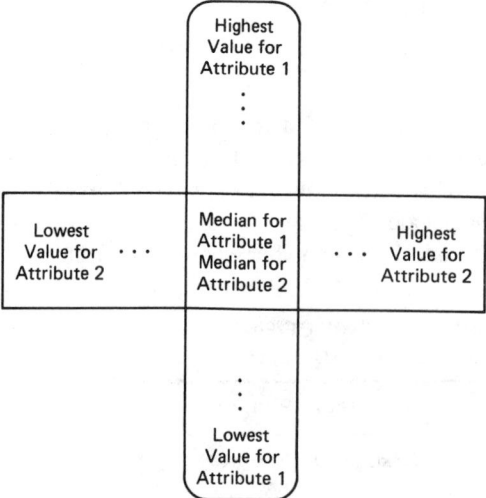

Figure 8.9   Intersecting Medians.

For example, in our sample data base, there are five males and three persons whose drug use value is 2. Arranged in order, these median values are shown in Table 8.5. Notice that Majors is the only name common to both lists and conveniently that name is in the middle of each list. Someone working at the Health Clinic might be able to find out that Majors is a white male whose drug use score is 2. That identifies Majors as the intersection of these two lists, and pinpoints Majors' financial aid as $2000. In this example, the queries

$$q = \text{median}(\text{AID where SEX} = \text{M})$$
$$p = \text{median}(\text{AID where DRUGS} = 2)$$

reveal the exact financial aid amount for Majors.

Tracker Attacks

As already explained, data base managers may conceal data where a small number of entries makes up a large proportion of the data revealed. A **tracker attack** can fool the data base manager into locating the desired data by using additional queries that produce small results. The tracker adds additional records to be retrieved for two different queries;

TABLE 8.5 INFERENCE FROM MEDIAN OF TWO LISTS.

Name	Sex	Drugs	Aid
Bailey	M	0	0
Dewitt	M	3	1000
Majors	M	2	2000
Groff	M	3	4000
Adams	M	1	5000
Liu	F	2	0
Majors	M	2	2000
Hill	F	2	5000

the two sets of records cancel each other out, leaving only the statistic desired. Instead of trying to identify a unique value, $n - 1$ other values are requested (where there are n values in the data base). Given n and $n - 1$, it is easy to compute the desired singleton element.

For instance, suppose we wish to know how many female Caucasians live in Holmes Hall. A query posed might be

```
count ((SEX=F) ∧ (RACE=C) ∧ DORM=Holmes))
```

The data base manager will consult the data base, find that the answer is 1, and refuse to answer that query because one record dominates the result of the query. However, further analysis of the query allows us to track sensitive data through nonsensitive queries.

The query

$$q = \text{count}((\text{SEX=F}) \wedge (\text{RACE=C}) \wedge (\text{DORM=Holmes}))$$

is of the form

$$q = \text{count}(a \wedge b \wedge c)$$

By algebra, this transforms to

$$q = \text{count}(a \wedge b \wedge c) = \text{count}(a) - \text{count}(a \wedge \neg(b \wedge c))$$

Thus, the original query is equivalent to

```
count (SEX=F)
```

minus

```
count ((SEX=F) ∧ (RACE≠C) ∧ (DORM≠Holmes))
```

Since $\text{count}(a) = 6$ and $\text{count}(a \wedge \neg(b \wedge c)) = 5$, it is easy to determine the suppressed value, $6 - 5 = 1$. Furthermore, neither 6 nor 5 is a sensitive count.

Linear System Vulnerability

A tracker is a specific case of a more general vulnerability. With a little algebra and a little more luck in the distribution of the data base contents, it may be possible to determine a series of queries that returns results relating to several different sets. For example, the following system of four queries does not overtly reveal any single c value from the data base. However, the queries (equations) can be solved for each of the unknown c values, revealing them all.

$$
\begin{aligned}
q_1 &= c_1 + c_2 + c_3 + c_4 + c_5 \\
q_2 &= c_1 + c_2 \quad\;\; + c_4 \\
q_3 &= \qquad\quad\;\; c_3 + c_4 \\
q_4 &= \qquad\qquad\quad\;\; c_4 + c_5 \\
q_5 &= \quad\; c_2 \qquad\quad\; + c_5
\end{aligned}
$$

By algebra $q_1 - q_2 = c_3 + c_5$, and $q_3 - q_4 = c_3 - c_5$. Thus, subtracting these two equations, we obtain $c_5 = \big((q_1 - q_2) - (q_3 - q_4)\big)/2$. From c_5 the others can be obtained.

In fact, this attack can also be used to obtain results in cases *other than* statistical attacks. Notice that the same algebraic properties occur with *and* ($\wedge$) and *or* ($\vee$), which are typical operators for data base queries. For example, each query might ask for precise data, instead of counts, with a request of the form

$$
q_1 = s_1 \vee s_2 \vee s_3 \vee s_4 \vee s_5
$$

The result is a set of records satisfying that query. By set algebra, individual results can be obtained by solving the system of linear set equations analogous to the numerical queries posed earlier.

Controls for Statistical Inference Attacks

The controls for all statistical attacks are similar. Denning and Schlörer [DEN83] present a very good survey of techniques for maintaining security in data bases. Essentially there are two ways to protect against inference attacks. Either controls are applied to the queries or controls are applied to individual items within the data base. As we have seen, it is difficult to determine whether a given query discloses sensitive data. Thus, query controls are effective primarily against direct attacks.

Two controls applied to data items are suppression and concealing. With **suppression**, sensitive data values are not provided; the query is rejected without response. With **concealing**, the answer provided is *close to* but not exactly the actual value.

These two controls reflect the contrast between security and precision. With suppression, any results provided are correct, yet many responses must be withheld in order to maintain security. With concealing, more results can be provided, although the accuracy of the results is lower. The choice between suppression and concealing depends on the context of the data base. Examples of suppression and concealing follow.

Limited Response Suppression

The n-item k percent rule eliminates certain low-frequency elements from being displayed. It is not sufficient to delete them, however, if their values can also be inferred. Consider Table 8.6, which shows counts of students by dorm and sex.

TABLE 8.6 STUDENTS BY DORM AND SEX.

	Holmes	Grey	West	Total
M	1	3	1	5
F	2	1	3	6
Total	3	4	4	11

With this table, the cells with counts of 1 should be suppressed because their counts are too revealing. But it does no good to suppress the Male-Holmes cell when the value 1 can be determined by subtracting Female-Holmes (2) from the total (3), to determine 1, as shown in Table 8.7.

TABLE 8.7 STUDENTS BY DORM AND SEX, WITH SUPPRESSION.

	Holmes	Grey	West	Total
M	–	3	–	5
F	2	–	3	6
Total	3	4	4	11

When one cell is being suppressed in a table with totals for rows and columns, it is necessary to suppress at least one additional cell on the row and one on the column to provide some confusion. By that logic, all cells (except totals) would have to be suppressed in this sample table. When totals are not provided, single cells in a row or column can be suppressed.

Combining Results

Another control combines rows or columns to protect sensitive values. For example, Table 8.8 shows several sensitive results which identify single individuals. (Even though these counts may not seem sensitive, they may be used to infer sensitive data such as NAME; therefore, we consider them to be sensitive.)

These counts, combined with other results such as sum, permit one to infer individual drug use values for the three males, as well as to infer that no female was rated 3 for drug use. To suppress such sensitive information, it is possible to combine the attribute values for 0 and 1, and also for 2 and 3, producing the less sensitive results shown in Table 8.9. In this instance, it is impossible to identify any single value.

TABLE 8.8 STUDENTS BY SEX AND DRUG USE.

	Drug Use			
Sex	0	1	2	3
M	1	1	0	3
F	2	2	2	0

TABLE 8.9 SUPPRESSION BY COMBINING VALUES.

	Drug Use	
Sex	0 or 1	2 or 3
M	2	3
F	4	2

Another way of combining results is to present values in ranges. Instead of releasing exact financial aid figures, results may be released for the ranges $0–1999, $2000–3999, and $4000 and above. Even if there is only one record represented by a single result, the exact value of that record is not known. Similarly, the highest and lowest financial aid values are concealed.

Yet another method of combining is by rounding. This is actually a fairly well-known example of combining by range. If numbers are rounded to the nearest 10, the ranges are 0–5, 6–15, 16–25, and so on. Actual values are rounded up or down to the nearest multiple of some base.

Random Sample

With random sample control, a result is not derived from the whole data base; instead the result is computed on a random sample of the data base. The sample chosen is large enough to be valid. Because the sample is not the whole data base, however, a query against this sample will not necessarily match the result for the whole data base. Thus a result of 5 percent for a particular query means that 5 percent of the records chosen for the sample for this query had the desired property. It is expected that approximately 5 percent of the entire data base will have the property in question, but the actual percentage may vary from 5 percent.

To prevent averaging attacks from repeated, equivalent queries, the same sample set should be chosen for equivalent queries. In this way, all equivalent queries will produce the same result, although that result will be only an approximation for the entire data base.

Random Data Perturbation

Another statistical control is to perturb the values of the data base by a small error. If x_i is the true value of data item i in the data base, ϵ_i is a random error term added to x_i

for statistical results. The ϵ values are both positive and negative, so that some reported values will be higher than their true values, and other reported values will be lower. Statistical measures such as sum and mean will be close, but not necessarily exact. Data perturbation is easier to use than random sample selection, since it is easier to keep all of the ϵ values in order to produce the same result for equivalent queries.

Query Analysis

A more complex form of security uses query analysis. Here, a query and its implications are analyzed to determine whether a result should be provided. As noted earlier, query analysis can be quite difficult. One approach involves maintaining a query history for each user and judging a query in the context of what inferences are possible given previous results.

Conclusion on the Inference Problem

There are no perfect solutions to the inference problem. The approaches to controlling it follow three paths. The first two methods can be used either to limit queries accepted or to limit data provided in response to a query. The last method applies only to data released.

1. *Suppress obviously sensitive information.* This can be done fairly easily. There is a tendency to err on the side of suppression, which restricts the usefulness of the data base.

2. *Track what the user knows.* Although possibly leading to the greatest safe disclosure, this approach is extremely costly. Information must be maintained on all users, even though most are not trying to obtain sensitive data. This approach seldom takes into account what any two people may know together.

3. *Disguise the data.* Random perturbation and rounding can inhibit statistical attacks that depend on exact values for algebraic manipulation. The users of the data base receive slightly incorrect or, worse, inconsistent results.

It is unlikely that research will reveal a simple, easy-to-apply measure that determines exactly which data can be revealed without compromising sensitive data.

A very effective control for the inference problem is just knowing that it exists. As with other problems in security, recognition of the problem leads to understanding of the purposes of controls for the problem and to sensitivity to the potential difficulties caused by the problem.

8.6 Multilevel Data Bases

So far, we have considered data only of two categories, either sensitive or nonsensitive. We have alluded to some data being more sensitive than others, but we have only allowed "yes" or "no" access. The presentation may have implied that sensitivity was a function of the *attribute*, the column in which the data appeared, although nothing we have done depended on this interpretation of sensitivity. Such a model appears in Figure 8.10. In that figure, two columns are identified as sensitive. However, sensitivity is not determined just by attribute.

The Case for Differentiated Security

Consider a data base containing data on U.S. government expenditures. Some of the expenditures are for paper clips, which is not sensitive information. Some salary expenditures are subject to privacy requirements. Individual salaries are sensitive, but the aggregate (for example, the total CIA payroll, which is a matter of public record) is not sensitive. Expenses of certain military operations are more sensitive, such as the total amount the U.S. spends for ballistic missiles, which is not public. There are even operations known only to a few people, and so the amount spent on these operations, or even the fact that anything was spent on such an operation, is highly sensitive.

For example, think about the data of Figure 8.10. Perhaps Davis is a temporary employee hired for a special project, and her whole record is of a different sensitivity. Perhaps the phone shown for Garland is his private line which is not available to the public. These refinements to the sensitivity of the data are shown in Figure 8.11.

NAME	DEPARTMENT	SALARY	PHONE	PERFORMANCE
ROGERS	TRAINING	43,800	4-5067	A2
JENKINS	RESEARCH	26,900	6-4281	D4
POLING	TRAINING	38,200	4-4501	B1
GARLAND	USER SVCS	54,600	6-6600	A4
HILTEN	USER SVCS	44,500	4-5351	B1
DAVIS	ADMIN.	51,400	4-9505	A3

Sensitive Attributes

Figure 8.10   Attribute-level Sensitivity

NAME	DEPARTMENT	SALARY	PHONE	RATING
ROGERS	TRAINING	43,800	4-5057	A2
JENKINS	RESEARCH	26,900	6-4281	D4
POLING	TRAINING	38,200	4-4501	B1
GARLAND	USER SVCS	54,600	6-6600	A4
HILTEN	USER SVCS	44,500	4-5351	B1
DAVIS	ADMIN.	51,400	4-9505	A3

Figure 8.11   Refined Sensitivity.

From this description, three characteristics of data base security emerge.

1. The security of a single element may be different from the security of other elements of the same record or from values of the same attribute. That is, the security of one element may be different from that of other elements of the same row or column. This situation implies that security should be implemented for each individual element.

2. Two levels—sensitive and nonsensitive—are inadequate to represent some security situations. Several grades of security may be needed. These grades may represent ranges of allowable knowledge, which may overlap. Typically, the security grades form a lattice.

3. The security of an aggregate—a sum, a count, or a group of values in a data base— may be different from the security of the individual elements. The security of the aggregate may be higher or lower than the individual elements.

These three principles lead to a model of security not unlike the military model of security encountered in Chapter 7, in which the security of an object is placed at one of n levels (in the military model $n = 4$) and is further separated into compartments by category. The military security model is an example of a **multilevel security model**. Multilevel secure data bases require two or more levels of security for both the data elements and the users of one data base.

Granularity

Recall that the military classification model applied originally to paper documents and was adapted to computers. It is fairly easy to classify and track a single sheet of paper or, for that matter, a paper file, a computer file, or a single program or process. It is entirely different to classify individual data items.

For obvious reasons an entire sheet of paper is classified at one level, even though certain words, such as "and," "the," or "of" would be innocuous in any context, and other words, such as codewords like "Manhattan project," might be sensitive in any context. But defining the security of each value in a data base is similar to applying a security level to each individual word of a document.

In fact, the problem is even more complicated. The word "Manhattan" by itself is not sensitive, nor is "project." However, the combination of these words produces the sensitive codeword "Manhattan project." A similar situation occurs in data bases. Therefore, not only does every element of a data base have a distinct sensitivity— every combination of elements may also have a distinct sensitivity. Furthermore, the combination can be more or less sensitive than any of its elements.

What is needed in order to associate a security level with each value of a data base? First, an access control policy must dictate which users may have access to what data. To implement this policy typically each data item is marked to show its access limitations. Second, a means is needed to guarantee that the value has not been changed by an unauthorized person. These two needs demonstrate the requirements for both security and integrity.

Security Issues

In Chapter 1 we introduced three general security concerns in computing: secrecy, integrity, and availability. In this section, we extend these concepts to include their special roles for multilevel data bases.

Integrity

Even in a single-level data base where all elements have the same degree of sensitivity, integrity is a tricky problem. In the case of multilevel data bases, integrity becomes both more important and more difficult to achieve. Because of the $*$-principle for access control, a process that reads high-level data is not allowed to write a file at a lower level. Applied to data bases, however, this principle says that a high-level user should not be able to write a lower-level data element.

The problem with this interpretation arises when the DBMS must be able to read all records in the data base and write new records for any of the following purposes: to do backups, to scan the data base to answer queries, to reorganize the data base according to a user's processing needs, or to update all records of the data base.

With people this deficiency is handled by trust and common sense. People who have access to sensitive information are careful not to convey that information to uncleared individuals. In a computing system there are two choices: Either (1) the process cleared at a high level cannot write to a lower level, or (2) the process must be a "trusted process," the computer equivalent of a person with a clearance. To date, no trusted DBMS has been developed, although work is underway to establish standards for and develop such a product.

Secrecy

Users trust that a data base will provide correct information, which means that it is consistent and accurate. As indicated earlier, some means of protecting sensitive data result in small changes to the data. Although these perturbations should not affect statistical analyses, they may produce two different answers representing the same underlying data value in response to two differently formed queries. In the multilevel case, two different users operating at two different levels of security might get two different answers to the same query. In order to preserve secrecy, accuracy is sacrificed.

Another result of this secrecy is unknowing redundancy. Suppose a personnel specialist works at one level of access permission. The specialist knows that John Q. Public works for the company. However, John's record does not appear on the retirement payment roster. The specialist assumes this is an error and creates a record for John.

The reason that no record for John appears is that John is a secret agent, and his employment with the company is not supposed to be public knowledge. There actually is a record on John in the file but, because of his special position, his record is not accessible to the personnel specialist. The creation of the new record means that there are now two records for John Q. Public: one sensitive and one not, as shown in Figure 8.12. This situation is called **polyinstantiation**, meaning that one record can appear (be instantiated) many times, with a different level of secrecy each time.

NAME	Sensitivity	Assignment	Location
Public, J.Q.	C		?
Public, J.Q.	TS	Secret Agent	South Bend

Figure 8.12   Polyinstantiated Records.

8.7 Proposals for Multilevel Security

It is premature to call the following sections "solutions" to the problems of multilevel security for data bases. The methods described here are very recent; some of them are only at the proposal stage, while others are prototypes or initial implementations. In five years some of them will have been tried and accepted, some may have been discarded, and other new approaches will certainly have been put forth. These proposals represent the current state of the art in an area that is not yet well understood.

Partitioning

The obvious control for multilevel data bases is partitioning. The data base is divided into separate data bases, each at its own level of security. This approach is similar to maintaining separate files in separate file cabinets. This control destroys a basic advantage of data bases: elimination of redundancy and improved accuracy through having only one field to update. Furthermore, it does not address the problem of a high-level user who needs to access some low-level data to be combined with high-level data.

Encryption

If sensitive data is encrypted, a user who accidentally receives sensitive data cannot interpret the data. Encryption has certain disadvantages, however.

First, a user can mount a chosen plaintext attack. Suppose party affiliation of REP or DEM is stored in encrypted form in each record. A user who achieves access to these encrypted fields can easily decrypt them by creating a new record with party=DEM and comparing the resulting encrypted version to that element in all other records. Worse, if authentication data is encrypted, the malicious user can substitute the encrypted form of his or her own data for that of any other user. Not only does this provide access for the malicious user, but it also excludes the legitimate user whose authentication data has been changed to that of the malicious user.

Using a different encryption for each record overcomes these defects. Each record's fields can be encrypted with a different key, or all fields of a record can be cryptographically linked, as with cipher block chaining. These possibilities are shown in Figure 8.13. The disadvantage, then, is that each field must be decrypted in order to perform standard data base operations such as "select all records with SALARY > 10,000." Decrypting the SALARY field, even on rejected records, increases the time to process a query. (Consider the query that selects just one record but that must decrypt and compare one field of each record to find the one that satisfies the query.)

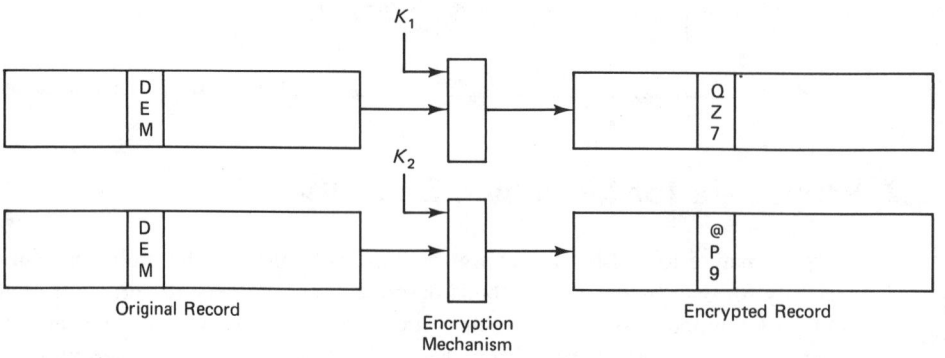

(a) Different Encryption Keys

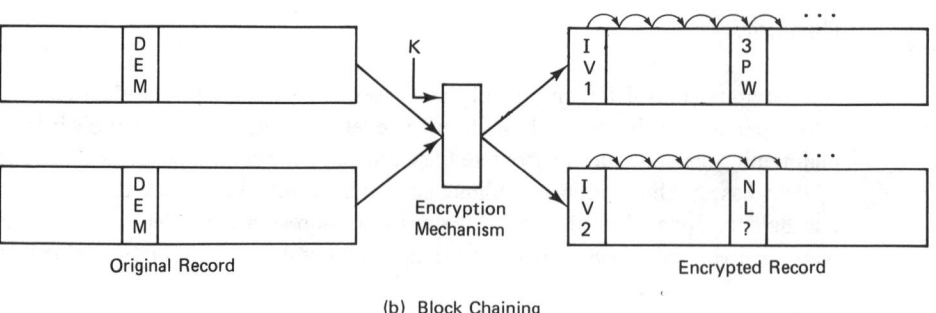

(b) Block Chaining

Figure 8.13   Cryptographic Separation.

Integrity Lock

The **integrity lock** was first proposed at the Air Force Summer Study on Data Base Security in 1982. The lock is a way to provide both integrity and limited access for a data base. The operation was nicknamed "spray paint," since each element is painted with a color that denotes its sensitivity. The coloring is maintained with the element, not in a master data base table.

A model of the basic integrity lock is shown in Figure 8.14. As shown in that figure, each data item consists of three pieces: the data itself, a label showing the sensitivity level of the data, and a checksum to prevent unauthorized modification of the data or its label. The data is stored in plaintext for efficiency, since the DBMS may need to examine many fields when selecting records to match a query.

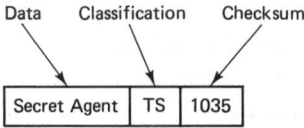

Figure 8.14 Integrity Lock.

The second component of an integrity lock is a label that indicates sensitivity to restrict the users who can access to the data. The sensitivity level should be

1. *unforgeable* so that a malicious subject cannot create a new sensitivity level for an element

2. *unique* so that a malicious subject cannot copy a sensitivity level from another element

3. *concealed* so that a malicious subject cannot even determine the sensitivity level of an arbitrary object

The third piece of the integrity lock for a field is an error-detecting code, called a cryptographic checksum. In order to guarantee that a data value or its security classification has not been changed, this checksum must be unique for a given element, and must contain both the element's data and something to tie that data to a particular position in the data base. As shown in Figure 8.15, an appropriate cryptographic checksum includes something unique to the record (the record number), something unique to this data field within the record (the field attribute name), the data of this element, and the security classification of the element. These four components guard against changing or moving the data. The checksum can be computed using a strong encryption algorithm such as DES.

Sensitivity Lock

The sensitivity lock shown in Figure 8.16 was designed by Graubert and Kramer [GRA84] to meet these principles. A **sensitivity lock** is a combination of a unique identifier (for example, the record number) and the security level. Because the identifier is unique, each integrity lock relates to one particular record. Many different elements will have

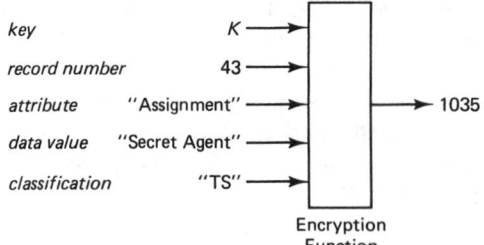

Figure 8.15   Cryptographic Checksum.

the same security level. A malicious subject should not be able to identify two elements having identical security levels just by looking at the security level portion of the integrity lock. Because of the encryption, the lock's contents, especially the security level, are concealed from plain view. Thus, the lock is associated with one specific record, and it protects the secrecy of the security level of that record.

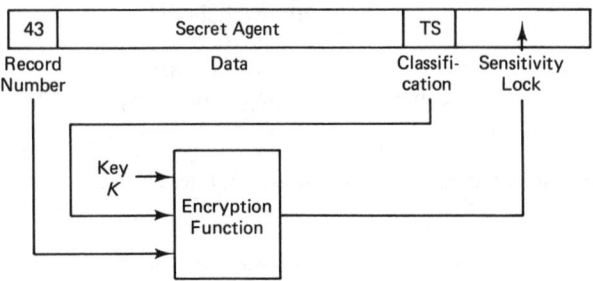

Figure 8.16   Sensitivity Lock.

Efficiency Analysis

The integrity lock was invented as a short-term solution to the problem of security in multilevel data bases. The intention was to be able to use any (untrusted) data base manager with a trusted procedure that handles access control. In this way, only the access procedure would need verification, since only it would be able to achieve or grant access to sensitive data. The structure of such a system is shown in Figure 8.17. The efficiency of integrity locks is a serious drawback. The space to store an element must be expanded to cover the sensitivity label. Since there are several pieces to this label, and there is one label for every element, the space required is not insignificant.

The processing time efficiency of an integrity lock is also problematic. The sensitivity label must be decoded every time the data is passed to the user in order to verify that the user's access is allowable. Also, each time a value is written or modified, the label must be recomputed. Thus, substantial processing time is consumed. If the data base file can be sufficiently protected, the data values of the individual elements can be left in plaintext. Doing so benefits select and project queries across sensitive fields, since an element need not be decrypted just to determine if it should be selected.

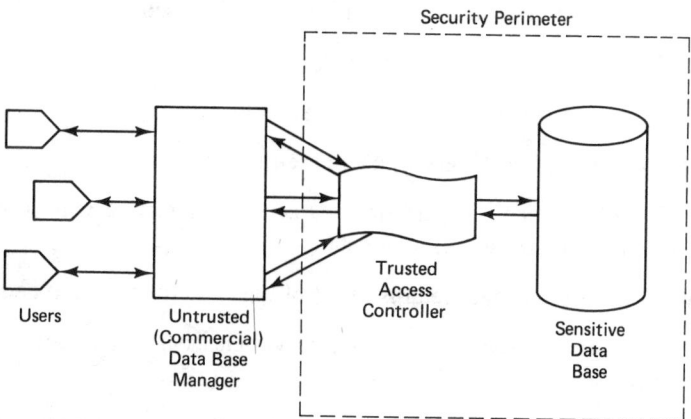

Figure 8.17   Trusted Data Base Manager.

Trusted Front-End

The model of a **trusted front-end** process is shown in Figure 8.18. A trusted front-end is also known as a **guard**; it operates much like the reference monitor of Chapter 7. The motivation for this approach is the recognition that many DBMSs have been built and put into use without consideration of multilevel security. The front-end concept enhances the security of these existing systems with minimal change to the system. This concept is explained in [GRA85]. The interaction between a user, a trusted front-end, and a DBMS involves the following steps.

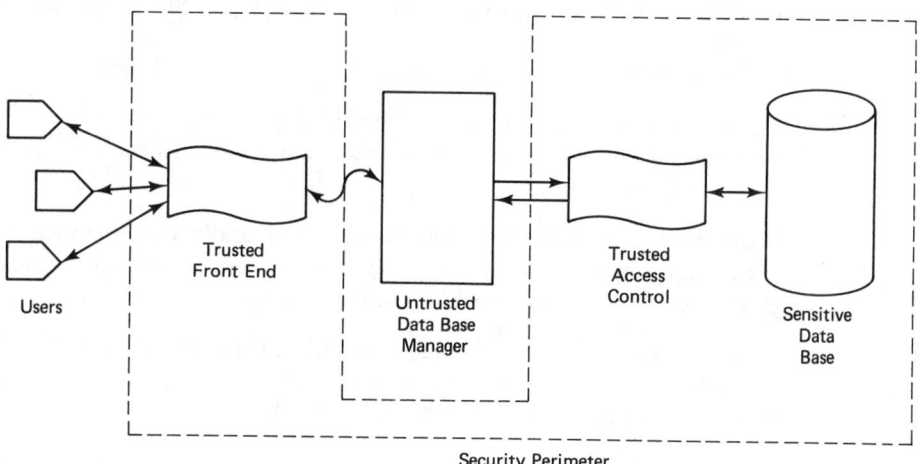

Figure 8.18   Trusted Front End.

1. User identifies self to front-end; front-end authenticates user's identity.

2. User issues a query to front-end.

3. Front-end verifies user's authorization to data.

4. Front-end issues query to data base manager.

5. Data base manager performs I/O access, interacting with low-level access control to achieve access to actual data.

6. Data base manager returns result of query to trusted front-end.

7. Front-end verifies validity of data via checksum and checks classification of data against security level of user.

8. Front-end transmits data to untrusted front-end for formatting.

9. Untrusted front-end transmits formatted data to user.

Commutative Filter

The notion of a commutative filter was proposed by Denning [DEN85] as a simplification of the trusted interface to the data base manager. Essentially, the filter screens the user's request, reformatting it if necessary, so that only data of an appropriate sensitivity level is returned to the user.

A **commutative filter** is a process that interfaces to both the user and a data base manager. However, unlike the trusted front-end process of Graubert, the filter tries to capitalize on the efficiency of most DBMSs. The filter reformats the query so that the data base manager does as much of the work as possible, screening out many unacceptable records. The filter then provides a second screening to select only that data to which the user has access.

Filters can be used for security at the record, attribute, or element level.

- When used at the record level, the filter requests desired data plus cryptographic checksum information; it then verifies the accuracy and accessibility of data to be passed to the user.

- At the attribute level, the filter checks whether all attributes in the user's query are accessible to the user and, if so, passes the query to the data base manager. On return, it deletes all fields to which the user has no access rights.

- At the element level, the system requests desired data plus cryptographic checksum information. When this is returned it checks the classification level of every element of every record retrieved against the user's level.

A simple example is the query

```
retrieve NAME where ((OCCUP=PHYSICIST) ∧ (CITY=WASHDC))
```

Suppose some physicists in Washington work on very sensitive projects, so that the current user should not be allowed to access their names. Suppose also that the current user is prohibited from knowing anything about any persons in Moscow. A conventional data base manager would have access to all records and would then pass the results of its query on to the user. However, as we have seen before, the user might be able to infer things about Moscow employees or Washington physicists working on secret projects without even accessing those fields directly.

The commutative filter reforms the original query in a trustable way so that sensitive information is never extracted from the data base. Our sample query would become

```
retrieve NAME where ((OCCUP=PHYSICIST) ∧ (CITY=WASHDC))
from all records R where (
    (NAME-SECRECY-LEVEL(R) ≤ USER-SECRECY-LEVEL) ∧
    (OCCUP-SECRECY-LEVEL(R) ≤ USER-SECRECY-LEVEL) ∧
    (CITY-SECRECY-LEVEL(R) ≤ USER-SECRECY-LEVEL))
```

The filter works by restricting the query to the data base manager and then restricting the results before they are returned to the user. In this instance, the filter would request NAME, NAME-SECRECY-LEVEL, OCCUP, OCCUP-SECRECY-LEVEL, CITY, and CITY-SECRECY-LEVEL values, and would then filter and return to the user only those that are of a secrecy level acceptable for the user. An example of this query filtering in operation is shown in Figure 8.19. The advantage of the commutative filter is that it allows query selection, some optimization, and some subquery handling to be done by the data base manager. This keeps the size of the security filter small, it reduces redundancy between it and the data base manager, and it improves the overall efficiency of the system.

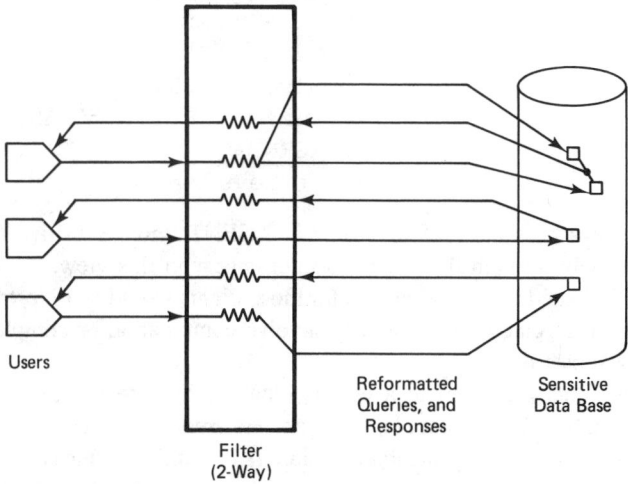

Users

Reformatted
Queries, and
Responses

Sensitive
Data Base

Filter
(2-Way)

Figure 8.19   Commutative Filters.

Window/View

An organizing principle for multilevel data base access is that of a **window** or a **view**. Denning *et al.* [DEN87] survey the development of views for multilevel data base security. A window is a subset of a data base, containing exactly the information that a user is entitled to access.

A view can represent a single user's subset data base, so that all of a user's queries access only that data base. This subset guarantees that the user does not access values outside the permitted amount, since nonpermitted values are not even in the user's data base. The view is specified as a set of relations in the data base, so that the data in the view subset changes as data in the data base changes.

For example, a travel agent might have access to part of an airline's flight information data base. Records for cargo flights would be excluded, as would the pilot's name and the serial number of the plane for every flight. Suppose the data base contained an attribute TYPE whose value was either CARGO or PASS (for passenger). Other attributes might be FLTNO, ORIG, DEST, DEP, ARR, SEATS, PILOT, and PLANENO.

Now suppose the airline created passenger flights that could only be booked directly through the airline. These flights might be represented as more sensitive information, unavailable to travel agents, by assigning their flight numbers a more sensitive rating. The whole data base, and the agent's view, would have the logical structure shown in Figure 8.20.

The travel agent's view of the data base above is expressed as

```
view AGENT-INFO
    FLTNO:=MASTER.FLTNO
    ORIG:=MASTER.ORIG
    DEST:=MASTER.DEST
    DEP:=MASTER.DEP
    ARR:=MASTER.ARR
    SEATS:=MASTER.SEATS
        where MASTER.TYPE='PASS'
    class AGENT
    auth retrieve
```

Since the access class of this view is AGENT, more sensitive flight numbers (flights booked only through the airline) do not appear in this view. An alternative that would have eliminated the entire records for those flights would be to restrict the record selection with a where clause. A view may involve computation or complex selection criteria to specify subset data.

The data presented to a user is obtained by **filtering** the contents of the original data base. Attributes, records, and elements are stripped away so that the user sees only acceptable items. Any attribute (column) is withheld unless the user is authorized to access at least one element. Any record (row) is withheld unless the user is authorized to access at least one element. Then for all elements that still remain, if the user is not authorized to access the element, it is replaced by UNDEFINED. This last step does not compromise any data, since the user knows the existence of the attribute (at least one

FLTNO	ORIG	DEST	DEP	ARR	SEATS	TYPE	PILOT	PLANENO.
362	JFK	BWI	0830	0950	114	PASS	DOSSER	2463
397	JFK	ORD	0830	1020	114	PASS	BOTTOMS	3621
202	LGA	LGW	1530	0710	183	PASS	JEVINS	2007
749	LGA	ATL	0947	1120	0	CARGO	WITT	3116
286	STA	SFO	1020	1150	117	PASS	GROSSMAN	4026
.								
.								
.								

(a) Airline Data Base

FLTNO	ORIG	DEST	DEP	ARR	SEATS
362	JFK	BWI	0830	0950	114
397	JFK	ORD	0830	1020	114
202	LGA	LGW	1530	0710	183
286	STA	SFO	1020	1150	117

(b) Travel Agent's View

Figure 8.20   (a) Airline Data Base, (b) Travel Agent View.

accessible element for the attribute exists) and the user knows the existence of the record (again at least one accessible element exists in the record).

In addition to elements, a view consists of relations on attributes. Furthermore, a user can create new relations from new and existing attributes and elements. These new relations are accessible to other users, subject to the standard access rights. A user can operate on the subset data base defined in a view only as allowed by the operations authorized in the view. As an example, a user might be allowed to retrieve records specified in one view or to retrieve and update records as specified in another view. Thus the airline example restricts travel agents to retrieving data.

The project described in [DEN87] is the basis for a system that will integrate with a trusted operating system to form a trusted data base manager. The layered implementation as described is shown in Figure 8.21. The lowest layer, the reference monitor, performs file interaction, enforcing the Bell-LaPadula access controls, and does user authentication. Part of its function is to filter data passed to higher levels. The second level performs basic indexing and computation functions of the data base. The third level translates views into the base relations of the data base. These three layers comprise the trusted computing base (TCB) of the system. The remaining layers implement normal DBMS functions and user interface.

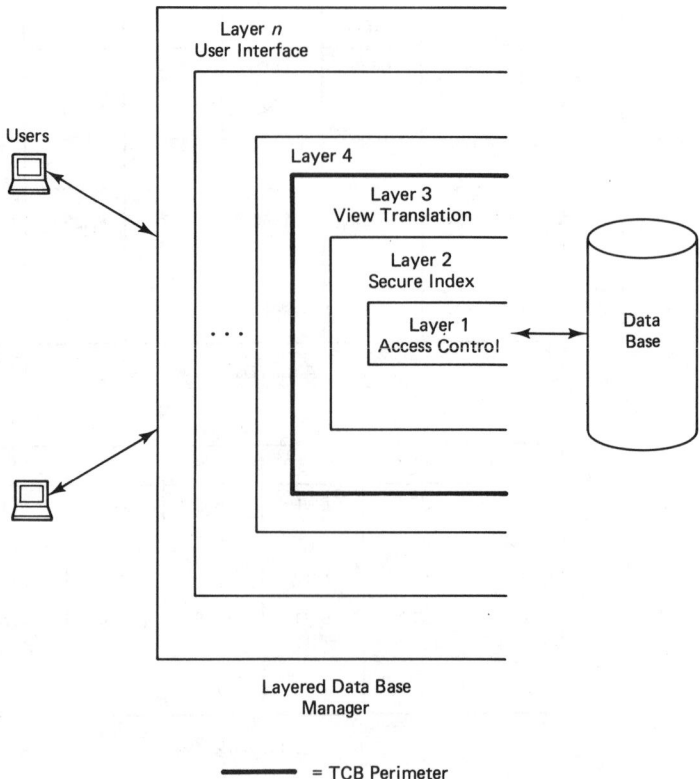

Figure 8.21   Secure Data Base Decomposition.

This layered approach makes views both a logical division of a data base and a functional one. The approach is an important step toward the design and implementation of a trustable data base management system.

Concluding Remarks

At the beginning of the section it was noted that the work in this section is still very fresh. The multilevel security problem for data bases has been studied for only a few years, and the solutions are still evolving. It is likely that in the next decade other approaches will augment or replace the approaches described here.

8.8 Summary of Data Base Security

This chapter has covered three aspects of security for data base management systems: (1) secrecy and integrity problems specific to data base applications, (2) the inference problem for statistical data bases, and (3) problems of including users and data of different sensitivity levels within one data base.

Both secrecy and integrity are important to users of data bases. Secrecy can be broken by indirect disclosure of a negative result or the bounds of a value. Integrity of the entire data base is a responsibility of the DBMS software; this problem is well addressed by most major commercial systems through backups, redundancy, change logs, and two-step updates. Integrity of an individual element of the data base is the responsibility of the data base administrator who defines the access policy.

The inference problem of a statistical data base arises from the mathematical relationships between data elements and query results. Controls studied to prevent statistical inference include limited response suppression, perturbation of results, and query analysis. One very complex control is monitoring all data provided to a user in order to prevent inference from independent queries.

Multilevel secure data bases must provide both secrecy and integrity. Integrity and access control can be implemented by use of an integrity lock. Three approaches for secrecy in multilevel secure data bases are views, trusted front-end with query modification, and commutative filters. Each of these solutions is just emerging from the prototype stage.

8.9 Terms and Concepts

data base management system (DBMS)
front-end
field
element
record
attribute
schema
subschema
relation
query
project
select
join
data base integrity
element integrity
access control
user authentication
auditability
availability
sensitive data
availability of data
access control decision
disclosure

exact disclosure
bounded disclosure
negative disclosure
probable value disclosure
disclosure of existence
security
precision
revealed data
retrieved data
requested data
allowed data
inference
direct inference
indirect inference
inference by sum
inference by count
inference by median
tracker inference
linear system inference
statistical inference
limited response suppression
combining results to suppress
revealing a random sample
random perturbation of data
restricting output by query analysis
multilevel data bases
granularity of control
response time
multilevel integrity
multilevel secrecy
polyinstantiation
partitioned data base
encryption
integrity lock
sensitivity lock
trusted front-end
query modification
commutative filter
window
view

8.10 Bibliographic Notes

Date [DAT81] addresses general topics of data base management, while the second volume [DAT83] covers recovery, integrity, concurrency, and security (secrecy). Fernandez and Wood [FER81] also cover basic security issues for data bases.

The inference problem dates back at least to [HOF70]. Denning and Schlörer [DEN83] survey the problems and controls for inference in data bases. Denning, Denning, and Schwartz [DEN79] describes tracker attacks. Access control is proposed by Stonebraker and Wong [STO74].

Multilevel security issues for data bases have been explored by Denning [DEN83], [DEN85], [DEN86], and [DEN87], and by Graubert [GRA84], [GRA85]. Two prototype implementations are described by Knode [KNO87], and Rougeau and Sturms [ROU87].

8.11 Exercises

1. In an environment where several users are sharing access to a single data base, how can indefinite postponement occur? Describe a scenario in which two users could cause the indefinite postponement of each other. Describe a scenario in which a single user could cause the indefinite postponement of all users.

2. Using the two-step commit presented in the beginning of this chapter, describe how to avoid assigning one seat to two people, as in the airline example. That is, list precisely which steps the data base manager should follow in assigning passengers to seats.

3. UNDO is a recovery operation for data bases. It is a command that obtains information from a transaction log and resets the elements of a data base to their values *before* a particular transaction is performed. Describe a situation in which an UNDO command would be useful.

4. The UNDO operation described in the previous exercise must be repeatable. That is, if x is the original value of a data base, and x' is an incorrectly modified version, we want

$$\text{UNDO}(x') = x,$$

but also

$$\text{UNDO}(x) = x$$

and

$$\text{UNDO}(\text{UNDO}(x')) = x.$$

(a) Why must $\text{UNDO}(x) = x$?
(b) Why must $\text{UNDO}(\text{UNDO}(x')) = x$?

5. Suppose a data base manager were to allow nesting of one transaction inside another. That is, after having updated part of one record, the DBMS would allow you to select another record, update it, and then perform further updates on the first record. What effect would nesting have on the integrity of a data base? Suggest a mechanism by which nesting could be allowed.

6. May a data base contain two identical records without a negative effect on the integrity of the data base? Why or why not?

7. Some operating systems perform "buffered I/O." In this scheme, an output request is accepted from a user, and the user is informed of the normal I/O completion. However, the actual physical write operation is performed later, at a time convenient to the operating system. Discuss the effect of buffered I/O on integrity in a DBMS.

8. A data base transaction implements the command set STATUS to 'CURRENT' in all records where BALANCE-OWED = 0. (a) Describe how that transaction would be performed using the two-step commit described in this chapter. (b) Suppose the relations from which that command was formed are (CUSTOMER-ID, STATUS) and (CUSTOMER-ID,BALANCE-OWED). How would the transaction be performed? (c) Suppose the relations from which that command was formed are (CUSTOMER-ID,STATUS), (CREDIT-ID,CUSTOMER-ID), (CREDIT-ID, BALANCE-OWED). How would the transaction be performed?

9. Show that if longitudinal parity is used as an error detection code, values in a data base can still be modified without detection. (Longitudinal parity is computed for the n-th bit of each byte; that is, one parity bit is computed and retained for all bits in the 0-th position, another parity bit for all bits in the 1-st position, etc.)

10. Suppose query $Q1$ obtains the median $m1$ of a set $S1$ of values. Suppose query $Q2$ obtains the median $m2$ of a subset $S2$ of $S1$. If $m1 < m2$, what can be inferred about $S1$, $S2$, and the elements of $S1$ not in $S2$?

11. Disclosure of the sum of all financial aid for students in Smith dorm is not sensitive, since no individual student is associated with an amount. Similarly, a list of names of students receiving financial aid is not sensitive, since no amounts are specified. However, the combination of these two lists reveals the amount for an individual student if only one student in Smith dorm receives aid. What computation would a data base management system have to perform in order to determine that the list of names might reveal sensitive data? What records would the data base management system have to maintain on what different users know in order to determine that the list of names might reveal sensitive data?

12. The response "sensitive value; response suppressed" is itself a disclosure. Suggest a manner in which a data base management system could suppress responses that reveal sensitive information without disclosing that the responses to certain queries are sensitive.

13. Cite a situation in which the sensitivity of an aggregate is greater than that of its constituent values. Cite a situation in which the sensitivity of an aggregate is less than that of its constituent values.

14. Explain the disadvantages of partitioning as a means of implementing multilevel security for data bases.

15. A data base management system is implemented under an operating system trusted to provide multilevel separation of users. (a) What security features of the operating

system can be used to simplify the design of the data base management system? (b) Suppose the operating system has rating r, where r is C2 or B1 or B3, and so on. State and defend a policy for the degree of trust in the data base management system, based on the trust of the operating system.

16. What is the purpose of encryption in a multilevel secure data base management system?

9
Personal Computer Security

A few years ago most computing was done on mainframe computers, and data processing centers were responsible for protection. Computing centers developed expertise in security, and they carried out many protection activities in the background, without users having to be conscious of protection needs and practices. Much sensitive computing is still done that way. Many of the security concepts we have studied relate to multiuser, shared-resource environments typical of large mainframe systems. It would be an overstatement to say that security problems in that context are "solved" or "trivial." Nevertheless, the security problems there are recognized and being dealt with effectively by the computing professionals who run computing centers.

More recently the use of personal computers has spread substantially, especially among professional, managerial, and clerical workers. We use the generic term **personal computer** to include microcomputers, office automation workstations, intelligent workstations, and even intelligent terminals. Each is a reasonably small machine, typically used by a single person at a time. A personal computer contrasts with a "mainframe computer," the more conventional, multiuser machine typical in major computing centers.

Personal computer users often do not recognize the risks they face, nor do they think of the simple measures that could contain those risks. A person who will carefully lock company confidential records in a safe will leave a personal computer on a secretary's or a manager's desk, where anyone walking past can retrieve confidential memoranda and data. A box of floppy disks may contain many times more data than a printed report, yet the report is an apparent, visible exposure, while the floppy disk is not obvious.

The basic security problems for personal computers are the same as for every other computer situation we have studied so far: applications require secrecy, integrity, and availability, as applied to the data, programs, and computing machinery. Security problems for personal computers are more serious than on mainframe computers for two reasons, one related to people, and one related to hardware and software.

Lack of Sensitivity.   People often do not understand the security risks associated with the use of personal computers.

In the mainframe environment, computing professionals are skilled and experienced. Computing is the principal concern for these people who can support and assist each other in security considerations. However, personal computer users may be much less skilled and experienced in computing. Often, users are not computer professionals. Instead, they use personal computing as a support tool in some other field, such as accounting, engineering, or office communication.

Lack of Tools.   The tools—hardware, software, and combinations of these—are fewer and less sophisticated than in the mainframe environment.

Many of the software and hardware facilities important in assuring security—facilities such as access control mechanisms, operating systems aids, supervisor mode, trusted computing bases, or professionally developed software—are inappropriate and unavailable in the personal computer environment.

In this chapter we consider security as it relates to personal computers. First we survey the problems of security for personal computers. Even though they have a different context, personal computer security needs and solutions often resemble solutions for mainframes. Thus, we focus on how personal computers are different from mainframes in their security capabilities. We identify some of the security facilities that are appropriate for users of personal computers. Finally, we consider the problem of copy protection and software distribution, since this issue, not often a mainframe security problem, has generated several controls unique to personal computers. Note that the emphasis of this chapter is on software solutions to security problems. In Chapter 12 we will consider physical security measures and additional devices that can be used to enhance security.

9.1 Contributors to Security Problems

Personal computers are essentially no different from the more general forms of computers studied extensively in Chapters 5–8. The major problems facing personal computer users involve secrecy, integrity and availability of programs, data, and machines, just as with mainframe computers. The standard controls, such as access control lists, protected memory, user authentication techniques, and trusted operating systems, should apply equally well to the small computer situation as the large.

Hardware Vulnerabilities

The difficulty with using classic mainframe controls is that most personal computers have no hardware-level protection. There is no protection of one memory space from another, even by a simple fence. There are no supervisory or privileged instructions available only to the operating system or a trusted kernel. Therefore, every user can execute every instruction, and can read and write every memory location. Although there may be software user authentication, a clever user can bypass the authentication code, or modify authentication data to avoid the authentication. The operating system may declare certain files as "system" files, but it cannot prevent a user from accessing them. Thus, the controls for personal computers are much less stringent than for mainframe computers. Certain new microprocessors, notably the Motorola 68020 and the Intel 80286, have stronger protection capabilities, but these capabilities are not yet fully exploited by operating systems.

Other Vulnerabilities

The machine is not the source of the security problem; the problem is *users* of the machine. The way people view the machine and their responsibilities for its use affect the security of personal computers. People must think about the potential vulnerabilities inherent in processing text and data on a microcomputer. Most users do not often consider these kinds of security risks. Thus, while the controls for personal computers are less powerful, the vulnerabilities are more numerous. The following list describes some of the vulnerabilities in personal computer security.

- *Low awareness of the problem.* Former mainframe users are used to passing responsibility for computer security to the data processing department. To many new, inexperienced users, a personal computer is an office tool, analogous to a calculator or a typewriter. People who are unaware of or insensitive to the other vulnerabilities in use of personal computers are themselves a vulnerability.

- *Few hardware controls.* Few personal computers have hardware features that simplify installation of security measures (such as a supervisor mode for sensitive instructions, hardware addressing limitation, or restricted access to I/O devices). Therefore, relatively unsophisticated attacks can overcome access control software or authentication techniques.

- *No audit trail.* If a problem arises, it is impossible to tell who has accessed a machine and when. Because unsophisticated attacks can defeat these machines, it is not even possible to determine what access occurred when trying to recover from an attack.

- *No unique responsibility.* If a machine is shared by several users, no one acknowledges individual responsibility for maintenance, supervision, or control of the machine.

- *Environmental attacks.* Smoke particles, food crumbs, beverages, power surges, and static electricity can all cause failures of personal computers. These factors are well controlled in major computer rooms but not with desktop personal computers.

- *Physical access.* Often a machine is left unattended and running in an office. The entire file structure is accessible to anyone who touches the keyboard.

○ *Care of media, components.* Floppy disks, containing the only copies of valuable software or data, are not consistently stored in a safe, appropriate environment.

○ *No backups.* Even experienced computer users are often remiss in making backup copies of important files. New users may not even appreciate the need for periodic full and partial backups.

○ *Questionable documentation.* Some software and hardware comes with complete, readable instructions for use, but some documentation is dreadful. Poor documentation leads to mistakes in use, which can be catastrophic.

○ *Amateur quality software.* Personal computer software is sometimes produced by amateurs, who may not practice the same rigorous testing as do professional software writers for mainframe computers. Similarly, users may be unaware of possible vulnerabilities in the use of untested or untrustworthy software.

○ *High portability.* A personal computer is highly vulnerable to theft, because of the same portability characteristics that make it desirable.

○ *Magnetic retention.* Typed or handwritten scratch copies are usually thrown away; computer scratch copy (or initial draft) media are often reused, sometimes for other files, and sometimes by other users. On many systems, the ERASE or DELETE command merely removes a file pointer; it does not erase or overwrite the file itself. This file can be retrieved by simple techniques, and it can be accessed by other users intentionally or through a user or system error.

○ *Combination of duties.* A classic principle in financial auditing is that no one person has full responsibility for performing a complete transaction. By contrast, most personal computer applications are designed for one user to perform all steps. Lack of checks and balances raises the possibility of malicious wrongdoing.

This list is long, but not complete; many other personal computer vulnerabilities can be identified. It may seem as if there is little that can be done to provide effective security. Fortunately, that is not the case: techniques affording some security for personal computers are not difficult to identify.

The National Computer Security Center (NCSC) is especially concerned with the vulnerability of personal computers. It has published a document describing vulnerabilities and controls for personal computers [NCS85]. Another useful document comes from the National Telecommunications and Information Systems Security Committee (NTISSC) [NTI87]. Various hardware vendors and security consulting firms have also published user guidelines. Some of the recommendations in this chapter are drawn from those documents.

9.2 Security Measures

Although the list of vulnerabilities is long and varied, the issues involved fall into four major classes: (1) user responsibility, (2) improper procedures for use, (3) hardware concerns, and (4) software concerns. In each area some controls are reasonably effective. Combinations of controls of two or more types can be especially effective. We consider what can be done in terms of these four classes.

Issues Addressed by User Awareness of Responsibility

Professionals who use computers must come to understand the vulnerabilities of computers in general and specifically of personal computers. This awareness may be developed from reading, from user awareness programs, or from a high-level assessment of the risks of computing. Unfortunately, awareness can also develop from unpleasant and costly experience. With luck, the material in this chapter can help to avoid some of those experiences.

Computing professionals must help managers and other users recognize and accept responsibility for security problems involving personal computers. From their experience, computer professionals are aware of many dimensions of general computer security problems. This experience can be applied to the personal computer environment.

Issues Addressed by Procedures for Use

Some of the vulnerabilities identified here can be controlled by administrative procedures. Sensible policies for the use of machines can reduce the risk associated with unattended machines, care of media, backups, the environment, magnetic residue, and separation of duties. Users who understand the vulnerabilities of their machines will appreciate and comply with sensible procedures for their use.

Several procedures can improve the security of use of personal computers.

- **Do not leave personal computers unattended if they contain sensitive information or are running sensitive computations.** Ease of use considerations for software have made it simple for unskilled users to learn how to use new packages. Similarly, many packages use a similar user interface to reduce learning time, and some companies have adopted one standard data base manager or one standard spreadsheet package, for example. These factors, which make it simple for users to learn new applications, also make it simple for unauthorized users to access sensitive data on unattended machines.

- **Do not leave printers unattended if they are printing sensitive output.** This restriction is especially important if one printer is shared by two or more computers, or if the printer is located in a public place.

- **Secure media as carefully as you would the equivalent confidential reports.** Floppy disks containing sensitive information should be locked up. Machines with hard disks containing sensitive information should be locked up. Turn off a personal computer after using it to clear volatile memory. Label each disk showing its contents and its sensitivity. Remember that data persists even after being erased. Overwrite spare disks at least three times, once with 0s, once with 1s, and once with a pattern of 0s and 1s, before releasing them for others to use. When a personal computer must be sent out for repair, understand that fixed disk systems may retain data; if the data on a disk is especially sensitive, either remove the disk or have the machine repaired by a trusted repair facility. If necessary, copy the contents of the hard disk to another medium and then overwrite the entire disk.

- **Do not allow eating, drinking, or smoking in any room containing a personal computer.** Crumbs and drinks can destroy hardware and media. Ash particles in smoke are large enough to ruin disk systems by becoming trapped between a read head and the medium.

- **Treat media with care.** The pressure from a ballpoint pen can damage a floppy disk. Write on disks only with a felt tip pen; preferably, write on the label before sticking the label to the disk. Keep the disk stored in its protective jacket, and store the disks in a hard case, away from dust and heat. Keep disks away from magnetic fields generated by sources such as telephones or large motors.

- **Perform periodic backups.** Depending on the criticality of the application, daily backups of changed files from a hard disk to a floppy disk or another device may be in order. In some cases, it may be better to back up a file every time it has been substantially changed. Also, make periodic (such as weekly or monthly) backups of all files so that a full system can be replaced in the event of a failure or so that backup copies are available of even supposedly insignificant files. Retain a full backup set, including system disks and software, in a building separate from the machine. This backup set will permit resumption of work on a new machine in case of fire, theft, or other catastrophe.

- **Practice separation of authority.** Design sensitive procedures so that no person alone has authority to affect sensitive data. For example, design accounting systems so that data is maintained on two systems by two people, and so that total figures must balance between the two systems. In this way, fraud requires the cooperation of two people.

Issues Addressed by Hardware Controls

As noted earlier, hardware controls are not as useful for personal computers as for mainframes. While personal computers have no privileged mode of execution or hardware memory protection, there are some controls that depend on hardware.

- **Secure the equipment.** Portability is a special advantage of personal computers, but that portability is also a vulnerability. Simple as it sounds, bolting the computer to a desk or securing it with an adhesive or mechanical lock provides good security against theft. A computer can be unlocked to be moved and then resecured at its new location. Several types of locks are listed in Chapter 12.

- **Consider using add-on security boards.** Different vendors have developed access control packages to run in the limited personal computer environment. Some of these packages offer only software controls, which are easily defeated or circumvented. Some more sophisticated packages combine hardware (usually an added board) with software. The board receives control every time the machine is initialized (booted), and it limits access to certain operating system commands, including file I/O, file directory maintenance (ERASE, DELETE, COPY, FORMAT), and any other desired commands. Although these solutions, too, can be circumvented, they do provide security against casual attack and untrusted software. These packages will be examined more completely in Chapter 12.

Issues Addressed by Software Controls

Common software vulnerabilities include the lack of audit trail, the use of software from untrusted sources, poor documentation, and the lack of operating system controls, such as reuse of file space or access control. As already noted, personal computers cannot provide true access control, including limited access by subjects to objects, proper auditing of accesses and secure identification and authentication of users.

Other than access control, protection against software vulnerabilities can include the following controls.

- **Use all software with full understanding of its potential threats.** Communications software can leak information that it transmits, programs can compute incorrect answers, and any software can damage or destroy files or other programs to which it has access.

- **Don't use software from dubious sources.**   Software from large, reliable manufacturers and distributors is less likely to exhibit the problems listed above than software from small, unknown companies, user groups, or public access to bulletin boards.

- **Be suspicious of all results.** Increasingly, applications are being developed by non-programmers. These developers know little about software engineering practices such as design methods, data validation, and thorough testing. Data produced by such programs may not be correct and may even corrupt correct data from other sources.

- **Maintain periodic complete backups of all system resources.** In the event of an incident due to faulty software, the only way to recover may be to reinstall the entire system from backup copies. With program flaws such as worms, it may be necessary to rebuild the system from a very old version because later versions may have been infected.

9.3 Protection for Files

In Chapter 6 we studied a general approach to file access control. That approach involved access control lists, an access control matrix, capabilities, and other techniques. Although very effective, these techniques are most appropriate for multiuser operating systems in situations where high security is important. In this chapter we will study the general problem of protection of personal computer files, which may contain either data or programs. In our discussion the whole file is the unit to be secured—a user either has access to the entire file or no access at all.

Essentially there are four types of protection applicable to personal computer files.

1. *Access control features*, provided either as a part of the operating system or as auxiliary packages

2. *Encryption* applied by the individual user

3. *Copy protection* to limit someone's ability to copy a file

4. *No protection*, which is really the case of having controlled the environment so that protection is not necessary

Access Controls

Most personal computer operating systems do not provide access controls to limit the access of people to files; where these controls are available, people do not always use them. This negligence results from the environment and the ease of use of a personal computer.

Personal Computer Users and Uses

The manufacturer of a piece of paper or a typewriter does not warn users that it is possible to type confidential data on the paper, and therefore appropriate security measures should be taken. It is assumed that the security risk is the user's responsibility. A similar assumption accompanies personal computers. Furthermore, the term "personal" is taken quite literally; that is, each machine is often used by one person, so that the environment does not seem to warrant comprehensive security systems. For this reason, personal computers seldom have protection analogous to the access control lists of multiuser operating systems.

Another reason for lack of access controls is ease of use. Many personal computer users access a small number of applications, such as word processing or spreadsheet calculation. Much thought has been given to the user interface for these packages to make them easy and pleasant to use. But that same ease of use can be at odds with access controls that require planning which individuals should have access to which files.

Why Access Control Mechanisms for Personal Computers?

Large-capacity disk drives, powerful operating systems, and networks are creating situations in which several users can productively share the use of one personal computer.

Even with only one user per machine, there are good reasons for access control mechanisms. Some of the motivations for access controls for personal computer files are listed here.

- o *Outside interference.* Even single-user systems are vulnerable to access by outsiders, such as coworkers, service and maintenance personnel, visitors, and others who could affect the contents of a file.

- o *Two users, one machine.* It is not uncommon for two coworkers to share a single machine. Although it may be reasonable to assume no malicious intent, one user can inadvertently destroy data or programs belonging to the other.

- o *Network access.* Even in a trustworthy office environment, as personal computers are networked, the number of users grows, and the ability to trust all users of a network declines. Furthermore, shared devices require some form of access control mechanism to ensure equitable sharing.

- o *Errors.* Access protection can limit the effect of errors by restricting the files that are accessible (that is, can be damaged) when certain applications are running.

- o *Untrusted software.* Personal computer software often does not have nearly the rigor of testing prior to release as does that for mainframe computers. Therefore, until a software package is known to be safe, it is prudent to run it in an environment where it can do only minimal damage.

- o *Separation of applications.* Access control mechanisms can facilitate logical separation of files by contents. Besides the protection advantages of this separation, it may be easier to keep track of files organized by category.

Features of Personal Computer Access Control Systems

Several companies have developed access control systems using a variety of hardware and software techniques. The packages all provide three basic features: user authentication, usually through password checking; file access limitation, such as read-only, execute-only, read-write, no access; and an audit log, a report showing who has accessed which files and when.

Additional features provided on individual systems include these.

- o *Transparent encryption.* The access mechanism can be useless if a user ever obtains access to the operating system, through programming, through an offline backup copy of important files, by exiting from a running program (for example, by pressing control-C), or from a flaw in the security system. Some systems automatically encrypt files so that even if they become accessible, their contents will not be evident.

- o *Time of day checking.* The security administrator can set up permissions for users allowing access only during certain times (for example, between 7:00 am and 6:00

pm), and only on certain days of the week (for example, Monday through Friday). This control ensures that employees or intruders cannot sneak into an office when the office is closed to try to defeat the system or to obtain furtive access.

o *Automatic timeout.* With this control activated, the system terminates the session of a user who fails to strike any keyboard key during a specified period (for example, 15 minutes). The system blanks the screen and requires a new user authentication to restart. If a user leaves a personal computer unattended, this control reduces the threat of an interceptor who walks past and finds an unoccupied but active machine.

o *Machine identification.* One system uses an added hardware device that responds with a unique serial number that can be read by applications software. Each hardware device thus identifies a unique machine. In this way a program can query the device to be sure that it is running on a particular authorized machine as a form of authentication.

Access control systems usually employ a combination of hardware and software to achieve their results. The hardware is often a board that plugs into the personal computer; this board is activated each time the machine is powered up or rebooted, thereby ensuring that the security mechanism will be in force any time the machine is used. The board contains memory, often a clock with which to maintain the correct time and date, and space for the program that enforces security. The code can be permanently installed at the factory on a read-only memory, or it can be loaded from a disk when the board is first installed. The advantage of installation from a disk is that the manufacturer can change the code easily by sending a new disk to the security administrator, who reinstalls the software. The disadvantage of this approach is that the security administrator, or anyone who could masquerade as the administrator, can install a different system, perhaps with a trapdoor. The more secure approach is to provide all instructions on a read-only memory from the factory; then changes require distributing and installing new chips.

User-Invoked Encryption

Encryption is a form of access control mechanism: Only users who know how to decrypt can obtain access to the plaintext of encrypted data. Any user can perform encryption; no complicated or expensive mechanism is required. Users of word processing systems and of personal computers would be wise to perform their own encryption. The techniques from Chapter 2 in this book can provide protection against casual observers, while the techniques of Chapter 3 are adequate for very sensitive information.

Several of the access control systems listed earlier provide automatic file encryption (not under user control). Others provide file encryption as an option, using a hardware implementation of the DES or by a proprietary encryption algorithm.

9.4 Copy Protection

Theft of software is another serious problem with the use of personal computers. With mainframe computers one copy of software is bought by a computing center, and all users can make use of one copy of the executable code of a program. With single-user systems, many more copies of software are needed, and it is important for software developers to provide users with ways to secure files containing their software.

There are two conflicting views of copy protection. First, the developers have a right to a fair return for their products. They price software at a level where they anticipate a reasonable profit for an expected number of sales; with fewer sales they lose money, and with more sales they make more. They lose money if they sell only half as many copies as they estimated. If the limited sales are due to overestimating the market or producing an inferior or noncompetitive product, that is the developers' fault. But if poor sales are because each legitimate purchaser makes one copy to give to a friend, the developers lose because they have produced a very good product. That does not seem fair.

The other side to consider is that of the consumers. Consumers have machines with hard disks, making it inconvenient to run programs from floppy disks. Users may also dedicate a portion of memory as a pseudo-disk that runs significantly faster. This pseudo-disk, also called RAM-disk, is effectively used for programs that make frequent disk accesses during execution. Of course, floppy disks occasionally fail. Buying one copy of software should entitle users to unlimited personal use of the software. Some software protection schemes do not permit copying a program to a hard disk. To address the backup problem, developers often offer to replace any defective disk returned, even long after the original sale, and even due to the purchaser's negligence (such as spilling a soft drink on the disk). The consumer counters that a replacement disk by mail is of no value if the program in question is needed within next day. The consumer is entitled to reliable and efficient use of the resources acquired legally.

The third party in this analysis, the software pirate, does not deserve consideration. Unfortunately, the skills of the pirate are what create the conflict between the interests of the developer and the legitimate consumer. In few other situations do we have the ability to make a functionally perfect copy of an object.

The solution most widely used now is copy protection. There are essentially three ways to prevent a file from being copied: (1) One can depend solely on software; (2) one can use a combination of software and a hardware device, and (3) one can use hardware alone.

Straight Software Techniques

Complete copy protection implemented in software is rare, since personal computers cannot prevent a user from circumventing a software protection scheme. Because such machines have no distinct supervisor mode, any user can write a program that does whatever is desired, in spite of any protection mechanisms. More often, copy protection is implemented with a software solution that is helped by hardware. To many software developers, "copy protected" means a disk that cannot be copied by ordinary software techniques.

In order to understand copy protection, it is necessary to understand the terminology of floppy disks. A floppy disk is composed of a number of concentric rings called **tracks**. Each ring is divided into pieces called **sectors**. Typically there are as many sectors on the outermost track as on the innermost, and the capacities of outer sectors are equal to those on the inside, even though the data must be more densely packed on the inner sectors (see Figure 9.1).

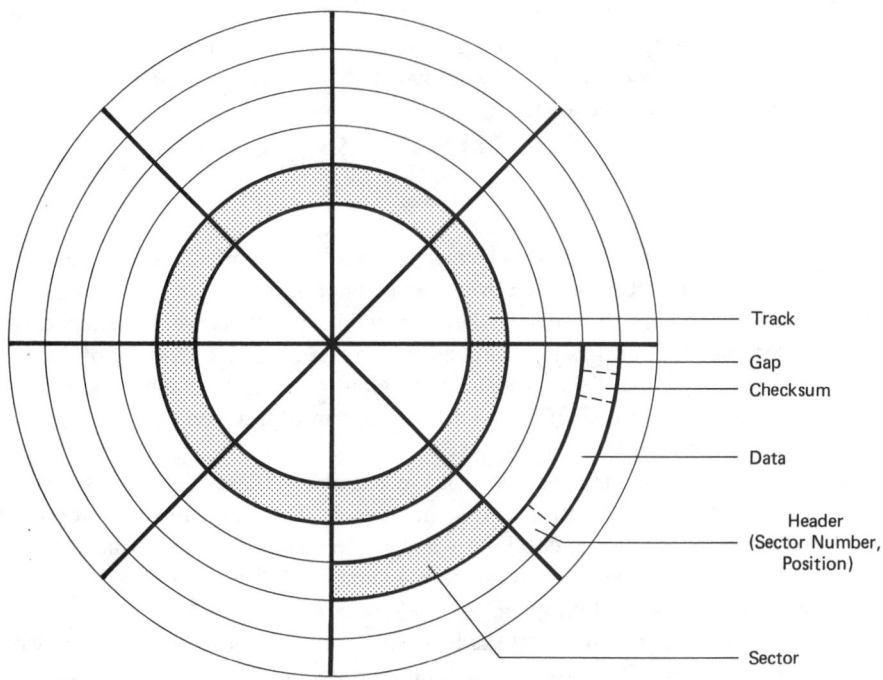

Figure 9.1   Floppy Disk Characteristics.

Each sector is **formatted** with a header block that indicates the sector number and its position. The space for data is followed by a **checksum** area, which holds a value used to detect flaws or errors in the recording process. Finally, a **gap** separates one sector from another.

Illegal Format

Because the sector address and the checksum pertain to the integrity of the data recorded on the disk, most copy utilities verify the legality of these as a disk is being copied. If something is incorrect, they refuse to copy the associated segment, or they try to correct the error and copy the corrected segment.

Early copy prevention schemes simply presented a disk with an error in one of these fields, so that copy utilities would not duplicate it. The program being protected would check during execution to see if the disk from which it was being executed contained a bad sector; if not, the program would conclude that the disk from which it was running was an illegal copy. This form of protection was easily defeated by writing programs that copy every bit from a disk, including bad data.

Other, more elaborate copy protection schemes involved writing tracks where there should be none (beyond the innermost track), writing tracks that spiral outwards at a predictable rate, writing tracks that are too long, writing tracks that do not line up to their expected positions, and writing tracks that are too wide. All of these "flawed" tracks can be detected by sending commands to the floppy disk access arm at the right moment, yet without knowing what flaw has been recorded on a disk, the copier cannot know what flaw to generate.

Failed Bits

Two more exotic protection schemes involve flaws on the recording medium. With one, the Prolok protection scheme from Vault, small scratches are made on the surface of the magnetic medium. These scratches produce bit positions where neither a 0 nor a 1 can be recorded, yet bit positions around them react normally. A copy of the failure pattern is recorded on the disk, so that the program can check whether the program disk has the failure pattern it should. If not, the program is assumed to be an illegal copy, and it refuses to execute.

Another scheme uses bits that are unstable. These bits hold no consistent value, sometimes being read as 1, and sometimes 0. The authentication program reads these locations several times, checking whether the results are inconsistent. If the results are consistent, the authentication program assumes the disk is an illegal copy and refuses to execute the protected program.

A third approach uses disks that have a unique serial number recorded in a nonre-producible form. The protected program written on this special disk includes a preamble to check that the program disk is correctly serial numbered. The programs and data on that disk can be copied to any other disk for backup purposes, but programs will execute only from the original program disk.

Software/Hardware Combinations

Most software security mechanisms other than the ones described so far must be created by hardware devices that operate predictably. These hardware devices can be calibrated carefully to produce errors or patterns of a precise type. The errors must also be detected by the relatively imprecise hardware of a personal computer, which may not even be properly calibrated for its application. It is difficult to develop recognizable patterns that can be detected by but not reproduced by personal computers.

Another security mechanism uses a hardware device in conjunction with a software test. Most frequently this device is a form of electronic "key" that plugs into one of the ports, such as the printer socket. The key will not interfere with normal operation of the printer. When a protected program runs, it sends a particular signal to that port. If the key is installed, it responds with a recognizable signal, which the software package recognizes as a sign to execute normally.

The difficulty with this is that a user with several such "keyed" software packages could need 10 or 20 keys plugged into a port. It is often inconvenient to plug in and remove these keys when changing from one program to another. However, one key might be incompatible with another program, or a ladder of keys plugged one into another might be physically unstable.

Hardware Techniques

Two of the access control devices described previously offer protection that can also prevent unauthorized copying of files. They operate by checking during execution that the machine in execution is the one for which the hardware is intended. One device provides a unique serial number and group number that appear in memory, so that the program can check that the machine is the expected one. Another goes one step farther: It encrypts executable files with an encryption that is unique to the specific machine. A file will then execute only on the machine on which it was encrypted.

In [ALB84] a proposal is made for development of a processor chip that has a decryptor as an integral part. The decryption key would be a part of the processor as well. Software would be distributed in encrypted form on unprotected disks. The distributed version of a piece of software would be encrypted with the intended user's unique key. Only as each instruction is executed would it be decrypted. In this way, the legitimate user could make an unlimited number of backup copies, could copy the program to a hard disk, or could place the program in RAM disk to execute. The decrypting processor could be a sealed unit, so that the end user might never know the actual decryption key sealed within the processor. In this way, the software could execute only on the machine registered for the authentic user. Decryption causes a degradation in speed, and the special decrypting processor is an added cost. However, neither of these disadvantages should be prohibitive factors.

No Protection

The final security approach for programs is to provide no protection for the files on the machine. This is, of course, the default position, and it is the simplest way out. It seems, however, as if it would be unacceptable. There are situations in which it can be quite appropriate.

Public Domain Software

A concept known as **public domain software** is one interesting method for distributing unprotected software. Certain works, including software or written materials that have been developed with U.S. government funds, cannot be copyrighted and may be distributed freely. Free software is distributed by firms that charge a small fee, typically under $10 per disk, to cover the cost of reproduction. Users are free to make backup copies and even to give copies to other users.

Other software authors have placed their packages with distribution companies, using the **shareware concept**. Shareware allows a potential user to try out a package before buying it, similar to taking a car for a test drive. The authors encourage free (both in the sense of liberal and in the sense of without charge) sharing of their software. Each such software package begins execution with a notice telling who the author is and suggesting that each user voluntarily contribute a reasonable sum, usually between

$10 and $100, to the author if the user is pleased. The software is thus distributed on a free, unlimited trial use basis. The software authors try to make it appealing to pay for the copy (called "registering"), by providing registered users benefits, such as printed documentation, offers of updates, access to service over the telephone, or reduced prices on other software.

There are now thousands of shareware or public domain software programs. Most of these are one-time projects developed by amateur software developers. A few of the larger firms, such as Jim Button (PC-File, PC-Calc, PC-Type) and Quicksoft (PC-Write) produce professional-quality software that rivals packages costing several hundred dollars more.

Site Licenses

A site license also permits the legal mass distribution of software. A large company with, say, 300 personal computers might not want to buy 300 copies of each piece of software. Certainly the cost of 300 copies of one package is a contributing factor. The company might also argue that of these 300 copies, only 30 would be in use at any time. (Notice, however, that if 20 people each need a typewriter ten percent of the time, 20 typewriters will usually be purchased.)

Another factor is that all 300 copies might not have been needed at the time the machines were acquired. One worker may have acquired a software package that no other users were expected to want or need. However, when the first worker starts explaining uses of the package to others, it becomes tempting for the worker to say, "I'll make you a copy of this disk so that you can use it too." The worker may not think of the legal issue involved, and it is almost impossible for the company to police or control such incidents.

As an alternative, some software package developers have negotiated site licenses with large installations. In this case, the developers receive a fee; in exchange the installation is allowed to make an unlimited number of copies for the use of people at the site.

A common example is a university where a professor may want to use a particular software package in class. The professor may not be able to justify the cost of a $200 or more software package for each student in the class, either as a cost to the university or to be paid by each student. With a mainframe computer one copy of the software would be shared by all students, but with personal computers each student requires an individual copy. A site license gives the university the legal right to distribute copies freely to students. Depending on the terms of the license, the students can make additional copies for other students, the university may be able to make copies for faculty and staff, and the students and faculty can use the package on computers at home, not just on campus.

By negotiating the site license, the software vendor makes it easy for the installation to meet both legal and moral restrictions. Furthermore, the license brings the vendor profit that would not have come had illegal copies been made. Finally, the installation takes over costs of distribution, advertising, and copying, which would have been expenses for the vendor. The site license concept is one that works because it provides something good for everyone involved.

9.5 Summary of Personal Computer Security

The demands of personal computer security are the same as those for other modes of computers; the difference is in the users' attitudes and the protection controls available. User attitude affects the understanding of and sensitivity to the problem and the willingness to spend money or use certain procedures in order to achieve some controls. Hardware and software controls are less useful than procedural ones in a personal computer environment.

Copy protection is an especially sensitive issue, since there are arguments on the user's side, as well as the software developer's side. The user is entitled to secure, convenient use of a package legitimately acquired, while the developer is entitled to fair compensation for distribution of a package. Legal controls are not especially effective, but are sometimes necessary, since software solutions can be broken, and hardware approaches are often cumbersome.

9.6 Terms and Concepts

personal computer
microcomputer
office automation workstation
intelligent workstation
intelligent terminal
user awareness
hardware controls
audit trail
responsibility for supervision, maintenance
environmental attacks
power surge
static electricity
physical access controls
care of media
backup copies
documentation standards
quality software development
portability
magnetic retention
division of duties
file protection
network access
encryption
access control hardware, software
copy protection
software piracy

track
sector
formatted disk
checksum
header
illegal format
failed bits
public domain software
site license

9.7 Exercises

1. In what ways is denial of service (lack of availability for authorized users) a vulnerability to users of single-user personal computers?

2. Identify the three most probable threats to a personal computing system in an office with fewer than ten employees. That is, identify the three vulnerabilities most likely to be exploited. Estimate the number of times each vulnerability is exploited per year; justify your estimate.

3. Perform the analysis of the previous exercise for a personal computing system located in a large research laboratory.

4. Perform the analysis of Exercise 2 for a personal computing system located in the library of a major university.

5. Explain why an audit trail is insecure in a personal computer without a privileged mode of execution.

6. Consider software packages, such as data base management systems or file managers, designed to run on single-user personal computers. Is it necessary for these packages to include features to mediate multiple concurrent accesses? Why or why not?

7. What is the purpose of a checksum on a floppy disk?

8. *Programming problem.* Write a procedure that performs file encryption and decryption for security. Estimate the amount of time that a dedicated interceptor would need in order to break your encryption. Perform a timing analysis of your program and derive a formula for its encryption and decryption speed.

9. *Programming problem.* Investigate the architecture of a particular personal computer and write a procedure to truly "delete" files by overwriting them with 0s when a file is deleted.

10. *Programming problem.* Investigate the architecture of a particular personal computer and write a procedure that blanks the screen if no key has been struck within the last 15 minutes.

11. *Design and programming problem.* Design a procedure for a particular personal computer that prompts for a user identification when the machine is booted. Then structure the file system so access is allowed only to system files and files of a single user who has been identified.

10

Computer Network Security

This chapter covers security in networks of computers. Although networks raise new issues in security, several familiar topics appear in the list of solutions to network security problems. The solutions include encryption, access controls, authentication, and protocols. In fact, networks can be viewed as more complex examples of computing systems, so that many of the same security concepts and controls for operating systems apply to networks as well.

This chapter considers only the network itself, not the media or devices through which network communications occur; that is the subject of the next chapter. For this chapter, we assume that a secure communications medium exists and is used throughout the network. This assumption is consistent with the general approach taken throughout this book, to separate security *design* and *policy* from its *implementation*. In fact, it should be possible to change the medium of a communications link in a network without reconsidering the security of the whole network. Ideally, changing one link should affect only the nodes to which it is connected.

This chapter begins with an analysis of networks, to determine what a network is and what about it is similar to and different from other computing systems. Second, the chapter turns to the security problems peculiar to networks. After exploring mechanisms that contribute to security in networks, the chapter concludes with two special cases of networks—local area networks (LANs) and multilevel security networks—and the security measures that are especially appropriate to each of them.

10.1 Comparison of Networks and Other Computing Systems

In order to study computer network security, it is necessary to understand what is meant by a network. The following definitions highlight the security aspects of a computing network.

Until now the term *computing system* has been used to refer to a single main processor, its peripheral devices, its data, and its software. Figure 10.1 shows a block diagram of a computing system. Such a system has a single operating system and one set of users. One characteristic of a computing system is *physical proximity*; all blocks of the computing system are located within a small distance, usually a few feet, of the rest of the system.

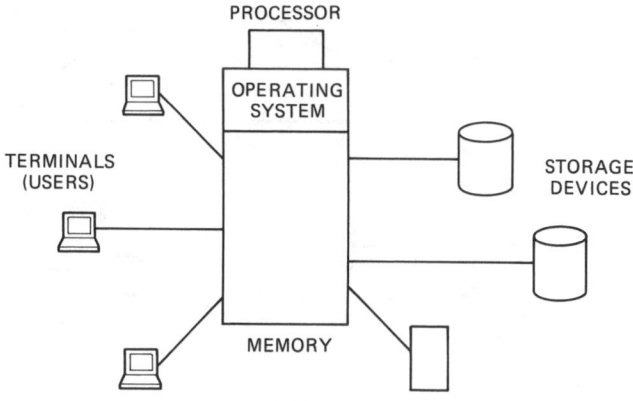

Figure 10.1   Computing System.

Notice that *size* is not a relevant characteristic in defining a computing system, since the security problems of microcomputers are very similar to those of large mainframes. Hardware and user characteristics dictate a different set of controls for microcomputers as opposed to mainframes. A second difference between security considerations for many microcomputers and for mainframes is *multiuser concurrent access*. These differences introduce new problems, but these problems are not related to the size of the system.

We define a **computing network** to be a computing environment with *more than one independent processor*. Essentially, a computing network is a collection of two or more independent computing systems. An example of a computing network is shown in the block diagram of Figure 10.2. Notice that the users access the network only indirectly—through a computing system.

The term "independent processor" in this definition is meant to exclude things like intelligent controllers for I/O devices; although they are processors in their own right, they are not used for computing by a separate group of users, and they do not significantly affect the security of the rest of the system. "Independent" also excludes multiprocessor systems or array processors, since these processors work cooperatively, under the control of one operating system.

Notice that *distance* does not enter into the definition of a computing network. It is true that the individual computing systems of a network are usually separated by some distance, and that in many computing networks distance is measured in miles or even thousands of miles. However, a network can consist of two systems standing side by

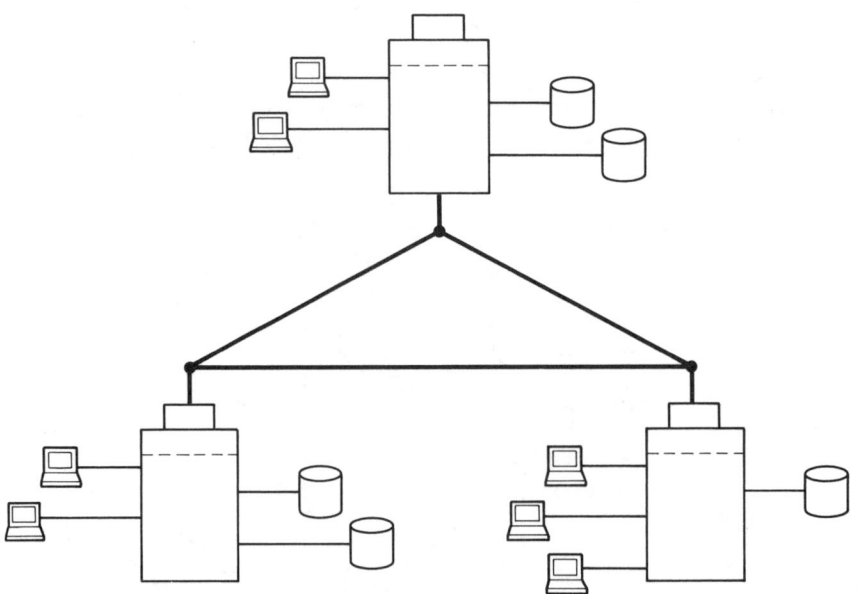

Figure 10.2 Computer Network.

side or in adjacent rooms. In any case, the security considerations of a computing network are generally unrelated to the distance between the component computing systems. Also, there is no minimum distance required for a computing environment to be called a network. Finally, distance is most important in determining whether or not certain communications media are appropriate for connecting the systems of a network. That consideration is one of implementation, not policy, and it will be addressed in the next chapter.

ISO Reference Model

The International Standards Organization (ISO) has developed a model of network communication using computers. This model is called the **Open Systems Interconnection** or OSI model. The model consists of seven layers ranging from a user or an application program (layer 7) through the physical medium (layer 1) by which a network communication occurs. The different layers are shown in Figure 10.3. The model describes a **peer-to-peer correspondence**, a relationship between corresponding layers of the sender and receiver sides. The communication is achieved through protocols of communication between those peers.

The layers represent different activities performed in the actual transmission of a message. Each layer serves a separate function; equivalent layers perform similar functions for the sender and receiver. For example, layer four of the sender affixes a header to a message, showing the sender, the receiver, and sequence information. On

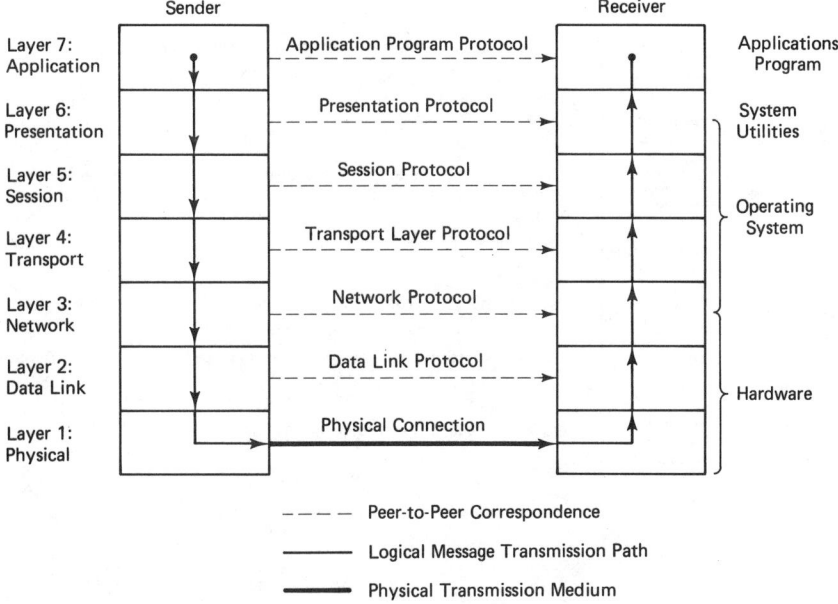

Figure 10.3   ISO OSI Network Model.

the receiving end, layer four verifies that it is the intended recipient and removes this header. Figure 10.4 shows the seven layers and the responsibility of each in message transmission and receipt.

Figure 10.5 shows a typical message that has been acted upon by the seven layers to prepare it for transmission. Layer 6 breaks the original message data into blocks. At the session layer (5), a session header is added to show the sender, the receiver, and some sequencing information. Layer 4 adds information concerning the logical connection between the sender and receiver. At the network layer (3) routing information is added; it also divides the message into units called "packets," which are the standard units of communication in a network. The data link layer (2) adds both a header and a trailer to ensure correct sequencing of the message blocks, and to detect and correct transmission errors. The individual bits of the message and the control information are transmitted on the physical medium by level 1. All of the additions to the message are checked and removed by the corresponding layer on the receiving side.

The OSI model really represents information interchange between pairs of corresponding levels. For example, if two programs at the applications layer exchange data, these programs are oblivious to the existence of lower layers in the model. At the same time, node routing information is added by layer three to the message to be communicated; level three of the receiver verifies that it is the correct node to have received the information and removes this routing information. Node routing does not depend on the data being exchanged by the application.

Layer 7 Application	User Program: Initiates message; optional encryption
Layer 6 Presentation	System Utilities: Blocking virtual terminal emulation, text compression; optional encryption
Layer 5 Session	Operating System: Establishes user-to-user session, message sequencing, recovery
Layer 4 Transport	Network Manager: Flow control, priority service
Layer 3 Network	Network Manager: Routing, message blocking into packets (e.g., 512 bytes)
Layer 2 Data Link	Hardware: Transmission error recovery, message separation into frames (e.g., bytes); optional encryption
Layer 1 Physical	Hardware: Physical signal transmission, by individual bits

Figure 10.4   Actions at Network Layers.

The OSI model is one of several models. Different network designers implement network activities in slightly different combinations, although there is always a clear delineation of responsibility. The OSI model is widely accepted, and so we use it here as a basis for our discussion. As we study security in networks, we consider at what points in the OSI model different security mechanisms are introduced.

Network Topology

A single computing system in a network is often called a **node**, and its processor (computer) is called a **host**. A connection between two hosts is known as a **link**, and the pattern of links in a network is called the **topology** of the network. Of course, network topology can affect security. Three typical topologies are shown in Figure 10.6. In one topology, the **bus** network, all nodes of the network are connected to a single connector (similar to the bus of a computer). The network hosts place messages on the bus. The addressees monitor the bus, taking off messages addressed to them.

An alternate arrangement is the **ring topology**. In this organization, each network host has two neighbors. Periodically one neighbor sends to another a collection of network messages. The neighbor takes any messages addressed to itself, and forwards the remainder of the messages along to the next neighbor.

The **star** topology uses a centralized host controller. All nodes wishing to communicate do so through the central host. The central host receives all messages, identifies the addressee, selects the link appropriate for that addressee, and forwards the message.

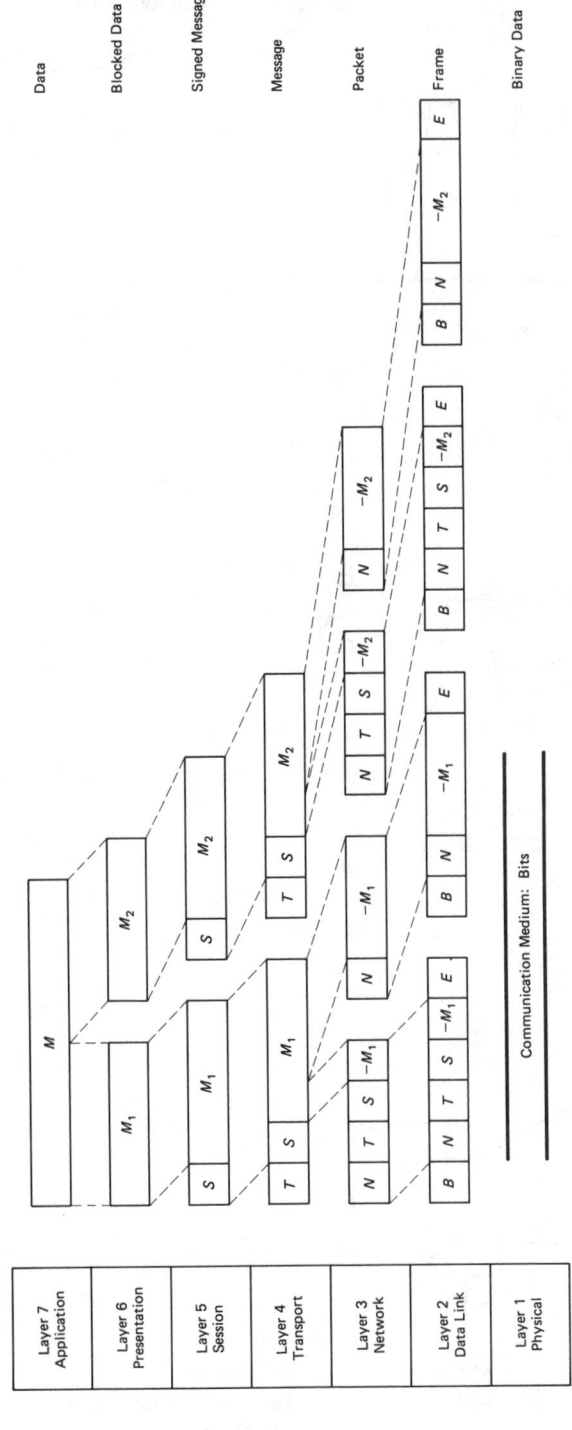

S: Session Header: Sequencing Information; Sender/Receiver Identification
T: Transport Header: Connection Information
N: Network Header: Routing Information
B: Data Link Header: Sequence Information
E: Data Link Trailer: Error Correction Information

Figure 10.5 Message Prepared for Transmission.

369

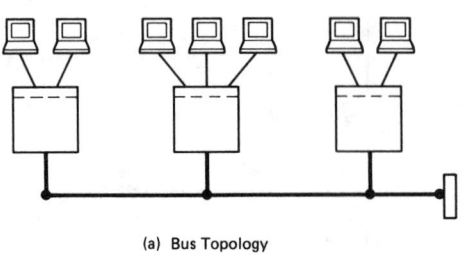

(a) Bus Topology

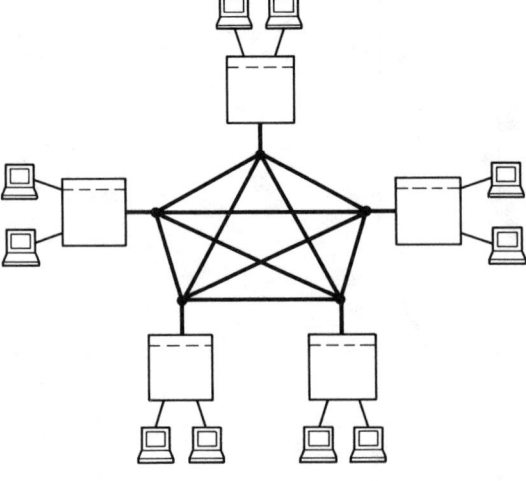

(b) Star Topology

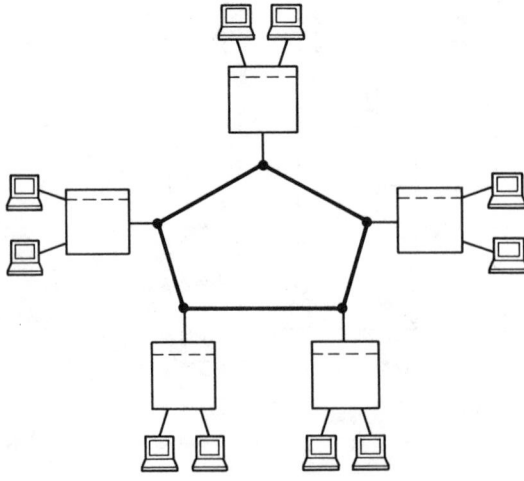

(c) Ring Topology

Figure 10.6 Examples of Three Network Topologies.

Networks are Systems, Too

The computing systems that we have considered up to now have been self-contained entities. A single set of security policies is associated with each computing system. Thus, each system is concerned with integrity of data, secrecy of data, and availability of service. A single operating system enforces its own security policies; hardware controls assist the operating system; and some users augment the controls from the operating system with security features in individual applications programs. Users trust the operating system to provide a certain level of protection.

Computing networks have similar characteristics. The network must ensure integrity of data, secrecy of data, and availability of service. Each user accesses the network through a single operating system, which also includes network interface responsibilities. Users still trust the individual operating systems to enforce the security policies of the network.

In a sense, then, a computer network is a large computing system containing other computing systems. From that perspective, a computing system resembles the block diagram of Figure 10.7 in which the processors of a computing network have been depicted as a single processor. Since size and distance are not important characteristics in defining computing systems or networks, this representation fits the definitions of both a computing system and a network.

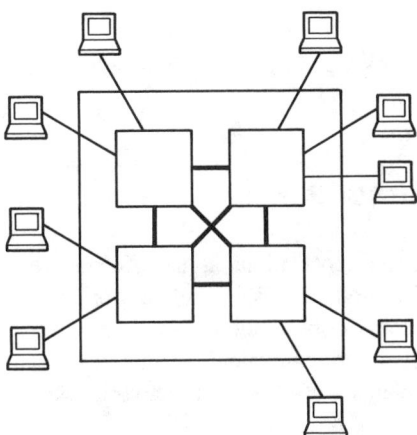

Figure 10.7 Distributed Computing System.

By treating a computing network as a system, we focus on users' accesses to the network, their processing within the system, and their output from the system. The internal processing consists of logical relationships among two systems of the network and the corresponding physical connections. However, we postpone study of the physical connections until the next chapter. In this chapter we consider user access, intersystem relationships, and output.

Advantages of Computing Networks

Computer networks offer several advantages over single-processor systems.

1. *Resource sharing.* Users of a network can access a variety of resources through the network. Usage may be too low to justify buying a specialized or expensive device for just one system. However, being able to share the device with many network users may justify its purchase. Furthermore, sharing common objects, such as data bases, reduces maintenance and storage costs while providing each user with improved access.

2. *Increased reliability.* Since a computing network consists of more than one computing system, the failure of one system or of just one component need not block users from continuing to compute. If similar systems exist, users can move their computing tasks to other systems when one system fails.

3. *Distributing the workload.* It is normal for the usage of a single system to vary as users join and leave a system. The degree of fluctuation of workload for a single system can be moderated in a network, so the workload can be shifted from a heavily loaded system to an underutilized one.

4. *Expandability.* Network systems can be expanded easily by adding new nodes. This expansion of the user base can occur without the manager of any single system having to take special action.

The advantages of using a network also bring security disadvantages, as described in the next section.

10.2 Network Security Issues

Users of networks have the same expectations as users of conventional computer systems. They expect delivery of accurate messages; delivery only to the intended recipient; protection from loss, modification, or observation of messages in transit; and reliable service. These are really just the network equivalents of integrity, secrecy, and availability. However, several security problems are inherent in network access and use.

Reasons for Network Security Problems

Networks have security problems for the following reasons.

1. *Sharing.* Because of the resource and workload sharing of networks, more users have the potential to access networked systems than single computers. Perhaps worse, access is afforded to *more systems,* so that access controls for single systems may be inadequate in networks.

2. *Complexity of system.* In Chapter 7 we observed that an operating system is a complicated piece of software. Rigorous security certification is difficult if not impossible on a large, existing operating system, especially a general-purpose one not designed specifically for security. A network combines two or more possibly dissimilar operating systems with mechanisms for interhost connection. Therefore, a network operating/control system is likely to be more complex than an operating system for a single computing system. This complexity deters certification of, or even confidence in the security of, a network.

3. *Unknown perimeter.* The expandability of a network also implies uncertainty about the network boundary. One host may be a node on two different networks, so that resources on one network are accessible to the users of the other network as well. Although wide accessibility is an advantage, this unknown or uncontrolled group of possibly malicious users is a security disadvantage. A similar problem occurs when new hosts can be added to the network. Every network node must be able to react to the possible presence of new, untrustable hosts. Figure 10.8 points out the problems in defining the boundaries of a network. Notice, for example, that a user on a host in network D may be unaware of the potential connections from users of networks A and B.

4. *Many points of attack.* A simple computing system is a self-contained unit. Access controls on one machine preserve the secrecy of data on that processor. However, when a file is stored in a network host remote from the user, the file may pass through many host machines to get to the user. While the administrator of one host may enforce rigorous security policies, that administrator may have no control over other hosts in the network. The user has to trust the access control mechanisms of all these systems.

5. *Unknown path.* As shown in Figure 10.9, there may be many paths from one host to another. Suppose that a user on host A1 wants to send a message to a user on host B3. That message might be routed through hosts A2 or B2 before arriving at host B3. Host A3 may provide acceptable security, but not A2 or B2. Network users seldom have control over the routing of their messages.

Security Exposures

The network security issues identified here give rise to several exposures specific to networks. These exposures are listed as follows:

1. *Privacy.* With many unknown users on a network, concealing sensitive data becomes more difficult.

2. *Data integrity.* Because more nodes and more users have potential access to a computing system, the risk of data corruption is higher. Types of corruption include modification of messages, insertion of bogus messages, deletion of messages, replay of messages, and reordering of messages. A "message" as used here may

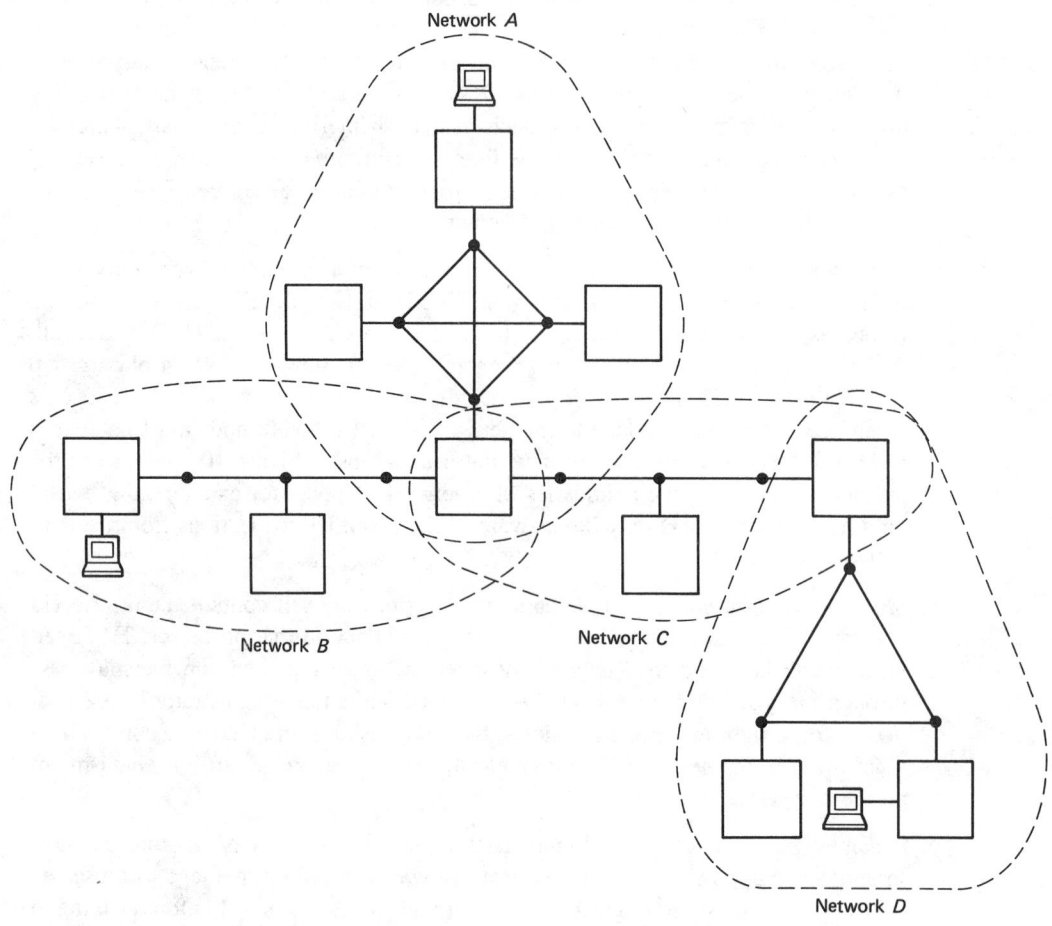

Figure 10.8   Unclear Network Boundaries.

be any communication on a network—a file, a command, a block of an encrypted transmission, and so forth.

3. *Authenticity*. It is difficult to assure the identity of a user on a remote system. One host may not trust the authentication a user performed by another host. In fact, the network may not even be able to trust the authenticity of hosts themselves.

4. *Covert channels*. Networks offer more possibilities for construction of covert channels for data flow, because there is so much data being transmitted in which to hide messages.

The following sections discuss controls for these exposures.

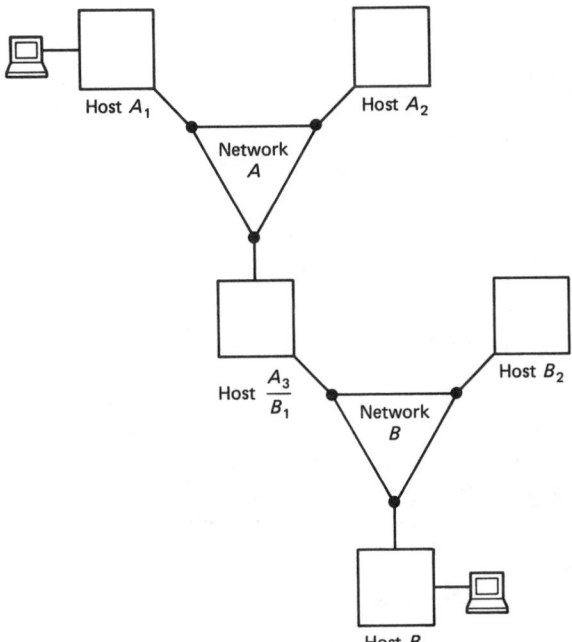

Figure 10.9   Message Routing in a Network.

10.3 Encryption in Networks

As shown before, encryption is a very powerful tool for providing privacy, authenticity, integrity, and limited access to data. Because of the greater risks involved, networks often secure data with encryption, perhaps in combination with other controls.

In network applications, encryption can be applied either between two hosts or between two applications, both of which we present in the following sections. Key distribution is always a problem with encryption. Encryption keys must be delivered to the sender and receiver in a secure manner. Techniques for safe key distribution in networks are also discussed. Finally, a secure cryptographic facility for a network computing environment will be described.

Link Encryption

In **link encryption** data is encrypted just before it is placed on the physical communications link. In this case, encryption occurs at layer 1 or 2 in the OSI model. Decryption occurs just as the communication enters the receiving computer. A model of link encryption is shown in Figure 10.10.

Encryption protects the message as it is in transit between two computers, but the message is in plaintext inside the hosts. (A message in plaintext is said to be "in the clear.") As shown in Figure 10.11, link encryption is especially vulnerable when a communication must pass through one or more additional hosts between sender and receiver.

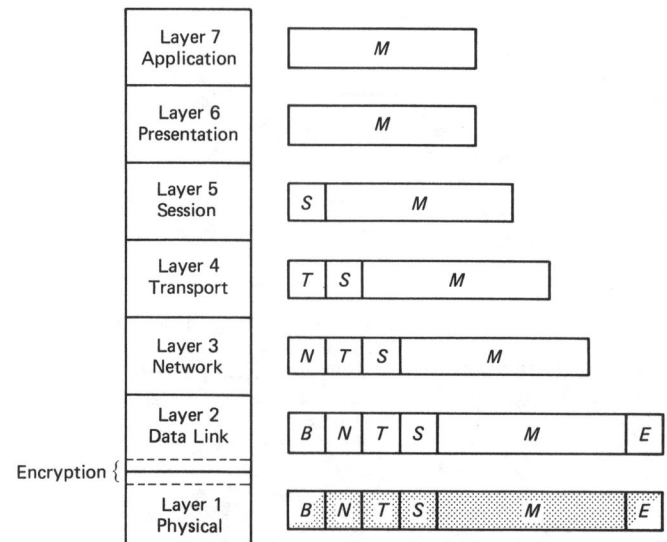

Figure 10.10   Link Encryption.

Suppose, for example, there is no direct link between hosts A and B of Figure 10.11, but there is a link between A and C, and one between C and B. A message may be adequately protected by hosts A and B, and encryption protects the message along the links. However, the message is in the clear in host C, and that host may not be especially trustworthy. If node C is compromised, all messages passing through C are exposed.

Link encryption is invisible to the user. Encryption becomes a transmission service performed by a low-level network protocol layer, just like message routing or transmission error detection. A typical link encrypted message is shown in Figure 10.12. There are devices that perform encryption quickly and reliably as a hardware function; in this case, link encryption is invisible to the operating system and the operator, too.

Link encryption is especially appropriate where the transmission line is the point of greatest vulnerability. If all hosts on a network are reasonably secure, but the communications medium is shared with other users or is not secure, link encryption is an easy control to use.

End-to-End Encryption

As its name implies, **end-to-end encryption** provides security from one end of a transmission through the other. The encryption can be applied by a hardware device between the user and the host. Alternately, the encryption can be done by software running on the host computer. In either case, the encryption is performed at the highest levels—either at layer 7 (application) or perhaps at layer 6 (presentation)—of the OSI model. A model of end-to-end encryption is shown in Figure 10.13.

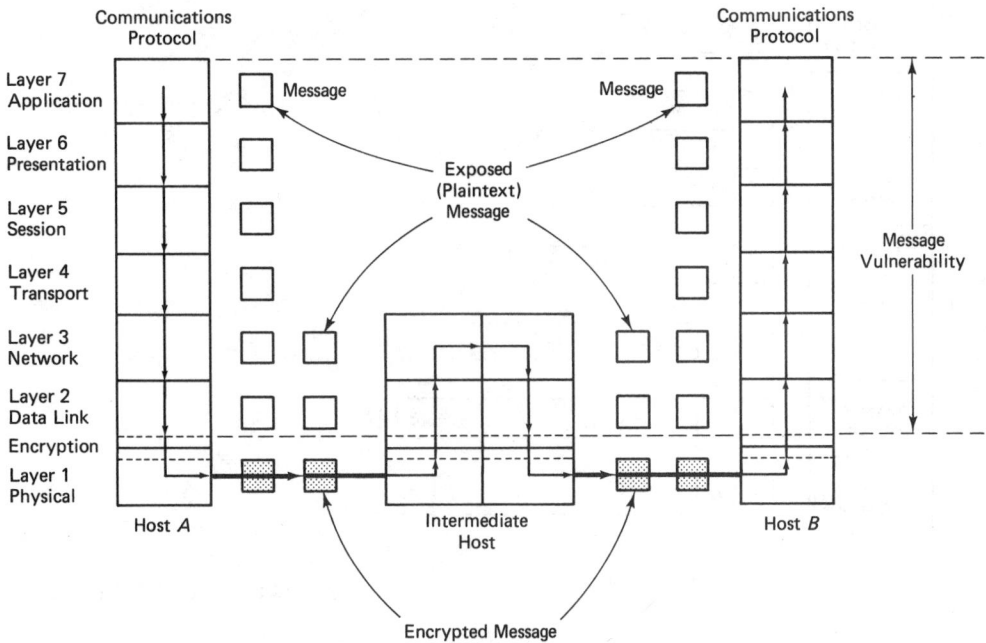

Figure 10.11   Link Encryption with Intermediate Hosts.

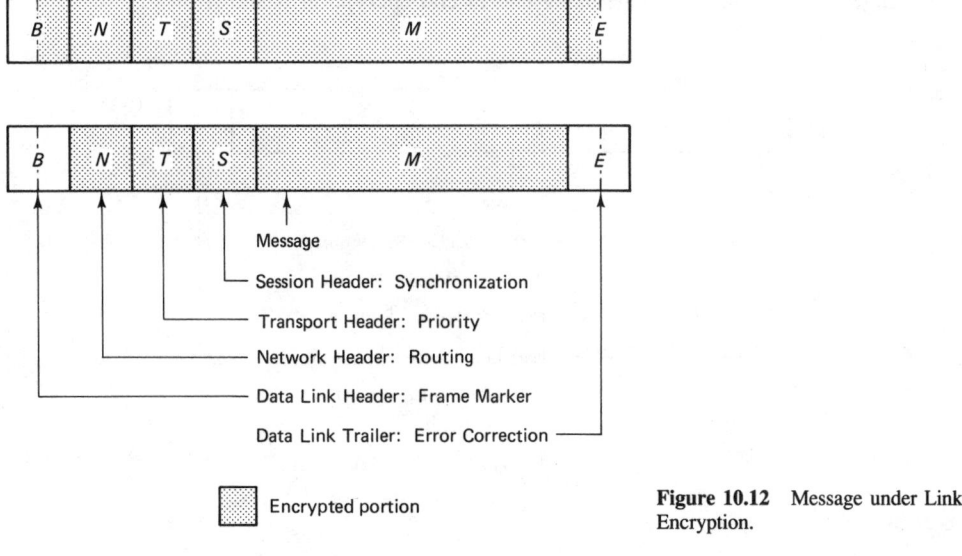

Message

Session Header: Synchronization

Transport Header: Priority

Network Header: Routing

Data Link Header: Frame Marker

Data Link Trailer: Error Correction

Encrypted portion

Figure 10.12   Message under Link Encryption.

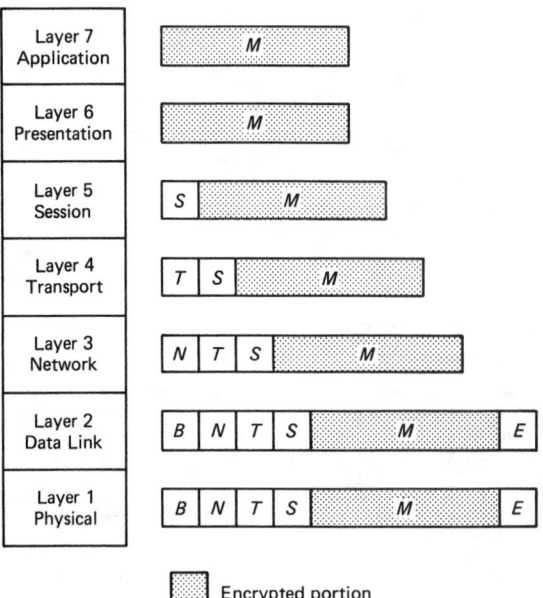

Encrypted portion

Figure 10.13 End-to-End Encryption.

Since the encryption precedes all routing and transmission processing of the layer, the message is transmitted in encrypted form throughout the network. The encryption covers potential flaws in lower layers in the transfer model. If a lower layer should fail to preserve security and reveal data it has received, the secrecy of that data is not endangered. A typical message using end to end encryption is shown in Figure 10.14.

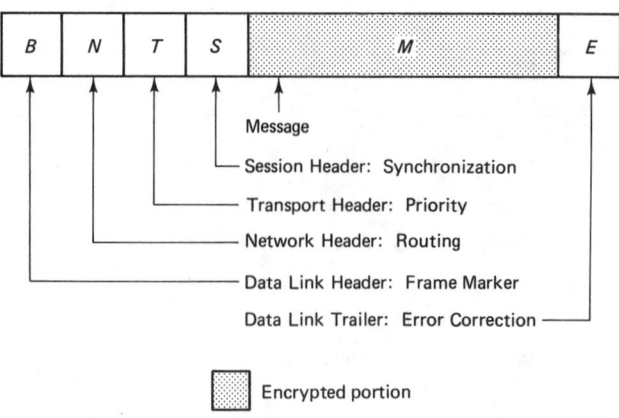

Encrypted portion

Figure 10.14   End-to-End Encrypted Message.

Messages sent through several hosts are protected. The data content of the message is still encrypted, as shown in Figure 10.15. Therefore, even though a message must pass through insecure node C on the path between A and B, the message is encrypted while in C.

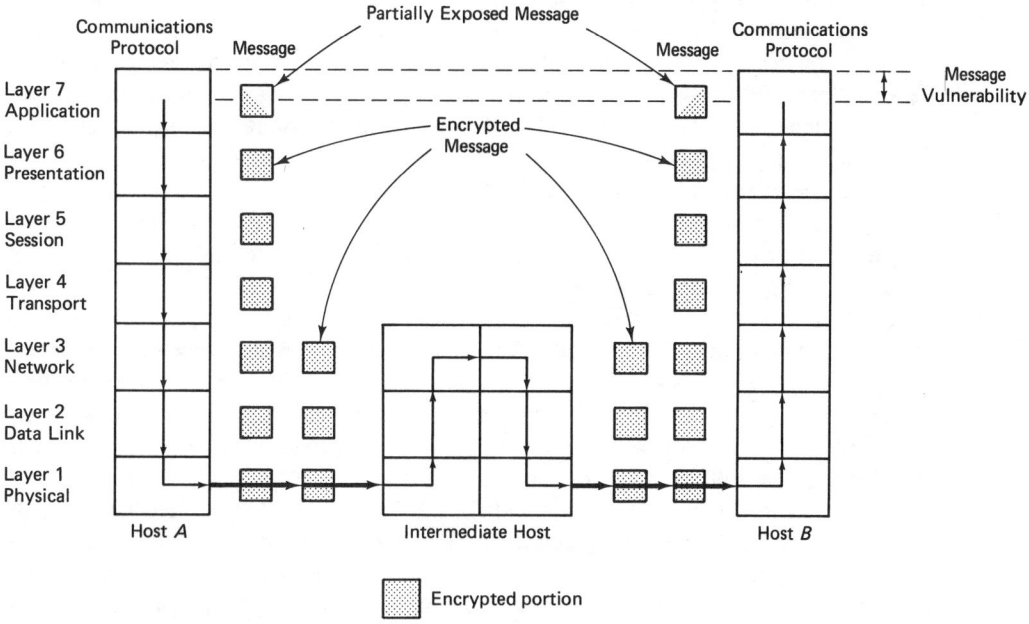

Figure 10.15   Encrypted Message Passing through a Host.

Comparison of Encryption Methods

Simply encrypting a message is not absolute assurance that the message will not be revealed during or after transmission. In many instances, however, the strength of encryption is adequate protection, considering the likelihood of the interceptor's breaking the encryption and the timeliness of the message.

With link encryption, the cryptographic facility is invoked for all transmissions along a particular link. Typically a host has only one link to a network, meaning that all network traffic will be encrypted by that host. This means, however, that every other host receiving these communications must also have a cryptographic facility in order to decrypt the messages. Furthermore, all hosts must share keys. Note that a message may pass through one or more intermediate hosts on the way to its final destination. Part of the advantage of encryption is lost if a message is encrypted along some links of a network but not along others. Therefore, link encryption is usually performed on all links of a network if it is performed at all.

By contrast, end-to-end encryption is applied to "logical links," which are channels between two processes. Since the intermediate hosts along a transmission path do not need to encrypt or decrypt a message, they have no need for cryptographic facilities. Thus, encryption is used only for those messages and applications where it is needed. Furthermore, the encryption can be done with software, so that it is easy to apply it selectively to one application or even to one message within a given application.

This selective advantage of end-to-end encryption is also a disadvantage with respect to encryption keys. Under end-to-end encryption there is a virtual cryptographic channel between each pair of users. In order to provide proper security, each pair of users should share a unique cryptographic key. The number of keys required is thus equal to the number of pairs of users, which is $n * (n - 1)/2$ for n users. This number increases rapidly as the number of users increases.

This count assumes that single key encryption is used. With a public key system, only one pair of keys is needed per recipient. Public key encryption, however, lacks the automatic authentication of single key systems. If A and B share a single encryption key, and the key has not been compromised, then any message B receives under that key must have come from A. With a public key system, A can provide secrecy for a message by encrypting it with B's public key. When B decrypts the message, however, B cannot be sure that it could have come only from A, since anyone in the network could have encrypted a message under B's public key. A and B must establish a signature protocol in order for them to have both privacy and authenticity.

By contrast, with link encryption, only one key per physical link is needed; typically very few hosts are directly connected to any single host, so the number of keys will be fairly small, as low as 1 for a remote node. The worst case occurs when each node has a link to every other node, and even then the number of keys is only $n * (n - 1)/2$ where n is the number of *nodes* not *users*.

Link encryption authenticates only the node, not the user. A communication received under the key of host A can be guaranteed to have come only from that host. The communication could have come from any user at host A, or it could even have been from a user at another host whose message was routed through A. Thus, link encryption does not provide user authentication.

Another advantage of end-to-end encryption is user trust. Link encryption is invisible to the user. With end-to-end encryption, the user can often see the result of the encryption applied to the data. Seeing the encrypted data instills confidence in the security of the application and reminds the user of the importance of maintaining security.

In summary, link encryption is faster, easier for the user, and uses fewer keys. End-to-end encryption is more flexible, can be used selectively, involves the user, and can be customized to the application. Neither form is uniformly "right." The characteristics of link and end-to-end encryption are summarized in Table 10.1.

Both forms of encryption can be applied within a single network. A user who doesn't trust the quality of link encryption provided in a system can apply end-to-end encryption as well. A system administrator who is concerned about the security of an end-to-end encryption scheme applied by an applications program can also install a link encryption device. If both encryptions are reasonably fast, this duplication of security will have little negative effect.

TABLE 10.1   LINK VERSUS END-TO-END ENCRYPTION.

Link Encryption	End-to-End Encryption
Security within Hosts	
message exposed in sending host	message encrypted in sending host
message exposed in intermediate nodes	message encrypted in intermediate nodes
Role of User	
applied by sending host	applied by sending process
invisible to user	user applies encryption
host maintains encryption	user must find algorithm
one facility for all users	user selects encryption
can be done in hardware	software implementation
all or no messages encrypted	user chooses to encrypt or not, for each message
Implementation Concerns	
requires one key per host pair	requires one key per user pair
provides node authentication	provides user authentication

Key Distribution

As just described, many keys are needed, especially for end-to-end encryption. Distributing keys in a secure manner can be difficult.

Keys can be distributed by using couriers. A human messenger is sent to each location with a new encryption key. As we have seen, changing keys periodically is prudent, since an intruder can collect a large body of ciphertext and begin to identify repeating characteristics of the encryption algorithm. However, frequent key distribution over long distance with couriers is not feasible. The problem, then, is to devise a secure method to distribute keys.

Secure Key Distribution Protocol

Ehrsam [EHR78] has proposed a key distribution method that uses one key to distribute other keys. Although the Ehrsam technique deals with distributing keys for the DES, the basic method works for any secret key cryptosystem. The method uses one key that is used only to distribute other keys.

The first key is called a **master key** and the others are called **session keys**. Since the master key is used only to encrypt session keys, an interceptor can obtain very little encrypted data (the keys). Therefore, the interceptor does not have the volume of ciphertext needed to perform statistical analysis in an effort to deduce the master encryption key. Consequently, the master key need not be changed very often.

To understand how the distribution protocol works, assume that A wants to establish a virtual communication channel with B; that is, A wants to exchange a certain amount of information with B. The amount of information might be as little as a single message, although it would more reasonably be a full file, the data resulting from a single execution of a process, or a single interactive computing session. Only A and B know the common master key, K_{AB} on which they have previously agreed.

User A picks a session key, K_S, through some process to determine encryption keys. This key is new, although it does not matter if an identical key happened to have been used for some previous communication, so long as there is no pattern to the reuse of keys. As shown in Figure 10.16, A sends to B $M_1 = E_{K_{AB}}(K_S)$, indicating that K_S

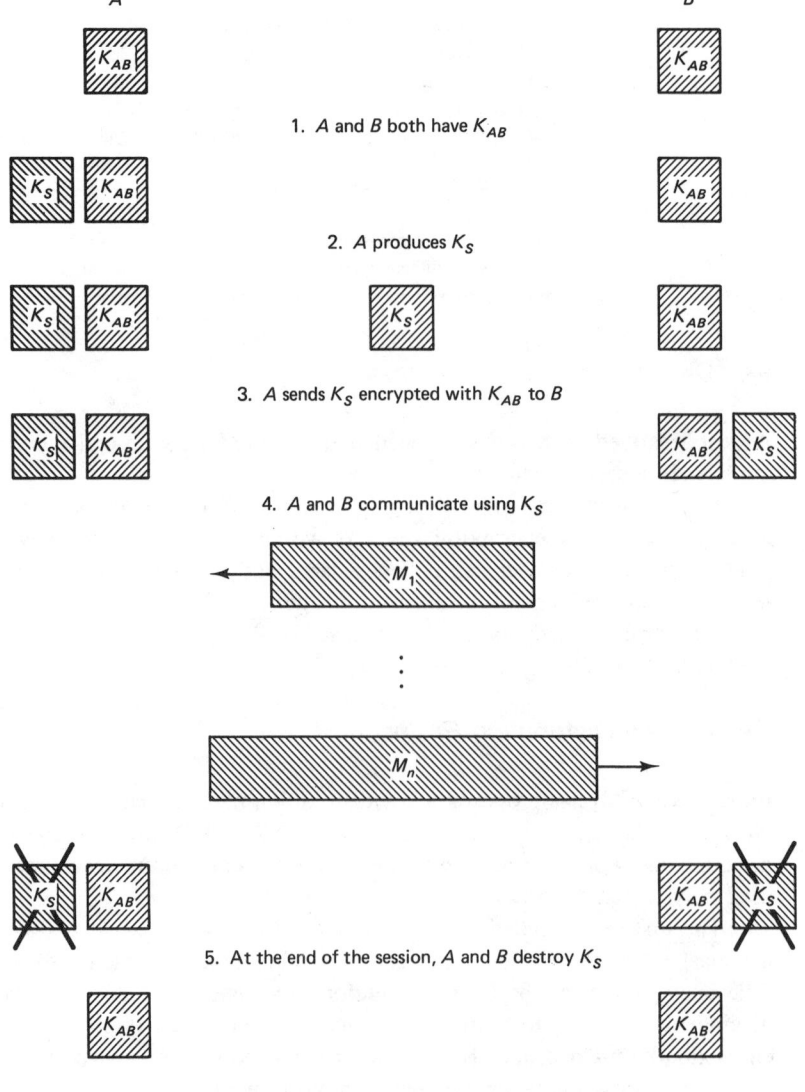

Figure 10.16   Two-Party Key Exchange.

is the session key both should use. Since B has K_{AB}, B can decrypt M_1, obtaining K_S, which is used for the session.

Since the keys are chosen at random, any good key will do, meaning that either A or B could select a key. The protocol is symmetric: Either A or B can initiate the session and choose the key. Finally, either party can discontinue using one key and announce a desire to change to a new key. The protocol assumes that the master key, K_{AB} is carefully concealed.

The assumption that A and B share a single key is very restrictive; in a system with many users, it is difficult to guarantee privacy of so many keys. Even without privacy concerns, it is difficult simply to keep track of many keys. Furthermore, as new users are added to the network, each existing user has to be given a different secure master key for the new user.

Key Server

A network **key server** is a process that distributes keys to users on request. The key server shares a unique key with each user. Let S_A be the key shared by A and the server, and let S_B be the key shared by B and the server.

Suppose again that A and B want to communicate. As shown in Figure 10.17, A calls the key server, saying that a session is desired between A and B. The key server generates a new key, K_S. It sends to A $M_A = E_{S_A}(K_S)$, and it sends to B $M_B = E_{S_B}(K_S)$. A and B decrypt M_A and M_B; both obtain K_S, and they transact their session using K_S. At the end of the session, both A and B destroy the key.

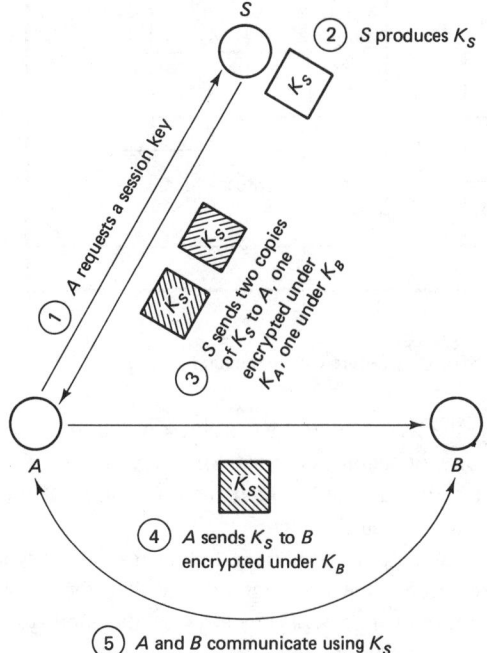

Figure 10.17 Session Keys with a Key Generator.

This facility can be used to provide end-to-end encryption without the massive number of keys normally needed. With a secure key generator, each user needs only one key by which to communicate with the key generator.

Secure Cryptographic Facility

An extension of the concept of a key server is a secure cryptographic facility, as described by Meyer and Matyas [MEY82]. The facility is a hardware device that performs secure encryption and decryption for users. (The fabrication of such a device is described by Weingart [WEI87].) A master key is permanently installed in the device. Operations the device can perform are encipher or decipher under the master key, accept a new working key, and encipher or decipher under the working key. A block diagram of such a facility is shown in Figure 10.18.

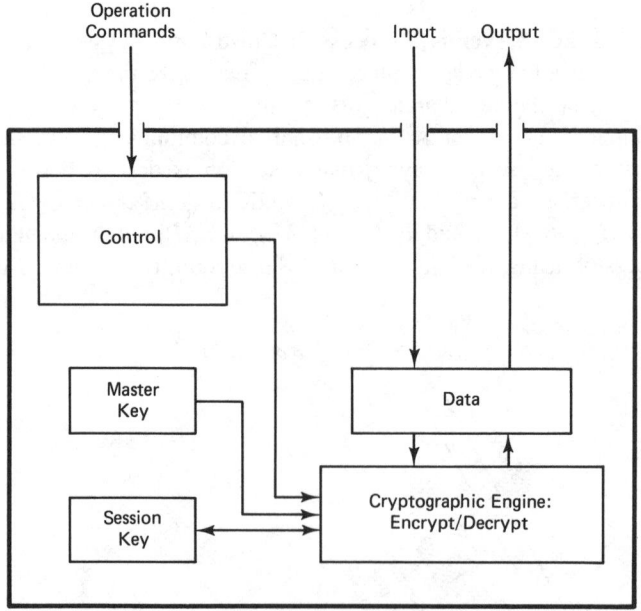

Figure 10.18   Secure Cryptographic Facility.

In order to use the facility, the user provides a session key that has been enciphered under the master key; this session key becomes the **working key**. In this way, the session key is not in plaintext; it is communicated only under the encryption of the master key. The session key is deciphered only inside the secure facility.

The user provides either plaintext or ciphertext to be en- or decrypted with the session key. As different users access the cryptographic utility, the operating system and/or the network controller must change working keys in the facility. The keys of waiting users can be encrypted for secure storage outside the facility.

This system provides a sharable, secure system for encryption and decryption. It handles secure storage and communication of session keys. As a separate device, it can be replaced if algorithms or master keys are to be changed. The security of this device is outside the user's control; therefore, the user does not have to be concerned with details of either physical security or implementation.

10.4 Access Control

Encryption is especially good for protecting data within a network. However, access to data, programs, and other resources of the network is also a serious concern in network security. In a single computing system, the number of authorized users may be limited because of the physical characteristics of the system. Often all users are within the same room or building, or they are affiliated with the same organization. However, when a computing system is part of a network, it is unclear what other users may be connected to the same network. Thus, in a network environment, access control must protect each single system of the network and also avoid allowing unauthorized users to pass through one system of a network to access other systems. Two aspects of network access control that we consider now are protecting access points and authenticating network nodes.

Port Protection

A serious vulnerability to a network system is dial-in port access. User authentication is difficult enough in a single computing system, but it becomes far more difficult when users can dial in from a telephone, literally anywhere in the world. (Telephones are now available even in airplanes.) Port protection is accomplished by several administrative and hardware techniques.

Automatic Call-Back

With an **automatic call-back** system, an authorized user dials a computer system. After the user identifies him- or herself, the computer breaks the communication line, effectively hanging up on the user. The computer then consults an internal table of telephone numbers and calls the user back at a predetermined number.

For example, if Cathy needed to access a computer from a terminal at her house, her home telephone number would be recorded on the list. An intruder accessing the computer and alleging to be Cathy would have to call in from Cathy's house in order to receive the return call.

This scheme works for people who expect to be at one number. If Cathy might be at, say, up to three different locations, she could list all three with the computer as legitimate locations. When she dials in, she identifies herself and gives the telephone number at which she expects to be called back. If the number she gives is one of the three registered for her, the computer calls her back there. If the number is not one of the three, the computer issues a warning to the security officer.

In a network this technique can also be used between two computers. The telephone number associated with a host computer seldom changes, so host computer A could have a table containing the phone number of host computer B. If host B wishes to establish a connection with A, it calls A at A's regular number. A determines that B wants to communicate, so A terminates the communication and calls B at B's regular number. B is reasonably well assured that A is calling if the call comes shortly after the first connection with A is terminated. A is sure to be communicating with B because it used the prescribed number for B. Clearly, the table of telephone numbers must be well protected against modification.

Differentiated Access Rights

Sensitive data can be protected by limiting the points from which access is allowed. People can be allowed to access the most sensitive data only from secure places; even though the individuals are trusted for more sensitive access, the access path is not trusted. For example, when dialing in, people might be allowed to obtain only less sensitive information. In this way, sensitive accesses must be made at the site, where it is more difficult to compromise data, or where it would be more noticeable if one were being forced to reveal the data. On a network, users with access to sensitive objects can do so only by direct connection, not through another network host. This restriction reduces the threat of malicious hosts in a network.

Differentiated access rights can be useful for people such as sales representatives who travel to many locations. These people can call their offices after making sales calls to send in sales data and to transfer nonsensitive electronic messages. Sensitive data, such as sales projections or pricing structures, could only be accessed at the office.

Silent Modem

The movie *War Games* publicized the penetration technique of systematic dialing of telephone numbers until a carrier tone (modem) is detected. The star of the movie had programmed a computer to dial numbers in series and create a file of those numbers that answered with a modem. If this trick was not widely known before the movie, it was after.

As explained in Chapter 6, a "loose lipped system" gives away information without obtaining assurance that its caller is legitimate. Typically, a computer receiving an incoming call establishes the connection by sending a modem signal. However, it can also wait silently until the *caller's* modem sends the first tone. In this way, the computer does not reveal that it is a computer until the caller has revealed that it is a computer.

This solution does not solve the problem of mutual suspicion, however; it merely forces the intruder to take a second step. A penetrator with a modem can send a modem tone to each telephone number dialed and wait for a modem tone in response. For this reason, authenticating nodes and remote users is very important for networked computing systems. We address these two topics in the next sections.

Node Authentication

A network node must be able to convince other nodes that is it authentic, that is, it is not the node of an impersonator masquerading as another node. Careful protocols, often involving encryption, are used to verify the identity of nodes. Even after authentication there is a possible exposure, for an intruder could wait until node B had been accepted by node A. After authentication, the intruder could tap the link between A and B and insert spurious messages, which A would presume came from B.

10.5 User Authentication

In this section we consider methods of user authentication. Chapter 6 presented the basic password protection mechanism. Passwords are very often used for authentication because they are easy to use and, used properly, they provide reasonable assurance. We also consider some other techniques that can increase security. Furthermore, some of these schemes are appropriate for authenticating computer-to-computer connections.

Authentication mechanisms are divided into three categories:

1. *What you know*, such as a password or an encryption key

2. *What you possess*, such as a token or a capability

3. *Something about you*, such as a picture or a fingerprint

We consider examples in each of these categories. For each example, we describe its specific use for a network.

Passwords

As presented in Chapter 6, passwords can offer reasonable security. A good password has the following characteristics. It is

1. *Composed of letters, digits, and other characters,* so that the base alphabet for an exhaustive attack is large

2. *Long,* so that there are many possibilities for an exhaustive attack

3. *Not a common word or name,* so that a dictionary attack will fail

4. *Unlikely,* not a characteristic related to the possessor, such as a spouse's name or a street address

5. *Frequently changed,* so that even in the event of someone's guessing it, the period of vulnerability is short

6. *Not written down,* so that it will not be found by outsiders

Some of these characteristics are appropriate for passwords used in network authentication and others are not. Here are some possibilities for passwords used on a network.

Group Password

With a group password, all users from a particular location or for a particular application use one password. For example, some systems provide a demonstration account for anyone to use to obtain an introduction to the use of the system. Obviously this practice is not very secure, since many people will not think the password is confidential. In another example, some network systems have one access password for all incoming network hosts. This choice relates to the problem of the number of encryption keys: Nodes connected to many other nodes have a substantial problem managing and securing lengthy password lists.

Unique Password

In a unique password situation, each password is distinct from that of *every* other user—no two system users have the same password. Therefore, one password establishes the user's identity and authenticates the user as well. Unique passwords are used primarily in very low-security situations, in which only casual intruders need to be excluded. For example, a physically secure word processing system may identify users by their three initials; the initials serve as both identifier and password. Any user could guess the identification of any other user, although the threat of a malicious user is judged to be minimal. It is presumed that physical security will exclude outsiders, or that any outsider will have only a very brief chance to try to access the system. Clearly, unique passwords are inadequate to control general access of people to systems.

Typically users need to be prompted for interaction with a system; a typical dialog with a user is "Enter name:, Enter password:." Whereas users need to be prompted for responses, two systems can communicate by well-understood protocol without prompting. Therefore, it is not uncommon for network hosts to establish both their identity and their authenticity with a single message (which is effectively a password).

The vulnerability of this approach occurs if system B contacts system A and passes a unique password, analogous to "I am B, password QWERTY246." Host B has just revealed all of its secret data, but B has no assurance that A is genuine. We will see a way around this problem in the exchange of secrets protocol below.

Not Necessarily Unique Password

Commonly, each user chooses a password, but it is not required to be unique. Thus two users may choose the same password, and neither knows that someone else has the same password. Such a password can only be used for authentication, not for identification.

Challenge-Response Systems

Passwords can be intercepted at the point of entry. Suppose while you type your password someone looks over your shoulder. Generally passwords are not displayed as they are entered, so an interceptor has to look at your fingers, not at the screen. Still, the interceptor may be able to pick up which letters you type, or at least the general pattern of movement of your fingers across the keys. Even such information as the pattern Right-

Left-Left-Shift-Right-Left-Number substantially narrows the field of possible passwords to try.

Passwords are in the clear from the moment they are entered until the moment they are accepted by the host computer. Therefore, someone who has tapped a communication line can intercept a user's password. Similarly, a user's password is vulnerable to a fake login attack perpetrated by a program that impersonates the operating system. The program paints a screen exactly like the login prompt and captures a user's name and password.

All of these problems occur because a password is static. Frequent change of passwords is desirable. To foil these kinds of attacks, the password has to be changed almost immediately after it is used. Few human users can handle passwords changed *very* frequently. However, two machines can have the effect of one-time passwords with a technique called a challenge-response system.

Challenge-response systems are essentially cryptosystems in which the host sends a message m and the user replies with $E(m)$. Both the message m and its encryption $E(m)$ may be obtained (by observation or by line tapping), but this loss will not reveal the encryption algorithm. Challenge-response systems were described in Chapter 6.

As with regular cryptosystems, challenge-response systems are subject to two weaknesses. First, someone who intercepts one plaintext message and its corresponding ciphertext may not be able to infer the encryption. Even with several messages in plaintext and ciphertext, the encryption may still be secure. However, the more plaintext or ciphertext becomes available about the encryption system, the more likely an interceptor is to be able to break the system. Therefore, a rather robust encryption system should be used. A robust system implies a complicated function which may be difficult for a user to compute by hand or to remember. But writing down or mumbling a key part of the formula defeats the security of such a system. Therefore, a solid challenge-response is most appropriate where each party has extensive computational power, such as computer-to-computer communication.

The second problem with encryption systems is the possibility of *replay* of an old message. One possible application of a challenge-response system is to assure a user of the authenticity of a host system. A fake login program could masquerade as a system in order to capture a user's password. To cover this vulnerability, a user might expect a system to send some secret as the login command. That is, both the challenge and the response would be secret.

As a simple example, suppose a user and a system share some private encryption system. The system sends a message like $M1 =$ "I am really host A. Send your password," except the message, $M1$, is in encrypted form. The user decrypts the message, concludes that the communication is really with host A, and enters the password.

This approach is insecure, because someone can intercept $M1$ and reuse it later. The interceptor might be able to retrieve one user's password at the same time message $M1$ is intercepted. Assume that the authentication encryption is the same for all users, that is, that each user receives the same message $M1$ as a proof that host A is authentic. The interceptor can then interject $M1$ into the line of any other user seeking to access host A. In this way, the interceptor can obtain the passwords of all users seeking access to this one system.

A more secure alternative is to use a message that cannot be reused. For example, the system might transmit the encryption of $M2$ = "It is Tuesday, April 10 at 8:47.05 am. I am really host A. Send your password." Because $M2$ depends on the current date and time, the message will be different for each use. A receiver can easily check that the date and time are current, and will refuse to respond if this message is a replay of a previous message. This same principle was used with block chaining and an initial chaining vector to prevent replays with regular encrypted text.

Exchange of Secrets Protocol

In the technique just developed, the host provides some secret but self-destructing piece of information. This leads to a protocol for exchange of secret information between two mutually suspicious parties. For example, two computing systems may wish to establish a communications link, but neither trusts that the other is genuine. In other words, both hosts know that an intruder could be at the opposite end of the communication line. Neither host wants to reveal private information until convinced of the authenticity of the other host.

If the two systems share an encryption key, the protocol is fairly simple:

> A sends $E(M2)$ to B.
> B sends $E(M2 + \text{password})$ to A.

Since E is known only to A and B, and $M2$ contains a time stamp, $E(M2)$ cannot be reused later. Therefore, $E(M2)$ assures B that the message came from A. But B has to prove that its response is also "live" (not a replay), so B can repeat $M2$ in its response. Also, B has to show something that only B would know, such as a password. In the form above, $E(M2 + \text{password})$ means some combination that depends on both message $M2$ and the password, such as a block-chained encryption.

If two systems do *not* share a common encryption key, the problem is more difficult. Demillo *et al.* [DEM83] present a protocol that uses a central authority, C, with whom A and B each share an encryption key. Following is a variation of that protocol. (A and B do not have to share the same key with C.)

> A sends $E_A(B, M2)$ to C.
> C generates a new session key K.
> C sends $E_A(M2, B, K, E_B(K, M2, A))$ back to A.
> A decrypts this to obtain $M2$, K, and $E_B(K, M2, A)$.
> A sends $E_B(K, M2, A)$ to B.

Only C and A know E_A, so C knows the first message comes from A as long as $M2$ has the current time. C has the private keys of both A and B, but C cannot give B's key to A without breaking that secrecy. Thus C gives A a message that A cannot understand, but which B will know immediately came from C; this message is $E_B(K, A)$. For secrecy, C encrypts the message under A's key.

After removing the decryption of E_A, A is convinced the message must be authentic from C. It contains $M2$, so the message is not a replay. A sends the message

$E_B(K, M2, A)$ to B. Even though A cannot read this message, A knows it will convince B that K is an acceptable session key.

B decrypts this message, and doing so informs B that the message is authentic from C. Since the message contains a current timestamp $(M2)$, the message is not a replay. Finally, the message contains A's name, so B is assured that this communication line is established with A. A and B then communicate for this session using K. The use of $M2$ to guarantee timeliness serves the same purpose as a one-time password.

Passphrases

Schemes such as those just described are fine for computers, which have essentially unlimited computing power at their disposal to perform encryption and other similar algorithms. Humans, however, need simpler authentication schemes that are still secure.

One form of authentication is a **passphrase**, which is just a longer version of a password. Passphrases are equivalent to passwords in their ability to authenticate. The argument about password length indicated that there are relatively few long passwords that people can remember easily. Examples of passphrases are a line from a song or a list of names of countries. The disadvantage of a long password is that it takes more computer memory to store.

Passphrases can be condensed, using a function whose result depends on every character of the passphrase. The computer condenses the entered passphrase for efficient storage. For example, a passphrase such as "roses are red; violets are blue" (including punctuation and spaces) could be encrypted with a block chained cipher, and only the last block would be stored. Any change to the phrase (such as "Roses are red..." with capital R) would disturb the bit pattern and would affect the encrypted result. With a cipher like DES, the result could be stored in 64 bits. Several different passphrases would encrypt the same as "roses are red...," but with a complex condensing function, there would be no obvious pattern to these other phrases.

Passphrases can also be used for a variable challenge-response system. Some banks use this technique to authenticate customers who want to make transactions by phone. A customer who opens an account with the bank reveals certain confidential information, such as name, employer, spouse's name, birth date, perhaps mother's maiden name, and so forth. The bank hopes that this information is not common knowledge (although clearly some of it could be pretty well known). When someone tries to make a telephone transaction, the bank asks for a piece of this secret information. The bank does not ask for the same piece of information each time. Therefore, an impersonator might not know all of the information to collect in advance. Also, a caller overhearing one end of the conversation would not know if the answer "Alma" was the name of a spouse, a mother's maiden name, or the name of a college.

Token or Smart Card

So far, all the examples have been of things people know. For human use, challenge-response systems have been rather limited, since the functions that humans can compute may be easy to cryptanalyze. Therefore, we would like a more complex challenge-response function that is still appropriate for human use.

A **token** is the general name for an object that authenticates its possessor. For example, royalty used to be authenticated by a signet ring, and in many applications people are authenticated by ID cards. In order to be useful, a token must be *unforgeable* and *unique*. In practice, ID cards can be forged, but they are still used for authentication.

The "magnetic stripe credit card" is one form of token for network communication. These cards are regular credit cards with certain information recorded in magnetic form on the back. The magnetic stripe is read by a sensing machine, often a machine that permits a customer to perform certain banking transactions at any time, day or night. These cards are not used as complete proof, since such a card might be lost or stolen. A user of the card also has to enter an identifying word or number in order to use the card.

A more complicated form of this card is called a **smart card** or **chip card**—which is similar, except it has a microprocessor embedded. Not only can the smart card retain information to identify the possessor, it can also hold information such as a bank or credit balance. Such a card is not merely a passive container of data. A smart card can actually perform computation, such as computing the response function of a challenge-response system, or performing link level encryption. Such a scenario might work like this.

Dave walks up to a terminal to initiate a login to a computing network. Dave enters his name on the terminal and receives the prompt for a password. Dave puts the smart card in a slot and types his password. Instead of the password being transmitted in the clear, the password is encrypted by the smart card. The remainder of the terminal session is encrypted by the smart card when it is transmitted and decrypted at the receiving end. In this way, Dave can carry on a secure session with a computing network from any place in the world.

Personal Characteristics

Some work is now being done on scanners that will recognize physical characteristics of people, such as fingerprints, pronunciation, and patterns of the retina of the eyes. These devices provide highly reliable assurance of authenticity. Furthermore, fingerprints or pronunciation cannot be lost or stolen; they are not inconvenient to carry around, they do not have to be kept secret, and they are virtually impossible to forge. Scanners to detect these types of patterns will be described in Chapter 12.

Summary of Authentication

Authentication depends on two factors: some piece of secret, unforgeable data, and a protocol for reliable transmission of that data. The conventional data has been the password, although some password systems provide very little security. However, a password system coupled with some form of encryption can enhance security dramatically.

The protocol for secure exchange of secrets is especially important in network situations. In a network, two hosts are mutually suspicious and need a means to assure authenticity of both. Cryptographic or one-way functions are important ways to generate authenticating data in networks.

10.6 Active Node Threats

An active intruder is another vulnerability in a network. With human-to-computer communication, the human is somewhat limited in speed and capacity. However, humans can program computers to impersonate network hosts. The use of computers to impersonate hosts has increased with the rise in use of personal computers. In this case, the host becomes an active participant in the network, not just an interceptor who reads data from a wiretap. In this section, we consider how networks are vulnerable to active attack from unauthorized hosts.

Playback of Previous Messages

We have already seen the problems associated with an active host that plays back a previous message. Encryption and time stamping can limit the likelihood of occurrence of this threat.

Disruption of Service

An active host can also tamper with the flow of messages on the network. For example, a host can flood a network with spurious messages, thereby blocking legitimate network traffic. Similarly, in some network topologies, a malicious host can alter routing information on messages, so that they are never received at the correct destination node. A host can disrupt service without even being able to determine the content of legitimate messages on the network. Both of these attacks deny service to users of the network.

An active attacker can disrupt service by intercepting and destroying messages destined for a particular user. Suppose a malicious host M wants to prevent messages from reaching host A. Host M may want to block some or all messages. (Blocking some messages at least reduces A's efficiency, as A determines certain messages have been lost and must ask for them to be retransmitted. Blocking some messages can seriously affect A's users if A does not use a communications protocol that lets A detect when a message is lost.)

One way to block messages for A is to remove them from the network. Periodically network communication links fail for hardware or software causes, so it is not unreasonable that a network host has become unreachable. If A and another host, B, recognize that they have not communicated recently, they may exchange a simple message just to be sure that the communication link is still operating correctly. If M intercepts all messages for A, other nodes in the network would receive no response from A and would conclude that the link to A had failed. With no acknowledgments to its messages, A also would assume that its link was defective. In this way, M could convince the entire network that A was unreachable, and all users on node A would be denied access to network service.

Alternatively, M can reroute messages destined for A. In a simple case, M can take all messages addressed to A, change the address A to another host, such as C, and put the messages back on the network. Host C will probably detect a message out of sequence and delete most of the spurious messages. If A realizes that a particular message has not been received, A can request a replacement, which also may or may not arrive. These requests and retransmittals increase the traffic on the network. These two attacks are shown in Figure 10.19.

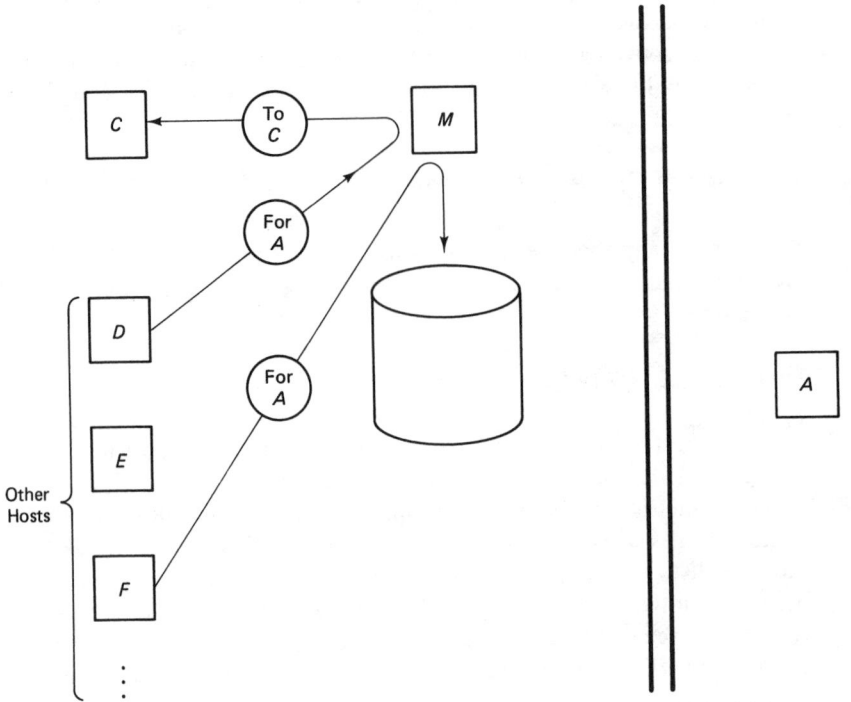

Figure 10.19   Malicious Disruption of Service.

Few controls can prevent these malicious network activities. The primary defense is preventing an untrustworthy node from being connected to the network in the first place. The attack just described can be practiced if A is connected by only one path and if the malicious intruder breaks into the link to A. Therefore, network topology including redundant communication links is a form of control.

Introduction of Spurious Messages

An intruder can damage network communications by generating spurious messages. These phony messages may appear authentic, or they may not even be similar to legitimate messages. Their essential purpose is to increase the traffic on the network, thereby degrading service to the users. Again, the primary control is to prevent unauthorized nodes from establishing a network connection.

10.7 Traffic Control

Because an interceptor can tap all blocks of messages passing through the network, the interceptor can determine who is communicating frequently with whom. Knowing that many messages are being transmitted between the personnel department and company management, a user might be able to infer that some substantial reorganization is about to occur. The military during wartime has trouble planning surprise offensives because a large volume of messages to a particular place may arouse the enemy's suspicion.

In both cases, the attack is called a **traffic analysis**. The standard control is introduction of many spurious messages between points of low traffic. In this way, communication between two sensitive points will not seem outstandingly heavy. Of course, this added traffic places an extra burden on the network, and service to all users may be degraded.

It is possible to establish a covert channel in a network by generating traffic, even spurious traffic as just described. The technique is to represent a binary 1 by a message to a single node, and a 0 by either no message or a message to another node. A listening interceptor observes the network traffic going to these one or two nodes and records the illicit data. The network tap does not require active participation from the listener. Furthermore, the traffic can appear innocuous if the spurious traffic is to a reasonable host, such as a file system. It is very difficult to detect, much less to prevent a process from creating such a covert channel.

Such traffic can permit a surprisingly high rate of data leakage. If confinement is a goal in a network, this covert channel must be denied. There are two possible ways to prevent users from employing the covert channel.

Pad Traffic

To deter a listener who is monitoring messages only from a particular host, the network administrator generates spurious messages for all possible pairs of hosts. A network administrator inserts random "noise" into the system by randomly sending messages to each node in the network. These messages must follow no pattern of frequency, source, or destination.

In this control, the administrator tries to add sufficient noise to the system so that the noise distorts the flow of information in the covert channel. The intended host must be able to recognize the messages as false messages so that they will not interfere with communication of a legitimate user. However, if an intended host can recognize these as false messages, the covert listener can, too. The administrator does not need to participate in the network traffic, other than to generate noise messages periodically.

Routing Control

As an alternative, the administrator can exercise active control of routing in the network. For example, if the covert channel were 1 for a message from A to B, and 0 for a message from A to C, the administrator might try to redirect messages. One possibility is to reroute messages from A to C to go from A *through* B and ultimately to C. In this way, an A–C message (0) would be converted to an A–B message (1) followed by a B–C message (no value).

An administrator can also periodically misroute messages, changing an A–B message into an A–C message, for example. If the message header contains information on its intended destination, C would detect that it had mistakenly received a message and would forward it to B.

If the network has a protocol to detect missing messages, the administrator can periodically delete messages. In this way, B might realize much later that a message from A had not been received. If so, B would ask for the message to be retransmitted. Repeating the message would not affect normal communication. It would disturb the flow of the covert channel, since other messages might have been transmitted already, and this message representing one bit would be transmitted out of sequence.

A third possibility is for the administrator to periodically delay a message. By delaying, the administrator hopes to destroy the synchronization between the sender and the listener, while not seriously affecting legitimate network traffic. This control is effective if the channel depends on the timing of messages.

All of these controls depend on an active network administrator who can perform network actions to destroy covert channels.

10.8 Data Integrity

The integrity of the data in a network is also a vulnerability. Integrity is a function of two things: correct generation of the data and correct storage and transmission. If we assume that data is correctly generated, our security concern is ensuring that data is correctly stored, communicated, and modified in the network.

Protocols

Network communication operates through protocols designed for reliable communication. These protocols must be able to detect duplicate messages, deleted pieces, pieces out of order, or modified pieces. Most transmission protocols use a numbering scheme to preserve order of message pieces. However, for security purposes this is inadequate, since a malicious intruder can modify the order number to interchange message pieces. For efficient routing and handling by low-level protocol layers, the order number may be transmitted in plaintext, but for integrity a second tamperproof copy should also accompany the message part.

Checksums

The cryptographic checksum is an important network guard against message tampering, as well as failures during message transmission. Normal message traffic on a network is subject to noise and occasional mistransmission of bits or data. Some network transmission protocols have additional check data built into a message to detect and perhaps correct failures. If a correction is impossible, the receiver will ask for the message to be retransmitted.

Parity

Error checking in network messages uses complex error detection and correction codes, but use of these codes can be demonstrated by using the simple example of parity. As a byte is transmitted, an additional bit is appended; this bit is set to 1 if the sum of the bits in the byte is even, and to 0 if the sum of the bits in the byte is odd. Parity can detect all errors involving the change of a single bit out of the byte; parity can also detect some multiple bit errors. As shown in Figure 10.20, parity can identify the byte, but not necessarily the bit in error. Parity also cannot identify the substitution of one byte (with correct parity) for another in a message.

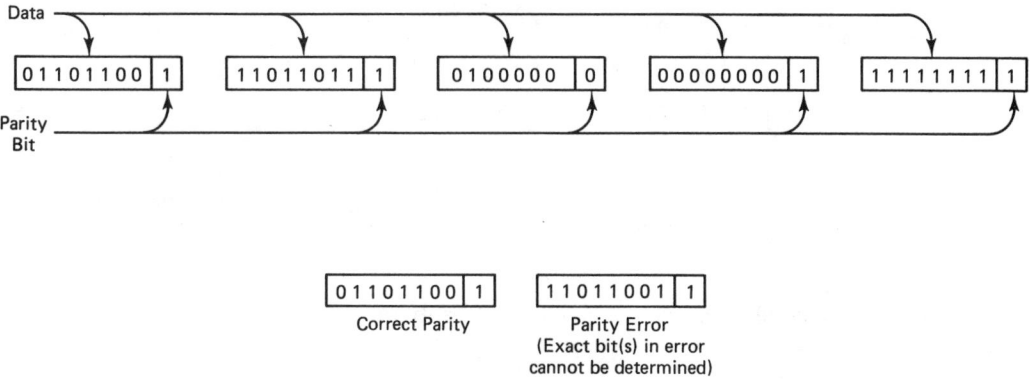

Figure 10.20   Use of Parity to Detect Errors.

Parity can also be used longitudinally; that is, parity can be computed for the 0th bit of all bytes, the 1st, the 2nd, and so on. This process yields eight more parity bits, one for each bit position in a message. With these longitudinal check bits, it is possible to determine the bit position, but not the exact byte of an error. An erroneous bit in a message will appear at the intersection of a byte parity error with a longitudinal parity error. Figure 10.21 shows how to locate an incorrect bit.

Byte parity and longitudinal parity together will detect changes to a message text. Network data error checking is added by a low layer in the transfer model; it is added to all messages, and its form is visible to anyone reading actual messages on the network. Because all messages are required to have error codes to ensure their integrity, the form, placement, and computation of error codes is a public matter known to all network hosts. A spurious host could modify network traffic so long as the check bits were modified accordingly. For example, to replace the first byte

01101100 1

with

10101100 1

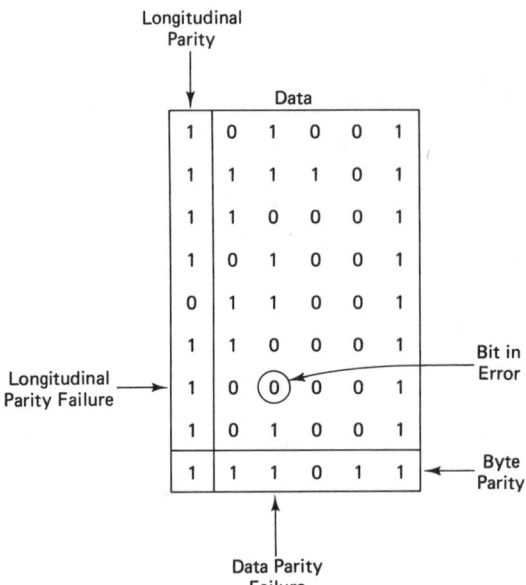

Figure 10.21 Use of Parity to Identify Exact Location of Error.

the host would also change the longitudinal parity to

$$00110111\ 1$$

A malicious host could replace a segment or an entire communication on a network.

More Sophisticated Error Codes

Parity is a rather simple code. It can be used to detect single-bit errors, but errors in pairs cancel each other. More sophisticated error codes permit detection of errors in two or more bits; some codes even allow correction. Standard network textbooks, such as Tanenbaum [TAN81], describe other error detection and correction codes used in networks.

Cryptographic Checksums

A more intricate function is needed to ensure the integrity of messages from modification by network hosts. At the application layer, a program may compute a **cryptographic checksum**. A cryptographic checksum is like any other error detection code, except that the formula used to compute it is not public and is not easily inferred from examples. A typical cryptographic checksum is the DES used in cipher block chaining mode. (Here, of course, the key is the secret part of the formula.) The final block encrypted is transmitted as the checksum. The recipient computes the same DES function and compares the result to the transmitted result. If the results are not the same, the recipient knows that the data received is not what was transmitted.

This cryptographic checksum scheme is flawed because two blocks can be interchanged without affecting the final result. The same thing would be true if a form of RSA encryption were used, since the RSA algorithm is commutative. A solution to this flaw is to combine a unique block number with each block as it is being encrypted. The combination might be done through block chaining or exclusive or ($\oplus$). This additional control would detect an exchange of blocks i and j, since $E(b_i \oplus j)$ is not the same as $E(b_i \oplus i)$ or $E(b_j \oplus j)$.

Digital Signatures

As we have already seen, a digital signature is a means to certify the authenticity of a set of data (which might represent a document, a message, a file, or something else). The person affixing the digital signature confirms that the data is authentic.

In a network, many unknown individuals have the ability to create transactions that can affect the integrity of data. For example, in an airline reservation system, numerous travel agents can generate commands that book seats on flights, thereby affecting the data base. Therefore, the data base application program needs to retain signed requests so that the source of any error can be determined and incorrect data can be corrected.

Notarization

Finally, a network authority can be called upon to attest to the authenticity of a message. The use of a cryptographic checksum requires that sender and receiver share a single encryption algorithm and key. A digital signature is most easily implemented where two users share either the public key of a two-key system or a single encryption key.

It is not reasonable to expect each pair of network users to share a key. Therefore, a protocol involving the services of a trusted notary is useful to ensure the integrity of messages in a network. The cryptographic checksum or digital signature just described can be implemented as an arbitrated protocol by using a notary to mediate the transmission between two network hosts.

10.9 Local Area Networks

The last two topics of this chapter concern security problems of two specific types of networks. In this section we consider the security problems of local area networks; the final section addresses security concerns in multilevel networks (networks performing computation for users having different security needs).

A local area network is scarcely differentiable from any other type of network. As the name implies, a **local area network** (or **LAN**) covers a small distance, typically within a single building. There is, however, no set maximum distance for a LAN. Usually a LAN connects several small computers, such as personal computers, as well as some printers and perhaps some dedicated file storage devices. Figure 10.22 shows the arrangement of a typical LAN. The primary advantage of a LAN is the opportunity for its users to share data and programs and to share access to devices such as printers.

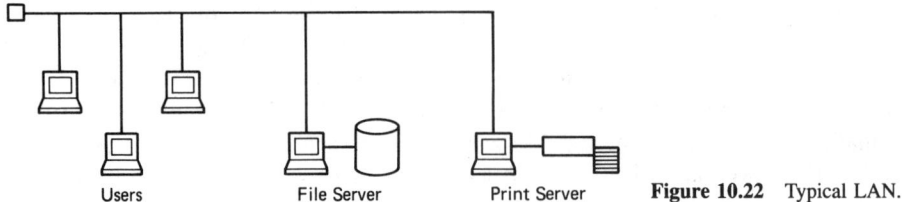

Users   File Server   Print Server   **Figure 10.22**   Typical LAN.

One security disadvantage is important in LANs. The users of LANs typically are professionals in fields other than computing, and they are apt not to be cognizant of security issues in computing. This disadvantage is somewhat moderated because LAN users tend to be business associates; the environment is thus one of trust. Therefore, the security needs of a local area network *may be* somewhat less than for other networks.

However, LANs often outgrow their initial designs, and so it is common to have one LAN connected to another, which may be connected to yet a third. For example, one LAN in the accounting department might be connected to another in the secretarial pool, so that financial planners can have their documents typed. Thus, the example of Figure 10.22 really looks more like Figure 10.23.

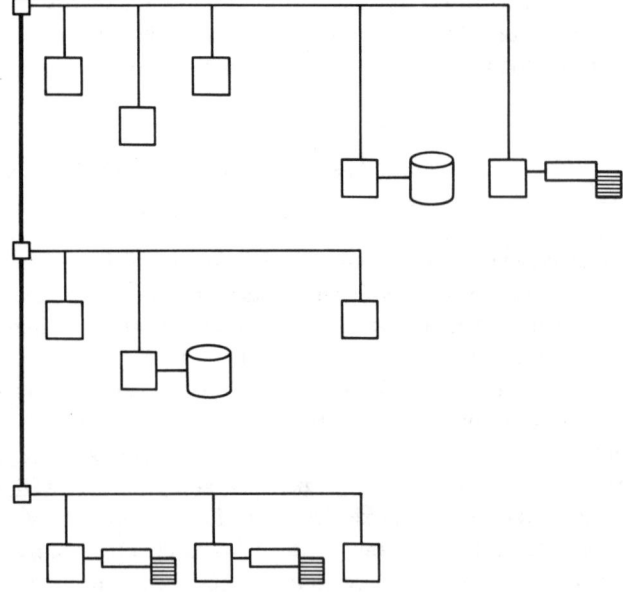

Figure 10.23   Typical LAN with Connections to Other LANs.

Topology

As described earlier in this chapter, the topology of a network can affect its security. We will study three topologies frequently employed in the design of local area networks. For reference, the earlier figure of network topologies is repeated as Figure 10.24.

Common Bus

Conceptually, a **common bus** is a wire to which each node of a LAN is connected. A network monitor provides timing signals on the bus to help the nodes communicate. This medium is especially convenient for LANs, since the configuration of offices changes frequently when new users are hired or old users change locations or duties. It is easy to add or delete nodes from the bus.

Each node is responsible for sending and retrieving all its communications. A host places a message on the bus at a time when no other process is using the bus. Hosts must also continually monitor the bus in order to retrieve communications destined for them. In that respect, every communication is accessible to every host, not just the designated addressee.

There is no central authority on a bus; each host acts cooperatively but autonomously. Therefore, no central node can control the routing of messages to processes. One node can insert sporadic noise into the network to limit the utility of covert channels, but no node can reroute transmissions through another node. Similarly, there is no central node to screen the authenticity of other nodes. If one node identifies itself as A, it is up to each individual node to verify the authenticity of that claim.

Star

In a **star** network, each node is connected to a central "traffic controller" node. All transmissions flow from the source node to the traffic controller and then from the traffic controller to the destination node. Such a central node is able to monitor and control traffic to defeat covert channels.

Each message is read only by the traffic controller (presumably for address only) and by the intended recipient. There is a unique path between any two nodes, and this path is inaccessible to any others. The exposure of a message to wrongful recipients is thus less than with the bus architecture.

Reliability is a problem with this topology, since there is only one path from a particular node to the central node. If that link fails, the peripheral node is unreachable. A node identifies itself to the central controller, which must have this information in order to route transmissions. The central controller can detect two nodes that identify themselves as the same node. Typically, however, the central controller does not perform any authentication of nodes. Each node is accepted to be whatever node it identifies itself to be.

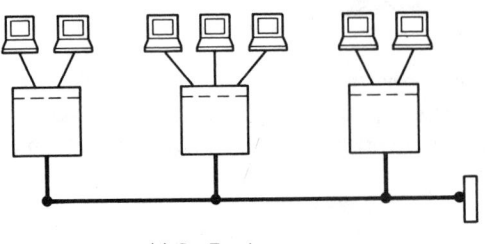

(a) Bus Topology

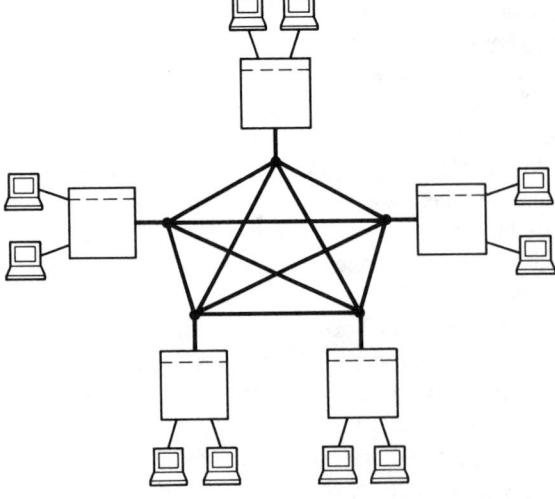

(b) Star Topology

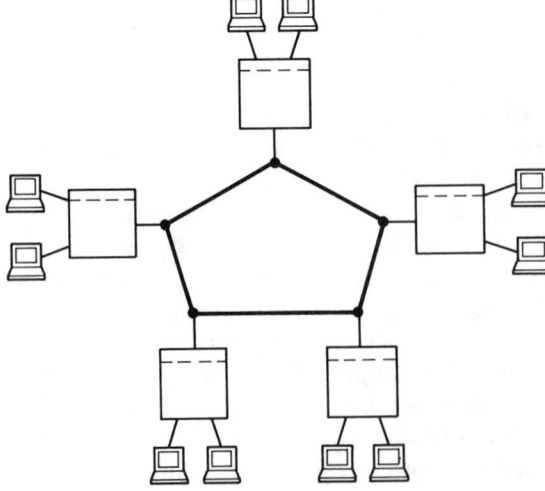

(c) Ring Topology

Figure 10.24 Network Topologies.

Ring

In a **ring topology**, each node receives many messages, scans each, removes ones designated for it, adds any more it wants to transmit, and sends the pack of messages to the next node. From a security standpoint, this means that each message is seen by other nodes, possibly by every other node. However, unlike the bus architecture where a node must capture a message as it goes past, in the ring architecture, one node can deny service to another by withholding or failing to forward messages.

No central authority can analyze traffic flow in order to detect covert channels. Likewise, no central authority verifies the authenticity of any node; a node can call itself anything it likes and take any messages that may or may not belong to it.

Other Security Concerns in Local Area Networks

Physical proximity is a convenient control in LANs. Often a LAN is installed within one building or within the boundaries of an office, department, or plant complex. Typically all users know all other users. This closeness provides a degree of physical security, although it is easy to overestimate the effectiveness of this control. If a LAN is connected to another remote LAN or to a wide area network, all such protection is gone.

Typically a LAN is established for a low security application, to enable users to share files, devices, data, and programs. The users are often trustworthy. However, the trust of the network users can be misleading. If a security problem arises, for example, because of a disgruntled employee, there is often no audit capability to detect the source of the problem or to identify the extent of the damage. Likewise, because there are fewer stringent access controls, an employee who becomes malevolent can cause serious damage. Finally, it can be difficult to convince users of the need for security procedures when these procedures were not needed previously.

Another vulnerability is created in LANs because file servers are active devices. In a conventional computing system, a disk drive cannot be used other than through its connected CPU. (We assume, of course, that physical controls prevent someone from carrying away a disk pack and installing it on another system.) A **file server** for a LAN is typically a separate computer with a large capacity disk for storage. This computer can be physically disconnected from the network. Then, not only are the files inaccessible to network users, but the secrecy and integrity of files are protected only by any access control inherent in the computer functioning as the file server. Many LANs use standard personal computers as file servers, which provide almost no control against offline access.

10.10 Multilevel Security on Networks

We have studied multilevel security in previous chapters, both as it applies to operating systems and to data bases. Many of the same principles—such as mandatory access control, labeling, and trust—apply to network situations as well. However, a multilevel security network has its own particular security properties. We consider the security of multilevel networks in this section.

With a **multilevel security network** two or more people wish to share network access. These people work on projects with different sensitivity levels. Thus, a hierarchy of security levels is imposed on the network. It is common to use the military security model, in which data is classified according to level of sensitivity and further identified by topic. Thus, only cleared people with a need to know have access to network data.

A multilevel secure network must preserve two properties of access to data:

1. The *simple security property* states that no user may read data at a level higher than that for which the person is authorized.

2. The *∗-property* states that no person may write data to a level lower than that the person has accessed.

These properties are the Bell-LaPadula security properties first presented in Chapter 7.

Size and complexity make it difficult to verify the security of an operating system. Certainly, few existing general-purpose operating systems can pass a rigorous security certification. Operating systems for more secure applications must be designed specifically with security in mind. Those operating systems designed for high-security certification have separated the operating system into an untrusted component and a trusted computing base. Simlarly, one attempt to achieve multilevel security certification of a computer network is to form a trusted network base, called the trusted network interface. This approach is described next.

Trusted Network Interface

Figure 10.25 shows graphically the structure of a trusted computing base for an operating system. Although the figure is usually presented as on the left, the right figure is more accurate in terms of user capabilities: Each user is isolated from the other users, and a user's access to resources or to other users is strictly controlled by the trusted computing base. There is actually only one trusted computing base (on a single machine), even though in the figure it appears to be duplicated for each user.

The trusted interface for networks is developed naturally, in a manner similar to operating systems, in Figure 10.26. Here each host has a distinct and possibly different version of the trusted network interface. Because each host is independent, each host must be cautious in case another host joins the network without having a trusted network interface. Each interface is responsible for maintaining the security of the resources that it controls.

The network and the network interfaces must provide the following things.

1. *Secure multilevel hosts.* Each network interface is responsible for preserving the security of its host.

2. *Labeled output.* A network host must label its output so that other hosts can be aware of the security level of the data, even if the output is passed from one host through several others to its final destination.

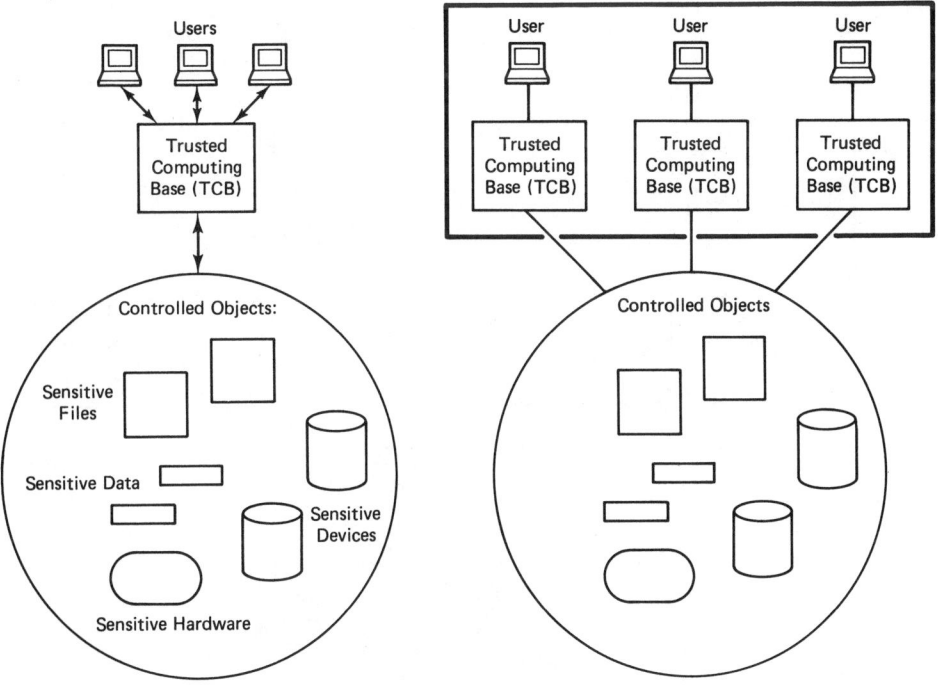

Figure 10.25   Trusted Computing Base for Operating Systems.

3. *Classification check before releasing data.* A host must be sure that it is releasing data to an approved recipient and that the recipient is authentic.

4. *Integrity of data.* The network host must take some measure, such as a cryptographic checksum, to ensure that data is not accidentally or intentionally modified during transmission.

5. *Confinement.* The interface must ensure that no host can leak information to another host.

6. *Protection from line compromise.* The network interface must ensure that a compromise of the links of the network will not compromise data.

Rushby and Randell [RUS83] present the design of such a secure system. In their example a number of UNIX systems form a local area network. The network design is shown in Figure 10.27. A basic premise for their work is that the host operating systems themselves should be unmodified; all security should be provided by the trusted network interface.

In the system proposed by Rushby and Randell, hosts encrypt all communications on the network. Each host operates at a specific security level, and all of its communications are protected under one key unique to that level. Therefore, there is little problem with

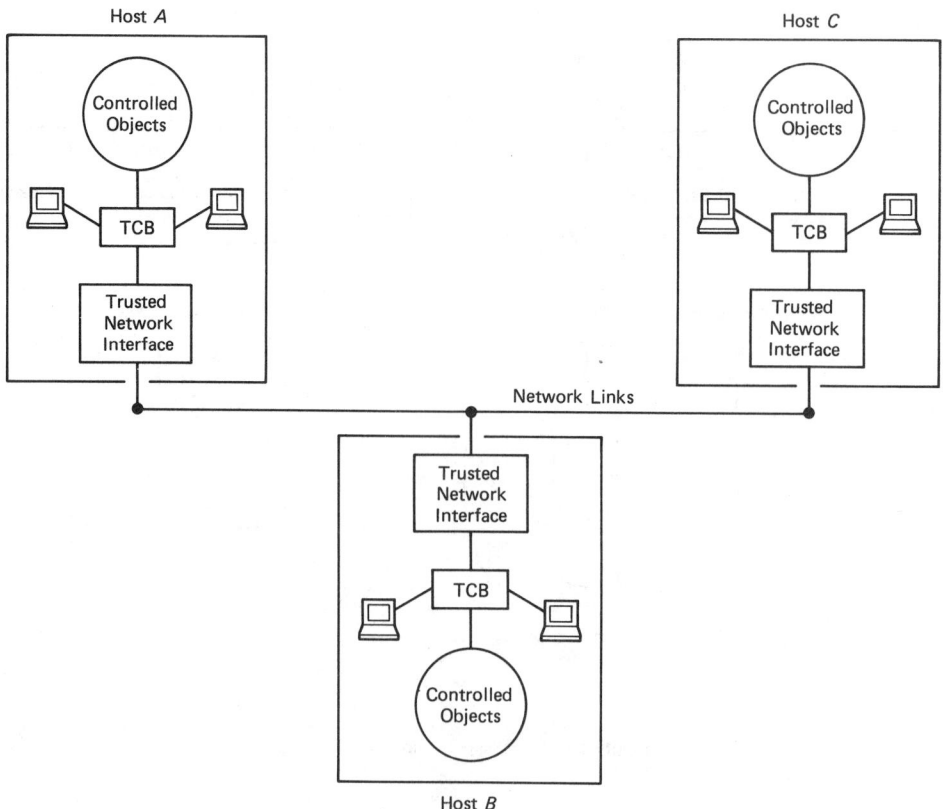

Figure 10.26   Trusted Network Interface.

unacceptable access between levels, since only those interfaces operating at a secret level, for example, could decrypt communications sent at the secret level.

Secure Communication

An alternate view of network security is presented by Walker [WAL85]. In this paper, Walker compares models of hosts at several security levels operating on the same network. As a simplification, assume there are three hosts connected to a network as shown in Figure 10.28. Hosts X and Y are trusted, in the sense of Chapter 7, at a level of B1 or higher. This means that they correctly implement a nondiscretionary access control policy limiting access of subjects to objects based on security levels. The network also contains an untrusted host, U.

In the first representation, the network does not enter into security considerations; all hosts are responsible for verifying the security of their own communications. Therefore, when process X1, running as a top secret process on host X, wishes to communicate with

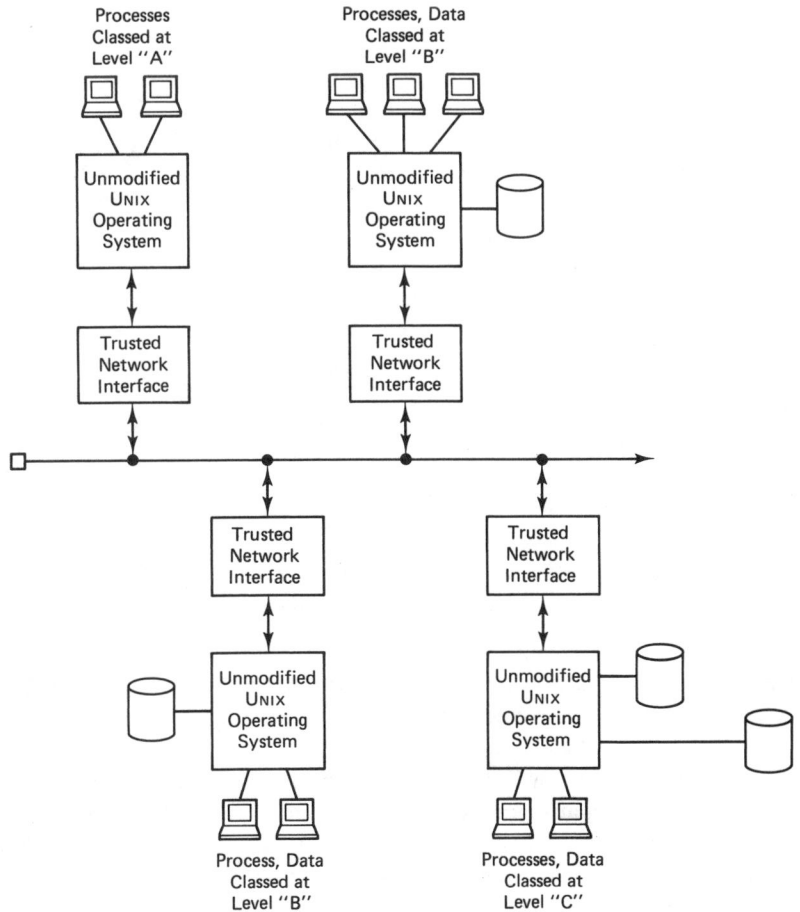

Figure 10.27   Secure Multilevel Network Design.

process Y1, running as a top secret process on host Y, hosts X and Y determine that this is an acceptable communication. When process X1 wishes to communicate with process Y2, running at secret level on host Y, host X prevents this communication because of the "no write-down" requirement of the *-principle.

Unreliable communications in networks cause a security problem. Process Y2, at secret level, can send a message to X1, at top secret level, because Y2 is allowed to write to any process whose security level is greater than or equal to the level of Y2. For example, Y2 might write a message to a high-security process X1 that maintains an audit log. Process X1 cannot reply to Y2, because that reply would constitute a write-down. Within a *single* system hardware and software are so reliable that Y2 does not need a reply to be confident that the message was received properly. However, suppose X1 is a process on another host in a network. Because of the unreliability of

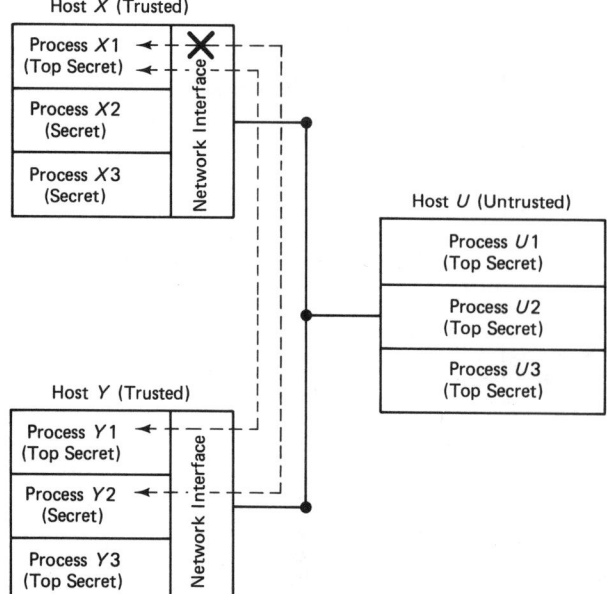

Figure 10.28   Multilevel Host Network.

network communications, Y2 wants assurance that the message has been received. This assurance, even a simple acknowledgment of message receipt, constitutes a write-down from X1 to Y2, which is not allowable.

A communications server on trusted host X can perform this service. Let XS be a secret-level communications server on X. Since XS and Y2 are at the same level, they can both read and write to each other. Thus Y2 can send its message to XS, and XS can respond that the message was successfully received at host X. XS will forward the message to X1 but, because of the difference in their levels, X1 will not acknowledge the receipt to XS. Y2 will accept an acknowledgment from XS to verify that X1 received the message since communications within a single host are reliable.

An untrusted host cannot use this technique, because the host cannot be relied upon to enforce an access policy on its processes. All processes on an untrusted host are assumed to operate at the same level, which becomes the level of the host. Suppose U is an untrusted host at level top secret and Y2 is a secret-level process on trusted host Y. Y2 wishes to send a message to process U1 on U. Although Y2 can send the message, it cannot be sure that the message was received by U or U1.

Walker describes a multilevel trusted network. As shown in Figure 10.29, a trusted network manager intervenes in communications. Thus, when Y2 wishes to send a message to U1 with reply, the network manager communicates with both U and Y to assure Y2 that the message was properly delivered.

The trusted network interface serves the same function as the trusted computing base of an operating system. A trusted computer base is allowed to violate the Bell-LaPadula *-property if it can be rigorously demonstrated that none of the information it reads from a high-level source is transferred to a lower-level object. Thus, a program can

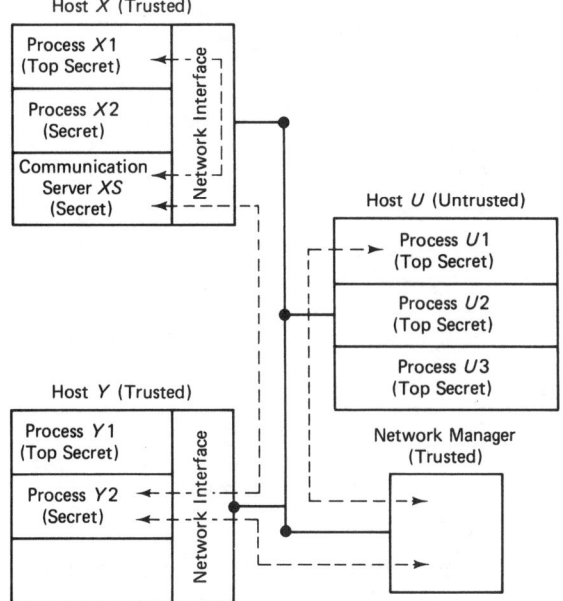

Figure 10.29   Multilevel Trusted Network Interface.

communicate with sources at different levels if a rigorous inspection of the code shows that the high-level data does not affect the output it produces for lower-level objects.

A model for security certification in multilevel networks is given in [NCS87]. This volume interprets the "orange book" [NCS85] policies for network implementations. It also specifies additional security properties, such as data integrity and availability of service.

Secure Network Interconnection

Rushby [RUS85] proposes dividing trusted network interfaces into domains with input and output sockets. It can be demonstrated whether or not data entering through one input socket can affect the output of another socket. A module demonstrating such separation is a true multilevel module. Its output socket can safely be connected to other modules (through their sockets) operating at lower security levels than the modules connected to the module's high security input sockets.

For example, module A in Figure 10.30 exhibits such channel separation; therefore, top secret modules can be connected to the input socket and secret modules to the output with no security leak. However, module B does not show this separation, and so the label of its input socket must be no higher than that of its output socket.

With the notion of channel separation, the output from a module can be separated into different security levels. If a module cannot enforce separation, all its output is at one level, the least upper bound of its input levels. Thus, a module reading from both secret and top secret levels would have all outputs classified as top secret, unless the module was known to enforce channel separation.

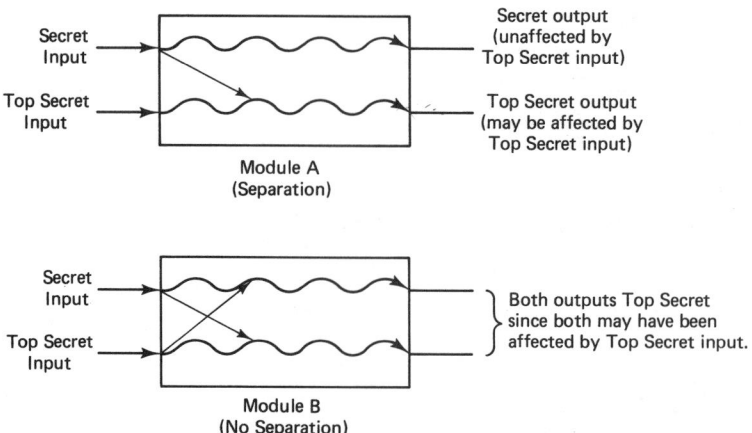

Figure 10.30   Channel Separation in Modules.

The classification label of a module output is also the level at which that output would be received as input to another module. For example, if a module produces top secret output and that output is taken as the input to another module, the level of the input is obviously top secret.

This labeling of inputs and outputs can also be used to determine allowable connections between processes in a network. Each process is a module that runs at a particular level. Each output may be connected only to inputs labeled at least as high. That is, an output classed secret may be connected to any input classed secret or top secret. If the connection between two processes is bidirectional, each connection handles both input and output, so that the labels of these processes must be the same. Therefore, a process producing secret output can be connected for two-way communication only to secret level processes. This situation is shown in Figure 10.31. The output from secret process U2 is labeled secret (A). Process U2 can thus be used as an input-only process to any process receiving input at level secret or higher (B, C, D, E, F). However, U2 can be connected for two-way communication only to inputs labeled secret (B, C, F).

This model describes secure connections in a multilevel network. Rushby uses these input and output labels to identify allowable connections in a multilevel network. According to his interpretation, "trust" relates to the ability of a module to separate its input from its output. Some network hosts also practice multilevel separation of user processes through a trusted operating system.

10.11 Summary of Network Security

In this chapter we have considered several security characteristics of networks. The network security issues of secrecy, integrity, authenticity, and availability have been studied. Networks possess many of the security vulnerabilities of other computing systems, although there are also weaknesses specific to networks.

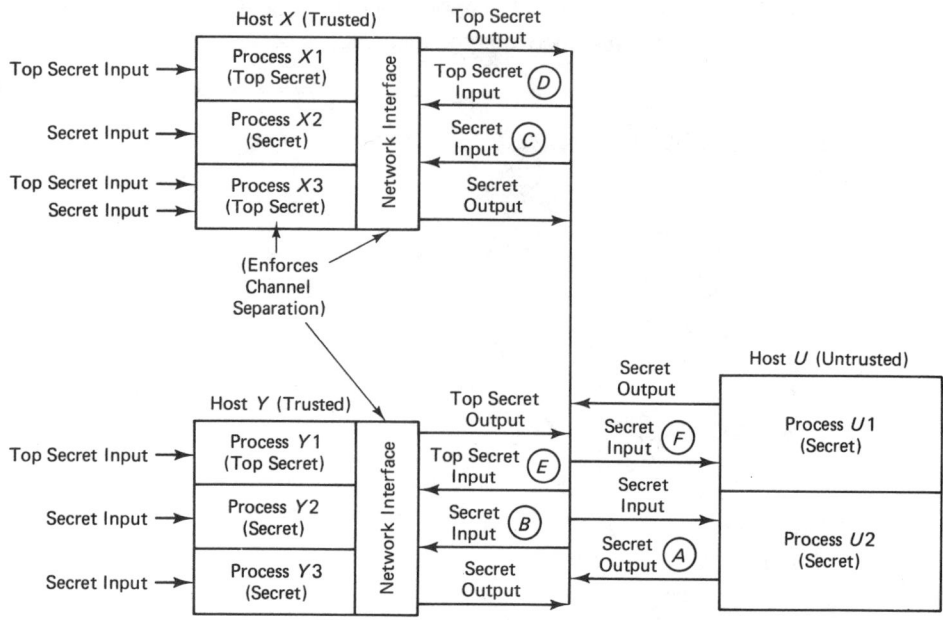

Figure 10.31   Multilevel Network with Channel Separation.

Encryption is a powerful tool in network security, although it is not the only tool, nor is it all-powerful. Link level encryption can be performed without the knowledge or participation of a user's process. Thus, link level encryption can be useful when users do not have the background to implement an appropriate encryption method. By contrast, with end-to-end encryption, the user is responsible for performing encryption. End-to-end encryption thus gives the user a choice of when to use encryption and which encryption algorithm to use.

The possible vulnerabilities of a network that have been studied include access by unauthorized users or nodes, as well as impersonation of authorized users or nodes. Access control and authentication techniques are similar to those for operating systems. A serious problem that remains in network security is establishing trust of a remote node, since a remote node can be impersonated, subverted, or replaced.

In network security integrity is an important issue that affects all users. Therefore, much attention has been devoted to developing network transmission protocols that ensure the integrity of the data being communicated.

Finally, we have examined two special classes of networks—the Local Area Network (LAN) and the multilevel network. We have discussed the security issues of both and have pointed out where existing controls are inadequate to control known vulnerabilities. The users of these systems need to be aware of these vulnerabilities in order to build appropriate controls into their applications and procedures, without relying solely on the network to enforce security. Work is currently in progress to develop an appropriate model for multilevel network security.

In the next chapter we will continue looking at network issues when we examine the actual media by which network communications occur.

10.12 Terms and Concepts

network
computing system
node
host
link
topology
ISO OSI model
layer
bus topology
ring topology
star topology
resource sharing
reliability (achieved by network)
distributed workload
expandability of network
message
message delivery
network boundary or perimeter
untrustable host
administrator of a host
line tap
intermediate node
link
network gateway
switch
message routing
host authenticity
message corruption
modification of message
bogus message
deletion of message
message replay
reordering message
covert network channel
link encryption
end-to-end encryption
authentication through encryption
key distribution

master key
session key
key server
port protection
automatic call-back
differentiated access rights
silent modem
mutual suspicion
node authentication
user authentication
password
challenge-response system
exchange of secrets protocol
passphrase
token
smart card
active node threat
playback
disruption of service
spurious messages
traffic analysis
covert channel through traffic
traffic volume padding
routing control
protocol for integrity control
checksum
error code
cryptographic checksum
digital signature
notary
local area network (LAN)
proximity
security level of LAN
active devices
active file server
multilevel network security
simple security property
∗-property
trusted computing base
trusted network base
trusted network interface
multilevel host
confinement
link security
secure network interconnection

10.13 Bibliographic Notes

The "network is a system" argument is continued very nicely in the paper by John Rushby [RUS85]; that paper pursues the argument that a network is a processing system which needs to be seen in relation to the rest of the world when analyzing the security of the system.

10.14 Exercises

1. What controls prevent a malicious user from inserting or deleting a new piece of hardware into a simple (*non*-network) computing system?

2. What assurance does an operating system in a simple (*non*-network) environment have of the authenticity of a component? That is, could a telephone line known internally as line 1 actually be cabled to line 2 without the knowledge of the operating system?

3. Are there network security problems that depend on distance? That is, are there problems that do not exist at, for example, 10 miles but do exist at 100 miles or more? If yes, what are these problems?

4. In the ISO model, peer processes communicate without regard for precise implementation of activities at other layers. For example, the application does not know or care what specific routing has been chosen by the network layer. What is the security effect of an application program's not knowing the routing selected for a particular message, or even a particular session?

5. A user wishes to establish a covert channel by control and analysis of the total traffic on the network. At what layer would this analysis have to be performed?

6. Can a single malicious node cause a denial of service fault to another node in a network with the bus topology? The ring topology? The star topology? Tell how or explain why not for each of these.

7. Network users can perform simple encryption to shield their messages. As presented in earlier chapters, simple encryptions are sensitive to volume: If an interceptor obtains a large amount of ciphertext, the likelihood of breaking the encryption increases. With what network topologies should users be concerned about availability of much ciphertext?

8. The network advantages of increased reliability and distributed workload are disadvantages to security, since more nodes have potential access to sensitive data or computations. What controls can allow distributed data or computing without sacrificing security?

9. Expandability is an advantage of network use; that is, new nodes can be added easily to a network. What security disadvantage does this present?

10. What is the security impact of the unknown perimeter of a network? Does it matter to user A if the network is also accessible to user B? to user C through a network shared with B and to user D through a network shared with C (and so on)?

11. Where (at what times during its transmission) is a message exposed if it is protected using link encryption? Where is a message exposed if end-to-end encryption is used?

12. Describe the vulnerabilities of the two-party key distribution protocol described in this chapter. That is, indicate each point at which a key compromise is possible, and explain how that compromise could be achieved.

13. Describe the vulnerabilities of the key server distribution protocol described in this chapter. That is, indicate each point at which a key compromise is possible, and explain how that compromise could be achieved.

14. Explain why node authentication is a continuous problem in a network. Describe a solution to this problem.

15. With the exchange of secrets protocol described in this chapter, (a) Why does C send $E_A(M2, B, K, E_B(-))$ back to A; that is, why can't C send just K to A? (b) Why does C send $E_B(-)$ to A; that is, why can't A compute that instead of receiving it from C?

16. What are two difficulties to producing timestamped messages in a network?

17. Suggest a control to prevent a covert channel via traffic analysis in a network without an administrator. That is, what control can an arbitrary user node provide against these kinds of covert channels?

18. Design a checking mechanism (other than parity) to ensure data integrity in a network communication.

19. In what circumstances can parity detect two-bit errors? Three-bit errors?

20. Integrity is an important network concern. Control information to ensure data integrity is a significant part of the information transmitted with messages. Are the Biba integrity properties (from Chapter 7) appropriate in a multilevel secure network? Why or why not?

21. Explain how output can be labeled on a multilevel security network. Why is it unsatisfactory to have a message saying, "The following message is classified top secret"?

11

Communications Security

The last chapter, on security in networks, concentrated on the network hosts by intentionally ignoring problems with the transmission media and their characteristics. That focus let us identify the security difficulties of allowing a possibly unbounded number of new users into a system. This chapter will show that not only do networks add to security concerns, but also the communications links between network hosts intensify these concerns. This chapter contains a brief introduction to communications media, with special emphasis on the security of communications.

The chapter begins with basic terminology from communications. We then consider different media used for communications and study the effect on security of choosing a particular medium. The chapter concludes by examining the two most common communications vulnerabilities—noise (loss of integrity) and active and passive wiretapping (loss of secrecy).

11.1 Communications Characteristics

This section opens by studying basic principles of communications, especially as related to digital computers. Signals and various methods of signal transmission are described.

Signals

In computer communications the goal is to transmit and receive binary data. A telegrapher's key transmits binary data as the presence or absence of current—a circuit that is either closed or open. Such a system is called a **switching circuit**. Because switching circuits are primarily mechanical, their speed is limited, too slow for most computing applications.

The speed of a transmission can be improved by converting a binary signal to a **wave**, a function that approximates the desired signal. In computer applications, signals are represented by electrical current, and so the value of the signal is **voltage**. The signal is represented by a **waveform**, the plot of the value of the signal against time.

Digital versus Analog

A signal can be either analog or digital. Figure 11.1 shows examples of these two signals. An **analog** signal is a smooth, continuous curve, at least over small amounts of time. An analog signal may have peaks and valleys, but there are no instantaneous changes in value. Let the value of a signal at time t_0 be $v(t_0)$, and the value at time t_1 be $v(t_1)$. If x is any value between $v(t_0)$ and $v(t_1)$, then there is some instant $t*$ between t_0 and t_1 when $x = v(t*)$. That is, the function passes through every value between $v(t_0)$ and $v(t_1)$. Figure 11.1 (a) shows an analog signal.

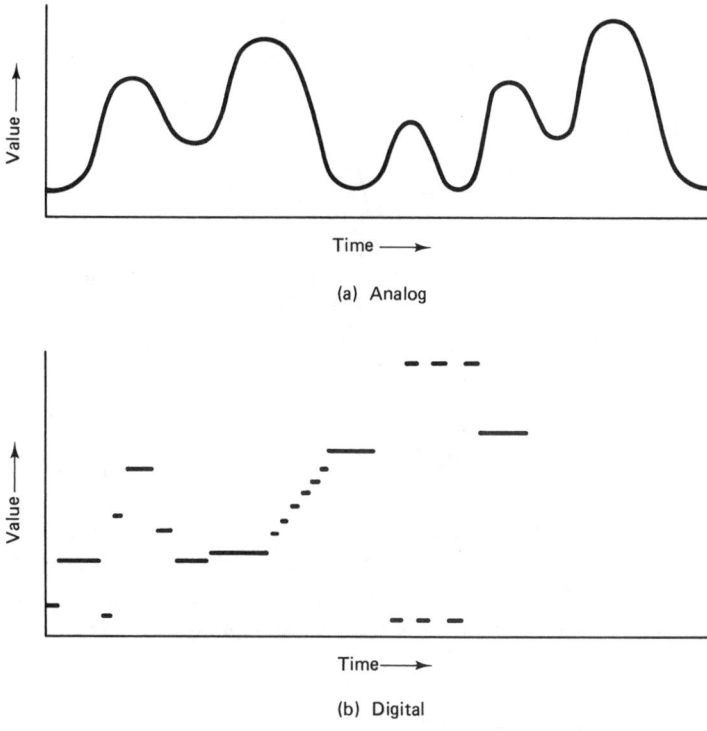

(a) Analog

(b) Digital

Figure 11.1   Examples of Signals: (a) Analog; (b) Digital.

The values of a **digital** or **discrete** signal form a finite set of distinct values. A change in value occurs instantaneously, not smoothly. For example, suppose a digital signal is being used to transmit the binary string 010. The value of the signal is 0 at t_0,

1 at t_1, and 0 at t_2. A digital representation of a signal changes immediately from one value to another. Thus, there is no time at which this digital signal has any value other than 0 or 1. By contrast, with analog signals there is a time $t*$ between t_0 and t_1 when $v(t*) = 0.5$, for example. Figure 11.1 (b) shows a digital signal.

    Computing applications usually involve digital values because computers operate on discrete, numeric items, such as bits or characters. These discrete values can be represented as either digital or analog signals. In the following sections, we study the representations of discrete values as analog and digital signals.

Representation of an Analog Signal

A digital signal can be represented as the sum of curves of the sine function. (These curves are called **waves** in communications.) The signal at time t is approximated by a repeating function of period T. The approximation is the sum of a set of n separate waves, called **harmonics**. Each harmonic is described by the equation

$$v(t) = \frac{1}{2}c + \sum_{n=1}^{\infty} a_n \sin\left(\frac{2\pi nt}{T}\right) + \sum_{n=1}^{\infty} b_n \cos\left(\frac{2\pi nt}{T}\right)$$

where

$$a_n = \frac{2}{T} \int_0^t v(t) \sin\left(\frac{2\pi nt}{T}\right) dt,$$

$$b_n = \frac{2}{T} \int_0^t v(t) \cos\left(\frac{2\pi nt}{T}\right) dt, \text{ and}$$

$$c = \frac{2}{T} \int_0^t v(t) \, dt.$$

Transmission of Signals

These equations give analog curves, which only approximate the digital signal to be transmitted. An example of this approximation is shown in Figure 11.2. Notice that with only one wave (one harmonic), the signal does not approximate the value of the signal very well, but as more waves are used, the approximation resembles the original curve more closely.

Reception of Signals

The last section of the Figure 11.2 shows how these approximations can be measured to determine the value represented by the function. The signal is sampled to determine if the value is high (1) or low (0). If the sampling occurs while the function value is rising or falling, the result may be inconclusive or even false. However, due to variations in timing between the sender and receiver, it is difficult to sample at precisely the points

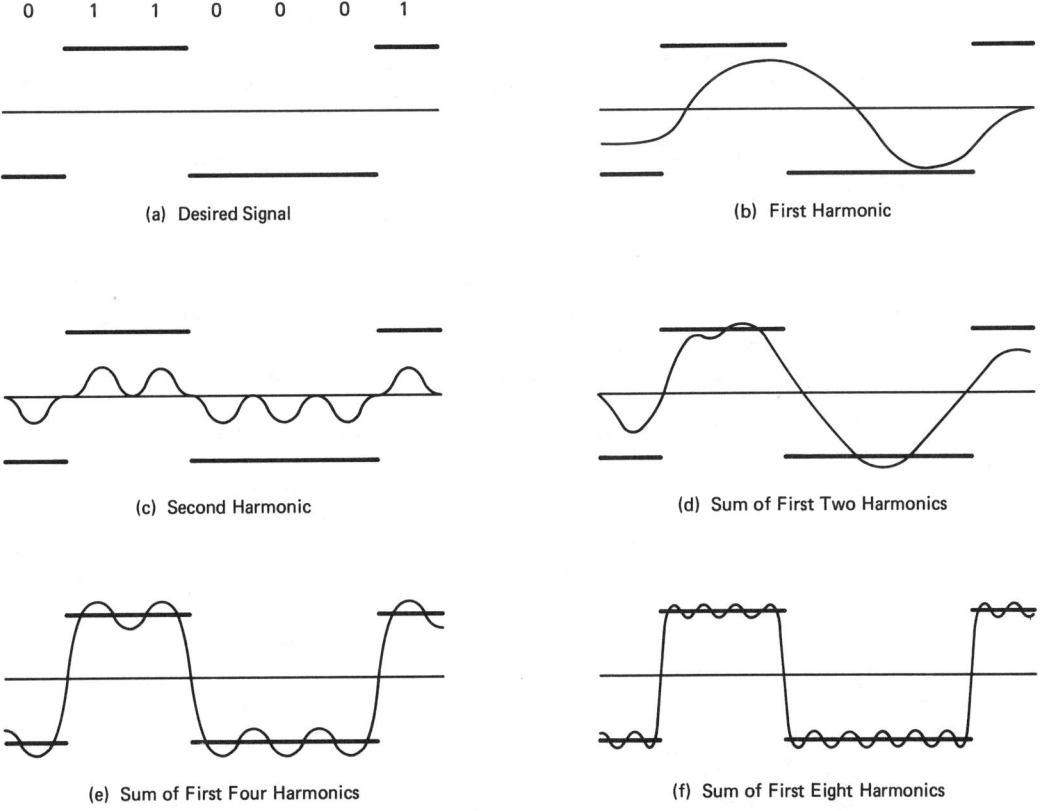

0   1   1   0   0   0   1

Figure 11.2   Approximation of a Signal by Sine Waves.

when a signal is high or low. Therefore, a tolerance is established: If a signal is within the accepted range for a high value, it is interpreted as 1, and similarly for 0.

If a signal is approximated with many harmonics, the approximation is closer to the actual value. That is, the signal is within the tolerance for a longer period of time, which means that the sampled value is more likely to be correctly interpreted as a 1 or 0. Therefore, an approximation using more harmonics is more likely to communicate without error. Unfortunately, the number of changes per second a line can accommodate is limited. The number of changes per second for a transmission line is rated in **baud**.

Suppose a system transmits 8-bit bytes. With a b baud line, the transmission rate is b bits per second, or $b/8$ bytes per second, and the first harmonic is at $b/8$ cycles per second. (Cycles per second is abbreviated Hz, and bits per second is written bps.) The harmonics repeat, so that the first harmonic is at $b/8$ Hz, the second at $2b/8$ Hz, and the n-th at $n * b/8$ Hz. With more harmonics, the approximation of a signal is better. These signals are in audible form, as tones or sounds.

Telephone Communication

Since telephone technology is a basic means of computer communication, we will discuss telephone systems first. An ordinary telephone line is called a **voice grade** line. **Bandwidth** is the range of frequencies allocated for a given transmission. A voice grade line has a bandwidth of 3000 Hz. This limit restricts the highest harmonic that can be carried on a line.

Table 11.1 shows the number of harmonics available for several different popular bit transmission frequencies. The figures in this table are for perfect transmission, with no noise on the line or distortion or decay of the signal. As this table shows, higher transmission rates mean fewer harmonics, which mean a less accurate approximation. This table helps to explain why most transmission is between 300–2400 bps, and transmissions of 4800 or 9600 bps are possible only on specially conditioned, low-noise lines.

TABLE 11.1   NUMBER OF HARMONICS FOR VARIOUS BIT RATES.

Bits per Second	First Harmonic at $(b/8)$ Hz	Number of Harmonics $\leq$ 3000 Hz
300	37.5	80
600	75	40
1200	150	20
2400	300	10
4800	600	5
9600	1200	2
19200	2400	1
38400	4800	0

Multiplexing

Transmission media are actually capable of carrying a wider frequency range than the 3000 Hz bandwidth of a voice grade line. A common voice connection is combined with other connections on high-capacity **trunk** lines. For example, a simple wire trunk line has a frequency range of about 36,000 Hz. At that range, 12 separate 3000 Hz telephone conversations can be carried on a single line.

The 36,000 Hz band is seen as a horizontal strip, carrying all frequencies from 0 to 36,000 Hz at a time. That strip is then cut into 12 stripes, as shown in Figure 11.3. A single voice channel is shifted by adding a constant factor to the frequency of the signal. This technique, called **multiplexing**, lets one line carry several separate communications. The different media have different bandwidths and can allow different amounts of multiplexing.

Digital Signal Transmission

A binary digital signal is transmitted as one of two possible values. These values are represented as two different voltage levels. As shown in Figure 11.4, a voltage level

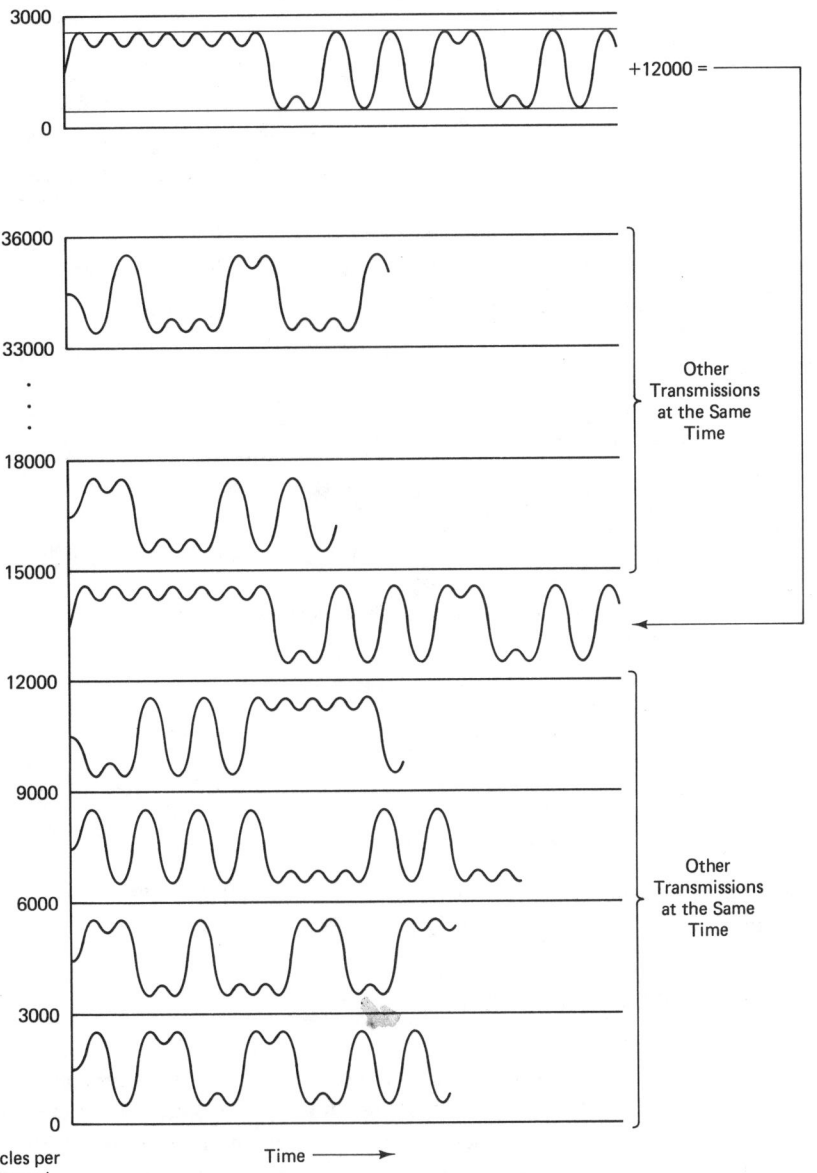

Figure 11.3   Frequency Multiplexing.

does not change instantaneously, but rather it rapidly moves *close to* the desired level, and then the rate of change decreases.

Because a digital signal may not have reached its peak at the time it is to be sampled, a digital signal is represented by **threshold values**. If a voltage is above the

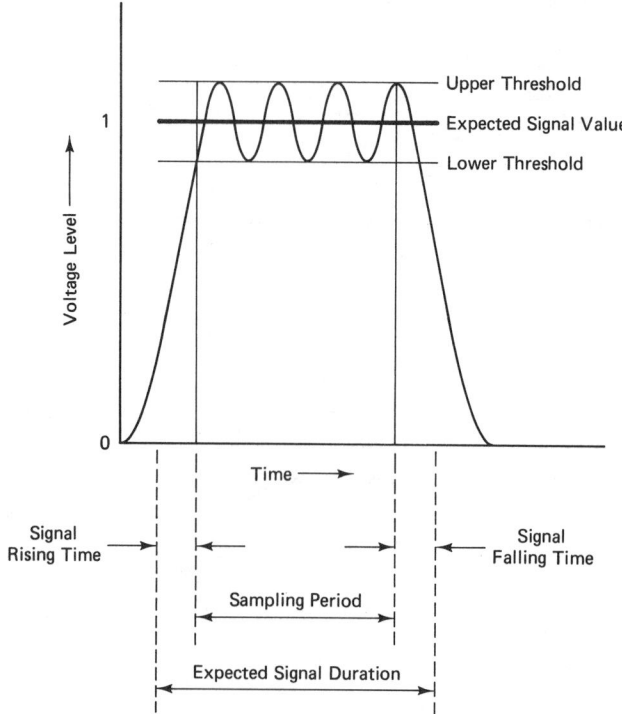

Figure 11.4   Digital Signal Approximated by a Voltage Level.

upper threshold value, it is taken to be a 1; if it is below the lower threshold, it is taken to be a 0.

Dedicated versus Switched

A telephone customer can obtain two different kinds of telephone lines. The standard telephone in most homes is a **switched line**. A customer with a switched line can call anyone connected to the telephone network. A line runs from the home telephone to a local switching office. As someone dials, the switching office interprets the signals of the number dialed and establishes a connection to the destination. With a switched line, a customer rents the ability to access the shared facilities of the telephone network.

If someone in New York calls California, the call might be routed via lines to Ohio, Minnesota, Oregon, and California; or it might be routed through Georgia, Texas, and Arizona to California. Now it is quite likely that the call will be sent by media other than plain wire, media such as microwave or satellite. Two similar calls might be sent on different routes at different times. Assuming the quality of all of these connections is the same, the customer never knows or cares what route the call took. The call will also probably be multiplexed with calls from other people.

A customer who rents a switched line is paying for part of the cost of the entire switching network. The customer subsidizes the cost of periods of low volume and the telephone company's need to have excess capacity, so that peak demand will not saturate the system, or even one link.

Consider a company that has an office in New York and an office in California, with substantial communication between those two offices. The company is not interested in calling any possible phone; it wants to be able to communicate only between its New York and California offices. The company does not want to underwrite the costs associated with capacity or volume of other parts of the network.

The telephone companies can provide a private line, called **dedicated service**, which is a direct line between the New York and California offices. Only the company's two offices have access to that line. The line does not pass through the normal switching network, so that extra noise due to switching circuitry is eliminated. The clarity of the line can be "conditioned," so that distortion on the line is reduced. For these reasons, a dedicated line is especially appropriate for transmission of data.

Digital versus Analog—Again

Earlier we looked at the difference between digital and analog *signals*. There are also digital and analog *communications facilities*.

Analog transmission is, surprisingly, the more common form of data transmission. To transmit data by analog signals, the binary data must first be converted to an analog signal (tone) by a device called a **modem** (which stands for *mo*dulator/*dem*odulator). A modem electronically reshapes a signal from a square, discrete, binary signal to its approximation as an analog frequency curve that fits within the prescribed bandwidth. A single bit may be the combination of several harmonics, so it will be transmitted as a series of different frequencies; on a telephone line these are audible tones. A modem at the receiving end converts this analog signal back to its discrete binary form.

By contrast, **digital** transmission progresses by sampling over time. Each bit is transmitted as a series of distinct coded symbols. The process is more difficult, because it requires closer time synchronization between the sender and receiver. Because of the precision required, digital transmission equipment is substantially more expensive than analog. This price difference is true both for the equipment owned by the telephone company and that owned by the customer.

The two principal advantages to digital communication are high transmission speed and low error rate. Data rates in excess of 1.5 *million* bits per second are possible on a high-grade digital line, while a standard analog line can carry 9600 bps at best. Furthermore, since each signal received should be either a 0 or a 1, noise that doesn't look like either of these two signals can be filtered easily. By contrast, noise adds to an analog transmission, and the noise may be enough to make a signal unrecognizable. We consider the problem of noise more fully later in the chapter.

Common Carrier

In the United States, telephone communication is handled by private industry. A long distance customer can subscribe to service to one of several different companies; these companies sometimes maintain their own equipment and sometimes lease equipment from other companies. In many other countries, especially in Europe, the telephone company is a government-owned or government-controlled monopoly, similar to the postal service in the United States.

Both here and abroad, customers *share* telecommunications access with other customers. One call may be combined with the calls of other customers, through multiplexing. In theory this combining is not noticeable, but in practice it is common to hear bits of other conversations during a long distance call on a switched line.

Thus, a common carrier is a *shared* medium. With a common carrier, a user loses control of the medium, the routing, and the security of the communication. Not only is there no control, but the common carrier does not assume responsibility for security or privacy. Therefore, the user must secure the contents of a transmission before delivering it to a common carrier.

Summary of Communications Techniques

Digital data, such as data produced by a computer, can be transmitted as either a digital or an analog signal. A digital signal is transmitted as a high or low voltage, represented by 0 or 1, respectively. Digital values are converted to analog approximations, represented as superimposed tones, to be transmitted as analog signals.

Digital transmission is expensive, but offers high speed and low error rates. Analog transmission is widely available: Nearly all homes and businesses have access to voice grade dial telephone lines.

Both digital and analog transmission are typically multiplexed with many other simultaneous transmissions.

11.2 Communications Media

With this background, we are now ready to consider the different media over which telecommunications transmissions occur. This brief survey of the capabilities of the different media will enable us to examine the security properties of each for computer communications.

Cable

The most common communication medium is **wire**. The medium most often used inside homes and offices is a pair of insulated copper wires, called a **twisted pair**. Copper has good transmission properties at a relatively low cost. Unfortunately, the bandwidth of such a system is rather limited, so that it is impossible to multiplex a large number of communications on a single line. For this reason, single twisted pair service is most often used locally, within a building or up to a local exchange office. Multiple pairs of wires are often strung within a single jacket, but size, weight, and difficulty to install and maintain limit the number of cable pairs that are put in a single sheath.

A **coaxial (coax) cable** has greater capacity. Whereas twisted pair transmission is limited to about a dozen voice grade circuits, one coax cable can carry more than 10,000 circuits. One or two dozen coax cables can be combined in the same sheath, putting the number of circuits per cable in the range of 10^5.

The signal quality of both twisted pairs and coax cable tends to degrade over distance. **Repeaters** are spaced periodically along the cable to pick up the signal, amplify it, and retransmit it. For paired cables, repeaters must be located about every 17 miles, but with coax cable the signal must be strengthened every mile. The added capacity of coax cable comes with the added cost and complexity of frequent repeaters. Since repeaters are components that can fail, the cost to maintain a coax system is quite high.

Security Considerations

Both twisted pair and coax cables are subject to wiretapping. **Wiretapping** means either that someone extracts a communication from the cable without damaging the cable, or that someone cuts the jacket and splices onto a wire from the cable. **Passive wiretapping** is just listening, whereas **active wiretapping** is injecting something into the communication. Without cutting into the cable only passive wiretapping is possible, but by direct contact with the wire either passive or active wiretapping is possible.

Any wire cable medium is subject to wiretapping. The large concentration of communication that flows through any major long distance cable makes it quite unlikely that it will be tapped. In order to extract one individual communication, an intruder would have to know not just which cable but also which of many channels on that cable carried the communication. The routing techniques for switched communications are unpredictable. Thus, it is unlikely that someone would tap a long distance line to obtain a specific communication.

A leased line, however, is often (although not always) assigned to the same channel of the same cable. Thus it is possible, although somewhat unlikely, for a wiretapper to intercept communications on a leased New York to California line from some point in Kansas.

An intruder is unlikely to extract one communication from many in Kansas if the communication can be obtained elsewhere more easily. The communication probably leaves the New York office on a single twisted pair cable until it joins a trunk line on a telephone pole somewhere nearby. Worse yet, many office buildings have an unlocked door leading to a small switching closet. All telephone connections pass through that closet on their way from a desk or computer room to the lines outside. These are places where an intruder can tap a single line that contains only one communication. The points of possible wiretap are shown in Figure 11.5. Because of the weakest point principle, the interceptor will try to access one transmission alone, rather than trying to extract it from a group of many multiplexed transmissions.

Wire is easily cut and spliced. Telephone circuits carry a particular resistance level, which is monitored by the telephone company. A change in resistance can mean a break in a line, so repair crews attempt to isolate and repair the damage when they discover it. However, moisture, vibration, and other causes, as well as wire cutting or splicing, can upset the resistance level. The telephone company will not always investigate a change in resistance, which means that wiretapping may not be detected or investigated by the telephone company.

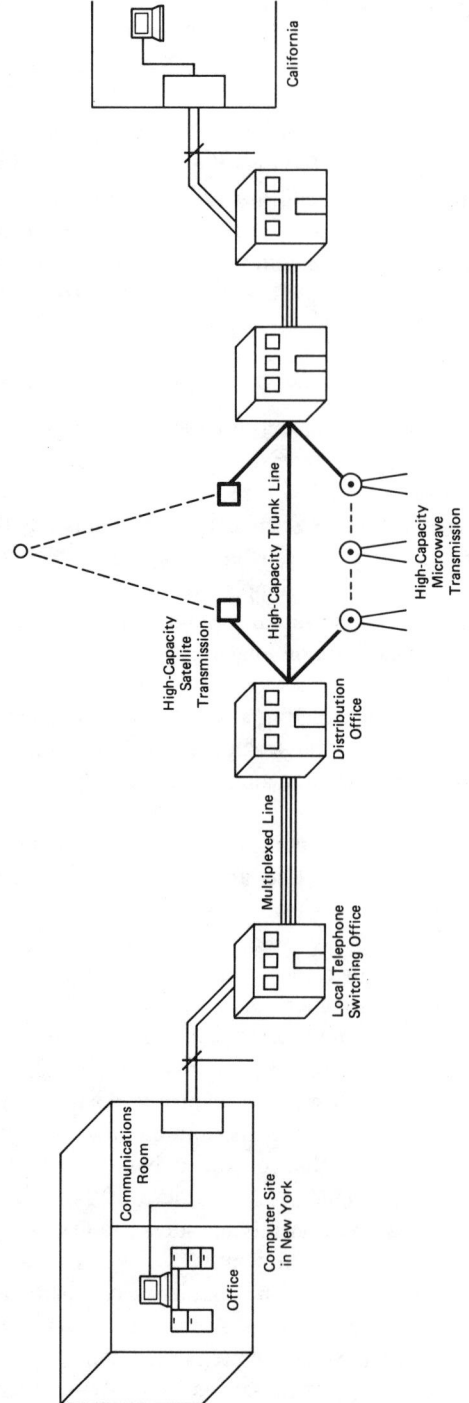

Figure 11.5 Wiretap Vulnerabilities.

Another problem is **inductance**. As current flows through a wire, it generates a magnetic field. This magnetic field can be detected by electronic circuitry that is close to, but not necessarily even in contact with, the wire. This field can be detected through the insulation around the cable. Electromagnetic leakage is a serious security vulnerability of all wire cable. Because of the problem of separating one transmission from another, inductance is less a problem in circuits carrying many communications than in ones with few. Inductance and magnetic emanations are considered in Chapter 12.

Microwave

Microwave has a channel capacity similar to coax cable. The principal advantage of microwave is that the signal is strong from its point of transmission to its point of receipt. Therefore, microwave signals do not need to be regenerated with repeaters, as do signals on cable.

However, a microwave signal travels in a straight line, while the earth curves. Microwave signals travel by line of sight: The transmitter and receiver must be in a straight line with one another, and there must be no intervening obstacles, such as mountains. As shown in Figure 11.6, a straight microwave signal transmitted between towers of reasonable height can travel a distance of only about 30 miles.

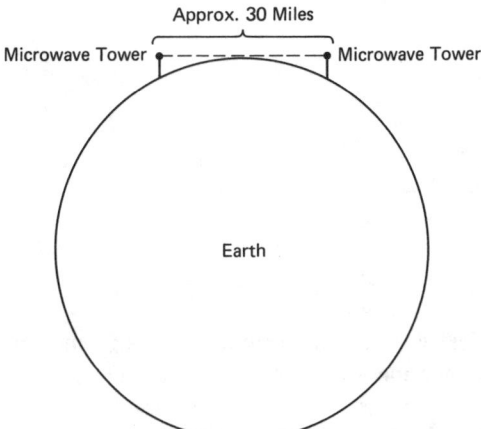

Figure 11.6   Microwave Transmission.

Security Concerns of Microwave

Microwave signals are shot through the air, available to anyone who wants to pick them up. A signal is not shielded or isolated to prevent interception. Microwave is therefore a very insecure medium. However, because of the large volume of traffic carried by microwave links, it is unlikely that someone will separate an individual transmission.

Since microwave signals are not carried along a wire, there is some problem with precision in aim. Typically a signal from a transmitter will be focused at its corresponding receiver, but the signal path will be fairly wide in order to be sure of hitting the receiver, as shown in Figure 11.7.

From a security standpoint, that situation is very undesirable. Not only can someone intercept a microwave transmission by interfering with the line of sight between sender and receiver, someone can also pick up an entire transmission from an antenna somewhere along the path but somewhat off the direct focus point.

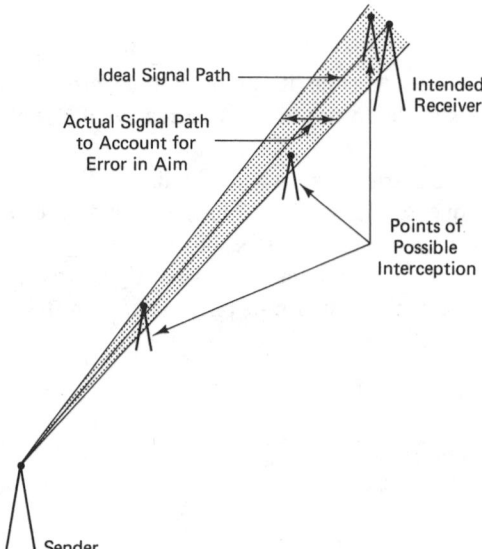

Ideal Signal Path

Intended Receiver

Actual Signal Path to Account for Error in Aim

Points of Possible Interception

Sender

Figure 11.7 Path of Microwave Signals.

Satellite

The communications companies own several satellites in orbit synchronized with the rotation of the earth. Although the medium is expensive to launch, once in space it is essentially maintenance-free. Furthermore, the quality of a satellite communication link is often better than an earth-bound wire cable.

These satellites receive and repeat signals; essentially the signal "bounces" off the satellite. In this way, a signal from the East coast travels 22,300 miles into the sky and the same distance back to a point on the West coast. The process of bouncing a signal off a satellite is shown in Figure 11.8.

In order to reduce the complexity of their circuitry, satellites act as "dumb" transponders; whatever they receive they broadcast out again. It is possible to project a signal to a satellite with reasonable accuracy, but the satellite is not expected to be able to duplicate this accuracy with its repeat of the signal. Thus, to reduce complexity and eliminate beam focusing, satellites typically spread their transmissions over a very wide area.

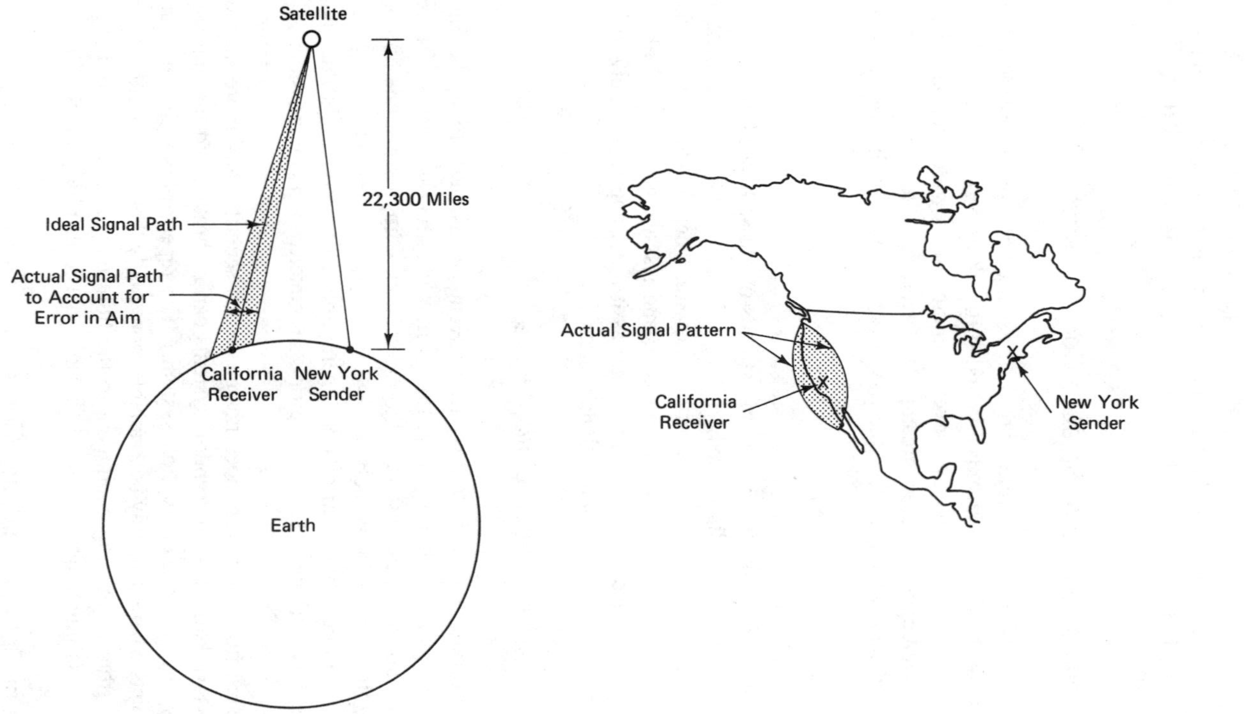

Figure 11.8 Satellite Communication.

A rather narrow angle of dispersion from the satellite's transmitter produces a fairly broad pattern on the surface of the earth—because of the 22,300 mile distance from the satellite to earth. A typical satellite transmission can be received over a path several hundred miles wide; in fact, some early ones could cover the width of the entire continental U.S. in a single transmission.

Security Considerations of Satellite Communication

Microwave signals on earth were described as insecure, since anyone could erect an antenna close to the line of transmission and still pick up a signal. A satellite communication can be picked up over an area several hundred miles wide and long. Therefore, the potential for interception is even greater. However, satellite communications are often heavily multiplexed, which reduces the risk of interception of any one communication.

Optical Fibre

A new form of cable is made of very thin strands of glass. Instead of carrying electrical energy, these fibres carry light energy. They do that very well. The bandwidth on optical fibre is generally higher than for copper wire. There is also less interference, less crossover between adjacent fibres, lower cost, and less weight. Optical fibre is a much better transmission medium than copper, and as it ages, copper is likely to be replaced by optical fibre in most communications systems.

Security Considerations of Optical Fibre

Optical fibre offers two significant security advantages as well. First, the entire optical network must be tuned carefully each time a new connection is made. Therefore, it is impossible to tap an optical system without detection. Clipping just one fibre in a bundle will destroy the balance in the network.

Secondly, optical fibre carries light energy, not electricity. Light does not induce a magnetic field as electricity does. Therefore, an inductive tap is impossible on an optical fibre cable.

Just using fibre, however, does not guarantee security, any more than does using encryption. (We know that encryption systems can be broken and that messages can be obtained by breaking the encryption system.) The repeaters, splices, and taps along a cable are points where data may be available more easily than in the fibre cable itself. The connections from computing equipment to the fibre may also be points for penetration. By itself, fibre is much more secure than cable, but it also has vulnerabilities.

Summary of Communications Media

Two points should be stressed about communications media and security. First, many communications signals are readily available in the air, near a microwave tower, or close to a copper telephone line. These communications can include voice conversations, data, and network commands. They can be tapped with devices ranging from a simple inductance coil (costing about $5 at an electronics store) to tuned antennas costing $1000 or more.

But second, although these signals are available, on a *switched* circuit it is unlikely that someone would be able to determine the route of a particular transmission and separate that communication from all the others with which it is multiplexed. This unpredictability is *not* true for dedicated (leased) lines. Worse, the predictability is 100 percent at the end points of communication—before a signal leaves the building in which it originates and after the signal reaches the destination building.

From a security standpoint, it is wise to assume that *all* communication links between network nodes can be broken. Encryption is the most solid defense against interception of a network transmission.

11.3 Loss of Integrity

So far, data communication has been described in an ideal network, one in which every transmission is received exactly as it was sent. Unfortunately this is seldom the case. Different factors cause loss of signals and introduction of spurious signals in communication. These errors constitute a lack of integrity in the communication system. We now consider how to control these losses.

Noise

The general term for spurious signals is **noise**. There are many possible causes of noise. For example, rain, humidity, and wind can cause components or connections to fail intermittently. Lightning strikes can disrupt transmissions with momentary surges of power along a line. Animals have been known to chew through cable coverings, and tree branches knock against lines, straining connections. Another source of noise is nearby generators of electromagnetic force, such as heavy motors. As more communications are sent through the same bundle of cables, there is a chance of **crosstalk**, leakage from one communication to another one in the same cable.

Regardless of the source, noise is a threat to the integrity of a transmission. For human voice communication, there is redundancy in language. Therefore, even if an occasional word or syllable is lost, a sentence is usually understandable. Furthermore, because of the pace of communication and the structure of sentences, one knows when an important word has been lost and can ask the other party to repeat it.

Computer communication travels at a much higher rate than voice communication. A slight pop that affects only part of a syllable in ordinary speech may affect hundreds of bits of a binary transmission. The common carriers that provide communication facilities try to filter out and correct noise that occurs during a communication. In this section we consider the detection and correction of noise in both analog and digital communication.

Noise in Analog Communication

As described previously, an analog signal uses harmonics of a sine wave to approximate underlying digital values. In order to increase the transmission speed, a signal is represented by few harmonics, so that the approximation to the true binary value may not be especially close. A pure binary signal might be approximated by the function shown in Figure 11.9.

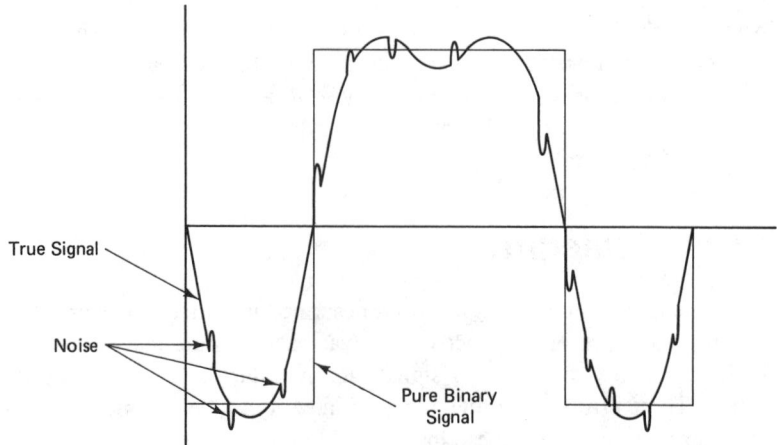

Figure 11.9   Analog Representation of a Digital Signal.

Noise, from whatever source, adds to that signal, so that the peaks and valleys of the signal may become distorted. If a noise factor extends a peak beyond the normal range for the communication, the new peak will be clipped, thereby losing both the noise and the correct signal. Furthermore, a small amount of noise can convert a wave that should represent 0 into one that is recognized as 1.

For analog signals, the problem is exacerbated by repeaters. Over distance, the strength of an analog signal sent by wire fades. As this occurs, the ratio of the signal strength to the strength of the background noise falls. Imagine trying to talk above the noise of heavy construction. When you first start to talk, your voice is strong and can overpower the construction noises. After talking loudly for a while, you become hoarse, and the strength of your voice diminishes relative to the constant noise of the construction. A repeater is like a microphone that is not very sensitive; thus, when your voice is strong, the microphone picks up your voice and amplifies it, to help you project over the noise. As you become hoarse, however, the microphone picks up more of the background noise along with your voice and amplifies both. An analog repeater repeats both noise and intended signals. After having been repeated several times, the noise level mixes with the signal so that it is difficult to separate the two.

Digital Noise

Digital signals are less sensitive to noise. A digital signal is either a 0 or a 1; anything above a certain limit is taken to be a 1, while anything below another limit is a 0. Each repeater is a **signal regenerator**, not an amplifier as used with analog communication. A digital regenerator analyzes the signal, determines whether a particular item is a 0 or a 1, and retransmits a correct version of a 0 or 1. If the voltage level has decayed through resistance, the regenerator constructs a new, strong signal to represent what it has just received. Therefore, while noise is amplified along with the signal in an analog transmission, in a digital transmission the noise is actually filtered out.

11.4 Wiretapping

Recall that the general term *wiretap* means any method of illicitly accessing a communication from its point of origin to its destination. Thus a wiretap can apply to a wire, as the name applies, or to any other device along the communication path. There are two ways to tap a communication. With a physical connection, something is actually attached to the line between the transmission and receiving point. With an inductance connection, no physical connection is necessary.

Physical Connection

A physical wiretap requires actual contact with some part of the communication circuit. This contact may be in the sending or receiving device, along a communications line, or in a component along the path, such as a repeater or even a network host.

Physical security is the first defense against a physical wiretap. Prohibiting outsiders from accessing computing equipment secures many systems. However, very small devices can perform the tap, so that someone who repairs equipment, delivers supplies, or tours the facility may plant a wiretap in a very short time.

Physical security is less effective once a communication leaves a secure area. The computer room may be appropriately guarded, but the communications lines coming into the building may be more readily accessible before they reach the computer room. The lines themselves may be even more vulnerable between the building and the local telephone switching office.

The previous sections have described the security properties of various common carrier media. Using a secure transmission medium limits the success of a wiretap.

Dialup links are likely to be different for each connection, so that this uncertainty of link helps to preserve security. Of course, it is not feasible to change equipment or lines within an installation frequently, just to avoid interception.

Encryption is also an effective control. Although encryption will prevent interpretation of most transmissions, encryption must be coupled with secure key storage and regular key changes to ensure a high degree of secrecy.

Inductive Wiretap

An inductive wiretap does not even require physical contact in order to intercept a communication. Induction uses coils to pick up the radiation shed by a communications line, by a device, or by a communications component.

Encryption is a control in this case as well. The same management principles identified earlier apply here, as well. Shielding to prevent emanations is another control, especially at points where the signal flows must be protected. Devices such as terminals, video displays, printers, and computers must be shielded, as must all the cables and components along the line, such as taps for equipment connections and repeaters. Emanations control will be addressed in Chapter 12 in the discussion of "Tempest" testing.

11.5 Summary of Communications Security

Every communications medium, from wire to fibre to microwave to satellite, can be compromised in some way. Satellite and terrestrial microwave leak more than the others; optical fibre does not leak, but the nonfibre junctions and repeaters can be tapped. Therefore, the communications customer interested in security must choose a medium whose leakage is *small enough* for the application.

Every communications link in a computer network must be assumed to leak data. Communications links within a building can be controlled. However, once communications are turned over to a common carrier, there is no longer any control of medium, routing, multiplexing, or leakage. This lack of control is both good and bad. It is bad in that it is difficult to limit the exposure. It is good in that the unpredictability is equal for the would-be interceptor.

Before trying to intercept a transmission, an intruder must ask three questions:

1. *Is this the weakest link?* If there is an easier way to obtain the same data, the interceptor may try that first.

2. *Do I have the skills to intercept?* Some links are secure enough to inhibit even very skilled interceptors.

3. *Is it worth doing?* Will the value of the data retrieved be worth the cost (time, difficulty) of getting it?

To determine the most vulnerable points of a network, put yourself in the place of an interceptor as you analyze the communications system. Think of easy ways to access data (wastebaskets, bribery, theft), as well as network tapping, and make sure that all are secure. Then make sure that the difficulty to obtain the data far exceeds its value.

11.6 Terms and Concepts

signal
waveform
analog signal
digital signal
discrete signal
wave

baud
cycle
harmonic
voice grade telephone line
bandwidth
capacity of channel
multiplexer
trunk line
dedicated line
switched line
modem
common carrier
communications medium
cable
wire
twisted pair
coaxial (coax) cable
repeater
wiretapping
active wiretap
passive wiretap
inductance
optical fibre
microwave
satellite
wiretap

11.7 Exercises

1. Which communications security issues are important considerations in a local area network environment? Which are important in a conventional ("wide area") network? Which are important for communications strictly within a single building?

2. Is a signal transmitted by digital communication or by analog communication less susceptible to interception? Which is less susceptible to intentional modification? Which is less susceptible to unintentional modification? Why?

3. Is encryption an effective control against passive wiretapping? Against active wiretapping? Why?

4. Identify all points of exposure of a signal between its transmission from New York and its reception in California, assuming satellite communication is used for the major cross-country transmission.

5. Explain how the simple security and $*$—properties of the Bell-LaPadula security model relate to communications security.

6. Design a protocol for communication between two network hosts that guards against communications fabrication by an active wiretap. Your protocol should use encryption to ensure authenticity of each message transmitted.

7. Design a protocol for communication between two network hosts that guards against substitution of a malicious host for a legitimate one. Your protocol should not depend on encryption of each message.

8. Is it secure to transmit communications of different levels of sensitivity (in the sense of multilevel secure operating systems, data bases, or networks) simultaneously on one communications medium? Why or why not?

9. If digital communications facilities are used for a network communication, is there any need for error detection or correction codes in the messages communicated? If so, what is their purpose; if not, why not?

12

Physical Protection—Planning
and Products

In this chapter we cover two related topics—physical security controls and add-on security products. Physical security is the term used to describe protection provided outside the computer system. Typical physical security facilities are guards, locks, and fences to deter direct attacks, although protection against less direct disasters is also a part of physical security. Fortunately, many physical security measures result from just good common sense. As Mark Twain observed, "Common sense is a most uncommon virtue." Thus, this chapter describes some of the obvious aspects of physical security.

Entrepreneurs will develop products to fill any apparent need. We have considered many security vulnerabilities throughout this book. While some of these vulnerabilities can be controlled with procedures or system design, others are inherent weaknesses in certain kinds of computer systems or applications. As described in previous chapters, security features on some systems, especially personal computers, are likely to be rather limited. Therefore, some manufacturers have developed products that can be added to a computing system to enhance its security. The last half of this chapter contains a survey of these devices. This section is not a product endorsement, nor even a comprehensive review of all products to meet a certain need; it is simply an overview of some products that are available today.

12.1 Perils

Most security vulnerabilities described in this book have been exploited by people who broke encryptions, tapped lines, circumvented access controls, and wrote malicious programs. Although people may be the biggest source of security problems for computing systems, people are not the only source. This section contains a catalog of the different physical vulnerabilities to security.

Natural

Computers are subject to the same natural disasters that can occur to homes, stores, and automobiles. They can be flooded, burned, melted, hit by falling objects, and destroyed by earthquakes, storms, and tornados. Additionally, computers are sensitive to their operating environment, so that excessive heat or inadequate power is also a threat. Since many of these perils cannot be prevented or predicted, controls focus on limiting possible damage and recovering from a disaster. Issues to be considered include the cost of replacing equipment, the speed with which equipment can be replaced, the need for available computing power, and the cost or difficulty of replacing data and programs.

Human Vandals

Since computers and their media are rather sensitive, a vandal can do a great amount of destruction rather easily. Human attackers can be people off the street, disgruntled employees, bored operators, saboteurs, people seeking excitement, or unwitting bumblers. Crude attacks using axes or bricks can be very effective, but more subtle attacks can also be quite serious. An unskilled vandal may try the crude attack, but people carrying large or dangerous objects are often seen and stopped. People with only slightly more sophisticated knowledge can short circuit a computer with a car key or disable a disk drive with a paper clip. These implements would not attract attention until the attack has been completed.

Interception

Interception is a serious problem with computing systems. With $300 worth of parts from any local electronics shop, a person can construct a device to read the data from a computer screen several hundred feet away. This attack requires no direct connection. A person needs only a moderate knowledge of electronics for this attack.

Unauthorized Access and Use

Movies and newspaper reports exaggerate the ease of gaining access to a computing system. Still, as distributed computing systems become more prevalent, protecting the system from outside access becomes more difficult and more important. Interception is a form of unauthorized access; in this context, interception is a *passive* attack, but *active* use is also a concern. Protection is needed both to prevent unauthorized users from obtaining access to the system and to verify the identity of accepted users.

The following sections expand on these four vulnerabilities: natural perils, human intrusion, interception, and unauthorized access and use.

12.2 Natural Disasters

It is impossible to prevent natural disasters, but through careful planning it is possible to reduce the damage they inflict. Some measures can be taken to reduce their impact.

Flood

Floods come from two sources: rains, tides, and waves (the natural variety) and disasters such as broken water pipes (the artificial variety). Regardless of type, both can cause serious damage. Controls against floods must consider rising water (such as floods) and falling water (such as leaking roofs).

Rising Water

Water from a natural flood comes from ground level, rising gradually, and bringing with it mud and debris. There is generally time for an orderly shutdown of the computing system, losing at worst some of the processing in progress. The machinery may be destroyed or damaged by mud and water, but most computing systems are insured and replaceable by the manufacturer. Managers of unique or irreplaceable equipment who recognize the added risk sometimes obtain duplicate redundant hardware systems to ensure against disruption of service.

Thus, hardware is replaceable. The real concern is the data and programs stored on magnetic media. Time works in the favor of the computing center, since there is often adequate time to move critical data to higher ground. Typically even in an extensive tape library the lowest tape is several inches above the floor, and disk packs are often stored on shelves between waist and eye level.

Unfortunately, most computing centers do not have an easy way to identify the most important media. In case of a flood, personnel may be available to help with the removal of sensitive media, but these people may not be computer operators or may not have the time to locate the two hundred most important volumes from a media inventory of several thousand volumes. A simple scheme is to mark each volume with a colored label: red for most important, yellow for second, and so on. Volunteers can be told to take every volume with a red label first, then if there is time, to pick up ones with yellow labels, and so forth.

The entire problem of water rising from the floor can be prevented by locating a computing center above ground level. To make it easy to deliver equipment and supplies, a ground level loading dock may be convenient. In some cases, a ground level location may be required; if this is so, placing the building on a slight elevation offers some protection.

Falling Water

The opposite problem is water desending, either from a burst water pipe, from a sprinkler system, or from flood water seeping down to a below-ground computing center. Depending on the source and the volume of the water, there may not be concern with accumulation beyond a few inches at floor level. The major problem is to protect the equipment and media from this unwanted "rainfall."

Here, again, a simple measure can be quite effective. Every computing installation should have available a box or roll of large plastic bags (such as trash bags). Volunteers can quickly wrap important media and cover much equipment to prevent damage. Several rolls of tape are also helpful to seal odd-shaped components.

These same precautions apply to users of personal computers, as well as to managers of major computing centers. A plastic bag or cover should sit next to each personal computer (or workstation or terminal). Usually, however, the machine is far easier to replace than the programs and data. All important removable media should be kept in one closed box for easy rescue.

Fire

Fire is more serious than water, because often there is not as much time to react, and because human lives are more likely to be in immediate danger.

In 1984, a $138 million fire occurred at Tinker Air Base in Oklahoma City. The fire, which destroyed a large facility used to repair jet aircraft, burned for two days. A large computing center was located in an adjacent building. There was less concern over possible spread of fire than over collapse of the burning building.

Several hours were available for a safe shutdown of the system and even for removal of some components of the computing system. There was not time, however, to rescue the entire massive library of tapes. Volunteers were hindered because they could not quickly identify the most important tapes to rescue. A system of colored labels, as described earlier, would have helped in this situation, too.

Every computing center should have a plan for shutting down the system in an orderly manner. Such a process takes only a few minutes but can make recovery much easier. This plan should include individual responsibilities for all personnel, some to halt the system, others to protect crucial media, others to close doors on media cabinets. Provision should be made for persons not present, on account of illness, vacations, and so on.

Water is not a good fire protector for computer rooms. In fact, more destruction has been done by sprinkler systems trying to stop fires in computer rooms than by fires themselves. A fire sensor will activate many sprinklers, dousing an entire room for a fire in a wastebasket. Magnetic media and electronic equipment are sensitive to water and, in many cases, the fire being "doused" was under control so that it was not a threat to the computing equipment. Most computing centers use carbon dioxide extinguishers or an automatic system using a gas that smothers a fire but leaves no residue. Unfortunately, these gas systems displace oxygen, which chokes the fire but also affects humans. When these protection devices are activated, humans must leave, which stops efforts to protect media.

A defense against fire is careful placement of a computing facility. A windowless location with fire-resistant access doors and nonflammable full-height walls can prevent a fire from spreading from adjacent areas to the computing room. With a fire- and smoke-resistant facility, personnel merely shut down the system and leave, perhaps carrying out the most important media.

Fire prevention is quite effective, especially since most computer goods are not especially flammable. Advance planning, reinforced with simulation drills, can help to make good use of the small amount of time available before evacuation is necessary.

Power Loss

Computers need their food—electricity—and they require a constant, pure supply of it. With a direct power loss, all computation ceases immediately. Because of possible damage to media by sudden loss of power, many disk drives monitor the power level and quickly retract the recording head if power fails. For certain time-critical applications, loss of service from the system is intolerable; in these cases alternate complete power supplies must be instantly available.

Uninterruptible Power Supply

One protection against power loss is called an **uninterruptible power supply.** This device stores energy during normal operation so that it can return the backup energy if power fails. One form of uninterruptible power supply uses batteries that are continually charged when the power is on, and so can provide power when electricity fails. However, size, heat, flammability, and low output can be problems with batteries.

Some uninterruptible power supplies use massive wheels that are kept in continuous motion when electricity is available. When the power fails, the inertia in the wheels operates generators to produce more power. Size and limited duration of energy output are problems with this variety of power supply. Both forms of power supplies are intended to provide power for a limited time, just long enough to allow the current state of the computation to be saved so that no computation will be lost.

Surge Suppressor

Still another problem with power is its "cleanness." Although most people are unaware of it, a variation of 10 percent from the stated voltage of a line is considered acceptable, and some power lines vary even more. A particular power line may always be 10 percent high or low.

In many places lights dim momentarily when a large appliance, such as an air conditioner, begins operation. When a large motor starts, it draws an exceptionally large amount of current, which reduces the flow to other devices on the line. When a motor stops, the sudden termination of draw can send a temporary surge along the line. Similarly, lightning strikes may send a momentary large pulse. Instead of being constant, the power delivered along any electric line shows many brief fluctuations, called **drops** and **spikes** or **surges**. A drop is a momentary reduction in voltage, and a spike or surge is a rise. For computing equipment, a drop is less serious than a surge. Most electrical equipment is tolerant of rather large fluctuations of current.

These variations can be destructive to sensitive electronic equipment, however. Simple devices called "surge suppressors" filter spikes from an electric line, blocking fluctuations that would affect computers. These devices cost from $20 to $100 and should be installed on every personal computer, printer, or other connected component. More sensitive models are typically used on larger systems.

As mentioned earlier, a lightning strike can send a surge through a power line. To increase protection, personal computer users unplug the machine when it is not in use and during electrical storms. Another possible source of destruction is lightning striking a telephone line, so that the phone line should be disconnected from the modem during storms. These simple measures may save much work as well as valuable equipment.

Heat

Computing systems are very sensitive to heat, and loss of cooling is rather common due to mechanical failure or electrical disruption. Unfortunately, the only solution for loss of cooling is shutting down the system. Temperature rise is slow; a change of ten degrees in an hour is uncommon, and twenty degrees in two hours is highly unlikely. Therefore, there is usually adequate time to react before serious consequences occur.

Computing systems change gradually from "normal" to "too hot." The environment may exceed the manufacturer's recommended operating temperature with no obvious effect. If the temperature continues to rise, components may perform unpredictably, sometimes working correctly, sometimes working apparently well but producing faulty results, and sometimes showing their failure to cooperate. The most serious state is sometimes correct/sometimes incorrect, since this uncertainty can corrupt the entire system while it seems to continue to function. For this reason, only essential computations should be done in hot conditions, and the results of these computations should be suspect.

12.3 Resumption After a Crisis

The key to successful recovery is adequate preparation. Seldom does a crisis destroy irreplaceable equipment; most computing systems—personal computers to mainframes—are standard, "off the shelf" systems that can be easily replaced. Data and locally developed programs are more vulnerable, since these cannot be quickly substituted from another source. In this section we consider continuing work after a crisis.

Backup

In many computing installations some data items change frequently, while others seldom change. For example, a data base of bank account balances changes daily, while a file of depositors' names and addresses will change much less often. Also the number of changes in a period of time is different for these two files. These variations in number and extent of change relate to the amount of data necessary to reconstruct these files in the event of a loss.

A **backup** is a copy of all or part of a file to assist in reestablishing a lost file. In professional computing systems, periodic backups are performed. Everything on the system is copied, including system files, user files, scratch files, and directories, so that the system can be regenerated after a crisis. This type of backup is called a **complete backup**. It is done at regular times, such as every Monday morning.

Major installations may perform **revolving backups**, in which the last several backups are kept. Each time a backup is done, the oldest backup is replaced. Another form of backup is a **selective backup**, in which only files that have been changed (or created) since the last backup are saved. In this case, fewer files must be saved, so the backup can be done more quickly. A selective backup combined with an earlier complete backup gives the effect of a complete backup in the time needed for only a selective backup.

Associated with performing a backup is saving the means to move from the backup forward to the point of failure. In critical transaction systems this problem is solved by keeping a complete record of changes since the last backup. If a system handles bank teller operations, the individual tellers duplicate their processing on paper records; if the system fails, people can start with the backup version and reapply all changes from the collected paper copies.

Personal computer users often do not appreciate the need for regular backups. Even minor crises, such as a failed piece of hardware, can seriously affect personal computer users. With a backup, users can simply change to a similar machine and continue work.

Off-Site Backup

A backup copy is useless if it is destroyed in the crisis, too. Many major computing installations rent warehouse space some distance from the computing system, in some cases 15 or 20 miles away. As a backup is completed, it is transported to the backup site. Keeping a backup version separate from the system reduces the risk of its loss. Similarly, the paper trail is also stored somewhere other than at the main computing facility.

Personal computer users concerned with integrity can take home a copy of important disks as protection, or send a copy to a friend in another city. If both secrecy and integrity are important, a bank vault, or even a secure storage place in another part of the same building, can be used. The worst place to store a backup copy is where it usually is stored—right next to the machine.

Cold Site

Depending on the nature of the computation, it may be important to be able to recover from a crisis and resume computation quickly. A bank, for example, might be able to tolerate a four-hour loss of computing facilities during a fire, but it could not tolerate a ten-month period to rebuild a destroyed facility, acquire new equipment, and resume operation.

Most computer manufacturers have several spare machines of most models that can be delivered to any location within 24 hours in the event of a real crisis. Sometimes the machine will come straight from assembly, while at other times the system will have been in use at a local office. Machinery is seldom the problem. The question that arises is where to put this equipment in order to begin a temporary operation.

A **cold site** or **shell** is a facility with power and cooling available, where a computing system can be installed to begin immediate operation. Some companies maintain their own cold sites, while other cold sites can be leased from disaster recovery companies. These sites come with raised floors, fire prevention equipment, separate office space, telephone access, and other features. Typically, a computing center can have equipment installed and resume operation from a cold site within a week of a disaster.

Hot Site

If the application is more critical, or if the equipment needs are more specialized, a **hot site** may be more appropriate. A hot site is a computer facility with an installed and ready-to-run computing system. The system has peripherals, telecommunications lines, power supply, and even personnel ready to operate on short notice. Some companies maintain their own, while other companies subscribe to a service that has available one or more locations with installed and running computers. To activate a hot site, it is necessary only to load software and data from offsite backup copies.

As an example, Weyerhauser–Recovery Services offers hot sites equipped with IBM 3083 and 4341, HP 3000, Honeywell DPS 8/70, and Digital VAX systems. They provide diagnostic and system technicians, connected communications lines, and an operations staff. They will also assist with relocation by arranging transportation and housing, by obtaining needed blank forms, and by acquiring office space.

Because these hot sites serve as backups for many customers, most of whom will not need the service, the annual cost to any one customer is fairly low. The cost structure is like insurance: The likelihood of an auto accident is low, so the premium is reasonable, even for a policy that covers the complete replacement cost of an expensive car. Notice, however, that the first step in being able to use a service of this type is a complete and timely backup.

12.4 Intruders

Up to this point "preventing unauthorized access" has meant preventing knowledgeable users from obtaining access to protected objects. Another class of unauthorized access is the physical presence of people who are not even users. With good reason, banks and hospitals exclude total strangers; computing installations should do the same. Unauthorized visitors can cause three problems: theft of machinery or data, destruction of machinery, and viewing sensitive data.

Theft Prevention

It is difficult to steal a major mainframe computer, like a large IBM 308x or 43xx machine or a DEC VAX. Not only is carrying it away difficult, finding a willing buyer and arranging installation and maintenance also require special assistance. However, printed reports or tapes or disks can be carried easily. If done well, the loss may not be detected for some time, or it may initially be blamed on poor organization in the machine room.

Personal computers are designed to be small and portable. Floppy disks and tape backup cartridges are easily carried; in fact the new 3-1/2 inch disk size was chosen to fit in a shirt pocket. Computers and media that are easy to carry are also often easy to conceal.

Three approaches can be taken to prevent thefts: prevent access, prevent portability, or detect exit. The next three sections survey devices that prevent access, portability, and exit.

The oldest access control is a guard. Guards are traditional, well understood, and adequate in many situations. However, guards must be continuously on duty in order to be effective; providing breaks implies at least four guards for a 24-hour operation, with extras for vacation and illness. A guard must personally recognize someone, or recognize an access token, such as a badge. People can lose or forget badges; terminated employees and forged badges are also problems. Unless the guard makes a record of everyone who has entered a facility, there is no way to know who (employee or visitor) has had access in case a problem is discovered.

The second oldest access control is a lock. This device is even easier, cheaper, and simpler to manage than a guard. However, it too provides no record of who has had access, and there are difficulties of lost and duplicated keys. With computer facilities, there is the inconvenience of fumbling for a key when someone's hands are filled with tapes or disks, which might be ruined if dropped. There is also the possibility that one person will walk through the door that someone else has just unlocked. Still, guards and locks provide simple, effective security for access to facilities such as computer rooms.

More exotic access control devices employ cards with radio transmitters, magnetic stripe cards (similar to 24-hour bank cards), and cards with electronic circuitry that makes them difficult to duplicate. Since each of these interfaces with a computer, it is easy to produce a list of who entered and left the facility when and by which routes. Some of these devices operate by proximity, so that a person can carry the device in a pocket or clipped to a collar; the person obtains access even with a handful of things. Also, since these are computer controlled, it is easy to invalidate an access authority when someone quits or reports the access token lost or stolen.

Depending on the application, more or less strict methods of access control can be used. Access control can cooperate with computer authentication to provide a second level of assurance.

Preventing Portability

The simplest way to prevent theft is to lock the room containing a computer. This control is effective but reduces the ease of use for legitimate users. Also, it deters but does not prevent theft by breaking a window or a door lock.

Four ways to restrict portability are weight, glue, chains and locks, and alarms. All of these are used to prevent theft of computer goods.

Weight and glue are less desirable. Some degree of portability of computing devices is necessary. For example, a report glued to a table is useless if someone across the country needs to read the report. Even permanently affixing a personal computer to a table may not be appropriate if the machine needs to be moved for service or to be replaced.

One anti-theft device is a pad connected to cable—similar to those used to secure bicycles. The pad is glued to the desk top with super adhesive. The cables loop around the equipment and are locked in place. Releasing the lock permits the equipment to be moved. An alternative is to couple the base of the equipment to a secure pad, in much the same way that televisions are locked in place in hotel rooms. Yet a third possibility is a large, lockable cabinet in which the personal computer and its peripherals are kept.

Some people argue that cables, pads, and cabinets are unsightly and, worse, they make the equipment inconvenient to use.

Connexus Technologies Corp. uses a fiber optic cable to secure equipment. The cable is secured to each piece of equipment by a loop or with a clamp. A light source sends a beam of light through the cable; if the cable is cut or broken, an alarm sounds. The protection is the continuous cable, so it can be installed in any location, without needing to be fixed to a rigid object such as a desk top.

Detecting Exit

For devices like personal computers, printers, or terminals, it is adequate to prevent someone from carrying away these devices. However, chaining down a disk pack makes it unusable. The other approach to theft is to detect when someone tries to leave a protected area with the protected object. In this case, the protection mechanism should be small and unobtrusive.

One such mechanism is similar to the protection system used by many libraries. Each sensitive object (such as a floppy disk) is marked with a special label. Although the label looks like a normal pressure-sensitive label, it can be detected at the exit door. Similar security code tags are available for vehicles, people, machinery, and documents. Another manufacturer inserts radio transmitters in magnetic tape cartridges and mass storage media. All of these controls are sensed by a detector mounted by the exit from the room. The detector sounds an alarm, and someone must apprehend the person trying to leave with the marked object.

Controlling Human Access

The surest way to present theft is to keep the thief away from the equipment. However, thieves can be either insiders or outsiders. Therefore, access control devices both prevent access by unauthorized individuals and record access by those authorized. A record of accesses can help to identify who committed a theft.

12.5 Disposal of Sensitive Media

When disposing of a draft copy of a confidential report containing a company's sales strategies for the next five years, the company wants to be especially sure the report is not reconstructed. With computers there may be two or more copies of the report: one printed on paper and the others on magnetic media. Even the printer ribbon may disclose which characters were printed. This section considers ways to destroy data on all forms of media.

Shredders

Shredders have been in existence for a long time, as devices used by banks, government agencies, and others who have large amounts of confidential data to dispose of. Most data shredded is on paper. Shredders can also be used for floppy disks, printer ribbons, and some tapes. Shredders convert their input into thin strips or pulp; with enough volume it becomes infeasible for most people to try to piece the appropriate strands back together again. (Some organizations burn the shreds for added protection.)

Overwriting Magnetic Data

As described in Chapter 9, for magnetic disks the ERASE or DELETE command often just changes a directory pointer; the sensitive data is still recorded on the medium, and it can be recovered by simple analysis of the directory. A more secure way to destroy data on magnetic devices is to overwrite the data several times, using a different pattern each time. This process will remove enough magnetic residue to prevent most people from reconstructing the original file. However, a person using highly specialized equipment might be able to identify each separate message, almost like peeling off layers of wallpaper. Furthermore, cleaning a disk this way takes time.

Degaussers

Degaussers destroy magnetic fields. Passing a disk, or any other magnetic medium, through a degausser generates a magnetic flux so forceful that all magnetic charges are instantly realigned, thereby fusing all the separate layers. A degausser is a fast way to cleanse a magnetic medium, although there is still question as to whether it is adequate for use in the most sensitive of applications. (Media that have had the same pattern for a long time, such as a tape that is saved for archive purposes, may retain traces of the original pattern even after it has been overwritten many times or degaussed.) For most users, however, a degausser is a fast way to neutralize a disk or tape, permitting it to be reused by others.

Emanations Protection—Tempest

As noted earlier, computer screens give off emissions that can also be detected from a distance. However, any components, including printers, disk drives, and main processors, can emit information. The U.S. government has a program, called **Tempest**, under which computer equipment is certified as not emitting detectable signals. Basically there are two approaches to preparing a device for Tempest certification: enclosing the device and modifying the emanations.

Enclosure

The obvious solution to preventing emanations is to trap the signals before they can be picked up. Enclosing a device in a conductive case, such as copper, diffuses all the waves by conducting them throughout the case. Copper is a good conductor, and the waves will travel much better through copper than through the air outside the case, so that the emissions are rendered harmless.

This solution works very well with cable, which is then enclosed in a solid, emanation-proof shield. Typically the shielded cable is left exposed so that it is easy to inspect visually for any signs of tapping or other tampering. The shielding must be complete. That is, it does little good to shield a length of cable but not also shield the junction box where that cable is connected to a component. The line to the component and the component itself must be shielded, too.

The shield must enclose the device completely. If top, bottom, and three sides are shielded, emanations are prevented only in those directions. However, a solid copper shield is useless in front of a computer screen. Covering the screen with a fine copper mesh in an intricate pattern carries the emanation safely away. This approach solves the emanation problem while still maintaining the usability of the computer screen (or any other part that must be seen.)

Entire computer rooms can be shielded in copper, so that large computers inside do not leak sensitive emanations. The shielding has to be done carefully, since any puncture is a possible point of emanation. Furthermore, continuous metal pathways, such as water pipes or heating ducts, act as antennas to convey the emanations away from their source. A shielded room is inconvenient, however, since it is impossible to expand the room easily as needs change.

Emanations Modification

Emanations can also be designed in such a way that they cannot be retrieved. This process is similar to generating noise in an attempt to jam or block a radio signal. Using this approach, the emanations of a piece of equipment must be modified by adding spurious signals. Additional processors are added to Tempest equipment specifically to generate signals that will fool any interceptor. The exact Tempest modification methods are classified.

As might be expected, Tempest-enclosed components are larger and heavier than their unprotected counterparts. Tempest testing is a very rigorous testing program of the U.S. Department of Defense. Once a product has been approved, even a minor design change, such as changing from one manufacturer's power supply to an equivalent one from another manufacturer, will invalidate Tempest approval. Therefore, these components are costly, ranging in price from 10 percent to 300 percent more than similar non-Tempest products. They are most appropriate in situations where the data to be confined is of great value, such as top-level government data. Other groups with less dramatic needs can use other less rigorous shielding.

12.6 Port Protection

Dial-in modem ports are a substantial vulnerability in a computer system. Security controls for those vulnerabilities; include dial-back connections, complex authentication schemes handled before connection to the computer, and silent modems. This section includes descriptions of various devices that can be used to protect ports from unauthorized access.

Microframe, Inc. of Cranbury, New Jersey, produces a line of dial-up access control devices. The form of the devices is shown in Figure 12.1. The DataLOCK 4000 product connects both at the host and at the user ends of a connection.

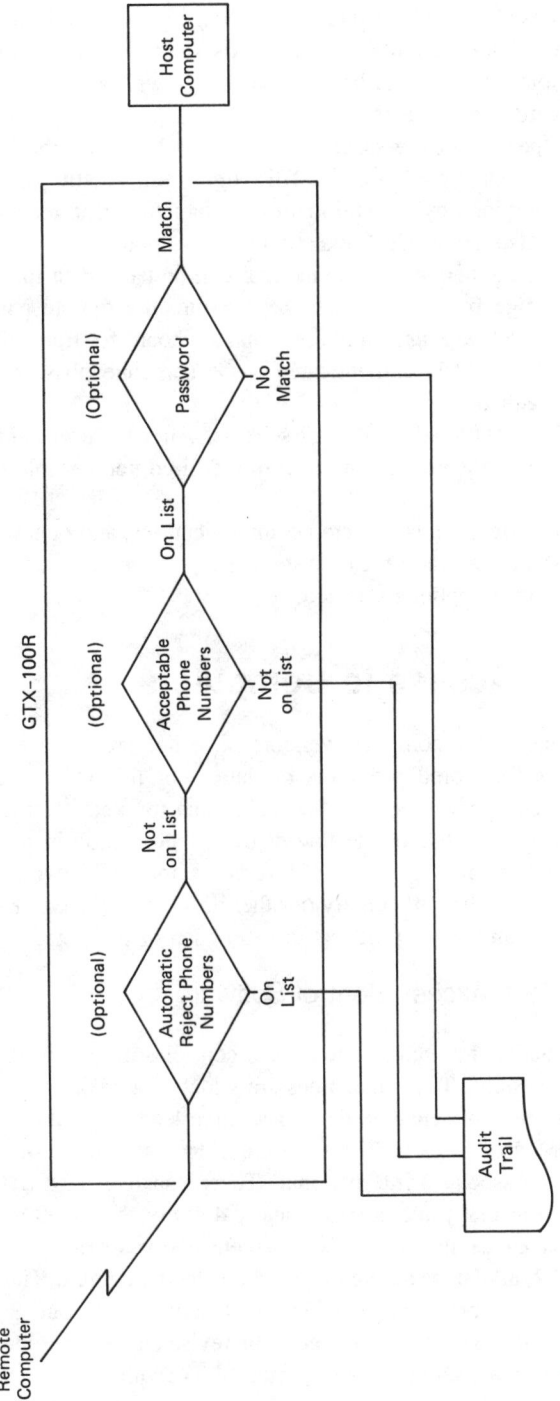

Figure 12.1 Data LOCK4000 Operating Modes.

The host end unit operates in any of four modes. In mode 1, a hardware device operates between the user and the user's modem. This device automatically computes a correct response to a 144-bit random challenge generated by the host station. Correct response to this challenge authenticates the user as operating from an accepted workstation. The remote device is further secured either with a metal key or with a magnetic stripe (credit card–type) reader.

Mode 4 operates in the same way as mode 1, except that after authentication all communication is encrypted with the DES algorithm. Again, further user security at the remote end is provided by a metal key or a magnetic stripe reader.

Mode 3 is also like mode 1, except that the response is computed in an unconnected "remote password generator," a device that can be carried in the user's hand. The user reads the challenge from the screen, keys it into the remote password generator, and enters the computed response on the terminal keyboard for transmission back to the host. In this mode, the user is authenticated to be someone possessing the correct remote password generator device.

Mode 2 is an automatic dial-back scheme. After the user is identified, the unit dials the user back at a predetermined number or a desired number that is on a list of approved numbers.

A complete log of calls, rejected communications, and operator actions is produced. The basic cost of the DataLOCK system, supporting 16 lines, ranges from $3000 to $4000, depending on options selected.

12.7 Control of Access to Computers

Traditionally the major computer vendors have not produced especially secure access control systems for stored programs or data. For this reason, add-on access control packages have been developed for the mainframe market. Microcomputers have access control difficulties because of the low degree of protection in the architecture. Finally, network access control is an entirely different problem: Network hosts need to be continually reassured of the authenticity of other hosts on the network. This section contains descriptions of examples of products to meet each of these needs.

Mainframe Data Access Control Software

The primary market for mainframe access control software is IBM machines with the MVS operating system. These machines are widely used commercially for massive computation and storage of sensitive data. The three leading products for access control are RACF, an IBM product, ACF2, from Cambridge Systems Group, and CA-Top Secret, from Computer Associates International. These packages cost $20,000–$40,000 per installation. Even at that price, approximately 4500 of the 10,000+ IBM installations use one of these packages, up from only 9 percent five years ago.

With ACF2, all data is automatically protected by default. The security administrator determines a security policy and decides which additional resources to protect. The policy is expressed in rules which do not need to be revised as new resources are acquired. New data and resources are automatically protected as acquired.

CA-Top Secret intercepts user sign-on activity to authenticate users. From that point, it limits each user to specific files, programs, access modes, and so forth. It logs attempted violations and can even selectively log authorized activity.

Microcomputer Access Control Hardware/Software

Mainframe computers have two or more modes of operation, so that the operating system can perform functions unavailable to users. Mainframe computers have hardware protected memory regions, so that values stored in certain locations are inaccessible to users. Finally, mainframe computers have I/O control so that users can perform I/O operations only with the intervention of the operating system. Therefore, mainframe computers have the facilities with which to implement access control.

Microcomputer access control software tries to provide the same security as access control systems for mainframe computers. Since microcomputers lack the important hardware advantages available on mainframe architecture, microcomputer access control systems are substantially more vulnerable than systems for mainframes. Although mainframe access control systems have been certified by the National Computer Security Center for nondiscretionary access control, to date no add-on system for a microcomputer has been certified.

The problems that microcomputer access control systems have to solve are:

1. Preventing the user from initiating use of the system other than through the access control system

2. Controlling the user's access to memory locations or other places where sensitive authentication data are stored

3. Restricting the user's I/O activity so that all I/O operations are handled by the control system

4. Preventing the user from circumventing access control by accessing files directly—on a removable medium, by program direct file access, or by network access from another machine

5. Protecting the access log from malicious modification by a user

This is not an easy list of goals to accomplish.

Some vendors offer a software-only access control system, but the safeguards against escaping from the system are generally not secure. Both the Comlok system from Computer Logics Ltd., Kansas City, Missouri, and Cortana by Cortana Systems Corp., Houston, Texas, offer hardware implementations of access control systems. Both authenticate users by means of passwords.

Cortana offers read, write, copy and delete access control for files and groups of files (subdirectories). Individual system commands, such as DELETE, FORMAT, and RECOVER can be restricted. Users can be prevented from accessing the system prompt in order to confine them to one application environment.

Comlok uses DES encryption to protect the access codes and system. This same encryption can be used to protect user files. Comlok can store over a year's worth of audit data.

Stored File Encryptors

Prime Factors, Inc. of Oakland, California, produces a variety of DES encryption programs. These software implementations encrypt files, records, or fields in real-time or batch mode. Versions are available in several programming languages, to run on both mainframes and microcomputers.

RSA Data Security, Inc. of Redwood City, California, produces a system that runs on IBM PCs and compatibles. The system uses the RSA algorithm for file encryption. Because RSA is a public key algorithm, both authentication and secrecy can be obtained with use of this one package. The implementation uses a custom chip to perform the time-consuming exponentiation required for the RSA algorithm. In addition to file security, this system can be used to form digital signatures; several government agencies are investigating use of this scheme to expedite processing of paper documents requiring many levels of approval.

Network Penetration Detectors

The LM 1009 product from Secom General Corp. of Southfield, Michigan, monitors a leased (private) communication line from its origin to the telephone company switching office. That part of the network is a good place to tap in order to intercept a communication, since that line is unique to the user. Once a communication reaches the switching office, it may be multiplexed with other communications or routed along any of numerous paths.

LM 1000 first tests the new line for normal conditions to determine a "fingerprint" for the line. Once the normal electrical pattern is recorded, any charge induced by a tap will alter the inductance of the line, and this will be detected. This technique is effective against active eavesdropping, although it cannot detect passive eavesdropping not connected to the line itself (through emanations collection, for example).

12.8 Authentication Devices

One final type of security device is an authentication process. As described in several chapters, users can be identified based on (a) what things they know (for example, passwords); (b) what objects they possess (for example, tokens); or (c) what characteristics they have (for example, fingerprints). Password security has been discussed at great length in Chapters 6 and 10. Devices for the other two kinds of authentication are considered in this section.

Smart Cards

A **smart card** is a small device, about the size of a credit card, that contains a microprocessor, memory, a limited input and output facility, and a power supply. The microprocessor is preprogrammed for a specific calculation which can be used as an authentication device. For example, the processor may compute an encrypted form of a number unique to the card and the current date and time, $E(\text{ID} + time)$. When used this way, the ID guarantees the authenticity of the card; if the card has not been taken by someone else, the card thus guarantees the authenticity of its owner. The *time value* guards against an interceptor trying to replay a previous authentication message.

Several vendors offer smart card systems. Security Dynamics of Cambridge, Massachusetts, manufactures SecurID, a system that generates a new unique password every 60 seconds. With that design, the card needs no input, so that it is a sealed token about the size of a credit card. Any attempt to investigate its internal design will destroy the card, rendering analysis impossible. The card costs about $50; the controlling logic at the mainframe end costs several thousand dollars.

Challenge-Response Systems

Two kinds of challenge-response systems appear on the market. The first type operates digitally; it functions much the same as a smart card, using a device like a pocket calculator. The user keys in the challenge, the device computes the reponse, and the user reads the response in a display and enters it into the computer keyboard. Such devices typically cost approximately $100.

The second available challenge-response system uses a hand-held reader. An example of this latter design is the product of Gordian Systems from Palo Alto, California. The host computer generates a random pattern of dots that it displays on the user's screen. The user holds the device up to the screen, and the device senses the dot pattern and converts it to a number. Such a pattern and its numeric conversion is shown in Figure 12.2. The device then computes a numeric response for the challenge pattern; from a display screen in the device, the user reads the response and keys it into the keyboard. The cost of the system is approximately $15,000 for the mainframe unit that generates the dot challenge pattern, plus $50–$100 for each reader.

Personal Characteristic Recognition

The third means of authentication is recognition of some personal (physical) characteristic of the user. Personal identification by means of fingerprints is well understood by law enforcement officials. Other biometric recognition systems depend on voice patterns, the blood vessels of the retina, palm prints, and handwriting characteristics.

Biometric devices are just being developed now. They are still classed as experimental so their uses are somewhat limited, and they are expensive. However, they show great promise for authentication, because the authenticating characteristic cannot be lost, stolen, forged, or forgotten.

An example is the EyeDentification System from EyeDentify, Inc. of Beaverton, Oregon. This sytem authenticates users by scanning the retina of the eye. The pattern

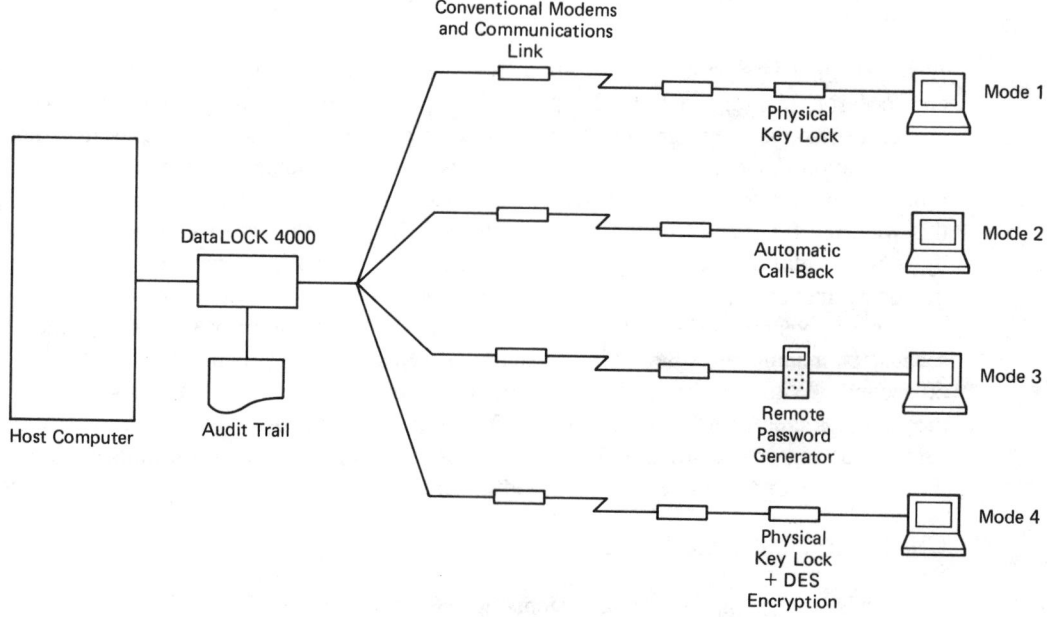

Figure 12.2   Challenge-Response Device.

of blood vessels in the retina is unique to an individual, just as is a fingerprint. A user's eye is scanned by an infrared camera, and a retina feature template is constructed. For subsequent access, the user's eye is scanned again, and the features of this new scan are compared against the old. A scan takes only a few seconds, and the manufacturer claims a false acceptance rate no higher than 0.0001 percent.

AT&T Information Systems is developing a speech recognition system. Each user has a ID number and a unique personal passphrase. The user enrolls in the system by speaking the passphrase several times. The essential features of the utterance are collected, and a template is built of the "average" form. To gain access with the system, the user enters the ID number and repeats the passphrase. If the passphrase matches the template, the authentication is achieved, and the template is modified to include any variations present in the new utterance. In this way, the system continues to learn about the user's speech pattern.

12.9 Personal Computer Copy Protection

Chapter 9 described copy protection for personal computers. Numerous techniques are available for copy protection on PCs. Software-only implementations are vulnerable to copying attacks by programs that duplicate the protection pattern. Hardware systems or hardware/software combinations are more cumbersome to use but are substantially harder to duplicate or circumvent. Several forms of protection were mentioned in that chapter, including a device that plugs into a computer to identify a legitimate user, as well as a method of recording on specially prepared disks. In this section we describe two examples of those systems.

The Iri-Lock protection scheme of I.S. (IRIS) International Software in Winnipeg, Canada, uses a nonduplicatable signature on a specially formatted diskette. The program to be protected is then installed on the diskette; installation involves a proprietary technique to conceal the program. When the program is run, a header first verifies that the signature is still on the disk before executing the program. The scheme works only with executable programs, not with source, text, or data files. The system requires that the original signed disk be in the disk drive in order for the program to run. Thus, there is no security against destruction of the diskette itself.

Rainbow Technologies of Irvine, California, produces the Software Sentinel, a hardware key that is used to unlock a matching software module. The key, which is about the size of a candy bar, plugs into a personal computer parallel port. During execution, the user's program sends periodic queries to the key, which computes and returns a response. Different queries generate different responses, which makes it difficult for anyone to predict the next response. With this device, unlimited backup copies can be made, but each can be run only on a machine with the key plugged into the parallel port. The price of such a module is between $25 and $50.

12.10 Conclusions

In this chapter we have surveyed the current marketplace for security products. Of course, this survey is just a listing of current products; new products are being developed constantly, and old products are being revised. The goal of the chapter has been to provide readers with examples of real products available on the market and to indicate their approximate prices, where those are available.

As you can see, the prices of products range from very low, for some products for PCs, to tens of thousands of dollars for access control mechanisms for mainframe computers. Some of these costs look high, although they may not be unreasonable when one considers the values of the assets they protect. In the next chapter we will use a method for comparing the price of protection to its expected benefit in order to predict its effectiveness.

12.11 Terms and Concepts

natural disasters
flood
fire
power loss
uninterruptible power supply
surge suppressor

heat
backup
revolving backup
selective backup
off-site backup
cold site
shell
hot site
theft prevention
preventing portability
detecting exit
human access control
guard
lock
token
shredder
degausser
Tempest certification
emanation
shield
port protection
callback modem
line encryption
remote password generator
computer access control
data access control
file encryptor
digital signature
smart card
challenge response device
personal characteristic recognition
retina scan
voice recognition
copy protection

13

Risk Analysis and Security Planning

This chapter contains a survey of two aspects of managing computer security: analyzing risks and developing a security plan. The subjects are appropriate both for computing professionals and managers who oversee the use of computers.

Security planning begins with risk analysis. Risk analysis is a process to determine the exposures and their potential harm. First, all exposures of a computing system are listed. Then, for each exposure, possible controls and their costs are listed. The last step of the analysis is a cost-benefit analysis: Does it cost less to implement a control or to accept the expected cost of the loss? This chapter contains a description of the risk analysis method and its strengths and weaknesses.

Risk analysis leads to a security plan which identifies responsibility for certain actions to improve security. The last half of this chapter describes how a security plan is written and what it should contain.

13.1 Risk Analysis

Risk analysis, as its name implies, is a study of the risks of doing something. Buying a lottery ticket is a form of risk, although most people think of it as a minor loss with a (very small) chance of large gain. Crossing streets, driving race cars, eating oysters, all involve some degree of risk. Each person considers the risk and chooses whether or not to do a particular thing.

Some risks are simply part of the cost of doing business—risks that must be taken as a part of normal operation. For example, there is a risk that a new technology will make gasoline-powered automobiles instantly obsolete. Every gas station owner accepts this risk. Similarly, every computer user accepts the risk that a storage device will fail, losing all the user's data.

Controls can reduce the seriousness of a threat. For example, a computer user can perform an independent backup of files as a defense against the possible failure of a file storage device. Large companies involved in extensive computing at many sites cannot easily determine the risks and controls of their computing installations. For this reason an organized approach to analyzing risks is necessary.

Reasons to Perform a Risk Analysis

Some of the benefits of careful analysis of risks are listed here:

- *Improve awareness.* Discussing issues of security can raise the general level of interest and concern among employees.

- *Identify assets, vulnerabilities, and controls.* Some companies are unaware of their computing assets and the vulnerabilities associated with those assets. A systematic analysis produces a comprehensive list of assets and risks.

- *Improve basis for decisions.* Controls reduce productivity through increased overhead and inconvenience to users. Some controls cannot be justified from the perspective of protection they provide. Also, some risks are so serious that they warrant a continuing search for more effective controls. In both of these situations, the seriousness of the risk affects the desirability of controls.

- *Justify expenditures for security.* Some security mechanisms are very expensive and have no obvious benefit. A risk analysis can help to identify instances that are worth the expense of a major security mechanism. It is often useful to identify the much larger risks from *not* spending for security.

Steps in Doing a Risk Analysis

Risk analysis is an orderly process adapted from practices in management. Following are the steps to analyzing the security risks in a computing system. Examples are shown of the kinds of questions asked during a risk analysis. Because any computing system is complex and distinctive, these points must be modified and expanded in an actual risk analysis.

The basic steps of risk analysis are listed here:

1. *Identify assets.*
2. *Determine vulnerabilities.*
3. *Estimate likelihood of exploitation.*
4. *Compute expected annual loss.*
5. *Survey applicable controls and their costs.*
6. *Project annual savings of control.*

These steps are described in the following sections.

Identify Assets

The first step of a risk analysis is to identify the assets of the computing system. The assets can be collected into categories, as in the following. The first three categories are familiar as the assets identified in Chapter 1 and described throughout this book. The remaining items are not strictly a part of a computing system, but are important to its proper functioning.

- *Hardware:* central processors, boards, keyboards, monitors, terminals, microcomputers, workstations, tape drives, printers, disk drives, cables, connections, communications controllers, communications media

- *Software:* source programs, object programs, purchased programs, in-house programs, utility programs, operating systems, systems programs (such as compilers), maintenance diagnostic programs

- *Data:* during execution, stored data, on magnetic media, printed data, archival data, update logs, audit records

- *People:* needed to run the computing system or specific programs

- *Documentation:* on programs, hardware, systems, administrative procedures, the entire system

- *Supplies:* paper, forms, ribbons, magnetic media, printer fluid

A risk analysis starts with a list of all the specific assets of a computing system. In a certain sense, this is an inventory of the system. Although in some computing systems, the inventory of hardware items may be done as an annual accounting exercise, at other places these inventories may be out of date. Furthermore, the annual inventory seldom includes intangibles such as data or human resources.

Identify Vulnerabilities of Assets

Listing the assets of a computing system is relatively easy, since many assets are tangible or easily identified. The next step of risk analysis is to determine the vulnerabilities of those assets. This step requires imagination in order to predict what damage might occur to the assets and from what sources.

The three basic goals of computer security are ensuring secrecy, integrity, and availability. A vulnerability is any situation that could cause loss of one of those three qualities. Possible vulnerabilities can be identified by considering situations that could cause loss of secrecy for a particular object, then loss of integrity, then loss of availability.

A chart, as shown in Table 13.1, can be used to organize the consideration of threats and assets. One vulnerability can affect more than one asset or cause more than one type of loss. The table is a guide to stimulate thinking, but its format is not rigid.

- What are the effects of natural and physical disasters? Consider fires, storms, floods, power outages, component failures.

TABLE 13.1 ASSETS AND VULNERABILITIES.

Asset	Secrecy	Integrity	Availability
Hardware			
Software			
Data			
People			
Documentation			
Supplies			

o What are the effects of outsiders? Consider network access, dial-in access, hackers, people walking through the building, people sifting through the trash.

o What are the effects of willfully malicious insiders? Consider disgruntled employees, bribery, curious browsers.

o What are the effects of unintentional errors? Consider typing the wrong command, typing the wrong data, mounting the wrong data pack, discarding the wrong listing, disposing of output insecurely.

Table 13.2 is a version of the previous table with some of the entries filled in. It gives a general idea of what can occur to the assets of a computing system. In a given installation it is necessary to determine what can happen to specific hardware, software, data items, and other assets.

Predict Likelihood of Occurrence

Step three of a risk analysis is determining how frequently each exposure will be exploited. Likelihood of occurrence relates to the stringency of the existing controls and the probability that someone or something will evade these controls. It may be impossible to predict the likelihood of occurrence of some events. However, there are ways by which to estimate the probability of an event. Here are some of them.

TABLE 13.2 ASSETS AND ATTACKS.

Asset	Secrecy	Integrity	Availability
Hardware		overloaded destroyed (maliciously or unintentionally) tampered with	failed, stolen destroyed unavailable
Software	stolen copied pirated	Trojan horse modified tampered with	deleted misplaced usage expired
Data	disclosed accessed by outsider inferred	damaged –software error –hardware error –user error	deleted misplaced destroyed
People			quit, retired terminated on vacation
Documentation			lost, stolen destroyed
Supplies			lost, stolen damaged

o **From observed data of the general population.** It is impossible to determine when a fire will strike a particular house. Insurance companies have collected massive amounts of data from which they can predict that, in a year, fires will strike n houses, with an average loss of $\$x$. Similar data are available on other natural disasters. Insurance companies also have data from which they can rate the likelihood of employee fraud, armed robbery, and so on. Manufacturers have data on the expected lifetimes of machinery. Professional organizations can also provide some guidance as to the likelihood of occurrence of other events, such as human errors of different sorts.

o **From observed data for a specific system.** Local failure rates are fairly easy to record. Operating systems can track data on hardware failures, failed login attempts, numbers of accesses, and sizes of data files.

o **Estimate of number of occurrences in a given time period.** The analyst is asked to approximate the number of times a described event has occurred in the last year, for example. Although the count is not exact, because the analyst will probably not have full information, the analyst may be able to select some reasonable estimates.

o **Estimate of likelihood from a table.** Several different risk analysis methodologies ask the analyst to estimate the likelihood of occurrence of an event, choosing one of the ranges in Table 13.3. Completing this analysis depends on the professional expertise of the rater. Instead of picking a number with no basis, however, the rater has a framework within which to consider each likelihood.

TABLE 13.3 RATINGS OF LIKELIHOOD.

Frequency	Rating
More than once a day	10
Once a day	9
Once every three days	8
Once a week	7
Once in two weeks	6
Once a month	5
Once every four months	4
Once a year	3
Once every three years	2
Less than once in three years	1

o Delphi approach. The **Delphi approach** is a technique in which several raters individually estimate the probable likelihood of an event. The estimates are collected, reproduced, and distributed to all raters. All raters are then asked if they wish to modify their ratings in light of values their colleagues have supplied. After a round of revisions, all values are collected. If the values are reasonably consistent, the final value is inferred. If the values are inconsistent, the raters meet to discuss the reason for the inconsistency and to select a final value.

Compute Uncovered Cost per Year (Annual Loss Expectancy)

Determining the cost of each incident is the next step in performing a risk analysis. As with likelihood of occurrence, this value is difficult to determine. Some costs, such as the cost to replace a hardware item, are simple to obtain. Even the cost to replace a piece of software can be approximated reasonably well from the initial cost to acquire it (design it, write it, buy it). However, the cost to others of the unavailability of a piece of hardware or software, or the cost of release of a piece of data is substantially harder to measure.

Some data needs to be protected for legal reasons. Personal data, such as police records, tax information, census data, and medical information, are so sensitive that there are criminal penalties for releasing the data to unauthorized persons. Other data is company confidential. Data on a new product, sales results, or certain financial information might give a competitor an advantage. Some financial data, especially adverse data, could seriously affect public confidence in a bank, an insurance company, or a stock broker. It is difficult to determine the cost of release of this data.

If a computing system, a piece of software, or a key person is unavailable, causing a particular computing task to be delayed, there are serious consequences. If a program that prints paychecks is delayed, employees' confidence in the company may be shaken, or some employees may face penalties from not being able to pay their own bills. If customers cannot make transactions because the computer is down, they may choose another company. For some time-critical services, such as life-support systems in a hospital or guidance systems for spacecraft with humans aboard, the costs of failure are infinitely high.

The following questions can lead to an analysis of the ramifications of a computer security failure. The answers to these questions will not produce precise cost figures, but they will help to identify possible tangible and intangible costs.

- What legal obligations are there to preserve the confidentiality or integrity of this data?

- Could release of this data cause a person or an organization harm? Would there be the possibility of legal action?

- Could unauthorized access to this data cause the loss of future business opportunity? Might it give a competitor an unfair advantage? What would be the estimated loss in sales?

- What is the psychological effect of lack of computer service? Embarrassment? Loss of credibility? Loss of business? How many customers would be affected? What is their value as customers?

- What is the value of access to data or programs? Could this computation be deferred? Could this computation be performed elsewhere? How much would have to be paid to a third party to have the computing done elsewhere?

- What is the value to someone else of access to data or programs? How much would a competitor be willing to pay for access?

- What problems would arise from loss of data? Could it be replaced? Could it be reconstructed? With what amount of work?

As mentioned earlier, these are not easy costs to evaluate. Nevertheless, they have to be evaluated in order to perform a thorough analysis of the risks in computing. Furthermore, the vulnerabilities in computer security are often considerably higher than managers expect. Realistic estimates of potential harm can raise concern for computer security and identify areas where attention is especially needed.

The cost of an incident is determined using the foregoing guidelines. That cost is then multiplied by the expected number of such incidents per year, to produce an estimate of the yearly loss (called the Annual Loss Expectancy, or ALE). For example, an event whose expected cost is $10,000 may have an expected frequency of three times per year, while another event whose cost is $1,000,000 may have an expected frequency of only once every five years (.2 times per year). The expected annual loss from the first event is $30,000, while the expected annual loss from the second is $200,000.

Survey New Controls

The computations just completed reflect the current situation. If the expected loss is unacceptably high, new controls must be investigated. For example, if the risk of unauthorized access is too high, access control hardware, software, and procedures need to be evaluated.

One way to identify additional controls is on a per-exposure basis. For example, a risk of data loss could be covered by periodic backups, by redundant data storage, by access controls to prevent unauthorized deletion, by physical security to keep someone from invading the machine room and stealing a disk pack, or by program development standards to limit the effect of programs on the data. The effectiveness of each of these controls is considered.

Another way to find additional controls is to review the material already covered in this book. We have described a number of types of controls, including

- cryptographic controls

- secure protocols

- program development controls

- program execution environment controls

- operating system protection features

- identification

- authentication

- secure operating system design and implementation

- data base access controls

- data base reliability controls

- data base inference controls

- multilevel security controls for data, data bases, and operating systems

- personal computer controls—procedural, physical, hardware, and software

- network access controls

- network integrity controls

- controls on telecommunications media

- physical controls

- physical devices

To identify controls for a particular exposure, it may be helpful to think of all the various aspects of computer security and to select controls to cover the specific exposure.

Project Savings

Finally, it is possible to compute the true cost or savings from implementing a new control. The effective cost is the cost of the control minus any reduction in annual loss expectancy from using the control. Thus, the true cost can even be negative if reduction in risk is greater than the cost of the control.

For example, suppose a department has had trouble with unauthorized access to (use of) the computing system. Although so far outsiders have succeeded only in accessing the system, it is feared that they might intercept or even modify sensitive data on the system. One approach is to install a more secure data access control program (software). Even though the cost of the access control program is high ($25,000), its cost is easily justified when compared to its value, as shown in Table 13.4. Since the entire cost of the package is charged in the first year, even greater benefits are expected for subsequent years.

TABLE 13.4 JUSTIFICATION OF ACCESS CONTROL SOFTWARE

Item	Amount
Risks: disclosure of company confidential data	
computation based on incorrect data	
cost to reconstruct correct data	
$1,000,000 @ 10% likelihood per year	$100,000
Effectiveness of access control software: 60%	−60,000
Cost of access control software	+25,000
Expected annual loss (100,000−60,000+25,000)	$65,000
Savings (100,000−65,000)	$35,000

In the next example, a company uses a common carrier to link to a network for certain computing applications. The company has identified risks of unauthorized access to data and computing facilities through the network. These risks can be eliminated by replacing network access by a machine operated on the company premises. The machine is not owned; a new one would have to be acquired. The economics of this example are not promising, as shown in Table 13.5.

As shown in these two examples, risk analysis can be used to evaluate the true costs of proposed controls and thus serves as an invaluable planning tool. The effectiveness of different controls can be compared on paper. Risk analysis can thus be used repeatedly in order to select an optimum set of controls.

13.2 An Example of Risk Analysis

RISKCALC[R] is a general purpose shell used to perform computer security risk analysis. RISKCALC directs the work of a security analyst and carries out routine computations to produce reports. Security analysts can also use RISKCALC to set up a risk model

TABLE 13.5 COST/BENEFIT ANALYSIS FOR REPLACING NETWORK ACCESS.

Item	Price
Risk: access to unauthorized data and programs	
$100,000 @ 2% likelihood per year	$2,000
unauthorized use of computing facilities	
$10,000 @ 40% likelihood per year	4,000
Expected annual loss	6,000
Effectiveness of network control: 100%	−6,000
Control cost: hardware (50,000 amortized over 5 years)	+10,000
software (20,000 amortized over 5 years)	+4,000
support personnel (each year)	+40,000
Annual cost	54,000
Expected annual loss (6,000−6,000 + 54,000)	54,000
Savings (6,000−54,000)	−48,000

which can then be distributed to other computing installations that fit the model. In this way, managers and users at the installations can complete a risk analysis without having to determine risk categories or set up the model.

The analyst using RISKCALC first develops a model of the risks of a computing environment. This model is set of risk categories and equations relating them. A feature of RISKCALC is that the analyst poses these risks as prose questions; the user then answers these questions to perform the risk analysis. An example of a risk model is shown in Figure 13.1.

As an example, consider as insurance office with a small personal computer. The hardware cost approximately $8000 and it has an expected life of five years. The expected uniform loss is 1/5 or 20 percent of the hardware cost each year. Software came from two sources: Some general packages (word processing, spreadsheet) were purchased, at a total cost of $1000. Also, some software was developed specifically for the office, at a cost of $5000. Since all software is backed up at an off-site location, the risk of loss or damage is figured at only one percent.

Data consists of a list of clients and their insurance amounts. Included with the customer data is personal information—such as income. The office figures there are three primary risks:

1. Loss of data, requiring it to be reentered manually from printouts.

2. Leakage of data to competitors, causing loss of business.

3. Diclosure of sensitive customer personal data, reducing customer confidence and perhaps causing loss of business.

The firm figures that it would require 80 hours for personnel to reenter lost data, at a cost of 80 ∗ $5.50 = $440. If customer data were leaked, the firm estimates that five

```
                        ─── ***    RiskCALC    *** ───
                    PROFILE ANALYSIS CORPORATION
                                                VERSION:    4.0
                        FIG13.RC
                           A              EVALUATION PACKAGE

      VARIABLE                       VALUE                PREVIOUS    %CHG
   1  Hardware Cost                    0                      0         0
   2  H/W Failure Prob.                0                      0         0
   3  Software Cost                    0                      0         0
   4  S/W Loss Prob.                   0                      0         0
   5  TOTAL TANGIBLE LOSS              0                      0         0
   6  Data Recovery Cost               0                      0         0
   7  Data Loss Prob.                  0                      0         0
   8  Data Leakage Loss                0                      0         0
   9  Data Discl. Loss                 0                      0         0
  10  Leak/Discl. Risk                 0                      0         0
  11  INTANGIBLES LOSS                 0                      0         0
  12  TOTAL EXPECTED LOSS              0                      0         0
```

Figure 13.1 Example Risk Model.

percent of its customers would change to a competitor, for a loss of five percent of net revenues, or $10,000. If personal data were disclosed, the firm figures that only two percent of the customers would discontinue their business, but that the customers likely to be offended would account for large sales; thus the expected loss is $6,000. Because the firm practices no backup procedures, the risk of data loss is estimated at 50 percent (one loss event every two years), while the risk of either form of disclosure is estimated at 20 percent. The primary source of disclosure is assumed to be a disgruntled employee.

After the user answers the questions posed, the system computes the annual loss expectation (A.L.E.) for the data as entered. RISKCALC then produces a narrative description, shown in Figure 13.2, of the risk as computed. The system also displays this information on the screen in a tabular format, as shown in the figure.

13.3 Insurance Office Risk Analysis

A significant advantage of using this package is the ability to enter "what if" scenarios. In these cases the user enters new values for significant variables and observes the effect of several changes to the data initially entered. Figure 13.3 depicts the effect of several changes to the data initially entered.

Based on the data you supplied, hardware has a replacement cost of $8,000 and a loss risk of 20 percent, and software has a replacement cost of $6,000 and a loss risk of 1 percent, for an expected annual loss of tangible assets of $1,660.

Lost data was estimated to cost $440 to replace, with a 50 percent likelihood of loss. The loss of business due to leakage of company confidential data was estimated at $10,000 and loss due to disclosure of private data was estimated at $6,000. The sources of these two losses are similar, and the likelihood of loss is estimated to be 20 percent.

```
 ―――――  ***   RiskCALC   ***  ―――――
              PROFILE ANALYSIS CORPORATION

                                    VERSION:    4.0

                    FIG13.RC

                     A          EVALUATION PACKAGE
```

	VARIABLE	VALUE	PREVIOUS	%CHG
1	Hardware Cost	8,000	0	HUGE
2	H/W Failure Prob.	20	0	HUGE
3	Software Cost	6,000	0	HUGE
4	S/W Loss Prob.	1	0	HUGE
5	TOTAL TANGIBLE LOSS	1,660	0	HUGE
6	Data Recovery Cost	440	0	HUGE
7	Data Loss Prob.	50	0	HUGE
8	Data Leakage Loss	10,000	0	HUGE
9	Data Discl. Loss	6,000	0	HUGE
10	Leak/Discl. Risk	20	0	HUGE
11	INTANGIBLES LOSS	3,420	0	HUGE
12	TOTAL EXPECTED LOSS	5,080	0	HUGE

Figure 13.2 Example of Computed Risk.

```
 ―――――  ***   RiskCALC   ***  ―――――
              PROFILE ANALYSIS CORPORATION

                                    VERSION:    4.0

                    FIG13.RC

                     A          EVALUATION PACKAGE
```

	VARIABLE	VALUE	PREVIOUS	%CHG
1	Hardware Cost	8,000	8,000	0
2	H/W Failure Prob.	20	20	0
3	Software Cost	6,000	6,000	0
4	S/W Loss Prob.	1	1	0
5	TOTAL TANGIBLE LOSS	1,660	1,660	0
6	Data Recovery Cost	440	440	0
7	Data Loss Prob.	10	50	-80
8	Data Leakage Loss	10,000	10,000	0
9	Data Discl. Loss	6,000	6,000	0
10	Leak/Discl. Risk	5	20	-75
11	INTANGIBLES LOSS	844	3,420	-75
12	TOTAL EXPECTED LOSS	2,504	5,080	-51

Figure 13.3 Example Revised Risk.

Total annual intangible losses are estimated to be $3,420.

The total annual loss expectancy (ALE) for this model is $5,080.

For example, the effect of careful hiring practices and activities to improve morale could reduce the risk of disclosure from 20 to 5 percent. The effect on the expected annual loss is shown. Weekly backup could reduce the risk of loss of data to 10 percent.

Since the system shows both old values and new, the user can monitor changes. This mode is not intended to dictate necessary or desired changes to the user. However, it allows the user to monitor the effect of possible changes and to see what changes have the greatest effect on expected loss.

Arguments Against Risk Analysis

Risk analysis is a well-known planning tool used by auditors, accountants, and managers. In spite of its common usage, there are arguments against its use. The arguments against risk analysis and their defenses are presented in the next sections.

Not Precise

The lack of precision of risk analysis is often cited as a deficiency. The values used in the method—the likelihood of occurrence and the cost per occurrence—are necessarily imprecise. Yet there are several different techniques for deriving reasonable approximations of these values.

The precision of the numbers is a red herring. Risk analysis is best used as a planning tool. One may not be able to differentiate between a loss that is expected once a year and one expected once in three years. Nevertheless, it is possible to distinguish that degree of risk from vulnerabilities expected to occur once every week. When risk analysis is used as a planning tool, it shows which security expenditures are likely to be most cost effective. This basis is important for deciding between controls when money available for security is limited.

False Sense of Precision

Another argument is that providing numbers yields a false sense of precision or security. Again, the numbers themselves are much less important that their relative sizes. Whether an expected loss is $100,000 or $150,000 is relatively unimportant. It is much more significant that the expected loss is far above the $10,000–20,000 category. A large potential loss deserves analysis for some control. Placing too much importance on the numbers is the fault of the user, not of the method.

Immutability

Risk analyses, like contingency plans and five-year plans, have a tendency to be filed and promptly forgotten. Ideally, the risk analysis should be updated annually. There is, however, a temptation to accept the figures of the previous year rather than analyze and justify them annually.

An important step in the annual review is considering what conditions have changed over the past year. What has significantly changed the likelihood of occurrence or the severity of a threat? It is important not to be too dependent on the old plan, but to use each review as an opportunity to rethink, and perhaps correct prior estimates based on recent experience. In this way, the values of the plan become more precise each time the analysis is done.

No Scientific Foundation

A final argument is that risk analysis does not depend on scientific theories and principles. This is not true. Risk analysis very much depends on principles of probability theory and statistical analysis.

Summary of Benefits of Risk Analysis

The previous discussion is not intended to glorify risk analysis as a precise, all-purpose planning tool. The results risk analysis provides are no more precise than the figures on which it operates, which are often mere guesses. Still, there are several benefits of a risk analysis, as already outlined. The list is repeated here for reference.

- *Improve awareness*

- *Identify assets, vulnerabilities, and controls*

- *Provide basis for decisions*

- *Justify expenditures for security*

A risk analysis forces a systematic study of the exposures in a computing system. As shown in the examples presented earlier, an expected loss often justifies spending the amount required for security. Sometimes it is necessary to decide between two controls or, because of limited funds, to invest in controls for only one vulnerability. A high-quality risk assessment can provide the basis for making these decisions. A risk analysis done with computer support can also be an excellent planning tool by allowing the user to work through several "what if" scenarios and by simulating the effects of instituting various controls. As such, it can allow the user to choose the most effective controls at the least cost. The discussion generated during risk analysis will improve general awareness of the need for security measures. A risk analysis is part of a general security plan, described in the next section.

13.4 Security Plan

A **security plan** is a document that describes how a company will address its security needs. The plan is subject to periodic review and revision as the security needs of the organization change. In this section we study how to define and implement a security plan. Three aspects of writing a security plan are described: what the plan should contain, who writes the plan, and how to acquire support for the plan.

Reasons for Creating a Security Plan

A security plan identifies and organizes the security activities for a computing system. The plan is both a description of the current situation and a plan for change. Every security plan must address six issues.

- *Policy:* A statement indicating the goals of a computer security effort and the willingness of personnel to work to achieve those goals

- *Current state:* A description of the status of security at the time of the plan

- *Recommendations:* Steps that will lead to meeting the security goals identified previously

- *Accountability:* A listing describing who is responsible for each security activity

- *Timetable:* A record identifying when different security functions are to be done

- *Continuing attention:* A statement specifying a structure for periodic review and revision of the security plan

A good security plan is an official documentation of current security practices, as well as a proposal for orderly change to improve those practices. A plan can thus be used later to measure the effect of any changes and to suggest further improvements. The impact of a security plan is important, too. A carefully written plan, supported by management officials, notifies employees that security is important to management (and therefore to everyone). Thus, both the content and the effect of the plan are important.

Content of a Security Plan

Every security plan contains the same basic material. The following sections describe the content of a security plan.

Policy

A security plan states a policy on security, which is one of the most difficult sections to write well. The policy statement should specify

- the organization's goals regarding security (for example, protect data from leakage to outsiders, protect against loss of data due to physical disaster, protect the integrity of data)

- where the responsibility for security lies (for example, with a small computer security group, with each employee, with relevant managers)

- the organization's commitment to security (for example, dollar expenditures, personnel assigned to task).

The more precise the policy statement, the easier it will be to interpret and implement.

Current Security Status

A risk analysis can form the basis of a description of the current status of security. The status includes a listing of the assets of the organization, the security threats to those assets, and the controls in place to protect those assets.

The plan should specify how data was gathered, how valuations were made, and what assumptions were made. As described earlier, a hard part of performing a risk analysis is valuing the assets and assessing the likelihood of security failure. In some cases, these figures are based on actual data, such as the cost to acquire hardware and software, or the wages of persons involved in reconstructing lost data. In other cases, the estimate is derived from a table of ranges of values. Since these two approaches affect the precision of the results, their use is described in the analysis of the current situation.

Finally, the plan should present a procedure for addressing a vulnerability that has not been considered. These vulnerabilities can arise from new equipment, new data, and new situations, or even from the oversights of security planners. Someone who identifies a new vulnerability should be instructed in how to integrate that vulnerability into the existing security procedures.

Recommendations

A comprehensive risk analysis identifies the exposures of greatest potential loss (raw cost, not modified by likelihood), the exposures of greatest expected loss, the controls that provide greatest total payoff, and the controls that provide greatest payoff per dollar invested. These four results are useful in deciding which areas require controls and in justifying allocation of funds for different security needs.

After identifying the areas of greatest risk and greatest potential savings, the security report should recommend controls. These controls should be listed in order of desirability, with the most desirable (covering greatest exposure or providing the greatest payback in investment) first. The projected savings and the feasibility of the recommended controls are also listed.

Some risks are too great or too diverse to cover, or the price of control is too high, or the risks are judged insignificant and not worth covering. In cases such as these, a conscious decision may be to leave a vulnerability uncovered. The security plan should identify these uncovered risks and explain why they are not covered. The plan should also describe what recovery actions should be taken in the event of exploitation of one of these risks.

Responsibility for Implementation

A section of the report should identify specific people responsible for the implementation. In this way, personnel understand their roles, and individuals who share responsibility know with whom they must coordinate. Furthermore, this section becomes a plan of accountability so that the responsible people can later be judged on the results they have achieved.

Some examples of groups with responsibilities for computer security are listed below.

o *Personal computer users* may each be responsible for their own machines, or a coordinator of personal computer security may be appropriate.

o *Data base administrators* may be responsible for the access to and integrity of data in their data bases.

o *Information officers* are being named in some organizations to oversee the creation and use of data; these officers may be responsible for retention and proper disposal of data.

o *Personnel staff members* may be responsible for security involving employees, such as screening potential employees for trustworthiness and arranging training programs for employees.

Timetable

If the controls are expensive or complicated, they may be acquired and implemented gradually. Similarly, procedural controls may require training of the staff or education to ensure that everyone understands and accepts the reason for the control. The plan should specify the order in which the controls are to be implemented, so that the most serious exposures are covered as soon as possible. A timetable also gives milestones by which the progress of the security program can be judged.

Continuing Attention

An important part of the timetable is establishing a date for evaluation and review of the security situation. As users, data, and equipment change, new exposures develop, and old means of control become obsolete or ineffective. Periodically the inventory of objects and the list of controls should be updated, and the risk analysis should be reviewed. The security plan should set a time for this periodic review.

The preceding six sections have outlined the major issues to be addressed in a security plan. The next two sections describe who should write this plan, and how support for the plan can be obtained.

Members of the Security Planning Team

Who performs the security analysis and recommends a security program? As with any large function, it will probably be done by a committee. The size of the committee depends on the size and complexity of the computing organization and the degree of commitment to security. From organizational behavior studies, the optimum size for a working committee is five to nine members. A larger committee may serve primarily as an oversight body to review and comment on the output of a working committee. A large committee might designate subcommittees to obtain the information for various sections of the plan.

A security planning team should represent each of the following groups. In some cases a group may be adequately represented by someone who is consulted at appropriate times, instead of having a committee member from each possible constituency.

The membership of a computer security planning team relates to the different aspects of computer security described in this book. Encryption, protocols, and security in operating systems and networks require the cooperation of the systems programming staff. Program security measures can be understood and recommended by applications programmers. Physical security controls are implemented by those responsibile for general physical security, both against human attacks and natural disasters. Finally, since controls will affect system users, the plan should encompass users' views of usability and desirability of controls. People from the following groups should be considered for assistance with security planning.

> computer hardware group
> systems programmers
> applications programmers
> data entry personnel
> physical security personnel
> representative users

Securing Commitment to a Security Plan

After the plan is written, it must be accepted and its recommendations carried out. Acceptance is a function of sensibility, understanding, and management commitment.

Education and publicity can help people to understand and accept a security plan. Remember the true case of the employee who went through 24 password changes at a time to get back to a favorite password; this particular system prevented use of any of the 23 most recently used passwords. Clearly the employee either did not understand or did not agree with the reason for restrictions on passwords. If people understand the need for controls and accept the recommended controls as sensible, they will use the controls. If people think the controls are bothersome, they will work to avoid them.

The other key to success is management commitment. Management commitment is obtained through understanding (knowing the cause and the potential effects of lack of security), cost effectiveness, and presentation of the plan.

Some managers do not understand computing and the special risks associated with it. Education that avoids technical jargon can help management to appreciate security in computing. Outside experts are often called in to justify to management the recommendations of a security plan.

Management is often reticent to allocate funds for controls until the value of those controls is explained. That is why risk analysis is such an excellent tool for communicating the benefits of implementing controls. Descriptions of vulnerabilities related to ordinary business activities (such as leakage of data to a competitor or an outsider) may help managers to understand the need for controls.

Finally, a well-organized, concise report that includes a plan of implementation is likely to be accepted. The sections establishing accountability, time for accomplishment, and continuing reevaluation are especially important.

13.5 Summary of Security Planning

This chapter has focused on two points: performing a risk analysis and developing a security plan. The risk analysis involves four primary steps: (1) identify assets, (2) determine exposures, (3) consider controls, and (4) compute benefits of implementing controls. Risk analysis highlights the weak spots in the security of a computing system and demonstrates where attention to security will have the biggest effect (that is, the most dramatic loss reduction).

A security plan includes six components: (1) statement of policy and goals, (2) description of the current situation, (3) analysis of risks and recommendations regarding controls, (4) list of persons responsible for implementing different aspects of the security mechanism, (5) timetable for implementation, and (6) plan for continuing review of security needs. A security plan is usually developed by a committee, including people from a computing group and appropriate users. The plan can be used to spearhead major computer security initiative in an organization and to secure the support of management.

13.6 Terms and Concepts

risk analysis
user awareness
inventory of assets
justification for security expenditures
identification of assets
classes of assets: hardware, software, data, people, documentation, supplies
classes of attacks: interrupt, intercept, fabricate, modify;
    secrecy, integrity, availability
exposures
natural disasters
outsiders
malicious insiders
unintentional errors
likelihood of occurrence
observed probability
estimated number of occurrences
estimated likelihood from table
Delphi approach
uncontrolled exposure
annual loss exposure
new controls: type, cost, effectiveness
cost/benefit analysis
security plan
priorities
accountability
timetable

review cycle
security policy
security team
management commitment

13.7 Bibliographic Notes

A basic work on risk analysis is the IBM-NBS report, which became FIPS PUB 65 [NBS79]. This technique is explained more fully by Parker [PAR81], Bequai [BEQ83], and Hoffman [HOF86]. A paper that provides a variation on the approach is by Miguel [MIG84].

14

Legal Issues in Computer Security

Not always do things resolve themselves pleasantly. Some people are going to think that they have been treated unfairly, and some people act unfairly. A current reaction to redress wrongs is to go to court. Typically people ask, "Isn't it illegal for them to treat me this way? Can't I get the police to arrest them? I'll sue!" The courts are seen as the ultimate arbiters and enforcers of fairness. As most lawyers will tell you, the courts' definition of *fair* may not coincide with yours. Even if you could be sure the courts would side with you, a legal battle is slow, costly, and emotionally draining. Our purpose in this chapter is to understand the legal system as it relates to computer security.

Law and computer security are related in several ways. First, both federal and state laws affect privacy and secrecy. These statutes often apply to the rights of individuals to keep personal matters private. Second, laws regulate the use, development, and ownership of data and programs. Patents, copyrights, and trade secrets are legal devices to protect the rights of developers and owners of programs and data. An aspect of computer security is controlling access to programs and data; that access control is supported by various legal mechanisms. Third, laws affect actions that can be taken to protect the secrecy, integrity, and availability of computer information and service. These basic concerns in computer security are both strengthened and confined by applicable laws. Thus, legal means coordinate with other controls to establish computer security.

However, as the introduction noted, the law does not always provide an adequate control, either in computer affairs or in any other area. The law is slowly evolving with regard to computers. Because computers are new, compared to houses or land or horses or money, their place in the law is not yet firmly established. As statutes are written and cases are decided, computers are becoming more defined in the law. However, laws do not yet cover all improper acts committed with computers. Finally, judges, lawyers, and police officers often do not understand computing, so that they cannot determine how computing relates to other more established parts of the law.

The laws of computer security affect programmers, designers, users, and maintainers of computing systems and computerized data banks. These laws provide protection, but they also regulate the behavior of people who use computers. Furthermore, computer professionals are among the best qualified to advocate changes in old laws and the creation of new ones regarding computers. Before recommending change, however, professionals must understand current legal practices with regard to computers. Therefore, we have three major goals in studying this chapter:

1. To know what protection the law provides for computers and data

2. To appreciate laws that protect the rights of others with respect to computers, programs, and data

3. To understand existing laws as a basis for recommending new laws to protect computers, data, and people

This chapter addresses the following aspects of computer security:

1. *Protection of code and data.* Copyrights, patents, and trade secrets are all forms of legal protection that can be applied to programs and sometimes to data. However, it is important to understand both the fundamental differences between the kinds of protection these three provide and how to obtain that protection.

2. *Protection of access to programs.* The law protects both programmers and people who employ programmers. Generally, programmers have only limited legal rights to access programs they have written while employed. This chapter contains a survey of the rights of employees and employers regarding programs written for pay.

3. *Protection of computing systems against criminals.* Computer criminals violate the principles of secrecy, integrity, and availability for computer systems. It is better to prevent the violation than to prosecute it after the fact. However, if other controls fail, legal action is necessary. In this chapter we study several representative laws in order to determine what acts are punishable under the law.

4. *Protection of private data about individuals.* Finally, we consider the rights of privacy. The private affairs of every individual are protected by laws. Computer security systems must be adequate to prevent unauthorized disclosure of sensitive data about individuals. The chapter concludes with a description of sensitive data that must be protected.

As a body of knowledge, computer law is very complex and subject to frequent changes. This chapter analyzes the current legal situation from the viewpoint of a layperson, not a lawyer. A lawyer who understands and specializes in computer law should be consulted in order to apply the material of this chapter to any specific case. And, as most lawyers will advise, it is far easier to acquire legal protection by doing things correctly from the beginning than to hire a lawyer to sort out a web of conflict after things have gone wrong.

14.1 Protecting Programs and Data

Shari has written a computer program to play a video game. She invited some friends over to play the game and gave them copies to play at home. Chuck took a copy and rewrote parts to improve the quality of the screen display. After Chuck shared the changes with her, Shari incorporated them into her program. Shari's friends now convince her that the program is good enough to sell, so she wants to advertise and offer the game for sale by mail.

Shari wants to know what legal protection she can apply to protect her software. Copyright, patent, and trade secret are all legal devices that protect computers, programs, and data. However, in some cases, precise steps must be taken to protect the work before anyone else is allowed access to it. We explain how each of these forms was originally designed to be used, and what is its current use in computing.

Copyrights

Copyrights are designed to protect the *expression of ideas*. Thus, a copyright applies to a creative work, such as a story, photograph, song, or pencil sketch. The right to copy an expression of an idea is protected by a copyright. Ideas themselves, the law alleges, are free; anyone with a bright mind can think up anything anyone else can, at least in theory. The intention of a copyright is to allow regular and free exchange of ideas.

The author of a book translates ideas into words on paper. This paper, the *expression* of those ideas, is the author's livelihood. That is, an author hopes to earn a living by presenting ideas in such an appealing manner that others will pay to have them. The law protects an individual's right to earn a living, while recognizing that exchange of ideas is the route to the intellectual growth of society. The copyright says that a particular way of expressing an idea belongs to the author. Copyright gives the author the *exclusive* right to make copies of the expression and sell them to the public. That is, only the author can sell copies of the author's book (except, of course, for booksellers or others working as the agents of the author).

Definition of Intellectual Property

A copyright can be registered for "... original works of authorship fixed in any tangible medium of expression, ... from which they can be perceived, reproduced, or otherwise communicated, either directly or with the aid of a machine or device" [USC78]. Again, the copyright does *not* cover the idea being expressed. "... In no case does copyright protection for an original work of authorship extend to any idea..." The copyright must apply to an *original* work, and it must be in some *tangible* medium of expression.

Only the originator of the expression is entitled to copyright; if an expression has no determinable originator, then copyright cannot be granted. Certain works are considered to be "in the public domain," owned by the public, by no one in particular. Works of the U.S. government are considered to be in the public domain and, therefore, not subject to copyright. Works generally known, such as the phrase "have a good day," or the joke about the travelling salesman who..., or the song "Happy Birthday to You," or a recipe for tuna noodle casserole, are also so widely known that it would be very difficult for someone to trace originality and claim a copyright. Finally, copyright lasts for only a limited period of time, so certain very old works, such as the plays of Shakespeare, are in the public domain, their possibility of copyright having expired.

The copyrighted expression must also be in some tangible medium. A story or art work must be written, printed, recorded (on a record), stored on a magnetic medium, or made concrete in some other way. Furthermore, the purpose of the copyright is to promote distribution of the work; therefore, the work must be distributed, even if a fee is charged for a copy.

Originality of Work

The work being copyrighted must be original to the author. As noted earlier, some expressions are general public knowledge and not subject to copyright. These generally known works are said to be in the **public domain**. A work can be copyrighted even if it contains some public domain material. The author does not even have to identify what is public and what is original.

For example, a music historian could copyright a collection of folksongs even if some are in the public domain. In order to be subject to copyright, something in or about the collection would have to be original. The historian might argue that collecting the songs, selecting which ones to include, and putting them in order was the original part. In this case, the copyright law would not protect the folksongs themselves (which would be in the public domain), but it would protect that specific collection. Someone selling a sheet of paper upon which one of the songs was written would likely not be found to have infringed on the copyright of the historian.

Fair Use of Material

The copyright law indicates that the copyrighted object is subject to "fair use." Specifically, the law allows "...fair use of a copyrighted work, including such use by reproduction in copies, ... for purposes such as criticism, comment, news reporting, teaching (including multiple copies for classroom use), scholarship or research..." The purpose of the use, and the effect of the use upon the potential market for or value of the work, affect the decision of what constitutes a fair use. The copyright law usually upholds the author's right to a fair return for the work, while encouraging others to use the underlying ideas.

Requirements for Registering a Copyright

The copyright is easy to obtain, and mistakes in securing a copyright can be corrected. The first step of registration is notice. Any potential user must be made aware that the work is copyrighted. Each copy must be marked with the copyright symbol ©, the word "Copyright", the year, and the author's name. This used to be followed by "All rights reserved" to preserve the copyright in certain South American countries. Adding the phrase now is unnecessary but harmless.

The order of the elements can be changed, and either © or "Copyright" can be omitted (but not both). Each copy distributed must be so marked, although the law will forgive failure to mark copies if a reasonable attempt is made to recall and mark any ones distributed without a mark.

The copyright must also be officially filed. A form is completed and submitted to the U.S. Copyright Office, along with a nominal fee and a copy of the work. Actually, the copyright office requires only the first 25 and the last 25 pages of the work, in order to help it justify a claim in the event of a court case. The filing must be done within three months after the first distribution of the work. The law allows filing up to five years late, but no infringements before the time of filing can be prosecuted.

A copyright now lasts for 50 years beyond the death of its author or last living coauthor, or a total of 75 years if it is considered a work done for hire (see the section "Work for Hire" later in this chapter.) These times are probably long enough for adequate protection of any computer works, which decrease in usefulness after only a few years.

Copyright Infringement

The holder of a copyright must go to court to prove that someone has infringed on the copyright. The infringement must be substantial, and it must be copying, not independent work. In theory, two people might write identically the same song independently, neither knowing the other. These two people would *both* be entitled to copyright protection for their work. Neither would have infringed on the other, and both would have the right to distribute their work for a fee. Again, copyright makes the most sense for works of fiction, since it is extremely unlikely that two people would express an idea with the same or similar wording.

The independence of nonfiction works is not nearly so clear. Consider, for example, an arithmetic book. Long division can only be explained in so many ways, so two independent books could use similar wording for that explanation. The number of possible alternative examples is limited, so that two authors might independently choose the same simple example. However, it is far less likely that two arithmetic textbooks would have the same pattern of presentation and the same examples from beginning to end.

Copyrights for Computer Works

The original copyright law envisioned protection for things such as books, songs, and photographs. It is fairly easy to detect when these items are copied. The separation between public domain and creativity is fairly clear. And the distinction between an idea (feeling, emotion) and its expression is pretty obvious. With works of nonfiction, there is understandably less leeway for independent expression. With computer programs, because of programming language constraints and speed and size efficiency, there is even less leeway.

Can a computer program be copyrighted? Yes. The 1976 copyright law was amended in 1980 to include an explicit definition of computer software. However, copyright protection may not be an especially desirable form of protection for computer works. To see why, consider the algorithm behind a program. The algorithm is the idea, and the statements of the programming language are the expression of that idea. Therefore, protection is allowed for the program statements themselves, but not for the design. The area of copyright protection applied to computer works is still new and subject to much interpretation by the courts. Therefore, it is not certain what aspects of a computer work are subject to copyright. One interesting case in the courts now is an argument that the design of a program's screen display and user interface are subject to copyright.

A second problem with copyright protection for computer works is the requirement that the work be published. A program may be published by distributing copies of its object code, for example, on a disk. However, if the source code is not distributed, it has not been published. An alleged infringer cannot have violated a copyright on source code if the source code was never published.

Copyright protection does not limit the kind of use of a work, only the distribution of copies. This restriction has an important implication for computer works. Suppose a single host on a network legally acquires a copy of a piece of software. That host can then allow any network user to access the software—so long as a new copy is not created—without infringing. A copyright controls the right to copy and distribute; it is not clear that allowing "distributed access" is a form of distribution.

Therefore, although copyright protection can be applied to computer works, the application of copyright law to software is still not clear. Moreover, copyrights do not address all the critical elements that require protection. For example, a programmer might want to protect an algorithm, not the way that algorithm was expressed in a particular programming language. Unfortunately, it may be very difficult to obtain copyright protection for an algorithm, at least as copyright law is currently interpreted.

Patents

Patents are unlike copyrights in that they protect inventions, not works of the mind. The distinction between patents and copyrights is that patents apply to the results of science, technology, and engineering, while copyrights cover works in the arts, literature, and writing. A patent can protect a "new and useful process, machine, manufacture, or composition of matter." The law excludes "newly discovered laws of nature ... [and] mental processes." Thus "$2 + 2 = 4$" is not a proper subject for a patent, since it is a law of nature. Similarly, that expression is in the public domain and would thus be unsuitable for a copyright. A patent is designed to protect the *device or process* for carrying out an idea, not the *idea* itself.

Requirement of Novelty

If two composers happen to compose the same song independently at different times, copyright law would allow both of them to have copyright. If two inventors devise the same invention, the patent goes to the person who invented it first, regardless of who filed the patent first. A patent can be valid only for something that is truly novel or unique.

An object patented must also be "nonobvious." If an invention would be obvious to a person ordinarily skilled in the field it cannot be patented. The law states that a patent *cannot* be obtained ". . . if the differences between the subject matter sought to be patented and the prior art are such that the subject matter as a whole would have been obvious at the time the invention was made to a person having ordinary skill in the art to which said subject matter pertains." For example, a piece of cardboard to be used as a bookmark would not be a likely candidate for a patent, since the idea of a piece of cardboard would be obvious to almost any reader.

Procedure for Registering a Patent

A copyright is registered by filing a form, marking a copyright notice on the creative work, and distributing the work. The whole process takes less than an hour.

In order to obtain a patent, an inventor must convince the U.S. Patent Office that the invention deserves a patent. For a fee, a patent attorney will research the patents already issued for similar inventions. This search accomplishes two things. First, it determines that the invention to be patented has not been previously created. Second, it can help to identify similar things that have been patented. These similarities can be useful when describing the unique features of the invention that make it worthy of patent protection. The Patent Office compares an application to those of all other similar patented inventions, and on that basis decides whether the application covers something truly novel and nonobvious. If the office decides the invention is novel, a patent is granted. The work is not over then, however.

Patent Infringement

A patent holder *must* oppose all infringement. With a copyright, the holder can choose which cases to prosecute, ignoring small infringements and waiting for serious infractions where the infringement is great enough to ensure success in court. However, failing to sue a patent infringement can mean losing the patent rights entirely. But, unlike copyright infringement, a patent holder does not have to prove that the infringer copied the invention; a patent infringement occurs even if someone independently invents the same thing, without knowledge of the patented invention.

Every infringement must be prosecuted. Prosecution is expensive and time-consuming, but even worse, suing for patent infringement can cause the patent *holder* to lose the patent. The potential infringer can argue all of the following points.

1. *This isn't infringement.* The infringer will claim that the two inventions are satis-factorily different.

2. *The patent is invalid.* If a prior infringement was not opposed, the patent rights may no longer be valid.

3. *The invention is not novel.* In this case, the infringer will try to persuade the judge that the Patent Office acted incorrectly in granting a patent and that the invention is nothing worthy of patent.

4. *The infringer invented the object first.* If so, the infringer, and not the original patent holder, is entitled to the patent.

The first defense does not damage a patent, although it can limit the novelty of your invention. However, the other three defenses can destroy patent rights. Worse, all four defenses can be used every time a patent holder sues someone for infringement. Finally, obtaining and defending a patent can incur substantial legal fees. Patent protection is most appropriate for large companies with substantial research and development (and legal) staffs.

Applicability of Patents to Computer Objects

The Patent Office has not encouraged patents of computer software. For a long time, computer programs were seen as the representation of an algorithm, and an algorithm was a fact of nature, which is not subject to patent. An early software patent case, *Gottschalk versus Benson*, involved a request to patent a process for converting decimal numbers into binary. The Supreme Court rejected the claim, saying it seemed to attempt to patent an abstract idea, in short, an algorithm. Nonetheless, most software developers would like to protect the algorithm by which their program works.

In 1981, two cases (*Diamond versus Bradley* and *Diamond versus Diehr*) won patents for a process that used computer software, a well-known algorithm, temperature sensors, and a computer to calculate the time to cure rubber seals. The court upheld the right to a patent since the claim was not for the software or the algorithm alone, but for the process that happened to use the software as one of its steps. An unfortunate inference is that using the software without using the other patented steps of the process would not be infringement.

The Patent Office has since issued software patents, but there have been few court challenges to uphold the legitimacy of patent rights. Patent protection does not seem appropriate for the underlying algorithms, which programmers really want to protect. In addition, because of the time and expense involved in obtaining and maintaining a patent, this form of protection may be unacceptable for a small-scale software writer.

Trade Secret

A trade secret is unlike a patent or copyright in that it must be kept a *secret*. The information has value only as a secret, and an infringer is one who divulges the secret. Once divulged, the information usually cannot be made secret again.

Characteristics of Trade Secrets

A **trade secret** is information that gives one company a competitive edge over others. For example, the formula for a soft drink is a trade secret, as is a mailing list of customers, or information about a product due to be announced in a few months.

The distinguishing characteristic of a trade secret is that it must always be kept secret. Employees and outsiders who have access to the secret must be required not to divulge the secret. The owner must take precautions to protect the secret, for example, by storing it in a safe, encrypting it in a computer file, or making employees sign a statement that they will not disclose the secret.

If someone obtains a trade secret improperly and profits from it, the owner can recover profits, damages, lost revenues, and legal costs. The court will do whatever it can to return the holder to the same competitive position it had while the information was secret. However, trade secret protection evaporates in the case of independent discovery. If someone else happens to discover the secret independently, there is no infringement, and trade secret rights are gone.

Reverse Engineering

Another way trade secret protection can vanish is by reverse engineering. Suppose a secret is the way to pack tissues in a cardboard box to make one pop up as another is pulled out. Anyone can cut open the box and study the process. Therefore, the trade secret is easily discovered. In **reverse engineering**, one studies a finished object to determine how it is manufactured or how it works.

Through reverse engineering someone might discover how a telephone is built; the design of the telephone is obvious from the components and how they are connected. Therefore, a patent is the appropriate way to protect an invention like a telephone. However, something like a soft drink is not just the combination of its ingredients. Making a soft drink may involve time, temperature, presence of oxygen or other gases, and similar factors that could not be learned from a straight chemical decomposition of the product. The recipe for a soft drink is a closely guarded trade secret. Trade secret protection works best when the secret is not apparent in the product.

Applicability to Computer Objects

Trade secret protection applies very well to computer software. The underlying algorithm of a computer program is novel, but its novelty depends on nobody else's knowing it. Trade secret protection allows distribution of the *result* of a secret (the executable program) while still keeping the program design hidden. Trade secret protection does not cover copying a product (specifically a computer program), so that it cannot protect against a pirate who sells copies of someone else's program without permission. However, trade secret protection makes it illegal to steal a secret algorithm and use it in another product.

Difficulty of Enforcement

Trade secret protection is of no help when someone infers a program's design by studying its output or, worse yet, decoding the object code. Both of these are legitimate (that is, legal) activities, and both will cause your trade secret protection to disappear.

The confidentiality of a trade secret must be ensured by adequate safeguards. If source code is distributed loosely, or if one fails to impress on people the importance of keeping the secret, any prosecution of infringement will be weakened. Employment contracts typically include a clause stating that the employee will not divulge any trade secrets received from the company, even after leaving a job. Additional protection, such as marking copies of sensitive documents or controlling access to computer files of secret information, may be necessary to impress people with the importance of secrecy.

Protection for Computer Objects

The previous sections have described three forms of protection—the copyright, the patent, and trade secret laws. Each of these provides a different form of protection for original products. In this section we consider different kinds of computer objects and describe which forms of protection are most appropriate for each kind.

Computer artifacts are very new, and they are not yet fully understood by the legal system. Perhaps in a decade the issue of what protection is most appropriate for what object will be more clearcut. Perhaps a new form of protection, or a new use of an old form, will apply specifically to computer objects. Until then, here are the kinds of protection that seem most appropriate today.

Protecting Hardware

Hardware, such as chips, disk drives, or floppy disk media, can all be patented. The medium itself can be patented, and then someone who invents a new process for manufacturing it can obtain a second patent.

Protecting Firmware

The situation is a little less clear with regard to microcode. Certainly, the physical devices on which microcode is stored can be patented. Also, a special-purpose chip that can do only one specific task (such as a floating-point arithmetic accelerator) can probably be patented. However, the data (instructions, algorithms, microcode, programs) contained in the devices are probably not patentable.

Can they be copyrighted? Are these the expression of an idea in a form that promotes dissemination of the idea? Probably not. And assuming these devices were copyrighted, what would be the definition of a copy that infringed on the copyright? Worse, would the manufacturer really want to register a copy of the internal algorithm with the Copyright Office? Copyright protection is probably inappropriate for computer firmware.

Trade secret protection seems appropriate for the code embedded in a chip. It is possible, but very time-consuming, to reverse engineer and infer the code from the behavior of the chip. The behavior of the chip does not reveal what algorithm is used to produce that behavior.

For example, Apple Computer is enforcing its right to copyright protection for an operating system embedded in firmware. The courts have affirmed that computer software *is* an appropriate subject for copyright protection, and that protection should be no less valid when the software is in a chip than in a conventional program. That decision is being appealed.

Protecting Object Code Software

Object code is usually copied so that it can be distributed for profit. The code is a work of creativity, and most agree that object code distribution is an acceptable medium of publication. Thus copyright protection seems appropriate.

The Copyright Office has not yet decided what is an appropriate medium in which to accept this code. A binary listing of the object code will be taken, but the Copyright Office does so without acknowledging that to be acceptable. The Office will accept a source code listing. Some people argue that a source code listing is not equivalent to an object code listing, in the same way that a French translation of a novel is different from its original language version. It is not clear *in the courts* that registering a source code version provides copyright protection to object code. However, someone should not be able to take the object code of a system, rearrange the order of the individual routines, and say that the result is a new system. Without the original source listings, it would be very difficult to compare two binary files and determine that one was the functional equivalent of the other simply through rearrangement.

Several court cases will be needed to establish acceptable ways of filing object code for copyright protection. Furthermore, these cases will have to develop legal precedents to define the equivalence of two pieces of computer code.

Protecting Source Code Software

Software developers selling to the mass market are reticent to distribute their source code. The code can be treated as a trade secret, although some lawyers also encourage that it be copyrighted. (These two forms of protection are possibly mutually exclusive, although registering a copyright will not hurt.)

Recall that the Copyright Office requires registering at least the first 25 and the last 25 pages of a written document. These pages are filed with the Library of Congress, where they are available for public inspection. This registration is to assist the courts in determining which work was registered for copyright protection. However, since they are available for anybody to see, they are not secret, and copyright registration can expose the secrecy of an ingenious algorithm. A copyright protects the right to distribute copies of the *expression* of an idea, not the idea itself. Therefore, a copyright does not prevent someone from reimplementing an algorithm, expressed through a copyrighted computer program.

As already noted, source code may be the most appropriate form in which to register a copyright for a program distributed in object form. It is difficult to register source code with the Copyright Office, while still ensuring its secrecy. A long computer program can be rearranged so that the first and last 25 pages do not divulge much of the secret part of a source program. Embedding errors or identifiable peculiarities in the source (or object) code of a program may be more useful in determining copyright infringement. Again, several court cases must be decided in order to establish procedures for protection of computer programs, in either source or object form.

Protecting Documentation

Copyright protection is effective and appropriate for documentation, since these manuals are essentially written works of nonfiction. Notice that the documentation is distinct from the program. A program and its documentation need to be copyrighted separately. Furthermore, copyright protection of the documentation may win a judgment against someone who illegally copies both a program and its documentation.

Protecting Data in a Data Base

The courts have had difficulty interpreting protection laws for application to data bases. Clearly data is not patentable. Trade secret protection does not seem appropriate for a large public data base, such as a bibliographic data base, because the underlying data is not at all secret.

However, copyright protection may not fit, either. The courts have applied three standards to determine suitability for copyright: hard work, creativity, and originality. A product should represent a substantial amount of work by the author; the author should do something creative in this work; and it should involve original thought by the author. These three tests are very difficult for a bibliographic data base to pass, since much of the work may have been done online or by machine. However, it is clear that a data base creator (its author) deserves fair compensation for the work of assembling and distributing the data base. The author was creative in designing the data base and did original thinking to decide how to obtain the data.

In cases where a written law is unclear or is not obviously applicable to a situation, the results of court cases serve to clarify or even extend the words of the law. As more unfair acts involving computer works are perpetrated, lawyers will argue for expanded interpretations of the law. The meaning and use of the law will continue to evolve through judges' rulings.

14.2 Rights of Employees and Employers

Employers hire employees to generate ideas and make products. Thus, the protection offered by copyrights, patents, and trade secrets applies to the ideas and products. However, considering the issue of who owns the ideas and products is much more complex. Ownership is an issue of computer security, since it relates to the rights of an employer to protect the secrecy and integrity of works produced by the employees. In this section we study the rights of employers and employees to computer products.

Ownership of Products

Suppose as a part of her job, Edye, who works for a computer software company, develops a program to manage windows for a computer screen display. The program belongs to her company, since they paid Edye to write it. Thus, Edye cannot market this program herself. The situation depends on the fact that Edye wrote the program as part of a work assignment. She could not sell the program even if she worked for a television company but developed the software as part of her job. Most employees understand this aspect of their responsibilities to their employer.

However, suppose that Edye develops this program in the evenings at home; it is not a part of her job. Edye tries to market the product herself. If Edye works as a programmer, her employer will probably say that Edye profited from training and experience gained on the job; at the very least, Edye probably conceived or thought about the project while at work. Therefore, the employer has an interest in (that is, owns at least part of) the rights to her program. However, the situation changes if Edye's primary job does not involve programming. If Edye is a television newscaster, her employer may have contributed nothing that relates to her computer product. If Edye's job does not involve programming, she may be free to market any computer product she makes.

Consider the legal position of a consultant. Suppose Edye is self-employed and, for a fee, she writes the program for the television station. She then wants to take the basis of the program, generalize it somewhat, and market it to others. Edye argues that she thought up, wrote, and tested the program; therefore, it is her work, and she owns it. The television station argues that it paid Edye to develop the program, and it owns the program, just as it would own a bookcase she might be paid to build for the station.

It is clear from the situations described here that the interpretation of laws of ownership is difficult. Each type of protection must be considered in turn.

Ownership of a Patent

The person who owns a work under patent or copyright law is the inventor; in the examples just described, the owner is the programmer. However, in patent law, it is important to know who files the patent application. If an employee lets an employer patent an invention, the employer is deemed to own the patent and, therefore, the rights to the invention.

The employer also has the right to the patent if the employee's job functions included inventing the product. In a large company a scientist may be hired to do research and development, and the results of this inventive work become the property of the employer. Even if an employee patents something, the employer can argue for a right to use the invention if the employer contributed some resources (such as computer time or access to a library or data base) in developing the invention.

Ownership of a Copyright

Ownership of a copyright is similar to ownership of a patent. The author (programmer) is the presumed owner of the work. The owner has all rights to an object. However, a special situation known as "work-for-hire" applies to many copyrights for development of software and to other products.

Work for Hire

In a work-for-hire situation, the employer, *not* the employee, is considered the author of a work. The relationship does not have to be that of a conventional employer to employee for work for hire to exist. Work for hire is not simple to identify. An employer may be in a work-for-hire relationship with an employee if the following conditions are true. No one of these conditions is decisive; however, the more of these conditions that are true, the more a situation resembles work for hire.

- The employer has a supervisory relationship, overseeing the manner in which the creative work is done.

- The employer has the right to fire the employee.

- The employer arranges for the work to be done before the work was created (as opposed to the sale of an existing work).

- A written contract between the employer and employee states that the employer has hired the employee to do certain work.

In the situation described earlier in which Edye develops a program on her job, her employer will certainly claim a work-for-hire relationship. Then the employer owns all copyright rights and should be identified in place of the author on the copyright notice.

Licenses

An alternative to a work-for-hire arrangement is licensed software. In this situation, the programmer develops and retains full ownership of the software. In return for a fee, the programmer grants to a company a license to use the program. The license can be for a definite or unlimited period of time, for one copy or for an unlimited number, to use at one location or many, to use on one machine or all, at specified or unlimited times. This arrangement is highly advantageous to the programmer, just as a work-for-hire arrangement is highly advantageous to the employer. The choice between work for hire and license is largely what the two parties will agree to.

Trade Secret Protection

A trade secret is different from either a patent or a copyright in that there is no registered inventor or author; there is no registration office for trade secrets. In the event a trade secret is revealed, the owner can prosecute the revealer for damages suffered. But first the owner has to be established, since only the owner can be harmed.

A company owns the trade secrets of its business as confidential data. As soon as a secret is developed, the company becomes the owner. For example, as soon as sales figures are accumulated, a company has trade secret rights to them, even if the figures are not compiled, totaled, summarized, printed, or distributed. As with copyrights, an employer may argue about having contributed to the development of trade secrets. If your trade secret is an improved sorting algorithm, and part of your job involves investigating and testing sorting algorithms, your employer will probably claim at least partial ownership of the algorithm you try to market.

Employment Contracts

Sometimes there is no contract between the software developer and a possible employer. However, it is common for an employment contract to spell out rights of ownership. Having a contract is desirable both for employees and employers so that both will understand their rights and responsibilities.

Typically an employment contract specifies that the employee is hired to work as a programmer exclusively for the benefit of the company. The company states that this is a work-for-hire situation. The company claims all rights to any programs developed, including all copyright rights and the right to market. The contract may further state that the employee is receiving access to certain trade secrets as a part of employment, and the employee agrees not to reveal those secrets to anyone.

More restrictive contracts (from the employee's perspective) assign to the employer rights to all inventions (patents) and all creative works (copyrights), not just those that follow directly from one's job. For example, suppose an employee is hired as an accountant for an automobile company. While on the job, the employee invents a more efficient way to burn fuel in an automobile engine. The employer would argue that the employee used company time to think about the problem, and therefore, it was entitled to this product. An employment contract transferring all rights of inventions to the employer would strengthen the case even more.

An agreement not to compete is sometimes included in a contract. The employee states that simply having worked for one employer will make the employee very valuable to a competitor. The employee agrees not to compete by working in the same field for a set period of time after termination. For example, a programmer who has a very high position involving the design of operating systems would understandably be familiar with a large body of operating systems design techniques. The employee might memorize the major parts of a proprietary operating system and be able to write a similar one for a competitor in a very short time. To prevent this, the employer might require the employee not to work for a competitor (including working alone). Agreements not to compete are not always enforceable in law; in some states the employee's right to earn a living takes precedence over the employer's rights.

14.3 Computer Crime

The law related to contracts and employment is difficult, but at least employees, objects, contracts, and owners are fairly standard entities for which legal precedents have been developed. The definitions in copyright and patent law are strained when applied to computing, because old forms must be made to fit new objects; for these situations, however, cases being decided now are establishing legal precedents. But crimes involving computers are an area of the law that is even less clear than the other areas. In this section we study computer crime and consider why new laws are needed to address some of its problems.

Why a Separate Category for Computer Crime?

There are certain recognized categories of crimes, including such terms as "murder," "robbery," and "littering." We do not separate crime into categories for different objects, such as "gun crime" or "knife crime." We separate subjects of crime into "people" and "other objects," but driving into your neighbor's picture window is as bad as driving into his evergreen tree or pet sheep. An example will explain why we need special laws relating to computers as subjects and objects of crime.

Rules of Property

A case related by Parker [PAR84] describes a theft of a trade secret proprietary software package. The theft was across state boundaries by means of a telephone line. The California Supreme Court ruled that this software acquisition was not "theft" because

> Implicit in the definition of "article" in Section 499c(a) is that it must be something *tangible*...Based on the record here, the defendant did not carry any tangible thing...from the computer to his terminal unless the impulses which defendant allegedly caused to be transmitted over the telephone wire could be said to be tangible. *It is the opinion of the Court that such impulses are not tangible and hence do not constitute an "article."*

The legal system has explicit rules of what constitutes property. Generally, property is tangible, unlike magnetic impulses. To a computer professional, taking a copy of a software package without permission is clearcut theft. However, the courts have not yet accepted a definition of property that is so different from its traditional meaning.

A similar problem arises with computer services. We would generally agree that unauthorized access to a computing system is a crime. Unauthorized use of a neighbor's lawn mower constitutes theft, even if the lawn mower was returned in essentially the same condition as when it was taken. However, because access is not a physical object, the courts are reticent to punish that as the crime of theft.

Rules of Evidence

Computer printouts have been used as evidence in many successful fraud prosecutions. However, the legal system has not yet consistently accepted such widely used media as magnetic tapes and disks as adequate evidence. Under the rules of evidence, courts prefer an original source document over a copy, under the assumption that the copy may be inaccurate. Magnetic media are interpreted by the courts as a repository for a copy of some paper document rather than an original.

However, magnetic and optical media are becoming the primary means of storing data. In some instances, the magnetic copy is the *only* copy; there is no paper copy. Thus, as technology advances, devices such as smart cards, optical disks, and memory chips will have to be accepted as evidence. Courts are understandably reluctant to change their procedures, because varying the rules of evidence to accommodate computer media may create a precedent to accept some less desirable medium.

Threats to Integrity and Confidentiality

The integrity and the secrecy of data are also issues in many court cases. Parker [PAR84] describes a case in which a trespasser acquired remote access to a computing system. The computing system contained confidential records about people, and the integrity of the data was important. The prosecution of this case had to be phrased in terms of theft of computer time and valued as such, even though that was insignificant compared to loss of privacy and integrity. Why? Because the law as written recognized theft of computer time as a loss, but not loss of privacy or destruction of data.

Several Federal and state laws recognize the privacy of data about individuals. For example, it is a crime to disclose grades or financial information without permission. These laws prevent computing center employees from disclosing data, but the laws do not apply to someone who acquires access without permission.

Value of Data

In another computer crime, a person was found guilty of having stolen a substantial amount of data from a computer data bank. However, the court determined that the "value" of that data was the cost of the paper on which it was printed, which was only a couple of dollars. Because of that value, this crime was classified as a misdemeanor, a minor crime.

Paper money is accepted as a valuable commodity, even if the paper it is printed on is worth only a few cents. Cash is easy to value—a dollar bill is worth one dollar. The assets of a credit bureau are its files. Banks and insurance companies willingly pay $20 or more for a credit report, even though the paper itself is worth less than a dollar. For a credit bureau, the amount a willing customer will pay for a report is a fair estimate of the report's value; this estimate is called the "market value" of the report. However, a confidential list of clients has no market value that can be established. The value of confidential information relates to the loss suffered when the secret information is revealed. Although these methods of valuation are accepted in civil suits, they have not yet been widely accepted in criminal prosecution.

Acceptance of Computer Terminology

Another area in which law is lagging behind technology is the acceptance of definitions of terms in computing. For example, according to a Federal statute, it is unlawful to commit arson within a federal enclave (18 USC 81). Part of that act relates to "machinery or building material or supplies" in the enclave, but court decisions have ruled that a motor vehicle located within a federal enclave at the time of the burning was not included under this statute. Because of that ruling, it is not clear whether or not computer hardware constitutes "machinery" in this context; "supplies" almost certainly does not include software. Computers and their software, media, and data need to be understood and accepted by the legal system.

Why Computer Crime is Hard to Define

From the examples cited, it is clear that the legal community has not accommodated to advances in computers as rapidly as the rest of society has. Some people in the legal process do not understand computers and computing, so that these people cannot treat crimes involving computers properly. Creating and changing laws are slow processes, intended to involve substantial thought about the effects of proposed changes. This deliberate process is very much out of pace with a technology that is progressing as fast as computing is.

Added to the problem of a rapidly changing technology is the fact that a computer can perform many roles in a crime. A particular computer can be the subject, object, or medium of a crime. A computer can be attacked (attempted unauthorized access), used to attack (impersonating a legitimate node on a network), and used as a means to commit crime (Trojan horse or fake login). Computer crime statutes have to include all of these evils.

Why Computer Crime is Hard to Prosecute

Even when it is acknowledged that a computer crime has been committed, there are several reasons why computer crime is hard to prosecute.

- *Understanding.* Neither courts nor juries or police necessarily understand computers. Many judges began practicing law before the invention of computers, and most began before the widespread use of the personal computer.

- *Fingerprints.* Police and courts have for years depended on tangible evidence, such as fingerprints. As readers of Sherlock Holmes know, seemingly miniscule clues can lead to solutions to the most complicated crimes (or so Doyle would have you believe). But with many computer crimes there simply are no fingerprints, no physical clues.

- *Forms of Assets.* We know what cash is, or diamonds, or even negotiable securities. But are 20 invisible magnetic spots really equivalent to a million dollars? Is computer time an asset? What is the value of stolen computer time if the system would have been idle during the time of the theft?

- *Juveniles.* Many computer crimes involve juveniles. Society understands immaturity and can treat even very serious crimes by juveniles as being done with less understanding than when the same crime is committed by an adult. A more serious, related problem is that many adults see juvenile computer crimes as childhood pranks, the modern equivalent of tipping over an outhouse.

As Bequai [BEQ83] points out, prosecutors may avoid the more complicated cases, ones that will take much preparation before going to trial. If the law does not quite fit the crime, or if an inappropriate statute has to be stretched to include a computer crime, the likelihood of conviction is narrower. Even if the law fits, there may be so little evidence that a conviction is dubious.

Conventional murder cases are easier to understand and, for the elected prosecutor, easier to justify. Computer crimes seldom involve "popular victims," with whom the public immediately sympathizes; more typically the victim of a computer crime is a large corporation, which the public thinks can probably afford to lose a large sum of money. For all these reasons, prosecutors may avoid computer crimes if the workload is heavy.

Then, too, the victim may not want to prosecute because of the possibility of arousing negative feelings due to the publicity. Banks, insurance companies, investment firms, the government, and health care groups fear the public's trust will be diminished if a vulnerability in their computer system is exposed. They may also fear repetition of the same crime by others.

For all these reasons computer crimes are not often prosecuted.

Examples of Statutes

Computer crime laws are rather recent, having been enacted at the state level since 1980. Almost every state now has such a law. Although the state bills are similar, there is no model computer crime statute; such a statute could make prosecution of computer crime cases and interchange of computer crime data and evidence easier. There is also a Federal crime statute, although it covers only Federal computers.

U.S. Computer Crime Statute

The primary Federal statute, which is 18 USC 1030, was enacted on October 12, 1984. This statute prohibits

1. unauthorized access to a computer containing data directly related to national defense or foreign relations

2. unauthorized access to a computer containing certain banking or financial information

3. unauthorized access, use, modification, destruction, or disclosure of a computer or information in a computer operated on behalf of the U.S. Government

Penalties range from $5,000 to $100,000 or twice the value obtained by the offense, whichever is higher, or imprisonment from 1 year to 20 years, or both.

Colorado Computer Crime Bill

To date, most state statutes first define various computer terms and then prohibit certain acts. The statutes are similar to the Colorado statute, reprinted here. Note that the definitions of computer objects have been drawn broadly to include everything that would typically be called a "computer" or related part. Notice that two crimes have been specified: access to a computer to defraud, and use or damage to a computer system. As is typical with statutes involving property, low-valued crimes are classified as misdemeanors (small crimes typically carrying light punishment) and higher-valued crimes are classified as felonies. Classes of misdemeanors and felonies further delineate the crimes.

Colorado Computer Crime Bill

18-5.5-101. *Definitions.* As used in this article, unless the context otherwise requires:

1. To "use" means to instruct, communicate with, store data in, retrieve data from, or otherwise make use of any resources of a computer, computer system, or computer network.

2. "Computer" means an electronic device which performs logical, arithmetic, or memory functions by the manipulation of electronic or magnetic impulses, and includes all input, output, processing, storage, software, or communications facilities which are connected or related to such a device in a system or network.

3. "Computer network" means the interconnection of communication lines (including microwave or other means of electronic communication) with a computer through remote terminals, or a complex consisting of two or more interconnected computers.

4. "Computer program" means a series of instructions or statements, in a form acceptable to a computer, which permits the functioning of a computer system in a manner designed to provide appropriate products from such computer system.

5. "Computer software" means computer programs, procedures, and associated documentation concerned with the operation of a computer system.

6. "Computer system" means a set of related, connected or unconnected, computer equipment, devices, and software.

7. "Financial instrument" means any check, draft, money order, certificate of deposit, letter of credit, bill of exchange, credit card, debit card, or marketable security.

8. "Property" includes, but is not limited to, financial instruments, information, including electronically produced data, and computer software and programs in either machine or human readable form, and any other tangible or intangible item of value.

9. "Services" includes, but is not limited to, computer time, data processing, and storage functions.

18-5.5-102. *Computer crime.*

1. Any person who knowingly uses any computer, computer system, computer network, or any part thereof for the purpose of: devising or executing

any scheme or artifice to defraud, obtaining money, property, or services by means of false or fraudulent pretenses, representations, or promises, or committing theft, commits computer crime.

2. Any person who knowingly and without authorization uses, alters, damages, or destroys any computer, computer system, or computer network described in section 18-5.5-101 or any computer software, program, documentation, or data contained in such computer, computer system, or computer network commits computer crime.

3. If the loss, damage, or thing of value taken in violation of this section is less than fifty dollars, computer crime is a class 3 misdemeanor; if fifty dollars or more but less than two hundred dollars, computer crime is a class 2 misdemeanor; if two hundred dollars or more but less than ten thousand dollars, computer crime is a class 4 felony; if ten thousand dollars or more, computer crime is a class 3 felony.

18-8-115. *Duty to report a crime.* It is the duty of every corporation or person who has reasonable grounds to believe that a crime has been committed to report promptly the suspected crime to law enforcement authorities. When acting in good faith, such corporation or person shall be immune from civil liability for such reporting.

Colorado is unusual in that it requires reporting of suspected computer crimes. If suspected computer crimes are reported, repeated or more serious instances of a crime can be prevented. A pattern of suspected crimes can be useful in tracking an unknown criminal. Finally, some computer criminals move from one position of trust to another, simply because one company is happy for the criminal to leave without the negative publicity of a crime committed by an employee. If suspected crimes were reported, these criminals would be unable to continue their crimes undetected.

Federal Statutes Related to Computing

Several Federal statutes relate to common applications of computing. These are the Freedom of Information Act, the Privacy Act of 1974, and the Fair Credit Reporting Act. These laws control uses of data; since most of this data is gathered, stored, organized, or processed by means of computers, the laws affect many computer applications.

Freedom of Information Act

The Freedom of Information Act provides public access to information collected by the Executive branch of the Federal government. The act requires disclosure of any available data, unless the data fall under one of several specific exceptions, such as national security or personal privacy. The original intention of the law was to release to individuals any information the government had collected on them. However, more corporations than individuals file requests for information as a means of obtaining information about the workings of the government. Foreign governments can even file for information. This act applies only to government agencies, although similar laws could require disclosure from private sources. The effect of this law is to require increased classification and protection for sensitive information.

Privacy Act of 1974

The Privacy Act of 1974 protects the privacy of personal data collected by the government. An individual is allowed to determine what data has been collected on him or her, for what purpose, and to whom such information has been disseminated. An additional use of the law is to prevent one government agency from accessing data collected by another agency for another purpose. This act requires diligent efforts to preserve the secrecy of private data collected.

Fair Credit Reporting Act

The Fair Credit Reporting Act applies to private industry. The law governs what types of data may be collected on individuals, and to what purposes the data may be used. For example, commercial credit bureaus collect data on credit history (payment records, bankruptcy proceedings, unpaid liens, and so forth). This information can legitimately be distributed to concerned parties on behalf of individuals seeking credit, employment, insurance, and for other business needs. The act limits what data may be stored and how long certain forms of data may be maintained (for example, most adverse information, like arrest records, bankruptcies, and lawsuits cannot be maintained longer than seven years). The consumer has a right to know the contents of the information collected about him or her and, if the information is incorrect, the law gives a means for having the information corrected. Thus integrity of the data is legally required. Finally, the law gives penalties for unauthorized disclosure of information by the collector.

Other Statutes

These laws have been passed partially in response to the growing use of computers to maintain information about individuals. They all support the individual's right to privacy and demand that groups collecting data maintain that privacy. Other similar laws are likely to assure the privacy of financial, medical, and other types of personal records. All of these situations will place an even greater emphasis on proper computer security measures in both the public and private sector.

What Computer Crime Does Not Address

Even with the definitions included in the statutes, it is up to the courts to interpret what is a "computer." Legislators cannot define precisely what a computer is because computer technology is used in many other devices, such as robots, calculators, and medical instruments. More importantly we cannot predict what kinds of devices may be invented ten or 50 years from now. Therefore, the language in each of these bills indicates the kinds of devices the legislature seeks to include as computers, and leaves it up to the court to rule on a specific case. Unfortunately, it takes a while for courts to build up a pattern of cases, and different courts may rule differently in similar situations. The interpretation of each of these terms will be unsettled for some time to come.

Value presents a similar problem. As noted in some of the cases cited, the courts have trouble separating the intrinsic value of an object (such as a sheet of paper with writing on it) from its cost to reproduce. The courts now recognize that a dollar bill is worth more than the cost of the paper and printing. But the courts have not agreed on the value of printed computer output. The cost of a blank computer tape is about $10, but it may require hours of data gathering and hours of machine time to produce the data encoded on the tape. The courts are still striving to compute the fair value of a recorded tape.

The value of a person's privacy and secrecy of data about a person are even less settled. In the next chapter we will consider how ethics and individual morality take over where the law stops.

14.4 Summary of Legal Issues in Computer Security

This chapter has described three aspects of the relationship between computing and the law. First, the legal mechanisms of copyright, patent, and trade secret were presented as means to protect the secrecy of computer hardware, software, and data. These mechanisms were designed before the invention of the computer, and so their applicability to computing needs is somewhat limited. However, program protection is especially desired, and software companies are pressing the courts to extend the interpretation of these means of protection to include computers.

The second topic considered in this chapter was the relationship between employers and employees, especially as this applies to writers of software. Well-established laws and precedents control the acceptable access an employee has to software written for a company.

Third, this chapter presented some of the difficulties in prosecuting computer crime. Several examples showed how breaches of computer security are treated by the courts. In general, the courts have not yet been able to evaluate the worth of computers, software, and data, nor the seriousness of computer crime. The legal system is moving cautiously in its acceptance of computers. Several important pieces of computer crime legislation were described.

14.5 Terms and Concepts

protecting programs and data
copyright
intellectual property
originality

fair use
registering a copyright
copyright of program versus protection of design
requirement to publish
limitation on distribution
limitation on use
patent
non-patentable objects
requirement of novelty
registering a patent
patent infringement
invalid patent
patentability of computer objects
trade secret
protecting hardware
protecting firmware
protecting object code
protecting source code
protecting documentation
protecting data
rights of employees; rights of employers
ownership of products
work for hire
employment contract
license
computer crime
understanding computer crime
computer evidence
forms of assets
computer offenses by juveniles
statutes
definitions of computer items
value of computer items
privacy

15

Ethical Issues in Computer Security

This final chapter will help to clarify thinking about the ethical issues involved in computer security. The chapter offers no answers. Rather, after listing and explaining some ethical principles, it presents several case studies to which the principles can be applied. Each case is followed by a list of possible ethical issues involved, although the list is not necessarily all-inclusive nor conclusive. The primary purpose of this chapter is to explore some of the ethical issues associated with computer security and to show how ethics functions as a control in computer security.

15.1 The Law and Ethics are Not the Same

As explained in the last chapter, law is not always the appropriate way to deal with issues of human behavior. It is difficult to write a law which subsumes only those events we want it to. For example, a law that prevents animals in public places must be amended to *permit* seeing-eye dogs for the blind. It is hard to think of all the exceptions when drafting a law. Even when a law is well conceived and well written, its enforcement may be difficult. The courts are overburdened, and prosecuting relatively minor infractions may be excessively time-consuming relative to the benefit.

Thus, it is impossible or impractical to develop laws to describe and enforce all forms of behavior acceptable to society. Instead, society relies on **ethics** or **morals** to prescribe generally accepted standards of proper behavior. (In this chapter the terms "ethics" and "morals" will be used interchangeably.) An **ethic** is an objectively defined standard of right and wrong. Ethical standards are often idealistic principles, because they focus on one objective. In a given situation, however, several moral objectives may be involved, so that it is necessary for people to determine an action that is appropriate, considering all the objectives. Even though religious groups and professional organizations promote certain standards of ethical behavior, ultimately each person is responsible for deciding what to do in a specific situation. Therefore, through choices, each person defines a personal set of ethical practices. A set of ethical principles is called an **ethical system**.

An ethic is different from a law in several important ways. First, laws apply to everyone: One may disagree with the intent or the meaning of a law, but that is not an excuse for disobeying the law. Second, if two laws conflict, judicial process itself determines which law takes precedence. Third, the laws and the courts identify certain actions as "right" and others as "wrong." From a legal standpoint, anything that is *not illegal* is "right." Finally, laws can be enforced, and there are ways to rectify wrongs done by unlawful behavior.

By contrast, ethics are personal: Two individuals may have different frameworks for making moral judgments. What one person thinks is perfectly justifiable, another would never consider doing. Second, ethical positions can and often do come into conflict. As an example, the value of a human life is very important in most ethical systems. Most people would not advocate the sacrifice of a human life, but in the right context some would approve of sacrificing one person to save another, or one to save many others. The value of one life cannot be readily measured against the value of others, and it is precisely this ambiguity on which many ethical decisions must be founded. Yet, there is no arbiter of ethical positions: When two ethical goals collide, each person must choose which is dominant. Third, two people may assess ethical values differently; there is no universal standard of right and wrong in ethical judgments. Nor can one person simply look to what another has done as guidance for choosing the "right" thing to do. Finally, there is no enforcement for ethical choices. These differences are summarized in Table 15.1.

TABLE 15.1   CONTRAST OF LAW VERSUS ETHICS.

Law	Ethics
described by formal, written laws	described by unwritten principles
interpreted by courts	interpreted by individuals
established by legislature representing everyone	presented by philosophers, religions, professional groups
applicable to everyone	personal choice
priority determined by courts if two laws conflict	priority determined by individual if two principles conflict
court is final arbiter of "right"	no external arbiter
enforceable by police and courts	limited enforcement

15.2 Studying Ethics

The study of ethics is not easy because the issues are complex. Sometimes people confuse ethics with religion, since religion supplies a framework in which to make ethical choices. Religions supply several moral frameworks, but ethics can be studied apart from any religious connection. Difficult choices would be easier to make if there were a set of universal ethical principles to which everyone agreed. However, the variety of social, cultural, and religious beliefs makes the identification of such a set of universal principles impossible. In this section we explore some of the problems raised by a study of ethics and then consider how an understanding of ethics can help in dealing with issues of computer security.

Ethics and Religion

Ethics is a set of principles or norms for justifying what is right or wrong in a given situation. To understand what ethics *is* it is helpful to understand what it is *not*. Ethical principles are different from religious beliefs. Religion is based on personal notions about the creation of the world and the existence of controlling forces or beings. Many moral principles are embodied in the major religions, and the basis of personal morality is really a matter of belief and conviction, as it is with religious faith. However, two people with different religious backgrounds may develop the same ethical philosophy, while two exponents of the same religion might reach opposite ethical conclusions in a particular situation. Finally, it is possible to analyze a situation from an ethical perspective and reach ethical conclusions without appealing to any particular religious framework. Thus, it is important to distinguish ethics from religion.

Ethics is not Universal

Ethical values vary by society and also from person to person within a society. For example, the concept of privacy is very important in Western cultures. But in Eastern cultures, people associate privacy with having something to hide. Not only do Orientals not understand a Westerner's desire for privacy, they also interpret it negatively. Thus culture and background have a tremendous effect on people's attitudes.

Also, an individual's standards of behavior may be influenced by past events in life. A person who grew up in a large family may place greater emphasis on personal control and ownership of possessions than would an only child who seldom had to share. Major events or close contact with others can also shape one's ethical position. Despite these differences, however, the underlying principles of moral judgment are the same.

Nonetheless, ethics is not founded on basic principles all can accept. Thus there is a measure of distrust, often from people with a scientific or technical background who expect precision and universality.

Ethics Does not Provide Answers

Ethical pluralism is recognizing or admitting that more than one position may be ethically justifiable in a given situation. Pluralism is another way of noting that two people may legitimately disagree on issues of ethics. We expect and accept disagreement in such areas as politics and religion.

However, in the scientific and technical fields, people expect to find unique, unambiguous, and unequivocal answers. In science one answer must be correct or demonstrable in some sense. Science has provided life with fundamental explanations. Ethics is rejected or misunderstood by some scientists because it is "soft," meaning that it has no underlying framework, or it does not depend on fundamental truths.

One need only study the history of scientific discovery to see that science itself is founded only on temporary truths. For many years the earth was believed to be the center of the solar system. Ptolemy developed a complicated framework of "epicycles," orbits within orbits of the planets, to explain the inconsistency of observed periods of rotation. Eventually his theory was superseded by the Copernican model of planets that orbit the sun. Similarly, Einstein's relativity theory opposed the traditional quantum basis of physics. Science is littered with theories that have fallen from favor as new explanations have been proposed. As each new theory is proposed, some people readily accept the new proposal, while others cling to the old.

But the basis of science is presumed to be "truth." A statement is expected to be provably true, provably false, or unproven, but a statement can never be both true and false. Scientists are uncomfortable with ethics because ethics does not provide these clean distinctions.

Worse, there is no higher authority of ethical truth. Two people may disagree about of the ethics of a particular situation, but there is no one to whom to appeal for a final determination of who is "right." However, conflicting answers need not deter one from considering ethical issues in computer security.

15.3 Ethical Reasoning

Most people make ethical judgments often, perhaps daily. (Is it better to buy from a home town merchant or from nationwide chain? Should I spend time with a volunteer organization or my friends? Is it acceptable to release sensitive data to someone who might not have justification for access to that data?) Since we all often make ethical choices, we should clarify how we do this, so that we can learn to apply the principles of ethics in professional situations, as we do in private life.

The study of ethics can yield two positive results. First, in those situations in which we already think we know what is right and what is wrong, ethics should help us justify our choice. Second, if we are not sure what is the ethical action to take in a situation, ethics can help us to identify the issues involved, so that we can make reasoned judgments.

Examining a Case for Ethical Issues

How, then, can issues of ethical choice in computer security be approached? There are several steps to making and justifying an ethical choice.

1. *Understand the situation.* Learn the facts of the situation. Ask questions of interpretation or clarification. Attempt to find out if there are any relevant forces that have not been considered.

2. *Know several theories of ethical reasoning.* To make an ethical choice, it is necessary to know how those choices can be justified.

3. *List the ethical principles involved.* What are the different philosophies that could be applied in this case? Do any of these include others?

4. *Determine which principles outweigh others.* This is a subjective evaluation. It often involves extending a principle to a logical conclusion, or determining cases in which one principle clearly supersedes another.

The most important steps are the first and third. Too often people judge a situation on incomplete information, which leads to judgments based on prejudice, suspicion, or misinformation. Considering all the different ethical issues raised forms the basis for evaluating the competing interests of step four.

Examples of Ethical Principles

In this section we present two different schools of ethical reasoning: One based on the good that results from actions, and one that is based on certain *prima facie* duties of people.

Teleology

The **teleological** theory of ethics focuses on the consequences of an action. The action to be chosen is that which results in the greatest future good and the least harm. For example, if a fellow student asks you to write a program he was assigned for a class, you might consider the good (he will owe you a favor) against the bad (you might get caught, causing embarrassment and possible discipline, plus the student will not learn the techniques to be gained from writing the program, leaving him deficient). The negative consequences clearly outweigh the positive, so you would refuse. Teleology is the general name applied to many theories of behavior, all of which focus on the *goal* or *outcome* of the action.

There are two important forms of teleology. **Egoism** is the form that says a moral judgment is based on the positive benefits to the person taking the action. An egoist weighs the outcomes of all possible acts and chooses the one that produces the most personal good with the least negative consequence. For example, an egoist trying to determine whether it is ethical to write shoddy computer code when pressed for time might argue as follows: "If I complete the project quickly, I will satisfy my manager, which will bring me a raise and other good things. The customer is unlikely to know enough about the program to complain, so there is no likelihood of my being blamed. Thus, it is justifiable to write shoddy code."

The principle of **utilitarianism** is also an assessment of good and bad results, but the reference group is the entire world. The utilitarian chooses that action that will bring the greatest collective good for all people with the fewest possible negative results for all. In the example cited, the utilitarian would assess personal good and bad, good and bad for the company, good and bad for the customer and, perhaps, good and bad for society at large (if the software were to monitor smokestack emissions, for example, so that everyone breathing would be affected). The utilitarian might perceive greater good to everyone by taking the time to write quality code, despite the negative personal consequence of displeasing management.

Deontology

Another ethical theory is the **deontological** theory, which is founded in a sense of duty. This ethical principle states that certain things are good in and of themselves. Good rules or acts require no higher justification. Something just *is* good, it does not have to be judged for its effect.

Examples (from William Frankena [FRA73]) of intrinsically good things are

- Truth; knowledge and true opinion of various kinds; understanding; wisdom

- Just distribution of good and evil; justice

- Pleasure, satisfaction; happiness; life; consciousness

- Peace, security, freedom

- Good reputation, honor, esteem; mutual affection, love, friendship, cooperation; morally good dispositions or virtues

- Beauty, aesthetic experience

Rule-deontology is the school of ethical reasoning that believes there are certain natural rules that specify our proper conduct. Certain basic moral principles are adhered to because of our responsibilities to one another; these principles are often stated as "rights": the right to know, the right to privacy, the right to fair compensation for work. Sir David Ross [ROS30] lists various duties incumbent on all human beings:

- *fidelity,* (truthfulness)

- *reparation,* (the duty to make recompense for a previous wrongful act)

- *gratitude,* (thankfulness for previous services or kind acts)

- *justice,* (distribution of happiness in accordance with merit)

- *beneficence,* (the obligation to help other people or to make their lives better)

- *non-maleficence,* (not harming others)

- *self-improvement,* (to become continually better, both in a mental sense and in a moral sense—for example, by not committing a wrong a second time)

Another school of reasoning is **act-deontology**. This form of reasoning says that certain acts are naturally right or wrong, without reference to any rule. For example, telling the truth is naturally good, not because there is a rule requiring people to tell the truth, but because truth-telling is a good act by itself. Act-deontologists practice **situation ethics**, meaning that one situation is different from another, and the naturally good action for a given situation cannot necessarily be determined by studying similar situations.

Applying Principles of Moral Reasoning

To be able to analyze how ethics affects professional actions, ethicists often study case situations. The remainder of this chapter consists of examples to analyze. These cases are modeled after ones developed by Parker [PAR79] as part of the AFIPS/NSF study of ethics in computing and technology. Each case study is designed to bring out certain ethical points, some of which are listed following the case. These cases are suitable for use in a class discussion, where other values will certainly be mentioned. Finally, each case reaches no conclusion, since each individual must assess the ethical situation alone. In a class discussion it may be appropriate to take a vote. Remember, however, that ethics is not determined by majority rule. Those siding with the majority are not "right," nor are the rest "wrong."

15.4 Case I: Use of Computer Services

This case concerns deciding what is appropriate use of computer time. Use of computer time is both a question of access by one person and of availability of quality of service to others. The person involved is permitted to access computing facilities for a certain purpose. Many companies rely on an unwritten standard of behavior that governs what people who have legitimate access to a computing system can do. The ethical issues involved in this case can lead to an understanding of that unwritten standard.

The Case

Dave works as a programmer for a large software company. He writes and tests utility programs such as compilers. His company operates two computing shifts: (1) During the day program development and online applications are run; (2) at night batch production jobs are completed. Dave has access to workload data and learns that the evening batch runs are complementary to daytime programming tasks; that is, adding programming work during the night shift would not adversely affect performance of the computer to other users.

Dave comes back after normal hours to develop a program to manage his own stock portfolio. His drain on the system is minimal, and he uses very few expendable supplies, such as printer paper. Is Dave's behavior ethical?

Values Issues

Some of the ethical principles involved in this case are listed below.

1. *Ownership of resources.* The company owns the computing resources and provides them for its own computing needs.

2. *Effect on others.* Although unlikely, a flaw in Dave's program could adversely affect other users, perhaps even denying them service because of a system failure.

3. *Universalism principle*. If Dave's action is acceptable, it should also be acceptable for others to do the same. However, too many employees working in the evening could reduce system effectiveness.

4. *Possibility of detection, punishment*. Dave does not know whether his action would be "wrong" or "right" if discovered by his company. If his company decided it was improper use, Dave could be punished.

What other issues are involved? Which principles are more important than others?

Analysis

The utilitarian would consider the total excess of good over bad for all people. Dave receives benefit from use of computer time, although for this application the amount of time is not large. Dave has a possibility of punishment, but Dave may rate that as unlikely. The company is neither harmed nor helped by this. Thus, the utilitarian could argue that Dave's use is justifiable.

The universalism principle seems as if it would cause a problem, however, since clearly if everyone did this, quality of service would degrade. A utilitarian would say that each new user has to weigh good and bad separately. Dave's use might not burden the machine, and neither might Ann's; but when Bill wants to use the machine, it is heavily enough used that Bill's use *would* affect other people.

Alternative Situations

Would it affect the ethics of the situation if

1. Dave began a business managing stock portfolios for many people for profit?

2. Dave's salary were below average for his background, implying that Dave was due the computer use as a fringe benefit?

3. Dave's employer knew of other employees doing similar things and tacitly approved by not seeking to stop them?

4. Dave worked for a government office instead of a private company, since the computer would then belong "to the people"?

15.5 Case II: Privacy Rights

In this case the central issue is the individual's right to privacy. This is both a legal and an ethical issue, because of the Federal Privacy Act of 1974, discussed in the previous chapter.

The Case

Donald works for the county health department as a computer records clerk, where he has access to files of patient records. For a scientific study, a researcher, Ethel, has been granted access to the medical portion—but not the corresponding names—of some records.

Ethel finds some information that she would like to use, but she needs the names and addresses corresponding with certain medical histories. Ethel asks Donald to retrieve the names and addresses in order to contact these people for more information and for permission to do further study.

Should Donald release the names and addresses?

Some Principles Involved

Here are some of the ethical principles involved in this case. What are other ethical principles? Which principles are subordinate to which others?

1. *Job responsibility.* Donald's job is to manage individual records, not to make determinations of appropriate use. Policy decisions should be made by someone of higher authority.

2. *Use.* The records are used for legitimate scientific study, not for profit or to expose sensitive data to unauthorized people.

3. *Possible misuse.* Although Ethel's motives are believed to be proper, they cannot be guaranteed to be so.

4. *Confidentiality.* Had Ethel been intended to have names and addresses, they would have been given initially.

5. *Tacit permission.* Ethel has been granted permission to access parts of these records.

6. *Propriety.* Since Ethel has no authority to obtain names and addresses, and since this represents confidential data, Donald should deny her request for access.

Analysis

The egoist would say that Donald gets minor good (Ethel's appreciation) from releasing the names. However, he could get into trouble with his superiors for unauthorized release of information. By not releasing the names and addresses no personal good occurs and only Ethel's displeasure occurs as a negative. Therefore, Donald is justified in not releasing the names since it brings him the most good (none) with the least bad (mild).

A rule deontologist would argue that privacy is an inherent good, and that one should not violate the privacy of another. Therefore, Donald should not release the names.

Extensions to the Basic Case

In this section we will consider several possible extensions to the scenario. These extensions probe other ethical issues involved in this case.

1. Suppose Donald were responsible for determining allowable access to the files. What ethical issues would be involved in his deciding whether or not to grant access to Ethel?

2. Should Ethel be allowed to contact the individuals involved? That is, should the health department release individuals' names to a researcher? What are the ethical issues for the health department to consider?

3. Suppose Ethel contacts the individuals to ask their permission, and one-third respond giving permission, one-third respond denying permission, and one-third do not respond. Ethel claims that at least one-half of the individuals are needed to make a valid study. What options are available to Ethel? What are the ethical issues involved in deciding which of these options to pursue?

15.6 Case III: Denial of Service

This case addresses issues related to the effect of one person's computation on other users. This is another situation involving people with legitimate access, so that standard access controls should not exclude these people. However, because of the actions of some individuals, others are denied legitimate access to the system. Thus, the focus of this case is on the rights of all users.

The Case

Charlie and Carol are students at a university in a computer science program. Each writes a program for a class assignment. Charlie's program happens to uncover a flaw in a compiler which, ultimately, causes the entire computing system to fail, causing users to lose the results of their current computation. Charlie's program uses acceptable features of the language; the compiler is at fault. Charlie did not suspect his program would cause a system failure. He reports the program to the computing center and tries to find ways to achieve his intended result without exercising the system flaw.

The system continues to fail periodically, for a total of ten times (beyond the first failure). When the system fails, sometimes Charlie is running a program, but sometimes Charlie is not. The director contacts Charlie, who shows all of his program versions to the computing center staff. The staff concludes that Charlie may have been inadvertently responsible for some, but not all, of the system failures, but that his latest approach to solving the assigned problem is probably safe, unlikely to lead to additional system failures.

On further analysis, the computing center director notes that Carol has had programs running each of the first eight (of ten) times the system failed. The director uses administrative privilege to inspect Carol's files and finds a file that exploits the same vulnerability as did Charlie's program. The director immediately suspends Carol's account, denying Carol access to the computing system. Because of this, Carol is unable to complete her assignment on time, she receives a D in the course, and she drops out of school.

Analysis

In this case the choices are intentionally not obvious. The situation is presented as a completed scenario, but in studying it you are being asked to suggest alternative actions the players *could have taken*. In this way, you build a repertoire of actions that you can consider in similar situations that might arise.

1. What additional information is needed?

2. Who has rights in this case? What rights are those? Who has a responsibility to protect those rights? (This step in ethical study is used to clarify who should be considered as the reference group for a deontological analysis.)

3. Has Charlie acted responsibly? By what evidence do you conclude so? Has Carol? Has the computing center director? (In this step you look for past judgments that should be confirmed, or wrongs that should be redressed.)

4. What are some alternate actions Charlie or Carol or the director could have taken that would have been more responsible?

15.7 Case IV: Ownership of Programs

In this case we consider who owns programs: the programmer, the employer, the manager, or all. From a legal standpoint, most rights belong to the employer, as presented in the previous chapter. However, this case expands on that position by presenting several competing arguments that might be used to support alternative positions. As described in the previous chapter, legal controls for secrecy of programs can be complicated, time-consuming, and expensive to apply. In this case we search for individual ethical controls that can prevent the need to appeal to the legal system.

The Case

Greg is a programmer working for a large aerospace firm, Star Computers, which works on many government contracts; Cathy is Greg's supervisor. Greg is assigned to program various kinds of simulations.

To improve his programming abilities, Greg writes some programming aids, such as a cross-reference facility and a program that automatically extracts documentation from source code. These are not assigned tasks for Greg; he writes them independently and uses them at work, but he does not tell anyone about them. Greg has written them in the evenings, at home, on his personal computer.

Greg decides to market these programming aids by himself. When Star's management hears of this, Cathy is instructed to tell Greg that he has no right to market these products since, when he was employed, he signed a form stating that all inventions become the property of the company. Cathy does not agree with this position, since she knows that Greg has done this work on his own. She reluctantly tells Greg that he cannot market these products. She also asks Greg for a copy of the products.

Cathy quits work for Star and takes a supervisory position with a competing company, Purple computers. She takes with her a copy of Greg's products and distributes it to the people who work with her. These products are so successful that they substantially improve the effectiveness of her employees, and Cathy is praised by her management and receives a healthy bonus. Greg hears of this, and contacts Cathy, who contends that since the product was determined to belong to Star, and since Star worked largely on government funding, the products were really in the public domain and therefore they belonged to no one in particular.

Analysis

This case certainly has major legal implications. Probably everyone could sue everyone else and, depending on the amount they are willing to spend on legal expenses, they could keep the cases in the courts for several years. A judgment would probably not be satisfying to all. Therefore, we want to explore the ethical positions involved, in order to determine who might have done what, and what changes might have been possible to prevent a tangle for the courts to unscramble.

First, let us explore the principles involved.

1. *Rights.* What are the respective rights of Greg, Cathy, Star, and Purple?

2. *Basis.* What gives Greg, Cathy, Star, and Purple those rights? What principles of fair play, business, property rights, and so forth are involved in this case?

3. *Priority.* Which of these principles are inferior to which others? Which ones take precedence? (Note that it may be impossible to compare two different rights, so the outcome of this analysis may yield some rights that are important but that cannot be ranked first, second, third.)

4. *Additional information.* What additional facts are needed in order to analyze this case? What assumptions are you making in performing the analysis?

Next, we want to consider what events led to the situation described and what alternative actions could have prevented the negative outcomes.

1. What could Greg have done differently before starting to develop his product? After developing the product? After Cathy explained that the product belonged to Star?

2. What could Cathy have done differently when she was told to tell Greg that his products belonged to Star? What could Cathy have done differently to avert this decision by her management? What could Cathy have done differently to prevent the clash with Greg after she went to work at Purple?

3. What could Purple have done differently upon learning that it had products from Star (or from Greg)?

4. What could Greg and Cathy have done differently after Greg spoke to Cathy at Purple?

5. What could Star have done differently to prevent Greg from feeling that he owned his products? What could Star have done differently to prevent Cathy from taking the products to Purple?

15.8 Case V: Proprietary Resources

In this case, we consider the issue of access to proprietary or restricted resources. Like the previous one, this case involves access to software. The focus of this case is the rights of a software developer in contrast with the rights of users, so that this case concerns determining legitimate access rights.

The Case

Suzie owns a copy of G-Whiz, a proprietary software package which she purchased legitimately. The package is copyrighted, and there is a license agreement in the documentation which says that the package is for use by the purchaser only. Suzie invites Mike to look at the package to see if it will fit his needs. Mike goes to Suzie's computer and she demonstrates the package to him. He says he likes what he sees, but he would like to try it in a longer test.

Extensions to the Case

So far the actions have all been ethically sound. The next steps are where ethical responsibilities arise. Take each of the following steps as independent; that is, do not assume that any of the other steps has occurred in your analysis of one step.

1. Suzie offers to copy the disk for Mike to use.

2. Suzie copies the disk for Mike to use, and Mike uses it for some period of time.

3. Suzie copies the disk for Mike to use, Mike uses it for some period of time and then buys a copy for himself.

4. Suzie copies the disk for Mike to try out overnight, under the restriction that he must bring the disk back to her tomorrow and must not copy it for himself. Mike does so.

5. Suzie copies the disk with the same restrictions, but Mike makes a copy for himself before returning it to Suzie.

6. Suzie copies the disk with the same restrictions, and Mike makes a copy for himself, but he then purchases a copy.

7. Suzie copies the disk with the same restrictions, but Mike does not return it.

For each of these extensions, describe who is affected, which ethical issues are involved, and which principles override which others.

15.9 Case VI: Fraud

In previous cases, we have dealt with people acting in situations that were legal or, at worst, subject to debate. In this case, we consider outright fraud, which is illegal. However, the case really concerns the actions of people who are asked to do fraudulent things.

The Case

Patty works as a programmer in a corporation. David, her supervisor, tells her to write a program to allow people to post entries directly to the company's accounting files ("the books"). Patty knows that ordinarily programs that affect the books involve several steps, all of which have to balance. Patty realizes that with the new program it will be possible for one person to make changes to crucial amounts, and there will be no way to trace who made these changes, with what justification, or when.

Patty raises these concerns to David, who tells her not to be concerned, that her job is simply to write the programs as he specifies. He says that he is aware of the potential misuse of these programs, but he justifies his request by noting that periodically a figure is mistakenly entered in the books, and they need a way to correct the inaccurate figure.

Extensions

First, let us explore the options Patty has. If Patty writes this program, she might be an accomplice to fraud. If she complains to David's superior, David or the superior might reprimand or fire her as a trouble-maker. If she refuses to write the program, David can clearly fire her for failing to carry out an assigned task. We do not even know that the program is desired for fraudulent purposes; David suggests an explanation that is not fraudulent.

She might write the program but insert extra code that creates a secret log of when the program was run, by whom, and what changes were made. This extra file could provide evidence of fraud, or it might cause trouble for Patty if there is no fraud but David discovers it.

At this point, here are some of the ethical issues involved.

1. Is a programmer responsible for the programs he or she writes? Is a programmer responsible for the results of those programs? (In contemplating this question, suppose the program were to adjust dosage in a computer-controlled medical application, and David's request were for a way to override the program controls to cause a lethal dosage. Would Patty then be responsible for the results of the program?)

2. Is a programmer merely an employee who follows orders (assigned tasks) unthinkingly?

3. What degree of personal risk (such as possible firing) is an employee obliged to accept for opposing an action he or she thinks is improper?

4. Would a program to manipulate the books as just described ever be justified? If so, in what circumstances would it be justified?

5. What kinds of controls can be placed on such programs to make them acceptable? What are some ways that a manager could legitimately ask an employee to write a program like this?

6. Would the ethical issues in this situation be changed if Patty designed and wrote this program herself?

Analysis of the Basic Case

The act-deontologist would say that truth is good. Therefore, if Patty thought the purpose of the program was to deceive, writing it would not be a good act. (If the purpose were for learning, or to be able to admire beautiful code, then writing it might be justifiable.)

A more useful analysis is from the perspective of the utilitarian. To Patty, writing the program brings possible harm for being an accomplice to fraud, with the gain of having cooperated with her manager. She has a possible item with which to blackmail David, but David might also turn on her and say the program was her idea. On balance, this option seems to have a strong negative slant.

By not writing the program her possible harm is being fired. However, she has a potential gain by being able to "blow the whistle" on David. This option does not seem to bring her much good, either. But fraudulent acts have negative consequences for the stockholders, the banks, and other innocent employees. Not writing the program brings only personal harm to Patty, which is similar to the harm she had above. Thus, it seems as if not writing the program is the more positive option.

There is another possibility. The program may *not* be for fraudulent purposes. If so, then there is no ethical conflict. Therefore, Patty might try to determine whether David's motives are fraudulent or not.

15.10 Case VII: Accuracy of Information

For our final case, we will consider responsibility for accuracy or integrity of information. Again, this is an issue addressed by operating systems and other access control mechanisms. However, as in previous cases, the issue here is access by an *authorized* user, so that access controls will not apply.

The Case

Emma is a researcher at an institute where Paul is a statistical programmer. Emma wrote a grant request to a cereal manufacturer to show the nutritional value of a new cereal, Raw Bits. The manufacturer funded Emma's study. Emma is not a statistician. She has brought all of her data to Paul to ask him to perform appropriate analyses and to print reports for her to send to the manufacturer. Unfortunately, the data Emma has collected seem to refute the claim that Raw Bits is nutritious, and in fact, they may indicate that Raw Bits is harmful.

Paul presents his analyses to Emma, but also indicates that some other correlations could be performed that would cast Raw Bits in a more favorable light. Paul makes a facetious remark about his being able to use statistics to support either side of any issue.

Ethical Concerns

Clearly, if Paul changed data values in this study he would be acting unethically. But is it any more ethical for him to suggest analyzing correct data in a way that supports two or more different conclusions? Is Paul obligated to present both the positive and the negative analyses? Is Paul responsible for the use to which others put his program results?

If Emma does not understand statistical analysis, is she acting ethically in accepting Paul's positive conclusions? His negative conclusions? Emma suspects that if she forwards negative results to the manufacturer, they will just find another researcher to do another study. She suspects that if she forwards both sets of results to the manufacturer, they will publicize only the positive ones. What ethical principles support her sending both sets of data? What principles support her sending just the positive set? What other courses of action has she?

15.11 Codes of Ethics

Because of ethical issues like the ones found in these cases, various computer groups have sought to develop codes of ethics for their members. Most computer organizations, such as the Association for Computing Machinery (ACM), the Institute of Electrical and Electronics Engineers Computer Society (IEEE-CS), and the Data Processing Management Association (DPMA), are voluntary organizations. Being a member of one of these organizations does not appreciably help in getting a job, nor does it certify a level of competence, responsibility, or experience in computing. For these reasons, codes of ethics in these organizations are primarily advisory.

The ACM code of professional conduct is representative of the ethical recommendations made by professional organizations. It states that

An ACM member should use his special knowledge and skills for the advancement of human welfare.

An ACM member should consider the health, privacy, and general welfare of the public in the performance of his work.

An ACM member, whenever dealing with data concerning individuals, shall always consider the principle of the individual's privacy and seek the following:

—to minimize the data collected
—to limit authorized access to the data
—to provide proper security for the data
—to determine the required retention period of the data
—to ensure proper disposal of the data

Although this standard is important, it is vague, subject to individual interpretation in specific situations, and lacking enforcement measures. Nevertheless, it does identify the kinds of ethical principles toward which computer professionals should strive.

15.12 Conclusion

In this overview of ethics, we have tried not to decide between right and wrong or even to brand certain acts as ethical or unethical. The purpose of this chapter is to stimulate thinking about ethical issues concerned with secrecy, integrity, and availability of data and computations.

The cases presented show complex conflicting ethical situations. The important first step in determining ethics in a situation is to obtain the facts, ask about any uncertainties, and acquire any additional information needed. In other words, first one must understand the situation.

The second step is to identify the ethical principles involved. Honesty, fair play, proper compensation, and respect for privacy are all ethical principles. Sometimes these conflict, and then it is necessary to determine which principles are more important than others. This may not lead to one principle that obviously overshadows all others. Still, a ranking to identify the major principles involved in needed.

The third step is choosing an action that meets these ethical principles. Making a decision and taking action is difficult, especially if there are evident negative consequences of the action. However, taking action based on a *personal* ranking of principles is necessary. The fact that other equally sensible people may choose a different action does not excuse one from taking some action.

This chapter is not trying to force the development of rigid, inflexible principles. Decisions may vary based on fine differences between two situations, or a person's views can change over time or in response to experience. Learning to reason about ethical situations is not quite the same as learning "right" from "wrong." Terms like "right" and "wrong" or "good" and "bad" imply a universal set of values, yet we know that even widely-accepted principles are overriden by some people in some situations. For example, the principle of not killing people may be superseded in the case of war or capital punishment. Few, if any, values are held by everyone or in all cases. Therefore, the purpose of this chapter has been to stimulate the recognition of ethical principles involved in cases related to computer security. Only by recognizing and analyzing principles can one act consistently, thoughtfully, and responsibly.

15.13 Terms and Concepts

law
ethical standard
religion
teleology
egoism
utilitarianism
deontology
rule-deontology
act-deontology
universalism

15.14 Bibliographic Notes

Two excellent and readable works on ethical reasoning are by Frankena [FRA73] and Harris [HAR86]. The work by Harris is especially recomended because it is written both clearly and concretely.

Bibliography

[ABR87a] ABRAMS, M., and PODELL, H. *Computer & Network Security–Tutorial*, IEEE Comp Soc Press 1987.

[ABR87b] ABRAMS, M., and JENG, A. "Network Security: Protocol Reference Model and the Trusted Computer System Evaluation Criteria." *IEEE Network*, v1 n2 Apr 1987, pp. 24-33.

[ADL82] ADLEMAN, L. "On Breaking the Iterated Merkle-Hellman Public-Key Cryptosystem." *Advances in Cryptology/Proc. Crypto 82*, Plenum Press 1982, pp. 303-308.

[ADL83] ADLEMAN, L. "On Breaking Generalized Knapsack Public Key Cryptosystems." *Proc. 15th ACM Symp. Theory of Computation*, pp. 402-412.

[AGN84] AGNEW, G. "Secrecy and Privacy in a Local Area Network Environment." *Advances in Cryptology/Proc. Eurocrypt 84*, Springer-Verlag 1985, pp. 349-357.

[AKL83] AKL, S. "Digital Signatures: A Tutorial Survey." *Computer*, v16 n2 Feb 1983, pp. 15-26.

[ALB84] ALBERT, D., and MORSE, S. "Combatting Software Piracy by Encryption and Key Management." *Computer*, v17 n4 Apr 1984, pp. 68-73.

[AME83] AMES, S. et al. "Security Kernel Design and Implementation: An Introduction." *Computer*, v16 n7 Jul 83, pp. 14-23.

[AND85] ANDERSON, J. "A Unification of Computer and Network Security Concepts." *Proc. 1985 IEEE Symp. Security & Privacy*, IEEE Comput Soc Press 1985, pp. 77-87.

[ATT76] ATTANASIO, C. et al. "A Study of VM/370 Integrity." *IBM System Journal*, v15 n1 1976, pp. 102-116.

[BAB86] BABICH, W. *Software Configuration Management*, Addison-Wesley 1986.

[BAL85] BALDWIN, R., and GRAMLICH, W. "Cryptographic Protocol for Trustable Match Making." *Proc. 1985 IEEE Symp. Security & Privacy*.

[BAL87] BALDWIN, R. "Rule Based Analysis of Computer Security." *Proc. 1987 COMPCON*, pp. 227-233.

[BAM82] BAMFORD, J. *The Puzzle Palace*, Houghton Mifflin 1982.

[BEC80] BECK, L. "A Security Mechanism for Statistical Data Bases." *ACM Trans Data Bases*, v5 n3 Sep 1980, pp. 316-338.

[BEL73] BELL, D., and LAPADULA, L. "Secure Computer Systems: Mathematical Foundations and Model." *MITRE Report MTR 2547*, v2 Nov 1973.

[BEL83] BELL, D. "Secure Computer Systems: A Retrospective." *Proc. 1983 IEEE Symp. Security & Privacy*, IEEE Comput Soc, pp. 161-162.

[BEN72] BENSOUSSAN, A. et al. "The Multics Virtual Memory: Concepts and Design." *Comm ACM*, v15 n5 May 1972, pp. 308-318.

[BEN84] BENZEL, T. "Analysis of a Kernel Verification." *Proc. 1984 IEEE Symp. Security & Privacy*, IEEE Comput Soc 1984, pp. 125-131.

[BEQ83] BEQUAI, A. *How to Prevent Computer Crime*, Wiley 1983.

[BER78] BERSTIS, T. et al. "System/38 Addressing and Authorization." *IBM System/38 Technical Development*, GS80-0237 1987, pp. 51-54.

[BIB77] BIBA, K. "Integrity Considerations for Secure Computer Systems." *US Air Force Electronic Systems Division*, 1977.

[BIR86] BIRRELL, A. et al. "A Global Authentication Service without Global Trust." *Proc. 1986 IEEE Symp. Security & Privacy*, IEEE Comput Soc 1986, pp. 223-230.

[BLA78] BLAKLEY, R., and BLAKLEY, G. "Security of Number Theoretic Public Key Cryptosystems against Random Number Attack, pt.1." *Cryptologia*, v2 n4 Oct 1978.

[BLA79] BLAKLEY, R., and BLAKLEY, G. "Security of Number Theoretic Public Key Cryptosystems against Random Number Attack, pt.2." *Cryptologia*, v3 n1 Jan 1979, pp. 29-42.

[BLA79a] BLAKLEY, R., and BLAKLEY, G. "Security of Number Theoretic Public Key Cryptosystems against Random Number Attack, pt.3." *Cryptologia*, v3 n2 Apr 1979, pp. 105-118.

[BLU83] BLUM, M. et al. "Reducibility Among Protocols." *Advances in Cryptology/Proc. Crypto 83*, Plenum Press 1983, pp. 137-146.

[BON81] BONYUN, D. "Role of a Well-Defined Auditing Proc. in Enforcing Private Policy." *Proc. 1981 IEEE Symp. Security & Privacy*, IEEE Comput Soc 1981, pp. 19-25.

[BOO81] BOOTH, K. "Authentication of Signatures Using Public Key Encryption." *Comm ACM*, v24 n11 Nov 1981, pp. 772-774.

[BRA73] BRANSTAD, D. "Privacy and Protection in Operating Systems." *Computer*, v6 n1 Jan 1973, pp. 43-46.

[BRA77] BRANSTAD, D. et al. "Report of the Workshop on Cryptography in Support of Computer Security." *NBSIR 77-1291*, Sept 1977.

[BRA78] BRANSTAD, D. "Security of Computer Communication." *IEEE Comm. Soc. Mag.*, v16 n6 Nov 1978, pp. 33-40.

[BRA79] BRANSTAD, D. "Hellman's Data Does Not Support His Conclusion." *IEEE Spectrum*, v16 n7 Jul 1979, p. 41

[BRA87] BRANSTAD, D. "Considerations for Security in the OSI Architecture." *IEEE Network*, v1 n2 Apr 1987, pp. 34-39.

[BRI82] BRICKELL, E. et al. "A Preliminary Report on the Cryptanalysis of Merkle-Hellman Knapsack." *Advances in Cryptology/Proc. Crypto 82*, Plenum Press 1982, pp. 289-303.

[BRI83] BRIGHT, H. "Modern Computational Cryptography." *Advances in Comp. Sec. Mgmt.*, Wiley 1983, pp. 173-201.

[BRI72] BRINCH HANSON, P. "Structured Multiprogramming." *CACM*, v15 n7 Jul 1972, pp. 574-577.

[BRO83] BROWNE, P., and TROY, E. "Designing Secure Data Processing Applications." *Advances in Comp. Sec. Mgmt. v2*, Wiley 1983.

[CHA86] CHALMERS, L. "An Analysis of the Differences between the Computer Security Practices in the Military and Private Sectors." *Proc. 1986 IEEE Symp. Security & Privacy*, IEEE Comput Soc 1986, pp. 71-74.

[CHA81] CHAUM, D. "Untraceable Electronic Mail, Return Addresses, and Digital Pseudonyms." *Comm ACM*, v24 n2 Feb 1981, pp. 84-88.

[CHA82] CHAUM, D. "Blind Signatures for Untraceable Payments." *Adv. in Cryptology/Proc. Crypto 82*, Plenum Press 1982, pp. 199-205.

[CHA85] CHAUM, D. "Security Without Identification: Transaction Systems to Make Big Brother Obsolete." *Comm ACM*, v28 n10 Oct 1985, pp. 1030-1044.

[CHE81] CHEHEYL, M. et al. "Verifying Security." *Comp Surveys*, v13 n3 Sept 1981, pp. 279-339.

[CHI87] CHILES, J. "Breaking Codes was This Couple's Lifetime Career." *Smithsonian*, v18 n3 Jun 1987, pp. 128-144.

[CHO85] CHOW, T. S. *Software Quality Assurance*, IEEE Com Soc Press 1985.

[CLA77] CLARK, R. *The Man Who Broke Purple*, Little-Brown 1977.

[COH84] COHEN, F. "Computer Viruses." *Computer Security, A Global Challenge*, Elsevier 1984, pp. 143-158.

[COO71] COOK, S. "The Complexity of Theorem-Proving Procedures." *Proc. 1971 ACM Symp. Theory of Computing*, ACM 1971, pp. 151-158.

[COR84] CORSINI, P. et al. "Distributing and Revoking Authorizations on Abstract Objects:." *Software-Practice and Experience*, v14 n10 Oct 1984, pp. 931-943.

[DAT81] DATE, C. *An Introduction to Data Base Systems, vol. 1, 3rd ed.*, Addison-Wesley 1981.

[DAT83] DATE, C. *An Introduction to Data Base Systems, vol. 2*, Addison-Wesley 1983.

[DAV78] DAVIDA, G. "Data Base Security." *IEEE Trans Software Engn*, vSE-4 n6 Nov 1978, pp. 531-533.

[DAV79] DAVIDA, G. "Hellman's Scheme Breaks DES in its Basic Form." *IEEE Spectrum*, v16 n7 Jul 1979, pp. 39.

[DAV80] DAVIDA, G. et al. "A System Architecture to Support a Verifiably Secure Multilevel Security System." *Proc. 1980 IEEE Symp. Security & Privacy*, IEEE Comput Soc 1980, pp. 137-144.

[DAV85] DAVIDA, G., and MATT, B. "Crypto-Secure Operating Systems." *AFIPS Proc. 1985 NCC*, pp. 577-581.

[DAV80a] DAVIES, D. "Protection." *Distributed Systems, An Advanced Course*, Springer-Verlag 1980.

[DAV81] DAVIES, D. *The Security of Data in Networks*, IEEE Comput Soc 1981.

[DAV82] DAVIES, D. "Some Regular Properties of the Data Encryption Standard Algorithm." *Advances in Cryptology/Proc. Crypto 82*, Plenum Press, pp. 89-97.

[DAV83] DAVIES, D. "Applying the RSA Digital Signature to Electronic Mail." *Computer*, v16 n2, Feb 1983, pp. 55-62.

[DAV83a] DAVIO, M. et al. "Propagation Characteristics of the Data Encryption Standard." *Advances in Cryptology/Proc. Crypto 83*, Plenum Press 1983, pp. 171-202.

[DAV84] DAVIES, D., and PRICE, W. *Security for Computer Networks*, Wiley 1984.

[DEA77] DEAVOURS, C. "Unicity Points in Cryptanalysis." *Cryptologia*, v1 n1 Jan 1977, pp. 46-68.

[DEA85] DEAVOURS, C. *Machine Cryptography & Modern Cryptanalysis*, Artech House 1985.

[DEM78] DEMILLO, R. ed *Foundations of Secure Computation*, Academic Press 1978.

[DEM78a] DEMILLO, R. et al. "Proprietary Software Protection." *Foundations of Secure Computation*, Academic Press 1978, pp. 115-132.

[DEM78b] DEMILLO, R. et al. "Combinatorial Inference." *Foundations of Secure Computation*, Academic Press 1978, pp. 27-38.

[DEM82] DEMILLO, R. et al. "Cryptographic Protocols." *Proc. 14th Symp. Theory of Computing*, 1982, pp. 383-400.

[DEM83] DEMILLO, R., and MERRITT, M. "Protocols for Data Security." *Computer*, v 16 n 2, Feb 1983, pp. 39-54.

[DEM83a] DEMILLO, R. et al. *Applied Crypt., Protocols, & Sec. Model*, Amer Math Soc 1983.

[DEN76] DENNING, D. "A Lattice Model of Secure Information Flow." *Comm ACM*, v19 n5 May 1976, pp. 236-243.

[DEN76a] DENNING, P. "Fault Tolerant Operating Systems." *Comput Surveys*, v8 n4 Dec 1976, pp. 359-389.

[DEN77] DENNING, D., and DENNING, P. "Certification of Programs for Secure Information Flow." *Comm ACM*, v20 n7 Jul 1977, pp. 504-513.

[DEN78] DENNING, D. "A Review of Research on Statistical Data Base Security." *Foundations of Secure Computation*, Academic Press 1978, pp. 15-25.

[DEN79] DENNING, D., and DENNING, P. "Data Security." *Comput Surveys*, v11 n3 Sept 1979, pp. 227-250.

[DEN79] DENNING, D. et al. "The Trackers: A Threat to Statistical Database Security." *ACM Trans DB Sys*, v4 n1 Mar 1979, pp. 76-96.

[DEN81] DENNING, D. "Restricting Queries That Might Lead to Compromise." *Proc. 1981 IEEE Symp. Security & Privacy*, IEEE Comput Soc 1981, pp. 33-40.

[DEN81] DENNING, D., and SACCO, G. "Timestamps in Key Distribution Protocols." *CACM*, v24 n8, pp. 533-536.

[DEN82] DENNING, D. *Cryptography and Data Security*, Addison-Wesley 1982.

[DEN83a] DENNING, D., and SCHLÖRER, J. "Inference Controls for Statistical Data Bases." *Computer*, v16 n7 Jul 1983, pp. 69-82.

[DEN83b] DENNING, D. "Protecting Public Keys and Signature Keys." *Computer*, v16 n2 Feb 1983, pp. 17-35.

[DEN83c] DENNING, D. "Field Encryption and Authentication." *Advances in Cryptology/Proc. Crypto 83*, Plenum Press 1983, pp. 231-247.

[DEN85] DENNING, D. "Commutative Filters for Reducing Inference Threats in Multilevel Database Systems." *Proc. 1985 IEEE Symp. Security & Privacy*, IEEE Comput Soc 1985, pp. 134-146.

[DEN86] DENNING, D. "An Intrusion-Detection Model." *Proc. 1986 IEEE Symp. Security & Privacy*, IEEE Comput Soc 1986, pp. 102-117.

[DEN87] DENNING, D. "Views for Multilevel Database Security." *IEEE Trans Software Engr*, vSE-13 n2 Feb 1987, pp. 129-140.

[DES84] DESMEDT, Y. et al. "Dependence of Output on Input in DES: Small Avalanche Characteristics." *Advances in Cryptology/Proc. Crypto 84*, Plenum Press 1984, pp. 359-376.

[DIF76] DIFFIE, W., and HELLMAN, M. "New Directions in Cryptography." *IEEE Trans. Info. Theory, IT-22*, v22 n6 Nov 1976, pp. 644-654.

[DIF77] DIFFIE, W., and HELLMAN, M. "Exhaustive Cryptanalysis of the NBS Data Encryption Standard." *Computer*, v10 n6 Jun 1977, pp. 74-84.

[DIF79] DIFFIE, W., and HELLMAN, M. "Privacy and Authentication." *Proc. IEEE*, v67 n3 Mar 1979, pp. 397-429.

[DIO81] DION, L. "A Complete Protection Model." *Proc. 1981 IEEE Symp. Security & Privacy*, IEEE Comput Soc 1981, pp. 49-55.

[DOD83] DOD (U.S. Dept of Defense) *Industrial Security Manual for Safeguarding Classified Information*, Sup of Document Jan 1983.

[DOD85] DOD (U.S. Dept of Defense) *Trusted Computing Sys. Evaluation Criteria*, DOD5200.28-STD Dec 1985.

[DOL82] DOLEV, D. et al. "On the Security of Ping-Pong Protocols." *Advances in Cryptology/Proc. Crypto '82*, Plenum Press 1982, pp. 177-186.

[DOW85] DOWNS, D. et al. "Issues in Discretionary Access Control." *Proc. 1985 IEEE Symp. Security & Privacy*, IEEE Comput Soc 1985, pp. 208-218.

[EHR78] EHRSAM, W. et al. "A Cryptographic Key Management Scheme for Implementing the Data Encryption Standard." *IBM Systems Journal*, v17 n2 1978, pp. 106-125.

[EST85] ESTRIN, D. "Non-Discretionary Controls for Inter-Organization Networks." *Proc. 1985 IEEE Symp. Security & Privacy*, IEEE Comput Soc 1985, pp. 56-61.

[EVA74] EVANS, A. et al. "A User Authentication Scheme not Requiring Secrecy in the Computer." *Comm ACM*, v17 n8 Aug 1974, pp. 437-441.

[EVE85] EVEN, S. et al. "A Randomizing Protocol for Signing Contracts." *Comm ACM*, v28 n6 Jun 1985, pp. 637-647.

[FAB74] FABRY, R. "Capability-Based Addressing." *Comm ACM*, v17 n7 Jul 1974, pp. 403-412.

[FEI70] FEISTEL, H. "Cryptographic Coding for Data Bank Privacy." *Tech Report RC2827 IBM TJ Watson Res. Ctr-Yorktown Hts*, New York 1970.

[FEI75] FEISTEL, H. et al. "Some Cryptographic Techniques for Machine to Machine Data Communication." *Proc. IEEE*, v63 n11 Nov 1975, pp. 1545-1554.

[FER81] FERNANDEZ, E. et al. *Database Security and Integrity*, Addison-Wesley 1981.

[FOR84] FORTUNE, S., and MERRITT, M. "Poker Protocols." *Advances in Cryptology/Proc. Crypto 84*, Plenum Press 1984, pp. 454-464.

[FOS76] FOSDICK, L., and OSTERWEIL, L. "Data Flow Analysis in Software Reliability." *Comput Surveys*, v8 m3 Sep76, pp. 305-330.

[FOS82] FOSTER, C. *Cryptanalysis for Microcomputers*, Hayden 1982.

[FRA83] FRAIM, L. "Scomp: A Solution to the Multilevel Security Problem." *Computer*, v16 n7 Jul 1983, pp. 26-34.

[FRA73] FRANKENS, W. *Ethics*, Prentice-Hall 1973.

[FRI74] FRIEDMAN, T., and HOFFMAN, L. "Execution Time Requirements for Enrichment Programs." *Comm ACM*, v17 n8 Aug 1974, pp. 445-449.

[FRI76] FRIEDMAN, W. *Advanced Military Cryptography*, Aegean Park Press 1976.

[FRI76a] FRIEDMAN, W. *Elementary Military Cryptography*, Aegean Park Press 1976.

[FRI76b] FRIEDMAN, W. *Elements of Cryptanalysis*, Aegean Park Press 1976.

[GIF82] GIFFORD, D "Cryptographic Sealing for Information Secrecy and Authentication." *Comm ACM*, v25 n4 Apr 1982, pp. 274-285.

[GOG82] GOGUEN, J., and MESEGUER, J. "Security Policies and Security Models." *Proc. 1982 IEEE Symp. Security & Privacy*, IEEE Comput Soc 1982, pp. 11-20.

[GOG84] GOGUEN, J., and MESEGUER, J. "Unwinding and Inference Control." *Proc. 1984 IEEE Symp. Security & Privacy*, IEEE Comput Soc 1984, pp. 75-86.

[GOL77] GOLD, B. et al. "VM/370 Security Retrofit Program." *Proc. 1977 ACM Annual Conference*, ACM 1977, pp. 411-418.

[GOL84] GOLD, B. et al. "KVM/370 in Retrospect." *Proc. 1984 IEEE Symp. Security & Privacy*, pp. 13-23.

[GOO84] GOODMAN, R. et al. "A New Trapdoor Knapsack Public Key Cryptosystem." *Advances in Cryptology/Proc. Eurocrypt 84*, Springer-Verlag 1985, pp. 150-158.

[GOS85] GOSLER, J., "Software Protection: Myth or Reality." *Advances in Cryptology/Proc. Crypto 85*, Plenum Press 1985, pp. 140-157.

[GRA86] GRABER, G. *The Difference Between Right & Wrong*, unpublished manuscript 1986.

[GRA68] GRAHAM, R. "Protection in an Information Processing Utility." *Comm ACM*, v11 n5 May 1968, pp. 365-369.

[GRA72] GRAHAM, G., and DENNING, P. "Protection—Principles and Practice." *Proc. 1972 Spring Joint Comp. Conference*, pp. 417-429.

[GRA84] GRAMPP, F., and MORRIS, R. "Unix Operating System Security." *AT&T Bell Labs Tech Journal*, v63 n8 pt2 Oct 1984, pp. 1649-1672.

[GRA84a] GRAUBERT, R., and KRAMER, S. "The Integrity Lock Support Environment." *Computer Security*, Proc. 2nd IFIP Conference, pp. 249-268.

[GRA85] GRAUBERT, R., and DUFFY, K. "Design Overview for Retrofittting Integrity-Lock Architecture onto a Commercial DBMS." *Proc. 1985 IEEE Symp. Security & Privacy*, IEEE Comput Soc 1985, pp. 147-159.

[GRA83] GRAYSON, M. "Vulnerabilities of Data Telecommunications Systems." *Advances in Computer Security Management*, Wiley 1983, pp. 161-172.

[GRI81] GRIES, D. *Science of Programming*, Springer-Verlag 1981.

[HAN76] HANTLER, S., and KING, J. "An Introduction to Proving the Correctness of Programs." *Comput Surveys*, v8 n3 Sep 1976, pp. 331-353.

[HAR76] HARRISON, M. et al. "Protection in Operating Systems." *Comm ACM*, v19 n8 Aug 1976, pp. 461-471.

[HAR85] HARRISON, M. "Theoretical Issues Concerning Protection in Operating Systems." *Advances in Computers*, v24 1985, pp. 61-100.

[HAR86] HARRIS, C. *Applying Moral Theories*, Wadsworth 1986.

[HAS79] HASCALL, P. "Security and Privacy." *Software Engineering*, [JEN79], pp. 412-484.

[HEL77] HELLMAN, M. "An Extension of the Shannon Theory Approach to Cryptography." *IEEE Trans. Info. Thy. VIT-23*, May 1977, pp. 289-294.

[HEL78] HELLMAN, M. "An Overview of Public Key Cryptography." *IEEE Comm Soc Mag*, v16 n6 Nov 1978, pp. 24-32.

[HEL79] HELLMAN, M. "DES Will Be Totally Insecure Within Ten Years." *IEEE Spectrum*, v16 n7 July 1979, pp. 32-39.

[HEL79a] HELLMAN, M. "The Mathematics of Public Key Cryptography." *Scientific American*, v241 n2 Feb 1979, pp. 146-157.

[HOA74] HOARE, C. "Monitors, An Operating System Structuring Concept." *Comm ACM*, v17 n10 Oct 1974, pp. 548-557.

[HOF70] HOFFMAN, L., and MILLER, W. "Getting a Personal Dossier from a Statistical Data Bank." *Datamation*, v16 n5 May 1970, pp. 74-75.

[HOF77] HOFFMAN, L. *Modern Methods for Computer Security and Privacy*, Prentice-Hall 1977.

[HOF86] HOFFMAN, L. "Risk Analysis and Computer Security: Bridging the Cultural Gap." *Proc. 9th National Computer Security Conf, 1986*.

[HOR85] HORWITT, E. "Protecting your Network Data." *Business Computer Systems*, Jul 1985, pp. 44-53.

[HSI79] HSIAO, D. et al. *Computer Security*, Academic Press 1979.

[HUL62] HULL, T., and DOBELL, A., "Random Number Generators." *SIAM Review*, v4 n3 Jul 1962, pp. 230-254.

[IBM87] IBM (International Business Machines Corp.) *Good Security Practices for Information Systems Networks*, IBM 1987.

[ING86] INGRAM, D. "Investigating and Prosecuting Computer Crime and Network Abuse." *Proc. 13th Computer Security Conference*, Computer Security Institute Nov 1986.

[JAN82] JANARDAN, R., and LAKSHMANAN, K. "A Public-Key Cryptosystem Based on the Matrix Cover NP-Complete Problem." *Advances in Cryptology/Proc. Crypto 82*, Plenum Press 1982, pp. 21-39.

[JEN79] JENSEN, R., and TONIES, C. *Software Engineering*, Prentice-Hall 1979.

[JON75] JONES, A., and WULF, W. "Towards the Design of Secure Systems." *Software–Practice and Experience*, v5 n4 Oct-Dec 1975, pp. 321-336.

[JON78] JONES, A. "Protection Mechanism Models: Their Usefulness." *Foundations of Secure Computation*, Academic Press 1978, pp. 237-252.

[JON78] JONES, A., and LIPTON, R. "The Enforcement of Security Policies for Computation." *Journal of Computer and System Science*, v17 n1 Aug 1978, pp. 35-55.

[JON78a] JONES, A., and LISKOV, B. "A Language Extension of Expressing Constraints on Data Access." *Comm ACM*, v21 n5 May 1978, pp. 358-367.

[JUE83] JUENEMAN, R. et al. "Authentication with Manipulation Detection Code." *Proc. 1983 IEEE Symp. Security & Privacy*, IEEE Comput Soc 1983, pp. 67-175.

[KAH67] KAHN, D. *The Codebreakers*, Macmillan 1967.

[KAI86] KAIN, R., and LANDWEHR, C. "On Access Checking in Capability-Based Systems." *Proc. 1986 IEEE Symp. Security & Privacy*, IEEE Comput Soc 1986, pp. 95-100.

[KAM78] KAM, J., and DAVIDA, G. "A Structured Design of Substitution-Permutation Encryption Network." *Foundations of Secure Computation*, Academic Press 1978, pp. 95-114.

[KAR84] KARGER, P., and HERBERT, A. "An Augmented Capability Architecture to Support Lattice Security and Traceability of Access." *Proc. 1984 IEEE Symp. Security & Privacy*, IEEE Comput Soc 1984, pp. 2-12.

[KAR72] KARP, R. "Reducibility Among Combinatorial Problems." *Complexity of Computer Computations*, Plenum Press 1972, pp. 85-104.

[KEM86] KEMMERER, R. *Verification Assessment Study Final Report*, NCSC C3-CR01-86 National Computer Security Center Mar 1986.

[KEN77] Kent, S. "Encryption-Based Protection for Interactive User/Computer Communication." *Proc. 5th Data Comm. Symp.*, Sep 1977, pp. 5-7–5-13.

[KIE78] KIEBURTZ, R., and SILBERSCHATZ, A. "Capability Managers." *IEEE Trans Software Engn*, vSE-4 n6 Nov 1978, pp. 467-477.

[KNI78] KNIGHT, H. "Cryptanalyst's Corner." *Cryptologia*, v2 n1 Jan 1978, pp. 69.

[KNU69] KNUTH, D. E. *The Art of Computer Programming, vol 1*, Addison-Wesley 1969.

[KON80] KONHEIM, A. et al. "The IPS Cryptographic Programs." *IBM Systems Journal*, v19 n2 1980, pp. 253-283.

[KON81] KONHEIM, A. *Cryptography, A Primer*, Wiley, 1981.

[KUL76] KULLBACK, S. *Statistical Methods in Cryptanalysis*, Aegean Park Press 1976.

[LAG83] LAGARIAS, J. "Knapsack Public Key Cryptosystems and Diophantine Approximation." *Advances in Cryptology/Proc. Crypto 83*, Plenum Press 1983, pp. 3-23.

[LAM81] LAMPORT, L., "Password Authentication with Insecure Communication." *Comm ACM*, v24 n11 Nov 1981, pp. 770-771.

[LAM71] LAMPSON, B. "Protection." *Proc. 5th Princeton Symp.* in *Operating Systems Review*, v8 n1 Jan 1974, pp. 18-24.

[LAM76] LAMPSON, B., and STURGIS, H. "Reflections on an Operating System Design." *Comm ACM*, v19 n5 May 1976, pp. 251-266.

[LAM79] LAMPSON, B. "Dynamic Protection Structures." *Proc. 1969 AFIPS FJCC*, v35 1969, pp. 27-38.

[LAN81] LANDWEHR, C. "Formal Models for Computer Security." *Comput Surveys*, v13 n3 Sept 1981, pp. 247-278.

[LAN83] LANDWEHR, C. et al. "The Best Available Technologies for Computer Security." *Computer*, v16 n 7 Jul 1983, pp. 86-100.

[LAN84] LANDWEHR, C. et al. "A Security Model for Military Message Systems." *ACM Trans Comput Sys*, v2 n2 Aug 1984, pp. 198-222.

[LEC83] LECHTER, M. "Protecting Software and Firmware Devices." *Computer*, v16 n8 Aug 1983, pp. 73-82.

[LEI82] LEISS, E. *Principles of Data Security*, Plenum Press 1982.

[LEM79] LEMPEL, A. "Cryptology in Transition." *Computing Surveys*, v11 n4 Dec 1979, pp. 285-303.

[LEN78] LENNON, R. "Cryptography Architecture for Information Security." *IBM Systems Journal*, v17 n2 1978, pp. 138-150.

[LEV84] LEVY, H. *Capability-Based Computer Systems*, Digital Press 1984.

[LEX76] Lexan Corp. *An Evaluation of the DES*, Sept 1976.

[LIN76] LINDEN, T. "Operating System Structures to Support Security and Reliable Software." *Computing Surveys*, v8 n4 Dec 1976, pp. 409-445.

[LIP82] LIPNER, S. "Non-Discretionary Controls for Commercial Applications." *Proc. 1982 IEEE Symp. Security & Privacy*, IEEE Comput Soc 1982, pp. 2-10.

[LIP77] LIPTON, R., and SNYDER, L. "A Linear Time Algorithm for Deciding Subject Security." *JACM*, v24 n3 Jul 1977, pp. 455-464.

[LOB86] LOBEL, J. *Foiling the System Breakers*, McGraw-Hill 1986.

[LON82] LONGPRE, L. "The Use of Public-Key Cryptology for Signing Checks." *Advances in Cryptology/Proc. Crypto 82*, Plenum Press 1982, pp. 187-197.

[MAT85] MATLEY, B. "Computer Privacy in America: Conflicting Practices and Policy Choices." *Proc. 1985 IEEE Symp. Security & Privacy*, IEEE Comput Soc 1985, pp. 219-223.

[MAT86] MATLOFF, N. "Another Look at the use of Noise Addition for Database Security." *Proc. 1986 IEEE Symp. Security & Privacy*, IEEE Comput Soc 1986, pp. 173-180.

[MAT78] MATYAS, S., and MEYER, C. "Generation, Distribution and Installation of Cryptographic Keys." *IBM System Journal*, v17 n2 1978, pp. 126-137.

[McC79] McCAULEY, E., and DRONGOWSKI, P. "KSOS–The Design of a Secure Operating System." *AFIPS Proc. 1979 NCC*, pp. 345-353.

[MCD77] McDONALD, N., and IPPOLITO, P. "Study of Computer Safeguards." *PRC Info. Sci. Co. Tech. report R-2*, Planning Research Corp 1973.

[MEA86] MEADOWS, C. "A More Efficient Cryptographic Matchmaking Protocol." *Proc. 1986 IEEE Symp. Security & Privacy*, IEEE Comput Soc 1986, pp. 134-137.

[MER78a] MERKLE, R. "Secure Communication over Insecure Channels." *Comm ACM*, v21 n4 Apr 1978, pp. 294-299.

[MER78b] MERKLE, R., and HELLMAN, M. "Hiding Information and Signatures in Trapdoor Knapsacks." *IEEE Trans. Info. Thy.*, IT-24-5 Sep 1978, pp. 525-530.

[MER80] MERKLE, R. "Protocols for Public Key Cryptosystems." *Proc. 1980 IEEE Symp. Security & Privacy*, IEEE Comput Soc 1980, pp. 122-133.

[MER81] MERKLE, R., and HELLMAN, M. "On the Security of Multiple Encryption." *Comm ACM*, v24 n7 Jul 1981, pp. 465.

[MEY82] MEYER, C., and MATYAS, S. *Cryptography: A New Dimension in Computer Security*, Wiley 1982.

[MIG84] MIGUEL, J. "A Composite Cost/Benefit/Risk Methodology." *Computer Security: A Global Challenge*, Proc. IFIP Conf. 1984, pp. 307-312.

[MIL76] MILLEN, J. "Security Kernel Validation in Practice." *Comm ACM*, v19 n5 May 1976, pp. 243-250.

[MIL81] MILLER, J., and RESNICK, R. "Military Message Systems: Applying a Security Model." *CH1629*, IEEE Press 1981, pp. 101-111.

[MOR77] MORRIS, R. et al. "Assessment of the NBS Proposed Data Encryption Standard." *Cryptologia*, v1 n3 Jul 1977, pp. 281-291.

[MOR79] MORRIS, R., and THOMPSON, K. "Password Security: A Case History." *Comm ACM*, v22(11) Nov 1979.

[NAV86] NAVATHE, S. "Integrating User Views in Database Design." *Computer*, v19 n1 Jan 1986, pp. 50-61.

[NBS77] NBS (National Bureau of Standards) "Data Encryption Standard." *FIPS Publ. 46*, Washington DC Jan 1977.

[NBS79] NBS (National Bureau of Standards) *Guideline for Automatic Data Process*, US Government Printing Office 1979.

[NBS80] NBS (National Bureau of Standards) "DES Modes of Operation." *FIPS PUB81*, US Government Printing Office 1980.

[NCS87] NSCS (National Computer Security Center) *Trusted Network Interpretation*, NCSC-TG-005-ver1 1987.

[NCS85] NCSC (National Computer Security Center) *Personal Computer Security Consideration*, NCSCPub WA-002-85 1985.

[NCS85] NCSC (National Computer Security Center) *"Orange Book"*, same as [DOD85].

[NEE78] NEEDHAM, R., and SCHROEDER, M. "Using Encrpytion for Authentication in Large Networks of Computer." *Comm ACM*, v21 n12 Dec 1978, pp. 993-999.

[NES86] NESSETT, D. "Factors Affecting Distributed System Security." *Proc. 1986 IEEE Symp. Security & Privacy*, IEEE Comput Soc 1986, pp. 204-222.

[NEU82] NEUGENT, W. "Acceptance Criteria for Computer Security." *Proc. 1982 AFIPS NCC*, v51, pp. 443-448.

[NEU78] NEUMANN, P. "Computer System Security Evaluation." *Proc. 1978 AFIPS NCC*, v47, pp. 1087-1095.

[NTI87] NTISS (Natl Telecommunications and Information Systems Security Committee) *Advisory Memo: Office Automation Security Guide*, NTISS COMPUSEC/1-87.

[PAD79] PADLIPSKY, M. et al. "KSOS–Computer Network Applications." *AFIPS Proc. 1979 NCC*, pp. 373-381.

[PAR76] PARKER, D. *Crime by Computer*, Scribners 1976.

[PAR79] PARKER, D. *Ethical Conflicts in Computer Science & Technology*, AFIPS Press 1979.

[PAR81] PARKER, D. *Computer Security Management*, Reston 1981.

[PAR83] PARKER, D. *Fighting Computer Crime*, Scribners 1983.

[PAR84a] PARKER, D., and NYCUM, S. "Computer Crime." *Comm ACM*, v27 n4 Apr 1984, pp. 313-321.

[PAR84b] PARKER, D. "The Many Faces of Data Vulnerabvility." *IEEE Spectrum*, v21 n5 May 1984, pp. 46-49.

[PEL79] PELEG, S., and ROSENFELD, A. "Breaking Substitution Ciphers Using a Relaxation Algorithm." *Comm ACM*, v22 n11 Nov 1979, pp. 598-605.

[PER84] PERRY, T., and WALLICH, P. "Can Computer Crime Be Stopped?." *IEEE Spectrum*, v21 n5 May 1984, pp. 34-45.

[PFL87] PFLEEGER, C., and PFLEEGER, S. "A Transaction Flow Approach to Software Security Certification for Document Handling Systems." to appear in *Computers & Security*

[PFL87a] PFLEEGER, S. *Software Engineering*, Macmillan 1987.

[PLE77] PLESS, V. "Encryption Schemes for Computational Confidentiality." *IEEE Trans. Comput.*, vC-26 n11 Nov 1977, pp. 1133-1136.

[POP74] POPEK, G. "Protection Structures." *Computer*, v7 n6 Jun 1974, pp. 22-23.

[POP78] POPEK, G., and KLINE, C. "Encryption Protocols, Public Key Algorithms, and Digital Signatures in Computer Networks." *Foundations of Secure Computation*, Academic Press 1978, pp. 133-155.

[POP78a] POPEK, G., and KLINE, C. "Issues in Kernel Design." *AFIPS Proc. 1978 NCC*, pp. 1079-1086.

[POP79] POPEK, G., and KLINE, C. "Encryption and Secure Computer Networks." *Computing Surveys*, v11 n4 Dec 1979, pp. 331-356.

[POP79a] POPEK, G. et al. "UCLA Secure Unix." *AFIPS Proc. 1979 NCC*, pp. 355-364.

[PRE87] PRESSMAN, R. *Software Engineering, A Practitioner's Approach*, 2ed McGraw-Hill 1987.

[PUB81] Public Cryptography Study Group "Report of the Public Cryptography Study Group." *Comm ACM*, v24 n7 Jul 1981, pp. 434-450.

[PUR74] PURDY, G. "A High Security Log-In Procedure." *Comm ACM*, v17 n8 Aug 1974, pp. 442-445.

[PUR82] PURDY, G. et al. "A Software Protection Scheme." *Proc. 1982 IEEE Symp. Security & Privacy*, IEEE Comput Soc 1982, pp. 99-103.

[RAB78] RABIN, M. "Digitalized Signatures." *Foundations of Secure Computation*, Academic Press 1978, pp. 155-166.

[REE77] REEDS, J. "'Cracking' a Random Number Generator." *Cryptologia*, v1 n1 Jan 1977, pp. 20-26.

[REE84] REEDS, J., and WEINBERGER, P. "File Security and the Unix Operating System 'crypt' Command." *AT&T Bell Labs Tech. Journal*, v63 n8 pt2 Oct 1984, pp. 1673-1684.

[REI80] REISS, S. "Practical Data Swapping: The First Steps." *Proc. 1980 IEEE Symp. Security & Privacy*, IEEE Comput Soc 1980, pp. 38-45.

[RIT79] RITCHIE, D. "On the Security of UNIX." *Unix Programmer's Manual, secn. 2*, AT&T Bell Labs.

[RIV78] RIVEST, R. et al. "A Method for Obtaining Digital Signatures and Public-Key Cryptosystems." *Comm ACM*, v21 n2 Feb 1978, pp. 120-126.

[RIV82] RIVEST, R., and SHAMIR, A. "How to Reuse a Write-once Memory." *Information and Control*, v55 1982, pp. 1-19.

[ROS30] ROSS, W. *The Right and The Good*, Clarendon Press 1930.

[ROT87] ROTH, A. "'Networks Add to Security Risk,' Expert Says." *Government Computer News*, v6 n9 May 8 1987, pp. 72.

[RUS83] RUSHBY, J., and RANDELL, B. "A Distributed Secure System." *Computer*, v16 n7 Jul 1983, pp. 55-67.

[RUS85] RUSHBY, J. "Networks are Systems." *Proc. DOD Computer Security Ctr. Wksp. Network Security*, 1985, pp. 7-24–7-38.

[SAL74] SALTZER, J. "Protection and the Control of Information Sharing in MULTICS." *Comm ACM*, v17 n7 Jul 1974, pp. 388-402.

[SAL75] SALTZER, J. and SCHROEDER, M. "The Protection of Information in Computer Systems." *Proc. IEEE*, v63 n9 Sept 1975, pp. 1278-1308.

[SCH72] SCHRODER, M., and SALTZER, J. "A Hardware Architecture for Implementing Protection Rings." *Comm ACM*, v15 n3 Mar 1972, pp. 157-170.

[SCH77] SCHAEFER, M. et al. "Program Confinement in KVM/370." *Proc. ACM Annual Conference*, 1977, pp. 404-410.

[SCH83a] SCHELL, R. "A Security Kernel for a Multiprocessor Microcomputer." *Computer*, v16 n7 Jul 1983, pp. 47-53.

[SCH83b] SCHWEITZER, J. "Protecting Information in the Electronic Office." Butterworth Press 1983.

[SCH84] SCHAUMUELLER-BICHL, I., and PILLER, E. "A Method of Software Protection Based on the Use of Smart Cards." *Advances in Cryptology/Proc. Eurocrypt 84*, Springer Verlag 1985, pp. 446-454.

[SCH86] SCHELL, R., and DENNING, D. "Integrity in Trusted Database Systems." *Proc. 9th National Computer Security*, pp. 30-36.

[SHA78] SHAMIR, A. et al. "Mental Poker." *MIT Lab for Comp. Sci.*, Report TM-125 Nov 1978.

[SHA80] SHAMIR, A. and ZIPPEL, R. "On the Security of the Merkle-Hellman Cryptographic Scheme." *IEEE Trans. Info. Theory*, vIT-26 n3 May 1980, pp. 339-340.

[SHA81] SHAMIR, A. "How to Share a Secret." *Comm ACM*, v22 n11 Nov 1979, pp. 612-613.

[SHA82] SHAMIR, A. "A Polynomial Time Algorithm for Breaking the Basic Merkle-Hellman Cryptosystem." *Advances in Cryptology/Proc. Crypto 82*, Plenum Press 1982, pp. 279-288.

[SHA83] SHAMIR, A. "On the Generation of Cryptographically Strong Pseudorandom Sequences." *ACM Trans Comput Sys*, v1 n1 Feb 1983, pp. 38-44.

[SHA49] SHANNON, C. "Communication Theory of Secrecy Systems." *Bell Systems Technical Journal*, v28 Oct 1949, pp. 656-715.

[SHO82] SHOCK, J., and HUPP, J. "The 'Worm' Programs–Early Experience with a Distributed Computer." *Comm ACM*, v25 n3 Mar 1982, pp. 172-180.

[SHO83] SHOOMAN, M. *Software Engineering*, McGraw-Hill 1983.

[SIB87] SIBERT, W. et al. "Unix and B2: Are They Compatible?." *Proc. 1987 NBS/NCSC Computer Security Conference*, pp. 142-149.

[SIM77] SIMMONS, G., and NORRIS, M. "Preliminary Comments on the M.I.T. Public-Key Cryptosystem." *Cryptologia*, v1 n4 Oct 1977, pp. 406-414.

[SIM79] SIMMONS, G. "Symmetric and Asymmetric Encryption." *Computing Surveys*, v11 n4 Dec 1979, pp. 305-330.

[SIM82] SIMMONS, G., and HOI DRIDGE, D. "Forward Search as a Cryptographic Tool Against a Public Key Private Channel.' *Proc. 1982 IEEE Symp. Security & Privacy*, IEEE Comput Soc 1982, pp. 117-128.

[SIN66] SINKOV, A. *Elementary Cryptanalysis: A Mathematical Approach*, Math Assn Amer 1966.

[SMI84] SMITH, S., and LIM, J. "An Automated Method for Assessing Effectiveness of Computer Security Safeguards." *Computer Security: A Global Challenge*, Proc. IFIP Conf. 1984, pp. 321-328.

[SNY81] SNYDER, L. "Formal Models of Capability-Based Protection Systems." *IEEE Trans Comput*, vC-30 n3 Mar 1981, pp. 172-181.

[SOL81] SOLOMON, D. "Processing Multilevel Secure Objects." *Proc. 1981 IEEE Symp. Security & Privacy*, IEEE Comput Soc 1981, pp. 56-61.

[SOL77] SOLOVAY, R., and STRASSEN, V. "A Fast Monte-Carlo Test for Primality." *SIAM Journal Comp.*, v6 Mar 1977, pp. 84-85.

[STO74] STONEBRAKER, M., and WONG, E., "Access Control in a Relational Data Base Management System by Query Modification." *Proc. 1974 ACM National Conference*, 1974, pp. 180-186.

[STO81] STONEBRAKER, M. "Operating System Support for Database Management." *Comm ACM*, v24 n7 Jul 1981, pp. 412-418.

[STO81a] STOUGHTON, A. "Access Flow: A Protection Model which Integrates Access Control & Information Flow." *Proc. 1981 IEEE Symp. Security & Privacy*, IEEE Comput Soc 1981, pp. 9-18.

[SUG79] SUGARMAN, R. "On Foiling Computer Crime." *IEEE Spectrum*, v16 n7 Jul 1979, pp. 31-32.

[SWA85] SWAMINATHAN, K. "Negotiated Access Control." *Proc. 1985 IEEE Symp. Security & Privacy*, IEEE Comput Soc 1985, pp. 190-196.

[TAN81] TANENBAUM, A. *Computer Networks*, Prentice-Hall 1981.

[THO84] THOMPSON, K. "Reflections on Trusting Trust." *Comm ACM*, v27 n8 Aug 1984, pp. 761-763.

[TOM84] TOMPKINS, J. *Report on Computer Crime*, American Bar Assn. 1984.

[TUC79] TUCHMAN, W. "Hellman Presents no Shortcut Solutions to the DES." *IEEE Spectrum*, v16 n7 Jul 1979, pp. 40.

[TUR82] TURN, R. "Private Sector Needs for Trusted/Secure Computer Systems." *AFIPS 1982 NCC*, v51, pp. 449-460.

[ULL82] ULLMAN, J. *Principles of Database Systems*, Computer Science Press 1982.

[VAH82] VAHLE, M., and TOLENDINO, L. "Breaking a Pseudo Random Number Based Cryptographic Algorithm." *Cryptologia*, v6 n4 Oct 1982, pp. 319-328.

[VOE86] VOELCKER, J., and WALLICH, P. "How Disks are 'Padlocked'." *IEEE Spectrum*, v 23 n 6 Jun 1986, pp. 32-40.

[VOY83] VOYDOCK, V., and KENT, S. "Security Mechanisms in High-Level Network Protocols." *Computing Surveys*, v15 n2 Jun 1983, pp. 135-171.

[WAG82] WAGNER, N. "Shared Database Access Using Composed Encryption Functions." *Proc. 1982 IEEE Symp. Security & Privacy*, IEEE Comput Soc 1982, pp. 104-110.

[WAG83] WAGSTAFF, S. "How to Crack an RSA Cryptosystem." *Advances in Cryptology/Proc. Crypto 83*, Plenum Press 1983.

[WAL80] WALKER, B. et al. "Specification and Verification of the UCLA Unix Security Kernel." *CACM*, v23 n2 Feb 1980, pp. 118-131.

[WAL85] WALKER, S. "Network Security Overview." *Proc. 1985 IEEE Symp. Security & Privacy*, IEEE Comput Soc 1985, pp. 62-76.

[WAR84] WARE, W. "Information System Security and Privacy." *Comm ACM*, v27 n4 Apr 1984, pp. 316-321.

[WEI87] WEINGART, S. "Physical Security for the ABYSS System." *Proc. 1987 IEEE Symp. Security & Privacy*, IEEE Comput Soc 1987, pp. 52-58.

[WIS86] WISEMAN, S. "A Secure Capability Computer System." *Proc. 1986 IEEE Symp. Security & Privacy*, IEEE Comput Soc 1986, pp. 86-94.

[WOO77] WOOD, H. "The Use of Passwords for Controlling Access to Remote Computer Systems." *Proc. 1977 National Comp. Conf.*, pp. 27-32.

[WOO80] WOOD, C. et al. "Data Base Security: Requirements, Policies, Models." *IBM Systems Journal*, v19 m2 1980, pp. 229-252.

[WOO85] WOOD, P., and KOCHAN, S. *Unix System Security*, Hayden 1985.

[WUL74] WULF, W. et al. "Hydra: The Kernel of a Multiprocessor Operating System." *Comm ACM*, v17 n6 Jun 1974, pp. 337-345.

[YAC86] YACOBY, Y. "On Proving Privacy in Multiuser Systems." *Computer Science Department Technical Report 398*, Technion (Israel) Feb 1986.

[YAR31] YARDLEY, H. *The American Black Chamber*, Bobbs-Merrill 1931.

[YOU85] YOUNG, W. et al. "Proving a Computer System Secure." *Scientific Honeyweller*, July 1985, pp. 18-27.

[ZEL78] ZELKOWITZ, M. "Implementation of a Capability-Based Data Abstraction." *IEEE Trans. Software Engn.*, vSE-4 n1 Jan 1978, pp. 56-64.

[ZIM86] ZIMMERMAN, P. "A Proposed Standard Format for RSA Cryptosystems." *Computer*, v19 n9 Sep 1986, pp. 21-34.

[ZIP86] ZIPP, E., and SHANNON, T. "Restricted Access." *Digital Review*, Apr 1986, pp. 49-56.

Index